SSC

Combined Higher Secondary

(10+2) Level

Tier I

Postal/Sorting Assistant | Data Entry Operator
Lower Division Clerk
Examination 2019

25
Practice Sets

Includes
Solved Papers
2017 & 2018

G K Publications (P) Ltd

CL MEDIA (P) LTD.

Edition : 2019

© PUBLISHER

No part of this book may be reproduced in a retrieval system or transmitted, in any form or by any means, electronics, mechanical, photocopying, recording, scanning and or without the written permission of the publisher.

ISBN : **978-93-89573-90-9**

Typeset by : *CL Media DTP Unit*

Administrative and Production Offices

Published by : CL Media (P) Ltd.
A-45, Mohan Cooperative Industrial Area, Near Mohan Estate Metro Station, New Delhi - 110044

Marketed by : G.K. Publications (P) Ltd.
A-45, Mohan Cooperative Industrial Area, Near Mohan Estate Metro Station, New Delhi - 110044

For product information :
Visit *www.gkpublications.com* or email to *gkp@gkpublications.com*

Contents

EXAM PATTERN

Part	Subject	Number of Questions	Maximum Marks	Time
(I)	General Intelligence	25	50	
(II)	English Language	25	50	**60 Minutes**
(III)	Quantitative Aptitude	25	50	
(IV)	General Awareness	25	50	

SOLVED PAPER 2018

SSC–Combined Higher Secondary Examination

(2nd July)

GENERAL INTELLIGENCE

1. Select the option that is related to the third number in the same way as the second number is related to the first number.

   54 : 41 :: 32 : ____

   (1) 29   (2) 13

   (3) 17   (4) 11

2. A paper is folded and cut as shown in the following figures. How will it appear when unfolded?

   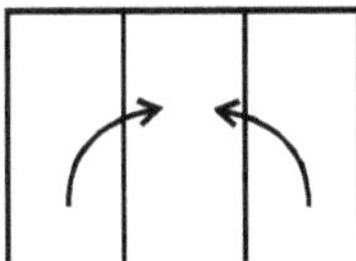 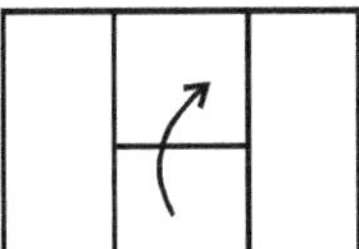 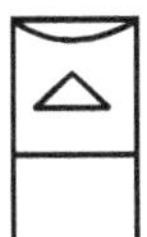

   (1) 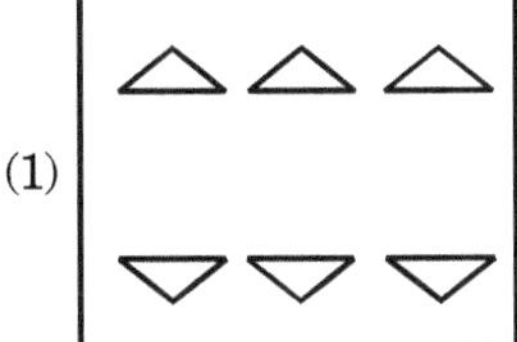

   (2) 

   (3) 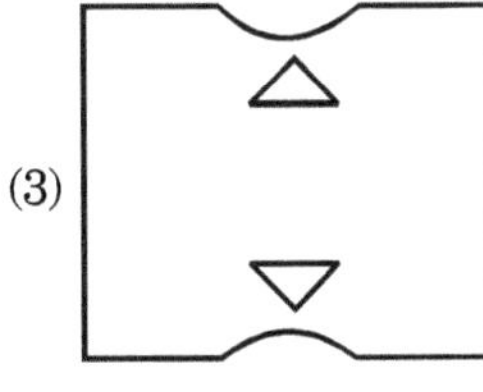

   (4) 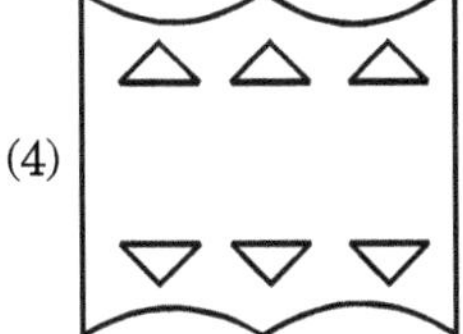

3. Select the correct mirror image of the given figure when the mirror is placed to the right of the figure.

   (1) 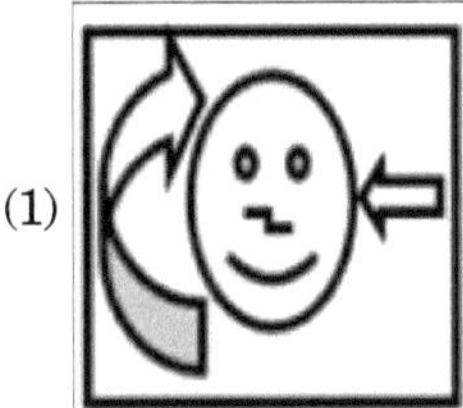

   (2) 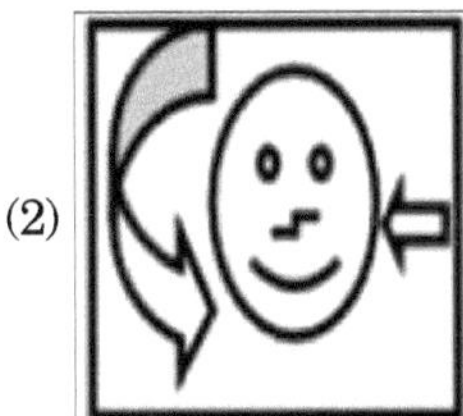

   (3) 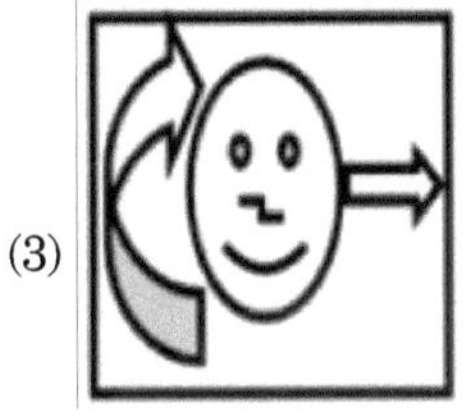

   (4) 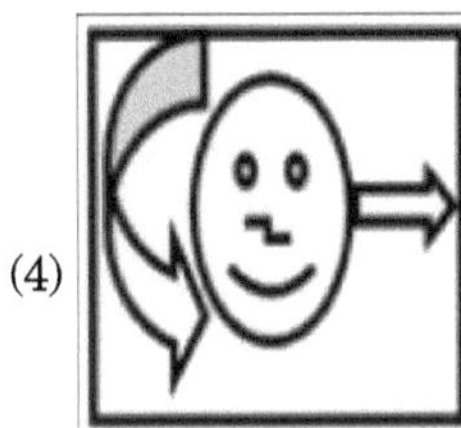

4. Which two signs should be interchanged in the following equation to make it correct?

   $24 \div 2 + 13 - 54 \times 2 = 34$

   (1) + and × (2) − and ×

   (3) × and ÷ (4) − and ÷

5. Arrange the following words in a logical and meaningful order.
   1. Promotion
   2. Application
   3. Job appointment
   4. Written test
   5. Merit list
   (1) 2, 5, 4, 3, 1 (2) 3, 2, 4, 1, 5
   (3) 4, 2, 5, 3, 1 (4) 2, 4, 5, 3, 1

6. How many triangles are present in the following figure?

   (1) 14 (2) 13
   (3) 10 (4) 12

7. Select the figure that will come next in the following figure series.

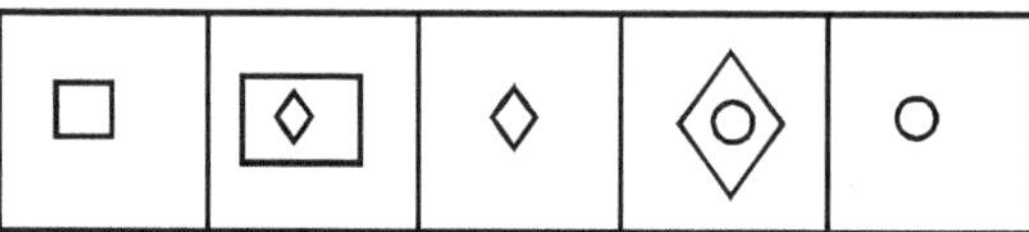

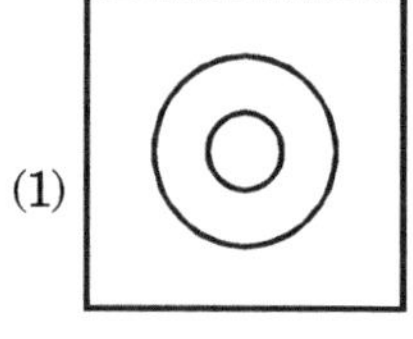
(1)

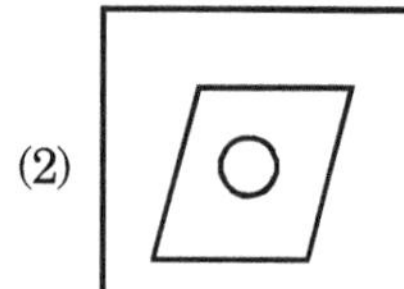
(2)

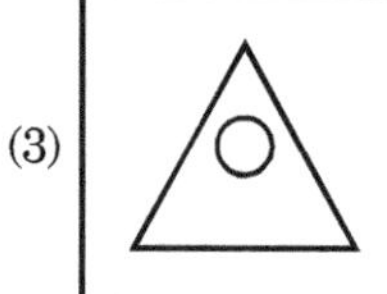
(3)

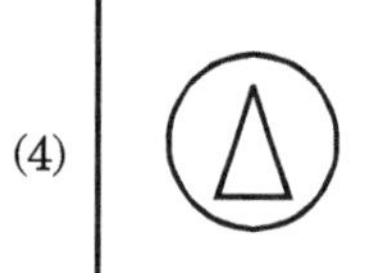
(4)

8. Three statements are given, followed by three conclusions numbered I, II and III. Assuming the statements to be true, even if they seem to be at variance with commonly known facts, decide which of the conclusions logically follow(s) from the statements.

   Statements:

   Some essays are poems.

   Some poems are directors.

   All directors are singers.

   Conclusions:

   I. Some directors are poems.

   II. Some singers are essays.

   III. Some singers are poems.

   (1) Only conclusions I and III follow.
   (2) Only conclusions II and III follow.
   (3) Only conclusions I and II follow.
   (4) Only conclusion I follows.

9. Rahul has Rs. 340 in the denominations of Rs. 2 notes, Rs. 5 notes and Rs. 10 notes. The number of notes of each denomination is equal. What is the total number of notes that Rahul has?

   (1) 40 (2) 60
   (3) 20 (4) 80

10. Which number will replace the question mark (?) in the following series?

    5, 9, 18, 43, 92, 213, 382, ?

    (1) 328 (2) 617
    (3) 382 (4) 671

11. Three of the following four letter-clusters are alike in a certain way and one is different. Pick the odd one out .

    (1) GSVE (2) LOPK
    (3) CXGT (4) MNQJ

12. In a code language, PERMUTATION is written as IBKFRMXMFLG. How will PUBLICSECTOR be written as in that language?

    (1) ICUFEVLBVNLK (2) ICUFEVLBVMLJ
    (3) IRUEFVLBVMLK (4) IRVEFVLBVMLK

13. Select the combination of letters that when sequentially placed in the gaps of the given letter series will complete the series.

    ab_ba_babd_acb_bdba_b

    (1) cdabc (2) dcbac
    (3) acbcd (4) dcabc

14. Select the venn diagram that best illustrates the relationship between the following classes.

Raw material, Labourers, Machines

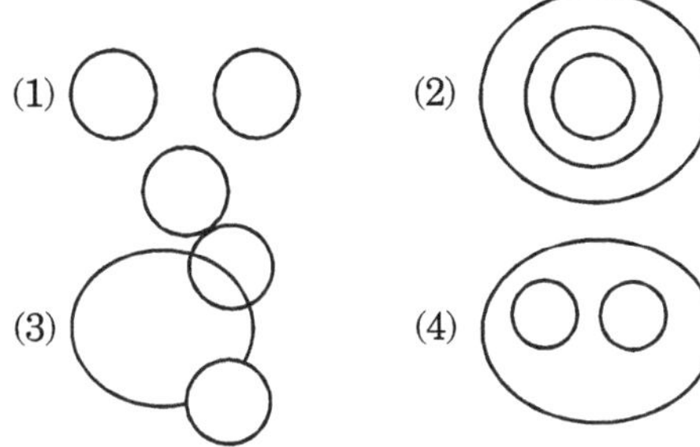

15. In a family of 5 members, X is the sister of Y. M has two children and he is the son of E, who is the father-in-law of H. H has only one son. Y is not the grand-daughter of E. How is X related to E?

(1) Sister (2) Daughter
(3) Grand-daughter (4) Grandson

16. Two different positions of the same dice are shown. Find the number opposite to the face having 4.

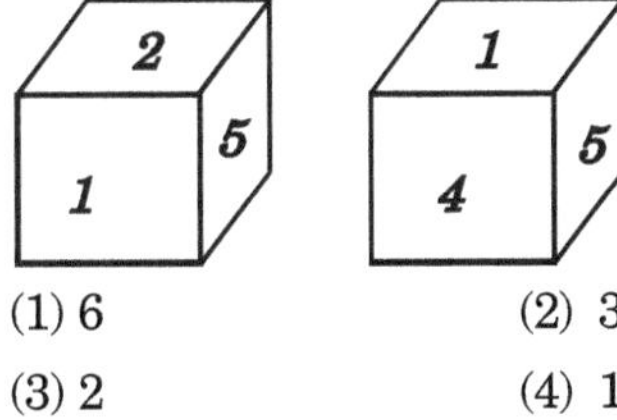

(1) 6 (2) 3
(3) 2 (4) 1

17. 'Cardiologist' is related to 'Heart' in the same way as 'Chiropractor' is related to '________'.

(1) Skin (2) Foot
(3) Chest (4) Joints

18. If MASTER is coded as 26138402536 and GOVIND is coded as 142254481288, then how will BACKSPACE be coded as?

(1) 4162238321625 (2) 5172339317125
(3) 4172393337125 (4) 5172933373215

19. Select the set in which the numbers are related in the same way as are the numbers of the following set.

(4, 10, 23)

(1) (7, 23, 49) (2) (3, 7, 17)
(3) (4, 12, 21) (4) (2, 6, 15)

20. Three of the following four words are alike in a certain way and one is different. Pick the odd word out.

(1) Bag (2) Suitcase
(3) Purse (4) Carpet

21. Select the option in which the given figure is embedded.

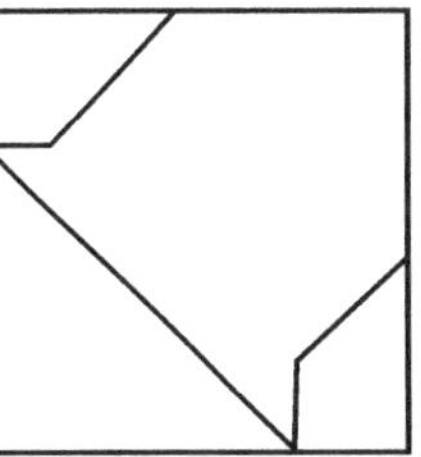

(1) 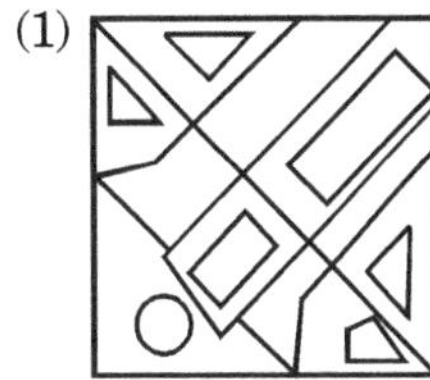 (2) 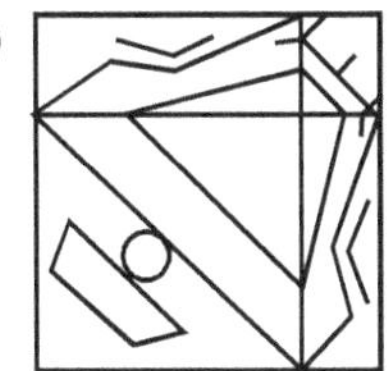

(3) 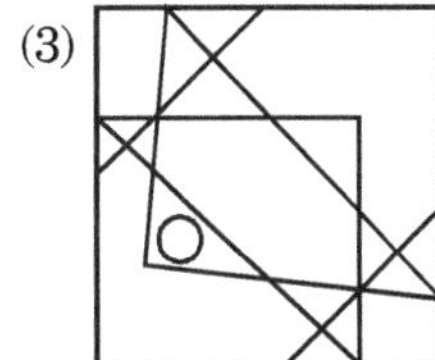 (4) 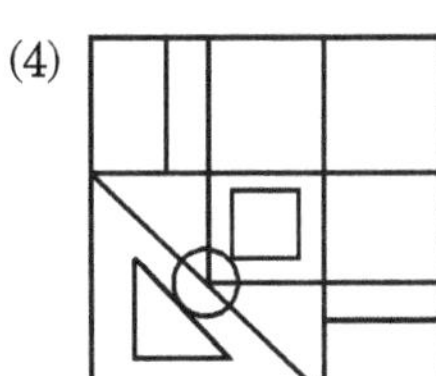

22. Select the option that is related to the third letter-cluster in the same way as the second letter-cluster is related to the first letter-cluster.

MARKET : IEONCV : : THERMO : ________

(1) PLBUKQ (2) JKCTKQ
(3) PLDSKQ (4) JLZUKQ

23. Three of the following four numbers are alike in a certain way and one is different. Pick the number that is different from the rest.

(1) 4147 (2) 8205
(3) 9368 (4) 7298

24. Select the set in which the numbers are related in the same way as are the numbers of the following set.

(5, 2, 30)

(1) (5, 1, 29) (2) (9, 2, 87)
(3) (4, 3, 28) (4) (7, 8, 114)

25. Select the word-pair in which the two words are related in the same way as are the two words in the following word-pair.

Spoke : Wheel

(1) Word : Sentence
(2) Printer : Computer
(3) Square : Side
(4) Tree : Branch

GENERAL AWARENESS

26. Who among the following was the first Sayyid ruler of Delhi?

    (1) Mubarak Shah   (2) Alam Shah

    (3) Muhammad Shah   (4) Khizr Khan

27. Who was the captain of the Indian women's Kabaddi team that won silver at the 2018 Asian Games?

    (1) Manpreet Kaur   (2) Ritu Negi

    (3) Shalini Pathak   (4) Payel Chowdhury

28. Which of the following states shares the longest boundary with China?

    (1) Sikkim

    (2) Arunachal Pradesh

    (3) Himachal Pradesh

    (4) Uttarakhand

29. Which of the following political parties was NOT an ally of the BJP-led NDA in 2019 Lok Sabha elections?

    (1) Shiromani Akali Dal

    (2) Asom Gana Parishad

    (3) AIADMK

    (4) DMK

30. Who among the following is the 2019 winner of the $100,000 Nine Dots Prize?

    (1) Annie Zaidi   (2) Chetan Bhagat

    (3) Shashi Tharoor   (4) Arundhati Roy

31. In June 2019, PepsiCo India proposed to invest $70 million to build a food manufacturing plant in:

    (1) Maharashtra   (2) Gujarat

    (3) Uttar Pradesh   (4) Madhya Pradesh

32. Who among the following won a silver medal in the equestrian event at the 2018 Asian Games?

    (1) Ashish Malik   (2) Fouaad Mirza

    (3) Rakesh Kumar   (4) Jitender Singh

33. Who is the director of the film 'PM Narendra Modi'?

    (1) Tigmanshu Dhulia

    (2) Omung Kumar

    (3) Rakeysh Omprakash Mehra

    (4) Hansal Mehta

34. On the occasion of 'World No Tobacco Day' on 31 May, which state banned e-cigarettes?

    (1) Assam   (2) Uttar Pradesh

    (3) Rajasthan   (4) Gujarat

35. The joint process of vapourisation and condensation is called:

    (1) Sublimation   (2) Chromatography

    (3) Distillation   (4) Crystallisation

36. Which of the following metals has an ore named Galena?

    (1) Nickel   (2) Copper

    (3) Iron   (4) Lead

37. The Bhupen Hazarika Setu, also called Dhola–Sadiya Bridge which connects Assam and —————.

    (1) Sikkim   (2) Meghalaya

    (3) West Bengal   (4) Arunachal Pradesh

38. Panchavati, a key part of the Valmiki Ramayana is located in which state of India?

    (1) Tamil Nadu   (2) Uttar Pradesh

    (3) Maharashtra   (4) Uttarakhand

39. In the new Union cabinet of 2019, the portfolio of Micro, Small and Medium Enterprises was allocated to:

    (1) Narendra Singh Tomar

    (2) Nitin Jairam Gadkari

    (3) Ramvilas Paswan

    (4) Sadananda Gowda

40. Rani-ki-Vav (the Queen's Stepwell), which is in the UNESCO World Heritage List, is located in:

    1. Madhya Pradesh   (2) Gujarat

    (3) Uttar Pradesh   (4) Rajasthan

41. During the passage of the Royal Titles Act 1876, the office of the British Prime Minister was occupied by:

    (1) William Ewart Gladstone

    (2) Arthur Balfour

    (3) John Russell

    (4) Benjamin Disraeli

42. What is the full form of GSTIN in relation to GST?

    (1) Goods and Services Tax Identification Note

    (2) Goods and Services Tax Identification Number

    (3) Goods and Services Tax Information Number

    (4) Goods and Services Taxation Income Number

43. Paan Singh Tomar, who was a seven-time national champion, was associated with which of the following sports?

    (1) Hockey   (2) Swimming

    (3) Shotput   (4) Steeplechase

44. In which year was Google incorporated as a private company?
    (1) 2000   (2) 2005
    (3) 2002   (4) 1998

45. In May 2019, the Government of India approved a new scheme which assures minimum monthly pension to all shopkeepers, retail traders and self employed persons after attaining the age of 60 years. How much is the pension amount?
    (1) Rs. 5,000   (2) Rs. 10,000
    (3) Rs. 3,000   (4) Rs. 7,000

46. Which of the following terms refers to the running down or payment of a loan in instalments?
    (1) Discounted cashflow
    (2) Credit creation
    (3) Backwardation
    (4) Amortisation

47. Which of the following are the highest-frequency electro magnetic waves?
    (1) Gamma Rays   (2) Radio Waves
    (3) Ultraviolet Rays   (4) Microwaves

48. Which of the following states separates Nepal from Bhutan?
    (1) Bihar   (2) Sikkim
    (3) Odisha   (4) Assam

49. A region of computer memory where frequently accessed data can be stored for rapid access is called:
    (1) Cookie
    (2) Plug-in
    (3) Token
    (4) Cache

50. Who among the following is the author of 'Kamayani', the epic poem that is considered as one of the greatest literary works in Hindi?
    (1) Mohan Rakesh
    (2) Jaishankar Prasad
    (3) Premchand
    (4) Ramdhari Singh Dinkar

QUANTITATIVE APTITUDE

51. If $\cos^2\theta - \sin^2\theta - 3\cos\theta + 2 = 0$, $0° < \theta < 90°$, then what is the value of $4\,\mathrm{cosec}\theta + \cot\theta$?
    (1) $3\sqrt{3}$ (2) 4
    (3) $4\sqrt{3}$ (4) 3

52. If $a^2 + 4b^2 + 49c^2 + 18 = 2(2b + 28c - a)$, then the value of $(3a + 2b + 7c)$ is:
    (1) 0   (2) 2
    (3) 1   (4) 3

53. Two trains of same length are running on parallel tracks in the same direction at 54 km/h and 42 km/h respectively. The faster train passes the other train in 63 seconds. What is the length (in metres) of each train?
    (1) 90   (2) 81
    (3) 105   (4) 210

54. Two concentric circles are of radii 15 cm and 9 cm. What is the length of the chord of the larger circle which is tangent to the smaller circle?
    (1) 24 cm   (2) 18 cm
    (3) 20 cm   (4) 25 cm

55. The simple interest on a certain sum for $3\frac{1}{2}$ years at 10% per annum is Rs. 2,940. What will be the compound interest on the same sum for $2\frac{1}{2}$ years at the same rate when interest is compounded yearly (nearest to a rupee)?
    (1) Rs. 2,272   (2) Rs. 2,227
    (3) Rs. 2,327   (4) Rs. 2,372

56. $\dfrac{(\sec\theta + \tan\theta)(1 - \sin\theta)}{\mathrm{cosec}\,\theta\,(1 + \cos\theta)(\mathrm{cosec}\,\theta - \cot\theta)}$ is equal to:
    (1) $\sin\theta$ (2) $\sec\theta$
    (3) $\cos\theta$ (4) $\mathrm{cosec}\,\theta$

57. After allowing a discount of 10% on the marked price of an article, it is sold for Rs. 360. Had the discount not been given, the profit would have been 25%. What is the cost price of the article?
    (1) Rs. 350   (2) Rs. 360
    (3) Rs. 320   (4) Rs. 325

58. The ratio of the incomes of A and B is 2 : 3 and that of their expenditures is 1 : 2. If 90% of B's expenditure is equal to the income of A, then what is the ratio of the savings of A and B?
    (1) 1 : 1   (2) 9 : 8
    (3) 8 : 7   (4) 3 : 2

59. A person sold an article at a loss of 8%. Had he sold it at a gain of 10.5%, he would have received Rs. 37 more. What is the cost price of the article?
    (1) Rs. 200   (2) Rs. 250
    (3) Rs. 240   (4) Rs. 210

60. The given Bar Graph presents the Target and Actual production of AC Machines (numbers in thousands) of a factory over five months.

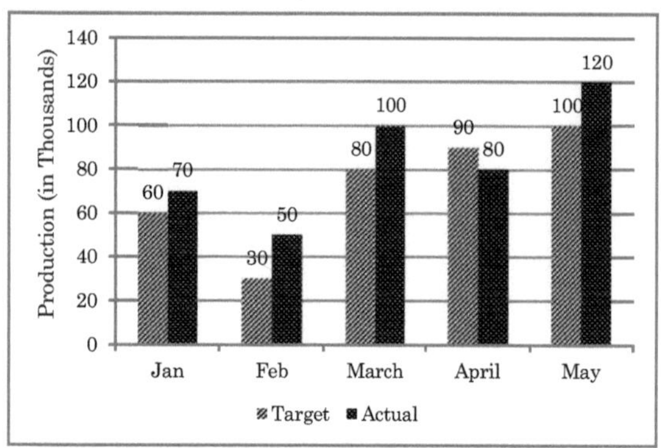

The ratio of the combined target production of AC Machines in January and April to that of the combined actual production of AC Machines in March and April was:

(1) 4 : 5

(2) 3 : 2

(3) 5 : 6

(4) 2 : 3

61. There are 90 students in a class, out of which 70% are from village A and others are from village B. The average score of students from village B in a test is 20% more than that from village A. If the average score of all the students is 53, then what is the average score of the students from village B?

(1) 54   (2) 60

(3) 64   (4) 50

62. A is 20% more than B, B is 25% more than C, C is 60% less than D and D is 20% more than E. Based on the above information, which of the following is true?

(1) D is 60% less than B.

(2) E is 28% more than A.

(3) A is 40% less than D.

(4) C is 24% less than A.

63. In $\triangle$ABC, D and E are the points on sides AB and AC, respectively, such that DE || BC. If DE : BC is 3 : 5, then (Area of $\triangle$ADE) : (Area of quadrilateral DECB) is:

(1) 9 : 16

(2) 3 : 4

(3) 9 : 25

(4) 5 : 8

64. In $\triangle$ABC, AB = 7 cm, BC = 24 cm and AC = 25 cm. If G is the centroid of the triangle, then what is the length (in cm) of BG?

(1) 10   (2) $8\dfrac{1}{3}$

(3) $8\dfrac{2}{3}$ (4) 9

65. If 30 persons take 10 days to complete a certain work working 8 hours a day, then 40 persons should work how many hours a day so that the work is completed in 6 days?

(1) 6   (2) 10

(3) 8   (4) 12

66. The volume of a right circular cone is 924 cm³. If its height is 18 cm, then the area of its base (in cm²) is:

(1) 154   (2) 132

(3) 176   (4) 198

67. The given Bar Graph presents the Target and Actual production of AC Machines (numbers in thousands) of a factory over five months.

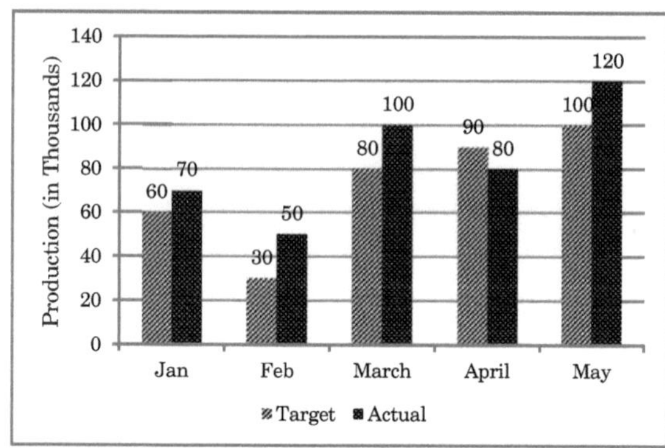

The total target production of AC Machines in February, April and May was what percentage less than the total actual production of AC Machines over all the five months (correct to one decimal place)?

(1) 46.2%   (2) 46.8%

(3) 47.1%   (4) 47.6%

68. If the eight-digit number 342x18y6 is divisible by 72, then what is the value of $\sqrt{9x + y}$, for the largest value of y?

(1) $2\sqrt{7}$ (2) $4\sqrt{7}$

(3) 8   (4) 6

69. if $\cot\theta = \dfrac{1}{\sqrt{3}}$, then the value of

$$\dfrac{2-\sin^2\theta}{1-\cos^2\theta} + \left(\cos ec^2\theta + \sec\theta\right) \text{ is:}$$

(1) 4   (2) 6

(3) 7   (4) 5

70. Two circles of radii 15 cm and 12 cm intersect each other, and the length of their common chord is 18 cm. What is the distance (in cm) between their centres?

(1) $18 + \sqrt{7}$ (2) $15 + \sqrt{7}$

(3) $12 + 2\sqrt{7}$ (4) $12 + 3\sqrt{7}$

71. The given Bar Graph presents the Target and Actual production of AC Machines (numbers in thousands) of a factory over five months.

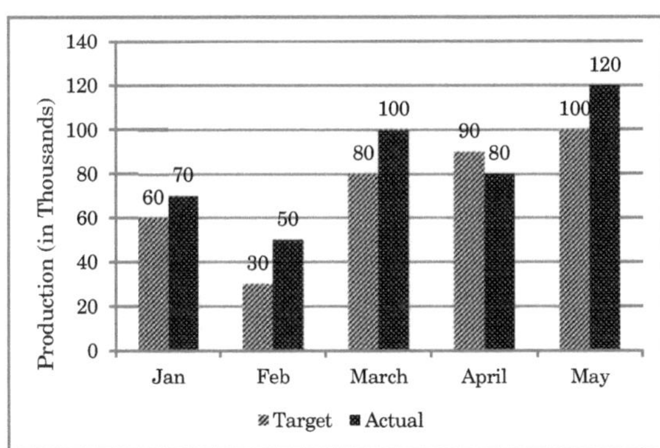

The actual production of AC Machines in April was what percentage more than the average target production of AC Machines over five months?

(1) $10\dfrac{1}{9}\%$ (2) $11\dfrac{1}{9}\%$

(3) 9%   (4) 10%

72. The value of $\dfrac{3 \div \left\{5 - 5 \div (6-7) \times 8 + 9\right\}}{4 + 4 \times 4 \div 4 \text{ of } 4}$ is :

(1) $\dfrac{1}{45}$ (2) $\dfrac{1}{18}$

(3) $\dfrac{1}{90}$ (4) $\dfrac{1}{3}$

73. If $a + b + c = 5$, $a^2 + b^2 + c^2 = 27$, and $a^3 + b^3 + c^3 = 125$, then the value of $4abc$ is:

(1) –20   (2) –15

(3) 15   (4) 20

74. If $3\sqrt{3}x^3 - 2\sqrt{2}y^3 = \left(\sqrt{3}x - \sqrt{2}y\right)$

$\left(Ax^2 - Bxy + Cy^2\right)$, then the value of $(A^2 - B^2 + C^2)$ is:

(1) 10   (2) 17

(3) 7   (4) 1

75. The given Bar Graph presents the Target and Actual production of AC Machines (numbers in thousands) of a factory over five months.

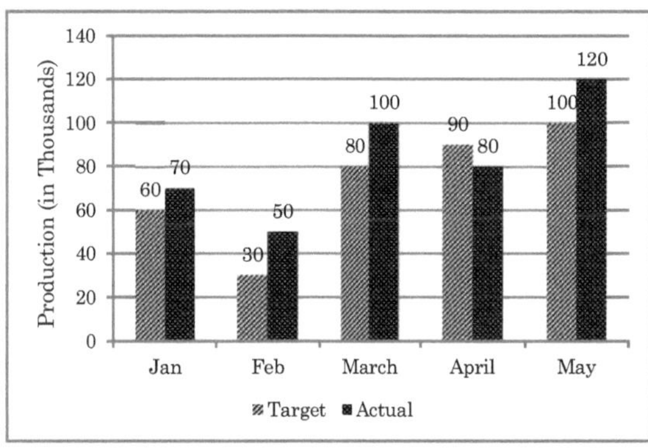

In which month the actual production of AC Machines was 25% more than the target production?

(1) February   (2) March

(3) January   (4) May

ENGLISH LANGUAGE

Direction for questions 76 to 80: In the following passage some words have been deleted. Fill in the blanks with the help of the alternatives given. Select the most appropriate option for each blank.

Big Ben is the UK's most iconic symbol. Since 2017, the Elizabeth Tower and the bell inside have been (76) ______ renovation. The structure is 160 years old and (77) ______ regular maintenance. (78) ______ many years, people had been painting the hands and numbers (79) ______ the clock black, but last Thursday, the workers (80) ______ the clock's original colour, Prussian Blue!

76. (1) undermining   (2) understanding

     (3) undergoing   (4) undertaking

77. (1) need

     (2) was needing

     (3) is needed

     (4) has needed

78. (1) About   (2) For

     (3) Before   (4) In

79. (1) to   (2) of
    (3) at   (4) for

80. (1) imparted   (2) invented
    (3) discovered   (4) concealed

81. Select the most appropriate option to substitute the underlined segment in the given sentence. If there is no need to substitute it, select No improvement.

    Oh, what a lovely necklace! You <u>need no buy</u> such an expensive gift.

    (1) hadn't needed to buy
    (2) needn't have bought
    (3) No improvement
    (4) didn't need to buying

82. Select the most appropriate antonym of the given word.

    EXOTIC

    (1) alien   (2) ordinary
    (3) colourful   (4) curious

83. In the sentence identify the segment which contains the grammatical error.

    I visited my friend to whom I had made an appointment.

    (1) I visited my friend
    (2) I had made
    (3) to whom
    (4) an appointment

84. Select the most appropriate option to substitute the underlined segment in the given sentence. If there is no need to substitute it, select No improvement.

    I hope never to have another <u>so experience as</u> I had in Puri during Cyclone Fani.

    (1) No improvement
    (2) such experience as
    (3) as experience as
    (4) same experience as

85. Select the most appropriate word to fill in the blank.

    People's will and determination can help them ______ most of the challenges of life.

    (1) overvalue
    (2) overdo
    (3) overview
    (4) overcome

86. Select the word which means the same as the group of words given.

    One who does not tire easily

    (1) infallible
    (2) indefatigable
    (3) inevitable
    (4) indelible

87. In the sentence identify the segment which contains the grammatical error.

    The Public Works Department has propose to construct an elevated corridor which will run parallel to the National highway.

    (1) to the National highway
    (2) The Public Works Department has propose
    (3) which will run parallel
    (4) to construct an elevated corridor

88. Select the word which means the same as the group of words given.

    A group of singers in a church

    (1) choir   (2) band
    (3) host   (4) troop

89. Select the wrongly spelt word.

    (1) berry
    (2) barren
    (3) berrel
    (4) barrier

90. Given below are four jumbled sentences. Out of the given options pick the one that gives their correct order.

    A. Most of them are in jail because of their circumstances.
    B. Not all prisoners are hardcore criminals.
    C. So, they deserve a chance to rehabilitate themselves.
    D. Therefore, learning a trade would help them reintegrate with society.

    (1) BDCA   (2) ABCD
    (3) DCBA   (4) BACD

91. Select the most appropriate meaning of the given idiom.

    to air dirty linen in public

    (1) to discuss private affairs in public
    (2) to hang out clothes in the open
    (3) to continue to complain
    (4) to stand up and fight

92. Select the most appropriate meaning of the given idiom.

    throw in the towel

    (1) face the situation

    (2) think of a solution

    (3) admit defeat

    (4) drop something

93. Given below are four jumbled sentences. Out of the given options pick the one that gives their correct order.

    A. He often asked questions which were strange and witty.

    B. Emperor Akbar was in the habit of putting riddles and puzzles to his courtiers.

    C. Once he asked a strange question that confused everyone.

    D. It took much wisdom to answer these questions.

    (1) BADC   (2) CABD

    (3) ABCD   (4) BACD

94. Select the most appropriate word to fill in the blank.

    In spite of being born in an ______ family, he chose to fight all odds and emerged as a notable statesman.

    (1) impeccable   (2) immaculate

    (3) intelligent   (4) impoverished

95. Select the most appropriate synonym of the given word.

    HIND

    (1) near   (2) rear

    (3) first   (4) front

96. Select the most appropriate synonym of the given word.

    INNUENDO

    (1) implication

    (2) evidence

    (3) verification

    (4) proof

97. Select the correct indirect form of the given sentence.

    Mrs. Gupta said to me, "Why are these boys standing in the sun?"

    (1) Mrs. Gupta told me why those boys are standing in the sun.

    (2) Mrs. Gupta asked me why those boys were standing in the sun.

    (3) Mrs. Gupta said to me that why are these boys standing in the sun.

    (4) Mrs. Gupta asked me why were these boys standing in the sun.

98. Select the wrongly spelt word.

    (1) assurence

    (2) assurable

    (3) assure

    (4) assuredly

99. Select the most appropriate antonym of the given word.

    SUCCINCT

    (1) pithy

    (2) terse

    (3) lengthy

    (4) curt

100. Select the correct passive form of the given sentence.

    The gardener has mowed the lawn.

    (1) The lawn was mowed by the gardener.

    (2) The lawn has been mowed by the gardener.

    (3) The lawn is mowed by the gardener.

    (4) The gardener has been mowed by the lawn.

ANSWERS

1. (2)	**2.** (2)	**3.** (2)	**4.** (3)	**5.** (4)	**6.** (2)	**7.** (4)	**8.** (1)	**9.** (2)	**10.** (4)
11. (1)	**12.** (3)	**13.** (2)	**14.** (1)	**15.** (3)	**16.** (3)	**17.** (4)	**18.** (1)	**19.** (4)	**20.** (4)
21. (3)	**22.** (1)	**23.** (4)	**24.** (4)	**25.** (1)	**26.** (4)	**27.** (4)	**28.** (2)	**29.** (4)	**30.** (1)
31. (3)	**32.** (2)	**33.** (2)	**34.** (3)	**35.** (3)	**36.** (4)	**37.** (4)	**38.** (3)	**39.** (2)	**40.** (2)
41. (4)	**42.** (2)	**43.** (4)	**44.** (4)	**45.** (3)	**46.** (4)	**47.** (1)	**48.** (2)	**49.** (4)	**50.** (2)
51. (1)	**52.** (2)	**53.** (3)	**54.** (1)	**55.** (1)	**56.** (3)	**57.** (3)	**58.** (3)	**59.** (1)	**60.** (3)
61. (2)	**62.** (3)	**63.** (1)	**64.** (2)	**65.** (2)	**66.** (1)	**67.** (4)	**68.** (4)	**69.** (4)	**70.** (4)
71. (2)	**72.** (3)	**73.** (1)	**74.** (3)	**75.** (2)	**76.** (3)	**77.** (4)	**78.** (2)	**79.** (2)	**80.** (3)
81. (2)	**82.** (2)	**83.** (3)	**84.** (2)	**85.** (4)	**86.** (2)	**87.** (2)	**88.** (1)	**89.** (3)	**90.** (4)
91. (1)	**92.** (3)	**93.** (1)	**94.** (4)	**95.** (2)	**96.** (1)	**97.** (2)	**98.** (1)	**99.** (3)	**100.** (2)

Reasoning

1. In the following question, select the related word pair from the given alternatives.

   Rabbit : Animal : : ? : ?
   - (1) Sun : Moon
   - (2) Pentagon : Figure
   - (3) Lion : Bird
   - (4) Animal : Cow

2. In the following question, select the related number pair from the given alternatives.

   63 : 36 : : ? : ?
   - (1) 94 : 49
   - (2) 35 : 54
   - (3) 47 : 72
   - (4) 73 : 39

3. In the following question, select the related letter/letters from the given alternatives.

   ACD : ZXW : : PMN : ?
   - (1) LMN
   - (2) MPN
   - (3) KOP
   - (4) KNM

4. In the following question, select the odd word from the given alternatives.
   - (1) Rhombus
   - (2) Cylinder
   - (3) Cone
   - (4) Sphere

5. In the following question, four number pairs are given. The number on left side of (–) is related to the number on the right side of (–) with some Logic/Rule/Relation. Three are similar on basis of same Logic/Rule/Relation. Select the odd one out from the given options.
   - (1) 14 – 18
   - (2) 42 – 46
   - (3) 22 – 28
   - (4) 24 – 28

6. In the following question, select the odd letter/letters from the given alternatives.
   - (1) UQMI
   - (2) SOKG
   - (3) MIEB
   - (4) PLHD

7. Arrange the given words in the sequence in which they occur in the dictionary.
   1. Exception
   2. Exceptional
   3. Exchanging
   4. Exchanged
   5. Excess
   - (1) 12543
   - (2) 21453
   - (3) 42531
   - (4) 32154

8. In the following question, select the missing number from the given series.

   11, 13, 17, 19, 23, ?
   - (1) 29
   - (2) 27
   - (3) 31
   - (4) 37

9. A series is given with one term missing. Select the correct alternative from the given ones that will complete the series.

   BEG, DGI, FIK, HKM, ?
   - (1) JNP
   - (2) NMO
   - (3) JMO
   - (4) KLO

10. Saurav, Mohit, Mukesh, Sumit and Bhim are arranged in descending order of their height from top to bottom. Saurav is at third place. Bhim is between Sumit and Saurav while Sumit is not at the top end. Who is at second place from the top?
    - (1) Mohit
    - (2) Mukesh
    - (3) Bhim
    - (4) Cannot be determined

11. From the given alternatives, select the word which CANNOT be formed using the letters of the given word.

    Contemptuous
    - (1) Con
    - (2) Tom
    - (3) Pretty
    - (4) Post

12. In a certain code language, "DRAPE" is written as "IWFUJ". How is "RIGID" written in that code language?
    - (1) CPLPK
    - (2) RVCVB
    - (3) WNLNI
    - (4) GTATK

13. In a certain code language, 'x' represents '+', '–' represents '×', '÷' represents '÷' and '+' represents '–'. Find out the answer to the following question.

    $4 \times 18 \div 5 - 10 + 8 = ?$
    - (1) 35
    - (2) 22
    - (3) 5
    - (4) 42

14. The following equation is incorrect. Which two signs should be interchanged to correct the equation?

    $12 - 16 \times 25 \div 80 + 10 = 7$
    - (1) ÷ and ×
    - (2) – and +
    - (3) × and –
    - (4) ÷ and –

15. If $6\alpha_1 = 70$, $2\alpha_3 = 50$ and $4\alpha_5 = 90$, then find the value of $1\alpha_4 = ?$
    - (1) 50
    - (2) 30
    - (3) 10
    - (4) 60

16. Which of the following terms follows the trend of the given list?

    BAAAAAAB, ABAAAAAB, AABAAAAB, AAABAAAB, AAAABAAB, _______________.

    (1) AAAAABAB   (2) AAAAAABB

    (3) BAAAAAAB   (4) ABAAAAAB

17. A shopper in a mart loads his trolley and walks 30 m through an alley which is going South, then he turns to his left and walks 10 m, then he turns North and walks another 10 m, then he turns West and walks 45 m and then he turns North and walks 20 m. Where is he now with reference to his starting position?

    (1) 35 m West   (2) 55 m West

    (3) 35 m East   (4) 55 m East

18. In the question two statements are given, followed by two conclusions, I and II. You have to consider the statements to be true even if it seems to be at variance from commonly known facts. You have to decide which of the given conclusions, if any, follows from the given statements.

    Statement I: All watches are ornaments

    Statement II: All clocks are watches

    Conclusion I: All ornaments are clocks

    Conclusion II: All clocks are ornaments

    (1) Only conclusion I follows

    (2) Only conclusion II follows

    (3) Both conclusions I and II follow

    (4) Neither conclusion I nor conclusion II follows

19. In the following figure, rectangle represents Physicians, circle represents Racers, triangle represents Writers and square represents Mothers. Which set of letters represents Mothers who are not Racers?

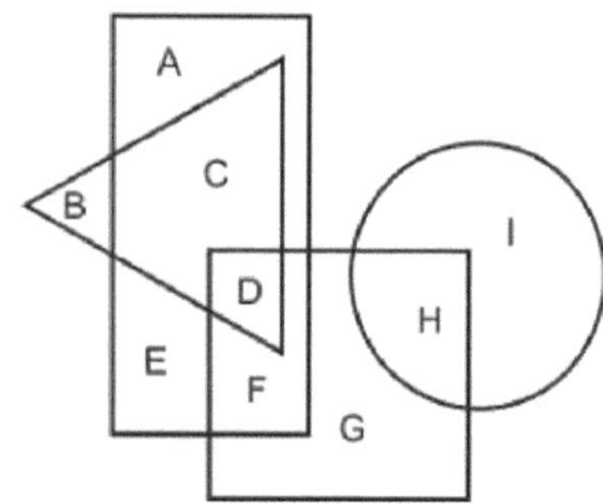

    (1) FGH   (2) ECA

    (3) DFG   (4) DGFI

20. A series is given with one term missing. Select the correct alternative from the given ones that will complete the series.

    GLN, HNQ, IPT, JRW, ?

    (1) KTZ   (2) KUY

    (3) LTY   (4) LUZ

21. In the following question, select the missing number from the given series.

    87, 62, 42, 27, 17, ?

    (1) 7   (2) 12

    (3) 8   (4) 10

22. In the following question, four groups of three numbers are given. In each group the second and third number are related to the first number by a Logic/Rule/Relation. Three are similar on basis of same Logic/Rule/Relation. Select the odd one out from the given alternatives.

    (1) (14, 29, 43)   (2) (11, 23, 34)

    (3) (15, 31, 46)   (4) (21, 42, 64)

23. If a mirror is placed on the line MN, then which of the answer figures is the right image of the given figure?

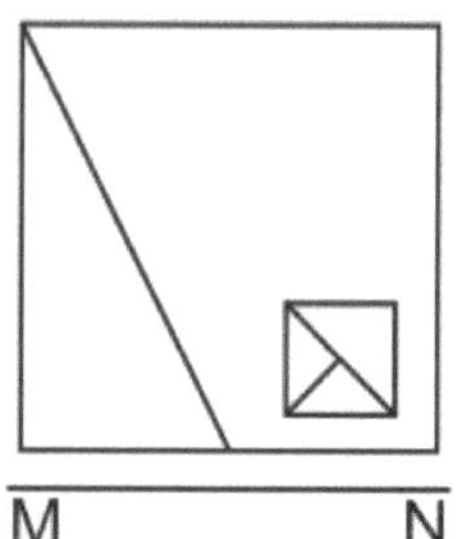

(1)
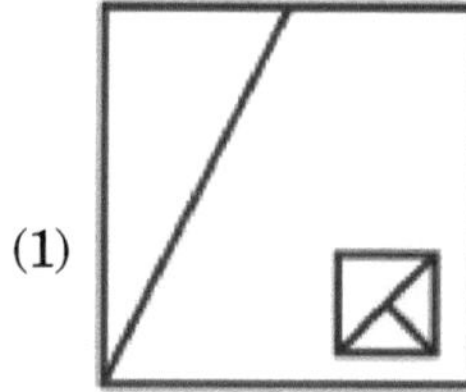

(2)
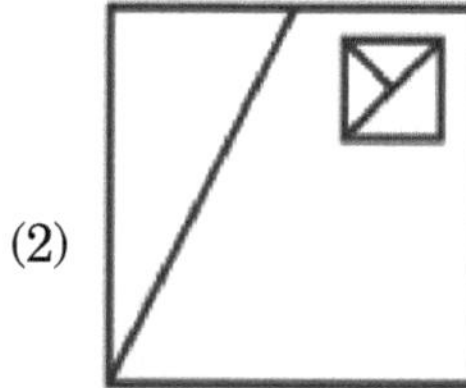

(3)
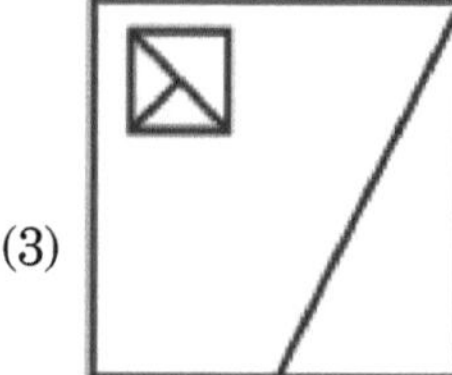

(4)
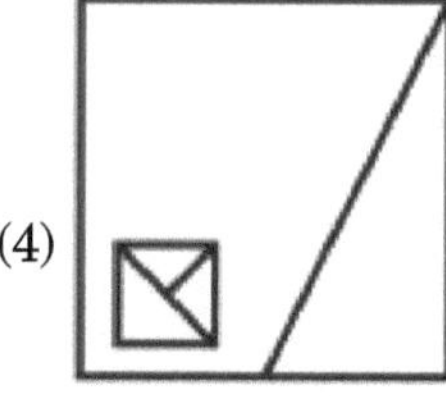

24. Which of the following cube in the answer figure cannot be maded based on the unfolded cube in the question figure?

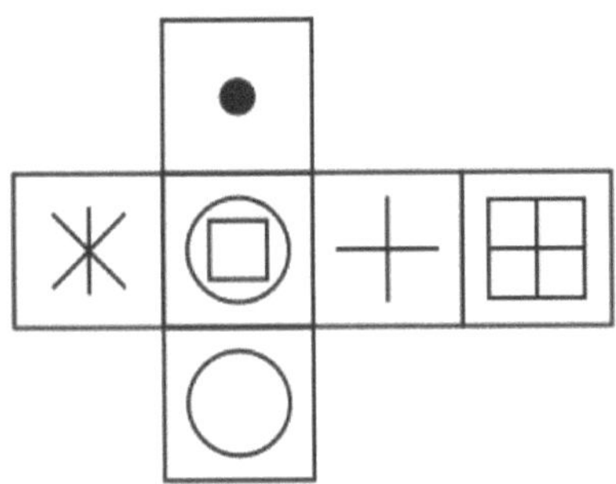

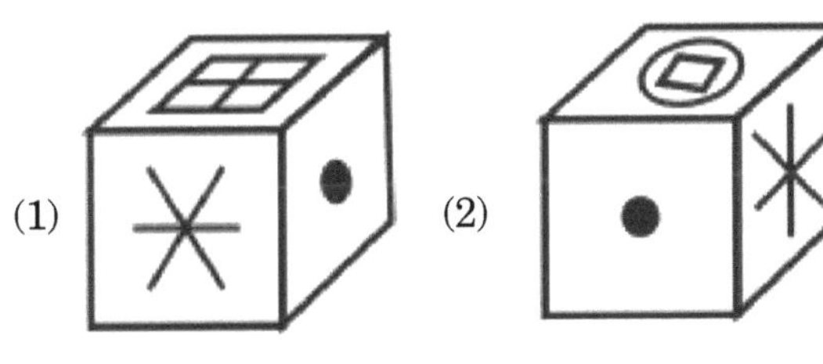

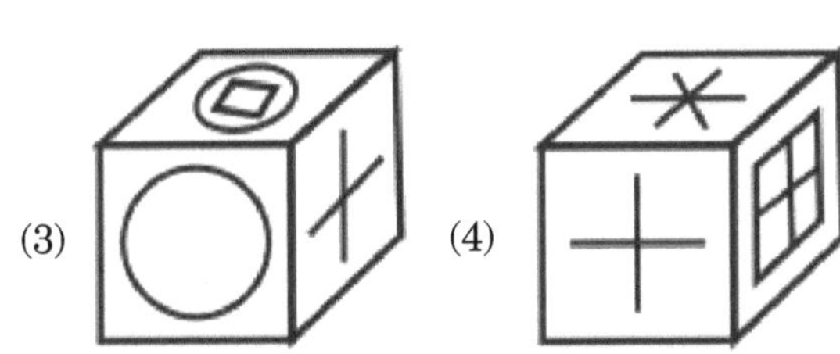

(1)   (2)

(3)   (4)

25. A word is represented by only one set of numbers as given in any one of the alternatives. The sets of numbers given in the alternatives are represented by two classes of alphabets as shown in the given two matrices. The columns and rows of Matrix-I are numbered from 0 to 4 and that of Matrix-II are numbered from 5 to 9. A letter from these matrices can be represented first by its row and next by its column, for example 'C' can be represented by 10, 34 etc and 'Q' can be represented by 85, 96 etc. Similarly, you have to identify the set for the word 'GOES'.

Matrix-I				
	0	1	2	3	4
0	A	A	J	M	G
1	C	J	H	G	J
2	H	B	L	M	D
3	I	J	L	I	C
4	E	E	D	M	L

Matrix-II				
	5	6	7	8	9
5	W	V	P	V	P
6	R	S	P	Z	U
7	R	Z	Z	O	T
8	Q	T	N	S	P
9	Y	Q	R	V	X

(1) 11, 75, 12, 77
(2) 32, 76, 44, 95
(3) 13, 78, 41, 66
(4) 33, 88, 21, 89

General Awareness

26. The agricultural price support program is an example of __________.
    (1) a price ceiling   (2) a price floor
    (3) equilibrium pricing (4) No option is correct.

27. Which was the first modern industry to develop in India?
    (1) Iron and Steel Industry
    (2) Cement Industry
    (3) Cottage Industry
    (4) Engineering Industry

28. Which of the following lake lies on the Equator in Africa continent?
    (1) Tanganyika   (2) Victoria
    (3) Nyasa lake   (4) Lake Kariba

29. Jog Falls is situated on which river?
    (1) Sharavati   (2) Cauvery
    (3) Narmada   (4) Chambal

30. Faizi lived in the court of _________.
    (1) Humayun
    (2) Dara Shikoh
    (3) Bahadur Shah Zafar
    (4) Akbar

31. Where did the leader of the Individual Satyagraha movement, Acharya Vinoba Bhave started this movement?
    (1) Nashik   (2) Poona
    (3) Pavnar   (4) Nagpur

32. The well-known dialogue between Nachiketa and Yama is mentioned in which Upanishada?
    (1) Chhandogyopanishad
    (2) Mundkopanishad
    (3) Kathopanishad
    (4) Kenopanishad

33. Which country, in January 2018 broke India's monopoly in providing Internet access to Nepal by becoming country's second Internet service provider?
    (1) South Korea   (2) China
    (3) Japan   (4) Indonesia

34. Which among the following is NOT a recipient of Sangeet Natak Akamemi's fellowships (Akademi Ratna)-2018?
    (1) Gajendra Chauhan
    (2) Ram Gopal Bajaj
    (3) Sunil Kothari
    (4) Arvind Parikh

35. When was the "Boxer Rebellion" happened in China?
    (1) 1895   (2) 1900
    (3) 1905   (4) 1909

36. What is formed when helium atom loses one electron?
    (1) Proton
    (2) Positive helium ion
    (3) Negative helium ion
    (4) Alpha particle

37. Apart from proposing atomic thoery, what did John Dalton researched on?
    (1) Plants
    (2) Colour blindness
    (3) Penicillin
    (4) Plastic

38. Which among the following is/are the unitary feature(s) of Indian Constitution?
    I. Single Constitution for State and Centre
    II. Single Citizenship
    III. Integrated Judiciary
    (1) Only I
    (2) Only II
    (3) Both I and II
    (4) All I, II and III

39. Article 360 of Indian Constitution, empowers whom to proclaim a Financial Emergency?
    (1) The Finance Minister of India
    (2) The Governor of Reserve Bank of India
    (3) The President of India
    (4) Defence Minister of India

40. Match the following:

Organism	**Feature of fission**
I. Amoeba	1. Many daughter cells by multiple fission
II. Leishmania	2. Fission takes place in definite orientation
III. Plasmodium	3. Fission can take place in any plane

    (1) I – 2, II – 3, III – 1
    (2) I – 1, II – 3, III – 2
    (3) I – 2, II – 1, III – 3
    (4) I – 3, II – 2, III – 1

41. What is the basis of classifying various plant tissues as meristematic tissue and permanent tissue?
    (1) Size
    (2) Dividing capacity
    (3) Location
    (4) No option is correct.

42. In December 2017, who launched project 'DARPAN' (Digital Advancement of Rural Post Office for a New India)?
    (1) Jayant Sinha
    (2) Manoj Sinha
    (3) Ravi Shankar Prasad
    (4) Prakash Javadekar

43. Botanical Survey of India has discovered a new species of parasitic flowering plant Gleadovia Konyakianorum named in the honour of which community?
    (1) Toda
    (2) Caddo
    (3) Nagas
    (4) Tobu

44. In October 2017, State Bank of India announced to set up Country's largest innovation centre in ______.
    (1) New Delhi
    (2) Bangalore
    (3) Navi Mumbai
    (4) Hyderabad

45. The Union Home Ministry will set up an Indian Cyber Crime Coordination Centre (14C), an apex coordination centre at which place to deal with cybercrimes?
    (1) Hyderabad
    (2) Pune
    (3) Bengaluru
    (4) New Delhi

46. A body of mass 6 kg accelerates from 6 m/s to 18 m/s in 3 seconds due to the application of a force on it. Calculate the magnitude of this force (in N).
    (1) 48
    (2) 60
    (3) 24
    (4) 96

47. We obtain average ______ by dividing the total energy consumed by the total time taken.
    (1) force
    (2) power
    (3) torque
    (4) momentum

48. Water covers ______% of the Earth's surface.
    (1) 95
    (2) 75
    (3) 55
    (4) 35

49. Which of the statements given below are correct?
    A. In 2017, Lewis Hamilton raced in Formula One for Mercedes.
    B. In 2018 IPL auctions, Mumbai Indians retained Hardik Pandya.
    C. Chen Meng won the Table Tennis 2017 ITTF World Tour Grand Finals Women's Singles.
    (1) Only A
    (2) Only B
    (3) Both B and C
    (4) A, B and C

50. ______ among the following is not an operating system.
    (1) Mozilla Firefox
    (2) Microsoft Windows
    (3) Linux
    (4) Apple MacOS

Quantitative Aptitude

51. Find the remainder in the expression
    $$\frac{557 \times 653 \times 672}{9}$$
    (1) 0
    (2) 3
    (3) 5
    (4) 6

52. Calculate the value of x, if $\sqrt{1 - \left(\dfrac{x}{529}\right)} = \left(\dfrac{16}{23}\right)$
    (1) 283
    (2) 276
    (3) 273
    (4) 374

53. How many solutions does a pair of linear equations will have, if the equations are $4x + 5y - 6 = 0$ and $16x + 20y + 20 = 0$?
(1) 0 (2) 1
(3) 2 (4) Infinite

54. Determine the value of m for which $4x + \dfrac{\sqrt{x}}{6} + \dfrac{m^2}{4}$ is a perfect square.
(1) $\dfrac{1}{24}$ (2) $\dfrac{1}{12}$
(3) 12 (4) 24

55. Consider the circle as shown in the figure and choose the CORRECT option for this case.

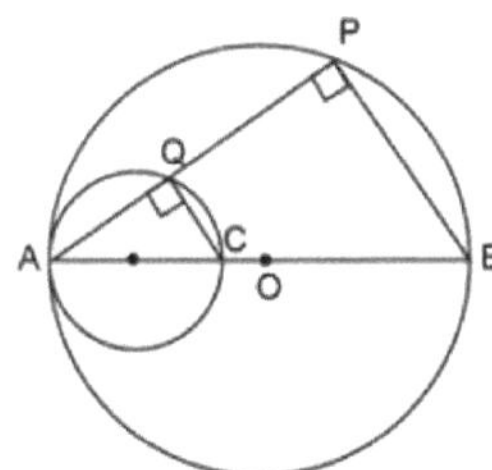

(1) QC ∥ PB
(2) QC is never parallel to PB
(3) $QC = \dfrac{1}{2}PB$
(4) $QC \parallel PB,\ QC = \dfrac{1}{2}PB$

56. The angle subtended by the chord of length 10 cm is 120° at the centre. Calculate the distance of the chord (in cm) from the centre.
(1) $\dfrac{5}{\sqrt{3}}$ (2) $\dfrac{6}{\sqrt{3}}$
(3) $\dfrac{4}{\sqrt{3}}$ (4) $\dfrac{5}{2\sqrt{3}}$

57. If $P : Q = 9 : 7$, then what is the value of $(P - Q) : (P + Q)$?
(1) $1 : 2$
(2) $1 : 8$
(3) $1 : 4$
(4) $2 : 13$

58. How much quantity (in kg) of wheat costing Rs 84 per kg must be mixed with 81 kg of wheat costing Rs 60 per kg so that on selling the mixture at Rs 75.9 per kg, there is a gain of 15%?
(1) 27 (2) 20.5
(3) 22.75 (4) 24

59. The average height of A, B and C is 148 cm. If the average height of A and B is 136 cm and that of B and C is 125 cm, then what is the height (in cm) of B?
(1) 56 (2) 78
(3) 112 (4) 130

60. Some part of Rs 17500 was lent at the rate of 24% per annum simple interest and the remaining part at the rate of 10% per annum simple interest. The total interest received after 5 years is Rs 13300. What is the ratio of money lent at the rate of 24% and 10%?
(1) $12 : 13$ (2) $3 : 4$
(3) $3 : 2$ (4) $13 : 22$

61. If 60% of total articles are sold at a loss of 50% and remaining articles are sold at a profit of 50%, then what will be the overall loss percentage?
(1) 20 (2) 15
(3) 25 (4) 10

62. If three successive discounts of 20%, 30% and 40% are given, then what will be the net discount (in percentage)?
(1) 80 (2) 87.6
(3) 90 (4) 66.4

63. Which of the following statement(s) is/are **TRUE**?
I. $\sqrt{676} + \sqrt{6.76} + \sqrt{0.0676} = 27.76$
II. $\sqrt{339 + \sqrt{36} + \sqrt{49} + \sqrt{81}} = 19$
(1) Only I
(2) Only II
(3) Neither I nor II
(4) Both I and II

64. R is 80% more efficient than S. If S alone can make a book in 90 days, then R alone can make the book in how many days?
(1) 65 (2) 60
(3) 50 (4) 70

65. Diameter of a car wheel is 21 cm. A car driver moving at the speed of 66 km/hr takes 36 seconds to reach a destination. How many revolutions will the wheel make during the journey?
(1) 1800
(2) 1500
(3) 1200
(4) 1000

66. What is the value of 88% of 1125 + 20% of 425?
(1) 1025
(2) 1125.2
(3) 1075
(4) 1055

Direction for questions 67 to 70: The HR department of a company prepared a report. The pie chart from this report shows number of employees in all the departments that the company has. Study the diagram and answer the following questions.

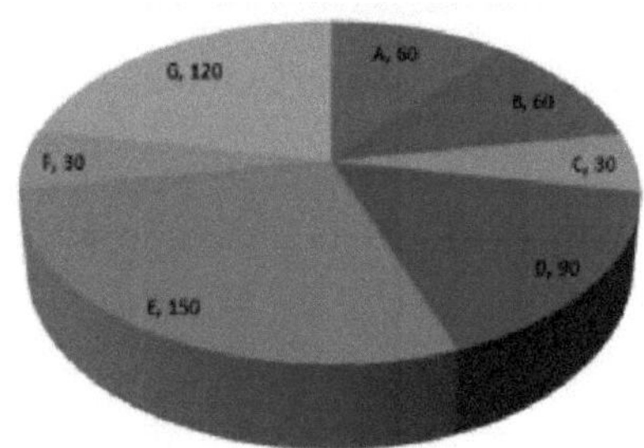

67. The most number of employees belong to which department?
    (1) E
    (2) F
    (3) G
    (4) A

68. What is the total number of employees of the company?
    (1) 400
    (2) 600
    (3) 480
    (4) 540

69. The measure of the central angle of the sector representing department B is ________ degrees.
    (1) 30
    (2) 40
    (3) 50
    (4) 60

70. If the average monthly salary of the employees of this company is Rs 20,000 then what is the total of the salaries (in Rs lakhs) paid to all the employees of this company?
    (1) 112
    (2) 120
    (3) 124
    (4) 108

71. The area of an equilateral triangle is $49\sqrt{3}$ cm². Find its side (in cm).
    (1) 7
    (2) 14
    (3) 28
    (4) 42

72. What is the measure of an exterior angle of a regular polygon of 6 sides?
    (1) 45°
    (2) 60°
    (3) 40°
    (4) 36°

73. The total surface area of a hemisphere is 1039.5 cm². Find its diameter (in cm).
    (1) 21
    (2) 10.5
    (3) 42
    (4) 31.5

74. ΔDEF is right angled at E. If $m\angle F = 30°$, then find the value of $\left(\cos D - \dfrac{1}{\sqrt{2}} \right)$.
    (1) $-\dfrac{1}{2}$
    (2) $\dfrac{(\sqrt{6}-1)}{\sqrt{3}}$
    (3) $\dfrac{(\sqrt{2}-2)}{2\sqrt{2}}$
    (4) $\sqrt{3}-2$

75. In ΔPQR measure of angle Q is 90o. If $\tan P = \dfrac{24}{7}$, and PQ = 14 cm, then what is the length (in cm) of side QR?
    (1) 50
    (2) 20
    (3) 26
    (4) 48

English Language

76. In the following question, some part of the sentence may have errors. Find out which part of the sentence has an error and select the appropriate option. If a sentence is free from error, select 'No Error'.

    I look up (1)/ after the blast (2)/ of light enveloped the park. (3)/ No error (4)
    (1) 1
    (2) 2
    (3) 3
    (4) 4

77. In the following question, some part of the sentence may have errors. Find out which part of the sentence has an error and select the appropriate option. If a sentence is free from error, select 'No Error'.

    According to the Copernican principle, the Earth does not (1)/ occupy a unique position in the Universe while (2)/ implies life on other planets can be a possibility. (3)/ No error (4)
    (1) 1
    (2) 2
    (3) 3
    (4) 4

78. In the following question, the sentence given with blank to be filled in with an appropriate word. Select the correct alternative out of the four and indicate it by selecting the appropriate option.

    The ______ age movies are quite popular.
    (1) come of
    (2) long
    (3) coming of
    (4) over

79. In the following question, the sentence given with blank to be filled in with an appropriate word. Select the correct alternative out of the four and indicate it by selecting the appropriate option.

    The love which is based on physical beauty is not ________.
    (1) imminent
    (2) deponent
    (3) remanent
    (4) permanent

Directions for questions 80 to 83: In the following questions, out of the given four alternatives, select the one which best expresses the meaning of the given word.

80. **Mollify**
    (1) Pacify
    (2) Agitate
    (3) Provoke
    (4) Worry

81. **Importune**
    (1) Appeal
    (2) Important
    (3) Imply
    (4) Purchase

82. **Rotund**
    (1) Fat   (2) Broad
    (3) Dumpy   (4) Slim

83. **Flamboyant**
    (1) Glamorous   (2) Modest
    (3) Colorful   (4) Sporty

84. Rearrange the parts of the sentence in correct order.

    Bringing equity

    P : for the rural population should be

    Q : a priority for the National Health Mission

    R : in access to the doctors and medicines

    (1) QRP   (2) RQP
    (3) PRQ   (4) RPQ

85. A sentence has been given in Active/Passive Voice. Out of the four given alternatives, select the one which best expresses the same sentence in Passive/Active Voice.

    The cat caught a rat.

    (1) A rat has been caught by the cat.

    (2) A rat was caught by the cat.

    (3) A rat is caught by the cat.

    (4) A rat had been caught by the cat.

86. A sentence has been given in Direct/Indirect Speech. Out of the four given alternatives, select the one which best expresses the same sentence in Indirect/Direct Speech.

    The wolf cried out to the hound, "A thought has just come into my head."

    (1) The wolf cried out that a thought had just came into his head.

    (2) The wolf cried out to the hound that a thought had just come into his head.

    (3) The wolf cried out about a thought into his head to the hound.

    (4) The wolf told hound about a thought into his head.

87. In the following question, a word has been written in four different ways out of which only one is correctly spelt. Select the correctly spelt word.

    (1) Caetegory   (2) Category
    (3) Cateigory   (4) Categoury

Direction for questions 88 to 92: In the following passage, some of the words have been left out. Read the passage carefully and select the correct answer for the given blank out of the four alternatives.

Let us examine the facts in the case more __________. First of all, language is no more __________ a medium; it is like air to the creatures of the land or water to fishes. If it is perfectly clear and pure, we do not notice it any more than we notice pure air when the sun is shining __________ a clear sky, or the taste of pure cool water when we drink a glass __________ a hot day. Unless the sun is shining, there is no brightness; unless the water is cool, there is __________ refreshment.

88. in the case more __________. First of all
    (1) closely   (2) close
    (3) closed   (4) closeness

89. no more __________ a medium;
    (1) then   (2) so
    (3) such   (4) than

90. sun is shining __________ a clear sky,
    (1) inside   (2) in
    (3) into   (4) inner

91. when we drink a glass __________ a hot day.
    (1) on   (2) onto
    (3) of   (4) for

92. there is __________ refreshment.
    (1) not   (2) no
    (3) none   (4) never

Directions for questions 93 and 94: In the following question, out of the four alternatives, select the alternative which best expresses the meaning of the idiom/phrase.

93. Don't put all your eggs in one basket
    (1) It is wise to have many baskets before you start collecting eggs.

    (2) The strength of the safe has to be in proportion to the value of goods it has to protect.

    (3) Have a fool proof plan before venturing on a risky mission.

    (4) Don't risk everything on the success of one venture.

94. Let your hair down
    (1) Behave uninhibitedly.
    (2) Accept your deeds.
    (3) Remove the mask.
    (4) Feel fresh and rejuvenated.

Direction for questions 95 and 96: In the following question, out of the four alternatives, select the alternative which is the best substitute of the words/sentence.

95. Senseless talk or writing
    (1) Astute
    (2) Balderdash
    (3) Sagacious
    (4) Prudent

96. Made or done in the traditional or original way
    (1) Authentic
    (2) Effigy
    (3) Archetype
    (4) Forge

Directions for questions 97 and 98: In the following question, out of the four alternatives, select the alternative which will improve the bracketed part of the sentence. In case no improvement is needed, select "no improvement".

97. At one time, the lock industry here flourished and locks (was exported) on a major scale.

    (1) is exported

    (2) were export

    (3) were exported

    (4) no improvement

98. The bliss of (oversleeping) cuddled up under a warm and cosy blanket is just other-worldly.

    (1) oversleep   (2) oversleeps

    (3) overslept   (4) no improvement

Directions for questions 99 and 100: The question below consists of a set of labelled sentences. Out of the four options given, select the most logical order of the sentences to form a coherent paragraph.

99. Students who

    A : intricacies of learning it

    B : subject know the

    C : study logic as a

    (1) CAB   (2) BCA

    (3) BAC   (4) CBA

100. In the following question, four words are given out of which one word is correctly spelt. Select the correctly spelt word.

    (1) scintillaters   (2) scintilators

    (3) scintillators   (4) scintilaters

ANSWER KEY

1. (2)	**2.** (1)	**3.** (4)	**4.** (1)	**5.** (3)	**6.** (3)	**7.** (1)	**8.** (1)	**9.** (3)	**10.** (4)
11. (3)	**12.** (3)	**13.** (3)	**14.** (2)	**15.** (1)	**16.** (1)	**17.** (1)	**18.** (2)	**19.** (3)	**20.** (1)
21. (2)	**22.** (4)	**23.** (2)	**24.** (4)	**25.** (3)	**26.** (2)	**27.** (1)	**28.** (2)	**29.** (1)	**30.** (4)
31. (3)	**32.** (3)	**33.** (2)	**34.** (1)	**35.** (2)	**36.** (2)	**37.** (2)	**38.** (4)	**39.** (3)	**40.** (4)
41. (2)	**42.** (2)	**43.** (3)	**44.** (3)	**45.** (4)	**46.** (3)	**47.** (2)	**48.** (2)	**49.** (4)	**50.** (1)
51. (4)	**52.** (3)	**53.** (1)	**54.** (2)	**55.** (1)	**56.** (1)	**57.** (2)	**58.** (1)	**59.** (2)	**60.** (4)
61. (4)	**62.** (4)	**63.** (2)	**64.** (3)	**65.** (4)	**66.** (3)	**67.** (1)	**68.** (4)	**69.** (2)	**70.** (4)
71. (2)	**72.** (2)	**73.** (1)	**74.** (3)	**75.** (4)	**76.** (1)	**77.** (2)	**78.** (3)	**79.** (4)	**80.** (1)
81. (1)	**82.** (4)	**83.** (2)	**84.** (4)	**85.** (2)	**86.** (2)	**87.** (2)	**88.** (1)	**89.** (4)	**90.** (2)
91. (1)	**92.** (2)	**93.** (4)	**94.** (1)	**95.** (2)	**96.** (1)	**97.** (3)	**98.** (4)	**99.** (4)	**100.** (3)

EXPLANATIONS

51. Remainder $\left(\dfrac{557 \times 653 \times 672}{9}\right)$

$= \text{remainder} \left(\dfrac{8 \times 5 \times 6}{9}\right) = 6.$

52. To solve this quesiton we can either square both sides of the given equation or can check the options for numerators of both sides.

On RHS, we have 16 so we need 256 in the numerator which we can get at x = 273.

53. Given equations are:

$4x + 5y = 6$ and $16x + 20y = -20$

Now we can see that,

$$\frac{4}{16} = \frac{5}{20} \neq \frac{6}{-20}$$

Hence, there will be no solution for the given pair of lines.

54. Given that: $4x + \dfrac{\sqrt{x}}{6} + \dfrac{m^2}{4}$

$$= \left(2\sqrt{x}\right)^2 + \left(\dfrac{m}{2}\right)^2 + 2 \times 2\sqrt{x} \times \dfrac{m}{2}$$

Now, $2 \times 2\sqrt{x} \times \dfrac{m}{2} = \dfrac{\sqrt{x}}{6}$

Hence, m $= \dfrac{1}{12}$

55. $\angle AQC = \angle APB = 90°$ (Corresponding angles) and AP is a transverse line. Hence, QC will be parallel to PB.

However, C is not the center of the diameter hence, the QC will not be half of PB.

56. Half of the angle subtended by the chord will be 60 degree and half the length of the chord will be 5 cm.

Now, $\tan 60 = \dfrac{5}{x}$

$\Rightarrow$ x (or the required distance) $= \dfrac{5}{\sqrt{3}}$ cm.

57. $(P - Q) : (P + Q) = (9 - 7) : (9 + 7)$

$= 2 : 16 = 1 : 8.$

58. CP (of the mixture) x 1.15 = 75.9

$\Rightarrow$ CP = Rs. 66

Now, $84x + 60 \times 81 = 66 \times (x + 81)$

Solving this, we get x = 27.

59. $A + B + C = 148 \times 3$ ....(i)

$A + B = 136 \times 2$ ....(ii)

$B + C = 125 \times 2$ ....(iii)

Now, (ii) + (iii) − (i) will give:

B = 78 cm.

60. Combined interest for 1 year

$= \dfrac{13300}{5} =$ Rs. 2660

$\therefore$ Combined interest rate

$= \dfrac{2660}{17500} \times 100 = 15.2\%$

Applying alligation we get the required ratio as:

$(15.2 - 10) : (24 - 15.2) = 13 : 22.$

61. Let the total articles be 5.

$\Rightarrow$ Required percent $= \dfrac{-50 \times 3 + 50 \times 2}{5} = -10\%$

Hence, there would be a loss of 10%.

62. Net value after successive discounts

$= 0.8 \times 0.7 \times 0.6$

$= 0.336$

Hence, net discount $= 100 - 100 \times 0.336 = 66.4\%$

63. Solving both equations I and II we get that only equation II is correct.

64. Let the work done by S in one day be 5 units such that the work done by R in one day is 9 units.

Hence, required time $= \dfrac{90 \times 5}{9} = 50$ days.

15. Distance covered by the car wheel

$= 66 \times \dfrac{5}{18} \times 36 = 660$ m

$\Rightarrow 2 \times \dfrac{22}{7} \times \dfrac{21}{2} \times n = 660 \times 100$

Hence, n (or the number of revolutions) = 1000.

66. $0.88 \times 1125 + 0.2 \times 425 = 1075.$

67. Department E has the most number of employees i.e. 150.

68. Total number of employees in the company

$= A + B + C + D + E + F + G$

$= 60 + 60 + 30 + 90 + 150 + 30 + 120$

$= 540.$

69. Required angle for department B

$= \dfrac{60}{540} \times 360 = 40°.$

70. Required salary = 20000 × 540 = 108 lakhs.

71. Given that:

$$\dfrac{\sqrt{3}}{4} x^2 = 49\sqrt{3}$$

Hence, x or the side of the equilateral triangle = 14 cm.

72. Measure of the exterior angle of the regular polygon with 6 sides = $\dfrac{360}{6} = 60°$.

73. Total surface area of the hemisphere = $3\pi r^2$

$\Rightarrow 3\pi r^2 = 1039.5$

Hence, r = 10.5 cm and diameter = 21 cm.

74. Given that: $\angle F = 30°$ so $\angle D = 60°$

Hence, $\cos D - \dfrac{1}{\sqrt{2}} = \dfrac{\sqrt{2}-2}{2\sqrt{2}}$

75. Given that $\tan P = \dfrac{24}{7} = \dfrac{QR}{PQ}$ and PQ = 14 cm.

Hence, QR = 48 cm.

PRACTICE SET – 1

GENERAL INTELLIGENCE

Directions : In the following question select the related letter/word from the given alternatives.

1. Baboon : Infant :: Beaver : ?

  (*a*) Kitten   (*b*) Kid

  (*c*) Joey   (*d*) Fawn

Directions: In question nos. **2** to **6**, a series is given, with one term missing. Choose the correct alternative from the given ones that will complete the series.

2. BGL, FKP, JOT, ___?___ .

  (*a*) MSY   (*b*) NSX

  (*c*) NRX   (*d*) MRY

3. BX, EU, HR, KO, ___?___ , QI, ___?___ .

  (*a*) NL and TF   (*b*) ML and TE

  (*c*) NK and TF   (*d*) MK and TE

4. 72, 46, 521, 612, 343, ___?___ .

  (*a*) 678   (*b*) 545

  (*c*) 215   (*d*) 154

5. W 5 K, T 12 M, Q 20 O, N 29 Q, ___?___ .

  (*a*) L 45 R   (*b*) K 39 S

  (*c*) K 37 S   (*d*) K 43 R

6. 17, 150, ___?___ , 1500, 1667, 15000, 16667.

  (*a*) 1607   (*b*) 1067

  (*c*) 167   (*d*) 177

Directions: In question nos. **7** and **8**, find the odd word/number from the given alternatives.

7. (*a*) French Beans

  (*b*) Gourd

  (*c*) Pumpkin

  (*d*) Jackfruit

8. (*a*) Solar energy   (*b*) Biomass

  (*c*) Fossil fuel   (*d*) Radiant energy

9. What is the least number that must be added to 2851 to make it a perfect square?

  (*a*) 55   (*b*) 65

  (*c*) 45   (*d*) 70

10. Karan is taller than Mukesh and is shorter than Anil. Rakesh is shorter than Sunil, who in turn is shorter than Anil. Who is the tallest?

  (*a*) Anil   (*b*) Sunil

  (*c*) Mukesh   (*d*) Karan

Directions : In the following question from the given alternatives select the word which cannot be formed using the letters of the given word.

11. ACCOUTREMENTS

  (*a*) ACCOUNTS   (*b*) TOURNAMENT

  (*c*) MOURNS   (*d*) TENETS

12. In the following question, the number of letters skipped in between adjacent letters in the series is consecutive odd numbers. Which of the following series observes this rule?

  (*a*) B D G J P   (*b*) C E I O V

  (*c*) D F J P X   (*d*) E G K P X

13. A man and his wife have four sons and three daughters. All four sons are married and have five children each. Find the total number of members in the family.

  (*a*) 33   (*b*) 25

  (*c*) 28   (*d*) 29

14. If 42 + 74 = 66 and 35 + 17 = 64, what is 57 + 21?

  (*a*) 68   (*b*) 36

  (*c*) 72   (*d*) 44

Directions: In question nos. **15** to **17**, select the missing number from the given responses.

15.

6	15	35
10	21	55
12	18	?

  (*a*) 45   (*b*) 28

  (*c*) 24   (*d*) 36

16. 7, 15, 30, 59, 116, ___?___

  (*a*) 197   (*b*) 189

  (*c*) 223   (*d*) 229

17.

13		21		54	
5	12	7	28	?	67

  (*a*) 13   (*b*) 9

  (*c*) 11   (*d*) 15

18. A and B started walking from a point 'X'. A walked 4 km towards North, then turned left walked for 4 km. B walked $4\sqrt{2}$ km towards South-west. In which direction is A with respect to B?

  (*a*) North-west   (*b*) North-east

  (*c*) South   (*d*) North

Directions : In the following question one/two statements are given followed by two/three conclusions I, II and III. You have to consider the statements to be true even if they seem to be at variance with commonly known facts. You are to decide which of the given conclusions can definitely be drawn from the given statements.

19. Statement:

People succeed when they work hard.

Conclusions:

I. Only hard work leads to success.

II. Honesty does not lead to success.

(a) Only conclusion I follows

(b) Only conclusion II follows

(c) Both conclusions I and II follow

(d) Neither conclusion I nor II follows

Directions : In the following question which answer figure will complete the question figure?

20. Question figure:

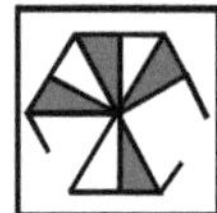

Answer figures:

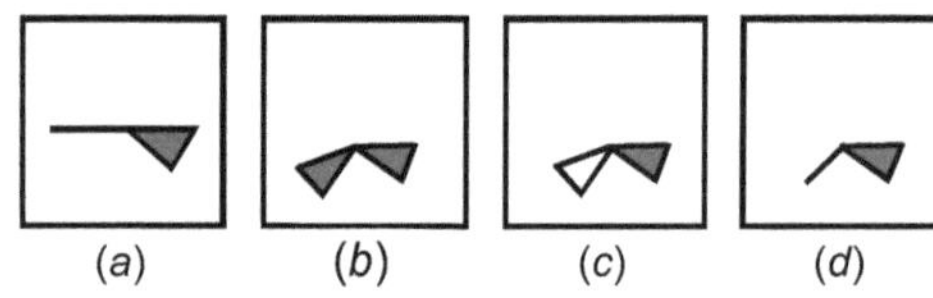

(a)   (b)   (c)   (d)

21. Which one of the following box can be created by folding the given key design?

Question figure:

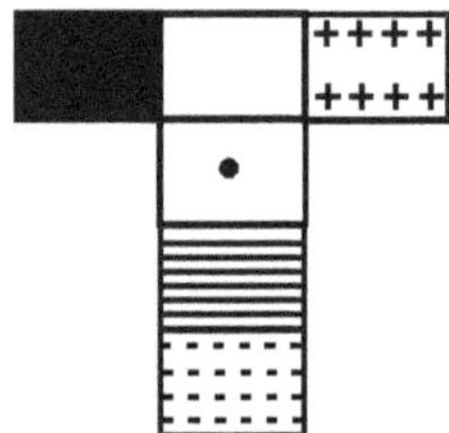

Answer figures:

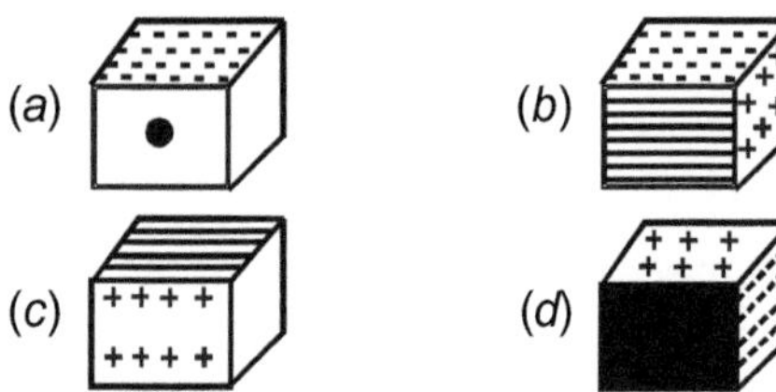

22. Choose from the following diagrams (a), (b), (c) and (d) the one that illustrates the relationships among three given classes:

Europe, London, United Kingdom

Answer figures:

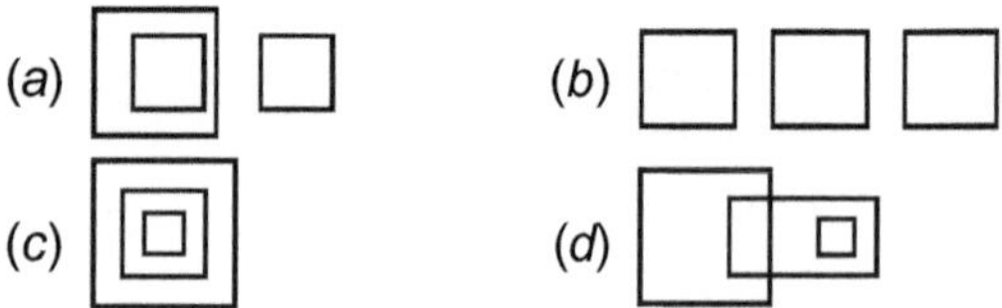

23. An unfolded cube is shown in figure. All the faces of the cube are numbered from 1 to 6. Select one figure which will result in a given cube when folded?

Question figure:

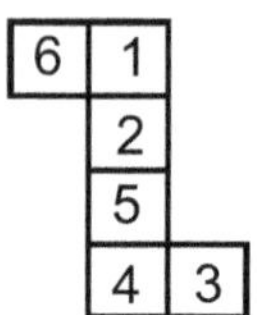

Answer figures:

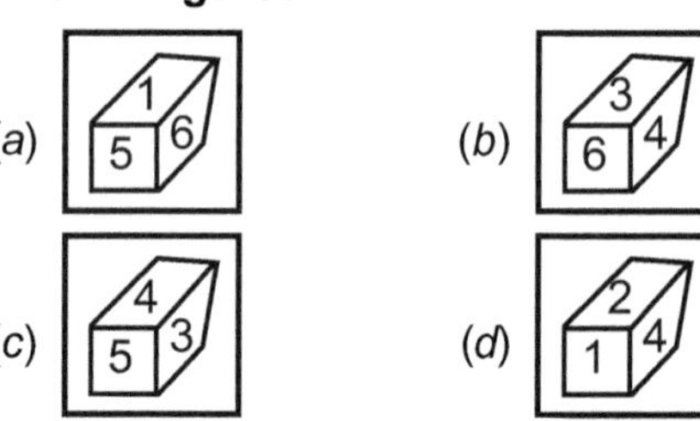

24. A piece of paper is folded and cut as shown below in the question figures. From the given answer figures, indicate how it will appear when opened.

Question figures:

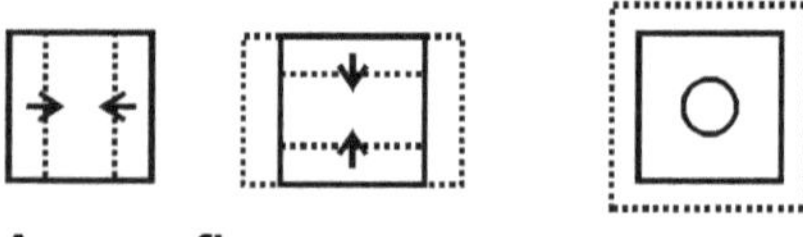

Answer figures:

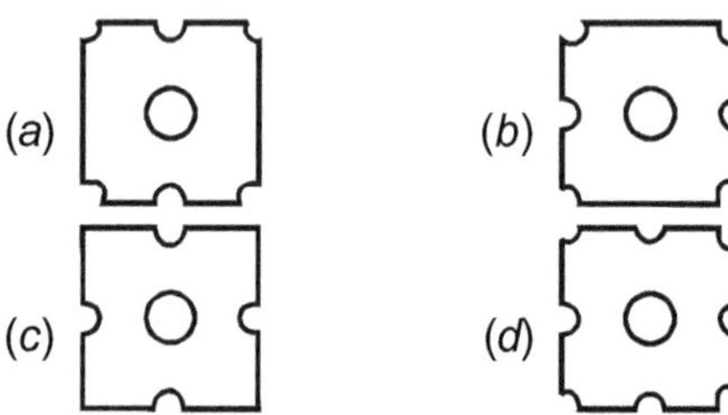

25. If a mirror is placed on the line MN, then which of the answer figures is the right image of the given figure?

Question figure:

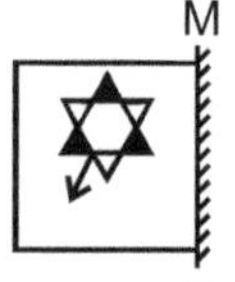

Answer figures:

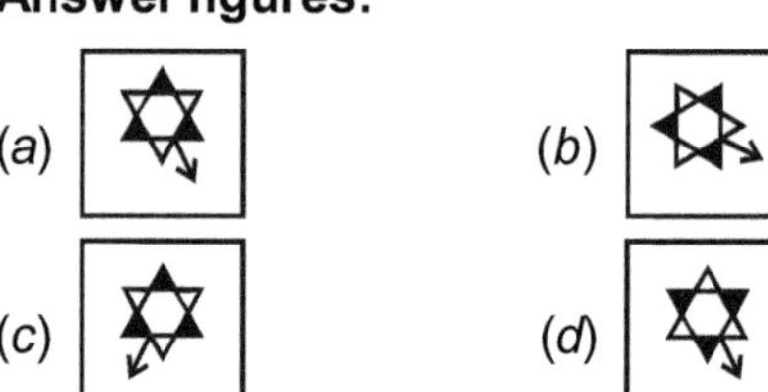

ENGLISH LANGUAGE

Direction : In the following question out of the four alternatives, choose the one which best expresses the meaning of the given word and mark it in the answer sheet.

26. Exude

   (*a*) Vent   (*b*) Seep

   (*c*) Pour   (*d*) Gush

27. Imperious

   (*a*) Dangerous   (*b*) Precious

   (*c*) Feeble   (*d*) Authoritarian

Directions: In question nos. **28** and **29**, choose the word opposite in meaning to the given word and mark it in the answer sheet.

28. Passive

   (*a*) Resigned   (*b*) Resistant

   (*c*) Yielding   (*d*) Forbearing

29. Incorrigible

   (*a*) Irredeemable   (*b*) Unruly

   (*c*) Reformable   (*d*) Inveterate

Directions: In question nos. **30** to **32**, Out of the four alternatives, choose the one which can be substituted for the given words/sentences.

30. Science of rearing of animals for farming

   (*a*) Aviculture   (*b*) Horticulture

   (*c*) Agriculture   (*d*) Apiculture

31. Bhawana always achieves her targets on time and she enjoys doing difficult tasks.

   (*a*) is narcoleptic   (*b*) is pyromaniac

   (*c*) is workaholic   (*d*) is glutton for work

32. Easy to understand

   (*a*) Confirmed   (*b*) Evident

   (*c*) Witty   (*d*) Chronic

Directions: In question nos. **33** to **35**, four alternatives are given for the idioms/phrases given below. Choose the alternative which best expresses the meaning of the given idiom/phrase.

33. He's been chasing his tail all week collecting data but the report is still not ready.

   (*a*) boot licking

   (*b*) working very hard

   (*c*) rushing around ineffectually

   (*d*) pushing oneself to work hard

34. The director of the school runs a tight ship.

   (*a*) organized and disciplined

   (*b*) haywire and upsetting

   (*c*) valueless and expensive

   (*d*) firmly and effectively

35. To catch some rays

   (*a*) To tan in the sun

   (*b*) To succeed

   (*c*) To rise with less efforts

   (*d*) To get promotion

Direction : In the following question out of four words only one word is spelt correctly. Find the correctly spelt word and mark your answer in the answer sheet.

36. (*a*) Casete   (*b*) Cassete

     (*c*) Casette   (*d*) Cassette

Directions: In question nos. **37** to **39**, some parts of the sentences have errors and some are correct. Find out which part of a sentence has an error and mark the answer corresponding to the appropriate letter (A,B,C). If a sentence is free from error, mark your answer as (*d*).

37. They're considering (*a*) / to making an appeal (*b*) / against the judgment. (*c*) / No error (*d*)

38. If I were working (*a*) / in Bandra, I will (*b*) / commute by the local train. (*c*) / No error (*d*)

39. My daughter pointed out last night (*a*) / that by next March, my nephew (*b*)/ shall be married for 10 years. (*c*) / No error (*d*)

Directions: In question nos. **40** to **42**, sentences are given with blanks to be filled with an appropriate word(s). Four alternatives are suggested for each question. Choose the correct alternative out of the four.

40. While the chicken is ______ way, you should prepare a rice mix and steam peas.

   (*a*) in   (*b*) on

   (*c*) under   (*d*) below

41. She asked her husband, "We should exercise daily, ______?"

   (*a*) shouldn't we   (*b*) should we

   (*c*) shall we   (*d*) should she

42. Tourists ______ on Niagara Falls after the giant waterfall froze. One of three waterfalls has frozen completely, while the Horseshoe Falls ______ to flow unimpeded.

   (*a*) disunited, continues   (*b*) disbanded, continued

   (*c*) converged, continues   (*d*) assembled, continued

Directions: In question nos. **43** to **45**, a sentence/part of the sentence is underlined. Beneath each sentence four different ways of phrasing the underlined part are given. Choose the grammatically correct option. In case no improvement is needed, your answer is option (*d*)

43. A lot of problems have arosen from her failure to meet the deadline.

   (*a*) arose   (*b*) arised

   (*c*) arisen   (*d*) No improvement

44. Fifteen years ago today, Sachin <u>was sitting</u> in the plane going to Australia.

   (*a*) sat

   (*b*) have been sitting

   (*c*) is sitting

   (*d*) No improvement

45. <u>They drove out of the country by car where they had been banished</u>.

   (*a*) They drove out of the country where they had been banished by car.

   (*b*) They drove where they had been banished out of the country by car.

   (*c*) They drove by car out of the country where they had been banished.

   (*d*) No improvement

Directions : In question no. 46 to 50, you have given a passage with 5 questions. Read the following passage carefully and choose the best answer to each question out of the four alternatives.

Wars, fought during the course of history, have been so destructive that they have left their marks on the world, and impacted the way things are today. The main idea of a war has either been to expand power, independence, or to join a war to help allies. World War I and World War II have both similarities and differences but both wars will be remembered as infamy.

Alliances of strong countries like Hungary, Germany, and Austria caused World War I because they decided to declare war on other countries. Allies of all the countries decided to join in, which made the war more damaging and made it worse. World War II was caused by Germany because Germany was unhappy with the Treaty of Versailles. So they decided to take matters into their own hands and invaded Poland which triggered the start of the war. In World War I, most of the battles were fought in trenches, and for the first time machine guns, tanks, flamethrowers, and mustard gas were introduced. But in World War II they used more advanced machinery. One of the World War II's famous weapon is the atom bomb. This was first introduced in World War II and was used as a threat during the Cold War. These wars have left so much destruction but in WWI there was far less damage than WWII. WWI caused approximately 24 million deaths, while WWII caused about 60 million deaths, which is about 2.5 times more deaths than WWII. At the end of WWI, the League of Nations was established. And at the end of WW2, there still was no peace because people were being executed from committing war related crimes.

46. Which, according to the passage, were the main reasons that led to wars during the course of history?

   (*a*) Expanding power, helping allies, Treaty of Versailles

   (*b*) Treaty of Versailles, helping allies, independence

   (*c*) Helping allies, independence, expanding power

   (*d*) Helping allies, independence, atom bomb

47. Find the word that is same in meaning to 'infamy'.

   (*a*) Infinity

   (*b*) Infamous

   (*c*) Shadiness

   (*d*) Blameworthiness

48. World War I was different from World War II because

   (*a*) WWI had more allies.

   (*b*) of the degree of the damage caused.

   (*c*) of the crimes that were caused during the war.

   (*d*) None of the above

49. World War II was triggered because

   (*a*) Allies of strong countries declared war on other countries.

   (*b*) it was a way to test the advanced machineries.

   (*c*) Germany threatened to use atom bomb during the cold war.

   (*d*) Germany took control of Poland against its wishes.

50. Which of the following weapons were used in WWI for the first time?

   (*a*) Trenches

   (*b*) Nuclear Bombs

   (*c*) Flame throwers

   (*d*) Riffles

QUANTITATIVE APTITUDE

51. A person borrows ₹33,000 at 20% compound interest. How much he has to pay equally at the end of each year, to settle his loan in two years?

   (*a*) ₹22,450

   (*b*) ₹21,600

   (*c*) ₹17,000

   (*d*) ₹19,600

52. If the expression $2x^2 - 6x + 5$ is written in the form $2\left(x - \dfrac{3}{2}\right)^2 + 2q^2$, then the possible values of q are

   (*a*) $\pm\dfrac{1}{2}$

   (*b*) $\pm\dfrac{2}{3}$

   (*c*) $\pm\sqrt{\dfrac{3}{2}}$

   (*d*) $\pm\sqrt{\dfrac{1}{2}}$

53. A faulty clock shows correct time at 6 a.m. It lags 1sec at the end of every 10 sec. What will be the time shown by the clock at 9 p.m.?

   (*a*) 7:00 p.m.

   (*b*) 7:30 p.m.

   (*c*) 8:00 p.m.

   (*d*) 8:30 p.m.

54. What is the value of x, if $x = \cfrac{1}{3 + \cfrac{3}{5 + \cfrac{4}{5 + \cfrac{7}{2}}}}$?

   (*a*) $\dfrac{31}{110}$

   (*b*) $\dfrac{31}{101}$

   (*c*) $\dfrac{41}{101}$

   (*d*) $\dfrac{3}{11}$

55. If $\dfrac{a}{b} = \dfrac{1}{4}$ and $\dfrac{b}{c} = \dfrac{2}{3}$, then $\dfrac{12a^2 - 8c^2}{33a^2 + c^2}$ is equal to

(a) −4   (b) −1

(c) 0   (d) $\dfrac{2}{17}$

56. Radius of two concentric circles C_1 and C_2 with centre O are 6 cm and 10 cm respectively. A tangent drawn to circle C_1 at point P meet the circle C_2 at points A and B. The area of the triangle AOB is

(a) 24 cm²   (b) 36 cm²

(c) 48 cm²   (d) 56 cm²

57. Amit goes 10 m North, then 15 m due West, then 14 m more due North. If he finally goes 8 m due East, then the distance between his initial and final position is

(a) 10 m   (b) 24 m

(c) 25 m   (d) 31 m

58. Two triangles ABC and PQR are such that $\angle ABC = \angle QPR$ and $\angle BCA = \angle PRQ$, then one can infer that $\triangle ABC \cong \triangle PQR$ when

(a) BC = PR   (b) $\angle BAC = \angle PQR$

(c) AB = PQ   (d) BC = QR

59. Two chords AB and CD of a circle with centre O intersect each other at P, $\angle DCA = 28°$ and $\angle APD = 62°$ then the $\angle CDB$ is

(a) 34°   (b) 62°

(c) 90°   (d) 118°

60. The difference of a number consisting of three different digits from the number formed by reversing the digits is always divisible by

(a) 9   (b) 10

(c) 11   (d) Both (a) and (c)

61. Pipe A can empty a tank in 12 minutes, pipe B can empty the tank in 18 minutes while the pipe C can empty the tank in 36 minutes. In how much time the tank will be empty if all three pipes are opened together?

(a) 22 minutes   (b) 10 minutes

(c) 6 minutes   (d) 5 minutes

62. Four men and ten women are assigned to complete a work. They complete one third of the work in 4 days, then 2 more men and 2 more women are also engaged to complete the work. They completed two-ninth of the work in next two days. If the remaining work is to be completed in 4 days, then how many more women must be employed?

(a) 60   (b) 75

(c) 90   (d) None of these

63. A conical vessel of base radius 9 cm and height 8 cm is filled with milk. If the milk leaks through a hole at the bottom of the conical vessel into a cylindrical jar of radius 3 cm, then find the level of the milk in the jar after the milk has leaked completely.

(a) 12 cm   (b) 15 cm

(c) 24 cm   (d) 27 cm

64. A shopkeeper sells an article at $12\dfrac{1}{2}\%$ loss. If he sells it for ₹51.80 more, then he gains 6%. What is the cost price of the article?

(a) ₹210   (b) ₹240

(c) ₹280   (d) ₹300

65. A shopkeeper gives 25% discount on buying an article and 15% additional discount if bought between 4 p.m. to 5 p.m. What will be the total discount offered to the customer?

(a) 40%   (b) 10%

(c) 36.25%   (d) 33.75%

66. A woman invested $\dfrac{2}{5}$ th of her saving at 6%, $\dfrac{1}{4}$ th at 9%, $\dfrac{3}{10}$ th at 10% and the remainder at 12%. If his annual income is ₹462, the saving is

(a) ₹4,400   (b) ₹5,000

(c) ₹5,600   (d) ₹6,000

67. Salary of a person on 01-01-2001 is ₹6,400 per month with increment ₹600 due on 01-09-2001, 01-09-2002, 01-09-2003, 01-09-2004 and 01-09-2005. If his monthly salary on 01-01-2006 increases by 40% of average monthly salary during last five years, what monthly salary did he draw in February 2006?

(a) ₹ 8,400   (b) ₹ 9,400

(c) ₹ 11,150   (d) ₹ 12,520

68. Radius of a right circular cone is decreased by 20%. To maintain the same volume, the height will have to be increased by

(a) 20%   (b) 40.75%

(c) 44%   (d) 56.25%

69. If $\mathrm{cosec}^2\theta + \cot^2\theta = 7$, then $\sin 3\theta$ is $(0° \le \theta \le 90°)$

(a) 1   (b) Undefined

(c) 3   (d) $\sqrt{3}$

70. The value of $(1 - \tan\theta + \sec\theta)(\cot\theta - 1 - \mathrm{cosec}\,\theta)$ is equal to

(a) −2   (b) −1

(c) 0   (d) 1

71. A pole stands vertically on a bank of a river. From a point on the other bank directly opposite the pole, the angle of elevation of the top of the pole is 60°. From another point 100 m further away on the line joining this point to the foot of the pole, the angle of elevation of the top of the pole is 30°. Find the height of the pole.

(a) $\dfrac{50}{\sqrt{3}}$ m　　　　　(b) $50\sqrt{3}$ m

(c) $\dfrac{100}{\sqrt{3}}$ m　　　　(d) $100\sqrt{3}$ m

72. 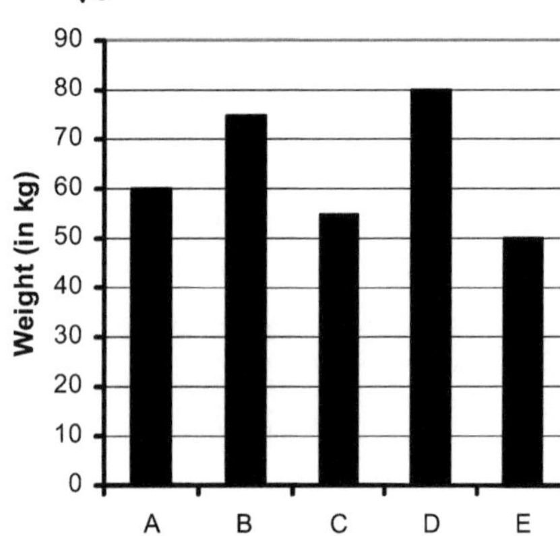

The above bar graph shows the weight (in kg) of the five persons – A, B, C, D and E. What is the average weight of the persons?

(a) 60 kg　　　　　(b) 55 kg

(c) 64 kg　　　　　(d) 72 kg

Directions: The pie chart shows the break-up of the cost of construction of a building. Study the graph and answer the question nos. **73** to **75**.

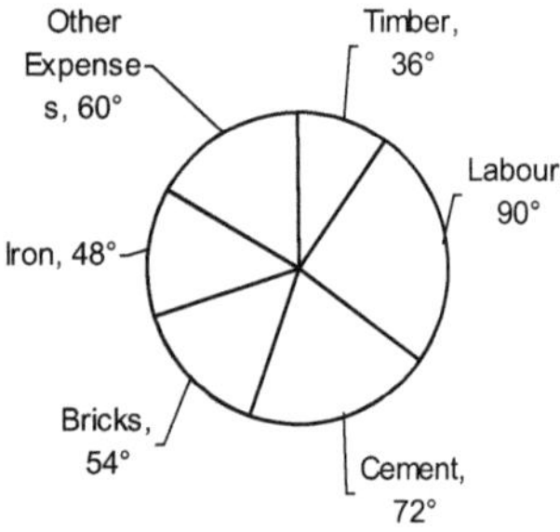

73. The amount spent on timber and bricks together is ₹4,50,000, the total amount spent on iron is

(a) ₹1,20,000　　　(b) ₹2,40,000

(c) ₹3,60,000　　　(d) ₹4,80,000

74. How much percent more is spent on cement than that on bricks?

(a) 25%　　　　　(b) 33.33%

(c) 37.5%　　　　(d) 40%

75. How much percent less is spent on Iron than that on other expenses?

(a) 15%　　　　　(b) 20%

(c) 25%　　　　　(d) 27%

76. Badminton player PV Sindhu recently won historic sliver medal in women's singles badminton event at Rio Olympics. Who won gold in the event?

(a) Wang Yihan　　　(b) Sain Nehwal

(c) Carolina Marin　　(d) Dolores Marco

77. The Hindi word 'rupiya' (Indian currency) is derived from Sanskrit word 'rupya' which literally means

(a) wrought iron　　　(b) wrought silver

(c) wrought aluminium　(d) wrought copper

78. Cracking in brass is caused by

(a) Ammonia　　　　(b) Nitric acid

(c) Hydrogen peroxide　(d) Sulphuric acid

79. Article 2 of the Indian constitution states

(a) Admission or establishment of new States

(b) Formation of new States and alteration of areas, boundaries or names of existing States

(c) a law that grants special autonomous status to Jammu and Kashmir

(d) deals with the failure of the Constitutional machinery of an Indian state

80. Which part of the human eye acts as an aperture?

(a) Retina　　　　　(b) Pupil

(c) Sclera　　　　　(d) Cornea

81. Which personality is mentioned in the Buddhist text 'Milinda Panha'?

(a) Nagasena　　　　(b) Chanakya

(c) Kalidas　　　　　(d) Hemachandra

82. Which coating of mucins gives them considerable water-holding capacity and makes them resistant to proteolysis?

(a) Fat coating　　　　(b) Sugar coating

(c) Protein coating　　(d) Glycoprotein coating

83. Which of the following are the possible outcomes after Quantitative easing?

1. Increase in Inflationary tendency in the economy.

2. Stimulus to the growth prospects of economy.

3. Availability of more credit in the market.

Correct code:

(a) 1 and 2 only　　　(b) 2 and 3 only

(c) 1 and 3 only　　　(d) 1, 2 and 3

84. The scientific method of dating based on the analysis of patterns of tree rings is known as

(a) Dendrology　　　(b) Dendrochronology

(c) Chronology　　　(d) Acanthochronology

85. Recently which Airport awarded Best Tourist Friendly Airport ?

(a) Nagpur　　　　　(b) Lucknow

(c) Goa　　　　　　(d) Tirupati

86. 'Making India Awesome' is a book authored by
    (a) Chetan Bhagat   (b) Arundhati Roy
    (c) V.S. Naipaul   (d) Amitav Ghosh
87. Which of the following is useful in ice-cream making?
    (a) Agar-Agar   (b) Algal extract
    (c) Algal bloom   (d) Algal excreta
88. Kushok Bakula Rimpochhe Airport is situated in
    (a) Assam   (b) Tripura
    (c) Jammu and Kashmir (d) Mizoram
89. Dengue is caused by the
    (a) Virus   (b) Bacteria
    (c) Nematode   (d) Protozoan
90. Where was the Asia's first export processing zone set up?
    (a) Mangalore   (b) Kandla
    (c) Howrah   (d) Gurgaon
91. Which Indian nationalist movement is also known as 'August Movement'?
    (a) Swadeshi Movement
    (b) Civil Disobedience Movement
    (c) Quit India Movement
    (d) Non-Cooperation Movement
92. Parasitic plants have a modified root known as
    (a) Haustorium   (b) Vellum
    (c) Prop roots   (d) Pneumatophore
93. The study of teeth is referred to as
    (a) Osteology
    (b) Archaeology
    (c) Opthalmology
    (d) Otolaryngology

94. Superconductivity was discovered by
    (a) Isaac Newton
    (b) Heike Kamerlingh Onnes
    (c) Albert Einstein
    (d) Joseph Rotblat
95. The Communal Award was made by the
    (a) Ramsay Macdonald   (b) Lord Irwin
    (c) Lord Macaulay   (d) Lord Ripon
96. Which treaty preserved the Finland's independence, ending the Soviet attempt to annex the country?
    (a) Moscow Peace Treaty
    (b) Paris Peace Treaty
    (c) Craiova Treaty
    (d) Treaty on the Final Settlement with Respect to Germany
97. Who is the ex-officio Chairman of Planning Commission?
    (a) Prime Minister   (b) President
    (c) Finance Minister   (d) Agriculture Minister
98. The rise in temperature in the stratosphere is caused by the absorption of
    (a) Ultra violet radiations
    (b) Infra red radiations
    (c) Visible spectrum
    (d) Ions present in the stratosphere
99. Nasonov pheromone is emitted by the
    (a) Ants   (b) Queen bees
    (c) Worker bees   (d) Drones
100. World Tourism Day observed on __________.
    (a) 24 September   (b) 25 September
    (c) 27 September   (d) 30 September

ANSWERS

1. (a)	**2.** (b)	**3.** (a)	**4.** (c)	**5.** (b)	**6.** (c)	**7.** (d)	**8.** (c)	**9.** (b)	**10.** (a)
11. (b)	**12.** (c)	**13.** (a)	**14.** (b)	**15.** (b)	**16.** (d)	**17.** (c)	**18.** (d)	**19.** (d)	**20.** (b)
21. (b)	**22.** (c)	**23.** (c)	**24.** (d)	**25.** (a)	**26.** (b)	**27.** (d)	**28.** (b)	**29.** (c)	**30.** (c)
31. (d)	**32.** (b)	**33.** (c)	**34.** (a)	**35.** (a)	**36.** (d)	**37.** (b)	**38.** (b)	**39.** (c)	**40.** (c)
41. (a)	**42.** (c)	**43.** (c)	**44.** (d)	**45.** (c)	**46.** (c)	**47.** (b)	**48.** (b)	**49.** (d)	**50.** (c)
51. (b)	**52.** (a)	**53.** (b)	**54.** (a)	**55.** (a)	**56.** (c)	**57.** (c)	**58.** (a)	**59.** (a)	**60.** (d)
61. (c)	**62.** (d)	**63.** (c)	**64.** (c)	**65.** (c)	**66.** (c)	**67.** (d)	**68.** (d)	**69.** (a)	**70.** (a)
71. (b)	**72.** (c)	**73.** (b)	**74.** (b)	**75.** (b)	**76.** (c)	**77.** (b)	**78.** (a)	**79.** (a)	**80.** (b)
81. (a)	**82.** (b)	**83.** (d)	**84.** (b)	**85.** (d)	**86.** (a)	**87.** (a)	**88.** (c)	**89.** (a)	**90.** (b)
91. (c)	**92.** (a)	**93.** (a)	**94.** (b)	**95.** (a)	**96.** (a)	**97.** (a)	**98.** (a)	**99.** (c)	**100.** (c)

EXPLANATIONS

1. The young one of a baboon is called an infant while the young one of a beaver is called a kitten. Hence, option (A) is the correct answer.

2.
```
B      G      L
↓+4    ↓+4    ↓+4
F      K      P
↓+4    ↓+4    ↓+4
J      O      T
↓+4    ↓+4    ↓+4
N      S      X
```

3.
```
B      X
↓+3    ↓−3
E      U
↓+3    ↓−3
H      R
↓+3    ↓−3
K      O
↓+3    ↓−3
N      L
↓+3    ↓−3
Q      I
↓+3    ↓−3
T      F
```

4. By reversing the digits of each term, the series will be:

   27, 64, 125, 216, 343.

   The series is formed by the cubes of consecutive numbers starting from 3. Hence, the next term in the series will be $8^3 = 512$ and by reversing the digits of the same, we get 215 as the next term in the series.

5.
```
W      5      K
↓−3    ↓+7    ↓+2
T      12     M
↓−3    ↓+8    ↓+2
Q      20     O
↓−3    ↓+9    ↓+2
N      29     Q
↓−3    ↓+10   ↓+2
K      39     S
```

6.
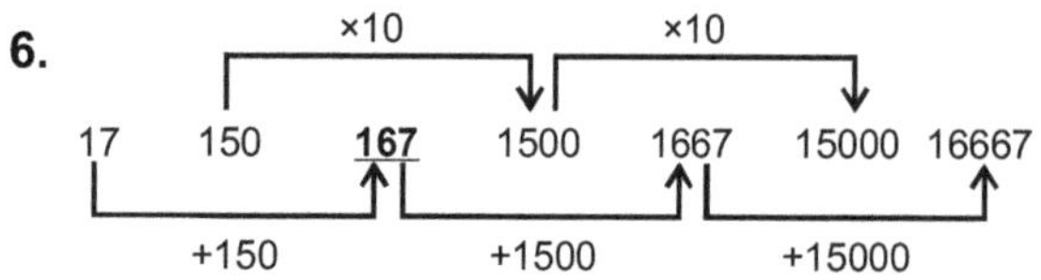

7. Gourd, Pumpkin and French Beans grow on vines while Jackfruit grows on trees. Hence, option (d) is the answer.

8. Fossil fuel is the answer since it is a non renewable source of energy, while energy resources in options (a), (b) and (d) are renewable energy sources.

9. As $(53)^2 < 2851 < (54)^2$

   ∴ The least number that must be added
   $$= (54)^2 - 2851 = 65.$$

10. The order of the heights of five given persons will be:

    Anil > Karan > Mukesh and Anil > Sunil > Rakesh

    Hence, Anil is the tallest among the five.

11. Option (b) is the answer since the given word has a single 'N' while TOURNAMENT uses 'N' twice.

12. In the series D F J P X the number of letters skipped between adjacent letters is consecutive odd numbers starting from 1.

    $$D \xrightarrow{+2} F \xrightarrow{+4} J \xrightarrow{+6} P \xrightarrow{+8} X$$

13. Total members = 2 + 3 + 4 × 2 + 4 × 5 = 33.

14. As (4 + 2) × (7 + 4) = 66 and (3 + 5) × (1 + 7) = 64

    Similarly, (5 + 7) × (2 + 1) = **36**.

15. In column 1,

    2 × 3 = 6, 2 × 5 = 10 ⇒ 2 + 3 + 2 + 5 = 12

    In column 2,

    3 × 5 = 15, 3 × 7 = 21 ⇒ 3 + 5 + 3 + 7 = 18

    Similarly, in column 3,

    5 × 7 = 35, 5 × 11 = 55 ⇒ 5 + 7 + 5 + 11 = **28**.

16.
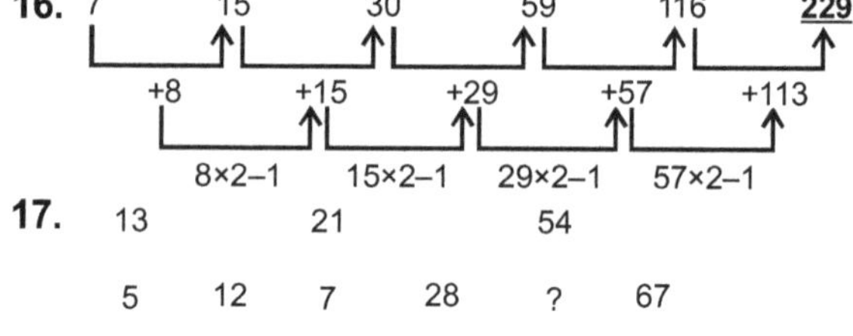

17.
```
13            21            54
5    12    7    28    ?    67
↓             ↓             ↓
```
Square root of   Square root of   Square root of
(13+12) = 25   (21+28) = 49   (54+67) = 121

∴ ? = 11.

18.

Hence, A is in North with respect to B.

19. The given statement shows a cause and effect relationship. It says that when people work hard, they succeed. Neither does the statement say anything about hard work being the only way to succeed nor does it say anything about any other way that will or

will not lead to success. Therefore, we can say that none of the conclusions follow. Hence, option (*d*) is the correct answer.

21. ∵ [dotted box] and [dot box] are opposite but in option (*a*) these are adjacent. Similarly, [striped box] and [blank box] are opposite but in option (*c*) they are adjacent. Similarly, [dark box] and [+++ box] are opposite but in option (*d*) they are adjacent. Hence, option (*b*) is correct.

22. London is a part of United Kingdom and United Kingdom is a part of Europe.

23. 1 and 5 are opposite but in option (*a*) they are adjacent. Similarly, 3 and 6 are opposite but in option (*b*) they are adjacent. Similarly, 2 and 4 are opposite but in option (*d*) they are adjacent. Hence, option (*c*) is correct.

26. 'Exude' means to flow out slowly, so does seep. Hence, option (*b*) is the correct answer. 'Gush', which means to flow out qickly, is the antonym of 'exude'.

27. 'Imperious' refers to someone who is fond of ordering people around. Hence, its synonym will be option (*d*), 'authoritarian'.

28. 'Passive' is used to describe someone who allows things to happen or accepts what other people decide for him. 'Resistant' is used to describe someone who is opposed to something. Hence, option (*b*) is the correct answer. Something or someone is called 'yielding' when it is not hard or rigid. 'Forbearing' is someone who avoids saying or doing something.

29. 'Incorrigible' is someone who is not able to be corrected or changed. 'Reformable' is someone who favours improvement. Hence, option (*c*) is the correct answer. 'Unruly' is someone who cannot be easily ruled, disciplined or managed. 'Inveterate' is someone who is often doing something specified.

30. 'Agriculture' deals with the science of growing plants and breeding animals for farming. Hence, option (*c*) is the correct answer. 'Aviculture' is concerned with the raising and caring of birds, especially of wild birds in captivity. 'Horticulture' deals with the study and science of flowers, fruits and vegetables. 'Apiculture' refers to keeping of bees especially on large scale.

31. 'Glutton for work' is a person who enjoys doing difficult and unpleasant tasks. Hence, option (*d*) is the correct answer. A 'narcoleptic' is a person who falls in deep sleep when he is in relaxing surroundings. A 'pyromaniac' is someone who enjoys making or watching fires. A 'workaholic' is a person who works very hard and finds it difficult to stop and relax.

32. 'Evident' means clear to sight or mind. Hence, option (*b*) is the correct option. 'Witty' means funny or clever.

'Confirmed' means not likely to change. 'Chronic' is something that exists frequently.

33. 'Chasing one's tail' means to run around ineffectually. Hence, option (*c*) is the correct answer.

34. 'To run a tight ship' means to run an organisation in an orderly and disciplined manner. Hence, option (*a*) is the correct answer.

35. 'To catch some rays' means to tan in the sun. Hence, option (*a*) is the correct answer.

36. The correct spelling is 'Cassette'. Hence, the correct answer is option (*d*)

37. The word 'considering' is not followed by any preposition. The preposition 'to' in part (*b*) is redundant. Hence, part (*b*) is the answer.

38. Clauses containing 'if' are like hypothesis, suppositions or desires and in such cases, we use past tense forms to talk about the present and the future. Therefore, the correct sentence will be 'If I were working in Bandra, I would commute by the local train'. Hence, the correct answer is part (*b*).

39. Future perfect continuous tense is used for actions which will be in progress over a period of time and will end in the future. In the sentence, 'shall be married', which is in future continuous tense, should be replaced by 'shall have been married'. Hence, part (*c*) is the answer.

40. 'Under way' means happening now. Hence, option (*c*) is the correct answer. Options (*a*), (*b*) and (*d*) will make the sentence erroneous.

41. If a statement is positive, then the question tag (short questions that we put at the end of sentences) is negative and vice-versa. Also, the question tag takes the same verb as used in the preceding part of the statement. For example: He did his homework, didn't he? Similarly, in the given sentence, the verb is 'should', which is referring to 'we'. Therefore, the correct question tag will be 'shouldn't we'. Hence, option (*a*) is the correct answer.

42. The sentence can suggest only two things; either people have stopped going to Niagara falls because it has frozen or even more people have started going to the falls to see the spectacle. So, the only words that can fit in the first blank would be 'converged' and 'assembled'. 'Disunited' means separated and 'disband' means to end an organisation. Both will make the sentence logically incorrect. Option (*d*) can be negated because 'continued' is incorrect for the second blank. We need a word, which shows an action that is ongoing and not something that has happened in the past. Hence, 'continues' would be the appropriate word to fill in the second blank. Thus, option (*c*) is the correct answer.

43. The underlined word should technically describe her 'problems'. Hence, the correct word to be used is option (c) - 'arisen', which is a past participle. A participle is an English verbal that functions as an adjective. 'Arosen' and 'arised' are incorrect words that do not exist in the dictionary.

44. The given sentence is correct in itself and hence, option (d) is the answer. The statement refers to an action that is going on at some time in the past. In such cases, the past continues tense is used.

45. The given statement is incorrect because it is not clear whether the place from where they had been banished was a country or a car. The grammatically correct sentence is given in option (c), where the modifier 'where they had been banished' is correctly placed beside 'country' making the place, where they were banished from, clear.

46. Refer to the third sentence of the passage. It says that the main idea of a war has either been to expand power, independence, or joining a war to help allies. Hence, option (c) is the correct answer.

47. 'Infamy' refers to the condition of being known for having done an evil or terrible act. 'Infamous' means well known for evil act. Hence, option (b) is the correct answer.

48. Option (a) is incorrect because we cannot infer from the passage which war had more allies. Option (b) says that the degree of damage caused made World War I different from World War II, which can be inferred from the third last sentence of the passage. Hence, option (b) is the answer. Option (c) is out of the scope of the passage.

49. What really triggered the war was Germany invading Poland. Refer to the following lines of the passage: 'So they decided …invaded Poland which triggered the start of the war'. Hence, option (d) is the correct answer.

50. The passage states that most of the war was fought in trenches. Flame throwers, tanks, etc. were used for the first time. Hence, option (d) is the correct answer. Nuclear bomb was first used in WWII. The passage makes no mention of the use of riffle in the wars.

51. Let the amount be ₹x. Then,

$$\left(33000\left(1+\frac{20}{100}\right)-x\right)\left(1+\frac{20}{100}\right)=x$$

$$\Rightarrow \frac{x\times 5}{6}+x=33000\times\frac{6}{5}$$

$$\Rightarrow x\times\frac{11}{6}=39600$$

$$\Rightarrow x=₹21,600.$$

52. $2x^2-6x+5=2x^2-6x+\dfrac{9}{2}+\dfrac{1}{2}=2\left(x-\dfrac{3}{2}\right)^2+2\left(\dfrac{1}{2}\right)^2$

$$\therefore q^2=\left(\frac{1}{2}\right)^2\Rightarrow q=\pm\frac{1}{2}.$$

53. Difference between the two time limits = 15 hrs. = 15 × 60 × 60 = 54000 sec

$\Rightarrow$ Lag at the end of 54000 sec = 5400 sec = 1 hr 30 min

Hence, the time shown = 7:30 p.m.

54. $x=\dfrac{1}{3+\dfrac{3}{5+\dfrac{4}{5+\dfrac{7}{2}}}}$

$\Rightarrow x=\dfrac{1}{3+\dfrac{3}{5+\dfrac{4}{\frac{17}{2}}}}\Rightarrow x=\dfrac{1}{3+\dfrac{3}{5+\dfrac{8}{17}}}$

$\Rightarrow x=\dfrac{1}{3+\dfrac{3}{\frac{93}{17}}}\Rightarrow x=\dfrac{1}{3+\dfrac{51}{93}}$

$\Rightarrow x=\dfrac{93}{330}=\dfrac{31}{110}.$

55. $\dfrac{a}{b}=\dfrac{1}{4}$ and $\dfrac{b}{c}=\dfrac{2}{3}\Rightarrow a:b:c=1:4:6$

$\therefore \dfrac{12a^2-8c^2}{33a^2+c^2}=\dfrac{12\times1^2-8\times6^2}{33\times1^2+6^2}=\dfrac{12(1-24)}{3(11+12)}=-4.$

56.

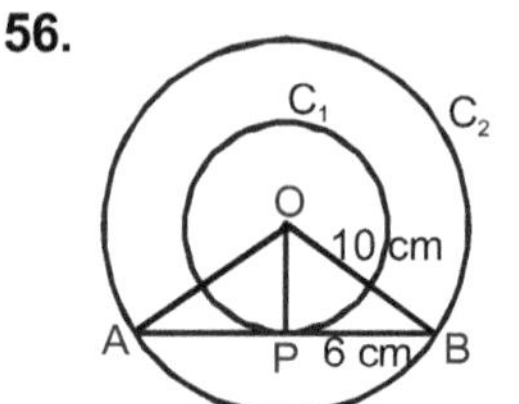

In $\triangle OPB$, $PB=\sqrt{OB^2-OP^2}=\sqrt{10^2-6^2}=8$ cm

Area of triangle AOB = Area of $\triangle POB$ + Area of $\triangle POA$

$= 2\times$ Area of $\triangle POB = 2\times\dfrac{OP\times PB}{2}=6\times8=48$ cm².

57.

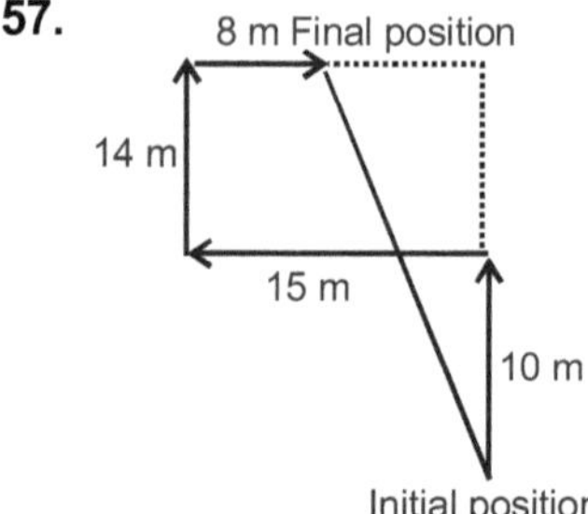

Hence, required distance

$$=\sqrt{(10+14)^2+(15-8)^2}=\sqrt{24^2+7^2}=25 \text{ m}.$$

58.

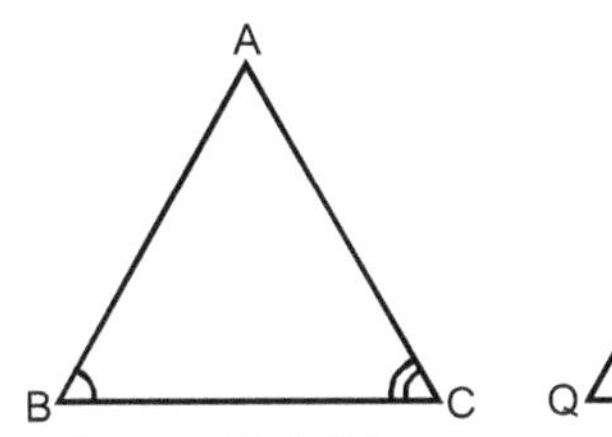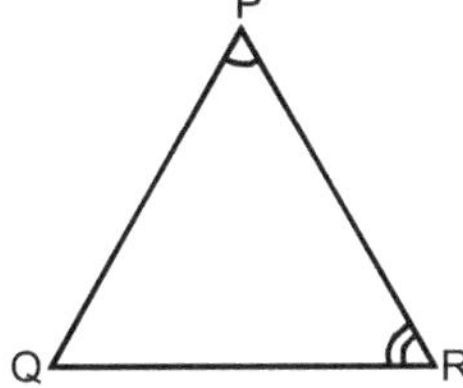

In ΔABC and ΔPQR,

∠ABC = ∠QPR and ∠BCA = ∠PRQ, then for ΔABC ≅ ΔQPR,

BC = PR (ASA property).

59.

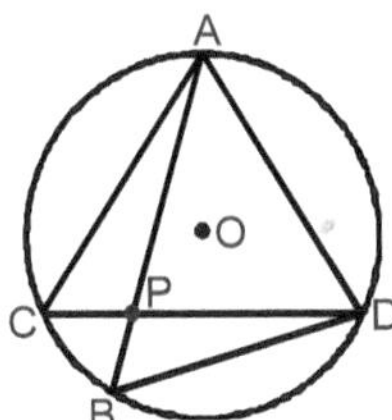

Let the point of intersection of CD and AB be P. Then,

∠DCA = ∠DBA = 28° (Angle in the same segment)

∠BPD = 180° − ∠APD = 180° − 62° = 118°

In ΔBPD,

∠PDB = 180° − (∠DBA + ∠BPD) = 180° − (28° + 118°) = **34°**.

60. Let the 3 digit number be 100x + 10y + z. Then,

(100z + 10y + x) − (100x + 10y + z) = 99(z − x) = 9 × 11 × a number.

61. Let the capacity of the tank be (LCM of 12, 18 and 36) 36 units. Then,

Pipe A empties $\frac{36}{12}$ = 3 units, pipe B empties $\frac{36}{18}$ = 2 units while pipe C empties $\frac{36}{36}$ = 1 unit from the tank in 1 minute.

Hence, required time = $\frac{36}{3+2+1}$ = 6 minutes.

62. Let the work done by a man and a woman in 1 day be 'm' and 'w' units and the total work be T units. Then,

(4m + 10w) × 4 = $\frac{T}{3}$

$\Rightarrow 2m + 5w = \frac{T}{24}$ ... (i)

Now, (6m + 12w) × 2 = $\frac{2T}{9}$

$\Rightarrow 2m + 4w = \frac{T}{27}$ ... (ii)

From (i) and (ii), we have

w = $\frac{T}{9 \times 24}$ and m = $\frac{T}{9 \times 12}$

Remaining work = T − $\frac{T}{3}$ − $\frac{2T}{9}$ = $\frac{4T}{9}$ units

Let 'n' be the number of required woman. Then,

(6m + (12 + n) w) × 4 = $\frac{4T}{9}$

$\Rightarrow$ n = 0.

63. Let the level of the milk in the jar be 'h'. Then, volume of the conical vessel = volume of the cylinder jar

$\Rightarrow \frac{1}{3}\pi(9)^2 \times 8 = \pi(3)^2 \times h$

$\Rightarrow$ h = 24 cm.

64. Let the cost price be ₹x. Then,

$\frac{(12.5 + 6)x}{100}$ = 51.80 $\Rightarrow$ x = 280.

65. Total discount = 15 + 25 − $\frac{15 \times 25}{100}$ = 36.25%.

66. Let her saving be 100x. Then, her annual income

= $\frac{2}{5} \times 100x \times \frac{6}{100} + \frac{1}{4} \times 100x \times \frac{9}{100} + \frac{3}{10} \times 100x \times \frac{10}{100}$

$+ \left(1 - \frac{2}{5} - \frac{1}{4} - \frac{3}{10}\right) \times 100x \times \frac{12}{100}$

$\Rightarrow 462 = \frac{12x}{5} + \frac{9x}{4} + 3x + \frac{3x}{5} = \frac{33x}{4}$

$\Rightarrow$ x = 56.

Hence, her saving is ₹5,600.

67. His total salary in 2001

= 6400 × 8 + (6400 + 600) × 4 = ₹79,200

His total salary in 2002

= 7000 × 8 + (7000 + 600) × 4 = ₹86,400

His total salary in 2003

= 7600 × 8 + (7600 + 600) × 4 = ₹93,600

His total salary in 2004

= 8200 × 8 + (8200 + 600) × 4 = ₹1,00,800

His total salary in 2005

= 8800 × 8 + (8800 + 600) × 4 = ₹108,000

Average salary during last 5 years

= $\frac{79200 + 86400 + 93600 + 100800 + 108000}{5 \times 12}$ = ₹7,800

His monthly salary in December 2005

= 8800 + 600 = ₹9,400

His monthly salary in February 2006

= $9400 + 7800 \times \frac{40}{100}$ = ₹12,520.

68. Let the height of the right circular cone be increased by x% and volume of the right circular cone = $\frac{1}{3}\pi r^2 h$ x

Then, $\frac{1}{3}\pi r^2 h = \frac{1}{3}\pi(0.8r)^2\left(1 + \frac{x}{100}\right)h$

$\Rightarrow \left(1 + \frac{x}{100}\right)$ = 1.5625

Hence, the required percentage = 56.25%.

69. $\csc^2\theta + \cot^2\theta = 1 + \cot^2\theta + \cot^2\theta = 7$

$\Rightarrow \cot^2\theta = 3$

$\Rightarrow \cot\theta = \sqrt{3}$

$\Rightarrow \theta = 30°$ (As $0° \le \theta \le 90°$)

$\therefore \sin 3\theta = \sin 90° = 1.$

70. $\left(1 - \dfrac{\sin\theta}{\cos\theta} + \dfrac{1}{\cos\theta}\right)\left(\dfrac{\cos\theta}{\sin\theta} - 1 - \dfrac{1}{\sin\theta}\right)$

$\Rightarrow \left(\dfrac{\cos\theta - \sin\theta + 1}{\cos\theta}\right)\left(\dfrac{\cos\theta - \sin\theta - 1}{\sin\theta}\right)$

$\Rightarrow \left(\dfrac{(\cos\theta - \sin\theta)^2 - 1^2}{\sin\theta \times \cos\theta}\right)$

$\Rightarrow \left(\dfrac{\cos^2\theta + \sin^2\theta - 2\sin\theta\cos\theta - 1}{\sin\theta \times \cos\theta}\right)$

$= \dfrac{-2\sin\theta\cos\theta}{\sin\theta\cos\theta} = -2.$

71.

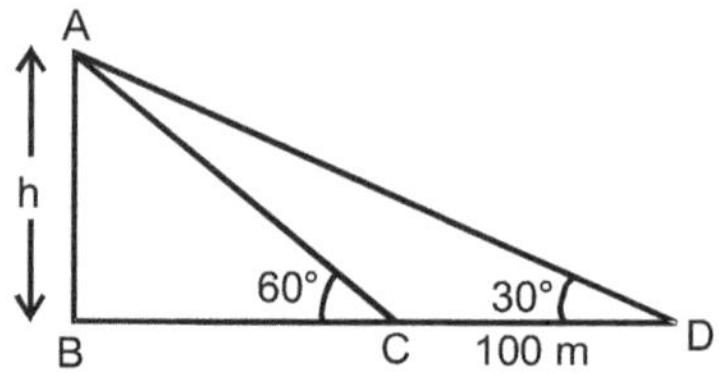

Let 'h' be the height of pole and BC be width of the river.

In $\triangle ABD$,

$\tan 30° = \dfrac{h}{BD}$

$\Rightarrow \dfrac{1}{\sqrt{3}} = \dfrac{h}{BD}$

$\Rightarrow BD = \sqrt{3}h$

In $\triangle ABC$,

$\tan 60° = \dfrac{AB}{BC} \Rightarrow BC = \dfrac{h}{\sqrt{3}}$

Now, DC = BD – BC

$\Rightarrow 100 = \sqrt{3}h - \dfrac{h}{\sqrt{3}} = \dfrac{3h - h}{\sqrt{3}} = \dfrac{2h}{\sqrt{3}}$

$\Rightarrow h = 50\sqrt{3}$ m.

72. The average weight of the persons

$= \dfrac{60 + 75 + 55 + 80 + 50}{5} = 64$ kg.

73. The total amount spent on iron

$= \dfrac{48}{36 + 54} \times 450000 = ₹2,40,000.$

74. Let x% more be spent on cement than that on bricks.

Then, $54\left(1 + \dfrac{x}{100}\right) = 72$

$\Rightarrow x = \left(\dfrac{72}{54} - 1\right) \times 100 = \dfrac{18}{54} \times 100$

$\Rightarrow x = 33.33.$

75. Let x% less be spent on iron than that on other expenses. Then, $60\left(1 - \dfrac{x}{100}\right) = 48$

$\Rightarrow x = \left(1 - \dfrac{48}{60}\right) \times 100$

$\Rightarrow x = 20.$

■■

GENERAL INTELLIGENCE

1. Select the related letter/word from the given alternatives.

   F-L : I-O :: P-V : ?

   (a) R-Y   (b) S-X

   (c) S-Y   (d) R-W

2. Which one set of letters when sequentially placed at the gaps in the given letter series will complete it?

   a_bab_aab_bcaa_abc

   (a) bbab   (b) bcab

   (c) abac   (d) acab

Directions: In the following question nos. **3** to **6**, a series is given, with one term missing. Choose the correct alternative from the given ones that will complete the series.

3. 7, 13, 25, 49, 97, ___?___ .

   (a) 194   (b) 184

   (c) 188   (d) 193

4. X T P L H D Z V R N J ? ? ? .

   (a) E B Y   (b) F B X

   (c) F B Y   (d) E C X

5. BSG, HQJ, NOM, ___?___ .

   (a) TMP   (b) SMO

   (c) TPN   (d) TMO

6. GJ XU MP RO ___?___

   (a) VS   (b) IM

   (c) LI   (d) SV

7. Certain numbers have symbols as given below.

   0 1 2 3 4 5 6 7 8 9

   + * ? $] # [& ^ @

   What is the number indicated by these symbols?

   &] ^ * [

   (a) 3 4 8 9 1   (b) 9 6 8 0 5

   (c) 7 6 8 1 4   (d) 7 4 8 1 6

Directions: In question nos. **8** to **9**, find the odd word/number from the given alternatives.

8. (a) 325   (b) 118

   (c) 272   (d) 253

9. (a) Man   (b) Whale

   (c) Hen   (d) Seal

10. Ravi and Rakesh start from their office and walk in opposite direction. Ravi travelled 8 km, then turned right and travelled for 6 km. Rakesh travelled 6 km, then turned right and travelled for 8 km. How far are they now from each other?

    (a) 14 km   (b) 28 km

    (c) 20 km $14\sqrt{2}$ (d) km

Directions: In question nos. **11** to **12** from the given alternatives select the word which cannot be formed using the letters of the given word.

11. TREMENDOUS

    (a) TREES   (b) MENTOR

    (c) TROUSER   (d) RESEND

12. CARNIVOROUS

    (a) SAVIOUR   (b) RACOON

    (c) RANCOR   (d) CAVERN

13. If < stands for multiplication, > stands for addition, – stands for division, = stands for subtraction, + stands for less than, ÷ stands for greater than and × stands for equal to, state which of the following is true?

    (a) 4 < 5 = 16 – 2 × 15

    (b) 5 < 3 = 10 ÷ 6 – 2 > 3

    (c) 12 – 4 > 5 + 4 < 5 = 10

    (d) 7 > 3 = 6 ÷ 4 < 5 – 2

14. If PLANET is written as THEJIP, how SQUARE will be written in that code?

    (a) OUQWVA   (b) WMYENI

    (c) OUQENI   (d) WMYWVA

Directions: In question nos. **15** to **17**, select the missing number from the given responses.

15. 1153, 1306, ___?___ , 2224

    (a) 1742   (b) 1750

    (c) 1612   (d) 1535

16.

25	49	81
144	196	256
30	49	?

    (a) 72   (b) 63

    (c) 56   (d) 68

17.

27	13	51	29	63	37
	7		11		?

    (a) 15   (b) 13

    (c) 9   (d) 17

18. Pipes A and B can fill an empty tank completely in 6 hours and 9 hours respectively. Pipe C can empty the same completely filled tank in 10 hours. Find the time taken to fill $3/4^{th}$ of the tank, if all the three pipes are opened together.

(a) 5 hours 37 minutes

(b) 4 hours 13 minutes

(c) 4 hours 20 minutes

(d) 5 hours 18 minutes

Direction: In the following question one/two statements are given followed by two/three conclusions I, II and III. You have to consider the statements to be true even if they seem to be at variance with commonly known facts. You are to decide which of the given conclusions can definitely be drawn from the given statements.

19. Statements:

   I.   All gloves are things.

   II. Some gloves are warm.

   Conclusions:

   I.   All gloves are warm.

   II. All warm are things.

   III. Some warm are things.

(a) Only conclusion III follows

(b) Only conclusion I follows

(c) Only conclusion II follows

(d) None follows

Directions: In question nos. **20** to **21**, which answer figure will complete the question figure?

20. Question figure:

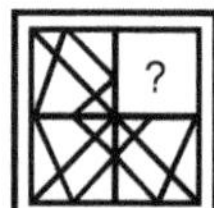

Answer figures:

 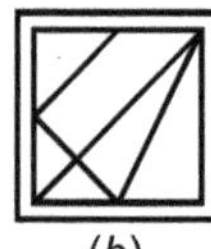 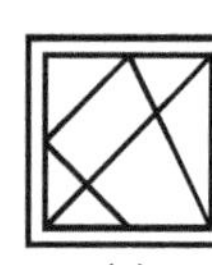 

    (a)   (b)   (c)   (d)

21. Question figure :

Answer figures:

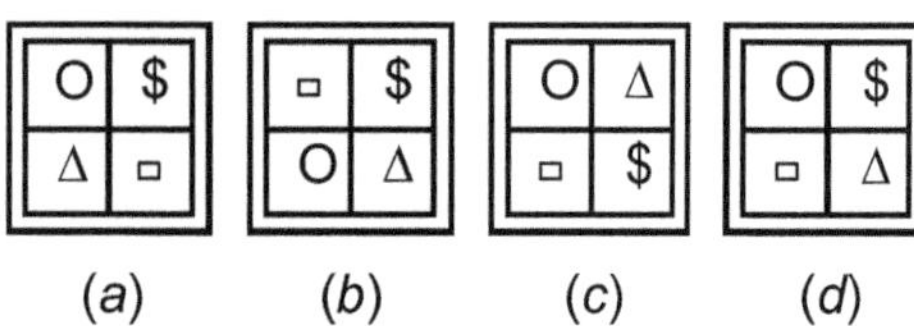

   (a)   (b)   (c)   (d)

22. Which figure represents the relationship among Universe, Planets, Galaxies?

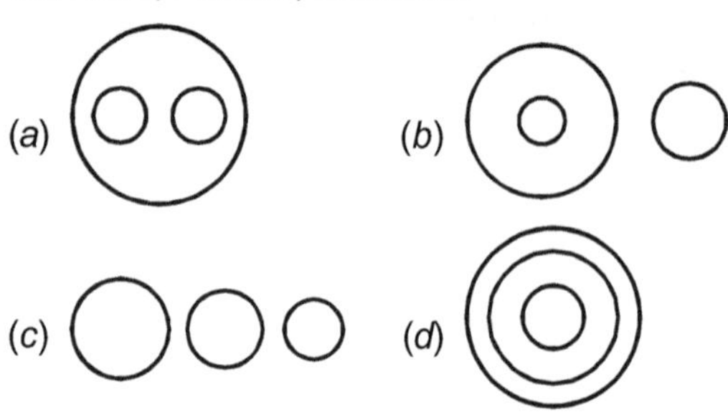

23. How many triangles are there in the following figure?

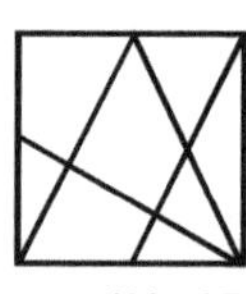

(a) 16   (b) 15

(c) 14   (d) 13

24. A word is represented by only one set of numbers as given in any one of the alternatives. The sets of numbers given in the alternatives are represented by two classes of alphabets as in the matrix given below. The columns and rows of Matrix are numbered from 0 to 6. A letter from the matrix can be represented first by its row and next by its column, e.g., 'S' can be represented by 11, 42, etc., and 'E' can be represented by 34, 65, etc. Similarly, you have to identify the set for the word 'BORN'.

Matrix

	0	1	2	3	4	5	6
1	S	T	K	A	Y	J	
2	G	R	C	Z	O	L	
3	V	H	N	E	P	T	
4	X	S	G	D	B	O	
5	L	A	N	M	Y	U	
6	C	B	R	I	E	J	

(a) 62, 25, 53, 33   (b) 45, 46, 63, 54

(c) 62, 46, 22, 53   (d) 45, 25, 34, 63

25. Which answer figure includes all the components given in the question figure?

Question figure:

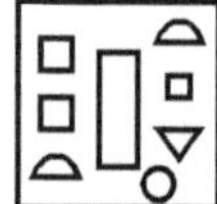

Answer figures:

(a) 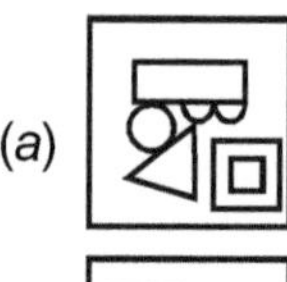   (b) 

(c) 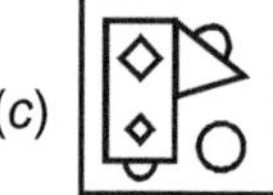   (d) 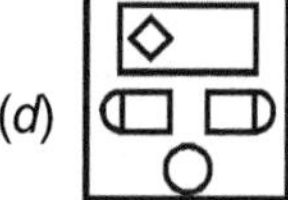

ENGLISH LANGUAGE

Directions: In question nos. **26** to **27**,out of the four alternatives, choose the one which best expresses the meaning of the given word and mark it in the answer sheet.

26. Awash

   (*a*) Swamp   (*b*) Arid

   (*c*) Dampish   (*d*) Soaked

27. Endue

   (*a*) Provide   (*b*) Divest

   (*c*) Strip   (*d*) Instill

Directions: In the following question choose the word opposite in meaning to the given word and mark it in the answer sheet.

28. Timid

   (*a*) Horrified   (*b*) Audacious

   (*c*) Aggressive   (*d*) Embarrassed

29. Precarious

   (*a*) Insecure   (*b*) Stable

   (*c*) Ambiguous   (*d*) Dangerous

Directions: In question nos. **30** to **32**, Out of the four alternatives, choose the one which can be substituted for the given words/sentences.

30. An agent who negotiates contracts of purchase and sale

   (*a*) Salesman   (*b*) Broker

   (*c*) Bargainer   (*d*) Moderator

31. A person who believes something is very important and should be followed all the time

   (*a*) Stickler   (*b*) Perseverer

   (*c*) Slacker   (*d*) Moral

32. A person who thinks that he is better than others and thinks and talks too much about himself

   (*a*) Immodest   (*b*) Egotist

   (*c*) Presumptuous   (*d*) Inordinate

Directions: In question nos. **33** to **35**, four alternatives are given for the idioms/phrases given below. Choose the alternative which best expresses the meaning of the given idiom/phrase.

33. With more clergy hooked up to computers, the demand for specialist software is growing.

   (*a*) associated   (*b*) dispersed

   (*c*) divorced   (*d*) snubbed

34. Good lawyers need to be able to think on their feet when pleading a case.

   (*a*) to be able to think and speak creatively

   (*b*) to be able to think and speak confidently

   (*c*) to be able to think and speak honestly

   (*d*) to be able to think and speak extemporaneously

35. Siddhant's comment about his friend's unethical activities was quite close to home.

   (*a*) a lucky guess

   (*b*) a relevant comment that makes one uncomfor-table

   (*c*) talking about something without coming to the point

   (*d*) speaking a lie without hesitating

Directions: In the following questionFour words are given in each question, out of which only one word is spelt correctly. Find the correctly spelt word and mark your answer in the answer sheet.

36. (*a*) Assasin   (*b*) Assassin

   (*c*) Asasin   (*d*) Asassin

Directions: In question nos. **37** to **39**, some parts of the sentences have errors and some are correct. Find out which part of a sentence has an error and mark the answer corresponding to the appropriate letter (A,B,C). If a sentence is free from error, mark your answer as (*d*).

37. Between you and me,(*a*) / it's Rahul's terrible habit that (*b*)/ both Somiya and me find annoying. (*c*) / No error (*d*)

38. I'm seeing Namit (*a*) / at 5 and then I am (*b*) / have dinner with Dikshant. (*c*) / No error (*d*)

39. I am reading (*a*) / this book for two months (*b*) / but I've only read half of it. (*c*) / No error (*d*)

Directions: In question nos. **40** to **42**, sentences are given with blanks to be filled with an appropriate word(s). Four alternatives are suggested for each question. Choose the correct alternative out of the four.

40. Paper airplane contest awards the flimsy fliers that are a cut _______ the rest.

   (*a*) through   (*b*) for

   (*c*) above   (*d*) among

41. Eating disorders are serious, potentially life-threatening _________that affect a person's emotional and physical health. People struggling with an eating disorder need to _________ professional help.

   (*a*) conditions, seek   (*b*) traits, seek

   (*c*) condition, take   (*d*) trait, take

42. They then heated the result in a ______, oxygen-free environment to distil out what they could in the form of oil.

   (*a*) pressurizing   (*b*) pressure

   (*c*) pressurized   (*d*) pressurizer

Directions: In question nos. **43** to **45**,a sentence/part of the sentence is underlined. Beneath each sentence four different ways of phrasing the underlined part are given. Choose the grammatically correct option. In case no improvement is needed, your answer is option (*d*)

43. The next flight is on time and will be arriving at five in the evening.

   (*a*) arrived   (*b*) arrives

   (*c*) has been arriving   (*d*) No improvement

44. He <u>is</u> playing since five o' clock.
    (a) has been   (b) would be
    (c) will be   (d) No improvement
45. If the dresses were cheaper, I <u>would buy</u> them.
    (a) would have bought (b) would be buying
    (c) will buy   (d) No improvement

Directions : In question nos. 46 to 50 You have given passage with 5 questions. Read the passage carefully and choose the best answer to each question out of the four alternatives.

They lived in well-planned cities, made exquisite jewelry, and enjoyed the ancient world's best plumbing. But the people of the sophisticated Indus civilization—which flourished four millennia ago in what is now Pakistan and western India—remain tantalizingly mysterious.

Unable to decipher the Indus script, archaeologists have pored over beads, slivers of pottery, and other artifacts for insights into one of the world's first city-building cultures.

Now scientists are turning to long-silent witnesses: human bones. In two new studies of skeletons from Indus cemeteries, researchers have found intriguing clues to the makeup of one city's population—and hints that the society was not as peaceful as it has been portrayed.

Peaceful or not, the Indus civilization accomplished great things. At its peak, its settlements spanned an area greater than that of ancient Egypt, a contemporary culture. Indus jewelry was so coveted that examples have been found as far as Mesopotamia, some 1,500 miles (2,500 kilometers) away. Indus cities boasted blocks of houses built on a grid pattern and drains that funneled sewage from homes to dumping grounds outside the city walls.

46. Which of the following adjectives best describe the people of Indus Civilization?
    (a) Hardworking and intelligent
    (b) Sophisticated and progressive
    (c) Peaceful and result oriented
    (d) Materialistic and boastful
47. Which of the following could be a reason that prompted the author to say "the society was not as peaceful as it has been portrayed"?
    (a) Archeologists have excavated weapons of destruction from the site of the civilization.
    (b) Scientists have found pottery depicting scenes from war.
    (c) Scientists feel that the Indus script points to the fact that the people were aggressive in nature.
    (d) Discoveries, which suggested the same, were made from the skeletal remains of the people of the Indus civilization.

48. The author calls the people of Indus Civilization as tantalizingly mysterious because
    (a) archeologists have been unable to decipher the Indus script.
    (b) archeologists have invested a lot of time in knowing about the civilisation, but to no avail.
    (c) all that is known about the civilization is not true.
    (d) they knew little about the people of Indus civilization.
49. What is the author's purpose in writing the last paragraph?
    (a) To show that the civilization covered a greater area than the Egyptian civilisation.
    (b) To show how great a culture Indus Civilization was.
    (c) To show how it was better than its contemporary.
    (d) To show that there is a dispute whether the civilization was peace loving or not.
50. Why does the author refer to the human bones as 'the long silent witnesses'?
    (a) The scientists could not get substantial clues from the skeletal remains for a long time.
    (b) The scientists did not try to dig clues from the skeletal remains earlier.
    (c) It is now that they have found the skeletons of the people of the civilization.
    (d) None of the above

QUANTITATIVE APTITUDE

51. A train starts running on a track on which an other train is running in the same direction. When second train starts running, first train is 360 meter ahead of it. If the first train runs 12 km in 8 minutes and the second train runs 24 km in 10 minutes, then what distance the second train travelled till it collided with first train?
    (a) 640 m   (b) 720 m
    (c) 960 m   (d) 1080 m
52. If $\dfrac{11+\sqrt{6}}{\sqrt{7+2\sqrt{6}}} = X + 2\sqrt{Y}$, then $5X + Y$ is
    (a) 1   (b) 43
    (c) 56   (d) 68
53. If $a^2 + 6a - 1 = 0$, then value of $\left(a+\dfrac{1}{a}\right)^2 - 5\left(a-\dfrac{1}{a}\right)$ is
    (a) 0   (b) 62
    (c) 30   (d) 70
54. $x^2 - y^2 = 60$. If $x = 6 + y$, then the average of x and y is
    (a) 10   (b) 6
    (c) 5   (d) 3

55. $\dfrac{1}{1+5\times 5^{2x-y}}+\dfrac{5}{5+5^{y-2x}}$ is equal to

(a) 5   (b) $\sqrt{5}$

(c) 1   (d) 0

56. AB is the diameter of the circle whose centre is O. If a chord CD is perpendicular to AB and the point of intersection of AB and CD is P, BP = 3 cm and DP = 4 cm, then find the radius of the circle.

(a) $\dfrac{16}{3}$ cm   (b) $\dfrac{32}{5}$ cm

(c) $\dfrac{25}{6}$ cm   (d) 5 cm

57. O is the incentre of the $\triangle$ABC. From point O a perpendicular is drop on side BC such that perpendicular meets BC at point P. If $\angle$BOP = 39°, then $\angle$ABC is

(a) 39°   (b) 78°

(c) 51°   (d) 102°

58. Length of the diagonal AC of a parallelogram ABCD is 24 cm. If O is the centroid of the $\triangle$BCD, then the length of AO is

(a) $8\sqrt{3}$ cm   (b) 16 cm

(c) 12 cm   (d) $6\sqrt{3}$ cm

59. The length (in cm) of the common chord of two circles of radii 36 cm and 48 cm whose centres are 60 cm apart, is

(a) 24   (b) 28.8

(c) 42.8   (d) 57.6

60. If the interior angles of a six-sided polygon are in the ratio of 3 : 5 : 4 : 3 : 5 : 4, then the measure of sum of the smallest two angles is

(a) 60°   (b) 120°

(c) 150°   (d) 180°

61. The number 851 has

(a) Four prime factors   (b) Three prime factors

(c) Two prime factors   (d) No prime factors

62. If a work can be completed by 24 women or 20 men in 30 days, the number of days required to complete the work by 8 women and 10 men is

(a) 24 days   (b) 36 days

(c) 30 days   (d) 32 days

63. A circle is inscribed in an equilateral triangle of side 6 cm. A square is inscribed in this circle, then the area of the square (in cm²) is

(a) 12   (b) 6

(c) 18   (d) 24

64. Two circles of radius 6 cm and 8 cm intersect each other such that centre of the circle of radius 8 cm lies on the circumference of the circle with radius 6 cm, then the length of the common chord is

(a) $\dfrac{8\sqrt{5}}{3}$ cm   (b) $\dfrac{16\sqrt{5}}{3}$ cm

(c) $4\sqrt{3}$ cm   (d) $3\sqrt{2}$ cm

65. A person buys an old cycle for ₹1,280 and spends ₹270 on repairing. If he wants to sell it for ₹2,325, as no one is ready to buy it on this price, he offers a discount of 20% and sells it. If he is able to sell it at 20% discount. His gain percent is

(a) 20   (b) 15

(c) 18   (d) 24

66. If volume of a right circular cylinder of base diameter 24 cm and height 9 cm is equal to the volume of a right circular cone of height 108 cm, then the base diameter of the right circular cone is

(a) 4 cm   (b) 6 cm

(c) 8 cm   (d) 12 cm

67. Average age of a man and his wife 7 years before at the time of their marriage was 28 years. At present they have two children. Their daughter is 2 years older than their son. One year after the birth of the daughter average age of the man, wife and their daughter is 21 years, then the present age of the son is

(a) 1 year   (b) 2 years

(c) 3 years   (d) 4 years

68. A retailer bought 96 cycles and sold 16 cycles at 10% profit, 25 cycles at 16% profit, 15 cycles at 18% profit and remaining 40 cycles at 22% profit. If the cost price of each cycle is ₹1,600, then his total profit is

(a) ₹ 16,440   (b) ₹ 18,720

(c) ₹ 27,360   (d) ₹ 30,860

69. Ramesh travelled from city A to city B, in which he travelled 42 km by motorcycle and $\dfrac{1}{4}$ th of the total distance by car. If the rest 40% of the distance is travelled in a bus, then what is the total distance?

(a) 100 km   (b) 120 km

(c) 140 km   (d) 160 km

70. If $\cos\left(50°-\psi\right)=\sin\left(70°-\theta\right)$, then the value of $\cot\left(\theta+\psi\right)$ is

(Assume that ψ and θ are both positive acute angles with $\psi < 50°$ and $\theta < 70°$)

(a) 1   (b) $\sqrt{3}$

(c) $\dfrac{1}{\sqrt{3}}$ (d) $\dfrac{\sqrt{3}}{2}$

71. If $\cos\theta + \sec\theta = 2$, then the value of $\cos^n\theta + \sec^n\theta$ is $(0° < \theta < 90°)$

(a) 2   (b) 2n

(c) 2^n (d) 2^{n+1}

72. If $\dfrac{2\tan\theta}{a} = \dfrac{3\sec\theta}{b}$, then $2\tan\theta + 3\sec\theta$ is equal to

(a) $\dfrac{a}{b} + \dfrac{b}{a}$ (b) $\dfrac{6(a+b)}{\sqrt{(2b)^2 - (3a)^2}}$

(c) $\dfrac{3b + 2a}{\sqrt{(2b)^2 - (3a)^2}}$ (d) $\dfrac{3b + 2a}{\sqrt{(2b)^2 + (3a)^2}}$

73.

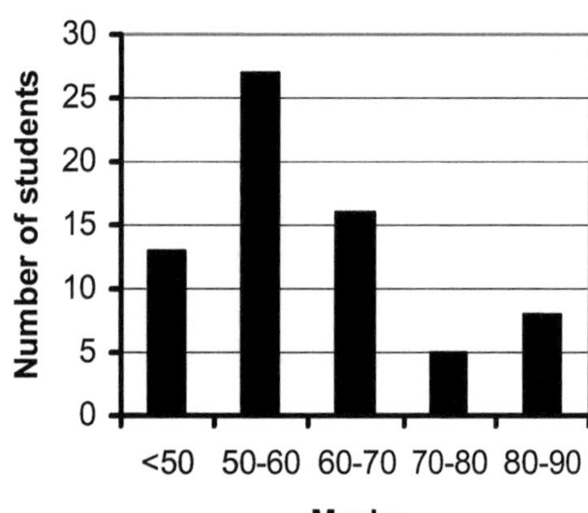

Study the bar graph carefully and answer the following question.

Which range of the marks is the most common?

(a) 60 - 70

(b) < 50

(c) 70 - 80

(d) 50 - 60

Directions: Study the following graph and answer the question nos. **74** and **75**.

The line graph given below shows the profile of a company during the period 2007 to 2012.

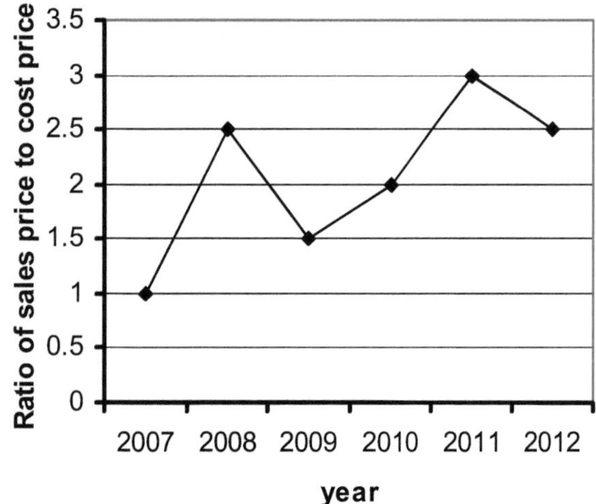

74. Find the percentage increase in sales price from 2007 to 2008.

(a) 150   (b) 75

(c) 25   (d) Data inadequate

75. If the cost price increases each year over previous year during the period 2007 to 2012, then in how many years sales price must increase in each year over previous year?

(a) 2   (b) 3

(c) 4   (d) 5

76. Where world's largest solar power plant opens recently?

(a) Neemuch, Madhya Pradesh

(b) Kamuthi, Tamil Nadu

(c) Sakri, Maharashtra

(d) Charanka village, Patan district, Gujarat

77. National Youth Day is celebrated on the birthday of

(a) Mahatma Gandhi

(b) Swami Vivekananda

(c) Jawaharlal Nehru

(d) Subhash Chandra Bose

78. 'ABO' blood group is known to be a 'Universal Recipient' because

(a) antibody A and B both are present in AB blood group

(b) no antigen is present in AB blood group

(c) antigen A and B both are present in AB blood group

(d) no antibody is present in AB blood group

79. Which logic gate is a 'universal gate'?

(a) NAND gate   (b) AND gate

(c) XOR gate   (d) OR gate

80. Strip cropping helps to stop

(a) Air pollution   (b) Soil erosion

(c) Water pollution   (d) Marine pollution

81. The manufacture of chlorofluorocarbon compounds has been phased out under the

(a) Kyoto protocol

(b) Montreal protocol

(c) Stockholm Convention on Persistent Organic Pollutants

(d) Protocol to the Convention on Long-range Transboundary Air Pollution on the Control of Emissions of Volatile Organic Compounds

82. Which battle resulted in a complete Macedonian victory and the annexation of the Punjab?
    (*a*) Battle of Trafalgar
    (*b*) Battle of Hydaspas
    (*c*) Battle of Wagram
    (*d*) Battle of Buxar

83. Who developed the synthetic polymer DOPA (dihydroxyphenylalanine)?
    (*a*) Messersmith
    (*b*) Henri Braconnot
    (*c*) Friedrich Ludersdorf
    (*d*) Nathaniel Hayward

84. Word Earth Day is celebrated on
    (*a*) April 22   (*b*) May 31
    (*c*) June 5   (*d*) July 30

85. International Translation Day observed across the world on __________.
    (*a*) 25 September   (*b*) 27 September
    (*c*) 30 September   (*d*) 2 October

86. Who can dissolve the Lok Sabha of Indian Parliament?
    (*a*) Speaker
    (*b*) President
    (*c*) Vice-president
    (*d*) Chairman of Rajya Sabha

87. Which of the following was not a member of the Simon Commission?
    (*a*) Clement Attlee   (*b*) George Lane-Fox
    (*c*) Vernon Hartshorn   (*d*) Lord Birkenhead

88. Which hormone regulates blood pressure and water (fluid) balance in human beings?
    (*a*) Rennin   (*b*) Renin-angiotensin
    (*c*) Thyroid   (*d*) Parathyroid

89. Who formed the Indian National Army in 1942?
    (*a*) S C Bose   (*b*) Mohan Singh
    (*c*) Shah Nawaz Khan   (*d*) P.K. Sahgal

90. Film and Television Institute of India (FTII) was very much in the news in 2015. It is located at
    (*a*) Pune   (*b*) Chennai
    (*c*) Mumbai   (*d*) Bhopal

91. Mohra is the hydro power project in
    (*a*) Himachal Pradesh   (*b*) Jammu and Kashmir
    (*c*) Assam   (*d*) Punjab

92. Asplenia refers to a non-functioning of
    (*a*) Liver   (*b*) Spleen
    (*c*) Lungs   (*d*) Gall bladder

93. 'Inferior goods' demand falls as consumer income
    (*a*) Decreases
    (*b*) Increases
    (*c*) Remains stagnant
    (*d*) Does not depend on the consumers income

94. Which strait connects Black Sea to the Marmara Sea?
    (*a*) Bosphorus Strait
    (*b*) Strait of the Dardanelles
    (*c*) Strait of Kerch
    (*d*) Strait of Malacca

95. Additional judges of Indian High Court are appointed by
    (*a*) Chief Justice of concerned High Court
    (*b*) Chief Justice of India
    (*c*) President
    (*d*) Supreme Court judges

96. Photography Exposure is measured in
    (*a*) Lux seconds   (*b*) Candela
    (*c*) Roentgen   (*d*) Decibels

97. In which of the following categories, Patrick Modiano received the Nobel Prize 2014?
    (*a*) Literature
    (*b*) Chemistry
    (*c*) Physiology
    (*d*) Physics

98. The Rainbow Coalition was founded in Chicago, Illinois by
    (*a*) Fred Hampton
    (*b*) Lyndon B. Johnson
    (*c*) Jose Cha Cha Jimenez
    (*d*) Puerto Rican

99. Article 51 A of Indian constitution deals with
    (*a*) Fundamental rights
    (*b*) Fundamental duties
    (*c*) Directive principles of state policy
    (*d*) President's rule

100. Name the Joint Military Training exercised has been launched at Uttarakhand to encourage the Indo-US Defence Co-operation?
    (*a*) Yudh Abhyas 2016
    (*b*) Yudh Karunya 2016
    (*c*) Yudha Marg 2016
    (*d*) Yudhavaisav 2016

ANSWERS

1. (c)	**2.** (d)	**3.** (d)	**4.** (b)	**5.** (a)	**6.** (d)	**7.** (d)	**8.** (c)	**9.** (c)	**10.** (d)
11. (c)	**12.** (d)	**13.** (c)	**14.** (d)	**15.** (c)	**16.** (a)	**17.** (b)	**18.** (b)	**19.** (a)	**20.** (c)
21. (d)	**22.** (d)	**23.** (c)	**24.** (c)	**25.** (b)	**26.** (d)	**27.** (a)	**28.** (b)	**29.** (b)	**30.** (b)
31. (a)	**32.** (b)	**33.** (a)	**34.** (d)	**35.** (b)	**36.** (b)	**37.** (d)	**38.** (c)	**39.** (a)	**40.** (c)
41. (a)	**42.** (c)	**43.** (b)	**44.** (a)	**45.** (d)	**46.** (b)	**47.** (d)	**48.** (d)	**49.** (b)	**50.** (b)
51. (c)	**52.** (a)	**53.** (d)	**54.** (c)	**55.** (c)	**56.** (c)	**57.** (d)	**58.** (b)	**59.** (d)	**60.** (d)
61. (c)	**62.** (b)	**63.** (b)	**64.** (b)	**65.** (a)	**66.** (d)	**67.** (c)	**68.** (c)	**69.** (b)	**70.** (c)
71. (a)	**72.** (b)	**73.** (d)	**74.** (d)	**75.** (b)	**76.** (b)	**77.** (b)	**78.** (d)	**79.** (a)	**80.** (b)
81. (b)	**82.** (b)	**83.** (a)	**84.** (a)	**85.** (c)	**86.** (b)	**87.** (d)	**88.** (b)	**89.** (b)	**90.** (a)
91. (b)	**92.** (b)	**93.** (b)	**94.** (a)	**95.** (c)	**96.** (a)	**97.** (a)	**98.** (a)	**99.** (b)	**100.** (a)

EXPLANATIONS

1.

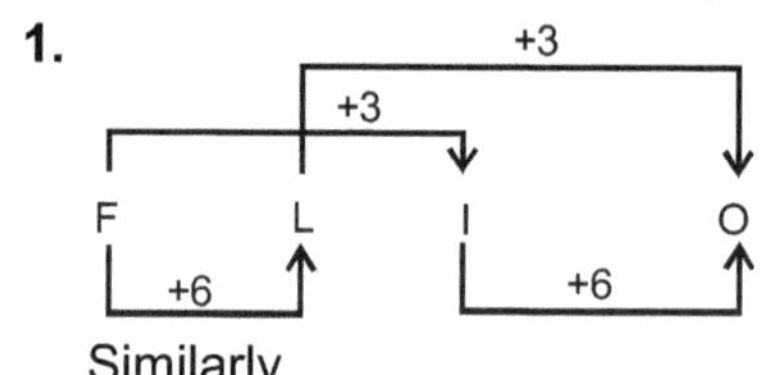

Similarly,

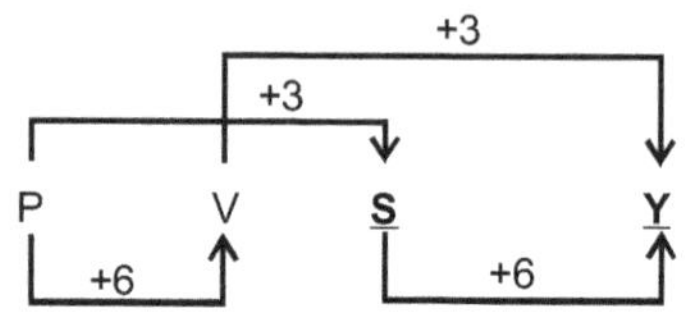

2. The series is a,ab,abc,a,ab,abc,…

3.

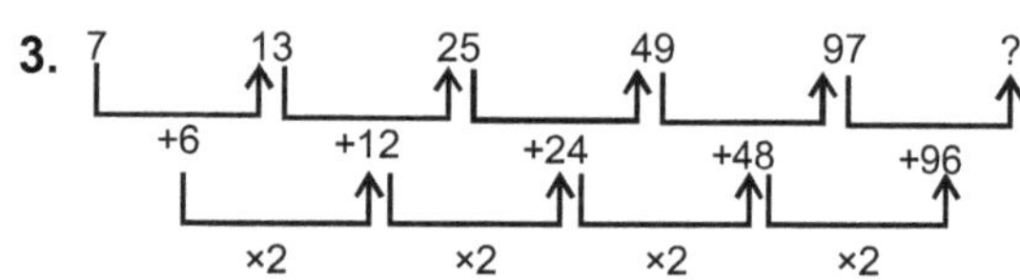

∴ ? = 97 + 96 = 193.

4. The letters in the series are moving four places back in the alphabetical series. So, the next letters in the series will be F B X.

5.
```
B      S      G
↓+6   ↓−2   ↓+3
H      Q      J
↓+6   ↓−2   ↓+3
N      O      M
↓+6   ↓−2   ↓+3
T      M      P
```

6.

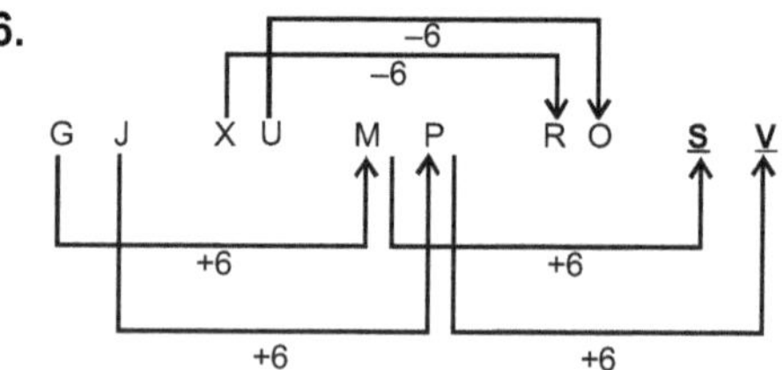

7. The number indicated by these symbols is 7 4 8 1 6.

8. Sum of the digits of 272 is 11. While in rest of the three options, sum of the digits of the numbers is 10.

9. Animals in options (a), (b) and (d) are mammals while hen is a bird. Hence, option (c) is the correct answer.

10.

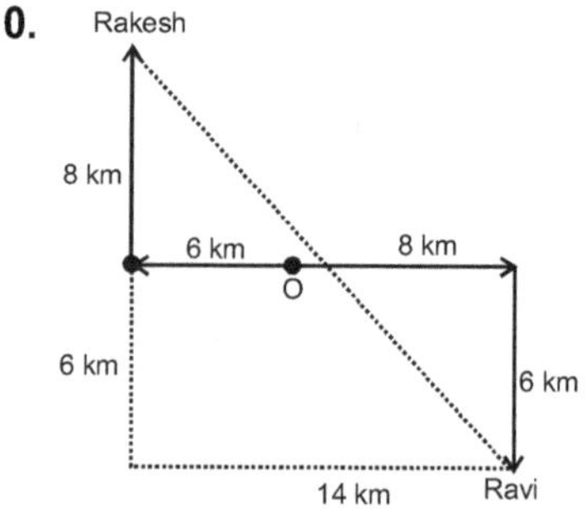

Let O be the initial position of Ravi and Rakesh.

Distance between Ravi and Rakesh

$$= \sqrt{14^2 + 14^2} = 14\sqrt{2} \text{ km.}$$

11. Option (c) is the answer since the given word has a single 'R' while TROUSER uses 'R' twice.

12. Option (d) is the correct answer since the given word does not have 'E', while CAVERN has an 'E' in it.

13. The given relation is true for option (c). Equation can be written as:

$12 \div 4 + 5 < 4 \times 5 - 10 \Rightarrow 8 < 10$, which is true.

14. $P(16) \xrightarrow{+4} T(20)$

$L(12) \xrightarrow{-4} H(8)$

$A(1) \xrightarrow{+4} E(5)$

$N(14) \xrightarrow{-4} J(10)$

$E(5) \xrightarrow{+4} I(9)$

$T(20) \xrightarrow{-4} P(16)$

Similarly,

$S(19) \xrightarrow{+4} W(23)$

$Q(17) \xrightarrow{-4} M(13)$

$U(21) \xrightarrow{+4} Y(25)$

$A(1) \xrightarrow{+4} W(23)$

$R(18) \xrightarrow{+4} V(22)$

$E(5) \xrightarrow{-4} A(1)$

15. The number formed from last three digits is added to the number to get the next term.

$1153 + 153 = 1306$

$1306 + 306 = \underline{\textbf{1612}}$

$1612 + 612 = 2224$.

16. In column 1,

$5^2 = 25,\ 12^2 = 144 \Rightarrow 5 \times 12 \div 2 = 30$

In column 2,

$7^2 = 49,\ 14^2 = 196 \Rightarrow 7 \times 14 \div 2 = 49$

Similarly, in column 3,

$9^2 = 81,\ 16^2 = 256 \Rightarrow 9 \times 16 \div 2 = \underline{\textbf{72}}$.

17. 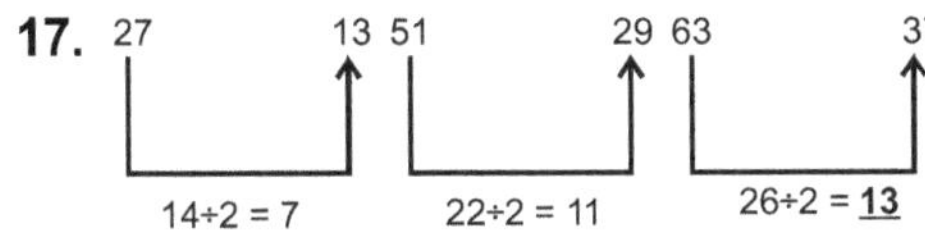

18. Let the capacity of the tank be LCM (6, 9, 10) = 90 units.

Number of units filled by pipe A alone in one hour

$= \dfrac{90}{6} = 15$

Number of units filled by pipe B alone in one hour

$= \dfrac{90}{9} = 10$

Number of units emptied by pipe C in one hour $= \dfrac{90}{10} = 9$

Number of units filled in one hour when all three pipes are opened together $= 15 + 10 - 9 = 16$

Hence, $\dfrac{3}{4}$th of the tank can be filled in

$\dfrac{3}{4} \times \dfrac{90}{16} \approx 4$ hours 13 minutes.

19. 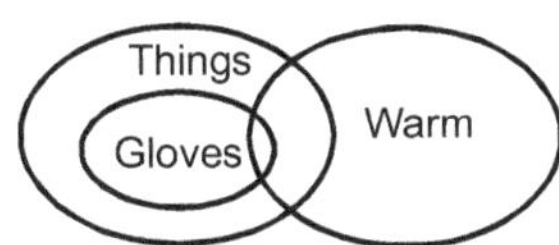

As is clear from the Venn diagram, only conclusion (III) follows. Hence, option (a) is the correct answer.

22. Universe contains millions of galaxies and each galaxy contains millions of stars and planets.

24. From matrix,

B – 45, 62

O – 25, 46

R – 22, 63

N – 33, 53

From options,

BORN→ 62, 46, 22, 53.

26. 'Awash' means flooded in large amount of water or any other liquid. 'Soaked' means to make someone or something wet with a large amount of water or any other liquid. Hence, option (d) is the correct answer. 'Swamp' refers to the land that is always wet and often covered in water. 'Arid' means very dry. 'Dampish' refers to the slight wetness in the air.

27. 'Endue' means to provide. Hence, option (a) is the correct answer.

28. A person is called 'timid' when he shows lack of courage or confidence. 'Audacious' is used to describe someone who is very bold and confident. Hence, option (b) is the correct answer. A person is described as 'aggressive' when he shows aggression and uses forceful methods to succeed.

29. 'Precarious' refers to something that is not safe, strong or steady. Hence, its antonym will be option (b), stable.

30. An agent who negotiates contracts of purchase and sale is called a 'broker'. The contracts can be contracts of securities, commodities, real estate, etc. Hence, option (b) is the correct answer. A 'salesman' is a person whose job is to sell things. A 'bargainer' is a negotiator of the terms of a trade. A 'moderator' is someone who leads a discussion in a group and tells each person when to speak.

31. A person who believes that a particular type of behaviour is important is called a 'stickler'. Hence, option (a) is the correct answer. 'Perseverer' is a persistent person. Someone who is lazy and avoids work is called a 'slacker'. Person who has certain social values is said to be 'moral'.

32. 'Egotist' refers to a person who feels that he is too important. Hence, option (b) is the correct answer. 'Immodest' means having too high opinion of oneself. 'Presumptuous' means being too confident in a way that shows lack of respect. 'Inordinate' means going beyond what is usual or proper.

33. 'Hooked up' means to connect. 'Associate' means to make a connection between people or things in your mind. Hence, option (*a*) is the correct answer. 'Disperse' means to move apart in different directions. 'Snub' means to ignore someone deliberately.

34. 'To think on one's feet' means to be able to think and speak effectively without any preparation. Hence, option (*d*) is the correct answer.

35. If a remark is 'close to home', it means that it is accurate and it makes you feel uncomfortable and embarrassed. Hence, option (*b*) is the correct answer.

36. The correct spelling is 'Assassin'. Hence, option (*b*) is the correct answer.

37. The given sentence is correct. A preposition such as 'between' should be followed by an objective pronoun (such as me, him, her and us) rather than a subjective pronoun (such as I, he, she and we). In part (*c*), the correct expression is 'Somiya and me' since it is the object of the sentence. Hence, part (*d*) is the correct answer.

38. There is a parallelism error in the sentence. The correct sentence should be "…I'm having dinner with Dikshant". Hence, part (*c*) is the correct option.

39. The sentence is in present perfect continuous tense since the action (reading book) started in the past, i.e., two months back, and is continuing in the present. Therefore, 'I am' in part (*a*) should be 'I have been', making part (*a*) the answer.

40. 'To be a cut above the rest' means to be better than other things or people. Hence, option (*c*) is the correct answer. Options (*a*), (*b*) and (*d*) will make the sentence grammatically incorrect.

41. Since 'eating disorders' is plural, the blank will take a plural verb. Therefore, options (*c*) and (*d*) are incorrect. Moreover, eating disorders are not traits; they are life-threatening conditions. 'Trait' is a quality that makes one different from another. Hence, option (*a*) is the correct answer.

42. Option (*c*) is the correct answer. The blank needs to be filled in with an adjective that would describe the noun 'pressure'. The other forms of the word will make the sentence grammatically incorrect.

43. Simple present tense is used for official timetables and programmes. Hence, the correct answer is option (*b*). 'Will be arriving' is future continuous tense that talks about things that will be in progress at a time in the future. The sentence does not suggest this and is therefore, incorrect.

44. The given sentence is incorrect. Past perfect continuous is used to denote when an action began in the past and is still continuing. Hence, option (*a*) is the correct answer.

45. In order to express the unreal, the hypothetical, the speculative, or imagined, we move time one step backward. In such cases two verbs are involved: one in the clause stating the condition (the "if" clause) and one in the result clause. Here **present unreal** event is used, so we will put the verb in the condition clause one step back, i.e., into the past. Hence, the given sentence, option (*d*) is the correct answer.

46. The Indus Civilization can be best described as sophisticated and progressive. From the second sentence of the passage we can infer that the people of Indus civilization were sophisticated. The civilization can be said to be progressive since it was then adept at plumbing, it was one of the worlds first city building cultures and had a well planned sewage system. Hence, option (*b*) is the correct answer.

47. The passage says that the scientists found hints that suggested that the people of Indus civilization were not as peaceful as they are portrayed to be. Hence, option (*d*) is the correct answer.

48. Option (*d*) is the correct answer. It can be inferred from the passage that scientists are trying to learn more about the civilization. Hence, option (*d*) is the correct answer.

49. The last paragraph says that the civilization accomplished great things and then goes on to list its accomplishments. Hence, option (*b*) is the correct answer.

50. The passage says that the scientists are 'now' trying to unravel the mysteries of the civilization through human bones. This means that earlier attempts were not made to know about the civilization through bones. Hence, option (*b*) is the correct answer.

51. Speed of the first train $= \dfrac{12 \times 1000}{8 \times 60} = 25$ m/sec

and speed of the second train $= \dfrac{24 \times 1000}{10 \times 60} = 40$ m/sec

Let after 'x' meter second train catch the first train. Then,

$$\frac{x}{40} = \frac{x - 360}{25}$$

$\Rightarrow 3x = 2880$

$\Rightarrow x = 960$ m.

52. $\dfrac{11 + \sqrt{6}}{\sqrt{7 + 2\sqrt{6}}} = \dfrac{11 + \sqrt{6}}{\sqrt{\left(\sqrt{6}\right)^2 + 2\sqrt{6} + 1}} = \dfrac{11 + \sqrt{6}}{\sqrt{6} + 1} = \dfrac{11 + \sqrt{6}}{\sqrt{6} + 1} \times \dfrac{\sqrt{6} - 1}{\sqrt{6} - 1}$

$= \dfrac{-5 + 10\sqrt{6}}{5} = -1 + 2\sqrt{6}$

$\therefore$ X = –1 and Y = 6

Hence, 5X + Y = 5(–1) + 6 = 1.

53. $a^2 - 1 = -6a$

$\Rightarrow a - \dfrac{1}{a} = -6$

Now, $\left(a + \dfrac{1}{a}\right)^2 - 5\left(a - \dfrac{1}{a}\right) = \left(\left(a - \dfrac{1}{a}\right)^2 + 4\right) - 5\left(a - \dfrac{1}{a}\right)$

$= \left(\left(-6\right)^2 + 4\right) - 5 \times -6 = 40 + 30 = 70.$

54. Given $x - y = 6$ and $x^2 - y^2 = 60$, therefore, $x + y = 10$

Hence, the average of x and $y = \dfrac{x+y}{2} = \dfrac{10}{2} = 5$.

55. $\dfrac{1}{1 + 5 \times 5^{2x-y}} + \dfrac{5}{5 + 5^{y-2x}} = \dfrac{1}{1 + 5^{2x-y+1}} + \dfrac{1}{1 + \dfrac{1}{5^{2x-y+1}}}$

$= \dfrac{1}{1 + 5^{2x-y+1}} + \dfrac{5^{2x-y+1}}{1 + 5^{2x-y+1}} = 1$.

56. 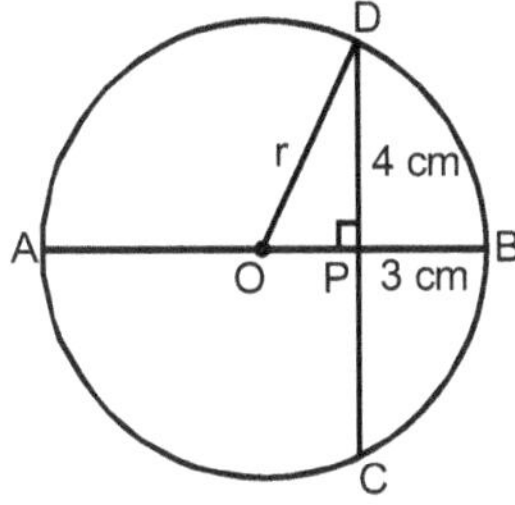

Let 'r' be the radius of the circle. Then,

$$OP = r - 3$$

In $\triangle OPD$, $OD^2 = OP^2 + PD^2$

$\Rightarrow r^2 = (r-3)^2 + 4^2 \quad \Rightarrow r^2 = r^2 + 9 - 6r + 16 \quad \Rightarrow r = \dfrac{25}{6}$ cm.

57. 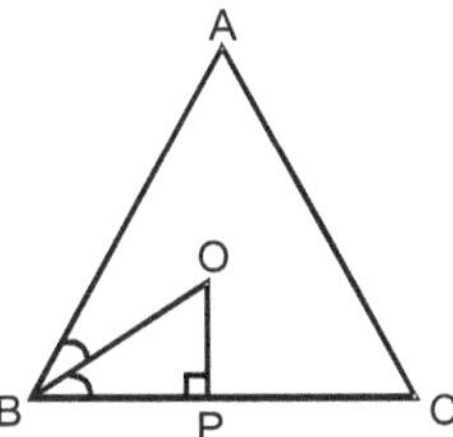

$\angle ABO = \angle OBP = \dfrac{\angle ABC}{2}$ and

$\angle OBP = 90° - \angle BOP = 90° - 39° = 51°$

Hence, $\angle ABC = 2 \times 51° = 102°$.

58. 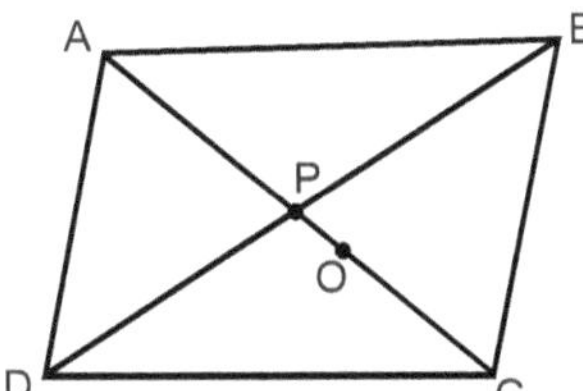

Let P be the point of intersection of the two diagonals AC and BD. Then, AP = PC = 12 cm.

As point O is centroid of $\triangle BCD$, therefore, PO : OC = 1 : 2

$\Rightarrow PO = \dfrac{1}{1+2} \times PC = 4$ cm

Hence, AO = 12 + 4 = 16 cm.

59. 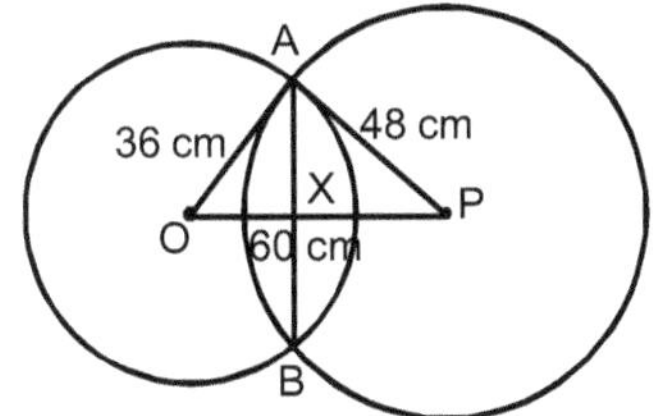

Let O and P be the centres of the circles with radii 36 cm and 48 cm respectively, AB be the common chord and X be the point of intersection of OP and AB. Then,

$\triangle OAP$ and $\triangle OXA$ are similar triangles, therefore,

$$\dfrac{AP}{OP} = \dfrac{AX}{OA}$$

$\Rightarrow \dfrac{48}{60} = \dfrac{AX}{36}$

$\Rightarrow AX = \dfrac{144}{5}$

$= 28.8$ cm

Hence, the length of the common chord

$= AB = 2 \times AX = 57.6$ cm.

60. Let the six angles be 3x, 5x, 4x, 3x, 5x and 4x. Then,

$3x + 5x + 4x + 3x + 5x + 4x = 720°$

$\Rightarrow x = 30°$

Hence, the sum of the smallest two angles = 3x + 3x = 6x = 6 × 30° = 180°.

61. $851 = 23 \times 37$

Hence, 851 has two prime factors.

62. Let the work done by a man and a woman in one day be m and w respectively. Then,

The total work = 24w × 30 = 20m × 30

$\Rightarrow 6w = 5m$

Hence, required number of days

$$= \dfrac{24 \times 30w}{8w + 10m} = \dfrac{24 \times 30w}{8w + 12w} = 36.$$

63. Let 'r' be the radius of the circle and 'a' be the length of the side of the square. Then, 'r' is the inradius of the equilateral triangle.

$\Rightarrow r = \dfrac{6}{2\sqrt{3}} = \sqrt{3}$ cm

$\Rightarrow$ Diameter = 2r = $2\sqrt{3}$ cm

$\because$ Diameter of the circle = Diagonal of the square

$\Rightarrow$ Diagonal of the square $= 2\sqrt{3}$ cm

$\Rightarrow$ Side of the square $= \dfrac{2\sqrt{3}}{\sqrt{2}} = \sqrt{6}$ cm

Hence, area of the square $= \left(\sqrt{6}\right)^2 = 6$ cm^2.

64. 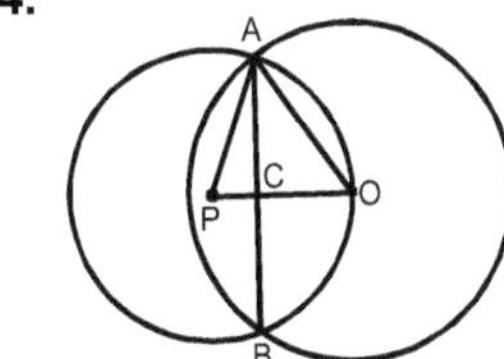

Let AB be the common chord, O and P be the centres of the circles of radius 8 cm and 6 cm respectively and OC be x cm. Then, in $\triangle AOC$,

$$AC^2 = OA^2 - OC^2 = 8^2 - x^2 \qquad \dots \text{(i)}$$

In $\triangle ACP$,

$$AC^2 = PA^2 - CP^2 = 6^2 - (6-x)^2 \qquad \dots \text{(ii)}$$

From (i) and (ii), we get $x = \dfrac{16}{3}$

$$\Rightarrow AC = 8^2 - \left(\dfrac{16}{3}\right)^2 = \dfrac{8\sqrt{5}}{3} \text{ cm}$$

Hence, length of the common chord

$$= 2 \times AC = \dfrac{16\sqrt{5}}{3} \text{ cm.}$$

65. Cost price of the cycle = 1280 + 270
$$= ₹1,550$$

Selling price = 2325 × 0.8 = ₹1,860

Hence, profit percent $= \dfrac{1860 - 1550}{1550} \times 100 = 20.$

66. Let the radius of the right circular cone be x cm. Then,

volume of a right circular cylinder = volume of a right circular cone

$$\Rightarrow \pi \times (12)^2 \times 9 = \dfrac{1}{3} \pi \times x^2 \times 108$$

$$\Rightarrow x = 6$$

Hence, the base diameter of the right circular cone

$$= 2x = 12 \text{ cm.}$$

67. Let the daughter be born 'x' years after their marriage. Then,

average age of the man, wife and their daughter one year after the birth of the daughter

$$= \dfrac{(28 + (x+1)) \times 2 + 1}{3} = \dfrac{59 + 2x}{3} = 21$$

$$\Rightarrow x = 2$$

∴ Present age of the daughter = 7 − 2 = 5 years

Hence, the present age of the son = 5 − 2 = 3 years.

68. Profit on 16 cycles = 1600 × 16 × 0.1 = ₹2,560

Profit on 25 cycles = 1600 × 25 × 0.16 = ₹6,400

Profit on 15 cycles = 1600 × 15 × 0.18 = ₹4,320

Profit on 40 cycles = 1600 × 40 × 0.22 = ₹14,080

Total profit = 2560 + 6400 + 4320 + 14080 = ₹27,360.

69. Let the distance between city A and city B be x km.

Then, $42 + \dfrac{x}{4} + \dfrac{2x}{5} = x$

$$\Rightarrow 42 + \dfrac{(5+8)x}{20} = x$$

$$\Rightarrow x = 120.$$

70. $\cos(50° - \psi) = \sin(90° - (50° - \psi)) = \sin(70° - \theta)$

$$\Rightarrow (90° - (50° - \psi)) = (70° - \theta)$$

$$\Rightarrow 40° + \psi = 70° - \theta$$

$$\Rightarrow \theta + \psi = 30°$$

$$\therefore \cot(\theta + \psi) = \cot 30° = \sqrt{3}.$$

71. $\cos\theta + \sec\theta = 2$

$$\Rightarrow \cos\theta + \dfrac{1}{\cos\theta} = 2$$

$$\Rightarrow \cos^2\theta - 2\cos\theta + 1 = 0$$

$$\Rightarrow (1 - \cos\theta)^2 = 0$$

$$\Rightarrow \cos\theta = 1$$

$$\therefore \cos^n\theta + \sec^n\theta = 1 + 1 = 2.$$

72. $\dfrac{2\tan\theta}{a} = \dfrac{3\sec\theta}{b}$

$$\Rightarrow \sin\theta = \dfrac{3a}{2b}, \text{ then } \tan\theta = \dfrac{3a}{\sqrt{(2b)^2 - (3a)^2}}$$

and $\sec\theta = \dfrac{2b}{\sqrt{(2b)^2 - (3a)^2}}$

$$\therefore 2\tan\theta + 3\sec\theta$$

$$= 2 \times \dfrac{3a}{\sqrt{(2b)^2 - (3a)^2}} + 3 \times \dfrac{2b}{\sqrt{(2b)^2 - (3a)^2}}$$

$$= \dfrac{6(a+b)}{\sqrt{(2b)^2 - (3a)^2}}.$$

73. The most common range of the marks is 50 − 60.

74. As the absolute values of sales price in both the years are not known.

Hence, the data is inadequate.

75. As the ratio of sales to cost price increases over previous year in the years 2008, 2010 and 2011, therefore, sales price must increase in each of these years over previous year.

■■

GENERAL INTELLIGENCE

Directions: In question nos. **1** & **2**, select the related letters /word /number from the given alternatives.

1. Vitamin A : Night blindness :: Vitamin C : ?

   (a) Nerve Contraction   (b) Rickets

   (c) Scurvy   (d) Goitre

2. H : 512 : : M : ?

   (a) 2197   (b) 1728

   (c) 2744   (d) 1566

3. If 462 * 3 = 18 and 564 * 2 = 12, then 617 * 4 =?

   (a) 13   (b) 14

   (c) 20   (d) 16

Directions: In the following question which one set of letters when sequentially placed at the gaps in the given letter series shall complete it?

4. a_bcabb_abc_aa_c

   (a) baab   (b) bccb

   (c) abac   (d) accb

Directions: In question nos. **5** to **6**, find the odd word/number / number-pair from the given alternatives.

5. 1, 9, 52, 94, 18, 57, 961

   (a) 18   (b) 961

   (c) 57   (d) 52

6. (a) Alfalfa   (b) Aloe Vera

   (c) Bonsai   (d) Lavender

Directions: In question nos. **7** to **9**, a series is given, with one term missing. Choose the correct alternative from the given ones that will complete the series.

7. ac, abd, eg, efh, ik, _?_ .

   (a) ikl   (b) ijl

   (c) jkm   (d) jkn

8. 10, 11, 24, 75,_?_ .

   (a) 345   (b) 304

   (c) 450   (d) 215

9. SPV : FCI :: LIO : ?

   (a) VZX

   (b) OLS

   (c) JGL

   (d) WTZ

10. Ram is the son of Geeta, who is the daughter of Dinesh. Suresh is the only son of Dinesh. How is Suresh related to Ram?

   (a) Cousin   (b) Uncle

   (c) Father   (d) Brother

11. Ankit told his wife Reena that Uma is his mother and Rohit is the son of his only sister. How is Uma related to Rohit?

   (a) Aunty   (b) Sister

   (c) Mother   (d) Grandmother

Directions: In the following question from the given alternatives, select the word which **cannot** be formed using the letters of the given word.

12. ACCOMPLISHMENTS

   (a) POLISH   (b) MOMENTS

   (c) COMPLIMENT   (d) COMMUTE

13. Which of the following interchanges of numbers would make the given equation correct?

$6 \times 3 + 96 \div 27 = 97$

   (a) 6, 96   (b) 3, 96

   (c) 6, 27   (d) 3, 27

14. Put the correct mathematical signs in the following equation from the given alternatives.

18 _?_19_?_ 3 _?_ 4 = 118

   (a) ÷ + –   (b) + + ÷

   (c) × ÷ +   (d) × + ÷

15. If the word SAMSUNG is coded as 14-6-8-24-16-19-2, how would you write LIBERTY?

   (a) 17-4-7-26-23-15-4   (b) 7-14-23-10-13-25-20

   (c) 7-4-23-26-13-15-20   (d) 17-14-7-10-23-25-4

Directions: In question nos. **16** and **17**, select the missing number from the given responses.

16.

16	24	18
8	32	27
32	18	?

   (a) 12

   (b) 24

   (c) 26

   (d) 16

17.

3	7	4
6	4	27
8	7	3
12	14	?

(a) 22 (b) 18

(c) 24 (d) 25

18. Aman walks 6 km towards North. Then turns 135° anticlockwise and walks for 10 km. Then he turns 45° anticlockwise and walks for 8 km and finally turned 90° clockwise and walks for 7 km. In what direction is Aman now?

(a) North-west (b) North-east

(c) South- west (d) South-east

Directions: In the following question one/two statements are given, followed by two/three conclusions. You have to consider the statements to be true, even if they seem at variance with commonly known facts. You are to decide which of the given conclusions can definitely be drawn from the given statements.

19. Statement : Children are God's gift to Earth.

Conclusions :

I. Adults are not God's gift.

II. God frequently sends gifts to Earth.

(a) Both conclusions I and II follow.

(b) Neither conclusion I nor II follows.

(c) Only conclusion I follows.

(d) Only conclusion II follows.

20. Which of the following diagrams best depicts the relationship between venomous, snakes and reptiles?

(a) 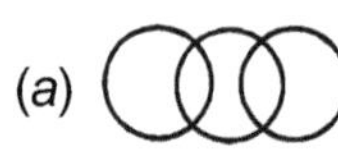 (b) 

(c)  (d) 

21. How many squares are there in the following figure?

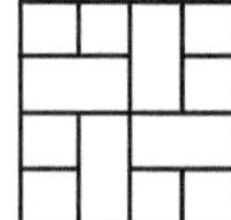

(a) 11 (b) 12

(c) 13 (d) 14

Directions: In In the following question in the given diagram, circle represents students playing cricket, square represents students playing football, triangle represents students playing tennis and rectangle represents students playing hockey. Different regions in the diagram are numbered 1 to 11.

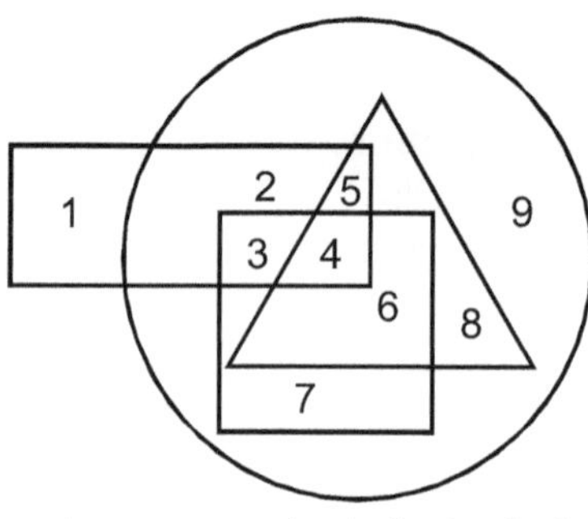

22. Which region represents students playing cricket and hockey but not tennis nor football ?

(a) 1

(b) 2

(c) 3

(d) 5

Directions : In question nos. **23**, which answer figure will complete the pattern in the question figure?

23. Question figure :

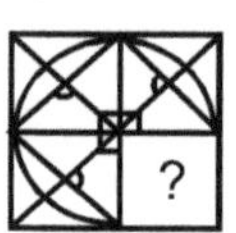

Answer figures :

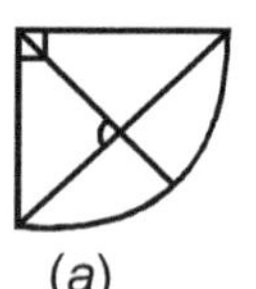 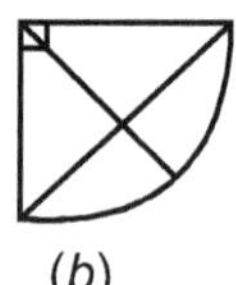 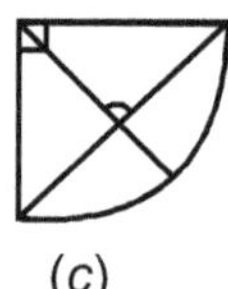 

(a) (b) (c) (d)

24. Which answer figure includes all the components given in the question figure?

Question figure :

Answer figures :

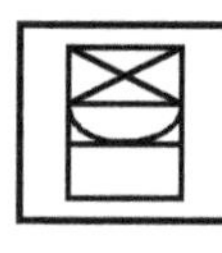   

(a) (b) (c) (d)

25. Choose the correct water-image of the question figure from given answer figures.

Question figure :

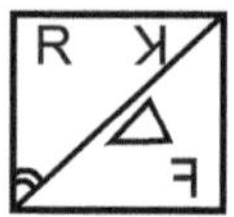

Answer figures :

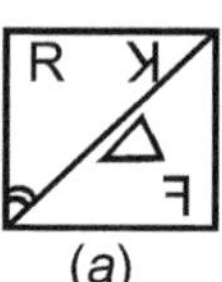 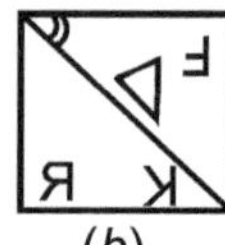 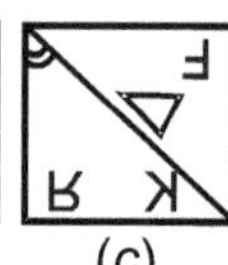 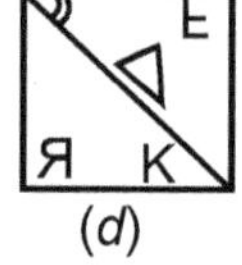

(a) (b) (c) (d)

ENGLISH LANGUAGE

Directions for question 26 to 27 : In the following question, a word is followed by four options. Select the option that best expresses the meaning of the given word.

26. Inferno

(a) Blaze (b) Mark

(c) Poison (d) Anger

27. Preposterous

(a) Realistic (b) Absurd

(c) Wise (d) Impulsive

Directions for questions 28 to 29 : In each of the following questions, a word is followed by four options. Select the option that is opposite in meaning to the given word.

28. Dovish

(a) Hawkish (b) Owlish

(c) Vulturous (d) Ravenous

29. Apposite

(a) Suitable (b) Harmonious

(c) Immaterial (d) Disagreeable

Directions: In question nos. **30** to **32**, Out of the four alternatives, choose the one which can be substituted for the given words/sentences.

30. I was under the wrong impression that the course was for complete beginners.

(a) fathomed (b) comprehended

(c) misapprehended (d) apprehended

31. They are celebrating their fifth wedding anniversary this year.

(a) triennial (b) quinquennial

(c) septennial (d) vicennial

32. A person who writes historical records

(a) Archaeologist (b) Annalist

(c) Radiologist (d) Genealogist

Direction for questions 33 to 35 : In the following question four alternatives are given for the idioms/phrases given below. Choose the alternative which best expresses the meaning of the given idiom/phrase.

33. Miss Jasmine kicked the bucket last week.

(a) had a fit (b) died

(c) retired (d) fired someone

34. Mr. Hyde was killed by a gangster because he was thought to be a stool pigeon.

(a) lazy person.

(b) spy for the police.

(c) forgetful person.

(d) burden.

35. To blow a fuse

(a) To be nervous

(b) To lose one's temper

(c) To act in boastful way

(d) To beat someone to death

Directions : In the following question groups of four different words are given below. In group, one word is correctly spelt. Find the correctly spelt word and mark your answer accordingly.

36. (a) Trapeese (b) Trapeze

(c) Trapeeze (d) Trapes

Directions for questions 37 to 39 : Read each of the following sentences to find out whether there is any grammatical error in it. The error, if any, will be in one part of the sentence. The number of that part is the answer. If there is 'No error' the answer is (d).

37. There's Sabu, whom (a)/ they say is the best (b)/ wrestler in the town. (c) / No error (d)

38. The play started by (a)/ the time Tenali Raman arrived (b)/ at the biggest theater in the world. (c)/ No error (d)

39. Our boss doesn't consent (a) / to us leaving work (b) / early on Saturday. (c)/ No error (d)

Directions for questions 40 to 42 : Each of the following sentences contains a blank to be filled in with an appropriate word. Choose the correct alternative out of the four given options.

40. Night came ______ . A full moon ______ high over the trees.

(a) by, risen (b) on, rose

(c) in, rise (d) by, raised

41. 'Feel free to contact me ______ my email address', said Flintstone.

(a) upon (b) on

(c) at (d) by

42. Even the president's own bipartisan commission can't agree ______ what to do.

(a) with (b) on

(c) to (d) at

Directions for questions 43 to 45 : In each of the following questions, a part of the sentence is underlined. Beneath each sentence four different ways of phrasing the underlined part are given. Choose the grammatically correct option. In case no improvement is needed, your answer is option (d).

43. If your child is thinking about a gap year, they can get good advice from this book.

(a) child is thinking about a gap year, he

(b) children is thinking about a gap year, they

(c) child think about a gap year, he

(d) No improvement

44. By next December, we <u>will have lived</u> here for 6 months.
   (a) shall have been living
   (b) will be living
   (c) shall be living
   (d) No improvement

45. Tarak writes with just the right mix of <u>disdain</u> and empathy.
   (a) admiration
   (b) favour
   (c) affection
   (d) No improvement

Directions for questions 46 to 50 : You have given passage with 5 questions. Read the passage carefully and choose the best answer to each question out of the four alternatives given.

The murders of Andrew Borden and Abby Borden shocked the community. Borden was one of the wealthiest—and most unpopular—men in town. Frugal to a fault, he was a self-made man who had become the head of one of the town's largest banks and a substantial property owner. The dour businessman had also made many enemies on his rise to the top, and rumors swirled that Andrew and Abby had perhaps been killed as revenge for Andrew's shady business dealings. For the police, their daughter, Lizzie, was the prime suspect of the case. However, there was no physical evidence linking her to the murders. A hatchet had been discovered in the basement of the Borden home, but its blade was clean and the handle had been broken off—by Lizzie, according to police. The police's reluctance to use any sort of forensic testing hampered the investigation.

46. Find an option that is opposite in meaning to the word given in bold.
   Dour
   (a) Hostile
   (b) Cold
   (c) Grim
   (d) Gentle

47. Andrew was not liked by many people in town because
   (a) people were jealous that he was a self made man.
   (b) he used his money carefully.
   (c) he indulged in mendacious business practices.
   (d) people were jealous of his wealth.

48. According to the passage, which of the following was not one of the reasons that held back the investigation?
   (a) The police was not comfortable with forensic testing.
   (b) Lizzie distorted the evidence that interfered with the investigation.
   (c) The police was unable to find any physical evidence linking Lizzie to the case.
   (d) Andrew Borden had many enemies and so it was difficult to determine who the murderer was.

49. Which of the following is not a trait describing Andrew Borden?
   (a) Unpopular
   (b) Affluent
   (c) Economical
   (d) Prudent

50. What was the rumor that surrounded the couple's death?
   (a) Somebody killed the couple in order to take revenge.
   (b) The couple's daughter, Lizzie, was the murderer.
   (c) Andrew Borden had many enemies.
   (d) Andrew Borden was killed over money.

QUANTITATIVE APTITUDE

51. The marked price of a jacket was ₹ 2,400. A man bought the same for ₹ 1,632 after getting two successive discounts, the 1st being 20%. What was the 2nd discount?
   (a) 12%
   (b) 10%
   (c) 20%
   (d) 15%

52. A person bought two chairs for ₹ 2,400 and sold the first at a profit of 25% and second at a loss of 10%. If he sold the first at 20% loss and second at 30% profit, he would get ₹ 280 more. The difference of the cost price of the chairs was
   (a) ₹ 600
   (b) ₹ 400
   (c) ₹ 800
   (d) ₹ 900

53. The diagonals of a rhombus shaped field are 21 cm and 32 cm. Find the cost of tiling it at the rate of ₹ 2.25 per sq. cm.
   (a) ₹ 856
   (b) ₹ 786
   (c) ₹ 836
   (d) ₹ 756

54. If PM is the bisector of $\angle QPR$, then which of the following relations is definitely true?
   (a) PM > PQ
   (b) PM > QM
   (c) PQ < MR
   (d) PQ > QM

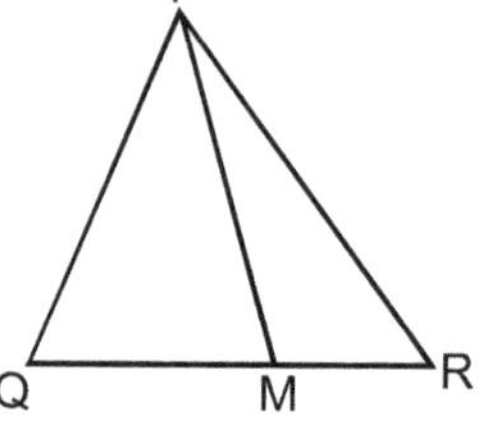

55. The cost price of an article was ₹1,540. If the dealer wanted to earn a profit of 10% after giving a discount of 30%, the marked price should be
   (a) ₹ 1,800
   (b) ₹ 2,400
   (c) ₹ 2,420
   (d) ₹ 2,200

56. If $\sec 43° = x$, then the value of

$$\frac{1}{\sec^2 47°} + \cos^2 43° + \cot^2 47° - \frac{1}{\cos^2 47° \csc^2 43°} \text{ is}$$

   (a) $x^2 - 1$
   (b) $\dfrac{1}{x^2 - 1}$
   (c) $\dfrac{1}{x^2 + 1}$
   (d) $x^2 + 1$

57. In a $\triangle PQR$, angles $P : Q : R = 2 : 2 : 1$. A line MN is drawn parallel to QR. Then difference between $\angle PMN$ and $\angle PNM$ is

(a) 72°　　　　　　　(b) 54°

(c) 36°　　　　　　　(d) 48°

58. The average age of a group of students in a school is 14 years. If 20% of them have an average age of 12 years and 40% have an average age of 16 years, then the rest students have an average age of

(a) 13.6 years　　　　(b) 12 years

(c) 13 years　　　　　(d) 12.5 years

59. If $p^2 + q^2 + 4r^2 + 3 = 2p - 2q + 4r$, then the value of $2p - 3q + 4r$ is (Assume that p, q, r are all real numbers.)

(a) 0　　　　　　　　(b) 1

(c) 5　　　　　　　　(d) 7

60. What is the product of

$$\left(2^{2^{222}} + 1\right) \text{ and } \left(2^{2^{223}} + 1 + 2.2^{2^{222}}\right)?$$

(a) $\left(2^{2^{222}} + 1\right)^2$　　　　(b) $\left(2^{2^{223}} + 1\right)^3$

(c) $\left(2^{2^{223}} + 1\right)^2$　　　　(d) $\left(2^{2^{222}} + 1\right)^3$

61. Forty five toffess are distributed among P, Q, R and S in such a way that S gets half of what P gets. Q gets 4/5 of what P and S get together. R gets 2/3 of what others are getting. What is the number of toffees with S?

(a) 5　　　　　　　　(b) 10

(c) 12　　　　　　　(d) 18

62. Three trains P, Q and R travel 90 km in 1.5 hr, 2 hr and 3 hr respectively. R starts from a station, at a certain time, Q starts from the same point 30 minutes later and P starts from the the same station 45 minutes later than R. Then P meets Q and R after

(a) 1 hr, 30 min　　　(b) 45 min, 45 min

(c) 45 min, 1 hr　　　(d) 1 hr, 45 min

63. Eighty one chocolates have to be distributed among four friends A, B, C and D. Which of the following could be the ratio in which the chocolates are divided?

(a) $\dfrac{1}{12} : \dfrac{1}{6} : \dfrac{1}{9} : \dfrac{1}{2}$　　　(b) $\dfrac{1}{4} : \dfrac{1}{6} : \dfrac{1}{5} : \dfrac{1}{3}$

(c) $\dfrac{1}{18} : \dfrac{1}{6} : \dfrac{1}{9} : \dfrac{1}{8}$　　　(d) $\dfrac{1}{12} : \dfrac{1}{18} : \dfrac{1}{9} : \dfrac{1}{2}$

64. A builder undertook to finish a work in 120 days and employed 250 men. After 90 days it was observed that only 2/3rd of the work is completed. How many men should be increased or reduced to complete the work on time?

(a) 100　　　　　　　(b) 75

(c) 125　　　　　　　(d) 120

65. What is the value of the expression $x^4 - 15x^3 + 15x^2 - 15x + 15$ at x = 14?

(a) 1　　　　　　　　(b) 0

(c) 2　　　　　　　　(d) 3

66. A retailer purchases a watch with an offer of 20% + 20% discount on the marked price. He sold it to the customer at a profit of 50%. The price at which the retailer sold the watch was what percent more/less than the marked price?

(a) 32% more　　　　(b) 4% less

(c) 36% less　　　　　(d) 4% more

67. A person has to cover a distance of 48 km in one hour. If he travels 16 km at a speed of 24 km/hr, what should be the speed for the remaining journey to complete it in scheduled time?

(a) 48 km/hr　　　　(b) 54 km/hr

(c) 96 km/hr　　　　(d) 64 km/hr

68. If the sum of $\dfrac{x}{y}$ and its reciprocal is 1, then the value of $x^6 - y^6$ will be

(a) 1　　　　　　　　(b) –1

(c) 0　　　　　　　　(d) 3

69. Two pipes P and Q can fill a tank in 10 hrs and 12 hrs respectively. If the two pipes are opened at 9 AM in the morning, at what time the pipe P should be closed to fill the tank exactly at 3.00 PM?

(a) 12:30 PM　　　　(b) 1:00 PM

(c) 2:00 PM　　　　　(d) 12:00 PM

70. By selling 75 kg of apples, a fruit seller gains the selling price of 15 kg apples. The gain percentage is

(a) 25%　　　　　　(b) 20%

(c) 16.66%　　　　　(d) 22.5%

Directions: In question nos. **71** to **75**, the bar graph given below shows the production of wheat for states–L, M and N–during the period 2005 to 2010. Study the bar graph and answer the questions.

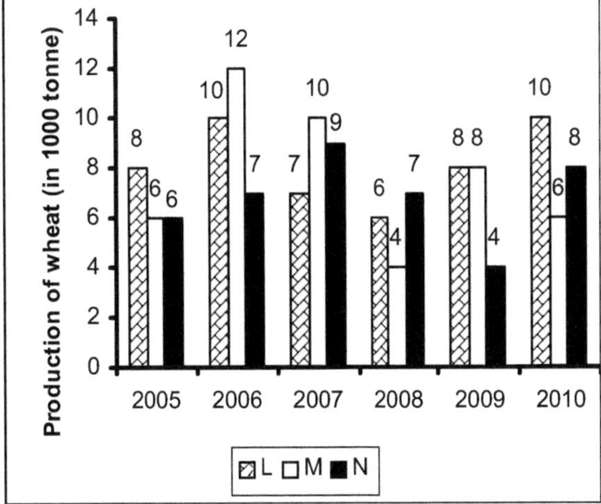

71. What is the difference between the total production of wheat for state M and state N during the given period?

(a) 5000 tonne   (b) 6000 tonne

(c) 7000 tonne   (d) 8000 tonne

72. What is the percentage increase in production of wheat in state M from 2005 to 2006?

(a) 25%   (b) 33.3%

(c) 50%   (d) 100%

73. In how many years production of wheat in state L shows an increment or decrement of more than 25% over the previous year?

(a) 4   (b) 5

(c) 2   (d) 3

74. The average annual production of wheat was maximum for which state(s)?

(a) M   (b) L

(c) N   (d) L and M

75. What is the difference between the average production of wheat in state M during 2008 to 2010, and that of state N during 2005 to 2007?

(a) 1333 tonne   (b) 3000 tonne

(c) 1500 tonne   (d) 500 tonne

GENERAL AWARENESS

76. Which phase of Technical Education Quality Improvement Programme has been approved by the Cabinet Committee on Economic Affairs?

(a) First Phase   (b) Second Phase

(c) Third Phase   (d) Fourth Phase

77. Noori, a cloned pashmina goat was created by which of the following countries?

(a) India   (b) Pakistan

(c) Israel   (d) Bangladesh

78. BCCI was formed in

(a) 1928   (b) 1938

(c) 1948   (d) 1958

79. Which of the following article of Indian constitution is related to right to information?

(a) Art 19   (b) Art 21

(c) Art 14   (d) Art 32

80. Which of the following odorant is added to LPG to detect its leakage?

(a) Ethane   (b) Methane

(c) Ethanethiol   (d) Ethanol

81. Ilbert Bill was introduced during the tenure of

(a) Lord Ripon   (b) Lord Macaulay

(c) Lord Dalhousie   (d) Lord Willington

82. Origin of which of the following musical instrument was not India?

(a) Conga   (b) Pakhavaj

(c) Talking drum   (d) Mridanga

83. A market form in which a market or industry is dominated by a small number of sellers is known as

(a) Oligopoly   (b) Monopoly

(c) Duopoly   (d) Monopsony

84. Which of the following religious groups were given special representation as 'minorities' in the constituent assembly of India?

(a) Sikhs & Muslims

(b) Sikhs & Christians

(c) Muslims & Christians

(d) Muslims & Parsis

85. Senior IFS officer Yashvardhan Kumar Sinha has been appointed as India's High Commissioner to which Country?

(a) United Kingdom   (b) Russia

(c) Sri Lanka   (d) canada

86. Who said "The truth comes as conqueror only because we have lost the art of receiving it as guest."?

(a) Mahatma Gandhi

(b) Jawaharlal Nehru

(c) Rabindranath Tagore

(d) Swami Vivekanand

87. Naujawan Bharat Sabha was founded in

(a) March, 1924   (b) March, 1926

(c) March, 1931   (d) March, 1942

88. Which one of the following is the most important & fundamental doctrine of Jainism?

(a) *Syâdvâda*   (b) *Anekantavada*

(c) *Nayavâda*   (d) Nirvana

89. Which one of the following hill stations is not a part of Shivalik range?

(a) Dalhousie   (b) Kullu

(c) Nanital   (d) Yelagiri hill

90. Fertigation is applied in

(a) Agriculture   (b) Fertilizer industry

(c) Mining   (d) Oil drilling

91. Langmuir precipitation is associated with

(a) Cloud burst   (b) Tsunami

(c) Heavy snowfall   (d) None of the above

92. Which of the following portion of human brain controls the thirst in human beings?

(a) Cerebellum   (b) Cerebrum

(c) Brain stem   (d) Hypothalamus

93. Which one of the type of diabetes is characterised by insulin resistance?

(a) Type 1   (b) Type 2

(c) both (a) & (b)   (d) none of these

94. "King Cotton" was a famous slogan used in which of the following historical events?

(a) American Civil War

(b) Indian struggle against British in 1857

(c) World War I

(d) World War II

95. A phenomenon of exactly zero electrical resistance and expulsion of magnetic fields occurring in certain materials when cooled below a characteristic critical temperature is known as

(a) Superconductivity

(b) Electrical conductivity

(c) Variable conductivity

(d) Thermal energy conversion

96. A COMSAT is an artificial satellite sent to space for the purpose of

(a) Telecommunications

(b) Weather forecasting

(c) Alien spaceship detector

(d) Checking space pollution

97. The surplus available for disposal with which the producer is left after his genuine requirements of the family consumption, payment of wages in kind, feed & seed have been met is known as

(a) Producer surplus   (b) Marketable surplus

(c) Consumer surplus   (d) None of the above

98. Respiration is a/an

(a) Catabolic process

(b) Anabolic process

(c) Both (a) & (b)

(d) Oxidation process

99. The active ingredient in Dettol that confers its antiseptic property is

(a) Chloroxylenol

(b) Hydrogen peroxide

(c) Inorganic iodine compounds

(d) Chlorhexidine

100. Who has been elected to assume his office as the new Chief Minister of Gujarat?

(a) Vijay Rupani

(b) Anandiben Patel

(c) Nithin Patel

(d) Ajay Rupani

ANSWERS

1. (c)	**2.** (a)	**3.** (c)	**4.** (d)	**5.** (c)	**6.** (c)	**7.** (b)	**8.** (b)	**9.** (d)	**10.** (b)
11. (d)	**12.** (d)	**13.** (c)	**14.** (c)	**15.** (b)	**16.** (a)	**17.** (b)	**18.** (c)	**19.** (b)	**20.** (d)
21. (c)	**22.** (b)	**23.** (c)	**24.** (b)	**25.** (c)	**26.** (a)	**27.** (b)	**28.** (a)	**29.** (c)	**30.** (c)
31. (b)	**32.** (b)	**33.** (b)	**34.** (b)	**35.** (b)	**36.** (b)	**37.** (a)	**38.** (a)	**39.** (b)	**40.** (b)
41. (c)	**42.** (b)	**43.** (a)	**44.** (a)	**45.** (d)	**46.** (d)	**47.** (c)	**48.** (d)	**49.** (d)	**50.** (a)
51. (d)	**52.** (c)	**53.** (d)	**54.** (d)	**55.** (c)	**56.** (a)	**57.** (c)	**58.** (c)	**59.** (d)	**60.** (d)
61. (a)	**62.** (b)	**63.** (d)	**64.** (c)	**65.** (a)	**66.** (b)	**67.** (c)	**68.** (c)	**69.** (c)	**70.** (a)
71. (a)	**72.** (d)	**73.** (c)	**74.** (b)	**75.** (a)	**76.** (c)	**77.** (a)	**78.** (a)	**79.** (a)	**80.** (c)
81. (a)	**82.** (a)	**83.** (a)	**84.** (a)	**85.** (a)	**86.** (c)	**87.** (b)	**88.** (b)	**89.** (d)	**90.** (a)
91. (a)	**92.** (d)	**93.** (b)	**94.** (a)	**95.** (a)	**96.** (a)	**97.** (b)	**98.** (a)	**99.** (a)	**100.** (a)

EXPLANATIONS

1. Night blindness is caused due to the deficiency of vitamin A. Similarly, scurvy is caused due to the deficiency of vitamin C. Hence, option (c) is the correct answer. Nerve contraction is caused due to the deficiency of calcium, rickets is caused due to the deficiency of vitamin D and goiter is caused due to the deficiency of iodine.

2. H(8) $\to 8^3$ = 512,

   Similarly, M(13) $\to 13^3$ = 2197.

3. 462 * 3 $\Rightarrow$ 462 × 3 = 1386 $\to$ 1 + 3 + 8 + 6 = 18

   564 * 2 $\Rightarrow$ 564 × 2 = 1128 $\to$ 1 + 1 + 2 + 8 = 12

   Similarly, 617 * 4 $\Rightarrow$ 617 × 4

   = 2468 $\to$ 2 + 4 + 6 + 8 = 20.

4. The series is aabc, abbc, abcc,....

5. Reversing the digits of the numbers in series, we get

   1, 9, 25, 49, 81, 75, 169

   All numbers are squares of odd consecutive numbers except 75.

   Hence, answer is 57.

6. Out of the given options, only bonsai is not a plant. Bonsai is a Japanese art form using miniature trees grown in containers. Hence, option (c) is the correct answer.

7. The series in numerical form can be written as 1-3, 1-2-4, 5-7, 5-6-8, 9-11. So, the next term in the series will be 9-10-12, i.e., ijl.

8. The series is 10, 10 × 1 + 1 = 11, 11 × 2 + 2 = 24, 24 × 3 + 3 = 75.

   So, the next term will be 75 × 4 + 4 = 304.

9. 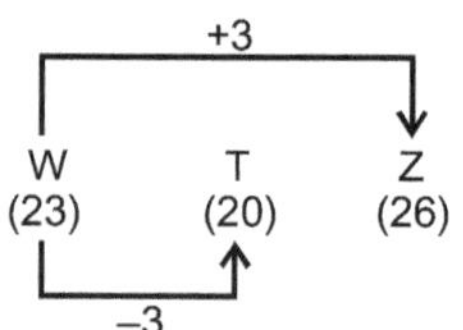

10. 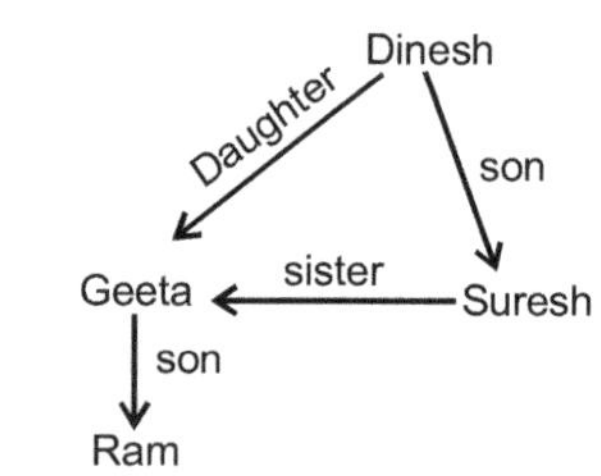

11. 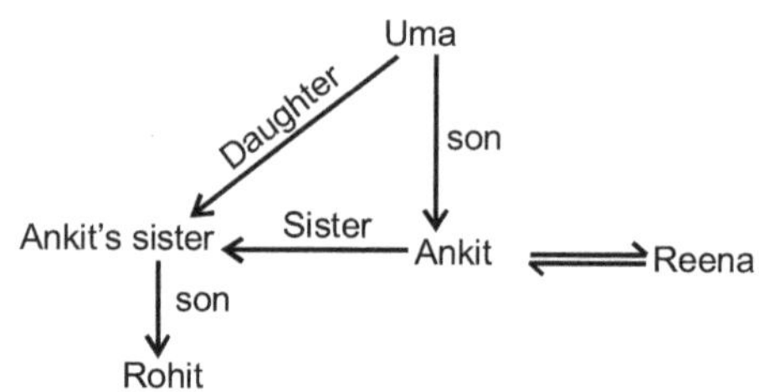

12. Option (d) is the correct answer since 'COMMUTE' requires a 'U' while the given word does not have a 'U'.

13. From option (c), we get

    27 × 3 + 96 ÷ 6 = 81 + 16 = 97

    Hence, answer is 6, 27.

14. The given equation is true for option (c). It can be written as:

    18 × 19 ÷ 3 + 4 = 118.

15.
S	A	M	S	U	N	G
(19)	(1)	(13)	(19)	(21)	(14)	(7)
−5	+5	−5	+5	−5	+5	−5
14	6	8	24	16	19	2

    Similarly,

L	I	B	E	R	T	Y
(12)	(9)	(2)	(5)	(18)	(20)	(25)
−5	+5	−5	+5	−5	+5	−5
7	14	23	10	13	25	20

16. In column 1,

    8 × 32 = 256 = 16^2

    In column 2,

    32 × 18 = 576 = 24^2

    Similarly, in column 3,

    27 × ? = $18^2 \Rightarrow$? = 12.

17. In column 1,

$$\sqrt{3 \times 6 \times 8} = 12$$

In column 2,

$$\sqrt{7 \times 4 \times 7} = 14$$

Similarly, in column 3,

$$\sqrt{4 \times 27 \times 3} = 18.$$

18.

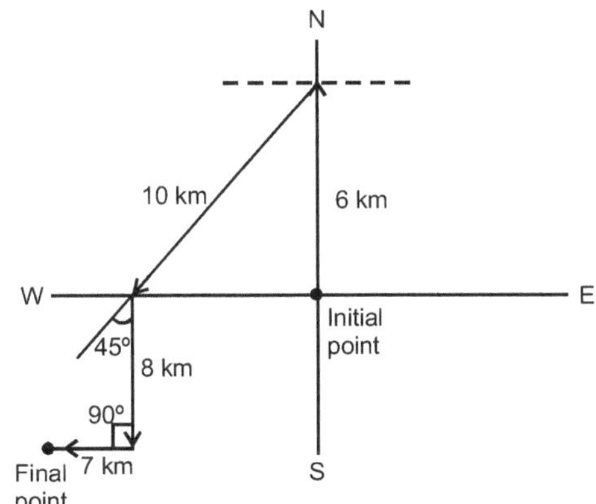

19. Neither of the conclusions follows. The statement does not say that children are the only gifts of God. Adults may or may not be god's gift. Also, the statement does not say anything about the frequency at which God sends gifts. Hence, option (*b*) is the correct answer.

20.

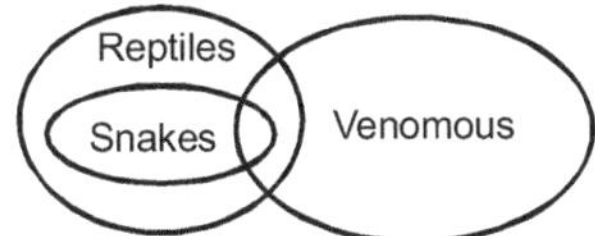

All snakes are reptiles. Some snakes are venomous and some reptiles other than snakes are also venomous. Similarly, some creatures that are not reptiles are also venomous. Hence, option (*d*) is the correct answer.

21. Number of squares = 8 + 4 + 1 = 13.

26. 'Inferno' refers to a very large and dangerous fire. 'Blaze' refers to an intensely burning fire. Hence, option (*a*) is the correct answer.

27. 'Preposterous' means very foolish or silly. Hence, option (*b*) is the correct answer.

28. 'Dovish' refers to a person who does not want war, but peace. 'Hawkish' is one who takes militant attitude. Hence, option (*a*) is the correct answer. 'Owlish' means resembling or suggesting an owl. 'Vulturous' means resembling a vulture especially in scavenging habits. 'Ravenous' means very hungry.

29. 'Apposite' means appropriate for a situation. 'Immaterial' means not important in a particular situation. Hence, option (*c*) is the correct answer.

30. 'Misapprehend' means to get a wrong idea about something. Hence, option (*c*) is the correct answer. 'Apprehend' means to notice and understand something. 'Fathom' means to understand the reason of something.

31. 'Quinquennial' refers to something that happens every five years. Hence, option (*b*) is the correct answer. 'Triennial' refers to something that happens every three years. 'Septennial' means happening every 7 years. 'Vicennial' means happening every 20 years.

32. An 'annalist' is a person who writes annals or historical records. Hence, option (*b*) is the correct answer. An 'archaeologist' is a person who deals with past human life. A 'radiologist' is a doctor trained in radiology. A 'genealogist' is someone who traces or studies the descent of persons or families.

33. 'Kick the bucket' means to die. Hence, option (*b*) is the correct answer.

34. A 'stool pigeon' is a criminal who helps the police to catch another criminal by spending time with them. Hence, option (*b*) is the correct answer.

35. 'To blow a fuse' means to lose one's temper. Hence, option (*b*) is the correct answer.

36. The correct spelling is 'Trapeze'. Hence, option (*b*) is the correct answer.

37. 'Who' is the subject of the verb and is used when we talk about the doer of the action. 'Whom' is the object and is used when we talk about the receiver of an object. In the sentence, Sabu is the doer of the action and therefore, the correct sentence will take 'who' instead of 'whom'. Hence, part (*a*) is the correct answer.

38. When two actions happened in the past, then past perfect tense is used for the one that happened before the other. In the sentence, the action (starting of the play) was completed before the second action (Tenali Raman's arrival). Thus, the correct sentence will be "The play had started by the time Tenali Raman arrived at the biggest theater in the world." Hence, part (*a*) is the correct answer.

39. The error is in part (*b*). The correct phrase should have been 'to our leaving work'. We use possessive form of pronoun before gerunds. Gerunds are verb forms that act as nouns. They end in –ing. Hence, option (*b*) is the correct answer.

40. The first sentence is in past tense. Therefore, the second blank will take a word that is in past tense. Thus, option (*c*) is incorrect. Option (*d*) is incorrect since 'raise' refers to lifting something manually. Option (*a*) is incorrect since 'risen' is always followed by 'had/have'. 'Rose' is simple past tense and is consistent with the structure of the sentence. 'Come on' means start to arrive or happen. Hence, option (*b*) is the correct answer.

41. Option (*c*), 'at', is the correct preposition to be filled in the blank. The preposition 'at' is used to indicate presence or occurrence, intended goal, the means, cause or manner, age or position in time, etc.

42. The correct preposition is 'on'. 'On' is used with 'agree' when we talk about an issue or a point of debate. Hence, option (*b*) is the correct answer. 'Agree with' is used when we accept the point of someone or something. 'Agree to' is used when we accept the demands or queries of a person. 'Agree at' is grammatically incorrect.

43. The given sentence is incorrect since 'child' is singular while 'they' refers to more than one. In option (*c*), 'child' is singular. Therefore, 'think', which is plural, should be replaced by 'thinks'. Option (*b*) is incorrect since 'children', which is plural, should be followed by 'are' and not 'is'. Only option (*a*) is correct since it takes one of the two prepositions (he or she) that go with 'child'.

44. Future perfect continuous tense is used for actions that will be in progress over a period of time and will end in future. Hence, option (*a*) is the correct answer. The given sentence is in future perfect tense, which is used to talk about actions that will be completed by a certain time in the future. Options (*b*) and (*c*) are in future continuous tense, which is used to talk about actions that will be in progress at a time in the future.

45. The given statement is correct. With 'empathy' we will use a word that contrasts with it since the sentence talks about the right mix of two things. 'Disdain' refers to a feeling of strong dislike or disapproval of someone or something you think does not deserve respect. 'Empathy', on the other hand, refers to the feeling that you understand and share another person's experiences and emotions. Hence, option (*d*) is the correct answer.

46. 'Dour' refers to someone who is serious and unfriendly. A person is called 'gentle' if he has a silent and kind nature. Hence, the correct answer is option (*d*) – gentle. 'Hostile' is someone who is not friendly. 'Grim' is someone who has serious appearance or manner. A person is described as 'cold' if he lacks normal human emotions, friendliness, compassion, etc.

47. Andrew was a self made man and was careful about spending money. But the reason why he was not liked by many people was that he engaged in dishonest business practices. Hence, option (*c*) is the correct answer. Option (*d*) is incorrect since people were not jealous of his wealth; rather he made some enemies while climbing the ladder to success.

48. Options (*a*), (*b*) and (*c*) are mentioned in the passage as a cause that hampered investigation. Although Andrew Borden had many enemies, it is nowhere stated that this posed a problem during the investigation. Hence, option (*d*) is the answer.

49. The passage does not suggest that Andrew Borden was careful while making judgments and decisions. Hence, option (*d*), prudent, is the correct answer. The passage says that he owned many properties. From this we can infer that he had a lot of money, i.e., he was affluent. The passage clearly says that he was 'frugal to a fault', which means that he spent his money carefully. This means that he was economical. The second sentence of the passage clearly states that he was unpopular.

50. Look at the line: "…rumors swirled that Andrew and Abby had perhaps been killed as revenge for Andrew's shady business dealings." Hence, option (*a*) is the correct answer.

51. Let the 2nd discount be 100x%.

Then, $2400 \times (1 - 0.2) \times (1 - x) = 1632$

$$\Rightarrow x = 1 - \frac{1632}{2400 \times 0.8} = 1 - 0.85 = 0.15$$

Hence, the second discount is 15%.

52. Let the cost price of first chair be ₹x and other chair be ₹(2400 – x).

Then,

$(x \times 0.8) + (2400 - x)1.3\} - \{(x \times 1.25)$
$\qquad\qquad\qquad + (2400 - x)0.9\} = 280$

$\Rightarrow 0.4(2400 - x) - 0.45x = 280$

$\Rightarrow 0.85x = 680$

$\Rightarrow x = ₹800$

Hence, the required difference = 2400 – x – x
$$= 2400 - 1600 = ₹800.$$

53. Area of the rhombus

$$= \frac{1}{2} \times 21 \times 32 = 21 \times 16 = 336 \text{ cm}^2$$

Hence, the cost involved in tiling = 2.25 × 336
$$= ₹756.$$

54. Let $\angle QPM = \angle RPM = x$

Also, $\angle PMQ = x + \angle MRP$ (Since exterior angle is equal to sum of interior opposite angles.)

Hence, $\angle PMQ > x$ i.e. $PQ > QM$ (Side opposite to greater angle is greater in a triangle.)

55. Let the marked price of the article be ₹x.

Then, $0.7 \times x = 1540 \times 1.1$

$\Rightarrow x = \dfrac{1540 \times 1.1}{0.7} = ₹2,420.$

56. We have,

$$\dfrac{1}{\sec^2 47°} + \cos^2 43° + \cot^2 47° - \dfrac{1}{\cos^2 47° \csc^2 43°}$$

$$= \cos^2 47° + \cos^2(90 - 47)° + \cot^2 47° - \sec^2 47° \sin^2 43°$$

$$= \cos^2 47° + \sin^2 47° + \cot^2 47° - \sec^2 47° \cos^2 47°$$

$(\because \sin^2\theta + \cos^2\theta = 1$ and $\sec\theta . \cos\theta = 1)$

$$= \cot^2 47° = \tan^2 43° = x^2 - 1.$$

57.

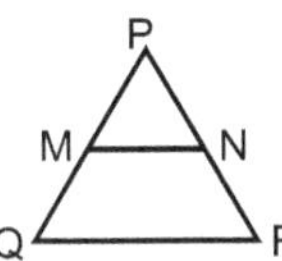

Let the angels of $\triangle PQR$ be 2x, 2x and x.

Then, $2x + 2x + x = 180°$

$\Rightarrow x = \dfrac{180°}{5} = 36°$

Since the line MN drawn is parallel to QR.

Hence, difference between $\angle PMN$ and $\angle PNM$ will be same as that of $\angle PQR$ and $\angle PRQ$.

i.e. $2x - x = 36°$.

58. Required average age

$$= \dfrac{(14 \times 100) - \{(12 \times 20) + (16 \times 40)\}}{40} = 13 \text{ years.}$$

59. We have, $p^2 + q^2 + 4r^2 + 3 = 2p - 2q + 4r$

$\Rightarrow p^2 - 2p + 1 + q^2 + 2q + 1 + 4r^2 - 4r + 1 = 0$

$\Rightarrow (p-1)^2 + (q+1)^2 + (2r-1)^2 = 0$

$\Rightarrow p = 1; q = -1$ and $r = \dfrac{1}{2}$

Hence, $2p - 3q + 4r = 7.$

60. Let $2^{2^{222}} = x.$

Then, $\left(2^{2^{222}} + 1\right)\left(2^{2^{223}} + 1 + 2.2^{2^{222}}\right)$

$= (x+1)(x^2 + 1 + 2x) = (x+1)^3 = \left(2^{2^{222}} + 1\right)^3.$

61. Let the number of toffees with R be r.

Then, $r = \dfrac{2}{3}(45 - r) \Rightarrow 5r = 90 \Rightarrow r = \dfrac{90}{5} = 18$

Let the number of toffees with P be p, then with S will be $\dfrac{p}{2}$ and with Q will be $\dfrac{6p}{5}$

By solving, we get p = 10, q = 12, r = 18 and s = 5. Hence, S will get 5 toffees.

62. Speed of train P = $\dfrac{90}{1.5} = 60$ km/hr

Speed of train Q = $\dfrac{90}{2} = 45$ km/hr

Speed of train R = $\dfrac{90}{3} = 30$ km/hr

Distance covered by train Q in 15 minutes will be 11.25 km and by train R in 45 minutes will be 22.5 km.

Time taken by P to meet Q

$$= \dfrac{11.25}{60 - 45}$$

$$= \dfrac{11.25}{15} \text{ hr} = 45 \text{ minutes}$$

Time taken by P to meet R = $\dfrac{22.5}{60 - 30}$

$$= 0.75 \text{ hr} = 45 \text{ minutes}$$

Hence, P meets Q and R after 45 minutes and 45 minutes respectively.

63. From option (*d*), we have A : B : C : D ≡

$$\dfrac{1}{12} : \dfrac{1}{18} : \dfrac{1}{9} : \dfrac{1}{2} \equiv 3 : 2 : 4 : 18$$

Hence, A, B, C and D will get 9, 6, 12 and 54 chocolates respectively.

64. Let the total units of the work be x.

Then, $\dfrac{2}{3}x = 90 \times 250$

$\Rightarrow x = 33750$ units.

Hence, number of men required to complete rest 1/3rd work in 30 days = $\dfrac{1}{3} \times \dfrac{33750}{30} = 375$ men.

Hence, extra men employed = 375 − 250 = 125 men.

65. The value of remainder by dividing the given expression with x − 14 will give the value of same at x = 14.

Also, $x^4 - 15x^3 + 15x^2 - 15x + 15 = (x - 14)$
$(x^3 - x^2 + x - 1) + 1$

Hence, the required value = 1.

66. Let the marked price of the watch be x.

Cost price for the retailer = $x \times 0.8 \times 0.8 = 0.64x$

Selling price of the retailer = $0.64x \times 1.5 = 0.96x$

Hence, required percentage

$$= \dfrac{x - 0.96x}{x} \times 100 = 4\% \text{ less.}$$

67. Let the speed to cover the remaining journey be s km/hr.

$$\therefore \frac{16}{24} + \frac{48-16}{s} = 1$$

$$\Rightarrow s = 96 \text{ km/hr.}$$

68. We have, $\frac{x}{y} + \frac{y}{x} = 1$

$$\Rightarrow x^2 + y^2 - xy = 0 \quad \dots(i)$$

Also, $x^6 - y^6 = \left(x^3\right)^2 - \left(y^3\right)^2 = \left(x^3 + y^3\right)\left(x^3 - y^3\right)$

$$= (x+y)\left(x^2 + y^2 - xy\right)(x-y)\left(x^2 + y^2 + xy\right)$$

Hence, from (i) the given expression will have value 0.

69. Let the capacity of tank be LCM (10,12) = 60 units

Hence, P can fill 6 units in an hour and Q can fill 5 units in an hour.

Tank filled by P and Q in 1 hour = 11 units.

If P is closed after 5 hours i.e. 2 PM, total work done = 11 × 5 = 55 units and the rest 5 units will be completed by Q in one hour.

∴ Pipe P should be closed at 2:00 PM.

70. Let the selling price of each kg of apple be x.

Selling price of 75 kg apples = 75x

∴ Gain = 15x

$$\therefore \text{Gain\%} = \frac{15x}{75x - 15x} \times 100 = 25\%.$$

71. Total production of wheat for state M

$$= (6 + 12 + 10 + 4 + 8 + 6) \times 1000$$
$$= 46000 \text{ tonne.}$$

Total production of wheat for state N

$$= (6 + 7 + 9 + 7 + 4 + 8) \times 1000$$
$$= 41000 \text{ tonne.}$$

Difference between the total production of wheat for state M and state N = 46000 – 41000 = 5000 tonne.

72. Increase in production of wheat in state M from 2005 to 2006 = 12000 – 6000 = 6000 tonne.

∴ Required percentage increase

$$= \frac{6000}{6000} \times 100 = 100\%.$$

73. In 2006, percentage change

$$= \frac{(10000 - 8000)}{8000} \times 100 = 25\%.$$

In 2007, percentage change

$$= \frac{(10000 - 7000)}{10000} \times 100 = 30\%.$$

In 2008, percentage change

$$= \frac{(7000 - 6000)}{7000} \times 100 = 14.28\%.$$

In 2009, percentage change

$$= \frac{(8000 - 6000)}{6000} \times 100 = 33.33\%.$$

In 2010, percentage change

$$= \frac{(10000 - 8000)}{8000} \times 100 = 25\%.$$

∴ In 2 years production of wheat in state L shows a change of more than 25%.

74. Total production of wheat in state L

$$= (8 + 10 + 7 + 6 + 8 + 10) \times 1000 = 49000 \text{ tonne}$$

Average annual production of wheat in state L

$$= \frac{49000}{6} \approx 8166 \text{ tonne}$$

Total production of wheat in state M

$$= (6 + 12 + 10 + 4 + 8 + 6) \times 1000 = 46000 \text{ tonne}$$

Average annual production of wheat in state M

$$= \frac{46000}{6} \approx 7666 \text{ tonne}$$

Total production of wheat in state N

$$= (6 + 7 + 9 + 7 + 4 + 8) \times 1000 = 41000 \text{ tonne}$$

Average annual production of wheat in state N

$$= \frac{41000}{6} \approx 6833 \text{ tonne.}$$

∴ Average annual production of wheat was maximum for state L.

75. Average production of wheat in state M during 2008 to 2010 $= (4 + 8 + 6) \times \frac{1000}{3} = 6000$ tonne.

Average production of wheat in state N during 2005 to 2007 $= (6 + 7 + 9) \times \frac{1000}{3} \approx 7333$ tonne.

∴ Required difference = 7333 – 6000 = 1333 tonne.

PRACTICE SET – 4

GENERAL INTELLIGENCE

Directions: In question nos. **1 & 2**, select the related letters /word /number from the given alternatives.

1. TALENT : VYNCPR :: NORMAL : ?

(a) PMYKBK   (b) PMTKCJ

(c) PMTLBJ   (d) PNTKDK

2. Sick : Dog :: Busy : ?

(a) Toad   (b) Crocodile

(c) Cuckoo   (d) Bee

3. Which one of the given responses would be a meaningful order of the following?

(1) Idea Generation and Screening

(2) Market Testing

(3) Concept Development/Testing

(4) Product Development

(5) Commercialization

(6) Analysis

(a) 1, 2, 4, 6, 5, 3   (b) 1, 2, 3, 4, 5, 6

(c) 1, 3, 6, 4, 2, 5   (d) 1, 4, 3, 2, 6, 5

Direction: In the following question which one set of letters when sequentially placed at the gaps in the given letter series shall complete it?

4. c_ba_bba_bbac_ba

(a) bbab   (b) bccb

(c) abac   (d) acab

Directions: In question nos. **5 to 7**, find the odd word/ number / number-pair from the given alternatives.

5. (a) Black gram   (b) Groundnut

(c) Wheat   (d) Fennel

6. (a) 253 – 351   (b) 478 – 692

(c) 123 – 22   (d) 971 – 816

7. (a) Primitive   (b) Protest

(c) Problem   (d) Project

Directions: In question nos. **8 to 9**, a series is given, with one term missing. Choose the correct alternative from the given ones that will complete the series.

8. ACE, GIK, MOQ, SUW, _?_, _?_.

(a) XZB, DFH   (b) YZB, DFH

(c) XZA, CEG   (d) YAC, EGI

9. 3 * 12 : 7 * 9 :: 6 * 8 : ?

(a) 6 * 9   (b) 5 * 7

(c) 7 * 12   (d) 9 * 11

10. Find the correct group of signs to solve the equation.

17 ? 13 ? 36 ? 6 ? 5

(a) = – × ÷   (b) – ÷ = +

(c) + = ÷ ×   (d) + – × ÷

11. Arun is older than Bhanu. Charu is older than Divya. Esha is older than Charu but younger than Bhanu. Who is the eldest among them?

(a) Arun   (b) Charu

(c) Esha   (d) Divya

Directions: In question nos. **12 to 13**, from the given alternatives, select the word which **cannot** be formed using the letters of the given word.

12. UNPARAGONED

(a) PRONE   (b) DAGGER

(c) ROPED   (d) ADORN

13. BIBLIOGRAPHIES

(a) GRAPES   (b) BRIBE

(c) PROBABLE   (d) SHARPER

14. If > stands for multiplication, × stands for addition, + stands for division, ÷ stands for subtraction, = stands for less than, – stands for greater than and < stands for equal to, state which of the following is true?

(a) 112 × 8 + 6 ÷ 10 < 5 (b) 15 ÷ 4 – 11 > 6 +2

(c) 11 > 2 < 51 + 3 × 4 (d) 34 × 52 + 4 – 27 ÷ 8

15. If each of the letters in the English alphabet is assigned an odd numerical value by giving A = 1, B = 3 and so on, what would be the total value of the letters for the word WATCH when similarly coded?

(a) 105   (b) 55

(c) 84   (d) 96

16. If the first and third letters in the word 'INSTRUMENTATIONS' were interchanged, also the second and fourth letters, fifth and seventh letters and so on, which letter would be eighth letter from your right?

(a) U   (b) S

(c) A   (d) R

Direction: In the following select the missing number from the given responses.

17.

112	96	224
7	8	4
12	?	4

(a) 40   (b) 16

(c) 24   (d) 28

18. A man starts from his home and walks straight for 5 km. Then he takes a right turn and walks for 4 km. Then he turns right again and walks for 2 km and then turns left and walks for 3 km. Then he turns left, walks for 6 km and finally he turns right and walks for 5 km. How far is he from the starting point?

(a) 20 km   (b) 18 km

(c) 15 km   (d) 25 km

Direction: In the following one/two statements are given, followed by two/three conclusions. You have to consider the statements to be true, even if they seem at variance with commonly known facts. You are to decide which of the given conclusions can definitely be drawn from the given statements.

19. Statements :

1. Some constellations are stars.

2. All stars are galaxies.

Conclusions :

I. All constellations are galaxies.

II. Some constellations are galaxies.

III. All galaxies are constellations.

(a) Only conclusion I follows

(b) Only conclusion II follows

(c) Only conclusions I and II follow

(d) Only conclusions I and III follow

20. There is a bowl and a rectangular mug. Four positions are shown below to keep them balanced. Which of the following will not get balanced easily?

Question figures :

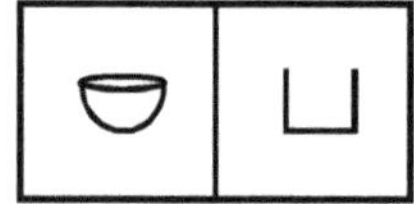

Answer figures :

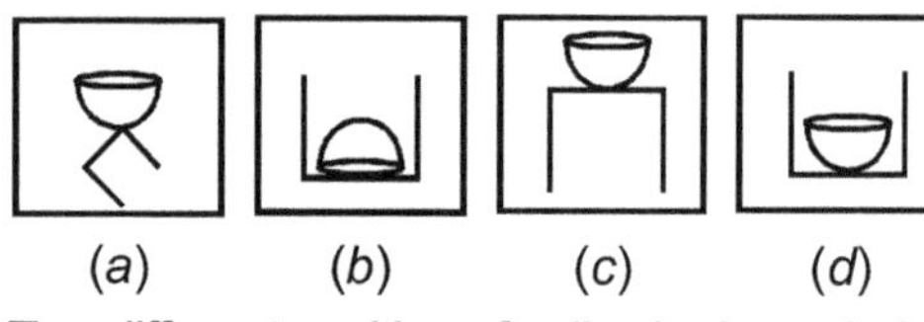

   (a)   (b)   (c)   (d)

21. Two different position of a dice is shown below. Which number is opposite to number 6?

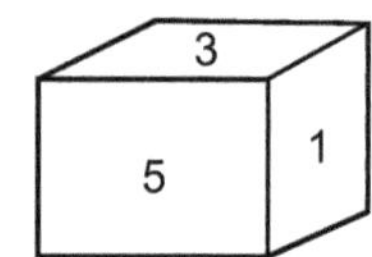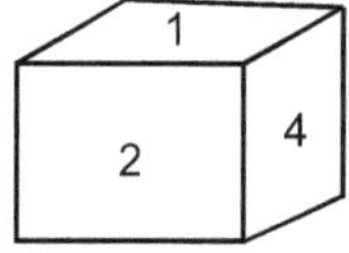

(a) 5

(b) 3

(c) 2

(d) 1

Direction: In the following in the given diagram, circle represents students playing cricket, square represents students playing football, triangle represents students playing tennis and rectangle represents students playing hockey. Different regions in the diagram are numbered 1 to 11.

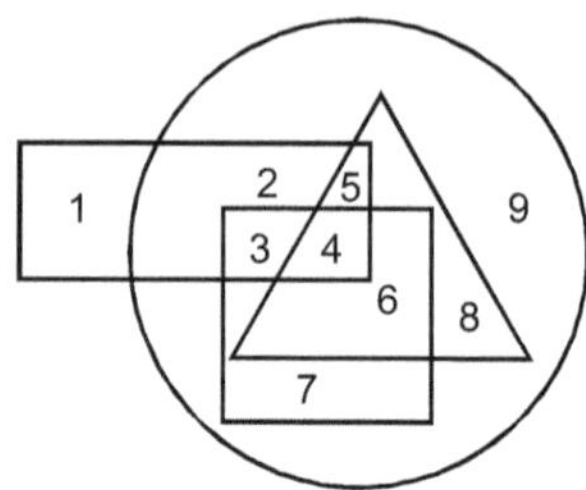

22. Which region represents students playing cricket, football and tennis but not hockey?

(a) 7   (b) 6

(c) 4   (d) 3

Directions: In question nos. **23**, which answer figure will complete the pattern in the question figure?

23. Question figure :

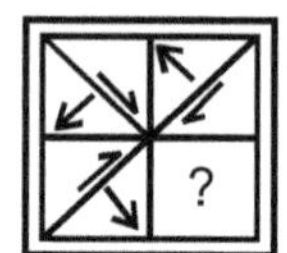

Answer figures :

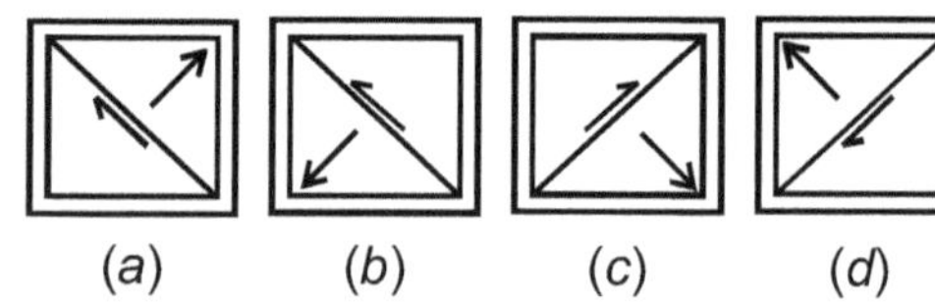

   (a)   (b)   (c)   (d)

24. A piece of paper is folded and cut as shown below in the question figures. From the given answer figures, indicate how it will appear when opened.

Question figures :

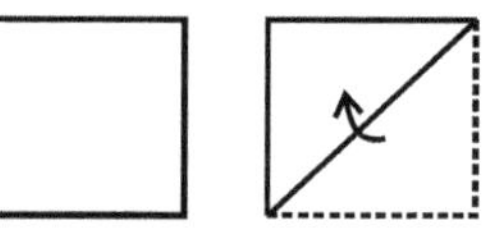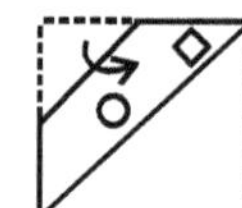

Answer figures :

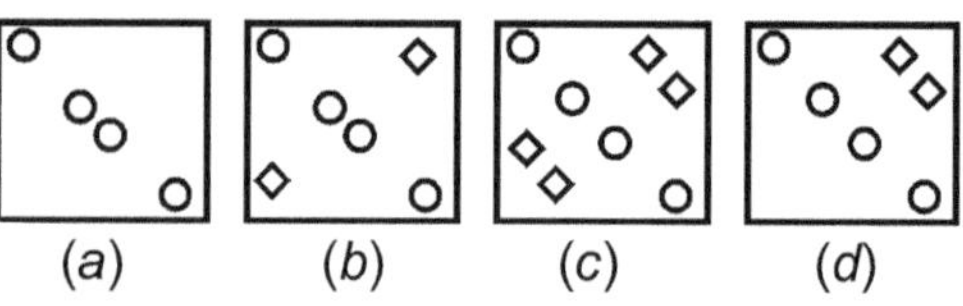

   (a)   (b)   (c)   (d)

25. A word is represented by only one set of numbers as given in anyone of the alternatives. The sets of numbers given in the alternatives are represented by two classes of alphabets as in two matrices given below. The columns and rows of **Matrix I** are numbered from 0 to 4 and that of **Matrix II** are numbered from 5 to 9. A letter from these matrices can be represented first by its row and next by its column, e.g., 'S' can be represented by 24, 41, etc., and 'A' can be represented by 55, 78, etc. Similarly, you have to identify the set for the word GLOW.

Matrix I						Matrix II				
	0	1	2	3	4		5	6	7	8	9
0	S	F	O	L	T	5	A	I	G	N	W
1	O	L	S	T	F	6	I	W	A	G	N
2	L	T	F	O	S	7	G	N	W	A	I
3	F	O	T	S	L	8	W	G	N	I	A
4	T	S	L	F	O	9	N	A	I	W	G

(a) 57, 02, 78, 66   (b) 03, 42, 56, 99

(c) 75, 34, 69, 44   (d) 68, 34, 23, 98

ENGLISH LANGUAGE

Directions for questions 26 to 27 : In each of the following questions, a word is followed by four options. Select the option that best expresses the meaning of the given word.

26. Pinnacle

(a) Bottom   (b) Crest

(c) Minimum   (d) Abyss

27. Sleuth

(a) Butcher   (b) Executioner

(c) Invigilator   (d) Investigator

Directions for questions 28 to 29 : In the following question, a word is followed by four options. Select the option that is opposite in meaning to the given word.

28. Detrimental

(a) Wicked   (b) Damaging

(c) Benign   (d) Indecisive

29. Nibble

(a) Devour   (b) Pester

(c) Gnaw   (d) Dull

Directions: In question nos. **30** to **32**, Out of the four alternatives, choose the one which can be substituted for the given words/sentences.

30. Mahatma Gandhi was <u>the one who advocated the removal of inequalities among people.</u>

(a) an egalitarian   (b) a federalist

(c) an absolutist   (d) a reformist

31. <u>A male servant who has charge of other employees</u>

(a) Assistant   (b) Minion

(c) Retainer   (d) Butler

32. The evidence suggests that he ran <u>an enterprise of embezzlement, bribery and blackmail.</u>

(a) a clatter   (b) a rumpus

(c) a racket   (d) a squabble

Directions for questions 33 to 35 : Four alternatives are given for the idioms/phrases given below. Choose the alternative which best expresses the meaning of the given idiom/phrase.

33. Until now, Aladdin couldn't figure out how to <u>get his foot in the door</u>, but now he has the perfect contact.

(a) enter an organisation as an initial step towards success

(b) enter into a competition that offers huge prize money

(c) step out of a difficult situation which involves money

(d) use the available opportunity for one's own good

34. Dr Jekyll, the chief of critical care at the hospital, said that the medical procedure was <u>in the home stretch.</u>

(a) time consuming.   (b) started.

(c) mid-way.   (d) nearly completed.

35. Hearing the train whistle gives me <u>itchy feet</u>.

(a) a feeling to move to a different place.

(b) a feeling of irritation.

(c) a desire to run away.

(d) a desire to stay at one place.

Direction : In the following group of four different words, one word is correctly spelt. Find the correctly spelt word and mark your answer accordingly.

36. (a) Bearucrat   (b) Beareaucrat

(c) Bureaucrat   (d) Bureacrat

Directions for questions 37 to 39 : Read each of the following sentences to find out whether there is any grammatical error in it. The error, if any, will be in one part of the sentence. The number of that part is the answer. If there is 'No error' the answer is (d).

37. 'Cheer up father, (a) / I'll go and will finish the (b)/ remaining work,' said Supandi. (c)/ No error (d)

38. Archie is one of (a)/ the cleverest boys that (b)/ has passed through the school. (c)/ No error (d)

39. Billu's taste in (a)/ comic books is (b)/ different than Pinky's (c)/ No error (d)

Directions for questions 40 to 42 : Each of the following sentences contains a blank to be filled in with an appropriate word. Choose the correct alternative out of the four given options.

40. Even _____ the price of gas is starting to come down now, many people _____ to take the bus or the train.

(a) if, had chosen   (b) though, had chosen

(c) if, are choosing   (d) though, are choosing

41. Tomorrow is Halloween, _____ everybody gets dressed up in a fancy costume. So we will go trick-or-treating _____ is a traditional practice for children in many countries.

(a) where, that   (b) where, which

(c) when, that   (d) when, which

42. I called _____ my professor when I last visited the town.

(a) to

(b) forth

(c) on

(d) after

Directions for questions 43 to 45 : In each of the following questions, a part of the sentence is underlined. Beneath each sentence four different ways of phrasing the underlined part are given. Choose the grammatically correct option. In case no improvement is needed, your answer is option (*d*).

43. Less than 20 children suffer from the disease each year.
(*a*) Less than 20 children suffer from the diseases each year
(*b*) Fewer than 20 children suffer from the disease each year.
(*c*) Fewer than 20 children suffers from the disease each year.
(*d*) No improvement

44. He found a blue small square photo-frame in the store room.
(*a*) blue square and small photo-frame
(*b*) small square blue photo-frame
(*c*) damaged small blue photo-frame
(*d*) No improvement

45. Pluto is the eldest dog in the pack.
(*a*) oldest
(*b*) older
(*c*) elder
(*d*) No improvement

Directions: In question nos. **46** to **50**, you have given a passages with 5 questions. Read the passage carefully and choose the best answer to each question out of the four alternatives.

One of the mysteries of Stonehenge is why our ancestors chose to use bluestones that had to be hauled hundreds of kilometres from the Preseli Hills in Pembrokeshire to the site in Wiltshire. But new research from London's Royal College of Art suggests sound might have played a role. Researchers tested thousands of stones on CarnMenyn in the Preseli Hills, and found a large number of the rocks ring when they are struck. Usually, stones produce a disappointing clunk when hit, with microscopic cracks making it difficult for vibrations to travel within the rock. But certain bluestones have the right microscopic structure - and sound like a metallic gong.

They also found a few of the rocks remaining at Stonehenge rang as well. The challenge they now face is providing good evidence that the bluestones were used for their musical quality. Sound is ephemeral, and disappears as soon as it is made, so it is difficult to know for sure that our ancestors used the stones as percussion instruments.

46. Which of the following cannot be inferred from the passage?
(*a*) The reason for using bluestones to create Stonehenge is still unknown.
(*b*) It is wrong to say that all the stones at Stonehenge produce a clunk sound when stuck together.
(*c*) Time has not been able to preserve the Stonehenge the way it was built by our ancestors.
(*d*) Scientists are performing tests to know more about Stonehenge.

47. Which of the following was suggested by the London's Royal College of Art?
(*a*) Ocular properties of the stone led our ancestors to choose to use bluestones.
(*b*) Acoustic properties of the stone led our ancestors to choose to use bluestones.
(*c*) Our ancestors liked the sound of bluestones over the sound of the other stones.
(*d*) Our ancestors knew that microscopic cracks in bluestones make it easy for the vibrations to travel.

48. Which of the following best expresses the meaning of the word 'ephemeral'?
(*a*) Brief
(*b*) Timeless
(*c*) Continuing
(*d*) Ancient

49. Which of the following is opposite in meaning to the word 'haul'?
(*a*) Lift
(*b*) Push
(*c*) Drag
(*d*) Carry

50. Why is it difficult for us to know for sure whether or not the stones were used as percussion instruments?
(*a*) There are no written records to conform our doubts.
(*b*) Researchers have not been able to find evidence suggesting that the stones were used for their musical ability.
(*c*) Sound does not last for a long period of time and disappears as soon as it is made.
(*d*) Since Stonehenge is not preserved in its original form, it is difficult to research on it.

QUANTITATIVE APTITUDE

51. The square root of $23 - 4\sqrt{15}$ is
(*a*) $\pm\left(\sqrt{5} - 2\sqrt{3}\right)$
(*b*) $\pm\left(2\sqrt{5} - \sqrt{3}\right)$
(*c*) $\pm\left(2\sqrt{5} + \sqrt{3}\right)$
(*d*) $\pm\left(\sqrt{5} + 2\sqrt{3}\right)$

52. What is the value of $\cot 3° \cot 6° \cot 9° ... \cot 93°$?
(*a*) undefined
(*b*) 0
(*c*) 1
(*d*) 93

53. The average age of 21 students and their teacher is 15 years. If the teacher's age is excluded, the average age reduces by 2. What is the teacher's age?
(*a*) 41 years
(*b*) 51 years
(*c*) 47 years
(*d*) 57 years

54. If the angle of elevation of the Sun changes from 30° to 60°, the length of the shadow of a tower decreases by 50 m. The height of the tower is
(*a*) 25 m
(*b*) $25\sqrt{3}$ m
(*c*) $\dfrac{25}{\sqrt{3}}$ m
(*d*) $\dfrac{50}{\sqrt{3}}$ m

55. If $x^2 - 4x + 1 = 0$, then the value of $x^3 + \dfrac{1}{x^3}$ will be

(a) 56   (b) 44

(c) 48   (d) 52

56. In the given figure, if MN is the diameter of the circle and $\angle MPQ = 120°$, then the value of $\angle QNM$ will be

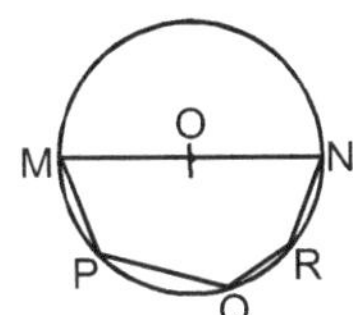

(a) 90°   (b) 120°

(c) 30°   (d) 60°

57. A square shaped field of edge 105 feet has to be fenced with wire. How many equal spaced supporting poles are required to fence it, if the poles should be fixed 7 feet apart?

(a) 60   (b) 64

(c) 62   (d) 56

58. If $a\cos\theta - b\sin\theta = c$, then the value of $a\sin\theta + b\cos\theta$ is

(a) $\pm\sqrt{a^2 - b^2 - c^2}$ (b) $\pm\sqrt{a^2 - b^2 + c^2}$

(c) $\pm\sqrt{-a^2 + b^2 + c^2}$ (d) $\pm\sqrt{a^2 + b^2 - c^2}$

59. If $a\$b = a - b + \dfrac{b^2}{a}$, then the value of 15\$3 is

(a) 87   (b) 12.6

(c) 11.6   (d) 12.4

60. If the length of the sides of a triangle are in the ratio of 3 : 4 : 5 and the circumradius of the triangle is 30 cm, then the length of the largest side is

(a) 60 cm   (b) 55 cm

(c) 40 cm   (d) 45 cm

61. A boy takes 2 minutes less time to cross a circular ground along its shortest path than to cover it once along the boundary. If his speed was 1.5 m/s, then the radius of the circular ground is

(Take $\pi = \dfrac{22}{7}$)

(a) 43.4 m   (b) 157.5 m

(c) 78.5 m   (d) 97.45 m

62. Ram gets 4 marks for each correct sum and loses 1 mark for each wrong sum. He attempts 40 sums and obtains 80 marks. The number of sums that was attempted wrong, is

(a) 22   (b) 20

(c) 18   (d) 16

63. A conveyor belt is attatched to two wheels of a machine of radius 7 cm and 2 cm. If the centres of the wheels are at a distance of 13 cm, then what is the total length (in cm) of the belt?

(a) $9\pi + 12$ (b) $9\pi + 24$

(c) $8\pi + 5$ (d) $8\pi + 3$

64. Two circles of equal radii 5 cm, intersect each other in such a way that a circle passes through the centre of the other circle. What is the area of the quadrilateral formed by joining the centers and the intersection points?

(a) $25\sqrt{2}$ cm² 		(b) $\dfrac{25\sqrt{3}}{2}$ cm²

(c) $25\sqrt{3}$ cm²   (d) $50\sqrt{3}$ cm²

65. If $\dfrac{\csc\theta - \cot\theta}{\csc\theta + \cot\theta} = \dfrac{1}{9}$, then the value of $\sin\theta$ is equal to

(a) $\dfrac{2}{5}$ (b) $\dfrac{4}{5}$

(c) $\dfrac{2}{3}$ (d) $\dfrac{3}{5}$

66. A cylindrical bucket of diameter 48 cm is filled with water to some height. If a solid spherical ball of diameter 24 cm is completely immersed, then increase in the height of water level in the bucket will be

(a) 1 cm   (b) 2 cm

(c) 3 cm   (d) 4 cm

67. If M is the midpoint of the side QR of a parallelogram PQRS such that $\angle MPS = \angle PQM$, then which of the following relation is true?

(a) PQ = QM   (b) PS = PQ

(c) RS = 2PS   (d) PQ = PM

68. What is the minimum value of $3\sin^2\theta + 5\cos^2\theta$?

(a) 4   (b) 5

(c) 3   (d) 1

69. Grass in a field can completely feed 20 cows or 30 goats for a day. The same field is sufficient to feed 10 cows and 12 goats for

(a) $1\dfrac{1}{2}$ days   (b) $1\dfrac{1}{3}$ days

(c) $1\dfrac{1}{9}$ days   (d) $1\dfrac{1}{4}$ days

70. If the length of the side of an equilateral triangle is $28\sqrt{3}$ cm, the area of the incircle of the triangle will be

(a) 616 cm²   (b) 1296 cm²

(c) 1336 cm²   (d) 1236 cm²

71. The population of a town is decreasing at a constant rate of 6% per year. What was the approximate population of that town in 2011 if population of that town was 1.6 million in 2013?

(a) 1.81 million

(b) 1.75 million

(c) 1.85 million

(d) 1.41 million

72. If $a^2 - 1 = a$ and $a > 0$, then the value of $a^3 - 2$ is

(a) $\sqrt{5}$

(b) $\sqrt{2}$

(c) 2

(d) 5

73. What is the area enclosed by straight line $2x + 4y = 12$ and coordinate axes?

(a) 18 sq. units

(b) 9 sq. units

(c) 12 sq. units

(d) 6 sq. units

74. The adjoining diagram is frequency polygon for the runs scored by Sachin against different teams. What is the total number of runs scored by Sachin?

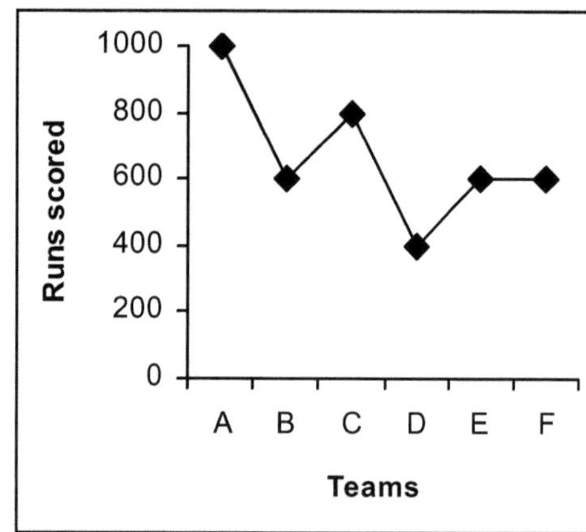

(a) 4500

(b) 2500

(c) 3000

(d) 4000

75. The pie chart given below shows the percentage distributions of the income of a family. The average income of a month is ₹ 21,200.

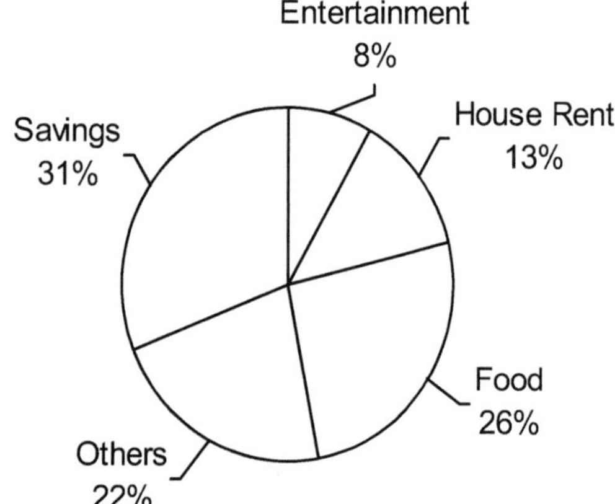

By what amount, expenditure on food is greater than that of entertainment in a year?

(a) ₹ 3,816

(b) ₹ 45,792

(c) ₹ 50,880

(d) ₹ 4,240

GENERAL AWARENESS

76. Who is named as the captain of the national team for the Rio Olympics by the Indian Hockey Federation?

(a) PR Ajees

(b) PR Murugesh

(c) PR Rajesh

(d) PR Sreejesh

77. Where is Kansai International Airport located?

(a) South Korea

(b) North Korea

(c) Japan

(d) China

78. Which of the following prize/award is also known as Asia's Nobel Prize?

(a) Ramon Magsaysay Award

(b) Simon Bolivar Prize

(c) Jnanpith Award

(d) Chameli Devi Award

79. Smog is a type of

(a) Air Pollution

(b) Water Pollution

(c) Soil Pollution

(d) Marine pollution

80. Which of the following is not true about Indian constitution?

(a) It is the longest written constitution of any sovereign nation.

(b) Jawaharlal Nehru is considered as the 'Father of Indian Constitution'.

(c) The constitution of India is federal in structure.

(d) Besides the English version, there is an official Hindi translation.

81. Barabati Stadium is situated at

(a) Kolkata

(b) Cuttack

(c) Chennai

(d) Karnataka

82. 74th amendment of Indian Constitution is associated with the

(a) Panchayati Raj Institutions

(b) Urban local Bodies

(c) Both (a) & (b)

(d) Reservation of women in Panchayat elections

83. Giffen goods are

(a) A product that people consume more often as the price rises

(b) A product that people consume more often as the price falls

(c) A product that people consume more or less in the same quantity irrespective of price changes

(d) None of the above

84. 'In the short run, especially during recessions, economic output is strongly influenced by aggregate demand.' This hypothesis was given by

(*a*) Paul Krugman (*b*) John Maynard Keynes

(*c*) Zoltan Acs (*d*) Franklin Allen

85. What is the name of the programme which is unveiled by the Union Urban Development Minister Venkaiah Naidu for 500 cities?

(*a*) Swachh Survekshan

(*b*) Swachh Surakshan

(*c*) Swachh Subikshan

(*d*) Swachh Sulokshan

86. Which of the following amendment of Indian constitution is known as 'Mini Constitution'?

(*a*) Ninth amendment, 1960

(*b*) Twenty first amendment, 1967

(*c*) Forty second amendment, 1976

(*d*) Forty fourth amendment, 1978

87. In which year 'Tana Bhagat Resistance Movement' started?

(*a*) 1910 (*b*) 1914

(*c*) 1918 (*d*) 1922

88. Which of the following year was not a part of 'Imperial Durbar' in India?

(*a*) 1877 (*b*) 1903

(*c*) 1911 (*d*) 1921

89. Which one of the following queen reigned Jammu & Kashmir?

(*a*) Rani Padmini

(*b*) Didda

(*c*) Rani Durgavati

(*d*) None of the above

90. Which one of the following is not true about the 'Golden Quadrilateral'?

(*a*) The largest highway project in India and the fifth longest in the world.

(*b*) It is the second phase of the National Highways Development Project (NHDP).

(*c*) The project was launched in 2001 by Atal Bihari Vajpayee under the NDA government and was planned to complete in January, 2012.

(*d*) The GQ project is managed by the National Highways Authority of India (NHAI) under the Ministry of Road, Transport and Highways.

91. Which of the following is not critically endangered bird species?

(*a*) Himalayan quail (*b*) Crow

(*c*) Sparrow (*d*) Pigeon

92. Pineal Gland is located in the

(*a*) Epithalamus (*b*) Thalamus

(*c*) Abdomen (*d*) Heart

93. Which of the following species contains Chlorocruorin?

(*a*) Marine Polychaetes (*b*) Hydra

(*c*) Earthworm (*d*) Squid

94. During World War I, which of the following was not a part of the Allied Powers?

(*a*) Romania (*b*) Belgium

(*c*) Greece (*d*) Bulgaria

95. Which one of the following layers of atmosphere affects the radio propagation?

(*a*) Mesosphere (*b*) Ionosphere

(*c*) Troposphere (*d*) Stratosphere

96. The electric potential needed for lightning may be generated by a

(*a*) Electric effect (*b*) Triboelectric effect

(*c*) Magnetic effect (*d*) Meissner effect

97. Who invented the electrical two-axis joystick?

(*a*) Douglas Engelbart (*b*) Charles Babbage

(*c*) C. B. Mirick (*d*) Robert Esnault-Pelterie

98. One molecule of water has two hydrogen atoms which are

(*a*) Covalently bonded to a single oxygen atom

(*b*) Covalently bonded to a double oxygen atom

(*c*) Covalently bonded to a triple oxygen atom

(*d*) Covalently bonded to a half oxygen atom

99. Which chemical additive encourages the suspension of one liquidin another?

(*a*) Gel (*b*) Emulsifier

(*c*) Gelatine (*d*) Pectin

100. How much money spended by Government of India as its contribution to the Atal Pension Yojana Scheme?

(*a*) Rs. 200 crore

(*b*) Rs. 160 crore

(*c*) Rs. 100 crore

(*d*) Rs. 120 crore

ANSWERS

1. (b)	**2.** (d)	**3.** (c)	**4.** (b)	**5.** (c)	**6.** (a)	**7.** (a)	**8.** (d)	**9.** (c)	**10.** (c)
11. (a)	**12.** (b)	**13.** (d)	**14.** (d)	**15.** (a)	**16.** (c)	**17.** (d)	**18.** (c)	**19.** (b)	**20.** (a)
21. (d)	**22.** (b)	**23.** (a)	**24.** (d)	**25.** (d)	**26.** (b)	**27.** (d)	**28.** (c)	**29.** (a)	**30.** (a)
31. (d)	**32.** (c)	**33.** (a)	**34.** (d)	**35.** (a)	**36.** (c)	**37.** (d)	**38.** (c)	**39.** (c)	**40.** (d)
41. (c)	**42.** (c)	**43.** (b)	**44.** (b)	**45.** (a)	**46.** (d)	**47.** (b)	**48.** (a)	**49.** (b)	**50.** (b)
51. (b)	**52.** (b)	**53.** (d)	**54.** (b)	**55.** (d)	**56.** (d)	**57.** (a)	**58.** (d)	**58.** (b)	**60.** (a)
61. (b)	**62.** (d)	**63.** (b)	**64.** (b)	**65.** (d)	**66.** (d)	**67.** (d)	**68.** (c)	**69.** (c)	**70.** (a)
71. (a)	**72.** (a)	**73.** (b)	**74.** (d)	**75.** (b)	**76.** (d)	**77.** (c)	**78.** (a)	**79.** (a)	**80.** (b)
81. (b)	**82.** (b)	**83.** (a)	**84.** (b)	**85.** (a)	**86.** (c)	**87.** (b)	**88.** (d)	**89.** (b)	**90.** (b)
91. (a)	**92.** (a)	**93.** (a)	**94.** (d)	**95.** (b)	**96.** (b)	**97.** (c)	**98.** (a)	**99.** (b)	**100.** (c)

EXPLANATIONS

1.

(20)	(1)	(12)	(5)	(14)	(20)
T	A	L	E	N	T
+2	−2	+2	−2	+2	−2
V	Y	N	C	P	R
(22)	(25)	(14)	(3)	(16)	(18)

Similarly,

(14)	(15)	(18)	(13)	(1)	(12)
N	O	R	M	A	L
+2	−2	+2	−2	+2	−2
P	M	T	K	C	J
(16)	(13)	(20)	(11)	(3)	(10)

2. This analogy is about the idioms which are used to draw comparisons. The idioms are as sick as a dog and as busy as a bee. Hence, option (d) is the correct answer.

3. The sequence shows the steps involved in a new product development. The correct answer is option (c), i.e., 1, 3, 6, 4, 2, 5.

4. The series is cbba, cbba, cbba,….

5. Wheat is a rabi crop while black gram, groundnut and fennel are kharif crops. Hence, option (c) is the correct answer.

6. $253 - 351 \Rightarrow 2 + 5 + 3 - (3 + 5 + 1) = 1$

$478 - 692 \Rightarrow 4 + 7 + 8 - (6 + 9 + 2) = 2$

$123 - 22 \Rightarrow 1 + 2 + 3 - (2 + 2) = 2$

$971 - 816 \Rightarrow 9 + 7 + 1 - (8 + 1 + 6) = 2$

Hence, $253 - 351$ is an odd pair.

7. Options (b), (c) and (d) have two vowels viz. 'o' and 'e'. Option (a) has 4 vowels, three 'i's and an 'e'. Hence, option (a) is the correct answer.

8. The series is A(1) C(3) E(5), G(7) I(9) K(11), and so on. So, the required terms will be Y(25) A(1) C(3), E(5) G(7) I(9).

9. $3 * 12 \Rightarrow 3 \times 12 = 36$

$7 * 9 \Rightarrow 7 \times 9 = 63$,

which is reverse of 36.

Similarly, $6 * 8 \Rightarrow 6 \times 8 = 48$

Then, $84 = 7 \times 12 \Rightarrow 7 * 12$.

10. From option (c), we get

$17 + 13 = 36 \div 6 \times 5$, which is true.

Hence, answer is option (c).

11. The sequence will be

Arun > Bhanu > Esha > Charu > Divya

Hence, Arun is the eldest.

12. Option (b) is the answer since the given word has a single 'G' while 'DAGGER' has two Gs.

13. Option (d) is the correct answer since 'SHARPER' has two 'Rs' while the given word has a single 'R'.

14. The given relation is true for option (d). Equation can be written as:

$34 + 52 \div 4 > 27 - 8 \Rightarrow 47 > 19$, which is true.

15. WATCH = $45 + 1 + 39 + 5 + 15 = 105$.

16. After interchanging the letters, the word will be:

STINMERUATNTNSIO

Hence, eighth letter from right will be A.

17. $112 = (7 \times 8) \times 2$

$96 = (4 \times 12) \times 2$

Similarly,

$224 = (? \times 4) \times 2 \Rightarrow ? = 28.$

18.

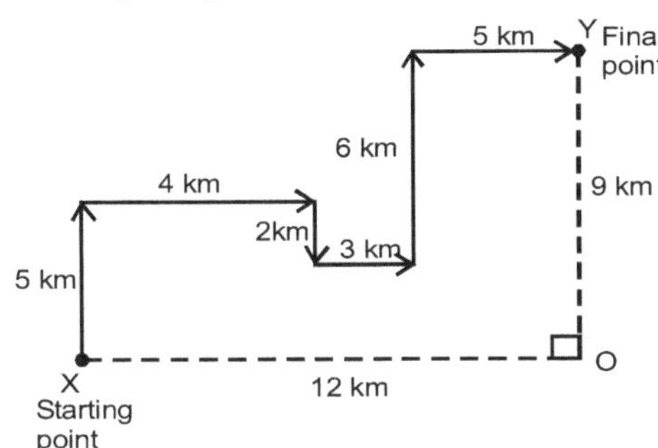

$XY^2 = XO^2 + YO^2$

$\Rightarrow XY^2 = 12^2 + 9^2$

$\Rightarrow XY = 15$ km.

19.

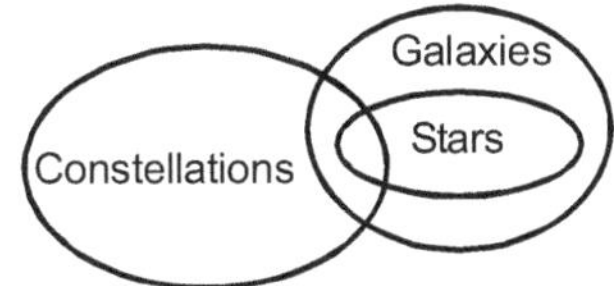

As shown in the diagram, only conclusion II follows. Hence, option (*b*) is the correct answer.

25. From matrix,

G – 57, 68, 75, 86, 99

L – 03, 11, 20, 34, 42

O – 02, 10, 23, 31, 44

W – 59, 66, 77, 85, 98

From options,

GLOW → 68, 34, 23, 98.

26. 'Pinnacle' means the highest point of something and so does 'crest'. Hence, option (*b*) is the correct answer. Options (*a*), (*c*) and (*d*) are the antonyms of 'pinnacle'.

27. 'Sleuth' is a person who looks for information to solve crimes. An 'investigator' does the same. Hence, option (*d*) is the correct answer.

28. 'Detrimental' means causing damage or injury. 'Benign' refers to something that is harmless. Hence, option (*c*) is the correct answer.

29. 'Nibble' means to eat slowly or gently. Hence, option (*a*), devour, is the correct answer. 'Devour' refers to eating of food hungrily or quickly.

30. 'Egalitarian' is a person who aims for equal wealth, status, etc., for all people. Hence, option (*a*) is the correct answer. 'Federalist' is a supporter of the federal system of government. 'Absolutist' is a person who believes that a ruler or government should have total power at all times. 'Reformist' is someone who wants to change political or social situations.

31. A 'butler' is the main male servant in the house of a wealthy person and has charge of other employees. Hence, option (*d*) is the correct answer.

32. 'Racket' refers to an illegitimate business or enterprise. Hence, it is the correct answer. Racket also means confused clattering noise. 'Clatter' means to make quick series of short loud sounds. 'Rumpus' refers to a noisy argument or fight. 'Squabble' is a noisy altercation or quarrel usually over petty matters.

33. 'To get one's foot in the door' means to manage to enter an organisation that could bring one success. Hence, option (*a*) is the correct answer.

34. 'In the home stretch' refers to the last part of an activity, etc. Hence, option (*d*) is the correct answer.

35. 'Itchy feet' means to want to travel or move to a different place; to want to do something different. Hence, option (*a*) is the correct answer.

36. The correct spelling is 'Bureaucrat'. Hence, option (*c*) is the correct answer.

37. The sentence does not have any grammatical error. Hence, part (*d*) is the correct answer.

38. When the subject of the verb is a relative pronoun ('that', in this case), then the verb agrees in number and person with the antecedent of the relative (boys). Therefore, 'has' in part (*c*) is grammatically incorrect, rendering part (*c*) the answer. The correct sentence should be 'Archie is one of the cleverest boys that have passed through the school.'

39. The preposition 'than' is used with 'different' when a noun is compared with a clause. For example: Her appearance was very different than I'd expected. When two nouns are compared, like in this case, then the preposition 'from' is used with 'different'. Hence, part (*c*) is the correct answer.

40. 'Even if' means whether or not and has to do with the conditions that may apply. 'Even though' means despite the fact. The sentence means the latter and therefore, options (*a*) and (*c*) are incorrect. The sentence says that the price of gas is starting to come down 'now'. The action is continuing to happen at present. Therefore, the second blank should logically take present continuous tense, i.e., 'are choosing'. Hence, option (*d*) is the correct answer.

41. The first blank will take 'when' because we are talking about a time. 'Where' is used when we talk of a place. The second blank will take 'that' and not 'which'. 'Which' is used if the sentence does not need the clause that the word in question is connecting. If it does, 'that' is used instead. Hence, option (*c*) is the correct answer.

42. 'Call on' means to visit someone for a short time. Hence, option (c) is the correct answer. 'Called to my professor' is grammatically incorrect. 'Call forth' means to produce a particular reaction. Since the sentence does not suggest that the professor is taken somewhere, option (b) can be negated. 'Call after' means to give a person the same name as someone else. For example: He was called after his great-grandfather.

43. 'Less' is used for uncountable nouns. For example: Less money, less time, etc. 'Fewer' is used for countable nouns. Since 'children' is a countable noun, we will use 'fewer' instead of 'less'. Option (c) is incorrect since 'suffers' is singular, while 'children' is plural. Hence, option (b) is the correct answer.

44. The sentence deals with the placement of adjectives. Generally, a noun is preceded by no more than three adjectives. These adjectives have to follow a certain order, which is: opinion, dimension/size/weight, age, shape, colour, country of origin, material and purpose. Only option (b) follows this order, i.e., dimension, shape, colour. Hence, option (b) is the correct answer.

45. 'Elder' and 'eldest' are used only for persons, not for animals or things. 'Older' and 'oldest' are used for both persons and things. 'Older' is used when we compare two things. For example: older than, older of the two, etc. 'Oldest' is used when more than two things are compared. Hence, option (a) is the correct answer.

46. Option (d) cannot be inferred from the passage since the option specifically states that it is the scientists who are performing the tests. The passage, however, does not suggest that the tests are performed by 'scientists'. Moreover, 'researchers', in the passage, refers to the researchers of London's Royal College of Art. Hence, option (d) is the correct answer. Option (a) can be inferred from the last line of the passage which says that it is difficult to say for sure that our ancestors used the stones as percussion instruments. This means that the reason for using bluestones is unknown. Option (b) can be directly inferred from the first line of the second paragraph - They also found a few of the rocks remaining at Stonehenge rang as well. The first sentence of the second paragraph states that a few rocks 'remaining' at Stonehenge cannot ring. From this we can infer that not all the stones that were originally put there could be preserved. Thus, option (c) can also be inferred.

47. 'Acoustic' is something that is related to sound. First paragraph clearly states that sound might have played the role. Hence, option (b) is the correct answer. 'Ocular' is something that is related to the eye and so, option (a) cannot be the answer.

48. 'Ephemeral' refers to something that lasts a very short time. Hence, option (a) is the correct answer.

49. 'Haul' means to move (something) with effort. Hence, its opposite will be option (b), push.

50. The last paragraph says that the challenge is providing good evidence that the bluestones were used for their musical ability. Hence, option (b) is the correct answer.

51.
$$23 - 4\sqrt{15} = \left(2\sqrt{5}\right)^2 + \left(\sqrt{3}\right)^2 - 2.2\sqrt{5}.\sqrt{3}$$
$$= \left(2\sqrt{5} - \sqrt{3}\right)^2$$

Hence, square root of $23 - 4\sqrt{15} = \pm\left(2\sqrt{5} - \sqrt{3}\right)$.

52. One of the terms in the given expression will be cot90° which is equal to zero. Hence, the value of the given expression is 0.

53. Sum of ages of the students and the teacher
= 22 × 15 = 330 years

Sum of ages of students only = 21 × 13 = 273 years

∴ Age of the teacher = 330 − 273 = 57 years.

54.
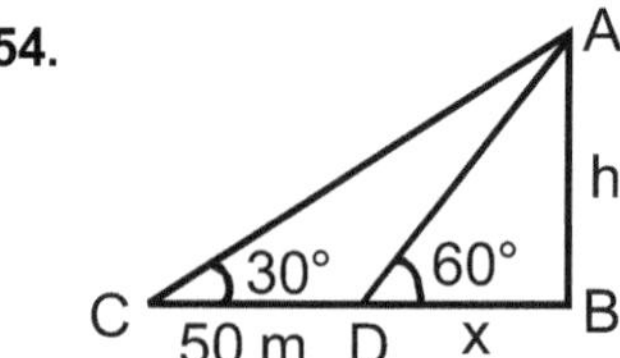

Let h be the height of the tower AB.

Then, in △ABD,

$$\tan 60° = \frac{h}{x}$$

$$\Rightarrow \sqrt{3} = \frac{h}{x}$$

$$\Rightarrow x = \frac{h}{\sqrt{3}} \qquad \dots (i)$$

In △ABC,

$$\tan 30° = \frac{h}{50 + x}$$

$$\Rightarrow \frac{1}{\sqrt{3}} = \frac{h}{50 + x}$$

$$\Rightarrow \sqrt{3}h = 50 + x \qquad \dots(ii)$$

From (i) and (ii),

$$h\sqrt{3} - \frac{h}{\sqrt{3}} = 50 \Rightarrow h = 25\sqrt{3} \text{ m}.$$

55. We have, $x^2 - 4x + 1 = 0$

$$\Rightarrow x + \frac{1}{x} = 4$$

Cubing both sides, we get

$$x^3 + \frac{1}{x^3} + 3.x.\frac{1}{x}\left(x + \frac{1}{x}\right) = (4)^3$$

$$\Rightarrow x^3 + \frac{1}{x^3} + 3(4) = 64$$

$$\Rightarrow x^3 + \frac{1}{x^3} = 52.$$

56. We have, $\angle MPQ = 120°$, $\angle MPN = 90°$ and $\angle MQN = 90°$

(As angle in a semi circle is a right angle.)

Hence, $\angle NPQ = 120° - 90° = 30°$

Also, $\angle NPQ = \angle NMQ$ (As angles in the same segment are equal.)

In $\triangle MQN$,

$$\angle QNM = 180° - (\angle MQN + \angle NMQ)$$

Hence, $\angle QNM = 180° - 90° - 30° = 60°$.

57. Total poles required on each edge other than corner poles

$$= \frac{105}{7} - 1 = 14$$

Hence, total number of poles including 4 corner poles

$$= 14 \times 4 + 4 = 60.$$

58. We have, $a\cos\theta - b\sin\theta = c$

By squaring both sides,

$$\left(a\cos\theta - b\sin\theta\right)^2 = c^2$$

$$\Rightarrow a^2\cos^2\theta + b^2\sin^2\theta - 2ab\sin\theta\cos\theta = c^2$$

$$\Rightarrow a^2(1 - \sin^2\theta) + b^2(1 - \cos^2\theta) - 2ab\sin\theta\cos\theta = c^2$$

$$\Rightarrow a^2\sin^2\theta + b^2\cos^2\theta + 2ab\sin\theta\cos\theta = a^2 + b^2 - c^2$$

$$\Rightarrow \left(a\sin\theta + b\cos\theta\right)^2 = a^2 + b^2 - c^2$$

Hence, $a\sin\theta + b\cos\theta = \pm\sqrt{a^2 + b^2 - c^2}$.

59. We have, $a\$b = a - b + \dfrac{b^2}{a}$

$$\Rightarrow 15\$3 = 15 - 3 + \frac{3^2}{15} = 12.6.$$

60. Let the length of the sides of the triangle be 3x, 4x and 5x.

Semi perimeter(s) = $\dfrac{3x + 4x + 5x}{2} = 6x$

Area of $\triangle$ = $\sqrt{6x(3x)(2x)(x)} = 6x^2$

Circumradius = $\dfrac{abc}{4 \times (\text{Area of } \triangle)}$

$$\Rightarrow 30 = \frac{3x \times 4x \times 5x}{4 \times 6x^2} \Rightarrow x = 12$$

Hence, the length of the largest side = 5x = 60 cm.

Alernate Method:

Given sides form a right angle triangle.

As, circumradius = $\dfrac{\text{hypotenuse}}{2}$

$\therefore$ Hypotenuse = $2 \times 30 = 60$ cm.

61. Let the radius of the circular ground be r m.

Time taken to cover the distance along the shortest path i.e. diameter = $\dfrac{2r}{1.5}$

And along the boundary = $\dfrac{\pi r}{1.5}$

$$\therefore \frac{\pi r}{1.5} - \frac{2r}{1.5} = 2 \times 60 \Rightarrow r\left(\frac{22}{7} - 2\right) = 2 \times 60 \times 1.5$$

$$\Rightarrow r = \frac{180 \times 7}{8} = 157.5 \text{ m.}$$

62. Let the total number of wrong sums be x.

$\Rightarrow$ Correct sum = 40 − x.

Then, $4(40 - x) - x = 80 \Rightarrow x = 16$.

63. Length of the conveyor belt = Sum of perimeters of semicircle + 2(length of direct common tangent)

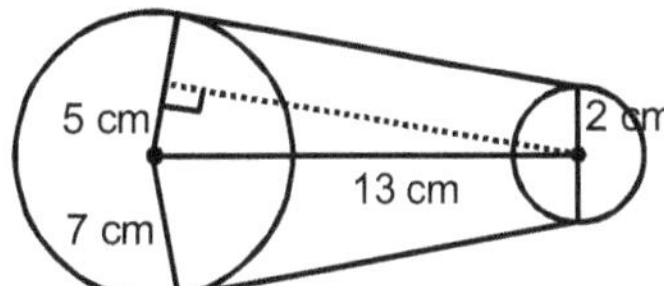

Perimeter of larger semicircle = 7π

Perimeter of smaller semicircle = 2π

Length of direct common tangent = $\sqrt{d^2 - \left(r_1 - r_2\right)^2}$

$$= \sqrt{13^2 - \left(7 - 2\right)^2} = 12 \text{ cm}$$

Hence, length of the conveyor belt (in cm) = $9\pi + 24$.

64.

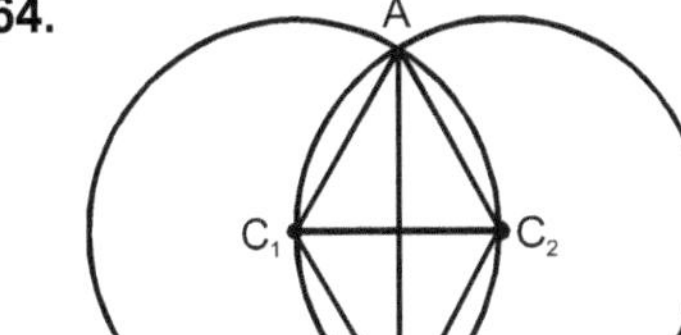

Let C_1 and C_2 be the centers of the two circles.

Here, AC_1C_2 and BC_1C_2 are equilateral triangles.

Hence, area of the quadrilateral AC_1BC_2

$$= 2 \times \frac{\sqrt{3}}{4} \times 5^2 = \frac{25\sqrt{3}}{2} \text{ cm}^2.$$

65. $\dfrac{\text{cosec}\,\theta - \cot\theta}{\text{cosec}\,\theta + \cot\theta} = \dfrac{1}{9}$

$$\Rightarrow \frac{\dfrac{1}{\sin\theta} - \dfrac{\cos\theta}{\sin\theta}}{\dfrac{1}{\sin\theta} + \dfrac{\cos\theta}{\sin\theta}} = \frac{1}{9} \Rightarrow \frac{1 - \cos\theta}{1 + \cos\theta} = \frac{1}{9}$$

$$\Rightarrow \cos\theta = \frac{4}{5}$$

Hence, $\sin\theta = \dfrac{3}{5}$.

66. We have, radius of the spherical ball = $\dfrac{24}{2} = 12$ cm

And radius of the bucket = $\dfrac{48}{2} = 24$ cm

Let the increase in height of water level be h.

Volume of the ball = volume of water raised

$$\dfrac{4}{3} \pi \times 12 \times 12 \times 12 = \pi \times 24 \times 24 \times h$$

Hence, h = 4 cm.

67. 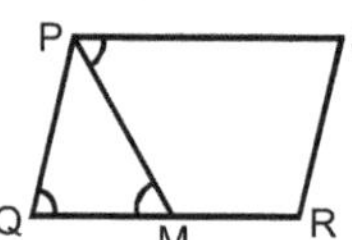

Here, $\angle MPS = \angle PQM$ (Given)

$\angle MPS = \angle PMQ$ (Alternate angles)

In $\triangle PQM$, $\angle PQM = \angle PMQ \Rightarrow PQ = PM$.

68. $3\sin^2\theta + 5\cos^2\theta = 3(\sin^2\theta + \cos^2\theta) + 2\cos^2\theta = 3 + 2\cos^2\theta$

Since minimum value of $\cos^2\theta$ is 0. Hence, the minimum value of the given expression will be 3.

69. We have, 20 cows $\equiv$ 30 goats

$$\Rightarrow 1 \text{ cow} \equiv \dfrac{3}{2} \text{ goats}$$

Also, 10 cows + 12 goats = $10 \times \dfrac{3}{2} + 12 \equiv 27$ goats

Hence, 27 goats can feed the same field for $\dfrac{30}{27} = 1\dfrac{1}{9}$ days.

70. Radius of the incircle = $\dfrac{a}{2\sqrt{3}} = \dfrac{28\sqrt{3}}{2\sqrt{3}} = 14$ cm

Hence, the area of the incircle

$$= \dfrac{22}{7} \times 14 \times 14 = 616 \text{ cm}^2.$$

71. Using, $P\left[1 + \dfrac{R}{100}\right]^n = A$

We get, $P\left[1 - \dfrac{6}{100}\right]^2 = 1.6$

$$\Rightarrow P = \dfrac{1.6 \times 100 \times 100}{94 \times 94} \approx 1.81 \text{ million}$$

$\therefore$ Population of town in 2011 was $\approx$ 1.81 million.

72. $a^2 - 1 = a$

$$\Rightarrow a - \dfrac{1}{a} = 1 \qquad \qquad \ldots \text{(i)}$$

Squaring both sides, we get

$$a^2 + \dfrac{1}{a^2} = 3$$

$$\Rightarrow a + \dfrac{1}{a} = \sqrt{5} \qquad \qquad \ldots \text{(ii)}$$

Cubing equation (i), we get

$$a^3 - \dfrac{1}{a^3} = 4 \qquad \qquad \ldots \text{(iii)}$$

Cubing equation (ii), we get

$$a^3 + \dfrac{1}{a^3} = 2\sqrt{5} \qquad \qquad \ldots \text{(iv)}$$

From equations (iii) and (iv), we get

$$a^3 = 2 + \sqrt{5}$$

$$\Rightarrow a^3 - 2 = \sqrt{5}.$$

73. 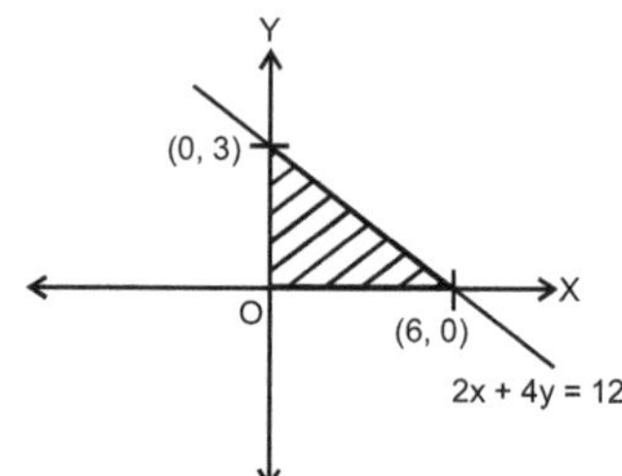

$\therefore$ Required area = $\dfrac{1}{2} \times 3 \times 6 = 9$ sq. units.

74. Total number of runs scored by Sachin

= 1000 + 600 + 800 + 400 + 600 + 600

= 4000 runs.

75. Required amount = $(26 - 8) \times \dfrac{21200}{100} \times 12 = ₹45,792.$

GENERAL INTELLIGENCE

Directions (Q. 1 - 2) : *In each of the following questions, select the related letters / word / number from the given alternatives.*

1. ACEG : TVXZ : : CEGI : ?

   (a) UWYZ   (b) VXZB

   (c) VYAC   (d) UVWX

2. PDZB : RGEI : : JSXA : ?

   (a) LVCH   (b) MVHB

   (c) LVBI   (d) MVHC

3. A piece of paper is folded and cut as shown below in the 'Question Figures'. From the given 'Answer Figures', indicate how it will appear when opened.

Question Figures:

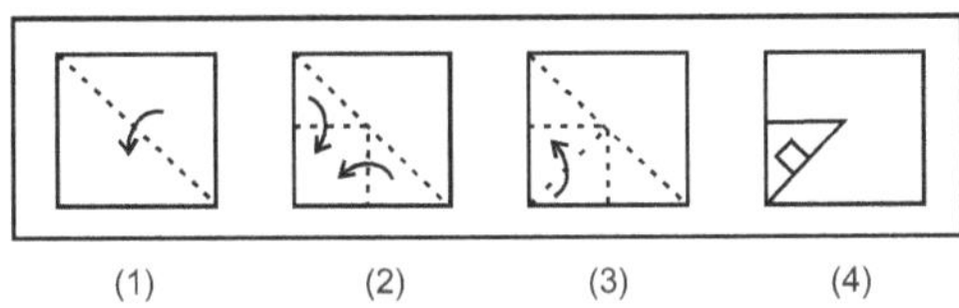

(1)   (2)   (3)   (4)

Answer Figures:

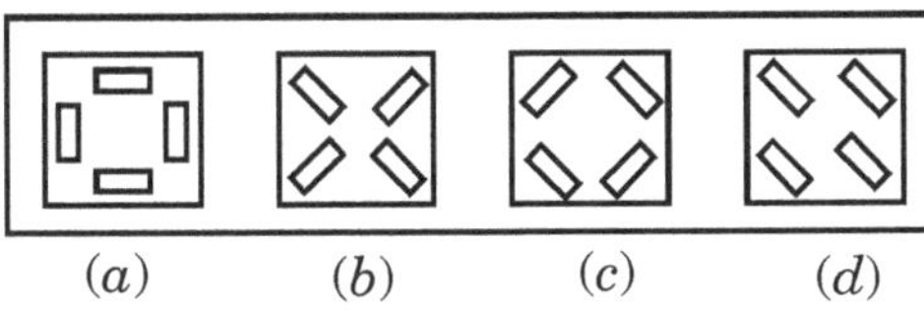

(a)   (b)   (c)   (d)

4. Find the missing element in the series given below.

19, 37, 61, 91, ?

   (a) 111   (b) 121

   (c) 127   (d) 131

Directions (Q. 5 - 6) : *Find the odd number / word from the given alternatives.*

5. (a) 111   (b) 5289

   (c) 687   (d) 442

6. (a) Defendant

   (b) Plaintiff

   (c) Attorney

   (d) Apologist

Directions (Q. 7 - 8) : *In each of the following questions, select the related word from the given alternatives.*

7. Table : Wood :: Notebook : ?

   (a) Iron   (b) Copper

   (c) Paper   (d) Water

8. Avert : Prevent :: Umbrage : ?

   (a) Satisfaction   (b) Offence

   (c) Mollification   (d) Appeasement

9. Age of B is 4/5th of A's age while age of C is 11/6th of B's age. Who among them is the oldest?

   (a) A   (b) B

   (c) C   (d) Cannot be determined

10. A statement is given followed by two assumptions,(1) and (2).You have to consider the statement to be true ,even if it seems to be at variance with commonly known facts. You are to decide which of the given assumptions can definitely be drawn from the given statement.

Statement:

Half of US teenagers are unfit for military service because of being overweight.

Assumptions:

1. Being fit is one of the criteria for induction in military service.

2. The rest half of the US teenagers are unfit for military service because of being underweight.

   (a) If only assumption 1 is implicit

   (b) If only assumption 2 is implicit.

   (c) If both 1 and 2 are implicit.

   (d) If both 1 and 2 are not implicit.

11. If START is coded as HGZIG in a code language, then how would FATAL be coded in the same code language?

   (a) UZKZL   (b) UZGZO

   (c) TZHZM   (d) TZKZL

12. If ACTIVE is coded as 549821 and PASSIVE is coded as 3577821 in a code language, then CATSCAN would be coded as

   (a) 5479544

   (b) 4597453

   (c) 5497544

   (d) 4579453

13. A man travels 10 km towards East and takes a left to travel 6 km. He again turns left to travel 2 km. How far is he from the starting point and in which direction is he moving?

   (a) 10 km North-East

   (b) 8 km East

   (c) 8 km North-West

   (d) 10 km East

14. Arrange the following words according to the dictionary:

A. Macaronic   B. Machiavellian

C. Macedonian   D. Machine

E. Macerate

(a) A,C,E,B,D   (b) A,E,C,B,D

(c) A,E,C,D,B   (d) A,C,E,D,B

15. A is the grandmother of C and D. B is the son of A. G is the father-in-law of E and husband of A. H, who is unmarried, is only sibling of B. Find the relation of H to C.

(a) Nephew   (b) Niece

(c) Uncle   (d) Cannot be determined

16. Choose the correct figure that represents relationship among English, Hindi and Urdu speaking people.

(a) 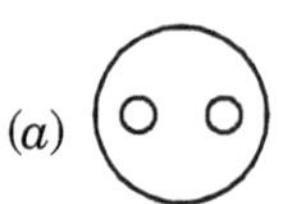   (b) 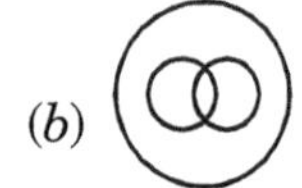

(c)    (d) 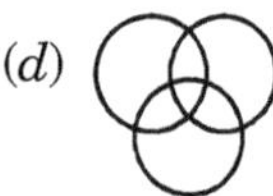

17. Find the missing number from the given responses.

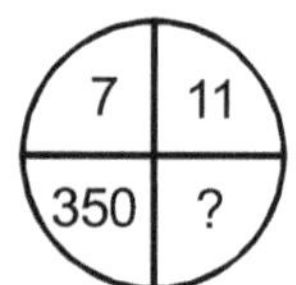

(a) 121   (b) 1331

(c) 1342   (d) 1050

18. If a mirror is placed on the line PQ, which one of the answer figures is the correct image of the given question figure?

Question Figure:

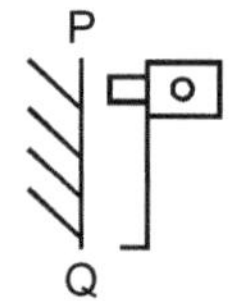

Answer Figure:

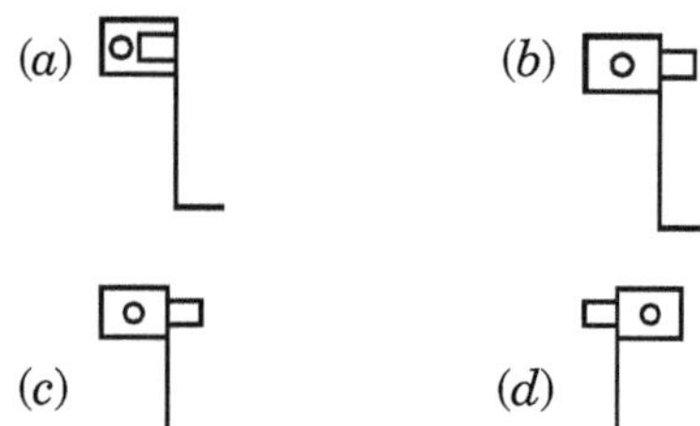

19. Which number will replace the question mark?

24	32	42
15	25	49
5	5	7
72	160	?

(a) 95   (b) 81

(c) 294   (d) 232

20. Which answer figure is the exact mirror image of the figure given in the question, when the mirror $M_1 M_2$ is placed as shown in the figure.

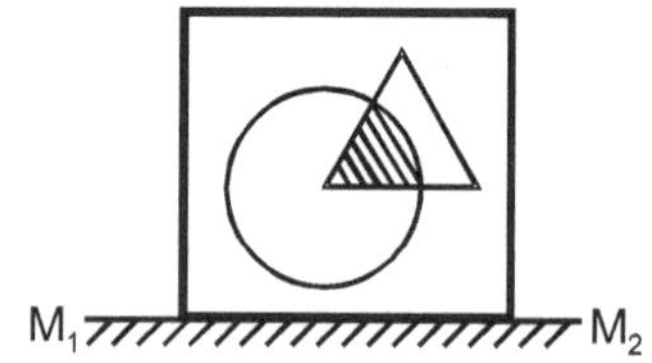

Answers figure

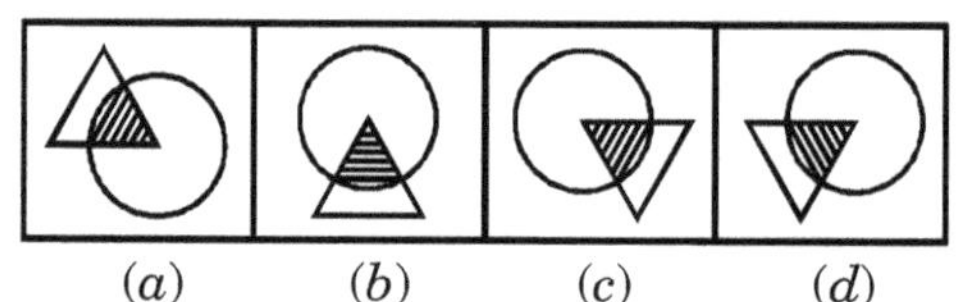

(a)   (b)   (c)   (d)

21. If '−' stands for multiplication, '+' stands for division, ' ' stands for addition and '÷' stands for subtraction, then which one of the following equation is wrong?

(a) $35 + 7 \times 39 \div 44 = 0$

(b) $33 - 3 + 11 \div 7 = 2$

(c) $125 + 25 \div 122 \times 131 = 17$

(d) $87 + 29 \times 11 - 3 = 36$

22. From the given alternative words, select the word which cannot be formed using the letters of the given word:

TABLATURE

(a) blurt

(b) lure

(c) turn

(d) table

23. From the given alternatives, select the word which can be formed using the letters of the given word:

REQUIREMENT

(a) Enquire

(b) Merriment

(c) Reign

(d) Reminder

24. In a survey conducted in an office of 100 employees, 23 like tea, 57 like coffee while 30 of them neither like tea nor coffee. What is the number of employees who like only coffee?

(a) 24   (b) 49

(c) 47   (d) 13

25. Two statements are given followed by four conclusions. You have to consider the statements to be true, even if they seem at variance with commonly known facts. You are to decide which of the given conclusions can definitely be drawn from the given statements.

Statements:

A. All hats are pigs.

B. All pigs are dirty.

Conclusions:

1. No pigs are dirty.

2. All hats are dirty.

3. Some hats are not dirty.

4. None of the hats are dirty.

(a) Only 2 follows

(b) Either 3 or 4 follow

(c) Either 1 or 3 follow

(d) All conclusions follow

ENGLISH LANGUAGE

Directions (Q. 26 - 27) : *In each of the following questions, a word is followed by four options. Select the option that best expresses the meaning of the given word.*

26. Cherubic

(a) Angelic   (b) Snobbish

(c) Restless   (d) Honest

27. Copious

(a) Powerful

(b) Delaying

(c) Plentiful

(d) Foolish

Directions (Q. 28 - 29) : *In each of the following questions, a word is followed by four options. Select the option that is opposite in meaning to the given word.*

28. Choleric

(a) Calm

(b) Ill-tempered

(c) Hygienic

(d) Sober

29. Harried

(a) Relaxed   (b) Harassed

(c) Instigated   (d) Pitch forked

Directions (Q. 30 - 32) : *Out of the four alternatives, choose the one which can be substituted for the given words.*

30. A person who is difficult to please

(a) Rhapsodic   (b) Fastidious

(c) Succulent   (d) Rambunctious

31. A cinema show, which is held in the afternoon.

(a) Proscenium   (b) Matinee

(c) Claire   (d) Dirge

32. A person who knows everything

(a) Omniscient   (b) Omnipresent

(c) Ignoramus   (d) Omnipotent

Directions (Q. 33 - 35) : *Four alternatives are given for the Idiom / Phrase. Choose the alternative which best expresses the meaning of the Idiom / Phrase.*

33. To crease something up

(a) to iron something

(b) to put things in order

(c) to disfigure something

(d) to wrinkle one's clothing

34. Skimp on something

(a) to use too little of something

(b) to gorge on a feast

(c) to skip some duty or task

(d) to do something easily

35. To die in harness

(a) to die while in service

(b) to die in prison

(c) to die lonely

(d) None of these

36. *Group of four words are given. One word is correctly spelt. Find the correctly spelt word.*

(a) Committment

(b) Comittment

(c) Commitment

(d) Comitment

Directions (Q. 37 - 39) : *Some of the sentences have errors and some are correct. Find out the part of a sentence which has an error. If there is no error, mark your answer is (d).*

37. He took to drink (a)/ to lessen (b)/ his mental worries (c)/. No error(d)

38. Despite of his protests (a)/ I decided to buy (b)/ the jeans which he did not like. (c) / No error(d)

39. The Poet and Scholar (a)/ have been(b)/ honoured. (c)/ No error(d)

Directions (Q. 40 - 42) : *Sentences are given with blanks to be filled in with an appropriate word. Four alternatives are suggested for each question. Choose the correct alternative out of the four.*

40. A bullet _________ his cheek.

    (*a*) glazed   (*b*) grazed

    (*c*) throttled   (*d*) amputated

41. Tourists forget their _________ ideas as soon as they visit our country.

    (*a*) preconceived   (*b*) ordained

    (*c*) gestalt   (*d*) ruffled

42. He has a reputation for being a _________ critic.

    (*a*) sacramental   (*b*) cyclopean

    (*c*) unleashed   (*d*) forthright

Directions (Q. 43 - 45) : *In the following questions a part of the sentence is **bold**. Below are given alternatives to the bold part at (a), (b) and (c) which may improve the sentence. Choose the correct alternative. In case no Improvement is needed your answer is (d).*

43. You are asked to copy this letter **word by word.**

    (*a*) word for word   (*b*) word with word

    (*c*) word to word   (*d*) No improvement

44. The weak man is a slave to his **sensuous** pleasures.

    (*a*) sensory

    (*b*) sensual

    (*c*) secondary

    (*d*) No improvement

45. As soon as she noticed the workmen, she asked them **what they have been doing**.

    (*a*) have done   (*b*) had been

    (*c*) are doing   (*d*) No improvement

Directions (Q. 46-50) : *Read the following passage carefully and choose the best answer to each question out of four alternatives and mark it the correct answer.*

The problem of water pollution by pesticides can be understood only in context, as part of the whole to which it belongs-the pollution of the total environment of mankind. The pollution entering our waterways comes from many sources, radioactive wastes from reactors, laboratories, and hospitals; fallout from nuclear explosions; domestic wastes from cities and towns; chemical wastes from factories. To these is added a new kind of fallout-the chemical sprays applied to crop lands and gardens, forests and fields. Many of the chemical agents in this alarming melange initiate and augment the harmful effects of radiation, and within the groups of chemicals themselves there are sinister and little-understood interactions, transformations, and summations of effect.

Ever since the chemists began to manufacture substances that nature never invented, the problem of water purification have become complex and the danger to users of water has increased. As we have seen, the production of these synthetic chemicals in large volume began in the 1940's. It has now reached such proportion that an appalling deluge of chemical pollution is daily poured into the nation's waterways. When inextricably mixed with domestic and other wastes discharged into the same water, these chemicals sometimes defy detection by the methods in ordinary use by purification plants. Most of them are so complex that they cannot be identified. In rivers, a really incredible variety of pollutants combine to produce deposits that sanitary engineers can only despairingly refer to as "gunk".

46. All the following words mean 'chemicals' except :

    (*a*) sands   (*b*) substances

    (*c*) pesticides   (*d*) deposits

47. The main argument of paragraph 1 is :

    (*a*) That there are sinister interaction in the use of chemicals

    (*b*) that there are numerous reasons for contamination of water supplies

    (*c*) that there are many dangers from nuclear fallout

    (*d*) that pesticides are dangerous

48. The word 'gunk' in the last line refers :

    (*a*) to the waste products deposited by sanitary engineers

    (*b*) to the debris found in rivers

    (*c*) to unidentifiable chemicals found in water

    (*d*) to the domestic water supplies

49. Water pollution can only be understood :

    (*a*) in relation to world contamination

    (*b*) by the whole human race

    (*c*) in context

    (*d*) in relation to the number of pesticides that exist

50. Water contamination has become serious :

    (*a*) since water pollution was difficult to assess

    (*b*) since nature has taken a hand in pollution

    (*c*) since chemists began to use new substances

    (*d*) since businessmen authorised the use of chemicals

QUANTITATIVE APTITUDE

51. Evaluate:

$$\sqrt[3]{21+\sqrt{28+\sqrt{59+\sqrt{13+\sqrt{144}}}}}$$

(a) 2   (b) 3

(c) 4   (d) 7

52. $\dfrac{(769+531)^2-(769-531)^2}{(769\times531)}=$

(a) 2   (b) 4

(c) 1300   (d) 238

53. If $x=7+4\sqrt{3}$, find the value of $\left(\sqrt{x}-\dfrac{1}{\sqrt{x}}\right)^2$.

(a) $2\sqrt{3}$ (b) $4\sqrt{3}$

(c) 12   (d) 14

54. The unit digit in the product $23 \times 29 \times 31 \times 37$ is

(a) 3   (b) 5

(c) 9   (d) 1

55. A train covers a certain distance at a speed of 90 km/hr in 8 hours. To cover the same distance in $5\dfrac{5}{6}$ hours, it must have a speed of

(a) 120 km/ hr

(b) $121\dfrac{3}{7}$ km/hr

(c) $123\dfrac{3}{7}$ km/hr

(d) 117 km/hr

56. Due to inflation, there is an increase of $33\dfrac{1}{3}\%$ in the price of bananas. If 3 less bananas are available for ₹24, the present rate of bananas per dozen is

(a) ₹30   (b) ₹32

(c) ₹34   (d) ₹36

57. Find the missing term in the series.

1, 6, 15, 28, 45, ...

(a) 56   (b) 57

(c) 66   (d) 63

58. The angles of a quadrilateral are in the ratio 3 : 2 : 4 : 6. The angles are respectively

(a) 72°, 48°, 96° and 144°

(b) 36°, 24°, 48° and 72°

(c) 90°, 60°, 30° and 180°

(d) None of these

59. The selling price of an article after giving a discount of 12% is ₹572. What is the cost price of the article, if the price is marked up by 30%?

(a) ₹475

(b) ₹500

(c) ₹525

(d) ₹540

60. The cost price of an article is ₹130. To gain 40% after allowing a 50% discount, the marked price of the article should be

(a) ₹364   (b) ₹400

(c) ₹520   (d) ₹650

61. Rupali and Swati can complete half of a piece of work in 10 days. Swati alone can complete the work in 30 days. In how many days can Rupali alone complete one fourth of the work?

(a) 20 days   (b) 15 days

(c) 18 days   (d) 24 days

62. The LCM of two numbers is 12 times the HCF. The sum of HCF and LCM is 403. If one of the numbers is 93, then the other number is :

(a) 134   (b) 124

(c) 128   (d) 310

63. A and B can complete a piece of work in 24 days and 30 days respectively when working alone. They start working together and after 10 days B left. The remaining work will be completed by A in

(a) 4 days   (b) 6 days

(c) 8 days   (d) None of these

Directions (Q. 64 - 66) : *Answer the questions on the basis of the information given below.*

The pie-chart given below shows the break-up of tudents pursuing different graduate courses from a college. Study the pie-chart and answer the following questions.

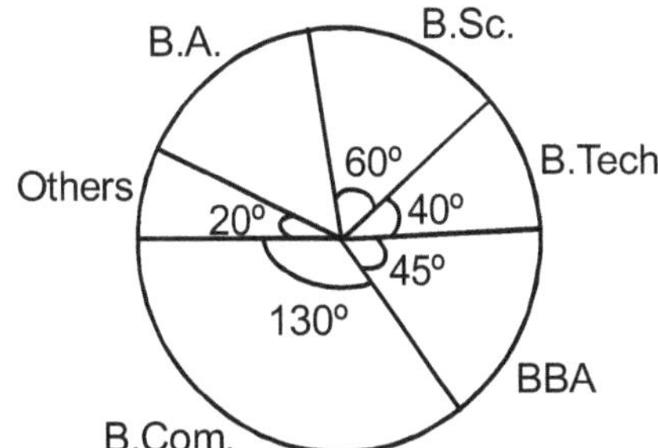

64. What is the approximate percentage of students who are pursuing B.A. from the college?

(a) 20%   (b) 18%

(c) 22%   (d) 25%

65. If the total number of students who are pursuing either B.Sc. or B.Tech. is 2,000, the total number of students in the college doing graduation is

(a) 3,600   (b) 7,200

(c) 5,400   (d) 8,400

66. If the total number of students who have taken admission under the graduate program are 3600, the difference between the number of students who are pursuing B.Tech. and those enrolled in BBA is

(a) 40   (b) 50

(c) 60   (d) None of these

67. The area of the largest circle that can be inscribed in a rectangle of length 19 cm and area 133 cm² is

(a) 35.5 cm^2 (b) 36.5 cm^2

(c) 37.5 cm^2 (d) 38.5 cm^2

68. What will be the gain percentage for a shopkeeper who sells 16 articles for the same price at which he bought 20 articles?

(a) 15%   (b) 20%

(c) 25%   (d) 40%

69. The average attendance of a class for the first four days is 47 and that for the first five days is 46. The number of students present on the 5th day is

(a) 41   (b) 42

(c) 43   (d) 44

70. By decreasing 15° of each angle of a triangle, the ratios of their angles are 2 : 3 : 5. The radian measure of greatest angle is :

(a) $11\pi/24$ (b) $\pi/12$

(c) $\pi/24$ (d) $5\pi/24$

71. The least value of $4 \csc^2\alpha + 9 \sin^2\alpha$ is :

(a) 14   (b) 10

(c) 11   (d) 12

72. If $\tan\theta - \cot\theta = a$ and $\cos\theta - \sin\theta = b$, then the value of $(a^2 + 4)(b^2 - 1)^2$ is

(a) 4   (b) 1

(c) 2   (d) 3

73. O is the circum centre of the triangle ABC with circumradius 13 cm. Let BC = 24 cm and OD is perpendicular to BC. Then the length of OD is :

(a) 7 cm   (b) 3 cm

(c) 4 cm   (d) 5 cm

74. The area of the largest triangle that can be inscribed in a semi circle of radius x in square unit is :

(a) $4x^2$ (b) x^2

(c) $2x^2$ (d) $3x^2$

75. D and E are the mid-points of AB and AC of ΔABC; BC is produced to any point P; DE, DP and EP are joined. Then,

(a) $\Delta PED = \dfrac{1}{4}\Delta ABC$ (b) $\Delta PED = \Delta BEC$

(c) $\Delta ADE = \Delta BEC$ (d) $\Delta BDE = \Delta BEC$

GENERAL AWARENESS

76. Which of the following women's team has claimed a record seventh International Hockey Federation (FIH) Champions Trophy title with a 2-1 win over reigning World and Olympic champions, the Netherlands recently?

(a) Argentina

(b) Brazil

(c) England

(d) USA

77. Who has authored the book "The Tin Drum"?

(a) Erin Morgenstern (b) Susan Nathan

(c) Gunter Grass   (d) Kiran Karnik

78. Directive Principles of State Policy in our constitution has been adopted from

(a) Thailand   (b) Japan

(c) Germany   (d) Ireland

79. Who signs the One-rupee note in India?

(a) Finance Minister (b) RBI Governor

(c) Finance Secretary (d) None of these

80. Which of the following is the capital of Kosovo?

(a) Juba   (b) Podgorica

(c) Pristina   (d) None of these

81. Tourette's syndrome is a disease that affects

(a) Nerves   (b) Lungs

(c) Gums   (d) Brain

82. Battle of Talikota was fought in which year?

(a) 1512 A.D.   (b) 1536 A.D.

(c) 1559 A.D.   (d) 1565 A.D.

83. Mir Bakshi in the regime of Akbar was required to look after:

(a) Revenue   (b) Law & Justice

(c) Military affairs   (d) None of these

84. Treaty of Srirangapatnam was signed between

(a) Tipu Sultan and Cornwallis

(b) Haider Ali and Elgin

(c) Tipu Sultan and Elgin

(d) None of these

85. Amuktamalyada, written by Krishna Deva Raya, was in which language?

(*a*) Kannada   (*b*) Telugu

(*c*) Malyalam   (*d*) Tamil

86. The uprising of 1857 was termed as first 'Indian war of Independence' by:

(*a*) R.C. Dutt   (*b*) V.D. Savarkar

(*c*) Dadabhai Naoroji (*d*) K.T. Telang

87. The layer of earth which is immediately below the crust is called:

(*a*) Outer mantle   (*b*) Outer core

(*c*) Inner mantle   (*d*) Inner core

88. Which of the following is the largest city in Latin America?

(*a*) Rio de Janeiro   (*b*) Bogota

(*c*) Caracas   (*d*) Mexico City

89. The Union government has appointed __________ as the Chief Executive Officer of National Investment and Infrastructure Fund (NIIF) Ltd.

(*a*) Sujoy Bose

(*b*) Ashok Lavasa

(*c*) NS Vishwanathan

(*d*) Gaurav Shah

90. Jayakwadi hydro electric project is on which river?

(*a*) Narmada   (*b*) Tapti

(*c*) Krishna   (*d*) Godavari

91. 'Satyameva Jayate' has been adopted from

(*a*) Katha Upanishad

(*b*) Mundak Upanishad

(*c*) Sam Veda

(*d*) None of these

92. Pine and cedar belongs to which of the following types?

(*a*) Gymnosperms   (*b*) Angiosperms

(*c*) Calciosperms   (*d*) None of these

93. What is the chemical name of the baking soda?

(*a*) Calcium Carbonate

(*b*) Sodium Carbonate

(*c*) Sodium Bicarbonate

(*d*) Calcium Sulphate

94. The Phenomena of absorption of ink by blotting paper is called

(*a*) Adsorption   (*b*) Osmosis

(*c*) Flexography   (*d*) Capillary action

95. Centre for cellular and molecular biology is located at:

(*a*) Hyderabad   (*b*) Pune

(*c*) Indore   (*d*) None of these

96. B.C. Roy award is given in which of the following fields?

(*a*) Sports   (*b*) Dance

(*c*) Medicine   (*d*) Literature

97. Which place is called the 'Light House of the Mediterranean?

(*a*) Alexandra   (*b*) Stromboli

(*c*) Gibraltar   (*d*) None of these

98. Yohan Bloke is a sprinter from which country?

(*a*) Jamaica   (*b*) USA

(*c*) Canada   (*d*) Brazil

99. Sensex is calculated on which basis?

(*a*) Free float market capitalization technology

(*b*) Market capitalization weights methods

(*c*) Wholesale Price Index

(*d*) None of these

100. Which of the following state government has launched a new scheme Kalinga Siksha Sathi Yojana with an aim to provide education loan at 1% interest to students for pursuing higher studies recently?

(*a*) Bihar   (*b*) Jharkhand

(*c*) Chhatisgarh   (*d*) Odisha

ANSWERS

1. (b)	**2.** (a)	**3.** (c)	**4.** (c)	**5.** (d)	**6.** (d)	**7.** (c)	**8.** (b)	**9.** (c)	**10.** (a)
11. (b)	**12.** (b)	**13.** (a)	**14.** (a)	**15.** (d)	**16.** (d)	**17.** (c)	**18.** (b)	**19.** (c)	**20.** (c)
21. (c)	**22.** (c)	**23.** (a)	**24.** (c)	**25.** (a)	**26.** (a)	**27.** (c)	**28.** (a)	**29.** (a)	**30.** (b)
31. (b)	**32.** (a)	**33.** (d)	**34.** (a)	**35.** (a)	**36.** (c)	**37.** (a)	**38.** (a)	**39.** (b)	**40.** (b)
41. (a)	**42.** (d)	**43.** (a)	**44.** (b)	**45.** (d)	**46.** (a)	**47.** (b)	**48.** (c)	**49.** (c)	**50.** (c)
51. (b)	**52.** (b)	**53.** (c)	**54.** (c)	**55.** (c)	**56.** (b)	**57.** (c)	**58.** (a)	**59.** (b)	**60.** (a)
61. (b)	**62.** (b)	**63.** (b)	**64.** (b)	**65.** (b)	**66.** (b)	**67.** (d)	**68.** (c)	**69.** (b)	**70.** (a)
71. (d)	**72.** (a)	**73.** (d)	**74.** (b)	**75.** (a)	**76.** (a)	**77.** (c)	**78.** (d)	**79.** (c)	**80.** (c)
81. (d)	**82.** (d)	**83.** (c)	**84.** (a)	**85.** (b)	**86.** (b)	**87.** (a)	**88.** (d)	**89.** (a)	**90.** (d)
91. (b)	**92.** (a)	**93.** (b)	**94.** (d)	**95.** (a)	**96.** (c)	**97.** (b)	**98.** (a)	**99.** (a)	**100.** (d)

EXPLANATIONS

1.

$$A \xrightarrow{+2} T,\quad C \xrightarrow{+2} V,\quad E \xrightarrow{+2} X,\quad G \xrightarrow{+2} Z$$

Similarly,

$$C \xrightarrow{+2} V,\quad E \xrightarrow{+2} X,\quad G \xrightarrow{+2} Z,\quad I \xrightarrow{+2} B$$

Hence, the correct option is (b).

2.

$$P \xrightarrow{+2} R$$
$$D \xrightarrow{+3} G$$
$$Z \xrightarrow{+5} E$$
$$B \xrightarrow{+7} I$$

Similarly,

$$J \xrightarrow{+2} L$$
$$S \xrightarrow{+3} V$$
$$X \xrightarrow{+5} C$$
$$A \xrightarrow{+7} H$$

Hence, the correct option is (a).

3. To find the final appearance of the paper, start unfolding it from the last question figure. On arriving the question figure 3, you see that the square cut will result into a rectangle such that the length of the rectangle will be twice of its breadth. Keep unfolding it till you arrive question figure 1. The final appearance of the paper will look like as given in option (c).

4.

$$19 \quad 37 \quad 61 \quad 91 \quad ? = 127$$
$$\ \ +18 \ \ +24 \ \ +30 \ \ +36$$

Hence, the correct option will be (c).

5. The numbers other than 442 has 3 as one of its factors.

Hence, the correct option is (d).

6. "Apologist" is a person who argues in defense or justification of something, such as a doctrine, policy, or institution. The rest of the words are concerned with legal proceedings.

7. Table is made from wood . Similarly, notebook is made from paper. Option (c) is the correct answer.

8. The meaning of avert is to prevent. The meaning of "umbrage" is to take offence. Mollification means to reduce in intensity. Appeasement means to soothe in temper or disposition.

9. Let A's age be x years.

$$\therefore \quad \text{B's age} = \frac{4x}{5}$$

and $\quad$ C's age $= \dfrac{11}{6} \times \dfrac{4x}{5} = \dfrac{22x}{15}$

$\therefore \quad$ A : B : C $= 1 : \dfrac{4}{5} : \dfrac{22}{15}.$

Hence, the correct option is (c).

10. Only assumption (1) is implicit as the statement says that half of US teenagers are unfit for military service. Hence it can be assumed that being fit is one of the criteria for induction in military service.

11. Similarly,

(19)S + (8)H = 27 $\qquad$ (6)F $\longrightarrow$ 21(U) = 27

(20)T + (7)G = 27 $\qquad$ (1)A $\longrightarrow$ 26(Z) = 27

(1)A + (26)Z = 27 $\qquad$ (20)T $\longrightarrow$ 7(G) = 27

(18)R + (9)I = 27 $\qquad$ (1)A $\longrightarrow$ 26(Z) = 27

(20)T + (7)G = 27 $\qquad$ (12)L $\longrightarrow$ 15(O) = 27

12. 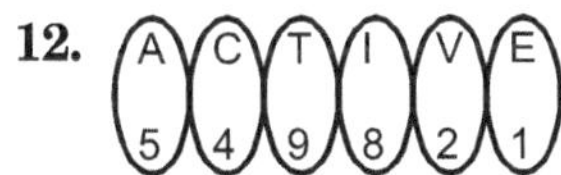

 C A T S C A N

4 5 9 7 4 5

Only option (b) satisfies the given condition.

$\therefore$ The correct answer is (b).

13. 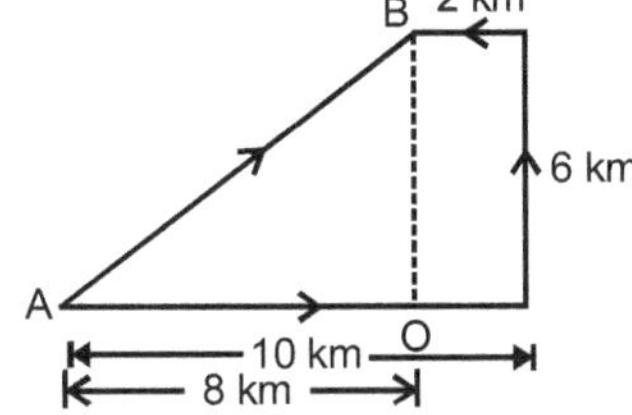

$$AB = \sqrt{AO^2 + OB^2}$$
$$= \sqrt{6^2 + 8^2} = 10 \text{ km.}$$

Therefore, the person is 10 km away from the starting point and is moving in North East direction.

14. The correct order is A,C,E,B,D according to the dictionary.

15. As the gender of H is not known, we cannot establish the relationship between H and C. Hence, it cannot be determined.

16. Some English speaking people speak Hindi, some Hindi speaking people speak Urdu and some Urdu speaking people speak English. Hence, correct option is (d)

17. Since, $350 = 7^3 + 7$

$\therefore ? = 11^3 + 11 = 1342.$

18. The figure in option (b) is the correct image of the question figure.

19. $24 \times (15 \div 5) = 72$

$32 \times (25 \div 5) = 160$

$42 \times (49 \div 7) = 294$

20. The object is inverted upside down in option (c).

21. If the given options are represented by actual algebraic signs, then,

$35 \div 7 + 39 - 44 = 0$

$33 \times 3 \div 11 - 7 = 2$

$125 \div 25 - 122 + 131 = 14$

$87 \div 29 + 11 \times 3 = 36$

Hence, (c) is the correct answer.

22. TURN is the only word that cannot be formed using the letters of the given word. The given word does not have the letter "N".

23. "Enquire" which is the British variant of the word "inquire" means to ask about. It can be formed from the given letters.

24. 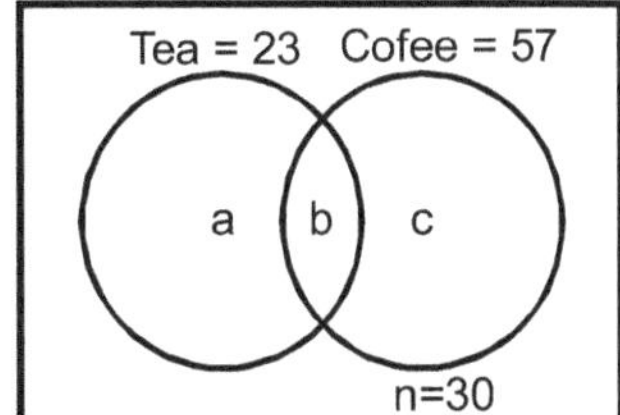

Number of employees who prefer tea $= a + b = 23$

Number of employees who prefer coffee $= b + c = 57$

Total number of employees who like either tea or coffee $= 100 - 30 = 70 = a + b + c$

$\therefore c = (a + b + c) - (a + b) = 70 - 23 = 47$

$\therefore$ Number of employees have preference for coffee only $= c = 47.$

25. 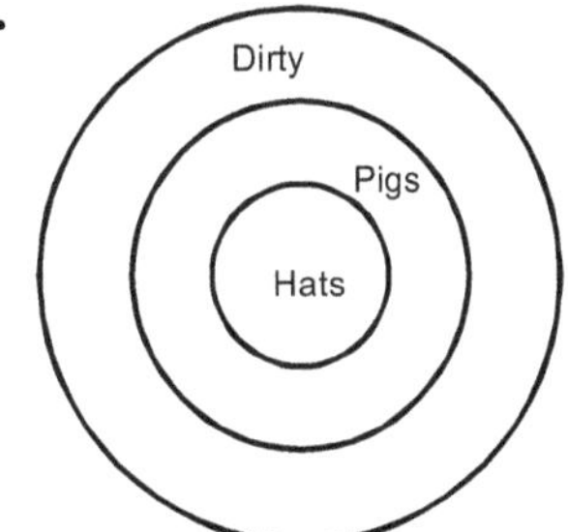

This implies all hats are dirty; thus only (2) follows.

26. "Cherubic" means a winged celestial being. "Angelic" is the word most similar in meaning to cherubic. "Snobbish" means pretentious. "Restless" means marked by a lack of quiet,

repose, or rest. "Honest" which means marked by or displaying integrity is inappropriate in the given context and thus negated.

27. "Copious" means yielding or containing plenty. "Plentiful" is the word most similar in meaning to the given word. "Powerful" means having or capable of exerting power. "Delaying" means to postpone until a later time. "Foolish" means lacking or exhibiting a lack of good sense or judgment.

28. "Choleric" means easily moved to often unreasonable or excessive anger. "Calm" is the word opposite in meaning to the given word. "Ill tempered" is negated as it is a synonym. "Hygienic" means having or showing good hygiene. "Sober" means not addicted to intoxicating drink.

29. "Harried" means beset by problems or harassed. "Relaxed" is the word most opposite in meaning to the given word. "Instigated" means provoked. "Pitchforked" means to thrust (someone) unwillingly into a position. "Harassed" is negated as it is a synonym.

30. "Rhapsodic" means extravagantly emotional and is thus negated. "Fastidious" which means having high and often capricious standards or difficult to please can be substituted for the given words. "Succulent" means full of juice. "Rambunctious" means marked by uncontrollable exuberance.

31. "Proscenium" which means the stage of an ancient Greek or Roman theater is negated. "Matinee" which means a musical or dramatic performance or social or public event held in the daytime and especially in the afternoon is the correct answer. "Dirge" means a funeral hymn or lament. "Claire" means a small enclosed pond for growing or observing the growth of oysters.

32. "Omniscient" which means having infinite awareness, understanding, and insight is the correct answer. "Omnipresent" means present everywhere simultaneously. "Ignoramus" means an ignorant person. "Omnipotent" means one having unlimited power or authority.

33. "To crease something up" means to wrinkle one's clothing.

34. "Skimp on something" means to use too little of something.

35. "To die in harness" means to die while actively engaged in work or duty.

36. "Commitment" is the correct spelling.

37. The correct sentence is "he took to drinking to lessen his mental worries". The gerund "drinking" is the object of the preposition "to".

38. The correct sentence is "despite his protests I decided to buy the jeans which he did not like." "Despite of" is idiomatically incorrect.

39. The correct sentence is "the poet and scholar has been honoured." Here the poet and the scholar refer to the same person; thus singular verb is used.

40. A bullet bruised his cheek. "Glazed" which means a substance coated with a layer of a vitreous substance is negated. "Grazed" which means an area of skin roughened or worn away by harsh rubbing against another surface is appropriate for the blank. "Throttled" means to keep (someone) from breathing by exerting pressure on the windpipe. "Amputated" means to cut off (a projecting body part), especially by surgery.

41. Tourist forget their biased ideas as soon as they visit our country. "Preconceived" which means to form (an opinion, for example) before possessing full or adequate knowledge is appropriate for the blank. "Ordained" means to establish or order by appointment, decree, or law. "Gestalt" is a German word for form or shape. "Ruffled" means troubled.

42. "Sacramental" means of, relating to, or having the character of a sacrament. "Cyclopean" means massive. "Unleashed" means to throw, shoot, or set in motion forcefully. "Forthright" which means straightforward is appropriate for the blank.

43. **word for word** means : In exactly the same words or when translated exactly equivalent words.

44. The word **sensual (Adjective)** means : connected with your physical feelings; giving pleasure to your physical senses; espe cially to sexual pleasures.

51. $\sqrt[3]{21+\sqrt{28+\sqrt{59+\sqrt{13+\sqrt{144}}}}}$

$= \sqrt[3]{21+\sqrt{28+\sqrt{59+\sqrt{13+12}}}}$

$= \sqrt[3]{21+\sqrt{28+\sqrt{59+5}}}$

$= \sqrt[3]{21+\sqrt{28+8}}$

$= \sqrt[3]{21+\sqrt{36}}$

$= \sqrt[3]{21+6}$

$= \sqrt[3]{27} = 3.$

52. $\dfrac{(769+531)^2-(769-531)^2}{769\times531}$

$= \dfrac{4\times769\times531}{769\times531} = 4 \ . \{(a+b)^2-(a-b)^2 = 4ab\}$

53. $x = 7 + 4\sqrt{3} \Rightarrow \dfrac{1}{x} = 7 - 4\sqrt{3}$

$$\left(\sqrt{x} - \dfrac{1}{\sqrt{x}}\right)^2 = \left(\sqrt{x}\right)^2 + \left(\dfrac{1}{\sqrt{x}}\right)^2 - 2\,\sqrt{x} \times \dfrac{1}{\sqrt{x}}$$

$$= x + \dfrac{1}{x} - 2$$

$$= 7 + 4\sqrt{3} + 7 - 4\sqrt{3} - 2$$

$$= 12.$$

54. The unit digit of the product $23 \times 29 \times 31 \times 37$ is same as that the unit digit of the product $3 \times 9 \times 1 \times 7$, which is 9.

55. Distance covered in both the cases is same i.e., $d_1 = d_2$.

$\Rightarrow s_1 \times t_1 = s_2 \times t_2$

$\Rightarrow 90 \times 8 = s_2 \times \dfrac{35}{6}$

$\therefore s_2 = \dfrac{90 \times 8 \times 6}{35} = \dfrac{864}{7} = 123\dfrac{3}{7}$ km/hr.

Hence, speed of the train should be $123\dfrac{3}{7}$ km/hr.

56. Let the price of a banana before inflation be ₹ x

$\therefore$ Number of bananas for ₹ 24 $= \dfrac{24}{x}$

Present price per banana $= x + 33\dfrac{1}{3}\%$ of $x = ₹\dfrac{4x}{3}$.

$\therefore$ Number of bananas for ₹ 24 $= \dfrac{24}{\dfrac{4x}{3}} = \dfrac{18}{x}$

According to the question,

$\dfrac{24}{x} - \dfrac{18}{x} = 3 \quad \Rightarrow \quad \dfrac{6}{x} = 3$

$\Rightarrow \quad x = 2$

$\therefore$ Rate of banana per dozen

$= 12 \times 2$

$= ₹24.$

$\therefore$ Present rate $= \dfrac{4x}{3} = \dfrac{4 \times 24}{3} = ₹32$ per dozen.

57. The given series is :

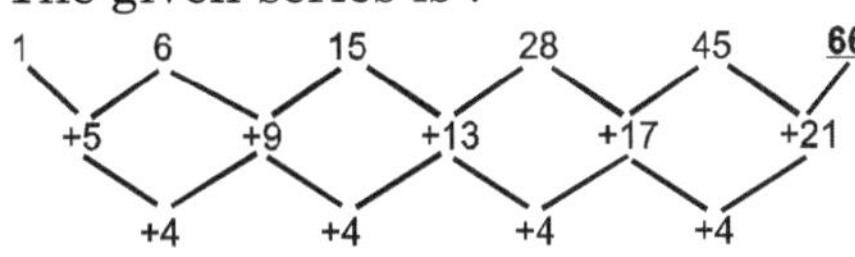

58. Let the angles of the quadrilateral be $3x$, $2x$, $4x$ and $6x$.

$\therefore 3x + 2x + 4x + 6x = 360°$

$\Rightarrow 15x = 360°$

$\Rightarrow x = \dfrac{360°}{15} = 24°$

$\therefore$ Angles are $72°$, $48°$, $96°$, and $144°$

59. MRP of the article $= \dfrac{572}{(1 - 0.12)} = \dfrac{572}{0.88} = ₹650$

$\therefore$ Cost price of the article, if profit is 30%

$= \dfrac{650}{(1 + 0.3)} = \dfrac{650}{1.3} = ₹500.$

60. Let the marked price of the article be ₹x.

$\therefore$ Selling price after 50% discount $= \dfrac{x}{2}$

Cost price $= \dfrac{\dfrac{x}{2}}{1 + 0.4} = \dfrac{x}{2(1.4)} = \dfrac{x}{2.8}.$

According to the question,

$\dfrac{x}{2.8} = 130$

$\Rightarrow \quad x = 2.8 \times 130 = ₹364.$

61. (Rupali + Swati)'s 1 day work $= \dfrac{1}{20}$

Swati's 1 day work $= \dfrac{1}{30}$

$\therefore$ Rupali's 1 day work

$= \dfrac{1}{20} - \dfrac{1}{30} = \dfrac{3 - 2}{60} = \dfrac{1}{60}$

$\therefore$ Rupali will take $\dfrac{60}{4} = 15$ days to complete $\dfrac{1}{4}th$ of the work.

62. Let HCF of two numbers be x.

$\therefore$ LCM $= 12x$.

$\therefore$ Product of numbers $=$ LCM $\times$ HCF $= 12x^2$

Also, sum of HCF and LCM $= 403$

$\Rightarrow 12x + x = 403$

$\Rightarrow 13x = 403$

$\therefore x = \dfrac{403}{13} = 31$

According to the question,

$93 \times$ second number $= 12 \times 31 \times 31$

$\therefore$ Second number $= \dfrac{12 \times 31 \times 31}{93} = 124.$

63. Let the total work be the LCM (24, 30) $= 120$ units.

Work done by A and B is 5 units and 4 units per day respectively.

Total work done in 10 days (when they work together) $= 10 \times (5 + 4) = 90$ units

Work left $= 120 - 90 = 30$ units.

This remaining work is completed by A in $\dfrac{30}{5} = 6$ days.

64. Percentage of students who are pursuing B.A.

$= \dfrac{65}{360} \times 100 = 18.05 \approx 18\%.$

65. Required total number of students

$$= \left(\frac{60 + 40}{360}\right) x = 2000$$

$\Rightarrow \qquad x = 7,200.$

66. The number of students who are pursuing

B.Tech. $= \dfrac{40}{360} \times 3600 = 400$

The number of students who are pursuing BBA

$= \dfrac{45}{360} \times 360 = 450$

$\therefore$ Required difference $= 450 - 400 = 50.$

67. Breadth of the rectangle $= \dfrac{133}{19} = 7\,\text{cm}$

Area of the circle $= \pi r^2$
(Maximum diameter = Breadth of the rectangle)

$= \dfrac{22}{7} \times \dfrac{7}{2} \times \dfrac{7}{2} = 38.5\,\text{cm}^2$.

68. Let C.P. of 20 articles be ₹100.

$\therefore$ C.P. of 16 articles = ₹80

$$\text{Profit \%} = \frac{\text{S.P.--C.P.}}{\text{C.P.}} \times 100\%$$

$$= \frac{100 - 80}{80} \times 100\%$$

$$= 25\% .$$

69. The number of students present on the 5th day
$= 46 \times 5 - 47 \times 4 = 42.$

70. $a + b + c = \pi$

$a - 15° : b - 15° : c - 15° = 2 : 3 : 5$

$$= 2x : 3x : 5x$$

$\Rightarrow a + b + c - 45 = 10x$

$\pi - 45 = 10x$

$\pi - \dfrac{\pi}{4} = 10x$

$\Rightarrow \quad 10x = \dfrac{3\pi}{4}$

$\qquad x = \dfrac{3\pi}{40}$

greatest$= c = 5x + 15°$

$$= \dfrac{3\pi}{8} + \dfrac{\pi}{12}$$

$$= \dfrac{9\pi + 2\pi}{24} = \dfrac{11\pi}{24}$$

71. $4\,\text{cosec}^2\alpha + 9\sin^2\alpha = \text{minum} = 12$

when, $4\text{cosec}^2\alpha = 9\sin^2\alpha$

$\Rightarrow \qquad \sin^2\alpha = \dfrac{2}{3}$

$\qquad \text{cosec}^2\alpha = \dfrac{3}{2}$

72. $a^2 = \tan^2\theta + \cot^2\theta - 2$

$b^2 = 1 - \sin 2\theta$

$\therefore (a^2 + 4)(b^2 - 1)^2 = (\sec^2\theta + \text{cosec}^2\theta).\sin^2 2\theta$

$$= 4(\sin^2\theta + \cos^2\theta)$$

$$= 4$$

73.

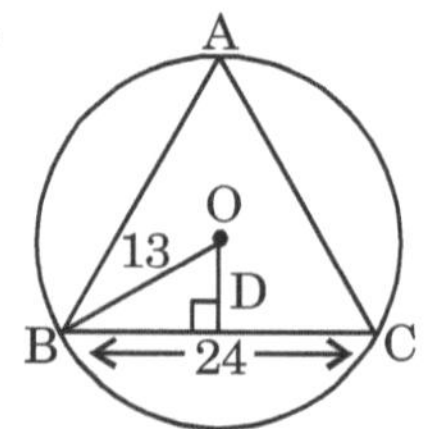

$(OD)^2 = (13)^2 - (12)^2$

$OD = 5$

74.

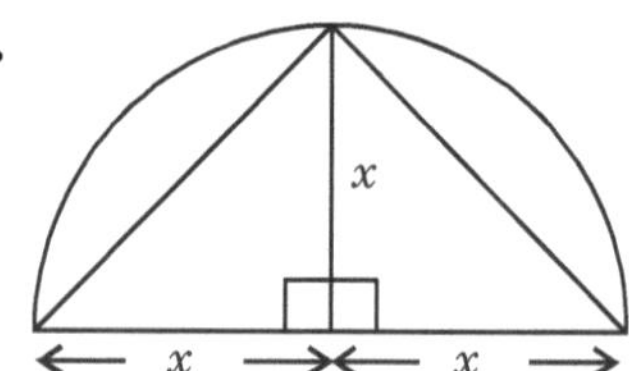

$\dfrac{1}{2} \times 2x \times x = x^2$

75.

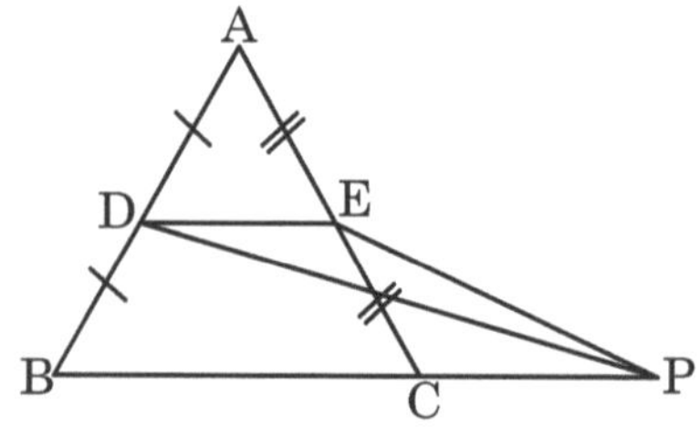

$\Delta PED = \Delta ADE$

$\&\ \Delta ADE = \dfrac{1}{4}\Delta ABC$

similar Δs due to same base and height.

■■

PRACTICE SET – 6

GENERAL INTELLIGENCE

1. If NOVELTY is coded as 5270813 and ESSAY is coded as 04463, then SEVEN will be coded as
   (a) 48785
   (b) 40085
   (c) 08285
   (d) 40705

2. 35% of 1180 + 65% of 860 = ? % of 8100
   (a) 8
   (b) 12
   (c) 15
   (d) 21

3. 'A' stands for multiplication, 'D' stands for equal to, 'B' stands for greater than, 'F' stands for subtraction, 'G' stands for less than, 'E' stands for addition and 'I' stands for division. In the following four alternatives, only one expression is correct according to the letter symbol. Identify that expression.
   (a) 18 I 6 E 4 G 30 F 11 A 2
   (b) 18 F 6 I 4 B 30 E 11 A 2
   (c) 18 F 6 I 4 E 30 G 11 A 2
   (d) 18 I 6 B 4 E 30 F 11 A 2

Directions : In question nos. **4** to **6**, find related word/number from the given alternatives.

4. Planet : Mercury :: Bone : ?
   (a) Femur
   (b) Stapes
   (c) Scapula
   (d) Tibia

5. Bear : Growl :: Doors : ?
   (a) Chime
   (b) Creak
   (c) Splatter
   (d) Jangle

6. Lion : Pride :: Geese : ?
   (a) Herd
   (b) Pack
   (c) Gaggle
   (d) Flock

Directions : In question nos. **7** to **9**, find the odd word/number/letters/number pair from the given alternatives.

7. (a) $\dfrac{4}{5}$
   (b) $\dfrac{6}{11}$
   (c) $\dfrac{3}{2}$
   (d) $\dfrac{8}{13}$

8. (a) CFIL
   (b) GJMP
   (c) KMQT
   (d) ORUX

9. (a) 2 - 5
   (b) 4 - 21
   (c) 6 - 41
   (d) 8 - 71

Directions : In question nos. **10** arrange the given words a meaningful and ascending order and select the option indicating the correct order.

10. 1. Fruit
    2. Root
    3. Stem
    4. Flower
    5. Leaves
    (a) 2, 3, 1, 4, 5
    (b) 5, 2, 3, 1, 4
    (c) 1, 4, 3, 5, 2
    (d) 2, 3, 5, 4, 1

11. Which one set of letters when sequentially placed at the gaps in the given letters series shall complete it?

    _ _ l l m _ l _ l _ m l
    (a) mlmlm
    (b) lmlml
    (c) lllmm
    (d) mmllm

Directions : In question nos. **12** to **14**, find the missing number from the given responses.

12. 99, 102, 51, 54, 27, 30, ?, ?
    (a) 12, 15
    (b) 15, 18
    (c) 10, 13
    (d) 18, 21

13. | 6 | 3 | 4 | 7 |
    |---|---|---|---|
    | 9 | 8 | 5 | 6 |
    | 4 | 8 | 12 | 14 |
    | 108 | ? | 120 | ? |

    (a) 64 and 147
    (b) 128 and 147
    (c) 96 and 294
    (d) 128 and 294

14. | 2 | 12 | 18 | 6 |
    |---|---|---|---|
    | 3 | 18 | 24 | 8 |
    | 5 | 30 | 36 | ? |

    (a) 14
    (b) 47
    (c) 42
    (d) 12

15. A watch reads 7:45. If the minute hand points East, then in which direction will the hour hand points?
    (a) South
    (b) North-east
    (c) South-west
    (d) South-east

Directions: In the following question from the given alternatives words, select the word which *cannot* be formed using the letters of the given word.

16. RATIFICATION

   (*a*) RATIO   (*b*) FICTION

   (*c*) TITAN   (*d*) FEST

17. Seven friends – A, B, C, D, E, F and G – are sitting in a row on a bench facing West. C is immediate right of D. B is sitting at one of the extreme ends and E is sitting at immediate next to him. G is sitting between E and F and no one is sitting between them. D is sitting third from North end. Who are sitting at the two extreme ends?

   (*a*) C and A   (*b*) A and B

   (*c*) C and B   (*d*) B and F

18. Priti walks 250 m towards North. She then turns towards her right and walks 350 m more. After that she turns left and walks 400 m. Now she turns by 135° in clockwise and walks 600 m. Now she turns 45° in anticlockwise and walks 300 m to reach at the gate of her college. Which direction is she facing now?

   (*a*) North   (*b*) South

   (*c*) West   (*d*) East

Directions: In the following question two statements are given which are followed by two/four conclusions I, II, III and IV. You have to consider the two statements to be true even if they seem to be at variance from commonly known facts. You have to decide which of the given conclusions, if any, follow from the given statements.

19. Statements:

   I. Kavya has four pairs of shoes.

   II. None of her siblings have four pairs of shoes.

   Conclusions:

   I. All her siblings have shoes.

   II. Only one sibling in the family has exactly four pairs of shoes.

   III. Kavya's siblings have less than four pairs of shoes.

   IV. Kavya is wealthier than her siblings.

   (*a*) Only conclusion I follows.

   (*b*) Only conclusion III follows.

   (*c*) Only conclusion II follows.

   (*d*) Only conclusion IV follows.

20. In the following figure △ represents cricketer, ◯ represents hockey player and ▢ represents footballer. Find the footballer and hockey player both but not cricketer.

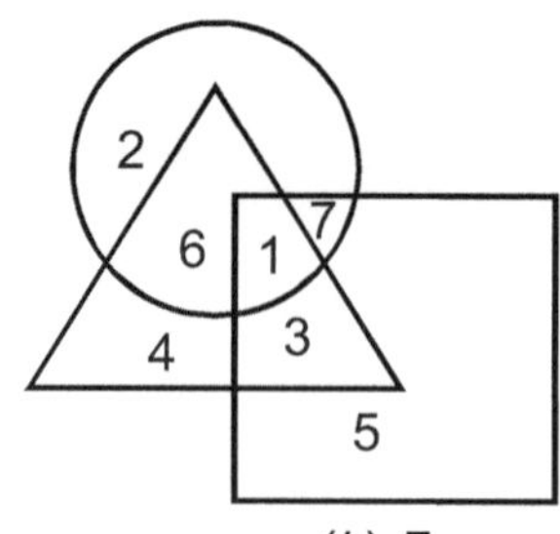

   (*a*) 2   (*b*) 7

   (*c*) 5   (*d*) 3

21.

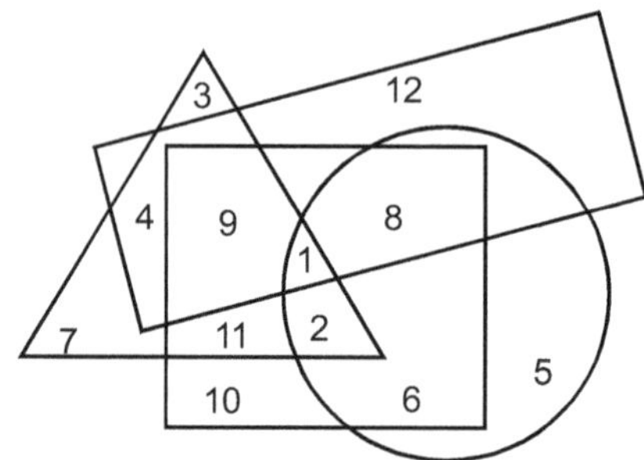

In the above figure, the square stands for authors, the circle stands for poets, the triangle stands for dramatists and the rectangle stands for teachers.

Which region represents teachers, authors and dramatists but who are not poets?

   (*a*) 1   (*b*) 8

   (*c*) 9   (*d*) 12

Directions: In the following question which answer figure will complete the pattern in the question figure?

22. Question figure

Answer figures

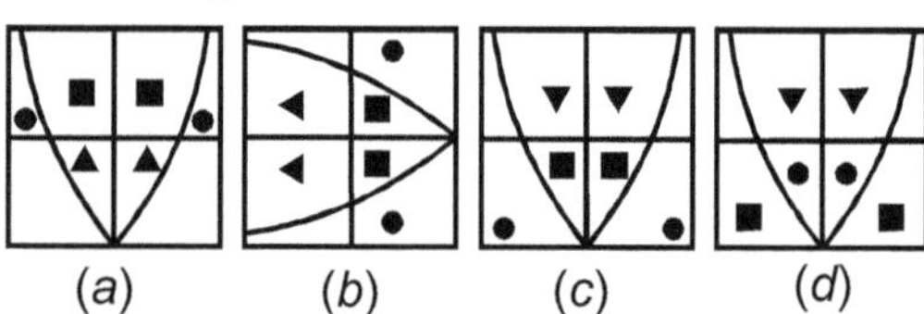

   (*a*)   (*b*)   (*c*)   (*d*)

23. From the answer figures, select the one in which the question figure is hidden/embedded.

Question figure

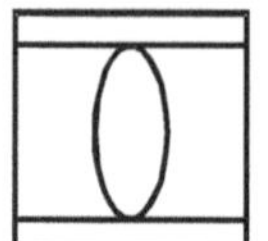

Answer figures

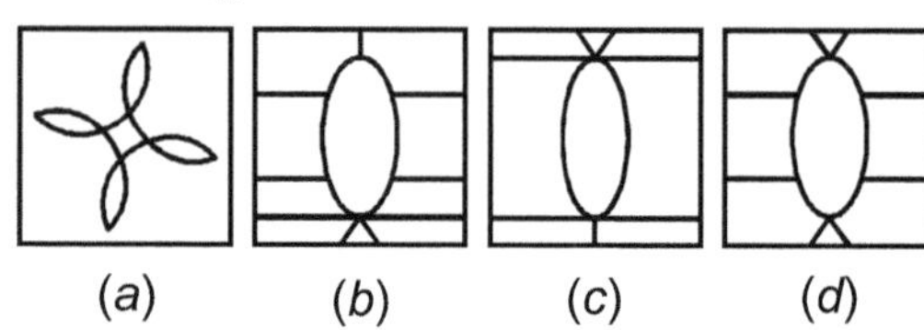

   (*a*)   (*b*)   (*c*)   (*d*)

24. From the answer figures, find out the figure which is the exact mirror image of the question figure, when the mirror is placed on the line 'MN'?

Question figure

Answer figures

(a)　　　(b)　　　(c)　　　(d)

25. A word is represented by only one set of numbers as given in any one of the alternatives. The sets of numbers given in the alternatives are represented by two classes of alphabets as in two matrices given below. The columns and rows of Matrix I are numbered from 0 to 4 and that of Matrix II are numbered from 5 to 9. A letter from these matrices can be represented *first by its row* and *next by its column*, e.g., 'B' can be represented by 12, 33, etc., and 'L' can be represented by 56, 79. etc. Similarly you have to identify the set for the word 'CAMP'.

Matrix I					
	0	1	2	3	4
0	E	C	A	D	B
1	A	D	B	E	C
2	C	B	D	A	E
3	D	E	C	B	A
4	B	A	E	C	D

Matrix II					
	5	6	7	8	9
5	O	L	M	P	N
6	P	M	N	L	O
7	M	N	P	O	L
8	N	O	L	M	P
9	L	P	O	N	M

(a) 01, 20, 88, 96

(b) 43, 66, 34, 89

(c) 32, 23, 75, 77

(d) 43, 02, 58, 88

ENGLISH LANGUAGE

Directions : In question nos. **26** to **27**: In the following question out of the four alternatives, choose the one which best expresses the meaning of the given word and mark it in the answer sheet.

26. Coercion

(a) Atrociousness　　　(b) Pressure

(c) Deceitfulness　　　(d) Misleading

27. Predicament

(a) Dilemma

(b) Situation

(c) Advantage

(d) Forecaster

Directions: In question nos. **28** to **29**, choose the word opposite in meaning to the given word and mark it in the answer sheet.

28. Conceit

(a) Analyzability　　　(b) Advancer

(c) Reproach　　　(d) Modesty

29. Opaque

(a) Unequivocal　　　(b) Coloured

(c) Ambiguous　　　(d) Dark

Directions: In question nos. **30** to **32**, out of the four alternatives, choose the one which can be substituted for the given words/sentences.

30. A narrow passage that helps end hunger

(a) Neck　　　(b) Stomach

(c) Throat　　　(d) Tongue

31. A word that carries within it a synonym of itself

(a) Joey word　　　(b) Kangaroo word

(c) Metaphor　　　(d) Acronym

32. A reservoir

(a) Sump　　　(b) Dump

(c) Lump　　　(d) Clump

Directions: In question nos. **33** to **35**, four alternatives are given for the idiom/phrase underlined in the sentence. Choose the alternative which best expresses the meaning of the given idiom/phrase.

33. We talked about everything <u>under the sun</u>.

(a) in an open area　　　(b) in existence.

(c) during the day　　　(d) about the planets.

34. She had to <u>go cap in hand</u> to the committee to get a grant for the proposal.

(a) to go somewhere excitedly to ask for a favour

(b) to go somewhere hastily to ask for a favour

(c) to nervously ask for a favour

(d) to ask for a favour which makes you feel ashamed

35. I had to do a <u>snow job</u> on my friend to make things work.

(a) To cover up things by making a false story

(b) To persuade someone to do something by praising them

(c) To deter a person from doing something by exhortation

(d) To change a persons' appearance

Directions: In the following question four words are given in each question, out of which only one word is spelt correctly. Find the correctly spelt word and mark your answer in the answer sheet.

36. (a) Judgmentally　　　(b) Judgementally

(c) Judgementaly　　　(d) Judgmentaly

Directions: In question nos. **37** to **39**, some parts of the sentences have errors and some are correct. Find out which part of the sentence has an error and mark the answer corresponding to the appropriate letter (A, B, C). If a sentence is free from error, mark your answer as (*d*).

37. I want you to apprise me (*a*)/ to any changes in the environment (*b*)/ that affect our business. (*c*)/ No error (*d*)

38. She has made it (*a*)/ clear that she feels superior than (*b*)/ me in every way. (*c*)/ No error (*d*)

39. I have eaten two burgers, four spoonsful (*a*) / of frosting, three packets of (*b*) / chips and I am loving it. (*c*)/ No error (*d*)

Directions: In question nos. **40** to **42**, sentences are given with blanks to be filled with an appropriate word(s). Four alternatives are suggested for each question. Choose the correct alternative out of the four.

40. Someone's been putting it ______ that you plan to shut down the organisation.

    (*a*) away   (*b*) up

    (*c*) aside   (*d*) about

41. There she ______!

    (*a*) went   (*b*) go

    (*c*) goes   (*d*) will go

42. Your brother hasn't yet ______ from the anaesthetic that the doctor gave him.

    (*a*) come about   (*b*) come out

    (*c*) come at   (*d*) come round

Directions: In question nos. **43** to **45**, a sentence / part of the sentence is underlined. Beneath each sentence four different ways of phrasing the underlined part are given. Choose the grammatically correct option. In case no improvement is needed, your answer should be option (*d*).

43. <u>Before he died, Raja, a theater artist, performed in this theatre.</u>

    (*a*) Raja, a theater artist, before he died performed in this theatre.

    (*b*) A theater artist, Raja, before he died performed in this theatre.

    (*c*) Raja, a theater artist, performed in this theatre before he died.

    (*d*) No improvement

44. You are late by a couple of seconds; he <u>have just left</u> for New York.

    (*a*) would have just left

    (*b*) had just left

    (*c*) has just left

    (*d*) No improvement

45. If I were you, I would plan <u>on</u> a big crowd at your open house.

    (*a*) in   (*b*) at

    (*c*) by   (*d*) No improvement

Directions: In question nos. **46** to **50**, you have given a passages with 5 questions. Read the passage carefully and choose the best answer to each question out of the four alternatives.

Le Moulin de la Galette depicts a windmill against a sunny sky above Montmartre in Paris. It was first shown in public in Amsterdam, 15 years after Van Gogh's death. Later it was the proud possession of the powerful American industrialist who inspired Ian Fleming to create his arch-villain Auric Goldfinger, the quintessential enemy of James Bond, whose closest companion was a fluffy white cat.

Van Gogh painted the work in April 1887 at a key point in the development of his vibrant, colourful style. During a two-year period, just after he had moved to Paris to live with his brother, Theo, the impoverished painter moved away from his customary dark studies of Dutch landscapes and his paintings took on some of the mannerisms of the impressionist movement in the hope that they might sell. Encouraged by Theo, he set up his easel by the windmills near their apartment in the artistic quarter above the French capital.

46. Which of the following can Le Moulin de la Galette possibly be?

    (*a*) Painting   (*b*) Film

    (*c*) Sketch   (*d*) Cannot be determined

47. Which of the following is closest in meaning to the word 'quintessential'?

    (*a*) Envious   (*b*) Strange

    (*c*) Worst   (*d*) Classic

48. Which of the following can most likely be inferred from the passage?

    (*a*) Van Gogh moved to Paris to live with his step-brother, Theo.

    (*b*) Theo encouraged Van Gogh to create Le Moulin de la Galette.

    (*c*) Van Gogh's art was in vogue in early 1887s.

    (*d*) Van Gogh's work came to light only after 15 years of his death.

49. Where was Le Moulin de la Galette first unveiled?

    (*a*) Paris   (*b*) Amsterdam

    (*c*) France   (*d*) Montmartre

50. Who bought Le Moulin de la Galette?

    (*a*) Auric Goldfinger

    (*b*) An American industrialist

    (*c*) Theo

    (*d*) Ian Fleming

QUANTITATIVE APTITUDE

51. Three number are in the ratio 2 : 3 : 5. By adding 10 to each of them, the new numbers formed are in the ratio 4 : 5 : 7. The numbers are
  (a) 12, 18, 30   (b) 10, 15, 25
  (c) 8, 12, 20   (d) 20, 25, 35

52. A man buys 4 shirts and 7 jeans for ₹6,900. Instead, if he would have bought 6 shirts and 11 jeans, he had to pay ₹3,800 more. Cost of one jeans is
  (a) ₹700   (b) ₹500
  (c) ₹400   (d) ₹600

53. Number of digits in the square root of 3548346624 is
  (a) 7   (b) 6
  (c) 4   (d) 5

54. In a company consisting of 20 employees, one employee retires and a new employee of age 25 years joins, resulting a decrease in average age of employees by 3. Find the age of retired employee.
  (a) 70 years   (b) 65 years
  (c) 85 years   (d) 80 years

55. What is the perpendicular distance between parallel lines $3x - y = 7$ and $9x - 3y = 17$?
  (a) $\dfrac{4}{3\sqrt{10}}$ units   (b) $\dfrac{4}{3}$ units
  (c) 3 units   (d) $\dfrac{4}{\sqrt{10}}$ units

56. The value of a car depreciates every year by 10%. If the value of the car after 2 years will be ₹81,000, then what is the present value of the car?
  (a) ₹ 90,000   (b) ₹ 1,00,000
  (c) ₹ 99,000   (d) ₹ 1,05,000

57. A, B and C can finish a work in 20, 30 and 60 days respectively working alone. If A and B started working together and after 5 days, B left the work and C joined to finish the remaining work with A. How many days did C work?
  (a) 8 days   (b) $8\dfrac{1}{2}$ days
  (c) $8\dfrac{3}{4}$ days   (d) $7\dfrac{3}{4}$ days

58. If 12 men or 20 women or 36 children can do a work in 12 months, then 5 men, 10 women and 15 children can do half of the work in
  (a) $5\dfrac{1}{2}$ months   (b) 4 months
  (c) 9 months   (d) $4\dfrac{1}{2}$ months

59. Find the quadratic equation whose roots are 2 more than the roots of the equation $x^2 - 2x - 24 = 0$.
  (a) $x^2 - 6x - 16 = 0$ (b) $x^2 - 8x - 16 = 0$
  (c) $x^2 + 12x - 36 = 0$ (d) $x^2 - 6x + 16 = 0$

60. A man buys two cows for ₹50,000. He then sold one cow at a loss of 10% and other cow at a profit of 10%, thereby gaining ₹500. Find the cost price of each cow.
  (a) ₹25,000, ₹25,000   (b) ₹20,000, ₹30,000
  (c) ₹22,500, ₹27,500   (d) ₹17,500, ₹32,500

61. Area of △ABC is 40 cm². If a line parallel to side BC cuts the sides AB and AC at points D and E respectively and also point D divides AB in the ratio 1 : 3, then the area of the quadrilateral BCED is
  (a) 30 cm²   (b) 24 cm²
  (c) 36 cm²   (d) 37.5 cm²

62. Train A of length 100 m crosses a pole in 4 seconds. Train B approaching towards train A with a speed of 15 m/sec crosses it in 7.5 seconds. Find the length of train B.
  (a) 100 m   (b) 200 m
  (c) 250 m   (d) 300 m

63. If $\dfrac{a}{x} = \dfrac{x}{a} - \dfrac{1}{x}$, then the value of $a^2 + a$ is
  (a) x   (b) x^2
  (c) $-x$ (d) $\dfrac{1}{x^2}$

64. Marked price of an article is ₹200. After giving two successive discounts of 20% and 10%, shopkeeper loses 4%. What is the cost price of that article?
  (a) ₹ 154.50   (b) ₹ 160
  (c) ₹ 150   (d) ₹ 148.50

65. The sides of a triangle T_1 are equal to the medians of the triangle T_2. If the area of triangle T_1 is 30 sq. units, then what will be the area of triangle T_2?
  (a) 120 sq. units   (b) 40 sq. units
  (c) 30 sq. units   (d) 90 sq. units

66. The unit digit of $(413)^{243}$ is
  (a) 7   (b) 1
  (c) 3   (d) 9

67. The marked price of an article is 20% more than its cost price, what should be the discount offered if the shopkeeper wants to earn 8% on that article?
  (a) 12%
  (b) 10%
  (c) 8%
  (d) 6.67%

68. Two circles of radius 8 cm and 5 cm touches each other externally. If tangents are drawn from the center of bigger circle to smaller circle, then what will be the area of quadrilateral made by tangents and perpendiculars drawn from the center of smaller circle to the tangents?

(a) 120 sq. units   (b) 60 sq. units

(c) 30 sq. units   (d) 240 sq. units

69. The perimeter of base of a right circular cone is 10π cm. If the height of the cone is 12 cm, then its curved surface area is

(a) 32π cm²   (b) 45π cm²

(c) 56π cm²   (d) 65π cm²

70. If $\cot\theta = 2$, then $\cos 2\theta$ will be

(a) $\dfrac{2}{3}$ (b) $\dfrac{3}{5}$

(c) $\dfrac{4}{5}$ (d) $\dfrac{2}{\sqrt{5}}$

71. The value of $\cos^2 36° + \cos^2 54°$ is

(a) $\dfrac{1}{\sqrt{3}}$ (b) $\dfrac{2}{\sqrt{3}}$

(c) 1   (d) 0

Directions: In question nos. **72** to **75**, study the two pie-charts and answer the questions given below.

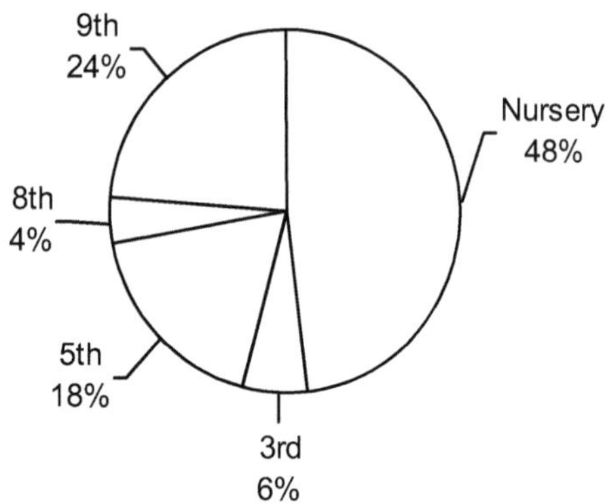

Total number of students taken admission in the school in 2012 = 1500

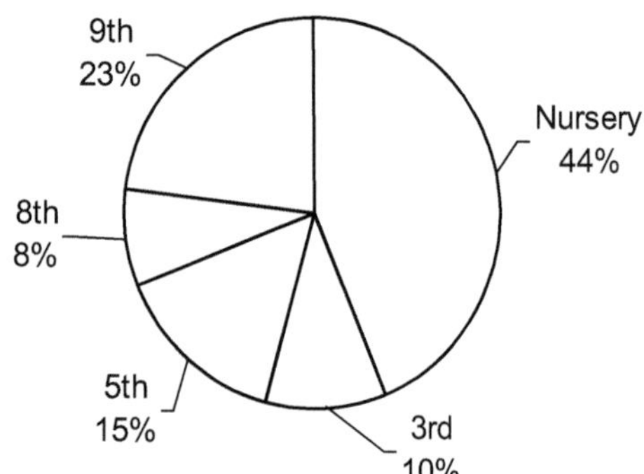

Total number of students taken admission in the school in 2013 = 2200

72. What is the percent increase in number of admissions in class Nursery from 2012 to 2013?

(a) 42.84 %   (b) 36.32 %

(c) 45.54 %   (d) 34.44 %

73. Ratio of the number of students admitted in 5th class in 2012 to the number of students admitted in 8th class in 2013 is

(a) 35 : 188   (b) 188 : 35

(c) 88 : 135   (d) 135 : 88

74. Number of students admitted in 3ʳᵈ and 9ᵗʰ class in 2013 are

(a) 220 and 506   (b) 270 and 759

(c) 330 and 575   (d) 528 and 689

75. Average number of students admitted in 3ʳᵈ, 5ᵗʰ and 8ᵗʰ class in 2012 is

(a) 120   (b) 140

(c) 170   (d) 180

GENERAL AWARENESS

76. Who has won the 20th Commonwealth Chess championship crown 2016 in Colombo, Sri Lanka?

(a) Abhijeet Gupta   (b) Viswanathan Anand

(c) Pentala Harikrishna   (d) Tania Sachdev

77. Which of the following treaty was signed at the end of the First World War?

(a) Treaty of Versailles   (b) Maastricht Treaty

(c) Treaty of Lisbon   (d) Treaty of Rome

78. Which of the following does not belong to the reptilian class?

(a) Lizard   (b) Snake

(c) Crocodile   (d) Frog

79. Who discovered the relationship between a changing magnetic field and the electric field?

(a) Michael Faraday   (b) Graham Bell

(c) Albert Einstein   (d) Isaac Newton

80. Lokpriya Gopinath Bordoli International Airport is located in which of the following cities?

(a) Tejpur   (b) Silchar

(c) Guwahati   (d) Gangtok

81. Which of the following element is used in the filament of bulb?

(a) Mercury   (b) Tungsten

(c) Cadmium   (d) Silicon

82. A row of trees planted to protect an area from the wind is known as

(a) Windbreak   (b) Shelterbelts

(c) Both (a) and (b)   (d) Contour farming

83. Strabismus is associated with

(a) Ear   (b) Eye

(c) Nose   (d) Skin

84. Poona Pact was signed in which of the following years?

(a) 1932   (b) 1934

(c) 1936   (d) 1938

85. Who has been appointed as new Chairman of the Airport Authority of India?

(a) Guruprasad Mohapatra

(b) Manoranjan Mahopatra

(c) Rajeev Ganguly

(d) Manohar Sukla

86. Ukai Power Project is situated in

(a) Maharashtra   (b) Gujarat

(c) Madhya Pradesh   (d) Andhra Pradesh

87. The main elements of carbohydrates are

(a) Carbon   (b) Hydrogen

(c) Oxygen   (d) All of these

88. Rust of iron is due to presence of

(a) Moisture   (b) Oxygen

(c) Air   (d) All of the above

89. Government of India Act 1909 is also known as

(a) Communal Representation Act

(b) Federalism Act

(c) Responsible Government Act

(d) All of the above

90. Which of the following erstwhile formulated five-year plans in India?

(a) Planning commission

(b) Finance Commission

(c) Both (a) and (b)

(d) National Development Council

91. Home Rule League was started in Maharashtra by

(a) Annie Besant   (b) Bal Gangadhar Tilak

(c) Both (a) and (b)   (d) Jawaharlal Nehru

92. Who is known as the 'Father of the Computer'?

(a) Charles Babbage

(b) Allen Turin

(c) Albert Einstein

(d) Michael Faraday

93. Arrange these in the order of descending wavelength

(a) Radio waves, microwaves, visible radiation, ultraviolet rays

(b) Microwaves, radio waves, visible radiation, ultraviolet rays

(c) Visible radiation, radio waves, ultraviolet rays, microwaves

(d) Ultraviolet rays, visible radiation, radio waves, microwaves

94. SEZ Act in India was passed in

(a) 2005   (b) 2006

(c) 2007   (d) 2008

95. Omega-3 fatty acids are present in

(a) Fish   (b) Frog

(c) Rice   (d) Wheat

96. National Voter's Day is celebrated on

(a) 25 Jan   (b) 26 Jan

(c) 14 Aug   (d) 15 Aug

97. What is the change in the total cost that arises when the quantity produced has an increment by unit?

(a) Marginal cost   (b) Average cost

(c) Unit cost   (d) All of these

98. Who was the first Chief Justice of India?

(a) P Sathasivam

(b) H J Kania

(c) Mehr Chand Mahajan

(d) Altamas Kabir

99. Fundamental rights of Indian Constitution were taken from the

(a) US Constitution

(b) UK Constitution

(c) Ireland Constitution

(d) Weimar constitution

100. The Ministry for Water Resources has constituted committee to restructure the Central Water Commission (CWC) and the Central Ground Water Board (CGWB). Which is headed by ?

(a) Mihir Shah

(b) Gopal Mukherjee

(c) Amitabh Kant

(d) Madhav Chitale

ANSWERS

1. (d)	**2.** (b)	**3.** (a)	**4.** (b)	**5.** (b)	**6.** (c)	**7.** (c)	**8.** (c)	**9.** (b)	**10.** (d)
11. (b)	**12.** (b)	**13.** (c)	**14.** (d)	**15.** (d)	**16.** (d)	**17.** (b)	**18.** (d)	**19.** (c)	**20.** (b)
21. (c)	**22.** (c)	**23.** (c)	**24.** (c)	**25.** (c)	**26.** (b)	**27.** (a)	**28.** (d)	**29.** (a)	**30.** (c)
31. (b)	**32.** (a)	**33.** (b)	**34.** (d)	**35.** (b)	**36.** (a)	**37.** (b)	**38.** (b)	**39.** (c)	**40.** (d)
41. (c)	**42.** (d)	**43.** (c)	**44.** (c)	**45.** (d)	**46.** (a)	**47.** (d)	**48.** (b)	**49.** (b)	**50.** (b)
51. (b)	**52.** (a)	**53.** (d)	**54.** (c)	**55.** (a)	**56.** (b)	**57.** (c)	**58.** (d)	**59.** (a)	**60.** (c)
61. (d)	**62.** (b)	**63.** (b)	**64.** (c)	**65.** (b)	**66.** (a)	**67.** (b)	**68.** (b)	**69.** (d)	**70.** (b)
71. (c)	**72.** (d)	**73.** (d)	**74.** (a)	**75.** (b)	**76.** (a)	**77.** (a)	**78.** (d)	**79.** (a)	**80.** (c)
81. (b)	**82.** (c)	**83.** (b)	**84.** (a)	**84.** (a)	**86.** (b)	**87.** (d)	**88.** (d)	**89.** (a)	**90.** (a)
91. (b)	**92.** (a)	**93.** (a)	**94.** (a)	**95.** (a)	**96.** (a)	**97.** (a)	**98.** (b)	**99.** (a)	**100.** (a)

EXPLANATIONS

1. Coding follows as :

   N → 5
   O → 2
   V → 7
   E → 0
   L → 8
   T → 1
   Y → 3

   and

   E → 0
   S → 4
   S → 4
   A → 6
   Y → 3

   Hence, the code for SEVEN is 40705.

2. Let 'x' be the required percentage. Then,

   $$\frac{35}{100} \times 1180 + \frac{65}{100} \times 860 = 413 + 559 = 972 = \frac{x}{100} \times 8100$$

   $$\Rightarrow x = \frac{97200}{8100} = 12.$$

3. Option (a): $18 \div 6 + 4 < 30 - 11 \times 2$ (Correct)

   Option (b): $18 - 6 \div 4 > 30 + 11 \times 2$ (Not correct)

   Option (c): $18 - 6 \div 4 + 30 < 11 \times 2$ (Not correct)

   Option (d): $18 \div 6 > 4 + 30 - 11 \times 2$ (Not correct)

4. The smallest planet in our solar system is 'mercury'. Similarly, the smallest bone in the human body is 'stapes'. Hence, option (b) is the correct answer.

5. The sound made by a bear is called 'growl'. 'Creak' refers to the sound made by an old door when it is opened. Hence, option (b) is the correct answer. 'Chime' is the sound made by bells. 'Splatter' is the sound of wet object hitting something hard. 'Jangle' refers to a harsh ringing sound.

6. A group of lions is called 'pride'. Similarly, a group of geese on land is called 'gaggle'. Hence, option (c) is the correct answer. When in flight, it is called 'skein'.

7. In all the fractions except (c), the numerator is less than the denominator.

8. In all the options except (c), letters follow the rule:

   1st letter + 3 = 2nd letter

   2nd letter + 3 = 3rd letter

   3rd letter + 3 = 4th letter

9. $2 \times 3 - 1 = 5$

   $4 \times 5 - 1 = 19$

   $6 \times 7 - 1 = 41$

   $8 \times 9 - 1 = 71$

10. The correct meaningful order of words is 2, 3, 5, 4, 1.

11. The series is

    I m I—I m I—I m I—I m I

12. 99 + 3 = 102

    102 ÷ 2 = 51

    51 + 3 = 54

    54 ÷ 2 = 27

    27 + 3 = 30

    30 ÷ 2 = **15**

    15 + 3 = **18**

13. $\dfrac{6 \times 9 \times 4}{2} = 108$

$\dfrac{3 \times 8 \times 8}{2} = \mathbf{96}$

$\dfrac{4 \times 5 \times 12}{2} = 120$

$\dfrac{7 \times 6 \times 14}{2} = \mathbf{294}$

14. 2; 2 × 6 = 12;

12 + 6 = 18;

18 ÷ 3 = 6

3; 3 × 6 = 18;

18 + 6 = 24;

24 ÷ 3 = 8

5; 5 × 6 = 30;

30 + 6 = 36;

36 ÷ 3 = **12**

15.

Hence, the hour hand points towards South-east.

16. The word RATIFICATION niether has an 'E' nor a 'S'.

17. The arrangement will be:

↑West B E G F D C A

Hence, A and B are sitting at two extreme ends.

18.

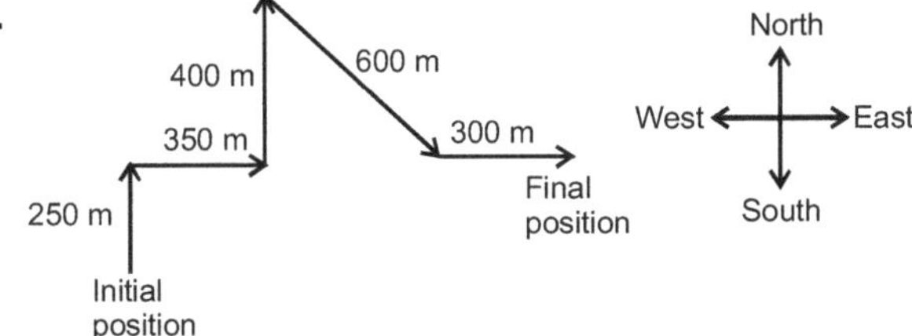

Hence, she is finally facing East.

19. Since only Kavya has four pairs of shoes, it can be correctly concluded that she is the only sibling in the family who has exactly four pairs of shoes.

20. Footballer: 1, 3, 5 and 7

Footballer and hockey player both: 1 and 7

Footballer and hockey player both but not cricketer: 7

21. Teachers: 1, 4, 8, 9 and 12

Teachers and authors: 1, 8 and 9

Teachers, authors and dramatists: 1 and 9

Teachers, authors and dramatists but who are not poets: 9.

22. Both the solid circle should be in lower corner parts.

23. Ellipse lies between the lines such that both the lines touch the ellipse.

25. From matrix,

C can be represented as: 01, 14, 20, **32**, 43

A can be represented as: 02, 10, **23**, 34, 41

M can be represented as: 57, 66, **75**, 88, 99

P can be represented as: 58, 65, **77**, 89, 96

Hence, answer is 32, 23, 75, 77.

26. 'Coercion' means getting something by force or threats. Hence, option (*b*), pressure, is the correct answer. 'Atrocious' means evil or cruel.

27. 'Predicament' refers to a difficult or an embarrassing situation that is difficult to deal with. 'Dilemma' refers to a situation in which you have to make a difficult choice. Hence, option (*a*) is the correct answer.

28. 'Conceit' means having or showing too much pride. 'Modesty' is the quality of not being too proud. Hence, option (*d*) is the correct answer. 'Reproachful' refers to something that causes shame or disgrace.

29. 'Opaque' refers to something that is difficult to explain; something that is not transparent. 'Unequivocal' means very strong and clear. Hence, option (*a*) is the correct answer. 'Coloured' and 'dark' are the synonyms of opaque. 'Ambiguous' means not expressed or understood clearly.

30. The correct answer is option (*c*), throat. It is a passage in the neck through which food and air pass on their way into the body. 'Neck' is the front part of throat.

31. A 'kangaroo word' is a word that contains letters of another word. The two words are synonyms of each other. A 'joey word' is a word that is contained in a kangaroo word. For example: 'alone' is a kangaroo word while 'one', which is formed by using the letters of the word 'alone', is a joey word. Hence, option (*b*) is the answer. A 'metaphor' is a figure of speech that describes a subject by asserting that it is, on some point of comparison, the same as another otherwise unrelated object. 'Acronym' is a word formed from the first letters of the words that make up the name of something. For example: SARS is an acronym of severe acute respiratory syndrome.

32. 'Sump' is a low part or area where liquid collects when it drains from something. Hence, option (*a*) is the correct answer. 'Dump' means to put down in a careless or untidy way. 'Lump' refers to a hard or solid piece that does not have a particular shape. 'Clump' is the sound made by somebody putting their feet down very heavily.

33. 'Under the sun' means on earth. It is used to emphasise that you are talking about a large number of things that are in existence. Hence, option (*b*) is the correct answer.

34. 'Go cap in hand' means to ask somebody for something in a polite manner that makes you feel less important or ashamed. Hence, option (*d*) is the correct answer.

35. 'Snow job' refers to an act of deception by persuading someone to do something by flattery. Hence, option (*b*) is the correct answer.

36. The correct spelling of the word is 'Judgmentally'. Hence, option (*a*) is the correct answer.

37. The preposition 'to' in part (*b*) is incorrect. You apprise someone 'of' something, which means to inform someone about something. Hence, part (*b*) is the correct answer.

38. Generally 'than' is used to compare two things. However, words like superior, inferior, senior, junior, etc. take 'to' instead of 'than'. Hence, part (*b*) is the correct answer.

39. Certain verbs like verbs of emotions, verbs of perception, verbs of thinking, etc. are not used in continuous tense. They are used in simple present tense. Hence, 'I am loving it' is incorrect, making part (*c*) the correct answer.

40. 'Put (something) about' means to give people some news or information that may be false. Hence, option (*d*) is the correct answer. 'Put (something) away' means to keep something back in its place. 'Put up' means to suggest an idea for other people to discuss. For example: put up an idea, put up a case, etc. 'Put aside' means to put away or to stop using

41. Simple present tense is used for exclamatory sentences beginning with 'here' and 'there' to express what is taking place in the present. 'Go' is incorrect since it is plural while the subject is singular.

42. 'Come round/around' means to become conscious again. Hence, option (*d*) is the correct answer. 'Come about something' means to arrive somewhere in order to get something.

43. There is a modifier error in the given sentence. From the clause 'before he died' it is difficult to understand whether it refers to Raja or to a different person altogether. Options (*a*) and (*b*) are incorrect because if we remove the parenthetical information, the sentences do not make any sense. Hence, option (*c*) is the correct answer.

44. Present perfect tense is used for actions that have been completed in the immediate past. The given sentence is incorrect since in the second clause, the subject (he) is singular while the verb (have) is plural. Hence, option (*c*) is the correct answer.

45. The given sentence is correct. 'Plan on something' means to anticipate about something; to prepare for something. Hence, option (*d*) is the correct answer. Options (*a*), (*b*) and (*c*) will make the sentence incorrect.

46. Le Moulin de la Galette is a painting. The first sentence of the second paragraph clearly states that Van Gogh painted the work in April 1887. Hence, option (*a*) is the correct answer.

47. 'Quintessential' means representing the most perfect or typical example of a quality or class. Hence, its synonym will be option (*d*), classic.

48. Option (*a*) is incorrect because the passage does not suggest that Van Gogh was Theo's step brother. Option (*c*) is incorrect because the passage states that April 1887 was a key point in the development of his artistic style. We do not know if his art was in vogue in early 1887. Option (*d*) is incorrect because the particular painting talked about in the passage is the one that came to public light 15 years after his death. Only option (*b*) can be inferred from the passage. The passage begins by telling the readers that Le Moulin de la Galette depicts a windmill against a sunny sky above Montmartre in Paris and the last sentence of the passage states that Theo encouraged him to set up his frame by the windmills in the French capital. These two sentences refer to the same painting, Le Moulin de la Galette. Hence, option (*b*) is the correct answer.

49. The second sentence of the passage states that the painting was first shown in public in Amsterdam. Hence, option (*b*) is the correct answer.

50. Le Moulin de la Galette was brought by an American industrialist. Hence, option (*b*) is the correct answer.

51. Let the numbers be 2x, 3x and 5x.

Then, 2x + 10, 3x + 10 and 5x + 10 will be in the ratio 4 : 5 : 7

Now, $\left(\dfrac{2x+10}{3x+10}\right) = \dfrac{4}{5}$

$\Rightarrow 5(2x+10) = 4(3x+10)$

$\Rightarrow x = 5$

So, the numbers are 10, 15 and 25.

52. Let the price of one shirt be ₹x and price of one jeans be ₹y.

Then, 4x + 7y = 6900   ...(i)

6x + 11y = 10700   ...(ii)

Multiply (i) by 3 and (ii) by 2 and then subtract (i) from (ii), we get

22y – 21y = 21,400 – 20,700

$\Rightarrow$ y = 700

Hence, cost of one jeans is ₹700.

53. Square root of $3548346624 \approx \sqrt{35 \times 10^8} \approx 6 \times 10^4$

So, the total number of digits will be 5.

54. Let the age of retired employee be 'x' years and average age of employees when the retired employee is working be 'y' years.

Then, $20y - x + 25 = 20(y - 3)$

$\Rightarrow x = 85$

Hence, age of retired employee = 85 years.

55. Distance between parallel lines

$$= \frac{|c_1 - c_2|}{\sqrt{a^2 + b^2}} = \frac{\left|7 - \frac{17}{3}\right|}{\sqrt{3^3 + 1^2}} = \frac{4}{3\sqrt{10}} \text{ units.}$$

56. Let the present value of the car be ₹P.

Then, $P\left(1 + \frac{(-10)}{100}\right)^2 = 81000$

$\Rightarrow P = 100000$

Hence, the present value of the car is ₹1,00,000.

57. Let the total work be LCM (20, 30, 60) = 60 units.

So, A will do $\frac{60}{20} = 3$ units, B will do $\frac{60}{30} = 2$ units and C will do $\frac{60}{60} = 1$ unit work in a day.

A and B working together for 5 days, work completed = 25 units

Remaining work = 60 − 25 = 35 units

$\Rightarrow$ A and C worked for $= \frac{35}{4} = 8\frac{3}{4}$ days

Hence, C worked for $8\frac{3}{4}$ days.

58. 12 men ≡ 20 women ≡ 36 children

$\Rightarrow$ 1 man ≡ $\frac{5}{3}$ women ≡ 3 children

Now, 5 men, 10 women and 15 children will be equivalent to 48 children.

As 36 children can do the work in 12 months, so the time taken by 48 children

$$= \frac{36 \times 12}{48} = 9 \text{ months.}$$

Hence, half of the work will be completed in $4\frac{1}{2}$ months.

59. Roots of equation $x^2 - 2x - 24 = 0$ are −4 and 6.

$\Rightarrow$ Roots of the required equation are −2 and 8

∴ Required equation is $x^2 - 6x - 16 = 0$ {∵ Quadratic equation is $x^2 - Sx + P = 0$, where S = sum of roots and P = product of roots}.

60. Let the cost price of one cow be ₹x.

So, cost price of other cow = ₹(50000 − x)

Now, $0.9x + 1.1(50000 - x) = 50500$

$\Rightarrow x = 22500$

Hence, cost price of the cows are ₹22,500 and ₹27,500.

61.

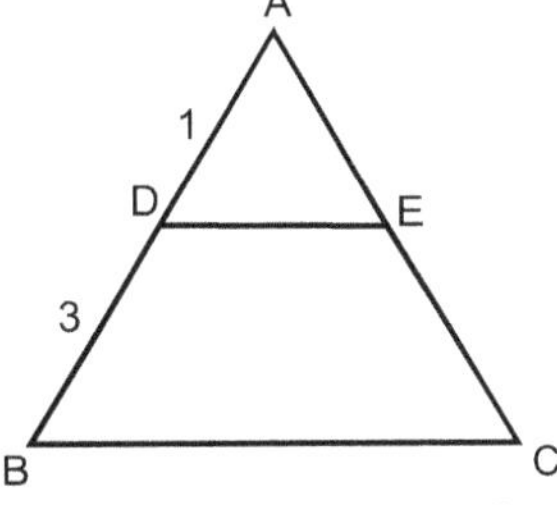

As DE is parallel to BC, so

$$\frac{AD}{AB} = \frac{AE}{AC} = \frac{DE}{BC} = \frac{1}{4}$$

$$\frac{\text{Area of } \Delta ADE}{\text{Area of } \Delta ABC} = \left(\frac{AD}{AB}\right)^2 = \frac{1}{16}$$

$\Rightarrow$ Area of $\Delta ADE = \frac{40}{16} = 2.5$ cm²

$\Rightarrow$ Area of quadrilateral BCED = 40 − 2.5 = 37.5 cm².

62. Let the length of train B be 'd' m.

Speed of train A $= \frac{100}{4} = 25$ m/sec

Now, time taken by train B to cross train A

$$= \frac{100 + d}{25 + 15} = 7.5$$

$\Rightarrow d = 200$ m

Hence, length of train B = 200 m.

63. $\frac{a}{x} = \frac{x}{a} - \frac{1}{x}$

$\Rightarrow \frac{a}{x} + \frac{1}{x} = \frac{x}{a}$

$\Rightarrow a(a + 1) = x^2$

∴ $a^2 + a = x^2$.

64. Selling price of the article = 0.8 × 0.9 × 200 = ₹144

∴ Cost price of the article $= \frac{144}{0.96} = ₹150$.

65. Area of triangle T_2 will be $\frac{4}{3}$ times to that of area triangle T_1.

Hence, area of triangle $T_2 = \frac{4}{3} \times 30 = 40$ sq. units.

66. Unit digit of $(413)^{243}$ is same as the unit digit of 3^{243}.

The cyclicity of 3 is 4.

∴ $3^{243} = 3^{240} \times 3^3$

$\Rightarrow$ Unit digit of $(413)^{243} = 1 \times 7 = 7$.

67. Let the cost price of article be ₹x.

Then, marked price = ₹1.2x

Selling price = ₹1.08x

$\Rightarrow$ Percentage of discount offered

$$= \frac{1.2x - 1.08x}{1.2x} \times 100 = 10\%.$$

68.

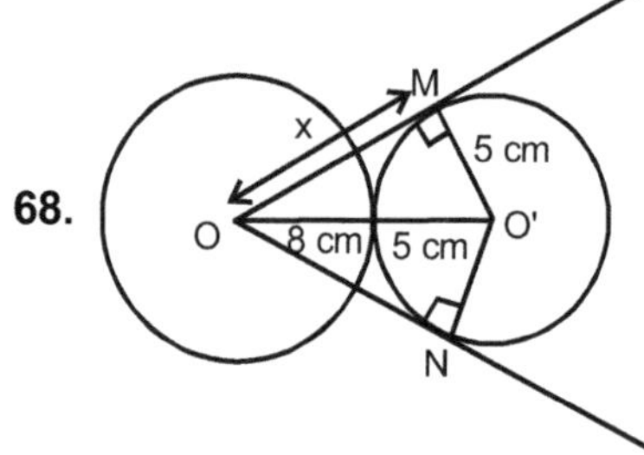

Let the length of tangents to the smaller circle with centre O' at points M and N be 'x' cm.

Then, $x^2 + 5^2 = 13^2$

$\Rightarrow x = 12$ cm

$\therefore$ Area of quadrilateral MONO'

$$= \frac{1}{2} \times 12 \times 5 + \frac{1}{2} \times 12 \times 5 = 60 \text{ sq. units.}$$

69.

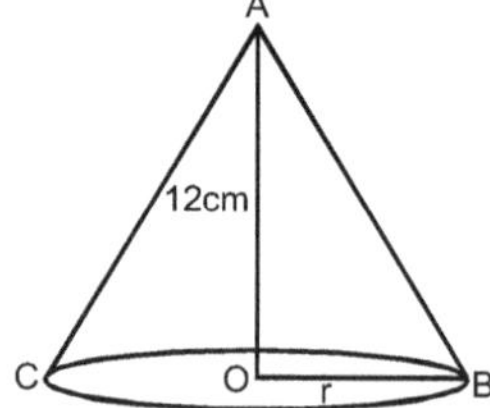

Let the radius of the base be 'r' cm and lateral height be 'l' cm.

Perimeter = $10\pi = 2\pi r$

$\Rightarrow r = 5$ cm

In $\triangle AOB$,

$AO^2 + OB^2 = AB^2$

$\Rightarrow l^2 = 12^2 + 5^2$

$\Rightarrow l = 13$ cm

Hence, curved surface area $= \pi \times r \times l$

$= \pi \times 5 \times 13 = 65\pi$ cm^2.

70. $\cot\theta = 2 \Rightarrow \tan\theta = \dfrac{1}{2}$

$$\cos 2\theta = \frac{1 - \tan^2\theta}{1 + \tan^2\theta}$$

$$\Rightarrow \cos 2\theta = \frac{1 - \left(\dfrac{1}{2}\right)^2}{1 + \left(\dfrac{1}{2}\right)^2} = \frac{3}{5}.$$

71. $\cos^2 36° + \cos^2 54° = \cos^2 36° + \cos^2(90° - 36°)$

$= \cos^2 36° + \sin^2 36° = 1.$

72. Number of admissions taken in Nursery in 2012

$$= \frac{48}{100} \times 1500 = 720$$

Number of admissions taken in Nursery in 2013

$$= \frac{44}{100} \times 2200 = 968$$

$\therefore$ Required percent increase

$$= \frac{968 - 720}{720} \times 100 \approx 34.44\%.$$

73. Number of admissions taken in 5th class in 2012

$$= \frac{18}{100} \times 1500 = 270$$

Number of admissions taken in 8th class in 2013

$$= \frac{8}{100} \times 2200 = 176$$

$\therefore$ Required ratio = 270 : 176 = 135 : 88.

74. Number of admissions taken in 3rd class in 2013

$$= \frac{10}{100} \times 2200 = 220$$

Number of admissions taken in 9th class in 2013

$$= \frac{23}{100} \times 2200 = 506.$$

75. Number of students admitted in 3rd, 5th and 8th class in 2012 = (6 + 18 + 4)% of 1500

$$= \frac{28}{100} \times 1500 = 420$$

$\therefore$ Required average $= \dfrac{420}{3} = 140.$

GENERAL INTELLIGENCE

Directions (Q. 1- 3): *Select the related letters / word / number from the given alternatives.*

1. CFIL : ORUX : : DGJM : ?

   (a) HJLN   (b) NQST

   (c) PSVY   (d) RTVX

2. 24 : 60 : : 120 : ?

   (a) 160   (b) 220

   (c) 300   (d) 108

3. Ecstasy : Gloom : : ?

   (a) Congratulations : Occasion

   (b) Diligent : Successful

   (c) Measure : Scale

   (d) Humiliation : Exaltation

Directions (Q. 4 -5) : *Find the odd number / letters / word from the given alternatives.*

4. (a) PQXZ   (b) BCQN

   (c) ABDF   (d) MNPR

5. (a) 5720   (b) 6710

   (c) 2640   (d) 4270

Direction (Q. 6) : *From among the given alternatives select the one in which the set of numbers is most like the set of number given in the question.*

Given Set: (4, 25, 81)

6. (a) (4, 36, 79)   (b) (9, 48, 81)

   (c) (16, 64, 100)   (d) (9, 49, 143)

Direction: *Which one of the given responses would be a meaningful order of the following?*

7. 1. Ocean   2. Rivulet

   3. Sea   4. Glacier

   5. River

   (a) 5, 2, 3, 1, 4   (b) 4, 2, 5, 3, 1

   (c) 5, 2, 3, 4, 1   (d) 4, 2, 1, 3, 5

Direction: *Arrange the following words as per order in the dictionary.*

8. 1. Preposition   2. Preparatively

   3. Preposterous   4. Preponderate

   5. Prepossess

   (a) 2, 4, 1, 5, 3

   (b) 1, 5, 2, 4, 3

   (c) 5, 4, 2, 3, 1

   (d) 4, 2, 5, 1, 3

9. Which one set of letters when sequentially placed at the gaps in the given letter series shall complete it?

   ac_cab_baca_aba_aca_

   (a) acbcc   (b) aacbc

   (c) babbb   (d) bcbba

Direction (Q. 10) : *A series is given, with one / two term(s) missing. Choose the correct alternative*

10. ______, DREQ, GUHT, JXKW

   (a) EFRS   (b) TGSP

   (c) JWVI   (d) AOBN

11. Find the wrong number in the series.

   6, 12, 21, 32, 45, 60

   (a) 6   (b) 12

   (c) 21   (d) 32

12. Ramesh ranks 13th in a class of 33 students. There are 5 students below Suresh rankwise. How many students are there between Ramesh and Suresh?

   (a) 12   (b) 14

   (c) 15   (d) 16

13. In a survey, 70% of those surveyed owned a car and 75% of those surveyed owned a TV. If 55% owned both a car and a TV. What percent of those surveyed did not own either a car or a TV?

   (a) 25%   (b) 20%

   (c) 10%   (d) 5%

14. If LOSS is coded as 1357 and GAIN is coded as 2468, what do the figures 84615 stand for?

   (a) NAILS   (b) SNAIL

   (c) LANES   (d) SLAIN

15. A statement is given followed by four alternative arguments. Select the alternative which is most appropriate.

   Statement : Is it necessary that education should be job oriented?

   I.   Yes, the aim of education is to prepare persons for earning.

   II.   Yes, educated person should stand on his own feet after completion of education.

   III. No, education should be for sake of knowledge only.

   IV. No, one may take up agriculture where education is not necessary.

(a) Only I and II arguments are strong

(b) Only III and IV arguments are strong

(c) Only I arguments is strong

(d) Only I and III arguments are strong

16. Sudha travels 8 km to the South. Then 8 km turns to the right and walks 4 km. The again she turns to her right and moves 8 km forward. How many km away is the from alerting point?

(a) 7

(b) 6

(c) 4

(d) 8

17. From the given alternatives words, select the word which can be formed using the letter of the given word

       'MULTIPLACATION'

(a) MUTUAL

(b) LIMITATION

(c) APPLICATION

(d) NOTION

Direction (Q. 18) : *Select the missing number from the given responses.*

18.

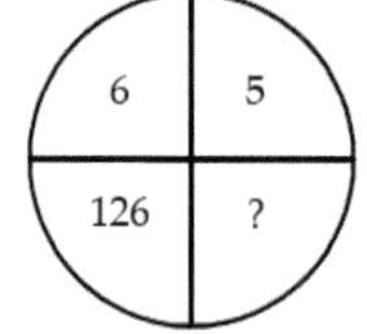

(a) 127

(b) 31

(c) 217

(d) 328

19. If '-' stands for division, '+' stands for subtraction, '÷' stands for multiplication, '×' stands for addition, then which one of the following equation is correct?

(a) $70 \div 2 - 4 \times 5 + 6 = -34$

(b) $70 \div 2 - 4 \times 5 \times 6 = 21$

(c) $70 - 2 + 4 \div 5 \times 6 = 341$

(d) $70 - 2 + 4 \div 5 \times 6 = 98$

20. Which diagram correctly represents the relationship between politicians, poets and women?

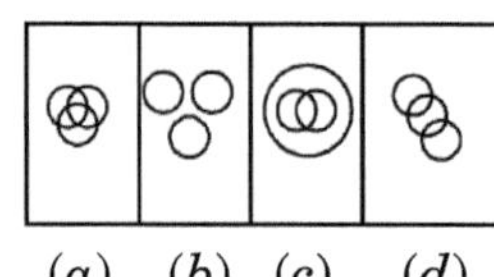

  (a)   (b) (c)   (d)

21. How many triangles are there in the following figures?

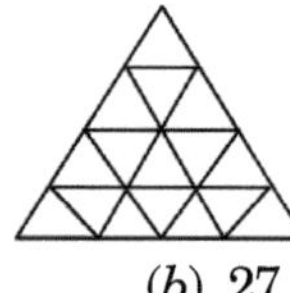

(a) 29

(b) 27

(c) 23

(d) 30

22. Some equations are solved on the basis of a certain system. Find the correct answer for the unsolved equation on that basis.

If $324 \times 289 = 35$, $441 \times 484 = 43$.

$625 \times 400 = 45$, find the value of 256×729.

(a) 33

(b) 35

(c) 43

(d) 34

Direction: *From the given answer figures select the one in which the question figure hidden / embedded.*

23. Question figure

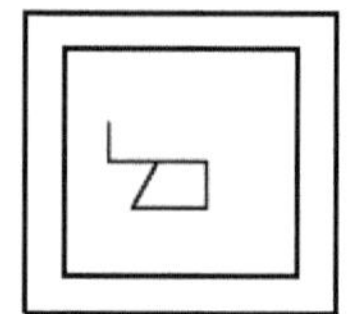

Answer figures:

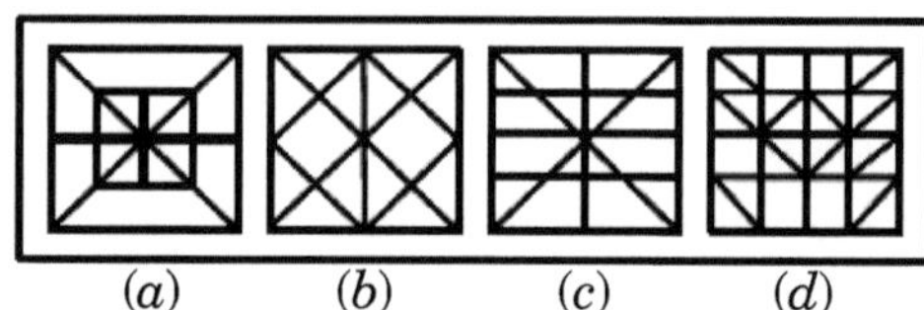

  (a)   (b)   (c)   (d)

Direction: *If a mirror is placed on the line MN, then which of the answer figures is the correct image of the given question figure?*

24. Question figure :

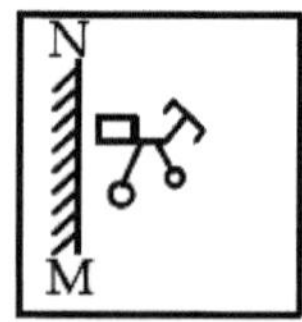

Answer figures:

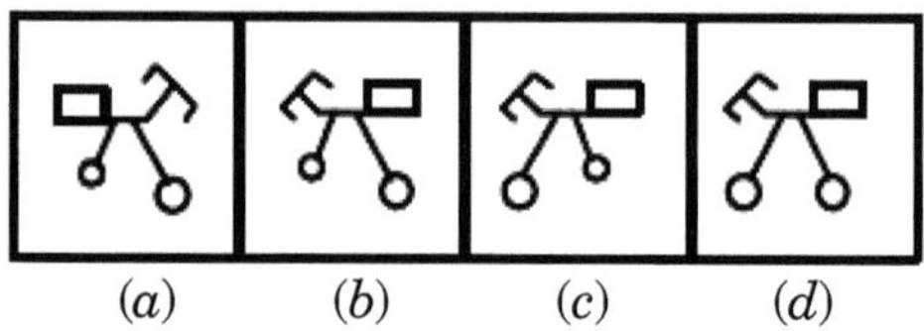

  (a)   (b)   (c)   (d)

Direction: *A piece of paper is folded and cut as shown in the question figures. From the given answer figures, indicate how it will appear when opened.*

25. Question figures:

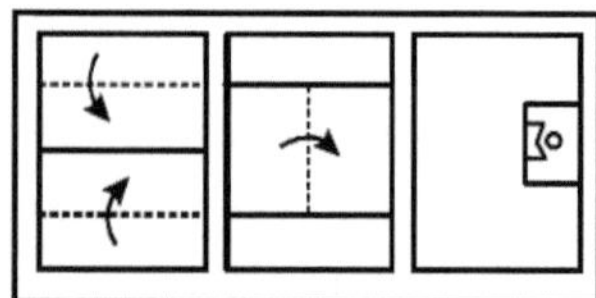

Answer figures:

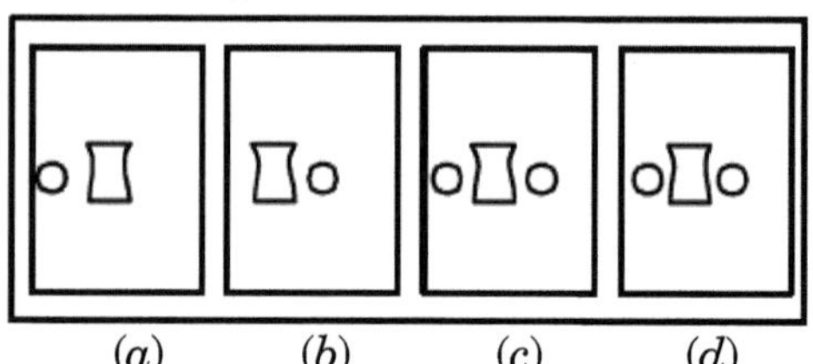

  (a)   (b)   (c)   (d)

ENGLISH LANGUAGE

Directions (Q. 26-27): *Out of the four alternatives, choose the one which best expresses the meaning of the given word and mark it in the Answer Sheet.*

26. LUCIDITY
    - (a) Fluidity
    - (b) Politeness
    - (c) Clarity
    - (d) Fluency

27. INDICT
    - (a) Implicate
    - (b) Elude
    - (c) Charge
    - (d) Manifest

Directions (Q. 28-29): *Out of the four alternatives, choose the word opposite in meaning to the given word and mark it in the Answer Sheet.*

28. INVINCIBLE
    - (a) Small
    - (b) Invisible
    - (c) Vulnerable
    - (d) Reachable

29. INOFFENSIVE
    - (a) Sensitive
    - (b) Organic
    - (c) Sensible
    - (d) Rude

Directions (Q. 30-32): *Out of four alternatives, choose the one which can substituted, for the given words/sentence an indicate it by blackening the appropriate rectangle [▭] in the Answer Sheet.*

30. Code of diplomatic etiquette and precedence
    - (a) Statesmanship
    - (b) Diplomacy
    - (c) Hierarchy
    - (d) Protocol

31. To renounce a high position of authority control
    - (a) Abduct
    - (b) Abandon
    - (c) Abort
    - (d) Abdicate

32. Not to be moved by entreaty
    - (a) Rigorous
    - (b) Negligent
    - (c) Inexorable
    - (d) Despotic

Directions (Q. 33-35): *Four alternatives are given for the meaning of the given Idiom/phrase. Choose the alternative which best expresses the meaning of the Idism/Phrase and mark in the Answer Sheet.*

33. To take the heart
    - (a) to be encouraged
    - (b) to grieve over
    - (c) to like
    - (d) to hate

34. Yeoman's service
    - (a) medical help
    - (b) excellent work
    - (c) social work
    - (d) hard work

35. To face the music
    - (a) to enjoy a musical recital
    - (b) to bear the consequences
    - (c) to live in a pleasant atmosphere
    - (d) to have a difficult time

Direction(Q. 36): *Groups of four words are given. In each group, one word is correctly spelt. Find the correctly spelt word and mark your answer in the Answer Sheet.*

36.
    - (a) mandatary
    - (b) circulatary
    - (c) temporary
    - (d) regulatory

Directions (Q. 37-39): *Some of the sentences have errors and some are correct. Find out which part of a sentence has an error blacken the rectangle [▭] corresponding to the appropriate letter (a, b, c). If a sentence is free from errors, blacken the rectangle corresponding to (d) in the Answer Sheet.*

37. A senior doctor (a) / expressed concern (b) / about physicians recommended the vaccine. (c) / No error. (d)

38. We have discussing (a) / all the known mechanisms (b) / of physical growth. (c) / No error. (d)

39. Children enjoy listening to (a) / ghost stories (b) / especially on Halloween night. (c) / No error. (d)

Directions(Q. 40-42): *Sentences are given with blanks to the filled in with an appropriate word. Four alternatives are suggested for each question. Choose the correct alternative out of the four and indicate it by blackening the appropriate rectangle [ ] in the Answer Sheet.*

40. The building is not safe and must be _____ down.
    - (a) pull
    - (b) pulling
    - (c) pulled
    - (d) pulls

41. There is something wonderful _____ him.
    - (a) of
    - (b) about
    - (c) for
    - (d) inside

42. The song is the play cannot be deleted as it is _____ to the story.
    - (a) intervened
    - (b) innate
    - (c) exacting
    - (d) integral

Directions(Q. 43-45): *A sentence or underlined part thereof is given which may need improvement. Alternatives are given at (a), (b) and (c) below, which may be a better option. In case no improvement is needed, blacken the rectangle [▭] corresponding to (d) in the Answer Sheet.*

43. The man whom I thought was thoroughly honest proved to be a swindler.

   (a) The man whom I thought was thoroughly honest proved a swindler.

   (b) The man who I thought was thoroughly honest proved to be a swindler.

   (c) The man to whom I thought was thoroughly honest proved to be a swindler.

   (d) No improvement

44. No sooner had the dividend been declared, the notices were sent out.

   (a) The company had hardly declared the dividend till the notices were sent for mailing.

   (b) They had no sooner declared the dividend then the notices were sent out.

   (c) Hardly had the dividend been declared than the notices were sent-out.

   (d) No improvement.

45. Riding upon his horse, the tiger jumped at him.

   (a) Riding upon the tiger, this horse jumped at him.

   (b) The tiger jumped at him while he was riding upon his horse.

   (c) The tiger rode at him while he was jumping upon his horse.

   (d) No improvement

Directions: *In question nos. 46 to 50, you have a passage with 5 questions in it. Read the passage carefully and choose the best answer to each question.*

In September 1620, a small ship called the Mayflower left Plymouth, England, carrying 102 passengers — an assortment of religious separatists seeking a new home where they could freely practice their faith and other individuals lured by the promise of prosperity and land ownership in the New World. After a treacherous and uncomfortable crossing that lasted 66 days, they dropped anchor near the tip of Cape Cod, far north of their intended destination at the mouth of the Hudson River. One month later, the Mayflower crossed Massachusetts Bay, where the Pilgrims, as they are now commonly known, began the work of establishing a village at Plymouth.

Throughout that first brutal winter, most of the colonists remained on board the ship, where they suffered from exposure, scurvy and outbreaks of contagious disease. Only half of the Mayflower's original passengers and crew lived to see their first New England spring. In March, the remaining settlers moved ashore, where they received an astonishing visit from an Abenaki Indian who greeted them in English. Several days later, he returned with another Native American, Squanto, who shared their pain. Squanto taught the Pilgrims, weakened by malnutrition and illness, how to cultivate corn, extract sap from maple trees, catch fish in the rivers and avoid poisonous plants. He also helped the settlers forge an alliance with the Wampanoag, a local tribe, which would endure for more than 50 years and tragically remains one of the sole examples of harmony between European colonists and Native Americans.

46. Find a word in the passage which is the opposite of 'unimpressive'.

   (a) Boring   (b) Unsurprising

   (c) Ordinary   (d) Astonishing

47. The phrase 'forge an alliance' means

   (a) A forced kinship

   (b) Developing a hoaxed liaison

   (c) Creating a successful relationship

   (d) Having bitter feelings

48. What is the meaning of the word 'brutal' in the given context?

   (a) Harsh   (b) Cold

   (c) Light   (d) Monstrous

49. As per the passage, which of the following is not an activity that the Pilgrims were tught?

   (a) Extraction of Sap (b) Fishing

   (c) Poultry   (d) Cultivation

50. Which of the following is a synonym of the word 'endure' as used in the passage?

   (a) Suffer   (b) Experience

   (c) Last   (d) Feel

QUANTITATIVE APTITUDE

51. If p = 124, $3\sqrt{p\left(p^2 + 3p + 3\right) + 1} = ?$

   (a) 5   (b) 7

   (c) 123   (d) 125

52. If $\sqrt{1 - \dfrac{x^3}{100}} = \dfrac{3}{5}$ then x equals

   (a) 2   (b) 4

   (c) 16   (d) $(136)^{1/3}$

53. $\sqrt{8 + \sqrt{57 + \sqrt{38 + \sqrt{108 + \sqrt{169}}}}} = ?$

   (a) 4   (b) 6

   (c) 8   (d) 10

54. The value of $\dfrac{2+\sqrt{3}}{2-\sqrt{3}} + \dfrac{2-\sqrt{3}}{2+\sqrt{3}} + \dfrac{\sqrt{3}+1}{\sqrt{3}-1}$ is

   (a) $16 + \sqrt{3}$ (b) $4 + \sqrt{3}$

   (c) $2 - \sqrt{3}$ (d) $2 + \sqrt{3}$

55. Simplify

$$\frac{0.0347 \times 0.0347 \times 0.0347 + (0.9653)^3}{(0.0347)^2 - (0.0347)(0.9653) + (0.9653)^2}$$

  (*a*) 0.9306   (*b*) 1.0009

  (*c*) 1.0050   (*d*) 1

56. A copper wire is bent in the form of an equilateral triangle and has area $121\sqrt{2}$ cm². If the same wire is bent into the form of a circle, the area (in cm²) enclosed by the wire is $\left(\text{Take } \pi = \dfrac{22}{7}\right)$

  (*a*) 364.5   (*b*) 693.5

  (*c*) 346.5   (*d*) 639.5

57. A child reshapes a cone make up of clay of height 24 cm and radius 6 cm into a sphere. The radius (in cm) of the sphere is

  (*a*) 6   (*b*) 12

  (*c*) 24   (*d*) 48

58. Water flows into a tank which is 200 m long and 150 m wide, through a pipe of cross-section 0.3 m × 0.2 m at 20 km/hour. Then the time (in hours) for the water level in the tank to reach 8 m is

  (*a*) 50   (*b*) 120

  (*c*) 150   (*d*) 200

59. Two equal vessels are filled with the mixtures of water and milk in the ratio of 3 : 4 and 5 : 3 respectively. If the mixtures are poured into a third vessel, the ratio of water and milk in the third vessel will be

  (*a*) 15 : 12   (*b*) 53 : 59

  (*c*) 20 : 9   (*d*) 59 : 53

60. I am three times as old as my son. After 15 years hence, I will be twice as old as my son. The sum of our ages is

  (*a*) 48 years   (*b*) 60 years

  (*c*) 84 years   (*d*) 72 years

61. A and B can do a work in 12 days, B and C can do the same work in 15 days, C and A can do the same work in 20 days. The time taken by A, B and C to do the same work it

  (*a*) 5 days   (*b*) 10 days

  (*c*) 15 days   (*d*) 20 days

62. A is 60% as efficient as B. C does half of the work done by A and B together. If C alone does the work in 20 days, then A, B and C together can do the work in

  (*a*) $5\dfrac{2}{3}$ days   (*b*) $6\dfrac{2}{3}$ days

  (*c*) 6 days   (*d*) 7 days

63. The ratio of the volumes in water and glycerin in 240 cc of a mixture is 1 : 3. The quantity of water (in cc) that should be added to the mixture so that the new ratio of the volumes of water and glycerin becomes 2 : 3 is

  (*a*) 55   (*b*) 60

  (*c*) 62.5   (*d*) 64

64. The ratio of the income to the expenditure of a family is 10 : 7. If the family expenses are ₹ 10,500, then the savings of the family is

  (*a*) ₹ 4,500   (*b*) ₹ 10,000

  (*c*) ₹ 4,000   (*d*) ₹ 5,000

65. In an equilateral triangle ABC of side to the side BC is trisected at D. Then length (in cm) of AD is

  (*a*) $3\sqrt{7}$ (*b*) $7\sqrt{3}$

  (*c*) $\dfrac{10\sqrt{7}}{3}$ (*d*) $\dfrac{7\sqrt{10}}{3}$

66. When the price of an article was reduced by 20% its sale increased by 80%. What was the net effect on the sale?

  (*a*) 44% increase   (*b*) 44% decrease

  (*c*) 66% increase   (*d*) 75% increase

67. Walking as $\dfrac{3}{4}$ of his usual speed, a man is $1\dfrac{1}{2}$ hours late. His usual time to cover the same distance in hours, is

  (*a*) $4\dfrac{1}{2}$ (*b*) 4

  (*c*) $5\dfrac{1}{2}$ (*d*) 5

68. A man sold 20 apples for ₹ 100 gained 20%. How many apples did he buy ₹ 100?

  (*a*) 20   (*b*) 22

  (*c*) 24   (*d*) 25

69. If 78 is divided into three parts which are the ratio $1 : \dfrac{1}{3} : \dfrac{1}{6}$, the middle part is

  (*a*) $9\dfrac{1}{3}$ (*b*) 13

  (*c*) $17\dfrac{1}{3}$ (*d*) $18\dfrac{1}{3}$

70. The difference between simple interest and compound interest of a certain sum of money at 20% per annum for 2 years is ₹ 48. Then the sum is

  (*a*) ₹ 1,000   (*b*) ₹ 1,200

  (*c*) ₹ 1,500   (*d*) ₹ 2,000

71. Shri X goes to his office by scooter at a speed of 30 km/h and reaches 6 minutes earlier. If he goes at a speed of 24 km/h, he reaches 5 minutes late. The distance to his office is

(a) 20km (b) 21km

(c) 22km (d) 24km

72. A sum of money becomes eight times in 3 years, if the rate is compounded annually. In how much time will the same amount at the same compound rate become sixteen times?

(a) 6 years (b) 4 years

(c) 8 years (d) 5 years

Directions(Q. 73 – 75): *The pie chart given below shows the spending of a family on various heads during a month. Study the graph and answer questions.*

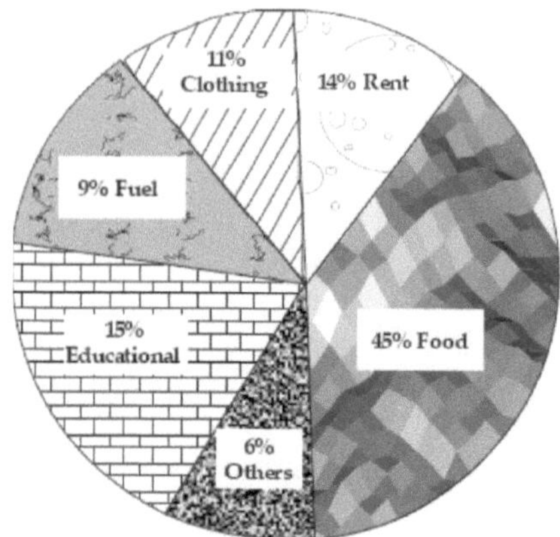

73. If the total income of the family is ₹ 25,000, then the amount spent of Rent and Food together is

(a) ₹ 17,250 (b) ₹ 14,750

(c) ₹ 11,250 (d) ₹ 8,500

74. What is the ratio of the expenses of Education to the expenses on Food?

(a) 1 : 3 (b) 3 : 1

(c) 3 : 5 (d) 5 : 3

75. Expenditure of Rent is what percent of expenditure of Fuel?

(a) 135% (b) 156%

(c) 167% (d) 172%

GENERAL AWARENESS

76. In which city, the 6th BRICS Agriculture Meeting on Agriculture and Agrarian Development would be held?

(a) Agartala (b) Shillong

(c) New Delhi (d) Imphal

77. The balance of payments of a country is in equilibrium when the

(a) demand for the domestic currency is the lowest

(b) demand as well as supply of the domestic currency are the highest

(c) demand for the domestic currency is equal to its supply

(d) demand for the domestic currency is the highest

78. Which was described by Dr. B.R. Ambedkar as the 'heart and soul' of the Constitution?

(a) Right to Equality

(b) Right against Exploitation

(c) Right to Constitutional Remedies

(d) Right to Freedom of Religion

79. In India, the concept-of single citizenship is adopted from

(a) England (b) U.S.A.

(c) Canada (d) France

80. Who had proposed partyless democracy in India?

(a) Jaya Prakash Narayan

(b) Mahatma Gandhi

(c) Vinoda Bhave

(d) S.A. Dange

81. Disinvestment in Public Sector is called

(a) Liberalisation (b) Globalisation

(c) Industrialisation (d) Privatization

82. Darwin finches refers to a group of

(a) Fishes (b) Lizards

(c) Birds (d) Amphibians

83. An individual's actual landward of living can be assessed by

(a) Gross National Income

(b) Net National Income

(c) Per Capita Income

(d) Disposable Personal Income

84. Which Sikh Guru called himself the 'Sacheha Badshah'?

(a) Guru Gobind Singh

(b) Guru Hargovind

(c) Guru Tegh Bahadur

(d) Guru Arjan Dev

85. The Civil Disobedience Movement was launched by Mahatma Gandhi in

(a) 1928 (b) 1930

(c) 1931 (d) 1922

86. What is the maximum strength prescribed for State Legislative Assemblies?

(a) 350 (b) 600

(c) 500 (d) 750

87. Fa-hien visited India during the reign of
(a) Chandragupta II (b) Samudragupta
(c) Ramagupta   (d) Kumaragupta

88. Which Indian Squash player won the U-19 Asian Junior Individual squash championship title in Kuala Lumpur, Malaysia on September 24, 2016?
(a) Senthil Murugan (b) Manikandan
(c) Velu Duraisamy   (d) Velavan Senthilkumar

89. Diu is an island off
(a) Daman   (b) Goa
(c) Gujarat   (d) Maharashtra

90. Which from the following is a land locked sea?
(a) Red Sea   (b) Timor Sea
(c) North Sea   (d) Aral Sea

91. Who gave the slogan "Inquilab Zindabad"?
(a) Chandrashekhar Azad
(b) Subhash Chandra Bose
(c) Bhagat Singh
(d) Iqbal

92. Troposphere is the hottest part of the atmosphere because
(a) it is closest to the Sun
(b) there are charged particles in it
(c) it is heated by the Earth's surface
(d) heat is generated in it

93. The outermost layer of the Sun is called
(a) Chromosphere   (b) Photosphere
(c) Corona   (d) Lithosphere

94. DNA fingerprinting is used to identify the
(a) Parents   (b) Rapist
(c) Thieves   (d) All the above

95. The normal cholesterol level in human body is
(a) 80-120 mg%   (b) 120-140mg%
(c) 140-180mg%   (d) 180-200mg%

96. Syrinx is the voice box in
(a) Amphibians   (b) Reptiles
(c) Birds   (d) Mammals

97. OTEC stands for
(a) Ocean thermal energy conservation.
(b) Oil and thermal Energy conservation.
(c) Oil and thermal Energy convention.
(d) Ocean thermal energy conversion.

98. 2018 FIFA World Cup would be held in
(a) Russia   (b) Qatar
(c) France   (d) Netherlands

99. Who discovered South Pole?
(a) Robert Peary   (b) Amundsen
(c) John Cabot   (d) Tasman

100. India along with which country has signed an agreement of about 7.87 billion euros for Rafale fighter jets?
(a) United States (b) France
(c) Bangladesh   (d) Afghanistan

ANSWERS

1. (c)	**2.** (c)	**3.** (d)	**4.** (b)	**5.** (d)	**6.** (c)	**7.** (b)	**8.** (a)	**9.** (b)	**10.** (d)
11. (a)	**12.** (b)	**13.** (c)	**14.** (a)	**15.** (d)	**16.** (c)	**17.** (b)	**18.** (c)	**19.** (a)	**20.** (a)
21. (b)	**22.** (c)	**23.** (a)	**24.** (b)	**25.** (c)	**26.** (c)	**27.** (c)	**28.** (c)	**29.** (d)	**30.** (d)
31. (d)	**32.** (c)	**33.** (b)	**34.** (b)	**35.** (b)	**36.** (c)	**37.** (c)	**38.** (a)	**39.** (b)	**40.** (c)
41. (b)	**42.** (d)	**43.** (d)	**44.** (c)	**45.** (b)	**46.** (d)	**47.** (c)	**48.** (a)	**49.** (c)	**50.** (c)
51. (d)	**52.** (b)	**53.** (a)	**54.** (a)	**55.** (d)	**56.** (c)	**57.** (a)	**58.** (d)	**59.** (d)	**60.** (b)
61. (b)	**62.** (b)	**63.** (b)	**64.** (a)	**65.** (c)	**66.** (a)	**67.** (a)	**68.** (c)	**69.** (c)	**70.** (b)
71. (c)	**72.** (b)	**73.** (b)	**74.** (a)	**75.** (b)	**76.** (c)	**77.** (c)	**78.** (c)	**79.** (a)	**80.** (a)
81. (d)	**82.** (c)	**83.** (d)	**84.** (b)	**85.** (b)	**86.** (c)	**87.** (a)	**88.** (d)	**89.** (c)	**90.** (d)
91. (d)	**92.** (c)	**93.** (c)	**94.** (d)	**95.** (d)	**96.** (c)	**97.** (d)	**98.** (a)	**99.** (b)	**100.** (b)

EXPLANATIONS

1. 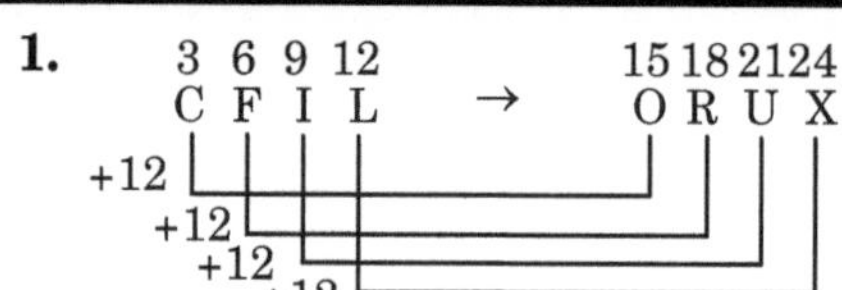

Similarly,

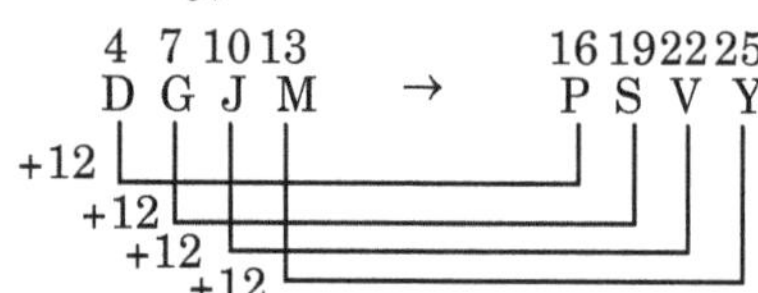

2. $\dfrac{24}{60} = \dfrac{120}{x}$

$x = \dfrac{60 \times 120}{24}$ $\qquad \therefore x = 300$

4. $P \xrightarrow{+1} Q \xrightarrow{+7} X \xrightarrow{+2} Z$

$B \xrightarrow{+1} C \xrightarrow{+14} Q \xrightarrow{-3} N \leftarrow$

$A \xrightarrow{+1} B \xrightarrow{+2} D \xrightarrow{+2} F$

$M \xrightarrow{+1} N \xrightarrow{+2} P \xrightarrow{+2} R$

5. In this, middle term is equal to the sum of left and right terms.

i.e. $\quad 5 + 2 = 7$

$\qquad 6 + 1 = 7$

$\qquad 2 + 4 = 6$

But, $\quad 7 + 4 \neq 2$

6. Given set : $(4, 25, 89) = (2^2, 5^2, 9^2)$

$\therefore (16, 64, 100) = (4^2, 8^2, 10^2)$

9. The correct sequence is

$aca\underline{c} / ab\underline{a}b / aca\underline{c} / aba\underline{b} / aca\underline{c}$

10. $\underset{1 \ 15 \ 2 \ 14}{A \ O \ B \ N} \xrightarrow{+3} \underset{4 \ 18 \ 5 \ 17}{D \ R \ E \ Q} \xrightarrow{+3}$

$\underset{7 \ 21 \ 8 \ 20}{G \ U \ H \ T} \xrightarrow{+3} \underset{10 \ 24 \ 11 \ 23}{J \ X \ K \ W}$

11. The series is as follows:-

$6 \xrightarrow{+6} 12 \xrightarrow{+9} 21 \xrightarrow{+11} 32 \xrightarrow{+13} 45 \xrightarrow{+15} 60$

12. Ramesh rank in class = 13th

Total number of student = 33

$\therefore$ Suresh rank in class = 33–5 = 28th

$\therefore$ Number of student between Ramesh and Suresh = 28 – (13 + 1) = 14.

13. 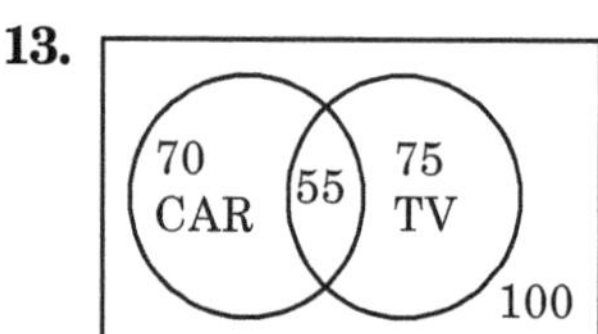

$\therefore$ Percentage of those surveyed did not own either a car or a tv

$= 100 - (70 + 75 - 55)$

$= 100 - (145 - 55) = 100 - 90 = 10\%$

14. $\underset{1 \ 3 \ 5 \ 3}{L \ O \ S \ S} \underset{\&}{} \underset{2 \ 4 \ 6 \ 8}{G \ A \ I \ N}$

$\therefore 8 \ 4 \ 6 \ 1 \ 5 \rightarrow N \ A \ I \ L \ S$

16. 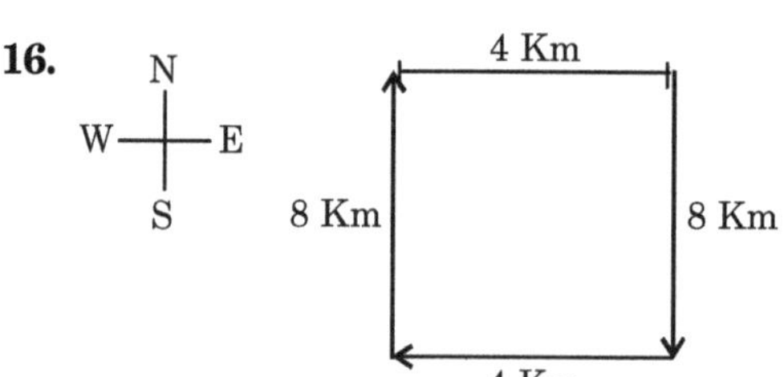

18. 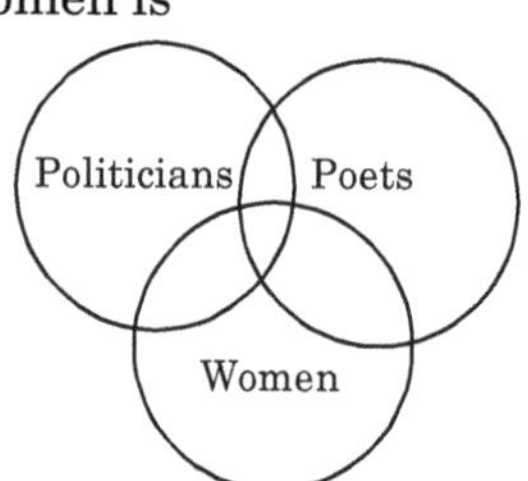

19. Given, $70 \div 2 - 4 \times 5 + 6 = 34$

According to question

$70 \times 2 \div 4 + 5 - 6 = 34$

$70 \times \dfrac{1}{2} + 5 - 6 = 34$

$35 + 5 - 6 = 34$

$34 = 34$

L.H.S = R.H.S

20. Diagram represents relation between politicians, poets and women is

22. Given pattern is

$324 \times 289 = 35$

i.e. $(17)^2 + (18)^2 = 17 + 18 = 35$

Similarly, $256 \times 729 = (16)^2 + (27)^2 = 16 + 27 = 43$

51. P = 124, we can write

$\sqrt[3]{P(P^2 + 3P + 3) + 1} = \sqrt[3]{P^3 + 3P^2 + 3P + 1}$

$= \sqrt[3]{(P + 1)^3} = P + 1$

$= 124 + 1 = 125$

52. $\sqrt{1-\dfrac{x^3}{100}}=\dfrac{3}{5}$

Squaring both side, we get

$1-\dfrac{x^3}{100}=\dfrac{9}{25}$

$\Rightarrow \quad 100-x^3=36$

$\Rightarrow \quad x^3=64$

$\Rightarrow \quad x=4.$

53. $\sqrt{8+\sqrt{57+\sqrt{38+\sqrt{108+\sqrt{169}}}}}$

$=\sqrt{8+\sqrt{57+\sqrt{38+\sqrt{108+13}}}}$

$=\sqrt{8+\sqrt{57+\sqrt{38+11}}}$

$=\sqrt{8+\sqrt{57+7}}=\sqrt{8+\sqrt{64}}=\sqrt{8+8}=4.$

54. $\dfrac{2+\sqrt{3}}{2-\sqrt{3}}+\dfrac{2-\sqrt{3}}{2+\sqrt{3}}+\dfrac{\sqrt{3}+1}{\sqrt{3}-1}$

$=\dfrac{(2+\sqrt{3})^2+(2-\sqrt{3})^2}{(2+\sqrt{3})(2-\sqrt{3})}+\dfrac{(\sqrt{3}+1)(\sqrt{3}+1)}{(\sqrt{3}+1)(\sqrt{3}-1)}$

$=\dfrac{4+3+4\sqrt{3}+4+3-4\sqrt{3}}{1}+\dfrac{3+2\sqrt{3}+1}{2}$

$=14+2+\sqrt{3}=16+\sqrt{3}$

55. $\dfrac{0.0347\times0.0347\times0.0347+(0.9653)^3}{(0.0347)^2-(0.0347)(0.9653)+(0.9653)^2}$

$=\dfrac{(0.0349)^3+(0.9653)^3}{(0.0347)^2-(0.0347)(0.9653)+(.9653)^2}$

$=(0.0347+0.9653)=1 \quad [a^3 b^3=(a+b)(a^2-ab+b^2)]$

56. Area of equilateral triangle $=\dfrac{\sqrt{3}}{4}a^2$ [where a is side of triangle]

$\therefore \quad \dfrac{\sqrt{3}}{4}a^2=121\sqrt{3}$

$a=22$ cm.

Perameter of triangle $=22\times3=66$ cm

Perameter of circle $=2\pi r$

i.e. $\quad 2\pi r=66$

$\Rightarrow \quad r=66\times\dfrac{7}{22\times2}=\dfrac{21}{2}$ cm

Now area of triangle $=\pi r^2$

$=\dfrac{22}{7}\times\dfrac{21}{2}\times\dfrac{21}{2}=346.5$ cm^2

57. Volume of cone $=\dfrac{1}{3}\pi r^2 h=\dfrac{1}{3}\times\dfrac{22}{7}\times6\times6\times24$

Volume of shpere $=\dfrac{4}{3}\pi r^3$

Hence, $\dfrac{4}{3}\pi r^3=\dfrac{1}{3}\times\dfrac{22}{7}\times6\times6\times24$

$r=6$ cm.

58. Volume of water to be filled in tank

$=200\times150\times8$ m^3

flow into tank per hour $=0.3\times0.2\times20\times1000$ m/hour

$\therefore$ Time required to fill 8 m water level in tank

$=\dfrac{200\times150\times8}{0.3\times0.2\times20\times1000}=20$ hours.

59. Let capacity of each vassel $=x$ ltr.

Then amount of water and milk in vassel one

$=\dfrac{3}{7}x$ and $\dfrac{4}{7}x$

Amount of water and milk in vessel two $=\dfrac{5}{8}x$

and $\dfrac{3}{8}x$.

Total amount of water

$=\dfrac{3}{7}x+\dfrac{5}{8}x=\dfrac{24+35}{56}x=\dfrac{59}{56}x.$

Similarly total amount of milk

$=\dfrac{4}{7}x+\dfrac{3}{8}x=\dfrac{32+21}{56}x=\dfrac{53}{56}x.$

Ratio of water and milk $=\dfrac{\dfrac{59}{56}x}{\dfrac{53}{56}x}=\dfrac{59}{53}.$

60. Let son's age $=x$ years, then my age $=3x.$

After 15 years

$\dfrac{3x+15}{x+15}=\dfrac{2}{1}\Rightarrow 2x+30=3x+15$

$x=15$

Sum of our ages $=3x+x=60$ years

61. Given, $\dfrac{1}{A}+\dfrac{1}{B}=\dfrac{1}{12}$ ...(1)

$\dfrac{1}{B}+\dfrac{1}{C}=\dfrac{1}{15}$ ...(2)

$\dfrac{1}{C}+\dfrac{1}{A}=\dfrac{1}{20}$ ...(3)

Adding equation (1), (2) and (3), we get

$2\left(\dfrac{1}{A}+\dfrac{1}{B}+\dfrac{1}{C}\right)=\dfrac{12}{60}$

$\Rightarrow \dfrac{1}{A}+\dfrac{1}{B}+\dfrac{1}{C}=\dfrac{1}{10}$ i.e. 10 days.

62. Given, $\dfrac{1}{A}=\dfrac{-6}{B}$ ... (1)

$\left(\dfrac{1}{A}+\dfrac{1}{B}\right)\dfrac{1}{2}=\dfrac{1}{C}=\dfrac{1}{20}$ ... (2)

$\dfrac{1}{A}+\dfrac{1}{B}+\dfrac{1}{C}=\dfrac{2}{C}+\dfrac{1}{C}=\dfrac{3}{C}=\dfrac{3}{20}$ i.e., $6\dfrac{2}{3}$ day.

63. 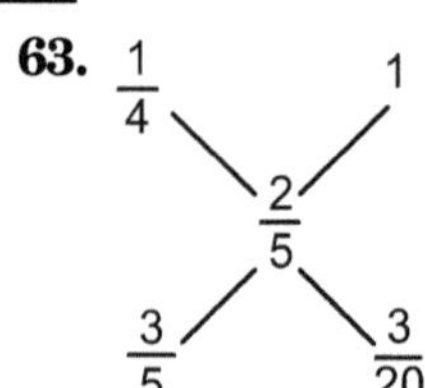

Hence, 60cc a water should be added to the mixture.

i.e 4 : 1;   i.e 240 : 60

64. $\dfrac{\text{Income}}{\text{Expenditure}} = \dfrac{10}{7}$

$\therefore$ Income $= \dfrac{10}{17}x$, expenditure $= \dfrac{7}{17}x$

$\therefore$ Saving = Income – Expenditure

$\qquad = \left(\dfrac{10}{17} - \dfrac{7}{17}\right)x = \dfrac{3}{17}x$

Given, $\dfrac{7}{17}x = 10500$

$\therefore \qquad \dfrac{3}{17}x = \dfrac{10500}{\dfrac{7}{17x}} \times \dfrac{3}{17}x = ₹\,4500$

66. Let initial price $= ₹\,x$

and initial sale $= y$

Then, according to question,

$\qquad 8x \times 1.8y = 1.44\,xy$

total movement on selling $= (1.44\,xy - xy) = .44\,xy$

Hence, 44% increment in sell.

67. Let usual speed $= 4$ km/h.

and usual time $= t$ hrs.

According to question,

$\Rightarrow \qquad ut = \dfrac{3}{4}u\left(t + \dfrac{3}{2}\right)$

$\Rightarrow \qquad \dfrac{4t}{3} = t + \dfrac{3}{2}$

$\Rightarrow \qquad \dfrac{1}{3}t = 3/2$

$\Rightarrow \qquad t = 9/2$ hr

68. Selling at ₹ 100, gained 20% for 20 apple

Let, cost price $= ₹\,x$ for 20 apple

$\therefore \qquad 1.2x = 100$

$\qquad x = ₹\,\dfrac{100}{1.2}$

Now, by unitary method,

$\because ₹\,\dfrac{100}{1.2}$ for 20 apple

$\therefore ₹\,100$ for $\dfrac{20}{100} \times 1.2 \times 100 = 24$ apple

69. $1 : \dfrac{1}{3} : \dfrac{1}{6}$, i.e. $x : \dfrac{x}{3} : \dfrac{x}{6}$

Now, $x + \dfrac{x}{3} + \dfrac{x}{6} = 78$

$\Rightarrow \qquad \dfrac{9x}{6} = 75$

$\Rightarrow \qquad x = \dfrac{78 \times 2}{3} = 52$

Then middle term $= \dfrac{x}{3} = \dfrac{52}{3} = 7\dfrac{1}{3}$

70. Compond interest $= P\left(1 + \dfrac{20}{100}\right)^2 - P = 0.44\,P$

Simple interest $= P \times \dfrac{20 \times 2}{100} = 0.4P$

difference $= 48 = 0.44P - 0.4P$

$\Rightarrow \qquad P = \dfrac{48}{0.04} = ₹\,1200$

71. Let distance to his office $= x$ km

and time taken to reach his office $= t$ hrs.

According to question,

$\dfrac{x}{30} = \left(t - \dfrac{6}{60}\right) \qquad …(1)$

$\dfrac{x}{24} = \left(t - \dfrac{5}{60}\right) \qquad …(2)$

$\rule{5cm}{0.4pt}$

$\dfrac{x}{24} - \dfrac{x}{30} = \dfrac{5}{60} + \dfrac{6}{60}$

(subtracting (1) from (2))

$\Rightarrow \qquad \dfrac{x}{120} = \dfrac{11}{60}$

$\qquad x = 22$ km.

72. $\qquad 8P = P\left(1 + \dfrac{2}{100}\right)^3$

$\therefore \qquad \left(1 + \dfrac{r}{100}\right) = 2$

Now, $\qquad 16 = 2 \qquad$ i.e. $\left(1 + \dfrac{r}{100}\right)^4$

So, time will be 4 years to become principle 16 times.

73. Amount spent on Rent and Food

$\qquad = 25000 \times \dfrac{59}{100} = ₹\,14750$

74. Ratio of expense to education to the expense on food

$\qquad = \dfrac{15\%}{45\%} = 1/3$

75. $\qquad \dfrac{14}{9} \times 100 = 155.55\% \simeq 156\%$

PRACTICE SET- 8

GENERAL INTELLIGENCE

1. If SMART is coded as RTASM, then UNDER is coded as
   - (a) NUDRE
   - (b) REDNU
   - (c) ERDUN
   - (d) RDENU

2. If STYLE is written as ELSTY, then FLIRT is written as
   - (a) LFRIT
   - (b) TRILF
   - (c) TRLFI
   - (d) TRFLI

3. Which of the following interchange of signs would make the given equation correct?

   $30 + 5 \times 4 \div 3 - 2 = 25$
   - (a) ÷ and −
   - (b) + and ×
   - (c) × and −
   - (d) + and ÷

4. Identify the symbols to be inserted to make the expression correct.

   16 Δ 2 Δ 9 Δ 3 Δ 4 Δ 5
   - (a) ÷ = + × +
   - (b) + = ÷ + ×
   - (c) ÷ + = × +
   - (d) + + ÷ = ×

Directions : In question nos. **5** to **7**, find related word/number from the given alternatives.

5. Plants : Cell Wall :: Animals : ?
   - (a) Ribosome
   - (b) Nucleus
   - (c) Lysosome
   - (d) Cell Membrane

6. Battery : Terminals :: Magnet : ?
   - (a) Charger
   - (b) Poles
   - (c) Power
   - (d) Ends

7. 15 : 65 : : 24 : ?
   - (a) 76
   - (b) 96
   - (c) 126
   - (d) 144

Directions : In question nos. **8** to **10**, find the odd word/number/letters/number pair from the given alternatives.

8. (a) Father
   (b) Wife
   (c) Mother
   (d) Son

9. (a) XTUQ
   (b) VRSP
   (c) TPQM
   (d) RNOK

10. (a) 42 - 51
    (b) 37 - 19
    (c) 12 - 30
    (d) 71 - 47

Directions : In the following question arrange the given words a meaningful and ascending order and select the option indicating the correct order.

11. 1. Coat   2. Mall
    3. Rack   4. Store
    5. Button
    - (a) 1, 2, 3, 5, 4
    - (b) 5, 3, 2, 4, 1
    - (c) 3, 2, 1, 5, 4
    - (d) 5, 1, 3, 4, 2

12. A series is given, with one term missing. Choose the correct alternative from the given ones.

    BDGK, PRUY, ?
    - (a) DFIM
    - (b) DGJN
    - (c) EGJN
    - (d) EGIM

Directions : In question nos. **13** and **14,** find the missing number from the given responses.

13. 7   17   11   13
    26   13   19   20
    15   8   6   ?
    61   54   46   69
    - (a) 11
    - (b) 13
    - (c) 15
    - (d) 17

14. 16   81   36
    36   25   49
    64   9   25
    6   7   ?
    - (a) 4
    - (b) 8
    - (c) 9
    - (d) 11

15. Gautam goes 10 km towards North, turns left and goes 4 km and then again turns right and goes another 5 km and then turns right and goes another 4 km. How many km is he from his original position?
    - (a) 23 km
    - (b) 19 km
    - (c) 15 km
    - (d) 5 km

Directions: In question nos. **16** and **17**, from the given alternatives words, select the word which **cannot** be formed using the letters of the given word.

16. TRANSFORMATION
    - (a) TRANSIT
    - (b) MISSION
    - (c) FIRST
    - (d) MOTION

17. PARLIAMENT
    - (a) PAST
    - (b) MINT
    - (c) NAME
    - (d) TERM

18. A is in the South-east of B, which is in the East of C. If D is in the North of C, then in which direction of A is D?

(a) North-west   (b) South-west

(c) North   (d) North-east

Directions: In the following question statements are given which are followed by two/four conclusions I, II, III and IV. You have to consider the two statements to be true even if they seem to be at variance from commonly known facts. You have to decide which of the given conclusions, if any, follow from the given statements.

19. Statements:

I. Some fruits are vegetables.

II. Flowers are fruits.

Conclusions:

I. Some vegetables are flowers.

II. No flower is a vegetable.

(a) Conclusion I follows.

(b) Conclusion II follows.

(c) Either conclusion I or II follows.

(d) Neither conclusion I nor II follows.

20. Three positions of a dice are given. Find out which number is found opposite to the number 1 in the given dice.

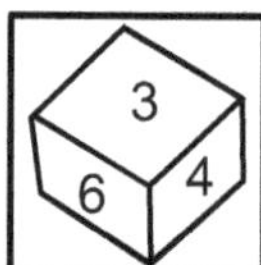 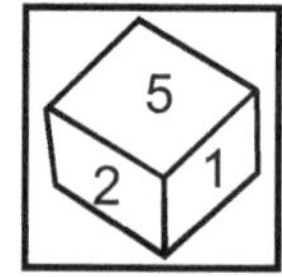 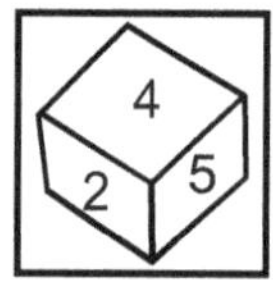

(a) 4   (b) 3

(c) 6   (d) 5

21. The below diagram shows the survey on a sample of 750 people in a society about their liking of Coffee, Tea and Lassi. How many people like Lassi and Tea both but not Coffee?

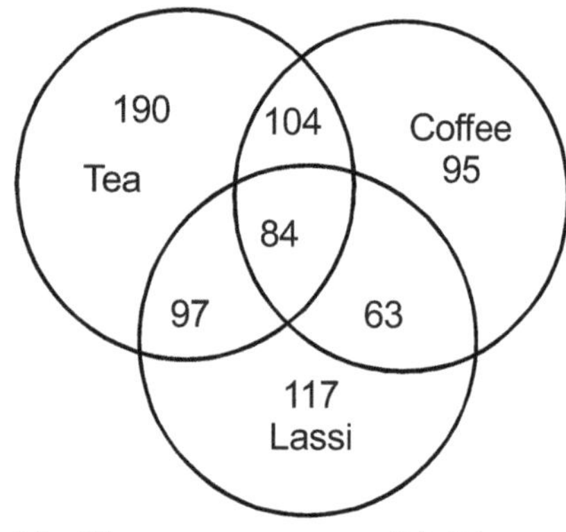

(a) 97   (b) 63

(c) 13   (d) 81

22. Identify the answer figures from which the piece given in question figure have been cut.

Question figure

Answer figures

  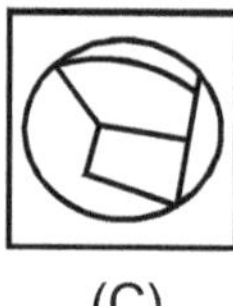 

(A)   (B)   (C)   (D)

Directions : In the following question which answer figure will complete the pattern in the question figure?

23. Question figure

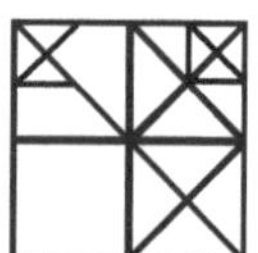

Answer figures

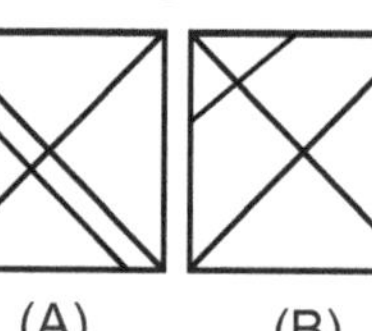 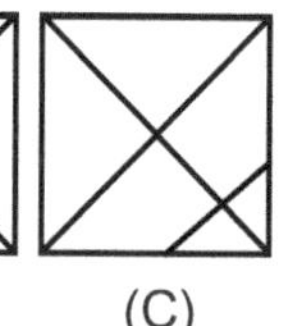 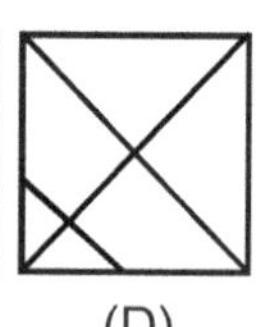

(A)   (B)   (C)   (D)

24. A piece of paper is folded and cut as shown below in the question figures. From the given answer figures, indicate how it will appear when opened.

Question figures

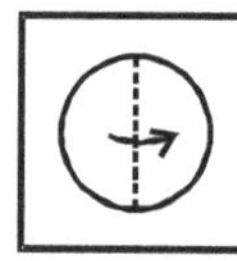  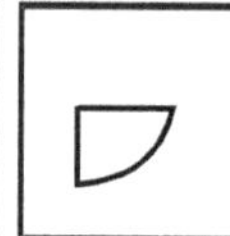 

Answer figures

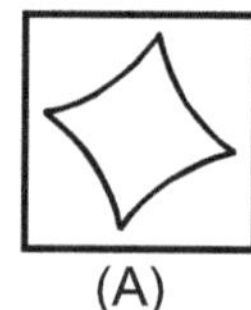 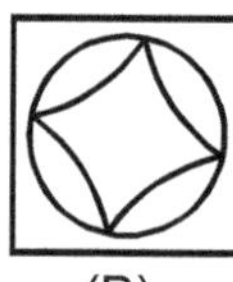  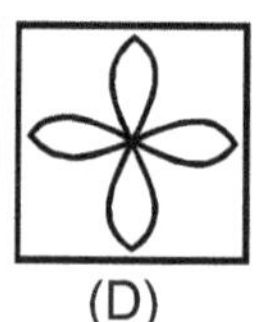

(A)   (B)   (C)   (D)

25. How many triangles are there in the given figure?

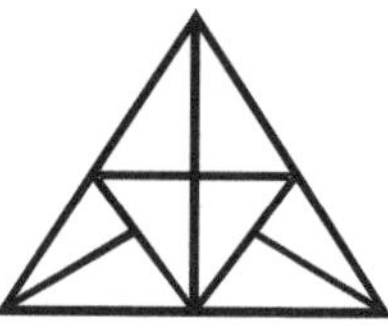

(a) 17   (b) 18

(c) 19   (d) 20

ENGLISH LANGUAGE

Directions: In question nos. **26** to **27**, out of the four alternatives, choose the one which best expresses the meaning of the given word and mark it in the answer sheet.

26. Assuage
- (*a*) Alleviate
- (*b*) Aggravate
- (*c*) Alter
- (*d*) Accumulate

27. Porch
- (*a*) Windowsill
- (*b*) Verge
- (*c*) Canopy
- (*d*) Veranda

Directions: In question nos. **28** to **29**, in the following question choose the word opposite in meaning to the given word and mark it in the answer sheet.

28. Gauche
- (*a*) Crude
- (*b*) Suave
- (*c*) Clumsy
- (*d*) Wet

29. Choose the word opposite in meaning to the given word and mark it in the answer sheet.

Purport
- (*a*) Gainsay
- (*b*) Acknowledge
- (*c*) Confess
- (*d*) Hush

Directions: In question nos. **30** to **32**, out of the four alternatives, choose the one which can be substituted for the given words/sentences.

30. Art of making movies
- (*a*) Cinema
- (*b*) Silver screen
- (*c*) Big screen
- (*d*) Show-biz

31. A study of rocks is called
- (*a*) Trichology
- (*b*) Ornithology
- (*c*) Gemology
- (*d*) Petrology

32. Two-legged animals
- (*a*) Bipartite
- (*b*) Bipedal
- (*c*) Biller
- (*d*) Bismuth

Directions: In question nos. **33** to **35**, four alternatives are given for the idiom/phrase underlined in the sentence. Choose the alternative which best expresses the meaning of the given idiom/phrase.

33. Eat one's heart out
- (*a*) To feel unhappy about something
- (*b*) To feel merry about something
- (*c*) To say disheartening words about someone
- (*d*) To quarrel with someone

34. It was not enough to just be heartbroken; you had to have egg all over your face too.
- (*a*) to be made to look stupid
- (*b*) to show that you are unhappy
- (*c*) to suffer injustice
- (*d*) to rely on a particular course of action

35. I grabbed the bull by the horns and opened my own business. I am a millionaire now.
- (*a*) assessed the situation thoroughly
- (*b*) took great risk by borrowing money from someone
- (*c*) faced difficult situation directly and with courage
- (*d*) took full charge of the situation

Directions: In the following question four words are given in each question, out of which only one word is spelt correctly. Find the correctly spelt word and mark your answer in the answer sheet.

36.
- (*a*) Missisippi
- (*b*) Mississippi
- (*c*) Misissippi
- (*d*) Misisippi

Directions: In question nos. **37** to **39**, some parts of the sentences have errors and some are correct. Find out which part of the sentence has an error and mark the answer corresponding to the appropriate letter (A, B, C). If a sentence is free from error, mark your answer as (*d*).

37. Smriti and I (*a*) / are thinking what you (*b*) / said yesterday was right. (*c*) / No error (*d*)

38. The waters of (*a*) / Yamuna cater to 408 people, (*b*)/ 147 households and 108 families. (*c*) / No error (*d*)

39. Every girl in group A and every (*a*) / boy in group B were (*b*) / assigned a task. (*c*) / No error (*d*)

Directions: In question nos. **40** and **42**, sentences are given with blanks to be filled with an appropriate word(s). Four alternatives are suggested for each question. Choose the correct alternative out of the four.

40. The people of both the nations are united _____ borders by religion and history.
- (*a*) through
- (*b*) by
- (*c*) in
- (*d*) across

41. Place the card _____ on the pile.
- (*a*) face up
- (*b*) face in
- (*c*) face on
- (*d*) face off

42. If you are planning to make an _____ commercial, you might go to one of the traditional animation houses.
- (*a*) animated
- (*b*) animate
- (*c*) animating
- (*d*) animation

Directions: In question nos. **43** to **45**, a sentence / part of the sentence is underlined. Beneath each sentence four different ways of phrasing the underlined part are given. Choose the grammatically correct option. In case no improvement is needed, your answer should be option (*d*).

43. The children were out playing games as I speak.
- (*a*) are out playing
- (*b*) had been out playing
- (*c*) will be out playing
- (*d*) No improvement

44. <u>If I was better at history, I will become an archeologist.</u>

(a) If I was better at history, I would have become an archaeologist.

(b) If I were better at history, I would become an archaeologist.

(c) If I were better at history, I will become an archaeologist.

(d) No improvement

45. The price of <u>these jeans are</u> reasonable.

(a) this jeans is

(b) these jeans is

(c) this jeans are

(d) No improvement

Directions: In question nos. **46** to **50**, you have given a passages with 5 questions. Read the passage and choose the best answer to each question.

"The beauty of the Japanese landscape is that it conveys philosophical message through each feature. The use of curving pathways rather than straight lines, for instance. This feature springs from the belief that only evil travels in straight lines, good forces tend to wander. Then odd number of plants or tress is used in these gardens because these numbers are considered auspicious. Even the plants are symbolic, for example, the cypress represents longevity and the bamboo symbolizes abundance," says Sadhana Roy.

In Japan, nature is said to be so closely intertwined with human life that parents actually plant a sapling in their garden when a child is born in the family, letting the growth of the child coincide with growth of the plant.

46. They refer curving pathways because

(a) they are inauspicious

(b) they can walk easily

(c) they stumble over straight ones

(d) good spirits walk on them

47. What is the meaning of "abundance" in the context of the passage?

(a) long life

(b) happiness

(c) plenty

(d) permanent

48. The Japanese parents plant sapling at time of birth because

(a) it is auspicious

(b) it is closely associated with growth of child

(c) it gives longevity to child

(d) it gives happiness to child

49. According to the passage, the Japanese are

(a) superstitious   (b) philosophical

(c) lover of nature   (d) lovers of numerology

50. The Japanese pathway tends to be

(a) symbolic   (b) beautiful

(c) curved   (d) straight

QUANTITATIVE APTITUDE

51. If $\left(\dfrac{4}{9}\right)^3 \left(\dfrac{3}{2}\right)^{-16} = \left(\dfrac{2}{3}\right)^{2x}$, then x is

(a) 6   (b) 10

(c) 11   (d) 8

52. If $x^2 + y^2 + z^2 + \dfrac{7}{2} = x - 2z - 3y$, then the value of $2x - 4y + 3z$ is

(a) 1   (b) 3

(c) 0   (d) 4

53. A chord of length 7 cm subtends an angle of 30° at a point on the circle. The diameter of the circle is

(a) 7 cm   (b) 14 cm

(c) 5 cm   (d) 10 cm

54. The ratio of inradius and circumradius of an equilateral triangle is

(a) 1 : 2   (b) 2 : 1

(c) $1 : \sqrt{2}$ (d) 1 : 3

55. What is the minimum value of $\sin^2\theta + \cos^2\theta + \sec^2\theta + \tan^2\theta + \cot^2\theta + \csc^2\theta$?

(a) 6   (b) 7

(c) 0   (d) 5

56. L and M are two points on a circle with centre at O. N is a point on the major arc of the circle, between the points L and M. The tangents to the circle at the points L and M meet each other at the point E. If $\angle LEM = 40°$, then $\angle LNM = ?$

(a) 75°   (b) 65°

(c) 80°   (d) 70°

57. In $\triangle ABC$, AB = AC and $\angle BAC$ is half of external angle at C. Then, $\angle BAC$ is

(a) 50°   (b) 60°

(c) 70°   (d) 45°

58. A boat can row 15 km upstream in 5 hours and the same distance downstream in 3 hours. Find the speed of the boat in still water.

(a) 4 km/hr
(b) 1 km/hr
(c) 3 km/hr
(d) 5 km/hr

59. The value of

$\cos 1° \sin 89° + \cos 2° \sin 88° + \cos 3° \sin 87° + \ldots + \cos 89° \sin 1°$, is

(a) 0
(b) 45
(c) 44.5
(d) 1

60. If $\tan\theta + \cot\theta = 3$, then the value of

$\tan^6\theta + \cot^6\theta$ is

(a) 196
(b) 322
(c) 224
(d) 1

61. A shopkeeper offers successive discounts of 20%, 10%, 5% respectively on a Titan watch which is marked at ₹1,500. He offers successive discounts of 20%, 20%, 10% respectively on a Ajanta watch which is marked at ₹2,000. What is the difference between their selling price?

(a) ₹152
(b) ₹126
(c) ₹26
(d) ₹0

62. The degree measure of 2 radian is

(Taking $\pi = \dfrac{22}{7}$)

(a) 114° 32' 44" (approx.)
(b) 57° 16' 22" (approx.)
(c) 114° 16' 44" (approx.)
(d) 57° 32' 16" (approx.)

63. If $\dfrac{a^{n-1} + b^{n-1}}{a^{n-2} + b^{n-2}}$ is arithmetic mean between a and b, then what will be the value of 'n'?

(a) 0
(b) 2
(c) 1
(d) – 1

64. ABC is an isosceles triangle with sides AB = AC = 15 cm and BC = 24 cm. AD is a median to base BC. Then the length of AD is

(a) 10 cm
(b) 13 cm
(c) 12 cm
(d) 9 cm

65. A sum of money amounts to ₹19,683 at 16% p.a. compounded semi-annually in $1\dfrac{1}{2}$ years. Find the interest accumulated on the sum for the same period.

(a) ₹4,058
(b) ₹5,004
(c) ₹4,506
(d) ₹3,435

66. AB and CD are two parallel chords of a circle such that AB = 6 cm and CD = 8 cm. If the chords are on the opposite sides of the centre and distance between them is 7 cm, then the sum of areas of triangles formed by the centre of the circle to the end points of the chords will be

(a) 18 cm²
(b) 12 cm²
(c) 24 cm²
(d) 16 cm²

67. If $x + \dfrac{1}{x+2} = 0$, then what is the value of $x^2 + \dfrac{1}{x^6}$?

(a) 0
(b) 1
(c) 2
(d) – 2

68. A's salary is 20% more than that of B and 30% less than that of C. If B's salary is 15% less than that of D's salary, then by what percent A's salary is less or more than that of D's salary?

(a) Equal
(b) 2% less
(c) 2% more
(d) 2.6% more

69. If $x + x^{-1} = 3$, then the value of

$x^2 + x^{-2} + x^6 + x^{-6}$ is

(a) 329
(b) 322
(c) 241
(d) 315

70. A circular track have a difference of 2 m between inner and outer radius. Also the area of circular track is 36π m². Find the radius of the outer circular boundary.

(a) 10 m
(b) 12 m
(c) 11 m
(d) 8 m

71. The angle of elevation to the top of a pole from a distance 450 m from its foot is 60°. The height of the pole is

(a) $150\sqrt{3}$ m
(b) $450\sqrt{3}$ m
(c) $225\sqrt{3}$ m
(d) $\dfrac{150}{\sqrt{3}}$ m

72. A contractor took a contract to complete a work in 90 days. To complete the work he employed 60 workers.

After 75 days, he found that only $\dfrac{4}{5}$th of the work was completed. To complete the contract on time, how many extra workers he should employee?

(a) 75
(b) 60
(c) 45
(d) 15

Directions: In question nos. **73** to **75**, the following pie-chart shows the distribution of motorcycles of different models sold by Kajaj in 2012-13. Study the chart and answer the questions given below.

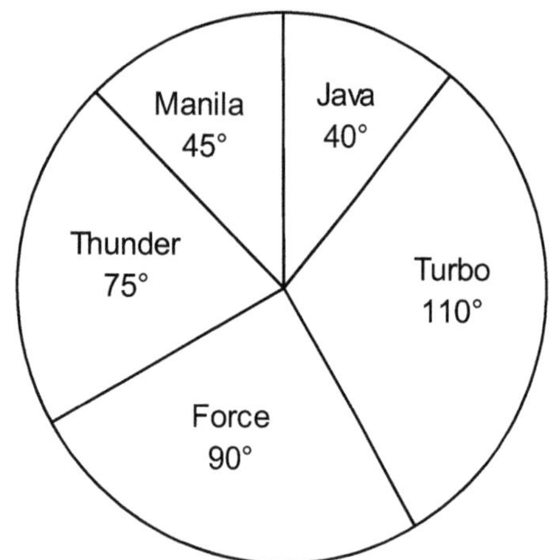

73. How many more motorcycles of model Thunder are sold than that of Manila, if the number of motorcycles of model Force sold is 20250?

(a) 4050   (b) 8100

(c) 12150   (d) 6750

74. If the number of motorcycles of model Force sold is 20250, what is the ratio between the number of motorcycles sold of model Force and Thunder?

(a) 9 : 5   (b) 6 : 5

(c) 11 : 9   (d) 9 : 7

75. If the number of motorcycles of model Force sold is 20250, then what is the total number of motorcycles sold of all the models together by Kajaj Enterprise?

(a) 37125   (b) 371250

(c) 81000   (d) 75000

GENERAL AWARENESS

76. Who founded the 'Indian National Union' during 1884?

(a) Firoz shah Mehta

(b) A O Hume

(c) Mary Carpenter

(d) Anand Mohan Bose

77. Recently Iram Sharmila Chanu ended her hunger strike, how many years she had done hunger strike?

(a) 16 years   (b) 14 years

(c) 13 years   (d) 10 years

78. Who gave the theoretical concept 'Survival of the Fittest'?

(a) Louis Pasteur   (b) Charles Darwin

(c) Ernst Haeckel   (d) Edward Jenner

79. Which of the following hormone is produced during pregnancy?

(a) Human Chorionic Gonadotropin

(b) Testosterone

(c) Aldosterone

(d) Somatotropin

80. Ghughua Fossil National Park is located in which of the following states?

(a) Madhya Pradesh   (b) Andhra Pradesh

(c) Himcahal Pradesh   (d) Nagaland

81. Which of the following is not a part of an ecosystem?

(a) Metro train   (b) Trees

(c) Soil   (d) Birds

82. Silver iodide is used in

(a) Photography   (b) Artificial rain

(c) Antiseptic   (d) All of the above

83. Which of the following airport is not situated in Asia?

(a) Aden International Airport

(b) Amami Airport

(c) Ahwaz airport

(d) El Dorado International Airport

84. Which of the following countries has launched world's biggest scanning project- Bio-bank imaging study?

(a) India   (b) Japan

(c) USA   (d) UK

85. Which of the following five-year plan was based on Mahalanobis model?

(a) First five-year plan

(b) Second five-year plan

(c) Third five-year plan

(d) Fourth five-year plan

86. Disguised unemployment is mostly associated with

(a) Agriculture sector

(b) Service sector

(c) Manufacturing sector

(d) None of the above

87. Golden Rice is a

(a) Transgenic crop

(b) Hybrid variety

(c) High Yielding Variety

(d) All of the above

88. The Vice President of India is elected

(a) Directly by the people

(b) Indirectly by the people

(c) By the cabinet ministers

(d) By the Parliamentary Committees

89. Filariasis is transmitted by
   (a) Mosquito   (b) Pigs
   (c) Cattles   (d) Bats

90. Ratnavali was composed by
   (a) Harsha   (b) Kalidas
   (c) Aryabhatta   (d) Ishwar Das Nagar

91. Project Elephant was launched in
   (a) 1992   (b) 1993
   (c) 1994   (d) 1995

92. Nails are composed of
   (a) Protein   (b) Carbohydrates
   (c) Fats   (d) All of the above

93. Bile is stored in
   (a) Liver   (b) Gallbladder
   (c) Pancreas   (d) Spleen

94. Which of the following is a stem parasite?
   (a) Cuscuta   (b) Cactus
   (c) Agaricus   (d) Agate

95. Which of the following is the author of the book "*Transcendence: My Spritual Experiences with Pramukh Swamiji*"?
   (a) Narendra Modi   (b) Lal Krishna Adavani
   (c) Tarun Vijay   (d) Abdul Kalam

96. Weather phenomena occur in the
   (a) Troposphere   (b) Stratosphere
   (c) Mesosphere   (d) Ionosphere

97. Finance commission was established under which of the following acts?
   (a) Art 279   (b) Art 280
   (c) Art 281   (d) Art 370

98. 'Look East Policy' was enacted during the period of
   (a) Rajiv Gandhi
   (b) Indhira Gandhi
   (c) P V Narasimha Rao
   (d) Jawaharlal Nehru

99. Which of the following represents the limit of FDI in single brand retail?
   (a) 26%   (b) 100%
   (c) 74%   (d) 49%

100. Recently who won the best actress award in India Film Festival of Melbourne 2016 (IFFM)?
   (a) Sonam Kapoor
   (b) Kareena Kapoor
   (c) Sonkshi Sinha
   (d) Anushka Sharma

ANSWERS

1. (c)	**2.** (d)	**3.** (d)	**4.** (c)	**5.** (d)	**6.** (b)	**7.** (c)	**8.** (b)	**9.** (b)	**10.** (d)
11. (d)	**12.** (a)	**13.** (d)	**14.** (a)	**15.** (c)	**16.** (b)	**17.** (a)	**18.** (a)	**19.** (c)	**20.** (a)
21. (a)	**22.** (d)	**23.** (d)	**24.** (c)	**25.** (a)	**26.** (a)	**27.** (d)	**28.** (b)	**29.** (a)	**30.** (a)
31. (d)	**32.** (b)	**33.** (a)	**34.** (a)	**35.** (c)	**36.** (b)	**37.** (b)	**38.** (d)	**39.** (b)	**40.** (d)
41. (a)	**42.** (a)	**43.** (a)	**44.** (b)	**45.** (b)	**46.** (d)	**47.** (c)	**48.** (b)	**49.** (b)	**50.** (c)
51. (c)	**52.** (d)	**53.** (b)	**54.** (a)	**55.** (b)	**56.** (d)	**57.** (b)	**58.** (a)	**59.** (c)	**60.** (b)
61. (b)	**62.** (a)	**63.** (b)	**64.** (d)	**65.** (a)	**66.** (c)	**67.** (c)	**68.** (c)	**69.** (a)	**70.** (a)
71. (b)	**72.** (d)	**73.** (d)	**74.** (b)	**75.** (c)	**76.** (b)	**77.** (a)	**78.** (b)	**79.** (a)	**80.** (a)
81. (a)	**82.** (d)	**83.** (d)	**84.** (d)	**85.** (b)	**86.** (a)	**87.** (a)	**88.** (b)	**89.** (a)	**90.** (a)
91. (a)	**92.** (a)	**93.** (b)	**94.** (a)	**95.** (d)	**96.** (a)	**97.** (b)	**98.** (c)	**99.** (b)	**100.** (a)

EXPLANATIONS

1. In the coding, letters of the word are reversed and then first two letters and last two letters exchange their positions. Hence, the code for UNDER is ERDUN.

2. Last two letters in reverse order become first two letters and remaining 3 letters come in the same order.

Hence, the code for FLIRT is TRFLI.

3. $30 \div 5 \times 4 + 3 - 2 = 6 \times 4 + 3 - 2 = 25.$

4. $16 \div 2 + 9 = 3 \times 4 + 5$

5. The outermost layer of a plant cell is called a cell wall. The outermost layer of an animal cell is called a cell membrane. Hence, option (D) is the correct answer.

6. The two ends of a battery are called terminals. Similarly, the two ends of a magnet are called poles. Hence, option (B) is the correct answer.

7. $(4 \times 4 - 1) : (4 \times 4 \times 4 + 1) : : (5 \times 5 - 1) : (5 \times 5 \times 5 + 1)$

Hence, required number is 126.

8. Other than wife all are blood relatives. Hence, option (B) is the correct answer.

9. In all the options except (B), letters follow the rule:

1st letter – 4 = 2nd letter

2nd letter + 1 = 3rd letter

3rd letter – 4 = 4th letter

10. In all the options except (B):

Sum of the digits on the left hand side = Sum of the digits on the right hand side.

11. The correct order is 5, 1, 3, 4, 2. A button is on a coat, which is in a rack. The rack is in a store that is in turn in a mall. Hence, option (D) is the correct answer.

12. B(2) + 2 = D(4)

D(4) + 3 = G(7)

G(7) + 4 = K(11)

K(11) + 5 = P(16)

P(16) + 2 = R(18)

R(18) + 3 = U(21)

U(21) + 4 = Y(25)

Y(25) + 5 = **D(4)**

D(4) + 2 = **F(6)**

F(6) + 3 = **I(9)**

I(9) + 4 = **M(13)**

13. 7 + 17 = 11 + 13

26 + 13 = 19 + 20

15 + 8 = 6 + ? ⇒ **? = 17**

61 + 54 = 46 + 69

14. $\sqrt{16} - \sqrt{36} + \sqrt{64} = 6$

$\sqrt{81} - \sqrt{25} + \sqrt{9} = 7$

$\sqrt{36} - \sqrt{49} + \sqrt{25} = \mathbf{4}$

15.

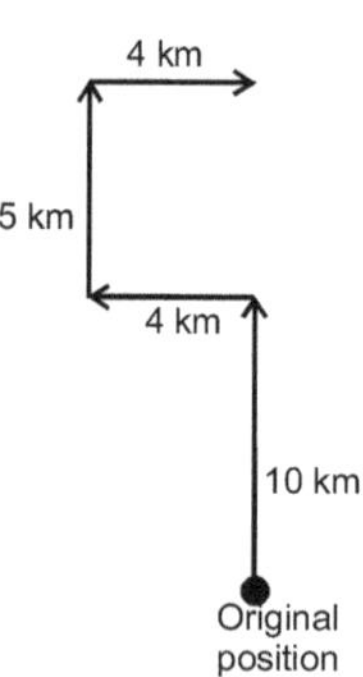

Hence, required distance = 10 + 5 = 15 km.

16. The word TRANSFORMATION has only 1 'S' and 1 'I'.

17. The word PARLIAMENT does not have a 'S'.

18.

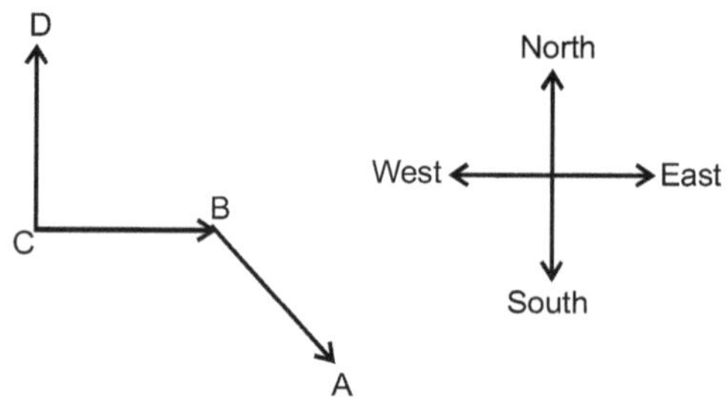

Hence, D is in the North-west of A.

19.

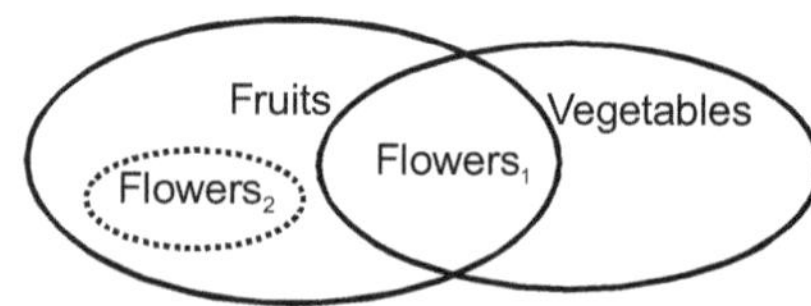

From the venn diagram it is clear that either of the conclusions can follow. Hence, option (C) is the correct answer.

20. Number 2, 5, 3 and 6 are on the adjacent faces of 4, therefore, 4 is on the opposite face of 1.

21. Number of people who like Lassi and Tea but not Coffee is 97.

23.

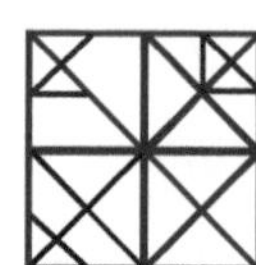

Answer will contain a line parallel to the diagonal in the left lower corner.

Hence, the answer is (D).

24. When it will be completely opened, then it will appear like this.

25.

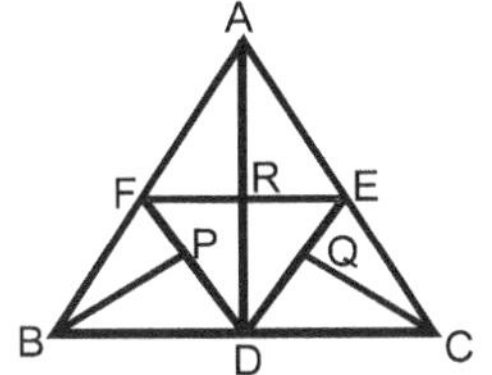

The triangles with 1 area part: ARF, ARE, BPF, BPD, CDQ, CEQ, FDR, DRE

The triangles with 2 area parts: AFE, BDF, CDE, DEF, AFD, ADE

The triangles with 4 area parts: ADB, ADC

The triangles with 8 area parts: ABC

26. 'Assuage' means to make something less painful or severe. 'Alleviate' means to reduce the pain or trouble of something. Hence, option (A) is the correct answer.

27. 'Porch' is a structure attached to the entrance of a building that has a separate roof. It may or may not have walls. 'Veranda' is a long, open structure on the outside of a building that has a roof. Hence, option (D) is the correct answer. 'Verge' is an area along the edge of a road, path, etc. 'Canopy' is a cloth that hangs over a throne, bed, etc.

28. 'Gauche' refers to someone who lacks social experience or grace. Hence, option (B) is the correct answer. Someone is described as 'suave' when they behave in a relaxed and confident way in social situations. 'Clumsy' and 'crude' are the synonyms of 'gauche'.

29. 'Purport' means to claim to do something when the claim may not be true. 'Gainsay' is used to show that something is not true; to deny with something. Hence, option (A) is the correct answer.

30. The art or technique of making movies is called 'cinema'. Hence, option (A) is the correct answer. A motion picture screen is called 'silver screen'. The motion picture medium often as contrasted to television is called 'big screen'. 'Show-biz' is the business of providing public entertainment.

31. 'Petrology' is defined as the study of rocks. Hence, option (D) is the correct answer. 'Trichology' deals with the scientific study of the health of hair and scalp. 'Ornithology' refers to the study of birds. 'Gemology' is the science of gems.

32. Two-legged animals like dinosaurs, crocodiles, etc. are called 'bipedal'. Hence, option (A) is the correct answer. 'Bipartite' refers to something that involves two parties. A 'biller' is a person who makes out bills. 'Bismuth' is a grayish-white metallic element that is used in alloys and drugs.

33. The idiom means to feel very unhappy, especially because you want somebody/something you cannot have. Hence, option (A) is the correct answer.

34. 'Have egg all over your face' means to be made to look stupid. Hence, option (A) is the correct answer.

35. 'Grab the bull by the horns' means to face a difficult or dangerous situation directly and with courage. Hence, option (C) is the correct answer.

36. The correct spelling of the word is 'Mississippi'. Hence, option (B) is the correct answer.

37. Certain verbs like verbs of thinking, verbs of appearing, etc., are not used in continuous form due to their meaning. Here, the correct sentence will be 'Smriti and I think what you said yesterday was right.' Hence, part (B) is the correct answer.

38. The sentence is grammatically correct. The plural 'waters' is used when we refer to a specific body of water. In the sentence since we are referring to a specific water body, Yamuna, we will use waters. Hence, part (D) is the answer.

39. Two nouns joined by 'and' take a plural verb. However, two nouns joined by 'each' or 'every' take a singular verb. Therefore, 'were' in part (B) is incorrect. It should have been 'was'. Hence, part (B) is the correct answer.

40. The sentence means that the people of both the nations are separated by borders but united by religion and history. 'Across' means from one side to the other side of something. Hence, option (D) is the correct answer. Options (A), (B) and (C) will render the sentence redundant. 'Through' means by means of. 'By' is usually used after a passive verb, to show who or what does, creates or causes something. 'In' means at a point within an area or space.

41. 'Face up' means with the front part or surface facing upwards. Hence, option (A) is the correct answer. 'Put your face on' means to put on makeup, which will render the given sentence meaningless.

42. Option (A) is the correct answer. The blank needs to be filled in with an adjective that would describe the noun 'commercial'. The other forms of the word will make the sentence grammatically incorrect.

43. Option (A) is correct since present continuous tense is used for an action that is going on at the time of speaking. The given sentence is incorrect as it is in past continuous tense, option (B) is in past perfect continuous tense and option (C) is in future continuous tense.

44. In case of wishful thinking, we use the past tense. Conditional expressions require that we use 'were' where we would otherwise have used another form of the verb 'be'. Only option (B) fulfills both the criteria and hence, is the correct answer.

45. 'Price' is singular. Therefore, 'are' should be substituted by 'is'. Words like jeans, scissors, pants, etc. are regarded as plural unless they are preceded by the phrase 'pair of'. Therefore, the correct phrase is 'these jeans'. Hence, option (B) is the correct answer.

46. Refer to the third sentence of the passage where the author says that good forces are inclined to travel in meandering lines. The other options are out of scope.

47. "Abundance" in the context of the passage means "plenty."

48. The author states that parents often plant a sapling in the garden when a child is born. They believe that the plant's growth will be closely associated with the growth of the child.

49. The very first sentence of the passage mentions that Japanese are "philosophical." Furthermore, their beliefs that good forces travel in meandering lines or a sapling is planted to coincide with the growth of a child are instances of philosophical perceptions. The author does not mention that the Japanese are superstitious and moreover, the word "superstitious" has a negative bearing. In the passage, the Japanese are never portrayed in a negative light. Additionally, we do not come across any reference – implicit or explicit that the Japanese are lovers of numerology or nature.

50. In the second sentence of the passage, the author talks about the use of "curving pathways."

51. $\because \left(\dfrac{4}{9}\right)^3 \left(\dfrac{3}{2}\right)^{-16} = \left(\dfrac{2}{3}\right)^6 \left(\dfrac{2}{3}\right)^{16} = \left(\dfrac{2}{3}\right)^{22}$

$\Rightarrow \left(\dfrac{2}{3}\right)^{22} = \left(\dfrac{2}{3}\right)^{2x}$

$\therefore x = 11.$

52. $x^2 + y^2 + z^2 + \dfrac{7}{2} = x - 2z - 3y$

$\Rightarrow \left(x^2 + \dfrac{1}{4} - x\right) + \left(y^2 + \dfrac{9}{4} + 3y\right) + (z^2 + 1 + 2z) = 0$

$\Rightarrow \left(x - \dfrac{1}{2}\right)^2 + \left(y + \dfrac{3}{2}\right)^2 + (z+1)^2 = 0$

$x = \dfrac{1}{2}, y = -\dfrac{3}{2}$ and $z = -1$

$\therefore 2x - 4y + 3z$

$= 2 \times \dfrac{1}{2} - 4 \times \left(-\dfrac{3}{2}\right) + 3(-1)$

$= 1 + 6 - 3 = 4.$

53. 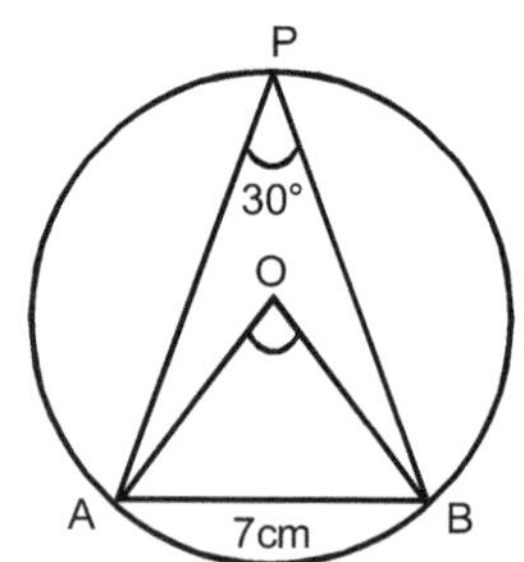

Let the chord of a circle be AB and center of a circle be O.

$\therefore \angle APB = 30°$

$\Rightarrow \angle AOB = 2 \times \angle APB = 60°$

Now, in $\triangle AOB$,

OA = OB {Radii of the circle}

$\Rightarrow \triangle AOB$ is an equilateral triangle.

$\therefore OA = OB = AB$

Hence, diameter of the circle = 14 cm.

54. 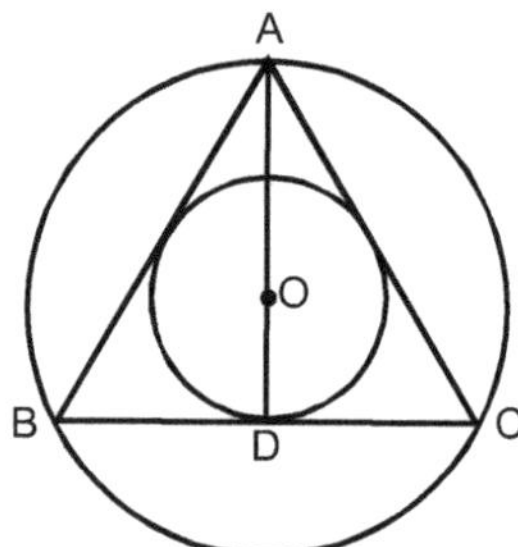

Let the side of an equilateral triangle be 'a' units.

Inradius = OD and circumradius = OA

In an equilateral triangle, the incentre is the point of intersection of medians of the triangle.

$\therefore \dfrac{OD}{OA} = \dfrac{1}{2}.$

55. $\sin^2 \theta + \cos^2 \theta + \sec^2 \theta + \cot^2 \theta + \tan^2 \theta + \text{cosec}^2 \theta$

$= 1 + 1 + 1 + 2(\tan^2 \theta + \cot^2 \theta)$

($\because$ Minimum value of $\tan^2 \theta + \cot^2 \theta = 2$)

$= 3 + 2 \times 2 = 7.$

56. 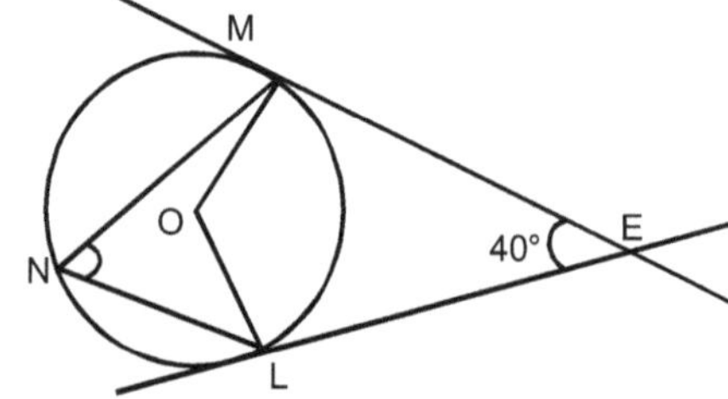

In quadrilateral MELO,

$\angle MOL + \angle OLE + \angle LEM + \angle EMO = 360°$

$\angle MOL = 140° (\because \angle OLE = \angle EMO = 90°)$

$\Rightarrow \angle LNM = 70°$ ($\because$ Angle made by arc at the center is double the angle made by same arc on the circle.)

57.

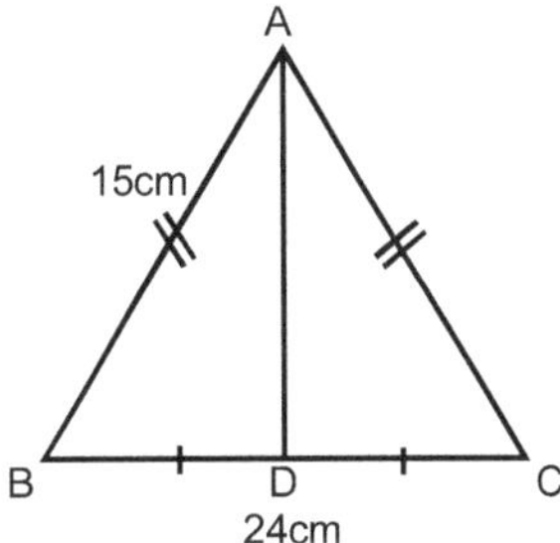

In $\triangle ABC$, let $\angle ABC = \angle ACB = x$ (As AB = AC)

$\Rightarrow \angle ACD = 180° - x$ (Linear pair)

As, $2\angle BAC = \angle ACD$

$\Rightarrow 2(180° - 2x) = 180° - x \Rightarrow x = 60°$

Hence, $\angle BAC = 60°$.

58. Let the speed of the boat in still water be 'x' km/hr and speed of stream be 'y' km/hr.

Time taken during upstream = $\dfrac{15}{x - y} = 5$

$\Rightarrow x - y = 3$ ...(i)

Time taken during downstream = $\dfrac{15}{x + y} = 3$

$\Rightarrow x + y = 5$ ...(ii)

From (i) and (ii), we get

x = 4 and y = 1

Hence, speed of the boat in still water is 4 km/hr.

59. We have, $\cos^2 1° + \cos^2 2° + \cos^2 3° + ... +$

$\cos^2 45° + \sin^2 44° + \sin^2 43° + ... + \sin^2 2° + \sin^2 1°$

$\because \cos(90° - \theta) = \sin\theta$ and $\sin(90° - \theta) = \cos\theta$

$= (\cos^2 1° + \sin^2 1°) + (\cos^2 2° + \sin^2 2°) + ... +$
$\qquad (\cos^2 44° + \sin^2 44°) + \cos^2 45°$

$= 1 + 1 + 1 + ... 44$ times $+ \dfrac{1}{2} = 44.5$.

60. $\tan\theta + \dfrac{1}{\tan\theta} = 3$

Squaring both sides, we get

$\tan^2\theta + \dfrac{1}{\tan^2\theta} = 7$

Cubing both sides, we get

$\tan^6\theta + \dfrac{1}{\tan^6\theta} = 322$

Hence, $\tan^6\theta + \cot^6\theta = 322$.

61. Selling price after successive discounts of 20%, 10%, 5% on Titan watch = 0.8 × 0.9 × 0.95 × 1500 = ₹1,026

Selling price after successive discounts of 20%, 20%, 10% on Ajanta watch = 0.8 × 0.8 × 0.9 × 2000 = ₹1,152

Hence, difference between selling price
$\qquad = 1152 - 1026 = ₹126$.

62. $\because \pi$ radian = 180°

$\Rightarrow 2$ radian $= \dfrac{180° \times 7 \times 2}{22} = 114\dfrac{6}{11}$

$\approx 114°32'44"$ {where 1° = 60' and 1' = 60"}.

63. Putting n = 2, we get, $\dfrac{a + b}{2}$, which is arithmetic mean of a and b.

64.

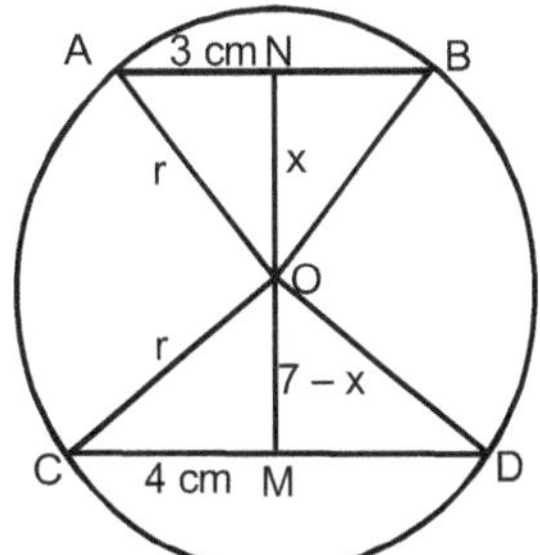

As AD is the median, BD = CD = 12 cm and $\angle ADB = 90°$

$\Rightarrow \triangle ABD$ is a right angled triangle.

$AD^2 + BD^2 = AB^2$

$\Rightarrow AD^2 = 15^2 - 12^2$

$\Rightarrow AD = 9$ cm.

65. Let the sum of money be ₹x.

Since $A = P\left(1 + \dfrac{\frac{r}{2}}{100}\right)^{2n}$

{$\because$ Interest compounded semi-annually}

$\therefore 19683 = x\left(1 + \dfrac{8}{100}\right)^3$

$\Rightarrow x = \dfrac{19683 \times 25 \times 25 \times 25}{27 \times 27 \times 27} = 15625$

$\therefore$ Interest = 19683 − 15625 = ₹4,058.

66.

Let M and N be the midpoints of chords AB and CD respectively.

Here, MN = 7 cm,

Let ON be 'x' cm, then OM = (7 − x) cm and 'r' be the radius of the circle.

Then, $r^2 = 3^2 + x^2$ ...(i)

And $r^2 = 4^2 + (7 - x)^2$ ...(ii)

Solving (i) and (ii), we get

$\quad$ r = 5 cm and x = 4 cm

$\Rightarrow$ Area of $\triangle$ABO + area of $\triangle$CDO $= \dfrac{1}{2} \times 6 \times 4 + \dfrac{1}{2} \times 8 \times 3$

$\quad = 24$ cm^2.

67. $x + \dfrac{1}{x+2} = 0$

$\Rightarrow x^2 + 2x + 1 = 0$

$\Rightarrow (x + 1)^2 = 0$

$\Rightarrow x = -1$

Then,

$x^2 + \dfrac{1}{x^6} = (-1)^2 + \dfrac{1}{(-1)^6} = 2.$

68. Let D's salary be ₹x.

Then, B's salary = ₹0.85x

and A's salary = 1.2 × 0.85x = ₹1.02x

∴ A's salary in comparison to D's salary is

$\quad = \dfrac{1.02x - x}{x} \times 100 = 2\%$ more.

69. $x + \dfrac{1}{x} = 3$

Squaring both sides, we get

$\Rightarrow x^2 + \dfrac{1}{x^2} = 7$ ...(i)

Cubing both sides, we get

$\Rightarrow x^6 + \dfrac{1}{x^6} = 322$ ...(ii)

Adding (i) and (ii), we get

$x^2 + x^{-2} + x^6 + x^{-6} = 7 + 322 = 329.$

70.

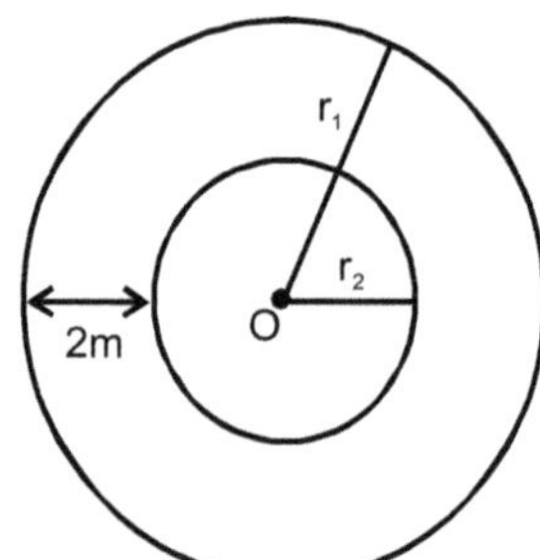

Let the radius of outer circle be 'r_1' m and radius of inner circle be 'r_2' m.

Now, $\pi r_1^2 - \pi r_2^2 = 36\pi$

$\Rightarrow r_1^2 - r_2^2 = 36$ ...(i)

And, $r_1 - r_2 = 2$ ...(ii)

Solving (i) and (ii), we get

$r_1 + r_2 = 18$ ...(iii)

Solving (ii) and (iii), we get

$r_1 = 10$

Hence, radius of outer circle = 10 m.

71.

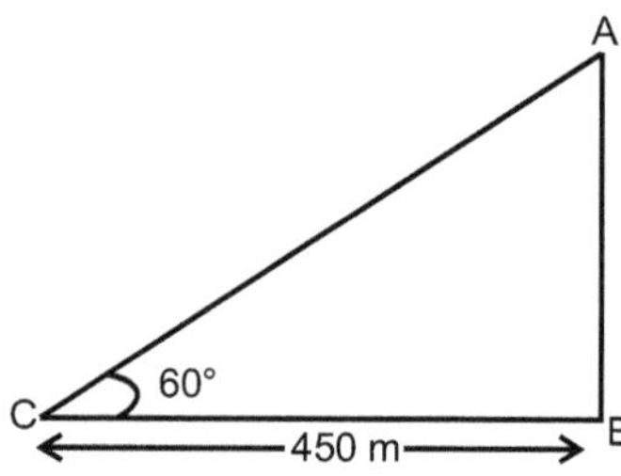

Let AB be the pole and C be the point 450 m away from the pole. Then,

$\tan 60° = \dfrac{AB}{BC} = \dfrac{AB}{450} \Rightarrow AB = 450\sqrt{3}$ m.

72. Let the total work done by a worker in 1 day be 1 unit and the total work be x units, then the work done by 60 workers in 75 days = 60 × 75 = 4500 units

Then, $\dfrac{4x}{5} = 4500 \Rightarrow x = 5625$

Total number of workers needed in last 15 days

$\quad = \dfrac{5625 - 4500}{15} = 75$

Hence, the number of extra employees = 75 − 60 = 15.

73. Difference between the angle made by Thunder and Manila

= 75° − 45° = 30° and angle made by Force = 90°.

As, 90° ≡ 20250

∴ 30° $\equiv \dfrac{90°}{3} \equiv \dfrac{20250}{3} \equiv 6750.$

74. Angle made by Force = 90° and angle made by Thunder = 75°.

∴ Required ratio = 90° : 75° = 6 : 5.

75. Angle made by Force = 90° and 90° ≡ 20250

Angle made by total number of motorcycles sold = 360° = 90° × 4

∴ Total number of motorcycles sold = 20250 × 4 = 81000.

■■

GENERAL INTELLIGENCE

Directions: In question no. 1 to 3, select the related word/letters/number from the given alternatives.

1. RDN : PBL : : NOS : ?

(a) LNQ   (b) KMR

(c) LMQ   (d) JNR

2. 15 : 225 : : 24 : ?

(a) 360   (b) 496

(c) 486   (d) 676

3. Tasty : Tastiness : : ?

(a) Vanturesome : Venturesomely

(b) Corrode : Corrodible

(c) Bureaucratic : Bureaucracy

(d) Hazard : Hazardous

Directions: In question nos. 4 and 5, find the odd word /number/letters from the given alternatives.

4. (a) SVY   (b) EMU

(c) KQW   (d) IMS

5. (a) SUXB   (b) NPSV

(c) LNQU   (d) DFIM

6. Which one of the given options would be a meaningful order of the following?

(i) Colour   (ii) Hang

(iii) Sketch   (iv) Frame

(a) (i), (iii), (iv), (ii)   (b) (iii), (i), (ii), (iv)

(c) (iii), (i), (iv), (ii)   (d) (iv), (iii), (i), (ii)

Directions: In question nos. 7 to 10, a series is given, with one term missing. Choose the correct alternative from the given ones.

7.

5	14	21
3	4	2
5	6	7
20	62	?

(a) 48   (b) 49

(c) 52   (d) 64

8. T, O, K, H, ?.

(a) E   (b) F

(c) G   (d) C

9. 14, 25, 51, 92, ?.

(a) 150   (b) 152

(c) 148   (d) 154

10.

49	36	64
81	121	144
16	17	?

(a) 19   (b) 20

(c) 22   (d) 21

11. A boy travels 26 km due South, then travels 18 km due East and further travels 2 km due North. How far is he from the starting point?

(a) 30 km   (b) 46 km

(c) 40 km   (d) 42 km

12. A is shorter than B. B is not as tall as C. A is not as short as D. Who is the tallest among them?

(a) C   (b) D

(c) B   (d) A

13. From the given alternatives, select the word which cannot be formed using the letters of the given word.

SARCASTIC

(a) CARATS   (b) CARCASS

(c) RACIST   (d) CROSS

14. If SLOT is written as TOLS, then KNOB will be written as

(a) BNOK   (b) BONK

(c) NOKB   (d) BKON

15. There are 30 students in a class. In an exam, 20 students passed in English. None of the students were there who did not pass in English or Hindi. Twelve students passed in Hindi. How many students were there who passed in both English and Hindi?

(a) 2   (b) 8

(c) 4   (d) 6

16. Which of the following interchange of sign would make the given equation **correct**?

$$12 + 6 - 3 \times 42 \div 7 = 89$$

(a) + and ×   (b) + and ÷

(c) ÷ and −   (d) − and ×

17. If '−' stands for addition, '÷' for multiplication, '×' for subtraction, and '+' for division, then which of the following is **correct**?

(a) $42 + 7 - 3 \div 8 \times 6 = 26$

(b) $36 + 9 - 5 \div 3 \times 2 = 17$

(c) $12 + 91 \div 7 - 6 \times 3 = 7$

(d) $31 - 12 \div 3 + 4 \times 7 = 55$

18. Shyam drove 12 km Northward from his office, then turned right and drove 6 km, again turned right and drove 6 km, finally turned left and drove 2 km. How many km will he have driven to reach home without taking any turn?

(a) 6 km
(b) 8 km
(c) 10 km
(d) 12 km

Directions: In the following question two statements are given followed by two conclusions I and II. You have to consider the statements to be true, even if they seem at variance from commonly known facts. You have to decide which of the given conclusions, if any, follow from the given statements.

19. Statement I: ABC Ltd, a subsidiary of XYZ Ltd, provides transportation facility to its employees.

Statement II: XYZ Ltd has a right to revoke the facility whenever it wishes to.

Conclusion I: XYZ Ltd gave ABC Ltd a right to provide transportation facility to its employees.

Conclusion II: XYZ Ltd did not assure transportation facility to ABC Ltd's employees.

(a) Only conclusion I follows
(b) Only conclusion II follows
(c) Both conclusions I and II follow
(d) Neither conclusion I nor conclusion II follows

20. Four positions of dice are given below. Which number will be opposite to 3?

(a) 1
(b) 4
(c) 5
(d) 6

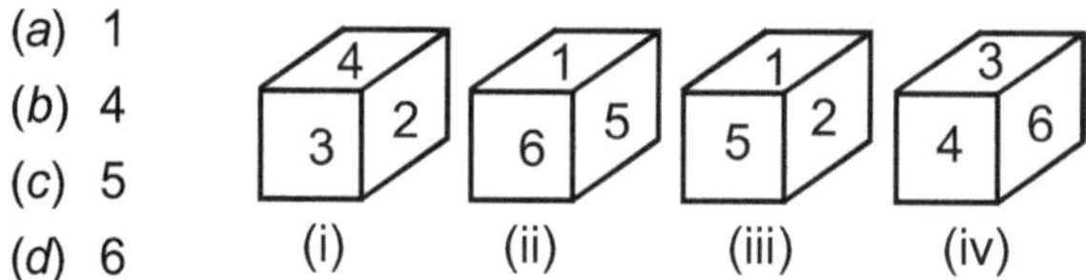

(i)   (ii)   (iii)   (iv)

21. In the given figure, circle represents persons who like Green color, triangle represents persons who like Red color, and square represents persons who like Blue color. Find the region where the persons like Blue and Red color but not Green?

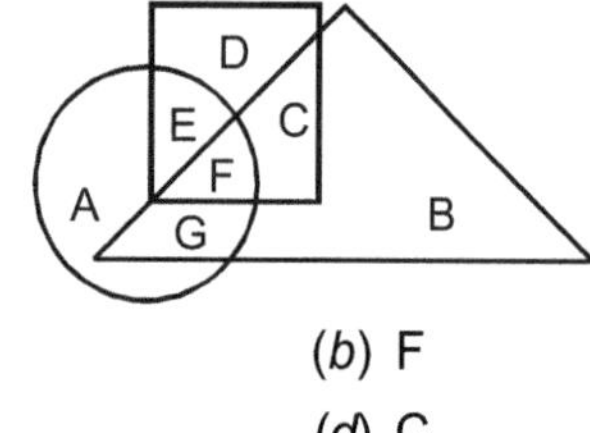

(a) E
(b) F
(c) G
(d) C

Directions: In question no. 22, study the following diagram carefully and answer the questions based on it.

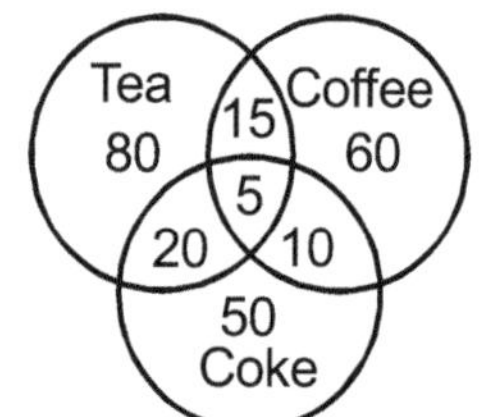

22. The diagram shows the survey of 250 students of the class with reference to their liking of Tea, Coffee and Coke. How many of them do not like any of the drinks?

(a) 5
(b) 20
(c) 10
(d) 15

Directions: In the following question which answer figure will complete the pattern in the question figure?

23. Question Figure:

Answer Figures:

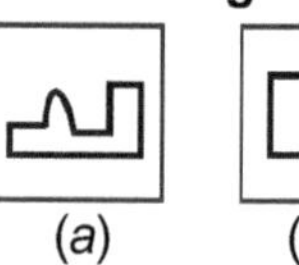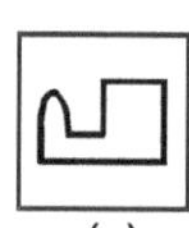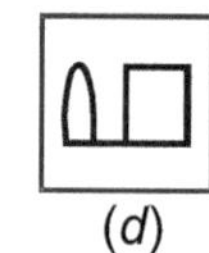

(a)   (b)   (c)   (d)

24. A word is represented by only one set of numbers as given in any one of the alternatives. The sets of numbers given in the alternatives are represented by two classes of alphabets as in two matrices given below. The columns and rows of Matrix I are numbered from 1 to 4 and that of Matrix II are numbered from 6 to 9. A letter from these matrices can be represented first by its row and next by its column, e.g. 'N' can be represented by 23, 87 etc. And 'Q' can be represented by 33, 88 etc. Similarly, you have to identify the set for the word 'SONAR'

Matrix – I				
	1	2	3	4
1	S	L	O	S
2	Q	M	N	R
3	N	T	Q	B
4	R	B	A	A

Matrix – II				
	6	7	8	9
6	Q	B	S	A
7	S	P	R	B
8	T	N	Q	M
9	B	A	O	P

(a) 14, 98, 23, 68, 78
(b) 14, 13, 87, 69, 79
(c) 76, 98, 31, 69, 24
(d) 76, 13, 24, 68, 78

25. If a mirror is placed on the line XY, then which of the answer figures is the right image of the given figure?

Question Figure:

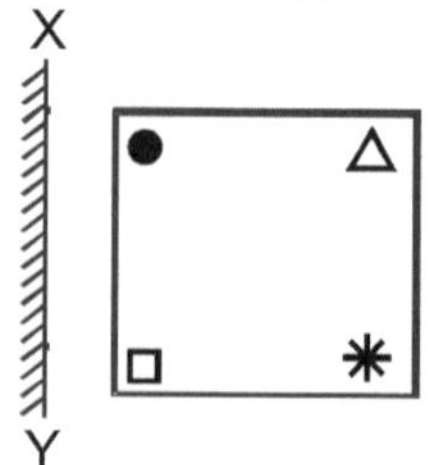

Answers Figures:

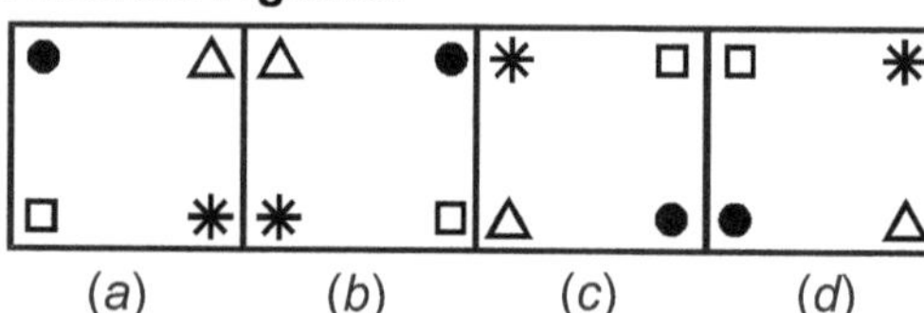

(a)   (b)   (c)   (d)

ENGLISH LANGUAGE

Directions: In the following question out of the four alternatives, choose the one which best expresses the meaning of the given word and mark it in the answer sheet.

26. Prolific

(a) Lush   (b) Efficient

(c) Scanty   (d) Hollow

27. Abysmal

(a) Shamless   (b) Dangerous

(c) Arazen   (d) Awful

Directions: In question nos. **28** to **29**, choose the word opposite in meaning to the given word and mark it in the answer sheet.

28. Privy

(a) Private   (b) Common

(c) Enthusiastic   (d) Crazy

29. Sovereign

(a) Absolute   (b) Limited

(c) Independent   (d) Paramount

Directions: In question nos. **30** to **32**, out of the four alternatives, choose the one which can be substituted for the given words/sentences.

30. Tasting good

(a) Fruitful   (b) Gluttonous

(c) Tempting   (d) Toothsome

31. A person who is hard to manage or control

(a) Factious

(b) Ruly

(c) Fractious

(d) Tractable

32. Uncontrollable craving for alcohol

(a) Pyromania

(b) Dipsomania

(c) Hypomania

(d) Megalomania

Directions: In question nos. **33** and **35**, four alternatives are given for the idiom/phrase underlined in the sentence. Choose the alternative which best expresses the meaning of the given idiom/phrase.

33. While other businesses are shutting down due to recession, pharmaceutical companies are <u>sitting pretty</u> with high profits.

(a) to be in an excellent situation

(b) to be in an advantageous position

(c) to be at the top

(d) to be in an unexpected state

34. The rescue team's arrival was like <u>manna from heaven</u> for the hostages.

(a) a person who needs help

(b) something that seems problematic at first but turns out to be good

(c) a way out

(d) unexpected help or aid

35. I <u>bent over backwards</u> to help her get out of the mess she was in.

(a) went out of my way

(b) devised a simpler plan

(c) gave her some money

(d) figured a laborious way

Direction: In the following question four words are given in question, out of which only one word is spelt correctly. Find the correctly spelt word and mark your answer in the answer sheet.

36. (a) Confete   (b) Confeti

(c) Confetti   (d) Confette

Directions: In question nos. **37** and **39**, some parts of the sentences have errors and some are correct. Find out which part of the sentence has an error and mark the answer corresponding to the appropriate letter (A,B,C). If a sentence is free from error, mark your answer as (d).

37. Army nurses travels from hospital (a) / to hospital, providing humane and efficient (b) / care for wounded, sick and dying soldiers. (c) / No error (d)

38. Neither does Prashant (a) / speak English nor do (b) / Pulkit speak French. (c) / No error (d)

39. "What kind of a car (a) / would you like to buy?", (b) / asked the car dealer. (c) / No error (d)

Directions: In question nos. **40** to **42**, sentences are given with blanks to be filled with an appropriate word(s). Four alternatives are suggested for each question. Choose the correct alternative out of the four.

40. No amount of populist pep talk can _______ the fact that Ulysses is a demanding book.

(a) obscure   (b) camouflage

(c) impersonate   (d) undrape

41. Charlemagne ______ on a mission to unite all Germanic peoples into one kingdom.

(a) plunged   (b) ceased

(c) embarked   (d) inaugurated

42. His eyes lighted ______ an insect that was lying in the shade of the peepal tree.

(a) down   (b) upon

(c) to   (d) by

Directions: In question nos. **43** to **45**, a sentence/ part of the sentence is underlined. Beneath each sentence four different ways of phrasing the underlined part are given. Choose the grammatically correct option. In case no improvement is needed, your answer should be option (*d*).

43. These poultries are fed almost entirely with potatoes boiled in steam.

   (*a*) poultry are fed

   (*b*) poultry are feeded

   (*c*) poultries are being fed

   (*d*) No improvement

44. Adolf Dassler didn't view the Berlin Games as a automobile for Nazi propaganda but as a chance to launch his humble athletic shoe business.

   (*a*) a bucket of bolts   (*b*) an automobile

   (*c*) a vehicle   (*d*) No improvement

45. In summers, people tend to buy less jackets.

   (*a*) fewer   (*b*) little

   (*c*) lesser   (*d*) No improvement

Directions: IIn question nos. **46** to **50**, you have given a passages with 5 questions. Read the passage and choose the best answer to each question.

A recent investigation by scientists at the university of geological survey shows that strange animal behaviour might help to predict future earthquakes. Investigators found such occurrences in a ten kilometre radius of the epicentre of a fairly recent earthquake. Some birds screeched and flew about wildly, dogs yelped and ran uncontrollably. Scientists believe that animals can perceive these environmental changes as early as several days before mishap.

In 1976, after observing the animal behaviour, the Chinese were able to predict a devastating earthquake. Although hundreds of thousands of people were killed, the government was able to evacuate millions of others thus keeping the death toll at a lower level.

46. If scientists can accurately predict earthquake there will be

   (*a*) fewer animals going crazy

   (*b*) a lower death rate

   (*c*) fewer people evacuated

   (*d*) fewer environmental changes

47. What prediction may be made by observing animal behaviour?

   (*a*) an impending earthquake

   (*b*) the number of people who will die

   (*c*) the ten kilometre radius of epicentre

   (*d*) ecological conditions

48. How can animal perceive these changes when humans cannot?

   (*a*) animals are smarter than humans

   (*b*) animals have certain instincts that humans don't possess

   (*c*) by running around they can feel the vibration

   (*d*) humans don't know where to look

49. Which of the following is NOT true?

   (*a*) some animals may sense approaching earthquake

   (*b*) observing animals, scientists can predict earthquake

   (*c*) the Chinese failed to predict earthquake

   (*d*) animals went wild before earthquake.

50. In this passage the word "evacuate" means

   (*a*) Remove   (*b*) Exile

   (*c*) Destroy   (*d*) Expel

QUANTITATIVE APTITUDE

51. If the total surface area of a right circular cone is 24π cm^2 and slant height of the cone is 5 cm, then the radius of the base of the cone is

   (*a*) 3 cm   (*b*) 4 cm

   (*c*) 5 cm   (*d*) $3\sqrt{3}$ cm

52. Evaluate: $(324)^{0.33} \times (324)^{0.17}$

   (*a*) 162   (*b*) 18

   (*c*) 9   (*d*) 324.50

53. A, B and C can do a piece of work in 15, 10 and 30 days respectively. In how many days can B do the work if he is assisted by C and A on every third day?

   (*a*) 24 days   (*b*) 18 days

   (*c*) 12 days   (*d*) 8 days

54. Divide ₹4,500 among A, B and C in the ratio $\dfrac{1}{3}:\dfrac{3}{4}:\dfrac{1}{6}.$

   (*a*) ₹800, ₹2,400, ₹900   (*b*) ₹900, ₹2,400, ₹600

   (*c*) ₹1,200, ₹2,700, ₹800 (*d*) ₹1,200, ₹2,700, ₹600

55. How much percent more than the cost price should a shopkeeper mark his goods so that after allowing a discount of 20% on the marked price, he gains 12%?

   (*a*) 32%   (*b*) 44%

   (*c*) 64%   (*d*) 40%

56. A person sells his bicycle at a discount of 20%. If the marked price is ₹625, then the selling price should be

   (*a*) ₹600   (*b*) ₹500

   (*c*) ₹450   (*d*) ₹400

57. A certain sum of money will be tripled in 18 years at the rate of simple interest per annum of

(a) $10\dfrac{1}{9}\%$ (b) 12%

(c) $11\dfrac{1}{9}\%$ (d) 6%

58. Average age of a family that consists of 8 members is 34 years. The youngest member of the family is 6 years old and the second youngest member is 10 years old. The average age of the family one year after the birth of the second youngest member was

(a) 27 years   (b) 29 years

(c) 31 years   (d) 32 years

59. In a class, 30% students will take Science in next class, 80% of remaining will take Commerce in next class and remaining 21 students will take Social Science in next class. Then the number of students in the class is

(a) 120   (b) 150

(c) 180   (d) 210

60. A person can row 10 km upstream in 20 minutes and 20 km downstream in 10 minutes. What is the speed of the stream?

(a) 30 km/hr   (b) 45 km/hr

(c) 60 km/hr   (d) 75 km/hr

61. In triangle ABC, $\angle CAB = 60°$, $\angle ABC = 30°$ and line BC is produced to D. If $\angle ACD = 3x°$, then $\dfrac{2x}{3}\%$ of 80° is

(a) 16°   (b) 20°

(c) 40°   (d) 90°

62. If $x = 2 - \sqrt{3}$, the value of $\left(x - \dfrac{1}{x}\right)^2$ is

(a) 12   (b) 16

(c) $10\sqrt{3}$ (d) $5\sqrt{3}$

63. If $x + \dfrac{3}{x} = 49$, then the value of $\dfrac{150x}{3x^2 + 78x + 9}$ is

(a) $\dfrac{5}{3}$

(b) $\dfrac{5}{9}$

(c) $\dfrac{2}{3}$

(d) $\dfrac{10}{9}$

64. If $a - (1 - b) = -(1 + c)$, then $\begin{pmatrix} \dfrac{2a}{b} & \dfrac{2b}{c} & \dfrac{2c}{a} \\ \dfrac{b}{c} & \dfrac{c}{a} & \dfrac{a}{b} \\ \dfrac{c}{a} & \dfrac{a}{b} & \dfrac{b}{c} \end{pmatrix}$ is

(a) 0   (b) 2

(c) 3   (d) 6

65. At a particular time on a sunny day in Delhi, the length of the shadow of a man is $\dfrac{1}{\sqrt{3}}$ times of his height. The angle of elevation of the sun at that moment is

(a) 60°   (b) 30°

(c) 90°   (d) 45°

66. If the diameter of the two circles are 6 cm and 10 cm and the length of the transverse common tangent is 6 cm, then the distance between the two centres is

(a) $6\sqrt{2}$ cm $5\sqrt{2}$ (b) cm

(c) 8 cm   (d) 10 cm

67. The circumcentre of $\triangle ABC$ is O. If $\angle CAB = 75°$ and $\angle CBA = 65°$, then $\angle CAO = ?$

(a) 25°   (b) 30°

(c) 35°   (d) 45°

68. Two circles with centres O_1 and O_2 have radii 8 cm and 5 cm respectively with $O_1O_2 = 15$ cm. A third circle with centre O_3 and radius r cm touches both the circles externally. If $\angle O_1O_3O_2 = 90°$, then find r.

(a) 2 cm   (b) 4 cm

(c) 5 cm   (d) 9 cm

69. Ratio of two angles of an isosceles triangle is 4 : 7 and the unequal angle is less than the equal angles. The difference between equal angle and unequal angle is

(a) 30°   (b) 40°

(c) 50°   (d) 70°

70. The numerical value of
$$\dfrac{1}{\sec^2\theta} + \dfrac{2}{1+\tan^2\theta} + \dfrac{3}{1+\cot^2\theta}$$ will be

(a) 0   (b) 1

(c) 3   (d) 6

71. The value of $\dfrac{5}{\csc^2\theta} + \dfrac{3}{1+\tan^2\theta} + 2\cos^2\theta$ is

(a) 2   (b) 3

(c) 4   (d) 5

Directions: Study the bar graph carefully and answer the question nos. **72 – 75.**

The bar graph shows the birth rate of 7 states of a country.

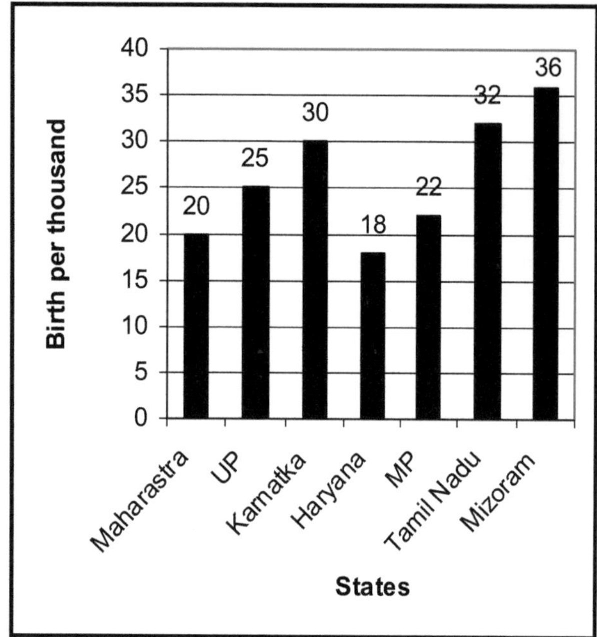

72. Birth rate of how many states are atleast 25% more than that of UP?

(a) 0　　　　　　　(b) 1

(c) 2　　　　　　　(d) More than 2

73. Birth rate of MP is what percent that of Tamil Nadu?

(a) 34.45　　　　　(b) 52.25

(c) 68.75　　　　　(d) 76.50

74. Birth rate of Karnatka is what times that of Haryana?

(a) 2　　　　　　　(b) 1.33

(c) 1.67　　　　　(d) 2.5

75. Approximate average birth rate of given 7 states is

(a) 26　　　　　　(b) 28

(c) 32　　　　　　(d) 34

GENERAL AWARENESS

76. Who has been awarded with Japan's Second Highest national award for his contribution towards Indo-Japan economic relations?

(a) PK Singh　　　(b) AK Singh

(c) NK Singh　　　(d) CK Singh

77. Labour demand refers to

(a) number of hours of hiring that an employer is willing

(b) increase in the demand of labour in the market

(c) decrease in the labour during peak period

(d) None of these

78. Special purpose entity is

(a) A legal entity

(b) A loan given to bank employees

(c) Low interest rate subsidy

(d) None of these

79. Name the mobile app for iOS and Windows Phone platforms launched by Ministry of External Affairs.

(a) mPort Seva　　　(b) myPassport Seva

(c) mPassport Seva　(d) mPass Seva

80. Niccole Machiavelli was a citizen of

(a) Italy　　　　　(b) Spain

(c) Greece　　　　(d) Russia

81. Recently which unit of Kudankulam Nuclear Power Plant dedicated to nation?

(a) Unit 2　　　　(b) Unit 1

(c) Unit 3　　　　(d) Unit 4

82. Which of the following diseases is related to immune system?

(a) AIDS/HIV　　　(b) Asthma

(c) Both (a) and (b)　(d) Cirrhosis

83. Seismometers are used for measuring

(a) Cyclone　　　　(b) Earthquakes

(c) Volcanic eruption　(d) Floods

84. Hudson Bay is located in

(a) North America　(b) South America

(c) Canada　　　　(d) Alaska

85. Khasis is the major tribal group of

(a) Jammu and Kashmir　(b) Meghalaya

(c) Manipur　　　　(d) Mizoram

86. Enzyme Rubisco is associated with the process of

(a) Urine formation　(b) Bile formation

(c) Photorespiration　(d) All of the above

87. Which of the following is the hardest part of human body?

(a) Teeth Enamel　(b) Bones

(c) Cartilage　　　(d) Muscles

88. Which of the following is a part of compound stomach?

(a) Omasum　　　(b) Abomasums

(c) Ileum　　　　(d) Both (a) and (b)

89. Magnetic declination is the

(a) Angle between the compass north and the true north

(b) Angle between the compass north and the true south

(c) Angle between the compass north and the compass south

(d) Angle between the compass south and the true north

90. Which of the following process is responsible for stars formation?

(*a*) Fusion

(*b*) Fission

(*c*) Thermodynamic reaction

(*d*) Exothermic reaction

91. French Open takes place at

(*a*) Lyon   (*b*) Marseille

(*c*) Roland Garros   (*d*) Bordeaux

92. Which of the following is not a colloid?

(*a*) Milk   (*b*) Blood

(*c*) Mist   (*d*) Water

93. Which of the following is a source of vitamin D?

(*a*) Sunlight   (*b*) Air

(*c*) Water   (*d*) None of the above

94. Which of the following is a waste management technique?

(*a*) Bioremediation   (*b*) Eutrophication

(*c*) Ozonolysis   (*d*) Biomagnification

95. Which of the following is not an example of frameshift mutation diseases?

(*a*) Tay Sachs   (*b*) Cystic fibrosis

(*c*) Thalessimia   (*d*) None of these

96. Where was the first Cricket World Cup organised?

(*a*) Australia   (*b*) India

(*c*) Melbourne   (*d*) England

97. Who was the first recipient of Jnanpith award?

(*a*) G Sankara Kurup

(*b*) Tarasankar Bandyopadhyay

(*c*) Kuppali Venkatappagowda Puttappa

(*d*) Umashankar Joshi

98. Which of the following river is wrongly matched with its city?

(*a*) Tirana   :   Bonn

(*b*) Danube   :   Belgrade

(*c*) Seine   :   Paris

(*d*) Perlovska   :   Sofia

99. When was the first Law Commission established in India?

(*a*) 1834   (*b*) 1839

(*c*) 1843   (*d*) 1853

100. Railway Ministry to set up two new Directorates and dialing service for Cancelling Train Ticket. What is the dialing service No.

(*a*) 109   (*b*) 129

(*c*) 138   (*d*) 139

ANSWERS

1. (*c*)	**2.** (*a*)	**3.** (*c*)	**4.** (*d*)	**5.** (*b*)	**6.** (*c*)	**7.** (*b*)	**8.** (*b*)	**9.** (*c*)	**10.** (*b*)
11. (*a*)	**12.** (*a*)	**13.** (*d*)	**14.** (*b*)	**15.** (*a*)	**16.** (*c*)	**17.** (*b*)	**18.** (*c*)	**19.** (*a*)	**20.** (*c*)
21. (*d*)	**22.** (*c*)	**23.** (*c*)	**24.** (*c*)	**25.** (*b*)	**26.** (*a*)	**27.** (*d*)	**28.** (*b*)	**29.** (*b*)	**30.** (*d*)
31. (*c*)	**32.** (*b*)	**33.** (*a*)	**34.** (*d*)	**35.** (*a*)	**36.** (*c*)	**37.** (*a*)	**38.** (*b*)	**39.** (*a*)	**40.** (*b*)
41. (*c*)	**42.** (*b*)	**43.** (*a*)	**44.** (*c*)	**45.** (*a*)	**46.** (*b*)	**47.** (*a*)	**48.** (*b*)	**49.** (*c*)	**50.** (*a*)
51. (*a*)	**52.** (*b*)	**53.** (*d*)	**54.** (*d*)	**55.** (*d*)	**56.** (*b*)	**57.** (*c*)	**58.** (*b*)	**59.** (*b*)	**60.** (*b*)
61. (*a*)	**62.** (*a*)	**63.** (*c*)	**64.** (*d*)	**65.** (*a*)	**66.** (*d*)	**67.** (*a*)	**68.** (*b*)	**69.** (*a*)	**70.** (*c*)
71. (*d*)	**72.** (*c*)	**73.** (*c*)	**74.** (*c*)	**75.** (*a*)	**76.** (*c*)	**77.** (*a*)	**78.** (*a*)	**79.** (*c*)	**80.** (*a*)
81. (*b*)	**82.** (*a*)	**83.** (*b*)	**84.** (*c*)	**85.** (*b*)	**86.** (*c*)	**87.** (*a*)	**88.** (*d*)	**89.** (*a*)	**90.** (*a*)
91. (*c*)	**93.** (*d*)	**93.** (*a*)	**94.** (*a*)	**95.** (*c*)	**96.** (*d*)	**97.** (*a*)	**98.** (*a*)	**99.** (*a*)	**100.** (*d*)

EXPLANATIONS

1.

R   D   N
↓ –2   ↓ –2   ↓ –2
P   B   L

Similarly,

N   O   S
↓ –2   ↓ –2   ↓ –2
L   M   Q

2. $225 = 15 \times 15$

Similarly, $24 \times 15 = 360$.

3. The given analogy is in the form of adjective: noun. Option (C) is the correct answer since 'Bureaucratic' is an adjective while 'bureaucracy' is a noun. Options (A) and (D) are in the reverse order. Option (B) is in the form of verb : adjective.

4. $S \xrightarrow{+3} V \xrightarrow{+3} Y$

$E \xrightarrow{+8} M \xrightarrow{+8} U$

$K \xrightarrow{+6} Q \xrightarrow{+6} W$

$I \xrightarrow{+4} M \xrightarrow{+6} S$

Hence, IMS is odd-one.

5. $S \xrightarrow{+2} U \xrightarrow{+3} X \xrightarrow{+4} B$

$N \xrightarrow{+2} P \xrightarrow{+3} S \xrightarrow{+3} V$

$L \xrightarrow{+2} N \xrightarrow{+3} Q \xrightarrow{+4} U$

$D \xrightarrow{+2} F \xrightarrow{+3} I \xrightarrow{+4} M$

Hence, NPSV is odd-one.

6. The correct sequence is (iii), (i), (iv), (ii). First you sketch a portrait and then you colour it. Once it is complete, it is framed and hanged on a wall. Hence, option (C) is the correct answer.

7. Here, $20 = 5 \times 3 + 5$; $62 = 14 \times 4 + 6$

Similarly, $? = 21 \times 2 + 7 = 49$.

8. $T \xrightarrow{-5} O \xrightarrow{-4} K \xrightarrow{-3} H \xrightarrow{-2} \underline{F}$

9.

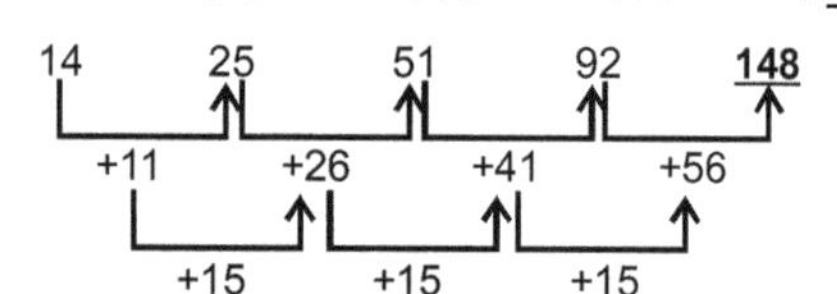

10. Here, $\sqrt{49} + \sqrt{81} = 16$, $\sqrt{36} + \sqrt{121} = 17$

Similarly, $? = \sqrt{64} + \sqrt{144} = 20$.

11.

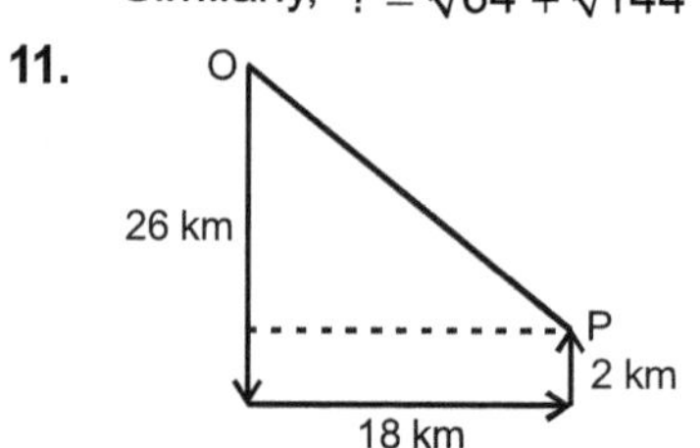

The boy travels a net distance of $(26 - 2) = 24$ km distance due South and 18 km due East. Hence, required distance from starting point,

$$OP = \sqrt{24^2 + 18^2} = 30 \text{ km}.$$

12. From the given information, we have A < B, B < C, A > D

Hence, C > B > A > D i.e., C is tallest among them.

13. The word 'CROSS' cannot be formed from the given word since the given word does not have the letter 'O'. Hence, option (D) is the correct answer.

14. $S \; L \; O \; T \xrightarrow{\text{Reverse order}} T \; O \; L \; S$

Similarly,

$K \; N \; O \; B \xrightarrow{\text{Reverse order}} B \; O \; N \; K$

15.

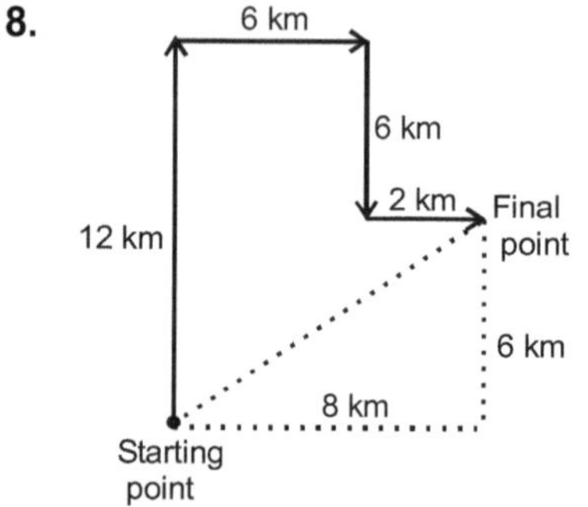

Required number of students = 20 + 12 – 30 = 2.

16. By interchanging the signs ÷ and –, we have,

$12 + 6 \div 3 \times 42 – 7 = 12 + 2 \times 42 – 7$
$= 12 + 84 – 7 = 89.$

17. In option (B), the given expression can be written as:

$36 \div 9 + 5 \times 3 – 2 = 4 + 15 – 2 = 17.$

18.

Required distance = $\sqrt{6^2 + 8^2} = 10$ km.

19. The statements say that transportation facility is provided by ABC Ltd and XYZ Ltd has a right to officially cancel that facility. This means that XYZ Ltd gave ABC Ltd a right to provide transportation facility to its employees. The statements do not say anything about XYZ Ltd giving assurance to the employees of ABC Ltd. Hence, option (A) is the correct answer.

20. From dice positions (i) and (iii), 3 is opposite to 5.

21. The region C represents persons who like Blue and Red color but not Green color.

22. Required number of students
    = 250 − (80 + 60 + 50 + 20 + 15 + 10 + 5)
    = 250 − 240 = 10.

24. S can be represented as, 11, 14, 68, **76**

    O can be represented as, 13, **98**

    N can be represented as, 23, **31**, 87

    A can be represented as, 43, 44, **69**, 97

    R can be represented as, **24**, 41, 78

    Hence, option (C) is correct.

26. 'Prolific' refers to something that produces a large amount of something. 'Lush' means having a lot of full and healthy growth or having a pleasingly rich quality. Hence, option (A) is the correct answer.

28. 'Privy' means private or belonging to one person. 'Common' means belonging to or shared by two or more people. Hence, option (B) is the correct answer.

29. 'Sovereign' means not limited. Hence, its antonym will be option (B), limited. Options (A), (C) and (D) are the synonyms of the word.

30. Something that tastes good is called 'toothsome'. Hence, option (D) is the correct answer. 'Fruitful' means producing many good results. 'Gluttonous' refers to a person who eats too much. 'Tempting' means attractive to an extent that people want to have it, do it, etc.

31. A person who is hard to manage or control is called 'fractious'. Hence, option (C) is the correct answer. 'Factious' is someone who is a part of a larger group and has different ideas and opinions than the rest of the group. 'Ruly' is someone who is obedient. Someone who can be easily managed or controlled is called 'tractable'.

32. 'Dipsomania' refers to the uncontrollable craving for alcoholic beverages. Hence, option (B) is the correct answer. 'Pyromania' is the mental illness that makes people have a strong desire to set things on fire. 'Hypomania' is a mild form of mania marked by elation and hyperactivity. 'Megalomania' is a strong feeling that you want to have more and more power.

33. 'Sitting pretty' means to be in a good situation, especially when others are not. Hence, option (A) is the correct answer.

34. 'Manna from heaven' means an unexpected help or comfort. Hence, option (D) is the correct answer.

35. 'Bend over backwards' means to work hard to accomplish something or to go out of one's way to do something for someone. Hence, option (A) is the correct answer.

36. The correct spelling is 'confetti'. It refers to the small pieces of brightly coloured paper that people throw at celebrations. Hence, option (C) is the correct answer.

37. 'Nurses' in part (A) is plural. Therefore, the verb should also be plural. 'Travels' is singular and should therefore, be replaced by its singular form, 'travel'. Hence, option (A) is the correct answer.

38. 'Does' is used when the subject is third person singular. For example: he does the work, she does the cooking everyday, etc. In other cases, 'do' is used. For example: Do you like cereal? Or Do I have to go there? In the given sentence, both 'Prashant' and 'Pulkit' is third person singular. Therefore, both will take 'does' and not 'do'. Hence, option (B) is the correct answer.

39. The error is in part (A). The correct phrase is "What kind of car". We use an article when we add an adjective to say that it belongs to a particular group. For example: If we add the word 'diesel' before 'car', then the use of article will be correct because then we will refer to a particular group of cars, i.e., diesel cars. Hence, option (A) is the correct answer.

40. The sentence means that no amount of encouraging speech can mask the fact that Ulysses is a demanding book. 'Camouflage' means to hide something by covering it up or making it harder to see. Hence, option (B) is the correct answer. 'Impersonate' means to pretend to be another person. 'Undrape' means to unveil. A fact that is already known to people cannot be undraped or unveiled. Same is the case with 'obscure', which means to make something difficult to understand or know.

41. The sentence means that Charlemagne set out for a mission to unite all peoples of Germany into one kingdom. 'Embark' means to begin a journey. Hence, option (C) is the correct answer. 'Ceased', 'plunged' and 'inaugurated' are incorrect since they do not take the preposition 'on'.

42. 'Light upon' means to find something by accident. Hence, option (B) is the correct answer.

43. Certain nouns like 'poultry', 'cattle', etc., though singular in form, are always used as plurals. Hence, option (A) is the correct answer. 'Feeded' is grammatically incorrect.

44. Option (C) is the correct answer. 'Vehicle for something' is used to express feelings or ideas as a way of achieving something. 'Bucket of bolts' refers to a piece of machinery that is not worth more than its scrap value.

45. 'Fewer' is used to refer to people or things in plural. 'Jackets' is plural. Hence, option (A) is the correct answer. 'Less' is used when something that cannot be counted is being referred to. 'Little' means small, which does not logically fit in the meaning of the sentence.

46. The author cites the earthquake of 1976 when the earthquake was predicted. The result was a lower death rate.

47. An impending earthquake can be predicted by observing animal behaviour. The author talks about the incident in China when an earthquake could be predicted by observing animal behaviour.

48. Refer to the last sentence of the first paragraph. Scientists believe that animals can perceive environmental changes even though humans don't.

49. The Chinese successfully predicted the earthquake. The author has mentioned this in the second paragraph. The other options are true.

50. In the passage, the word "evacuate" has been used to mean relocation of millions of people in China before the earthquake struck in 1976. The other options are out of scope in the passage.

51. Let 'r' be the radius of the right circular cone. Then, total surface area of the right circular cone = 24π

$$\Rightarrow \quad \pi r \times 5 + \pi r^2 = 24\pi$$
$$\Rightarrow \quad r(5 + r) = 24$$
$$\Rightarrow \quad r^2 + 5r - 24 = 0$$
$$\Rightarrow \quad r = 3 \text{ cm. (x cannot be negative)}$$

52. $(324)^{0.33} \times (324)^{0.17} = (324)^{0.33 + 0.17} = 0.5$
$$= (18)^{2 \times 0.5} = 18.$$

53. Let the total work be 30 (LCM of 15, 10 and 30) units. Then, in 1 day A, B and C do $\dfrac{30}{15} = 2$, $\dfrac{30}{10} = 3$

and $\dfrac{30}{30} = 1$ units respectively

Work done in first three days
$$= 3 \times 3 + (2 + 1) = 12 \text{ units}$$
Work done in first six days = 12 + 12 = 24 units
Remaining 6 units will be completed by B in 2 days
Hence, required number of days = 3 + 3 + 2 = 8.

54. Ratio of share of A, B and C = $\dfrac{1}{3} : \dfrac{3}{4} : \dfrac{1}{6} = 4 : 9 : 2$

$\therefore$ Share of A, B and C are $\dfrac{4}{4+9+2} \times 4500$

$$= ₹1,200, \quad \dfrac{9}{4+9+2} \times 4500$$
$$= ₹2,700$$

and $\dfrac{2}{4+9+2} \times 4500 = ₹600$ respectively.

55. Let the marked price be x% more than the cost price and let the cost price be ₹100. Then,

$$\text{Marked price} = 100\left(1 + \dfrac{x}{100}\right)$$
$$= ₹(100 + x)$$
$$\Rightarrow \quad (100 + x)\left(1 - \dfrac{20}{100}\right) = 112$$
$$\Rightarrow \quad 100 + x = 140$$
$$\Rightarrow \quad x = 40.$$

56. The selling price = 625 × 0.8 = ₹500.

57. Let the rate of interest be r% and the principal be ₹P. Then, the simple interest
$$= 3P - P = ₹2P$$
$$\therefore \quad 2P = \dfrac{P \times r \times 18}{100}$$
$$\Rightarrow \quad r = \dfrac{100}{9}$$
$$= 11\dfrac{1}{9}\%.$$

58. Sum of the ages of the family members
$$= 34 \times 8 = 272 \text{ years}$$
Age of the second youngest family member
$$= 10 \text{ years}$$
$\Rightarrow$ The number of family members one year after second youngest member's birth = 7

Sum of the ages of the family
$$= 272 - (9 \times 7) - (\text{age of the youngest member})$$
$$= 272 - 63 - 6 = 203$$

Average age = $\dfrac{203}{7} = 29$ years.

59. Let the total number of students in the class be x. Then,

$(x \times 0.7) \times 0.2 = 21$
$$\Rightarrow \quad 0.7x = 105$$
$$\Rightarrow \quad x = 150.$$

60. Let the speed of the boat in still water be x km/hr and the speed of the stream be y km/hr. Then,

$$(x - y) \times \frac{20}{60} = 10 \qquad \ldots(i)$$

$$(x + y) \times \frac{10}{60} = 20 \qquad \ldots(ii)$$

On solving (i) and (ii), we get

y = 45 km/hr.

61.

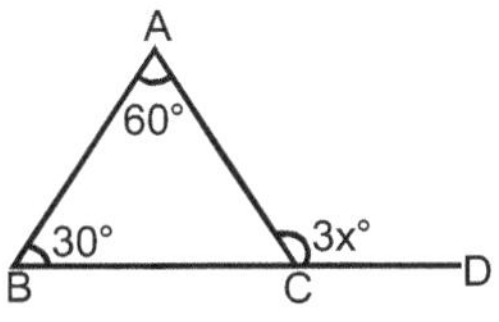

$$\angle ACD = \angle CAB + \angle ABC$$
$$= 60° + 30° = 90°$$
$$\Rightarrow \qquad 3x = 90$$
$$\Rightarrow \qquad x = 30$$
$$\Rightarrow \qquad \frac{2x}{3}\% \times 80° = \frac{20}{100} \times 80° = 16°.$$

62.
$$\frac{1}{x} = \frac{(2 + \sqrt{3})}{(2 - \sqrt{3})(2 + \sqrt{3})}$$

$$= (2 + \sqrt{3})$$

$$\therefore \qquad \left(x - \frac{1}{x}\right)^2 = \left(2 - \sqrt{3} - (2 + \sqrt{3})\right)^2$$

$$= \left(-2\sqrt{3}\right)^2 = 12.$$

63.
$$x^2 + 3 = 49x$$
$$\Rightarrow \qquad 3x^2 + 9 = 147x$$
$$\Rightarrow \qquad 3x^2 + 78x + 9 = 147x + 78x = 225x$$

$$\therefore \qquad \frac{150x}{3x^2 + 78x + 9} = \frac{150x}{225x} = \frac{2}{3}.$$

64.
$$a - (1 - b) = -(1 + c)$$
$$\Rightarrow \qquad a + b + c = 0$$

$$\left(\frac{2a}{\frac{b}{c}} + \frac{2b}{\frac{c}{a}} + \frac{2c}{\frac{a}{b}}\right) = 2\left(\frac{a^2}{bc} + \frac{b^2}{ac} + \frac{c^2}{ab}\right)$$

$$= 2\left(\frac{a^3}{abc} + \frac{b^3}{abc} + \frac{c^3}{abc}\right)$$

$$= 2\left(\frac{a^3 + b^3 + c^3}{abc}\right)$$

$$= 2 \times \frac{3abc}{abc} = 6.$$

(As a + b + c = 0, then $a^3 + b^3 + c^3 = 3abc$)

65.

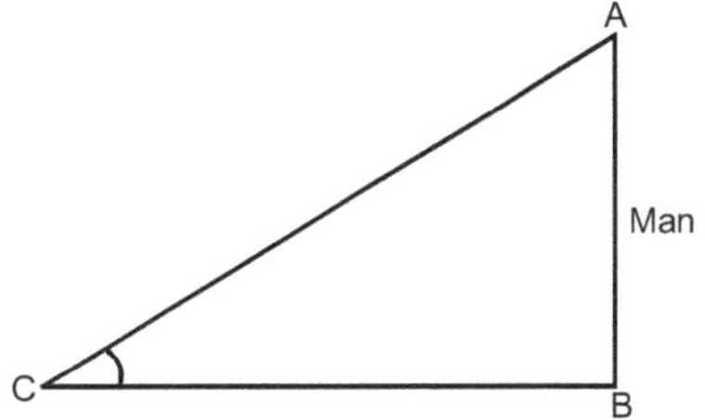

Let AB be the man and BC be its shadow. Then,

$$BC = \frac{AB}{\sqrt{3}}$$

$$\tan(ACB) = \frac{AB}{BC} = \sqrt{3}$$

$$\Rightarrow \qquad \angle ACB = 60°$$

Hence, the angle of elevation of the sun is 60°.

66. Let the distance between the two centres be x cm and r_1 and r_2 be the radii. Then,

Length of the transverse common tangent

$$= \sqrt{x^2 - (r_1 + r_2)^2}$$

$$\Rightarrow \qquad 6^2 = x^2 - (3 + 5)^2$$

$$\Rightarrow \qquad x = 10.$$

67.

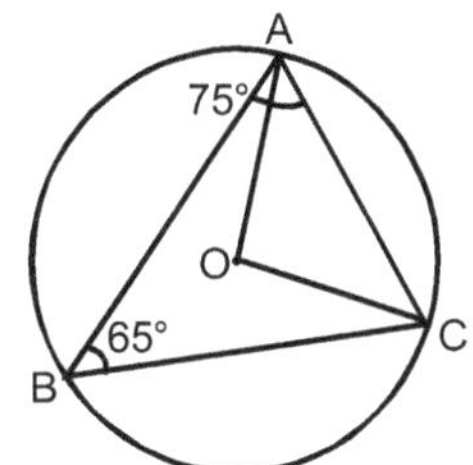

As $\angle CBA = 65°$, then $\angle AOC = 2 \times 65° = 130°$ and

$\angle ACO = \angle CAO = \theta$ (Let)

$$130° + \theta + \theta = 180°$$

$$\Rightarrow \qquad \theta = 25°.$$

68.

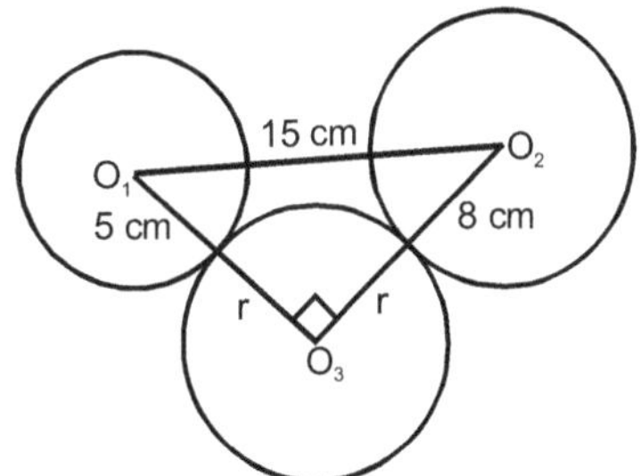

Let r be the radius of the third circle.

$\angle O_1 O_3 O_2 = 90°$, $O_1 O_2 = 15$ cm, $O_1 O_3 = (8 + r)$ cm and $O_2 O_3 = (5 + r)$ cm

From Pythagoras' Theorem,

$$(O_1 O_2)^2 = (O_1 O_3)^2 + (O_2 O_3)^2$$

$$\Rightarrow \qquad 15^2 = (8 + r)^2 + (5 + r)^2$$

$$\Rightarrow \qquad r^2 + 13r - 68 = 0$$

$$\Rightarrow \qquad r = 4 \text{ cm.}$$

69. Let each of the equal angle be 7x and the unequal angle be 4x. Then,

$$7x + 7x + 4x = 180°$$
$$\Rightarrow \quad x = 10°$$

Hence, the required difference $= 7x - 4x = 30°$.

70. $\dfrac{1}{\sec^2\theta} + \dfrac{2}{1+\tan^2\theta} + \dfrac{3}{1+\cot^2\theta}$

$$= \dfrac{1}{\sec^2\theta} + \dfrac{2}{\sec^2\theta} + \dfrac{3}{\operatorname{cosec}^2\theta}$$
$$= \cos^2\theta + 2\cos^2\theta + 3\sin^2\theta$$
$$= 3\cos^2\theta + 3\sin^2\theta = 3.$$

71. $\dfrac{5}{\operatorname{cosec}^2\theta} + \dfrac{3}{1+\tan^2\theta} + 2\cos^2\theta$

$$= \dfrac{5}{\operatorname{cosec}^2\theta} + \dfrac{3}{\sec^2\theta} + 2\cos^2\theta$$
$$= 5\sin^2\theta + 3\cos^2\theta + 2\cos^2\theta$$
$$= 5\left(\sin^2\theta + \cos^2\theta\right) = 5.$$

72. 25% more than birth rate of UP $= \left(1 + \dfrac{25}{100}\right) \times 25$

$$= 31.25$$

Birth rate of only two states (Tamil Nadu and Mizoram) are atleast 25% more than the birth rate of UP.

73. Birth rate of MP = 22 and Birth rate of Tamil Nadu

$$= 32$$

$\therefore$ Required percent $= \dfrac{22}{32} \times 100 = 68.75.$

74. Birth rate of Karnatka = 30 and birth rate of Haryana

$$= 18$$

$\therefore$ Required factor $= \dfrac{30}{18} \approx 1.67.$

75. Required average $= \dfrac{20 + 25 + 30 + 18 + 22 + 32 + 36}{7}$

$$= \dfrac{183}{7} \approx 26.$$

QUANTITATIVE APTITUDE

1. A man sells two articles at ₹6,300 each. He incurs a loss of 10% on the first article. At what profit percent should he sell the second article in order to gain 5% on the whole transaction?

(a) 20%

(b) 16.67%

(c) 26%

(d) 25%

2. If an article is marked 20% above its cost price and then sold at 25% discount, what is the overall gain or loss percentage?

(a) 10% loss

(b) 10% gain

(c) 15% loss

(d) 15% gain

3. If ABC is an isosceles right angled triangle, right angled at B, then what is the ratio of the length of side AB to that of AC?

(a) $1 : \sqrt{2}$

(b) $\sqrt{2} : 1$

(c) $\sqrt{3} : 1$

(d) $1 : \sqrt{3}$

4. In how much time will a sum of ₹8,000 become ₹13,824 at a rate of 20% compound interest?

(a) 3 years

(b) 2.5 years

(c) 2 years

(d) 4 years

5. If a train crosses a person in 15 seconds and a platform of length 600 m in 45 seconds, length of the train is

(a) 400 m

(b) 200 m

(c) 250 m

(d) 300 m

6. $1 \times 2 + 2 \times 3 + 3 \times 4 + 4 \times 5 + \cdots + 20 \times 21 = ?$

(a) 3120

(b) 3060

(c) 3080

(d) 3070

7. A's income is 20% more than B's income and C's income is 30% less than A's income. By what percentage is C's income more/less than B's income?

(a) 16% more

(b) 16% less

(c) 20% more

(d) 20% less

8. Which is the smallest among the following fractions?

$$\frac{16}{17}, \frac{17}{18}, \frac{9}{25} \text{ and } \frac{10}{26}$$

(a) $\frac{16}{17}$

(b) $\frac{17}{18}$

(c) $\frac{9}{25}$

(d) $\frac{10}{26}$

9. If the cost price of 10 articles is equal to the selling price of 8 articles, the profit percentage is

(a) 20%

(b) 25%

(c) 30%

(d) 16.67%

10. The average weight of A, B and C is 50 kg. The average weight of A and B is 57 kg while the average weight of A and C is 51 kg. Find the weight of A.

(a) 76 kg

(b) 66 kg

(c) 56 kg

(d) 57 kg

11. The length and the breadth of a rectangle is increased by 10% and 12% respectively. Find the percentage change in the area of the rectangle.

(a) 23.20%

(b) 24.12%

(c) 25%

(d) 22%

12. If $\dfrac{5\sqrt{3} + 2\sqrt{2}}{8\sqrt{3} + 2\sqrt{2}} = a + b\sqrt{6}$, find the value of a.

(a) $\frac{13}{42}$

(b) $\frac{14}{23}$

(c) $\frac{23}{14}$

(d) $\frac{42}{13}$

13. Food at a camp of 80 soldiers is sufficient for 'x' days. If twice of the existing soldiers also join the camp, the food will last for

(a) 24 days

(b) x days

(c) $\frac{x}{3}$ days

(d) $\frac{80}{3}$ days

14. How much angle will the hour hand sweep between 7 a.m to 9 p.m.?

(a) 120°

(b) 420°

(c) 360°

(d) 240°

15. A project is to be completed in 45 days. 18 men completed 60% of the project in 30 days. How many more men should be hired to complete rest of the work in the stipulated time?

(a) 4
(b) 5
(c) 6
(d) 7

16. Rajesh travelled a distance of 300 km in 5 hrs partly by train at 20 m/s and partly by bus at 10 m/s. Find the distance travelled by Rajesh in bus.

(a) 60 km
(b) 100 km
(c) 150 km
(d) 200 km

17. Abhay, Yogesh and Sumit enter into a partnership by investing ₹54,000 in a ratio 5 : 6 : 7 for a period of 12 months, 8 months and 6 months respectively. If ₹12,500 is the profit at the end of the year, then what is the difference of the amount received by Abhay and Sumit?

(a) ₹1,000
(b) ₹1,500
(c) ₹800
(d) ₹1,200

18. Simplify: $\dfrac{0.729 + 0.216}{0.81 - 0.54 + 0.36}$

(a) 0.945
(b) 0.513
(c) 1.5
(d) 0.3

19. What must be subtracted from both numerator and denominator of the fraction $\dfrac{11}{13}$, such that the resultant fraction becomes $\dfrac{4}{5}$?

(a) 5
(b) 2
(c) 3
(d) 4

20. A manufacturer gains 20% by selling an article after giving a discount of 40% on marked price. If marked price of the article is ₹80, then its cost price is

(a) ₹48
(b) ₹36
(c) ₹42
(d) ₹40

21. Raman bought a drum of paint, which is $\dfrac{4}{5}$ th full. After using 26 liters of paint, it is $\dfrac{3}{7}$ th full. The capacity (in liters) of the drum is

(a) 65
(b) 70
(c) 80
(d) 85

22. Walking at $\dfrac{3}{5}$ th of his usual speed, a man reaches his office $1\dfrac{1}{2}$ hours late. The usual time taken by him to reach his office is

(a) $2\dfrac{1}{4}$ hours
(b) 2 hours
(c) $2\dfrac{1}{2}$ hours
(d) 3 hours

Directions for questions 23 to 25 : *Answer the questions on the basis of the information given below.*

The bar graph given below shows the income and expenditure (in thousand ₹) of five households in the year 2011.

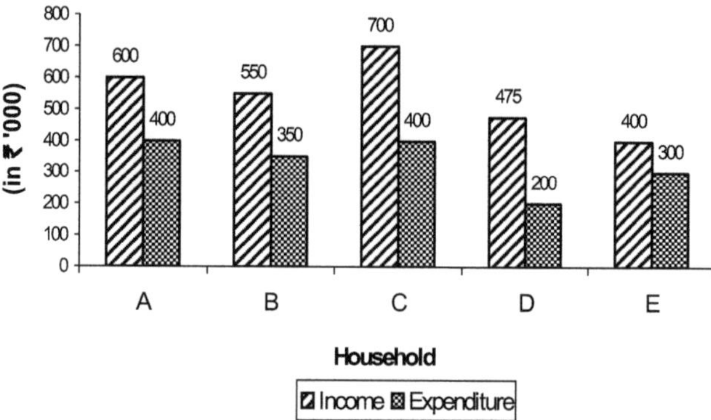

23. Which of the following households had the maximum savings in 2011?

(a) B
(b) D
(c) A
(d) C

24. What is the ratio of the expenditure of A and E together to the expenditure of B and C together?

(a) 17 : 13
(b) 13 : 17
(c) 14 : 15
(d) 14 : 11

25. The income of the household C is what percentage of the combined incomes of households A, B and E?

(a) 42.32%
(b) 43.8%
(c) 45.16%
(d) 41.26%

ENGLISH LANGUAGE

Directions for questions 26 to 27: *In each of the following questions, a word is followed by four options. Select the option that best expresses the meaning of the given word.*

26. Prudent

(a) Discretion
(b) Cheerless
(c) Wise
(d) Anxious

27. Incapable

(a) Hard
(b) Disagree
(c) Solicit
(d) Ineffective

Direction for questions 28 to 29: *In each of the following questions, a word is followed by four options. Select the option that is opposite in meaning to the given word.*

28. Immaculate

(a) Impure
(b) Selfish
(c) Destitute
(d) Unpopular

29. Approbation

   (*a*) Disapproval   (*b*) Blessing

   (*c*) Admiration   (*d*) Consent

Direction for questions 30 to 32: *Out of the four alternatives, choose the one which can be substituted for the given words.*

30. Giving good reason for being doubted, questioned

   (*a*) Equivocal   (*b*) Incontestable

   (*c*) Undeniable   (*d*) Clear

31. Very Pleasing to eat

   (*a*) Gastronome   (*b*) Gourmand

   (*c*) Toothsome   (*d*) None of these

32. Short speech at the end of play

   (*a*) Prologue   (*b*) Epilogue

   (*c*) Dialogue   (*d*) Bibliography

Directions for questions 33 to 35: *Four alternatives are given for the Idiom/Phrase. Choose the alternative which best expresses the meaning of the Idiom/Phrase.*

33. Apple of discord

   (*a*) Rotten apple   (*b*) Cause of dispute

   (*c*) Helpless condition (*d*) None of these

34. In cold blood

   (*a*) To murder in cold weather

   (*b*) A dangerous act

   (*c*) Temporary break

   (*d*) Ruthlessly

35. To bob and weave

   (*a*) Practically never

   (*b*) Pass the stage at which interest, activity is at its greatest

   (*c*) To make rapid bodily movements up and down and from side to side

   (*d*) None of these

Direction for question 36: Groups of four words are given. In each group, one word is correctly spelt. Find the correctly spelt word.

36. (*a*) Therapuetic   (*b*) Sudetorium

   (*c*) Caesarean   (*d*) Sufocate

Directions for questions 37 to 39: *Some of the sentences have errors and some are correct. Find out which part of a sentence has an error. If there is no error, your answer is (d)*

37. Despite being tried his best (*a*) / to persuade people to give up smoking (*b*)/, he could not attain success (*c*)./ No error (*d*)

38. He is taller(*a*) / than (*b*) / any student in his class (*c*). / No error (*d*)

39. A thousand rupees(*a*) / are (*b*) / all that he wants (*c*)./ No error (*d*)

Directions for questions 40 to 42: *Sentences are given with blanks to be filled in with an appropriate word. Four alternatives are suggested for each question. Choose the correct alternative out of the four.*

40. Concerned British Muslims, mostly of South Asian origin, want to ___ their religion to critical enquiry and debate.

   (*a*) open   (*b*) embark

   (*c*) restrict   (*d*) divulge

41. Perhaps the one positive aspect to an otherwise _____ story of chronic hunger in India is the more frequent public acknowledgement of this sorry state of affairs.

   (*a*) mild   (*b*) grim

   (*c*) unyielding   (*d*) unflinching

42. Research has ______that chronic maternal undernourishment leads to fetal deprivation.

   (*a*) establishes   (*b*) establish

   (*c*) established   (*d*) establishing

Directions: In question no. **43** to **45**, a sentence / a part of the sentence is underlined. Below are given alternatives to the underlined part at (A), (B), (C) which may improve the sentence. Choose the correct alternative. In case no improvement is needed, your answer is (D).

43. A number of applicants <u>who have been</u> interviewed.

   (*a*) are already been (*b*) has already been

   (*c*) have been   (*d*) No improvement

44. The more he shouted, <u>he was achieving less</u>.

   (*a*) the less he achieved

   (*b*) he achieved insufficiently

   (*c*) he did not achieve enough

   (*d*) No improvement

45. People all over the country are starving <u>in great numbers</u>.

   (*a*) great in numbers (*b*) in more numbers

   (*c*) more numerously (*d*) No improvement

Directions: In question nos. **46** to **50**, you have a passage with 5 questions in it. Read the passage carefully and choose the best answer to each question.

In September 1620, a small ship called the Mayflower left Plymouth, England, carrying 102 passengers — an assortment of religious separatists seeking a new home where they could freely practice their faith and other individuals lured by the promise of prosperity and land ownership in the New World. After a treacherous and uncomfortable crossing that lasted

66 days, they dropped anchor near the tip of Cape Cod, far north of their intended destination at the mouth of the Hudson River. One month later, the Mayflower crossed Massachusetts Bay, where the Pilgrims, as they are now commonly known, began the work of establishing a village at Plymouth.

Throughout that first brutal winter, most of the colonists remained on board the ship, where they suffered from exposure, scurvy and outbreaks of contagious disease. Only half of the Mayflower's original passengers and crew lived to see their first New England spring. In March, the remaining settlers moved ashore, where they received an astonishing visit from an Abenaki Indian who greeted them in English. Several days later, he returned with another Native American, Squanto, who shared their pain. Squanto taught the Pilgrims, weakened by malnutrition and illness, how to cultivate corn, extract sap from maple trees, catch fish in the rivers and avoid poisonous plants. He also helped the settlers forge an alliance with the Wampanoag, a local tribe, which would endure for more than 50 years and tragically remains one of the sole examples of harmony between European colonists and Native Americans.

46. Find a word in the passage which means 'a collection of things or people'.

(a) Bunch   (b) Bundle

(c) Assortment   (d) Pack

47. Which of the following is a disease that the colonists on board suffered from?

(a) Scurvy   (b) Rickets

(c) Beriberi   (d) Tuberculosis

48. Where did the ship stop at the end of 66 days of uncomfortable sailing?

(a) Plymouth

(b) England

(c) Massachusetts Bay

(d) Cape Cod

49. Which of the following, according to the passage, is a characteristic that is used to describe the pilgrims?

(a) Malnourished   (b) Deprived

(c) Old   (d) Obese

50. What does the phrase 'share someone's pain' means?

(a) To take away someone's pain

(b) To sympathise with someone's pain

(c) To deal with someone in pain

(d) To medically treat someone in pain

GENERAL INTELLIGENCE

51. If EDUCATION is coded as 543312965 in a code language, then what will be the code for WESTERN?

(a) 4532595   (b) 4512575

(c) 5512595   (d) 5512585

52. One morning after sunrise, Ajay was facing a pole whose shadow was on his left. Which direction was Ajay facing?

(a) North   (b) West

(c) East   (d) South

53. Find the missing number.

10	20	40
6	12	24
14	?	224

(a) 56   (b) 84

(c) 42   (d) 70

54. In the following question, number of letters is skipped by a particular rule. Which of the following observes the rule?

(a) ZUQNJ   (b) YURNJ

(c) ZUROI   (d) YUQMI

55. Which of the following set of letters when sequentially placed in the gaps in the given letter series shall complete it?

_ ba _ baba_ba_a_b

(a) aabba   (b) ababa

(c) aaabb   (d) aaaba

Directions for questions 56 to 57: *In each of the following questions a series is given with one term missing. Choose the correct alternative from the given options that will complete the series.*

56. 5, 7, 25, 49, 125, ?

(a) 245   (b) 625

(c) 346   (d) 343

57. hgf, kji, n??

(a) lp   (b) up

(c) oq   (d) ml

58. Which one of the following diagrams represents the correct relationship between Colleague, Enemy and Friend.

(a) 

(b) 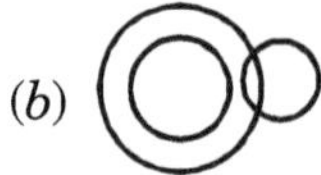

(c) 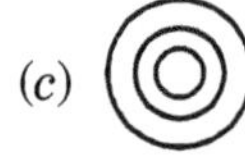

(d) 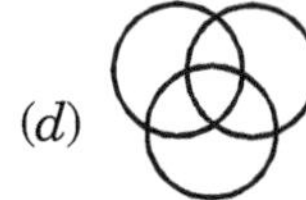

59. Which one of the given responses would be a meaningful order of the following words?

A. Infant
B. Adolescent
C. Child
D. Adult
E. Elderly

(a) A,C,B,E,D
(b) A,C,B,D,E
(c) A,C,D,B,E
(d) A,C,D,E,B

60. Arrange the following words according to the dictionary:

A. Jeremiad
B. Jersey
C. Jerky
D. Jerkin
E. Jeroboam

(a) A,D,C,E,B
(b) A,D,E,C,B
(c) A,D,E,B,C
(d) A,D,C,B,E

Directions for questions 61 : *In each of the following questions, find the odd numbers/letters from the given alternatives.*

61. (a) ADPS
(b) FISV
(c) ILPS
(d) MPOQ

62. From the given alternative words, select the word which can be formed using the letters of the given word:

DISCOURAGING

(a) discourse
(b) courage
(c) rage
(d) soaring

63. Find out the pair of numbers that does not belong to the group for lack of common property.

(a) 27-15
(b) 45 -15
(c) 279 - 93
(d) 108 - 36

64. In the figure given below, which part belongs to the persons who have been in all the three professions?

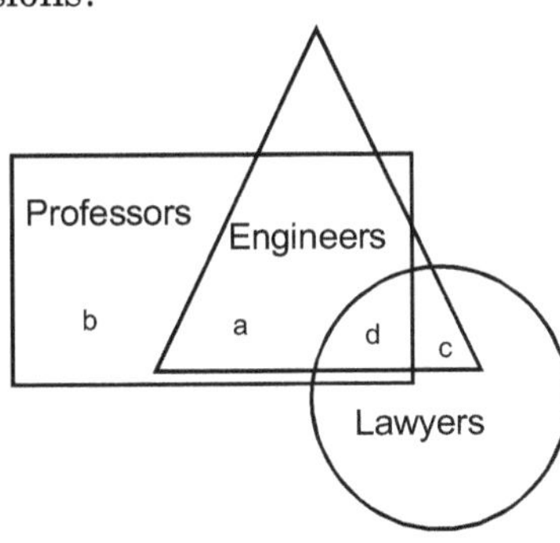

(a) a
(b) b
(c) c
(d) d

65. Three alarms ring at intervals of 3 min 10 sec, 6 min 20 sec and 9 min 30 sec respectively. If they together rang at 9 a.m., when will they ring together again?

(a) 19 minutes past 9
(b) 10 O' clock
(c) 14 minutes past 11
(d) 18 minutes past 11

66. Two statements are given below followed by four alternative inferences.

Select the most appropriate response.

Statements:

(i) All jokers are boys.

(ii) Some lazy are jokers.

Inferences:

1. Some jokers are lazy.

2. All lazy are jokers.

3. Some boys are lazy.

4. All boys are lazy.

(a) 1 and 2 only

(b) 1,2 and 3 only

(c) 1 and 3 only

(d) All of them

67. What will come in place of the question mark 9, 17, 30, 48, 71, ?.

(a) 111
(b) 99
(c) 102
(d) 94

68. Priyanka is older to Pratibha as well as Parul. Pratibha is younger to Priya. Parul is not the youngest among the four. The youngest among them is

(a) Priyanka
(b) Pratibha
(c) Priya
(d) Cannot be determined

69. In which of the answer figures is the question figure embedded?

Question figure

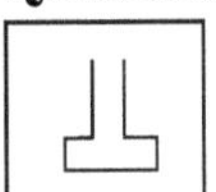

Answer figures

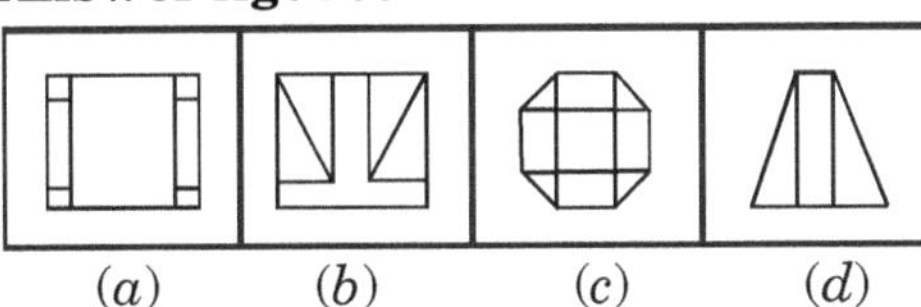

    (a)   (b)   (c)   (d)

70. Find the correct answer figure which could replace question mark (?) in the problem figure.

Problem figures

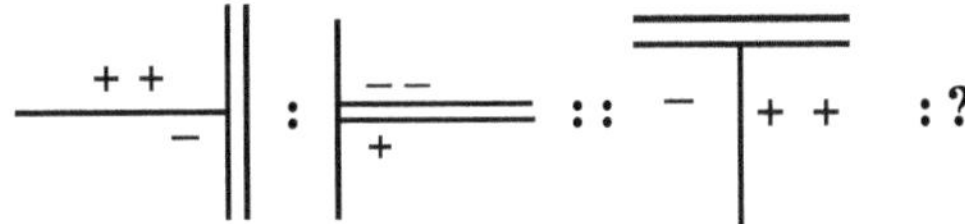

Answer figures

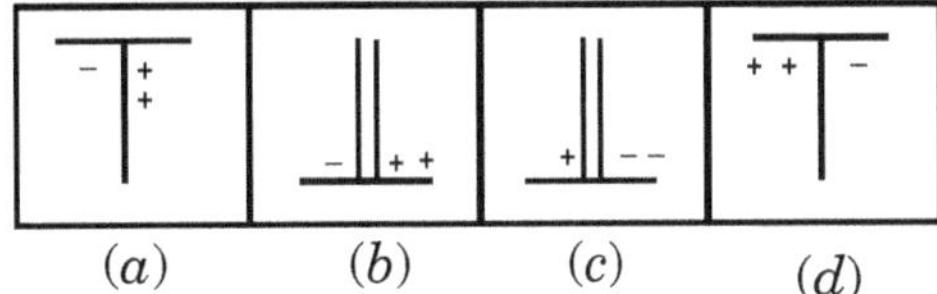

    (a)   (b)   (c)   (d)

71. Which 'Answer Figure' is the exact mirror image of the given 'Question Figure' when the mirror $M_1 M_2$ is placed as shown in the figure.

Question Figure

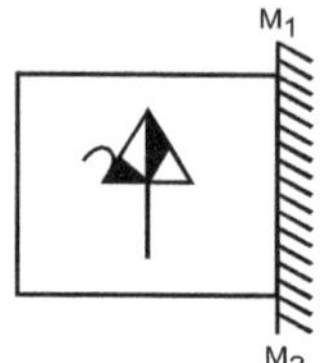

Answer Figures

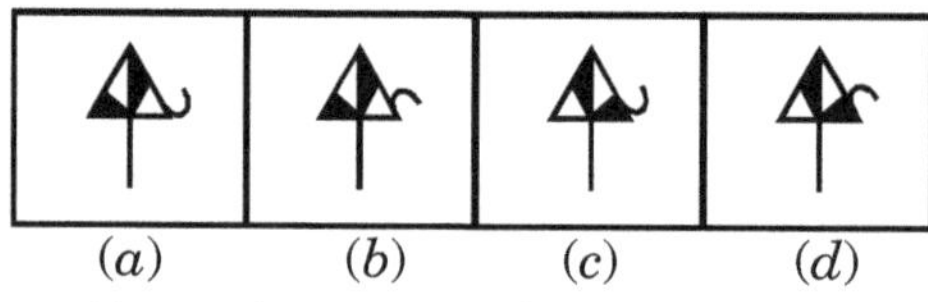

(a)   (b)   (c)   (d)

Directions for questions 72 : *In each of the following questions, select the related word from the given alternatives.*

72. Water : Rain :: Fur :

(a) ring   (b) coat

(c) spectacles   (d) bottle

73. From the given alternative words, select the word which cannot be formed using the letters of the given word:

TRANSPLANTED

(a) sand   (b) plant

(c) plain   (d) tread

74. Which of the following represents a relationship among Men, Doctors and Lecturers?

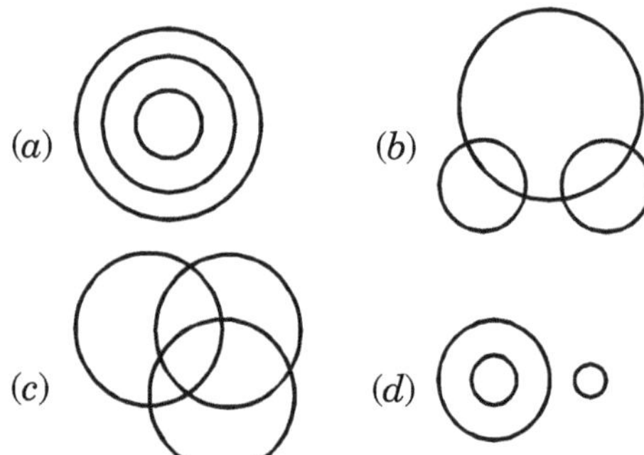

(a)   (b)   (c)   (d)

75. How many squares are there in the figure?

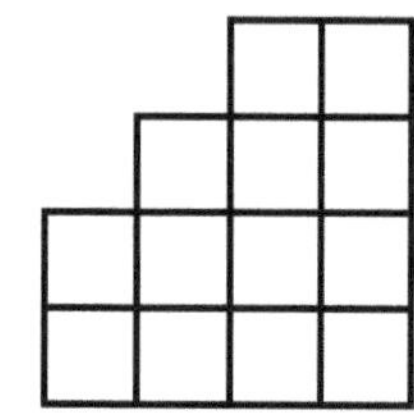

(a) 20   (b) 19

(c) 21   (d) None of these

GENERAL AWARENESS

76. Swachh helpline ____________ launched by PM Narendra Modi

(a) 1969   (b) 1996

(c) 1968   (d) 1987

77. The separation of which two countries has been termed as Velvet Divorce?

(a) Serbia and Montenegro

(b) Sudan and South Sudan

(c) Czech Republic and Slovakia

(d) None of these

78. National Institute of Virology is located at:

(a) Pune   (b) Mysore

(c) Bhopal   (d) Bilaspur

79. Magna Carta, the charter of Rights was signed in which year?

(a) 1215 A.D.   (b) 1252 A.D.

(c) 1362 A.D.   (d) 1402 A.D.

80. First Asian Games in 1951 was held at which of the following cities?

(a) Bangkok   (b) Kuala Lumpur

(c) Manila   (d) Delhi

81. Which of the following became the first state in India to launch health insurance for its entire people?

(a) Kerala   (b) Uttarakhand

(c) Goa   (d) Himachal Pradesh

82. 'The Scream' is a famous painting by:

(a) Tyeb Mehta   (b) Pallo Picasso

(c) Amrita Shergill   (d) Edvard Munch

83. Who of the following wrote 'Siddhant Siromani'?

(a) Aryabhatt   (b) Sushruta

(c) Charak   (d) Bhaskaracharya

84. Which of the following is going to be world's first carbon neutral country by 2020?

(a) New Zealand   (b) France

(c) Tuvalu   (d) Samoa

85. Who of the following was the first mayor of Delhi?

(a) Hiren Mukherjee

(b) Govind Vallabh Pant

(c) Lakshmi Sehgal

(d) Aruna Asaf Ali

86. Puszta is a temparate grassland of which country?

(a) Argentina   (b) Brazil

(c) Hungary   (d) Denmark

87. Which of the following is called the 'Key of the Baltic'?

(a) Copenhagen   (b) Vilnius

(c) Sochi   (d) None of these

88. Name the advanced indigenously built guided Missile Detroyer has been launched by the Indian Navy at Mumbai?

(a) Kochi   (b) Visakhapatnam

(c) Mumbai   (d) Mormugao

89. The latitude of a place denotes its angular position with respect to:

(a) Equator   (b) Poles

(c) Axis   (d) None of these

90. Muslim League was founded in which year?

(a) 1903   (b) 1906

(c) 1909   (d) 1916

91. Power of Supreme Court to decide the dispute between centre and states comes under the ambit of:

(a) Original jurisdiction

(b) Appellate jurisdiction

(c) Extraordinary jurisdiction

(d) Advisory jurisdiction

92. Railway staff college is locates at:

(a) Pune   (b) Vadodara

(c) Mathura   (d) Bareilly

93. Who is regarded as the 'Father of Geometry'?

(a) Pythagoras   (b) Euclid

(c) Aryabhatta   (d) Bhaskara

94. National youth day is observed on:

(a) 12th January   (b) 23rd March

(c) 18th August   (d) 8th September

95. Sindhi language was added in the eighth schedule of constitution by which amendment?

(a) 1st amendment

(b) 14th amendment

(c) 21st amendment

(d) 26th amendment

96. Which of the following high court was not established in 1862 A.D.?

(a) Bombay   (b) Calcutta

(c) Madras   (d) Allahabad

97. Iron and aluminium compounds dominate the composition of which type of soil?

(a) Laterite soil   (b) Alluvial soil

(c) Mountain soil   (d) Desert soil

98. Which of the following is the largest man made reservoir in India?

(a) Rihard Sagar   (b) Govind Vallabh Sagar

(c) Nagarjuna Sagar   (d) None of these

99. L M Singhvi committee was related to:

(a) Panchayati Raj Institutions

(b) Co-operatives

(c) Banking sector

(d) Digitalization of cable

100. Prime Minister launched irrigation and drinking water supply projects worth 4800 crore rupees in tribal areas of which state?

(a) Assam

(b) Arunchal Pradesh

(c) Tamilnadu

(d) Gujarat

ANSWERS

1. (c)	**2.** (a)	**3.** (a)	**4.** (a)	**5.** (d)	**6.** (c)	**7.** (b)	**8.** (c)	**9.** (b)	**10.** (b)
11. (a)	**12.** (b)	**13.** (c)	**14.** (b)	**15.** (c)	**16.** (a)	**17.** (b)	**18.** (c)	**19.** (c)	**20.** (d)
21. (b)	**22.** (a)	**23.** (d)	**24.** (c)	**25.** (c)	**26.** (c)	**27.** (d)	**28.** (a)	**29.** (a)	**30.** (a)
31. (c)	**32.** (b)	**33.** (b)	**34.** (d)	**35.** (c)	**36.** (c)	**37.** (a)	**38.** (c)	**39.** (b)	**40.** (a)
41. (b)	**42.** (c)	**43.** (c)	**44.** (a)	**45.** (d)	**46.** (c)	**47.** (a)	**48.** (d)	**49.** (a)	**50.** (b)
51. (c)	**52.** (a)	**53.** (a)	**54.** (d)	**55.** (d)	**56.** (d)	**57.** (d)	**58.** (a)	**59.** (b)	**60.** (a)
61. (d)	**62.** (d)	**63.** (a)	**64.** (d)	**65.** (a)	**66.** (c)	**67.** (b)	**68.** (b)	**69.** (b)	**70.** (c)
71. (d)	**72.** (b)	**73.** (c)	**74.** (c)	**75.** (a)	**76.** (a)	**77.** (c)	**78.** (a)	**79.** (a)	**80.** (d)
81. (c)	**82.** (d)	**83.** (d)	**84.** (a)	**85.** (d)	**86.** (c)	**87.** (d)	**88.** (d)	**89.** (d)	**90.** (b)
91. (a)	**92.** (b)	**93.** (b)	**94.** (a)	**95.** (c)	**96.** (d)	**97.** (a)	**98.** (c)	**99.** (a)	**100.** (d)

EXPLANATIONS

1. C.P. of the first article $= \dfrac{6300}{0.9} = ₹7,000$

Total C.P. of both the articles

$$= \dfrac{12600}{1.05} = ₹12,000$$

$\therefore$ C.P. of the second article

$$= 12000 - 7000$$

$$= ₹5,000$$

Profit on the second article

$$= 6300 - 5000$$

$$= ₹1,300$$

Profit percentage on the second article

$$= \dfrac{1300}{5000} \times 100 = 26\% .$$

2. Let C.P. of the article be $₹x$.

$\therefore$ Marked price $= x \times (1 + 0.2) = 1.2x$

Selling price after 25% discount

$$= (1.2\,x) \times (1 - 0.25)$$

$$= 1.2x \times 0.75$$

$$= 0.9x$$

Loss percentage $= \dfrac{\text{CP} - \text{SP}}{\text{CP}} \times 100$

$$= \dfrac{x - 0.9x}{x} \times 100$$

$$= 10\%.$$

3. $AC\,(\text{Hypotenuse}) = \sqrt{AB^2 + BC^2}$

$$= \sqrt{2AB^2} = \sqrt{2}\,AB$$

$$[\because AB = BC]$$

$\Rightarrow \quad \dfrac{AB}{AC} = \dfrac{1}{\sqrt{2}}$ i.e. $1 : \sqrt{2}$.

4. Let the time be 'n' years.

$\therefore \quad 13824 = 8000\left(1 + \dfrac{20}{100}\right)^n$

$\Rightarrow \quad \dfrac{13824}{8000} = \left(\dfrac{6}{5}\right)^n$

$\Rightarrow \quad \left(\dfrac{24}{20}\right)^3 = \left(\dfrac{6}{5}\right)^n$

$\Rightarrow \quad \left(\dfrac{6}{5}\right)^3 = \left(\dfrac{6}{5}\right)^n$

$\Rightarrow \quad n = 3$ years.

5. Let speed of the train be 's' m/s.

$\therefore$ Length of the train $= 15 \times s$

According to the question,

$$600 + 15s = 45s$$

$\Rightarrow \qquad 30s = 600$

$\Rightarrow \qquad s = 20$ m/s

$\therefore$ Length of the train $= 15s = 15 \times 20 = 300$ m.

6. $1 \times 2 + 2 \times 3 + 3 \times 4 + 4 \times 5 + \ldots + 20 \times 21$

$$= \sum_{n=1}^{20} n\,(n+1) = \sum_{n=1}^{20} (n^2 + n) = \sum_{n=1}^{20} n^2 + \sum_{n=1}^{20} n$$

$$= \dfrac{20 \times 21 \times 41}{6} + \dfrac{20 \times 21}{2}$$

$$\left[\sum n^2 = \dfrac{n(n+1)(2n+1)}{6} \text{ and } \sum n = \dfrac{n(n+1)}{2} \right]$$

$$= 2870 + 210 = 3080.$$

7. Let B's income be $₹\,x$.

$\therefore$ A's income $= ₹1.2x$.

Also, C's income $= 1.2x \times 0.7 = ₹0.84x$

Required percentage

$$= \dfrac{x - 0.84x}{x} \times 100$$

$$= 16\% \text{ less.}$$

8. $\dfrac{16}{17} = 0.941$, $\dfrac{17}{18} = 0.944$

$\dfrac{9}{25} = 0.36 \quad$ and $\quad \dfrac{10}{26} = 0.38$

$\therefore \dfrac{9}{25} < \dfrac{10}{26} < \dfrac{16}{17} < \dfrac{17}{18}$

Hence, $\dfrac{9}{25}$ is the smallest among the given fractions.

9. C.P. of 10 articles = S.P. of 8 articles

$$= ₹\,x \text{ (let)}$$

$\therefore$ C.P. of 1 article $= ₹\dfrac{x}{10}$

and S.P of 1 article $= ₹\dfrac{x}{8}$.

$\therefore$ Required profit percentage

$$= \frac{\dfrac{x}{8} - \dfrac{x}{10}}{\dfrac{x}{10}} \times 100$$

$$= \frac{\dfrac{x}{40}}{\dfrac{x}{10}} \times 100 = 25\%.$$

10. Total weight of A, B and C = $50 \times 3 = 150$ kg

Total weight of A and B = $57 \times 2 = 114$ kg

Total weight of A and C = $51 \times 2 = 102$ kg

$\therefore$ Weight of A = (A + B) + (A + C) − (A + B + C)

$$= 114 + 102 - 150 = 66 \text{ kg}.$$

11. Let the length and breadth of the rectangle be 'l' and 'b' respectively.

Area of rectangle = l × b

Length after an increment of 10% = 1.1 l

Breadth after an increment of 12% = 1.12b

New area of rectangle = 1.1 l × 1.12 b = 1.232 lb

Percentage change in area of the rectangle

$$\frac{1.232\,lb - lb}{lb} \times 100 = 23.20\%.$$

Alternate:

Required percentage increase

$$= 10 + 12 + \frac{10 \times 12}{100} = 23.20\%.$$

12. $\dfrac{5\sqrt{3} + 2\sqrt{2}}{8\sqrt{3} + 2\sqrt{2}} = a + b\sqrt{6}$

$\dfrac{5\sqrt{3} + 2\sqrt{2}}{8\sqrt{3} + 2\sqrt{2}} \times \dfrac{8\sqrt{3} - 2\sqrt{2}}{8\sqrt{3} - 2\sqrt{2}} = a + b\sqrt{6}$

$\Rightarrow \dfrac{5\sqrt{3}\left(8\sqrt{3} - 2\sqrt{2}\right) + 2\sqrt{2}\left(8\sqrt{3} - 2\sqrt{2}\right)}{\left(8\sqrt{3}\right)^2 - \left(2\sqrt{2}\right)^2} = a + b\sqrt{6}$

$\Rightarrow \dfrac{120 - 10\sqrt{6} + 16\sqrt{6} - 8}{192 - 8} = a + b\sqrt{6}$

$\Rightarrow \dfrac{112 + 6\sqrt{6}}{184} = a + b\sqrt{6}$

$\Rightarrow \dfrac{56 + 3\sqrt{6}}{92} = a + b\sqrt{6}$

$\therefore a = \dfrac{56}{92} = \dfrac{14}{23}.$

13. For 1 soldier, food lasts for $80x$ days

Total number of soldiers in the camp after joining of new soldiers

$$= 80 + 2 \times 80$$
$$= 240$$

$\therefore$ The food will last for $\dfrac{80x}{240} = \dfrac{x}{3}$ days.

14. Since, the hour hand sweeps $360°$ in 12 hours,

and the total duration between 7 a.m. to 9 p.m. is 14 hrs.

$\therefore$ Angle swept $= \dfrac{360}{12} \times 14 = 420°.$

15. Let a man complete a unit of work in a day.

$\therefore 18 \times 30 = 60\%$ of Total work

$\Rightarrow$ Total work $= \dfrac{18 \times 30 \times 100}{60} = 900 \text{ units}$

Let x men hired to complete the remaining work in the remaining 15 days.

$\therefore (18 + x) \times 15 = 900 - 18 \times 30$

$\Rightarrow x = \dfrac{900 - 540}{15} - 18 = 24 - 18 = 6.$

16. Let the distance travelled by Rajesh in bus be 'x' km.

$\therefore$ Distance travelled by Rajesh in train

$$= (300 - x) \text{ km}$$

Speed of the bus $= 10 \times \dfrac{18}{5} = 36$ km/hr.

Speed of the train $= 20 \times \dfrac{18}{5} = 72$ km/hr.

According to the question,

$$\dfrac{x}{36} + \dfrac{300 - x}{72} = 5$$

$\Rightarrow \dfrac{2x + 300 - x}{72} = 5$

$\Rightarrow x = 360 - 300 = 60 \text{ km}.$

17. Ratio of their profit sharing

$$= 5 \times 12 : 6 \times 8 : 7 \times 6$$
$$= 10 : 8 : 7$$

Amount received by

Abhay $= \dfrac{10}{25} \times 12500 = ₹5,000.$

Amount received by Sumit

$$= \dfrac{7}{25} \times 12500 = ₹3,500.$$

Required difference

$$= 5000 - 3500 = ₹1,500.$$

18. $\dfrac{0.729+0.216}{0.81-0.54+0.36} = \dfrac{(0.9)^3+(0.6)^3}{(0.9)^2-0.9\times0.6+(0.6)^2}$

$= 0.9+0.6 = 1.5.\,[a^3+b^3=(a+b)(a^2-ab+b^2)]$

19. Let x be subtracted from both numerator and denominator. Then,

$$\dfrac{11-x}{13-x} = \dfrac{4}{5}$$

$\Rightarrow \qquad 55-5x = 52-4x$

$\Rightarrow \qquad x = 3.$

20. S.P. of the article after discount of 40%

$$= 80 \times 0.6 = ₹48$$

∴ C.P. of the article for a profit of 20%

$$= \dfrac{48}{1+0.2} = ₹40.$$

21. Let the capacity of drum be 'x' liters.

According to the question,

$$\dfrac{4x}{5} - 26 = \dfrac{3x}{7}$$

$\Rightarrow \qquad \dfrac{28x-15x}{35} = 26$

$\Rightarrow \qquad x = 70 \text{ liters.}$

22. Let 's' be the usual speed and 't' be the usual time taken by the man.

$\therefore st = \dfrac{3s}{5}\left(t+\dfrac{3}{2}\right) \qquad$ [Since distance is constant]

$\Rightarrow \qquad t = \dfrac{3}{5}\left(\dfrac{2t+3}{2}\right)$

$\Rightarrow \qquad 10t = 6t+9$

$\Rightarrow \qquad t = \dfrac{9}{4} = 2\dfrac{1}{4} \text{ hours.}$

23. Saving of the household C is maximum.

24. Required ratio $= \dfrac{\text{Expenditure of (A+E)}}{\text{Expenditure of (B+C)}}$

$$= \dfrac{400+300}{350+400}$$

$$= \dfrac{700}{750} = 14:15.$$

25. Combined income of households A, B and E

$$= 600+550+400 = 1550$$

∴ Required percentage

$$= \dfrac{700}{1550}\times100 \approx 45.16\%$$

26. "Prudent" means marked by wisdom or judiciousness. "Wise" is most similar in meaning to "prudent". "Discretion" means individual choice or judgment. "Cheerless" means bleak or lacking qualities that cheer. "Anxious" means characterized by extreme uneasiness of mind.

27. "Incapable" means lacking capacity, ability, or qualification for the purpose or end in view. "Ineffective" which means not capable of performing efficiently or as expected is the word most similar in meaning to "incapable". "Hard" means not easily penetrated. "Disagree" means to fail to agree. "Solicit" means to approach with a request or plea.

28. "Immaculate" means pure or having no stain .The word most opposite in meaning to the given word is "impure". "Selfish" means concerned excessively or exclusively with oneself. "Destitute" means lacking possessions and resources. "Unpopular" means viewed or received unfavorably by the public.

29. "Approbation" means an act of approving formally or officially. The word most opposite in meaning to "approbation" is disapproval. "Blessing" means approval or encouragement . "Admiration" means an object of esteem . "Consent" means to give assent or approval.

30. "Equivocal" means uncertain or questionable in nature. Thus it can be substituted for the given words. Options $(b),(c)$ and (d) refer to something which cannot be disputed. These options are negated as these are antonyms.

31. "Gastronome" means a lover of good food. "Gourmand" means one who is heartily interested in good food and drink. "Toothsome" means of palatable flavor and pleasing texture. Thus it can be substituted for the given words. Option (d) is negated.

32. "Epilogue" means a speech often in verse addressed to the audience by an actor at the end of a play. "Prologue" is the preface or introduction to a literary work. "Dialogue" is a written composition in which two or more characters are represented as conversing. "Bibliography" is a list of works written by an author.

33. "Apple of discord" is a subject of dissension. This expression refers to the Greek myth in which a golden apple inscribed 'for the fairest' was contended for by the goddesses Hera, Athene and Aphrodite.

34. "In cold blood" means without feeling or mercy.

35. "To bob and weave" means to make rapid bodily movements up and down and from side to side.

36. The correct spelling for option (*a*) is "therapeutic". The correct spelling for option (*b*) is "sudatorium". The correct spelling for option (*d*) is "suffocate".

37. The correct sentence is "despite trying his best to persuade people to give up smoking he could not attain success." The verb form is incorrect.

38. The correct sentence is "he is taller than any other student in his class." In the original sentence it implies that he is taller than himself as he is also a student of the class.

39. The correct sentence is "a thousand rupees is all that he wants." Nouns such as rupees require a singular verb.

40. Concerned British Muslims, mostly of South Asian origin, want to turn their religion to critical enquiry and debate. "Open" is appropriate for the given blank. "Divulge" means to make public. "Restrict" means to confine within bounds. "Embark" means to make a start.

41. Perhaps the one positive aspect to an otherwise gloomy story of chronic hunger in India is the more frequent public acknowledgement of this sorry state of affairs. We need a word with a negative connotation as can be seen by the use of "sorry state of affairs". Option (*a*) is negated. "Unyielding" means characterized by firmness. "Unflinching" means uncompromising.

42. Research has established that chronic maternal undernourishment leads to fetal deprivation. The present perfect tense is used here. Present perfect tense consists of has and past participle.

43. Here 'applicants' is the subject which is plural. The sentence is in passive voice and hence, 'have been' should be used.

44. (A) is the correct option because it starts with 'the'- parallelism.

45. All the given options are grammatically incorrect. Hence, the correct answer is option (D).

46. The correct answer is option (C). A collection of things or people is called 'assortment'.

47. Refer to the first sentence of the second paragraph. It says that the colonists on board suffered from exposure, scurvy and outbreaks of contagious disease. Hence, option (A) is the correct answer.

48. Refer to the second sentence of the passage - 'After a treacherous and uncomfortable. lasted 66 days, they dropped anchor near the tip of Cape Cod.'.. Hence, option (D) is the correct answer.

49. The second paragraph of the passage clearly states that the pilgrims were "weakened by malnutrition and illness". Hence, option (A) is the correct answer.

50. 'To share someone's pain' means to understand and sympathize with someone's pain. Hence, option (B) is the correct answer.

51.
$$E = 5$$
$$D = 4$$
$$U = 21 \Rightarrow 2 + 1 = 3$$
$$C = 3$$
$$A = 1$$
$$T = 20 \Rightarrow 2 + 0 = 2$$
$$I = 9$$
$$O = 15 \Rightarrow 1 + 5 = 6$$
$$N = 14 \Rightarrow 1 + 4 = 5$$

Similarly,
$$W = 23 \Rightarrow 2 + 3 = 5$$
$$E = 5$$
$$S = 19 \Rightarrow 1 + 9 = 10 \Rightarrow 1 + 0 = 1$$
$$T = 20 \Rightarrow 2 + 0 = 2$$
$$E = 5$$
$$R = 18 \Rightarrow 1 + 8 = 9$$
$$N = 14 \Rightarrow 1 + 4 = 5.$$

Hence, the code of WESTERN is 5512595.

52.

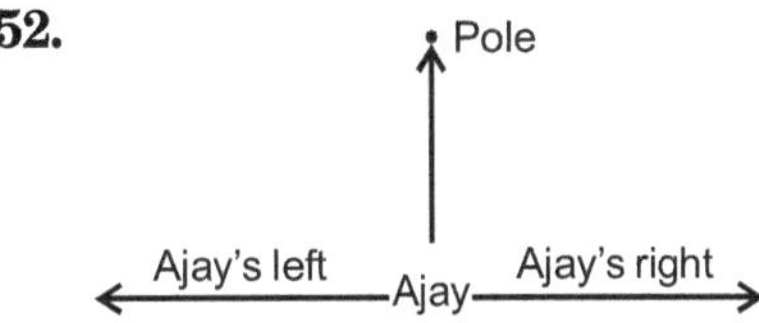

If the pole's shadow was on Ajay's left, it means that the left hand of Ajay was pointing towards West.

Hence, Ajay was facing North.

53. The numbers in the middle coloumn are square root of the product of the numbers in other two coloumns.

54. Three letters are skipped between every two consecutive letters.

55. The given series is abaab/abaab/abaab.

56. The given series is a combination of two alternate series 5, 25, 125… and 7, 49, 343, ...
Hence, required number is 343.

57. The pattern followed in the series is as follows:
$$h \xrightarrow{-1} g \xrightarrow{-1} f$$
and
$$k \xrightarrow{-1} j \xrightarrow{-1} i$$
$$\therefore \quad n \xrightarrow{-1} m \xrightarrow{-1} l$$

Hence, missing letters will be **ml**.

58. 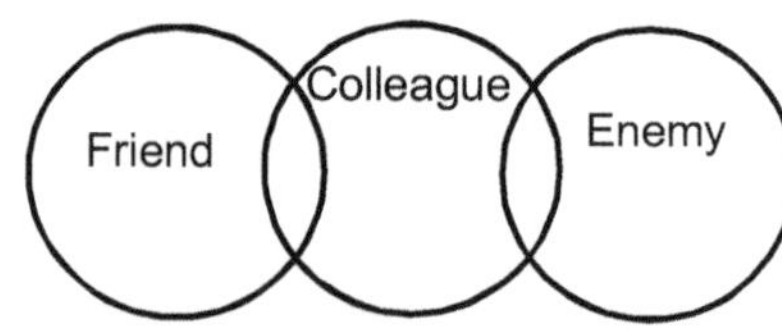

59. The correct order is A,C,B,D,E according to the stages in the life of a person.

60. The correct order of the words according to the dictionary is A,D,C,E,B

61. Position number of 2nd letter is 3 more than the position number of 1st letter and position number of 4th letter is 3 more than the position number of 3rd letter in every word.

62. "Soaring" is the only word which can be formed using the letters of the given word.

63. In all other options numbers are in the ratio of 3 : 1.

64. The required region is the common region of the triangle, rectangles and circle.

65. The alarm will ring together after 1140 sec

$$= 19 \text{ minute}$$

(LCM of 3 min 10 sec, 6 min 20 sec and 9 min 30 sec) Therefore, the three alarms will ring simultaneously again at 9: 19 a.m.

66. 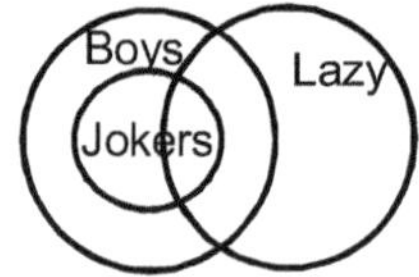

Only statements 1 and 3 are true.

67. 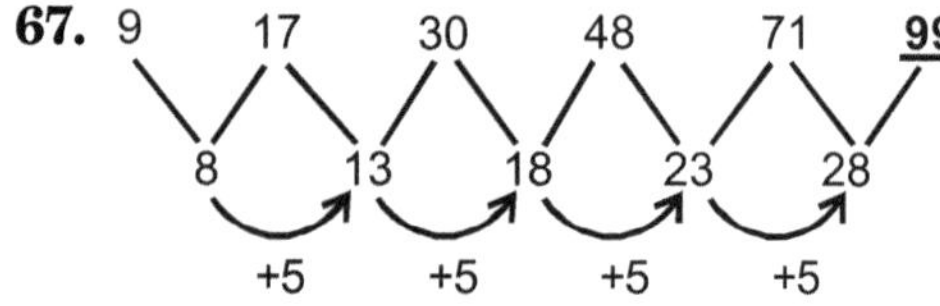

68. From the given information,

Priyanka > Pratibha

Priya > Pratibha

Priyanka > Parul

Since, Parul is not the youngest, so Pratibha is youngest of them.

69. 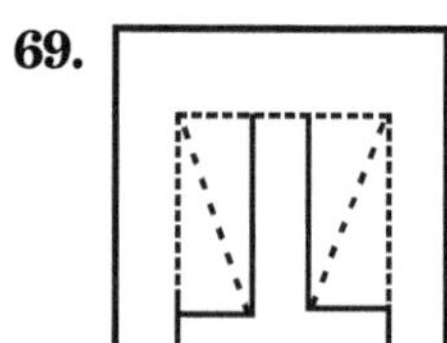

70. Number of vertical and horizontal lines get interchanged. Also number of '+' and '−' get interchanged and the whole figure is rotated by 180

71. On reflection, the L.H.S. of the question figure becomes the R.H.S of the answer figure and vice versa.

72. Rain is made of water. Coat is made of fur. The correct answer is option (*b*).

73. "Plain" cannot be formed using the letters of the given word. The given word does not have the letter "I"

74. 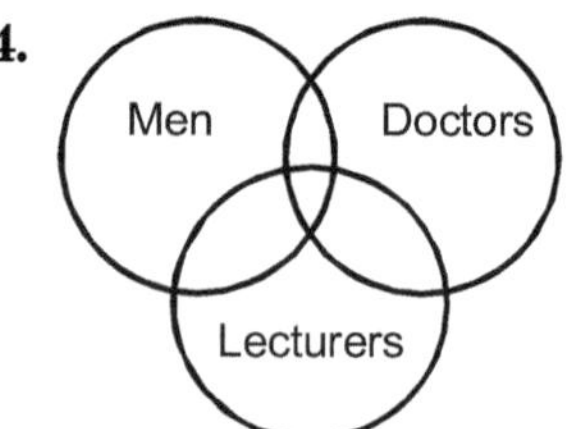

75. Number of 1 × 1 square = 13

Number of 2 × 2 square = 6

Number of 3 × 3 square = 1

∴ Total number of squares = 13 + 6 + 1 = 20

PRACTICE SET – 11

GENERAL INTELLIGENCE

Directions (Q. 1-2): *Select the related word / number from the given alternatives.*

1. Stethoscope : Heart beat : : ? : Temperature

   (a) Heat   (b) Mercury

   (c) Scale   (d) Thermometer

2. 520 : 738 : : ? : 350

   (a) 220   (b) 222

   (c) 230   (d) 248

Directions (Q. 3-4) : *Find the odd word / number or letter pair, from the given responses.*

3. (a) Play - Actor   (b) Building - Architect

   (c) Craft - Artisan   (d) Cloth - Skirt

4. (a) 357   (b) 581

   (c) 698   (d) 784

Direction : *From among the given alternatives, select the one in which the set of numbers is most like the set of numbers given in the question.*

5. Given set : (2, 10, 28)

   (a) (4, 20, 56)   (b) (7, 42, 49)

   (c) (12, 24, 48)   (d) (9, 27, 81)

Direction : *Which one of the given responses would be a meaningful order of the following words ?*

6. 1. Amoeba   2. Oyster

   3. Worm   4. Cow

   (a) 1, 3, 2, 4   (b) 1, 2, 3, 4

   (c) 4, 3, 2, 1   (d) 3, 2, 4, 1

7. Arrange the following words in a dictionary order :

   1. Intricate   2. Interview

   3. Intransigent   4. Interrogation

   5. Intravenous

   (a) 2, 4, 5, 3, 1   (b) 5, 3, 1, 2, 4

   (c) 4, 2, 3, 5, 1   (d) 3, 5, 2, 1, 4

Direction : *Which one set of letters when sequentially placed at the gaps in the given letter series-shall complete it ?*

8. a e b d _ fjgi _ koln _

   (a) cmh

   (b) chm

   (c) cgm

   (d) cjl

Directions (Q. 9-11) : *Find the missing number / letters / figure from the given responses.*

9. 5255, 5306, ..., 5408, 5459

   (a) 5057   (b) 5357

   (c) 2257   (d) 5157

10. Question Figures

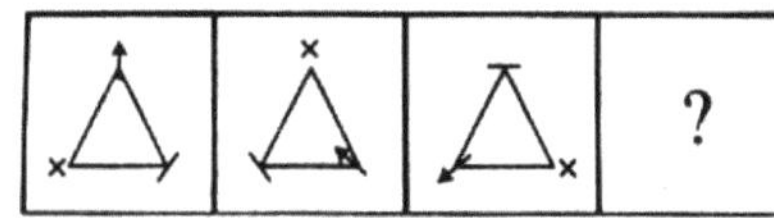

Answer Figures

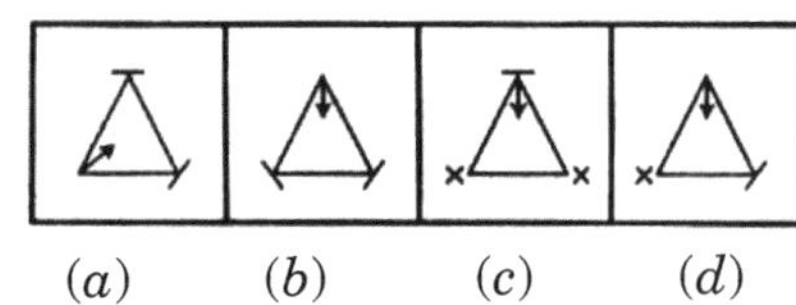

   (a)   (b)   (c)   (d)

11. $\dfrac{c}{6}, \dfrac{e}{10}, \dfrac{g}{14}, \dfrac{i}{18}, ?$

   (a) k/22   (b) k/11

   (c) p/22   (d) p/11

12 A father's age is one more than 5 times of his son's age. After 3 years, the father's age would be 2 less than four times the son's age. Find the present age of the father.

   (a) 30 years   (b) 40 years

   (c) 31 years   (d) 29 years

13. A is the father of B, C is the daughter of B, D is the brother of B, E is the son of A. What is the relationship between C and E ?

   (a) Brother and sister

   (b) Cousins

   (c) Niece and uncle

   (d) Uncle and aunt

Direction (Q. 14) : *From the given alternatives, select the word which **cannot** be formed using the letters of the given word.*

14. REPUBLICAN

   (a) CLIP   (b) PURE

   (c) ANKLE   (d) BANE

15. If SEVEN is coded as 23136 and EIGHT as 34579, what will be the code for NINE ?

   (a) 6463   (b) 6364

   (c) 6346   (d) 6436

16. Which one of the following is correct ?

$$96 * 6 * 8 * 2$$

(a) ÷, =, ×

(b) ×, =, ÷

(c) =, ÷ ×

(d) =, ×, ÷

17. Some equations are solved on the basis of certain systems. On the same basis find out the correct answer from amongst the four alternatives for the unsolved equation in the question.

$$a = 12(390) 8, b = 7 (134)5, c = 5(?) 12$$

(a) 299

(b) 289

(c) 279

(d) 280

Direction : *Find the missing number from the given responses.*

18.

1	3	7
2	4	4
4	5	9
3	2	3
50	70	?

(a) 23

(b) 115

(c) 118

(d) 220

19. My friend and I started simultaneously towards each other from two places 100 m apart. After walking 30 m, my friend turns left and goes 10 m, then he turns right and goes 20 m and then turns right again and comes back to the road on which he had started walking. If we walk with the same speed, what is the distance between us at this point of time ?

(a) 50 m

(b) 20 m

(c) 30 m

(d) 40 m

20. Choose from the four answer figures, the figure that will be formed when the question figure is folded into a box.

Question Figure

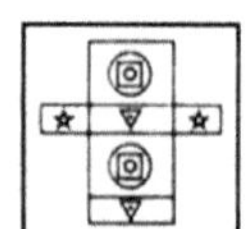

Answer Figures

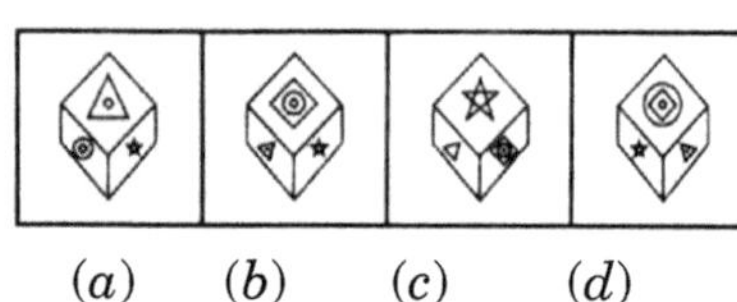

(a)   (b)   (c)   (d)

Direction (Q. 21) : *A statement is followed by two conclusions I and II. You have to consider the statement to be true, even if it seems to be at variance from commonly known facts. You are to decide which of the given conclusions can definitely be drawn from the given statements. Indicate your answer.*

21. Statement :

India is a multilingual country. Hindi is the national language of India.

Conclusions :

I. All Indians should learn many languages.

II. To be an Indian one needs to learn Hindi.

(a) Only I follows

(b) Only II follows

(c) Neither I nor II follows

(d) Both I and II follow

22. Which one of the following four diagrams represents correctly the relationship between Musicians, Instrumentalists, Violinists ?

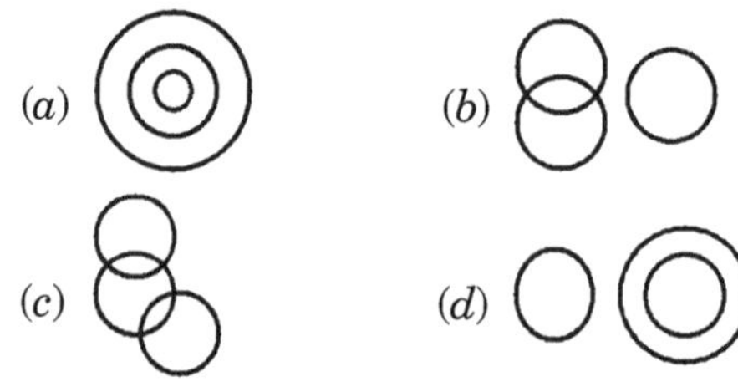

(a)   (b)

(c)   (d)

23. Which answer figure will complete the question figure ?

Question Figure

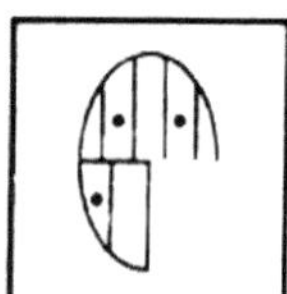

Answer Figures

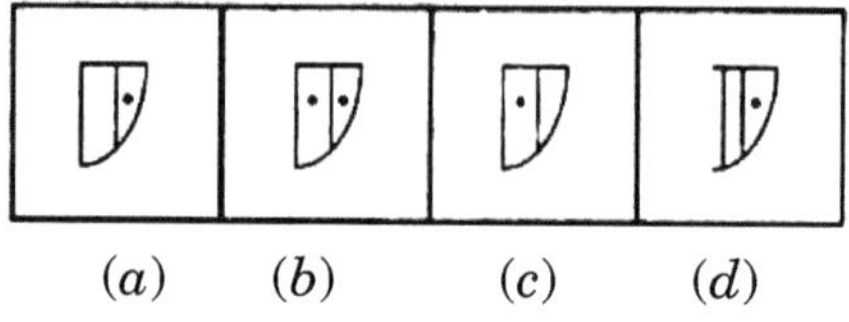

(a)   (b)   (c)   (d)

24. In the following figure in a garden, square represents the area where Jackfruit trees are grown; circle represents Mango trees and triangle represents Coconut trees. Which number represents the common area in which all types of trees are grown ?

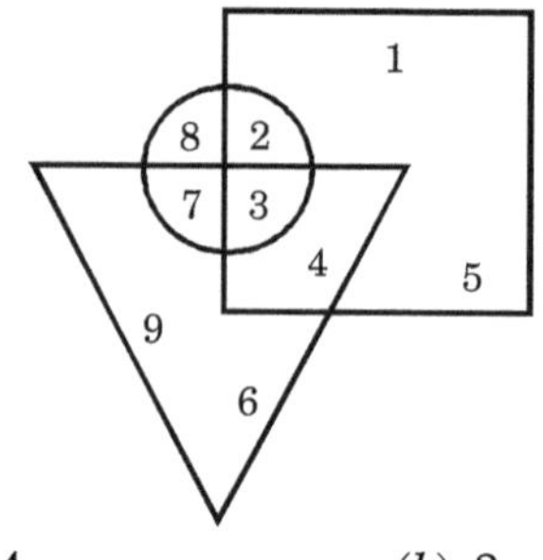

(a) 4

(b) 3

(c) 7

(d) 8

Directions: *From the given answer figures, select the one in which the question figure is hidden / embedded.*

25. Question Figure

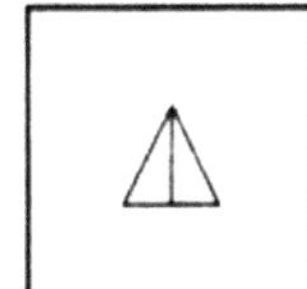

Answer Figures

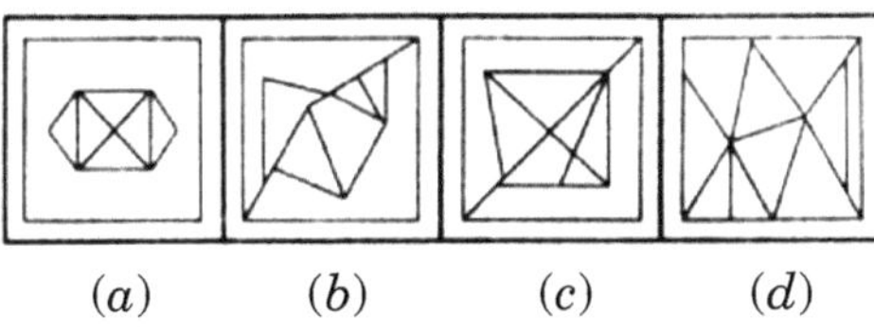

  (a) (b) (c) (d)

ENGLISH LANGUAGE

Directions(Q. 26-27): *Out of the four alternatives, choose the one which best expresses the meaning of the given word and mark it in the Answer Sheet.*

26. Benevolent
- (a) Beneficial
- (b) Kind
- (c) Helpful
- (d) Supportive

27. Ancestors
- (a) Extinct tribes
- (b) Relatives
- (c) Forefathers
- (d) Old people

Directions(Q. 28-29): *Choose the word opposite in meaning to the given word and mark it in the Answer Sheet.*

28. Gloomy
- (a) Radiant
- (b) Fragrant
- (c) Melodious
- (d) Illusory

29. Blessing
- (a) Dull
- (b) Curse
- (c) Hurt
- (d) Harsh

Directions(Q. 30-32): *Out of the four alternatives, choose the one which can be substituted for the given words / sentence and indicate it by blackening the appropriate rectangle [■] in the Answer Sheet.*

30. Instrument to measure atmospheric pressure
- (a) Metronome
- (b) Compass
- (c) Pedometer
- (d) Barometer

31. One who tends to take a hopeful view of life
- (a) Magnate
- (b) Creator
- (c) Pacifist
- (d) Optimist

32. Belonging to all parts of the world
- (a) Common
- (b) Universal
- (c) Worldly
- (d) International

Directions(Q. 33-35): *Four alternatives are given for the idiom / phrase underlined in the sentence. Choose the alternative which best expresses the meaning of the idiom / phrase and mark it in the Answer Sheet.*

33. Helena was <u>over head and ears</u> in love with Demetrius
- (a) Carefully
- (b) Completely
- (c) Brilliantly
- (d) Cautiously

34. Gopi works by <u>fits and starts</u>
- (a) Consistently
- (b) Irregularly
- (c) In high spirits
- (d) Enthusiastically

35. Naresh Goyal had <u>to stand on his feet</u> very early in his life
- (a) To be physically strong
- (b) To be independent
- (c) To stand erect
- (d) To be successful

Direction(Q. 36): *Groups of four words are given. In each group, one word is correctly spelt. Find the correctly spelt word and mark your answer in the Answer Sheet.*

36. (a) Onvelope
- (b) Envelope
- (c) Envelope
- (d) Envelap

Directions(Q. 37-39): *Some of the sentences have errors and some have none. Find out which part of a sentence has an error and blacken the rectangle [■] corresponding to the appropriate letter (a, b, c). If there is no error, blacken the rectangle [■] corresponding to (d) in the Answer Sheet.*

37. Last night I dream /I was a Sheikh on the 169th
  (a)   (b)
floor / of Burj Khalifa. No error.
  (c)   (d)

38. As soon as/ the lion saw the deer / he began to
  (a)   (b)   (c)
run after it. No error.
    (d)

39. The police asked us / about our movements
  (a)   (b)
/on a night of the crime. No error.
  (c)   (d)

Directions(Q.40-42): *Sentences are given with blanks to be filled in with an appropriate word(s). Four alternatives are suggested for each question. Choose the correct alternative and indicate it by blackening the appropriate rectangle [■] in the Answer Sheet.*

40. He travelled all..............the world when he was eight years old.

(*a*) in   (*b*) over

(*c*) with   (*d*) of

41. Dr. Sharma concluded his speech .... stressing on Buddha's teachings of the importance of charity.

(*a*) by

(*b*) with

(*c*) at

(*d*) in

42. Shivaji Maharaj fought............... every kind of aggression.

(*a*) against   (*b*) to

(*c*) with   (*d*) at

Directions(Q.43-45): *A part of the sentence is underlined. Below are given alternatives to the underlined part at (a), (b) and (c) which may improve the sentence. Choose the correct alternative. In case no improvement is needed your answer is (d).*

43. <u>The strong breeze</u> blew his hat away

(*a*) The strong air   (*b*) The strong breath

(*c*) The strong wind (*d*) No improvement

44. The Japanese are <u>hardly working</u> people

(*a*) A hard working people

(*b*) A hardly working people

(*c*) Hard working people

(*d*) No improvement

45. The monkey was seated at the <u>foot</u> of a tree

(*a*) Bottom   (*b*) End

(*c*) Root   (*d*) No improvement

Directions: In question nos. **46** to **50**, you have given a passage with 5 questions. Read the passage carefully and choose the best answer to each question out of the four alternatives.

Contrary to common assumption, major forms of large-scale organized political violence in sub-Saharan Africa are declining in frequency and intensity, and the region is not uniquely prone to the onset of warfare. African civil wars in the late 2000s were about half as common compared to the mid-1990s. The character of warfare has also changed. Contemporary wars are typically small-scale, fought on state peripheries and sometimes across multiple states, and involve factionalized insurgents who typically cannot hold significant territory or capture state capitals. Episodes of large-scale mass killing of civilians are also on the decline. That said other forms of political violence that receive less attention in the academic literature are increasing or persistent. These include electoral violence and violence over access to livelihood resources, such as land and water. In the twenty-first century both the volume and the character of civil wars have changed in significant ways. Civil wars are and have been the dominant form of warfare in Africa, but they have declined steeply in recent years, so that today there are half as many as in the 1990s.

46. What is the common assumption pertaining to the political violence in sub-Saharan Africa.

(*a*) Major forms of large scale organized political violence are decreasing in frequency and intensity.

(*b*) African civil wars in late 2000s were not as common as the civil wars in mid 1990s.

(*c*) The region is uniquely prone to the beginning of a war.

(*d*) Mass killing of civilians is declining in the region.

47. Which of the following is not a characteristic of contemporary wars according to the passage?

(*a*) Wars involved people that were part of a larger group.

(*b*) Wars were sometimes fought between the people of multiple states.

(*c*) Wars were generally fought on a small-scale.

(*d*) Wars were fought to capture state capitals.

48. Which of the following wars is the most powerful form of warfare in Africa?

(*a*) Contemporary wars

(*b*) Civil wars

(*c*) Small-scale wars

(*d*) Large-scale wars

49. Which of the following is the antonym of the word 'onset'?

(*a*) Whammy   (*b*) Ambusher

(*c*) Offensive   (*d*) Omega

50. Which of the following is the synonym of the word 'periphery'?

(*a*) Skirt   (*b*) Center

(*c*) Crest   (*d*) Ambit

QUANTITATIVE APTITUDE

51. If $\sqrt{2^x} = 256$, then the value of x is

(a) 14 (b) 16

(c) 18 (d) 20

52. If $a^4 + b^4 = a^2 b^2$, then $(a^6 + b^6)$ equals

(a) 0 (b) 1

(c) $a^2 + b^2$ (d) $a^2 b^4 + b^4 b^2$

53. A number, when divided by 221, leaves a remainder 64. What is the remainder if the same number is divided by 13?

(a) 0 (b) 1

(c) 11 (d) 12

54. If the selling price of 4 articles is equal to the cost price of 5 articles, the profit is

(a) 20% (b) $22\dfrac{1}{2}\%$

(c) 25% (d) 30%

55. $\dfrac{3.25 \times 3.25 + 1.75 \times 1.75 - 2 \times 3.25 \times 1.75}{3.25 \times 3.25 - 1.75 + 1.75}$

is simplified to

(a) 0.5 (b) 0.4

(c) 0.3 (d) 0.2

56. The next number of the sequence

3, 7, 15, 31, 63, ? is

(a) 95 (b) 111

(c) 123 (d) 127

57. $\left(\dfrac{1+\sqrt{2}}{\sqrt{5}+\sqrt{3}} + \dfrac{1-\sqrt{2}}{\sqrt{5}-\sqrt{3}} \right)$ simplifies to

(a) $\sqrt{5} + \sqrt{6}$ (b) $2\sqrt{5} + \sqrt{6}$

(c) $\sqrt{5} - \sqrt{6}$ (d) $2\sqrt{5} - 3\sqrt{6}$

58. $(0.9 \times 0.9 \times 0.9 + 0.1 \times 0.1 \times 0.1)$ is equal to

(a) 0.73 (b) 0.82

(c) 0.91 (d) 1.00

59. If 30% of $(B - A)$ = 18% of $(B + A)$, then the ratio $A : B$ is equal to

(a) 4 : 1 (b) 1 : 4

(c) 5 : 4 (d) 5 : 9

60. In an examination, a student has to obtain 33% of the maximum marks to pass. He got 125 marks and failed by 40 marks. The maximum marks were

(a) 500 (b) 600

(c) 800 (d) 1000

61. A's income is 10% more than B's income. How much per cent is B's income less than A's income ?

(a) 10% (b) 9%

(c) $11\dfrac{1}{9}\%$ (d) $9\dfrac{1}{11}\%$

62. Two successive discounts of 10% and 5% are equivalent to a single discount of

(a) 14% (b) 14.25%

(c) 14.50% (d) 15%

63. If the length of a rectangular plot of land is increased by 5% and the breadth is decreased by 10%, how much will its area increase or decrease ?

(a) 6.5% increase (b) 5.5% decrease

(c) 5.5% increase (d) 6.5 decrease

64. Two pipes, P and Q can fill a cistern in 12 and 15 minutes respectively. Both are opened together, but at the end of 3 minutes, P is turned off. In how many more minutes will Q fill the cistern ?

(a) 7 (b) $7\dfrac{1}{2}$

(c) 8 (d) $8\dfrac{1}{4}$

65. The speeds of two trains are in the ratio 6 : 7. If the second train runs 364 km in 4 hours, then the speed of first train is

(a) 60 km/hr (b) 72 km/hr

(c) 78 km/hr (d) 84 km/hr

66. Two trains, 80 metres and 120 metres long, are running at the speed of 25 km/hr and 35 km/hr respectively in the same direction on parallel tracks. How many seconds will they take to pass each other?

(a) 48 (b) 64

(c) 70 (d) 72

67. A sum of money becomes double in 3 years at compound interest Compounded annually. At the same rate, in how many years will it become four times of itself ?

(a) 4 (b) 6

(c) 6.4 (d) 7.5

68. The simple interest on a sum of money is $\dfrac{1}{9}$ of the principal and the number of years is equal to the rate per cent per annum. The rate of interest per annum is

(a) $1\dfrac{1}{9}\%$ (b) $2\dfrac{2}{3}\%$

(c) 3% (d) $3\dfrac{1}{3}\%$

69. In an examination, the average of marks was found to be 50. For deducting marks for computational errors, the marks of 100 candidates had to be changed from 90 to 60 each and so the average of marks came down to 45. The total number of candidates, who appeared at the examination, was

(a) 600   (b) 300
(c) 200   (d) 150

70. There are 50 students in a class. Their average weight is 45 kg. When one student leaves the class, the average weight reduces by 100 g. What is the weight of the student who left the class ?

(a) 45 kg   (b) 47.9 kg
(c) 49.9 kg   (d) 50.1 kg

71. A boat covers 24 km upstream and 36 km downstream in 6 hours, while it covers 36 km upstream and 24 km downstream in $6\dfrac{1}{2}$ hours. The speed of the current is

(a) 1 km/hr   (b) 2 km/hr
(c) 1.5 km/hr   (d) 2.5 km/hr

72. 30 pens and 75 pencils altogether were purchased for ₹ 510. If the average price of a pencil was ₹ 2, what was the average price of a pen ?

(a) ₹ 9   (b) ₹ 10
(c) ₹ 11   (d) ₹ 12

Directions : *Given here is a bar graph showing the number of cycles produced in a factory during five consecutive weeks. Observe the graph and answer questions number 73, 74 and 75.*

Graph showing the number of cycles produced in a factory in 5 consecutive weeks

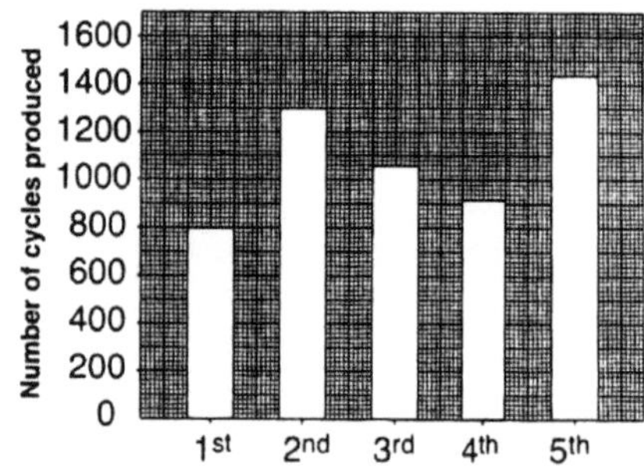

73. The number of cycles produced during third and fourth weeks together is

(a) 1060   (b) 1980
(c) 920   (d) 1900

74. The number of cycles produced in the 5th week is

(a) 1400   (b) 1300
(c) 1440   (d) 1600

75. Total number of cycles produced in five consecutive weeks is

(a) 5520   (b) 1600
(c) 7200   (d) 7000

GENERAL AWARENESS

76. Which state has announced to ban 15 year old petrol vehicles and 10 year old diesel vehicles to curb air pollution?

(a) Bihar   (b) Haryana
(c) Maharashtra   (d) Telangana

77. How many times was the term of the Lok Sabha extended upto 6 years ?

(a) Once   (b) Twice
(c) Thrice   (d) Never

78. Where did the practice of 'Shadow Cabinet' originate ?

(a) United States of America
(b) Great Britain
(c) Italy
(d) France

79. Sarkaria Commission was constituted to give its report on

(a) New pay scales for the government servants
(b) Centre - State relations
(c) Ram Janmabhoomi - Babri Masjid dispute
(d) Kaveri dispute

80. Which of the following Articles of the Constitution deals with the Fundamental Duties ?

(a) Article 39 C   (b) Article 51 A
(c) Article 29 B   (d) None of these

81. Poverty in less developed countries is largely due to

(a) voluntary idleness
(b) income inequality
(c) lack of cultural activities
(d) lack of intelligence of the people

82. Karl Marx's book 'Das Kapital' was published in

(a) 1857   (b) 1862
(c) 1867   (d) 1872

83. Among the tax revenues of the Union Government, the most important source is —

(a) Income Tax   (b) Customs Duty
(c) Corporation Tax   (d) Union Excise Duties

84. The headquarters of the Ghadar Party was at

(a) Karachi   (b) Moscow
(c) Berlin   (d) San Francisco

85. NITI AAYOG signed two year Statement Of Intent with which company to set up the first 10 Atal Tinkering Labs in India to foster curiosity, creativity and imagination among young innovators?

(a) Google　　　　(b) Yahoo

(c) CDAC　　　　(d) Intel

86. After the death of Rajaram in 1700 A.D., Marathas continued the war against the Mughals under his brave wife

(a) Tarabai　　　　(b) Lakshmibai

(c) Ramabai　　　　(d) Jijabai

87. Where is the satellite launching centre of India located ?

(a) Ahmedabad　　　　(b) Hassan

(c) Sriharikota　　　　(d) Thumba

88. Hardayal, an intellectual giant, was associated with

(a) Home Rule Movement

(b) Ghadar Movement

(c) Swadeshi Movement

(d) Non-Cooperation Movement

89. The song 'Jana-Gana-Mana' composed by Rabindra Nath Tagore was first published in January 1912 under the title of

(a) Jay He　　　　(b) Rashtra Jagriti

(c) Bharat Vidhata　　(d) Matribhoomi

90. In which case did the Supreme Court restore the priority of the Fundamental Rights over the Directive Principles of State Policy ?

(a) Golaknath Case

(b) Keshavananda Bharti Case

(c) Minerva Mills Case

(d) State of Madras vs. Champkam Dorairajan

91. When did India join the United Nations ?

(a) 1945　　　　(b) 1947

(c) 1950　　　　(d) 1954

92. Indian desert is called

(a) Gobi　　　　(b) Sahara

(c) Thar　　　　(d) Atacama

93. The animal which can tolerate more summer heat is

(a) Buffalo　　　　(b) Cow

(c) Goat　　　　(d) Donkey

94. According to Darwin's Theory of Evolution, long necks in giraffes

(a) arose because of constant attempt to reach leaves on tall trees, generation after generation

(b) do not give them any special advantage and is just an accident

(c) give them advantage in finding food, because of which those with long necks survive

(d) is a result of the special weather prevalent in African Savannah

95. Cooking gas is a mixture of

(a) methane and ethylene

(b) carbon dioxide and oxygen

(c) butane and propane

(d) carbon monoxide and carbon dioxide

96. Dry powder fire extinguishers contain

(a) sand

(b) sand and sodium carbonate

(c) sand and potassium carbonate

(d) sand and sodium bicarbonate

97. Which type of glass is used for making glass reinforced plastic ?

(a) Pyrex glass　　　　(b) Flint glass

(c) Quartz glass　　　　(d) Fibre glass

98. The most commonly used chemical in the artificial rainmaking or cloud seeding are

(a) Silver Iodide (AgI)

(b) Sodium Chloride (NaCl)

(c) Dry Ice (Frozen CO_2)

(d) All of these

99. Grammy Award is given in the field of

(a) Literature

(b) Music

(c) Science

(d) Inventions and Discoveries

100. Which bank announced partnership with Reliance Jio Money for One-Click payment service that will make payment ease for their customers?

(a) Yes Bank

(b) Indus Ind Bank

(c) Federal Bank

(d) HDFC Bank

ANSWERS

1. (d)	**2.** (b)	**3.** (d)	**4.** (a)	**5.** (a)	**6.** (a)	**7.** (c)	**8.** (b)	**9.** (b)	**10.** (d)
11. (a)	**12.** (c)	**13.** (c)	**14.** (c)	**15.** (a)	**16.** (a)	**17.** (c)	**18.** (b)	**19.** (b)	**20.** (d)
21. (c)	**22.** (a)	**23.** (a)	**24.** (b)	**25.** (b)	**26.** (b)	**27.** (c)	**28.** (a)	**29.** (b)	**30.** (d)
31. (d)	**32.** (b)	**33.** (b)	**34.** (b)	**35.** (b)	**36.** (b)	**37.** (a)	**38.** (d)	**39.** (c)	**40.** (b)
41. (a)	**42.** (a)	**43.** (c)	**44.** (c)	**45.** (a)	**46.** (c)	**47.** (d)	**48.** (b)	**49.** (d)	**50.** (a)
51. (b)	**52.** (a)	**53.** (d)	**54.** (c)	**55.** (c)	**56.** (d)	**57.** (c)	**58.** (a)	**59.** (b)	**60.** (a)
61. (d)	**62.** (c)	**63.** (b)	**64.** (d)	**65.** (c)	**66.** (d)	**67.** (b)	**68.** (d)	**69.** (a)	**70.** (c)
71. (b)	**72.** (d)	**73.** (b)	**74.** (c)	**75.** (a)	**76.** (b)	**77.** (a)	**78.** (b)	**79.** (b)	**80.** (b)
81. (b)	**82.** (c)	**83.** (d)	**84.** (d)	**85.** (d)	**86.** (a)	**87.** (c)	**88.** (b)	**89.** (a)	**90.** (d)
91. (a)	**92.** (c)	**93.** (a)	**94.** (a)	**95.** (c)	**96.** (d)	**97.** (d)	**98.** (a)	**99.** (a)	**100.** (c)

EXPLANATIONS

1. As Stethoscope measures Heart beats, similarly Thermometer measures temperature.

2. The sum of digits of second number is 2 more than the sum of the digits of first number.

4. Only 357 is exactly divisible by 3.

5. $2 \xrightarrow{\times 2} 4$

$10 \xrightarrow{\times 2} 20$

$58 \xrightarrow{\times 2} 56$

8. a e b d c, p j g i h, k o l n m

9. 5255 5306 5357 5408 5459
$+51$ $+51$ $+51$ $+51$

11. $\dfrac{c \;^{+2}\; e \;^{+2}\; g \;^{+2}\; i \;^{+2}\; k}{6 \;_{+4}\; 10 \;_{+4}\; 14 \;_{+4}\; 18 \;_{+4}\; 22}$

12. Let the present age of the son be x years

∴ The present age of the father

$$= 5x + 1 \text{ years}$$

∴ $\quad 5x + 1 + 3 = 4(x + 3) - 2$

∴ $\quad 5x + 4 = 4x + 12 - 2$

∴ $\quad x = 10 - 4 = 6$

∴ The present age of the father is 31 years.

13.

A • Father B Brother • → D
Son ↓   ↓ Daughter
E   C

E is the uncle of C and C is the niece of E.

14. K is not in the given word.

15. SEVEN = 23136

and EIGHT = 34579

∴ NINE = 6463

16. $96 \div 6 = 8 \times 2$

$16 = 16$

17. $(12 + 8)^2 = 400 \to 400 - 10 = 390$

$(7 + 5)^2 = 144 \to 144 - 10 = 134$

Similarly

$(5 + 12)^2 = 289 \to 289 - 10 = 279$

18. $1 + 2 + 3 + 4 = 10$

$\Rightarrow \quad 10 \times 5 = 50$

$3 + 4 + 5 + 2 = 14$

$\Rightarrow \quad 14 \times 5 = 70$

∴ $\quad 7 + 4 + 9 + 3 = 23$

$\Rightarrow \quad 23 \times 5 = 115$

∴ $\quad ? = 115$

19.

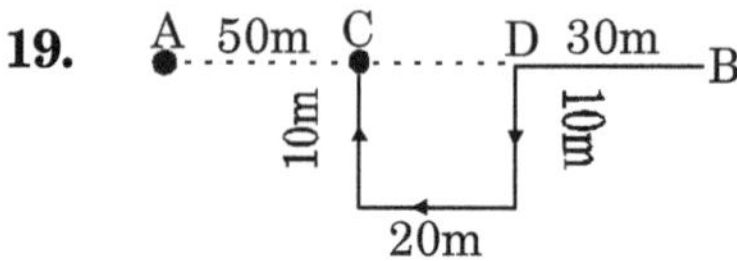

Distance travelled by the friend

$$= 30 + 10 + 20 + 10 = 70 \text{ m}$$

∴ I shall after travelling 70 m, reach at D.

∴ Required distance = 20 m

20.

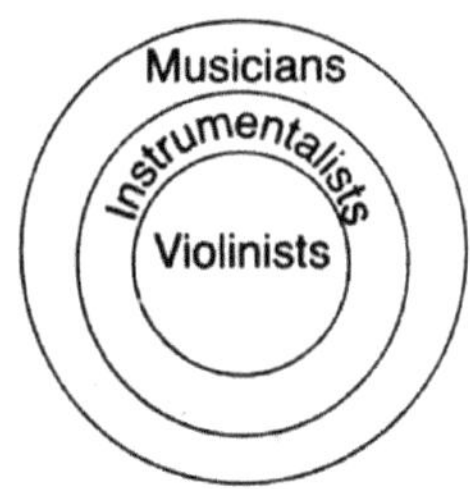

1 is opposite to 5, 21 is opposite to 4 and 3 is opposite to 6.

22. All of the violinists are instrumentailsts and all instrumentalists are musicians.

51.
$$\sqrt{2^x} = 256$$
$$2^{x/2} = (2)^8$$
$$\therefore \quad \frac{x}{2} = 8$$
$$\therefore \quad x = 16$$

52.
$$a^4 + b^4 = a^2 b^2$$
$$\Rightarrow a^4 + b^4 - a^2 b^2 = 0$$
$$\therefore a^6 + b^6 = (a^2 + b^2)(a^4 + b^4 - a^2 b^2) = 0$$

53. Required remainder = 12

54. Profit = $\dfrac{5-4}{4} \times 100 = 25$

55.
$$\frac{3.25 \times 3.25 + 1.75 \times 1.75 - 2 \times 3.25 \times 1.75}{3.25 \times 3.25 - 1.75 \times 1.75}$$
$$= \frac{(3.25)^2 + (1.75)^2 - 2 \times 3.25 \times 1.75}{(3.25)^2 - (1.75)^2}$$
$$= \frac{(3.25 - 1.75)^2}{(3.25 - 1.75)(3.25 + 1.75)}$$
$$= \frac{3.25 - 1.75}{3.25 + 1.75} = \frac{1.50}{5.00} = 0.3$$

56. 3, 7, 15, 31, 63, (127)

$\times 2 + 1$ $\times 2 + 1$ $\times 2 + 1$ $\times 2 + 1$ $\times 2 + 1$

57.
$$\frac{1+\sqrt{2}}{\sqrt{5}+\sqrt{3}} + \frac{1+\sqrt{2}}{\sqrt{5}-\sqrt{3}}$$
$$= \frac{(1+\sqrt{2})(\sqrt{5}-\sqrt{3}) + (1-\sqrt{2})(\sqrt{5}+\sqrt{3})}{(\sqrt{5}+\sqrt{3})(\sqrt{5}-\sqrt{3})}$$
$$= \frac{\sqrt{5}+\sqrt{10}-\sqrt{3}-\sqrt{6}+\sqrt{5}-\sqrt{10}+\sqrt{3}-\sqrt{6}}{5-3}$$
$$= \frac{2\sqrt{5}-2\sqrt{6}}{2} = \sqrt{5}-\sqrt{6}$$

58. $0.9 \times 0.9 \times 0.9 + 0.1 \times 0.1 \times 0.1$
$$= 0.729 + 0.001 = 0.730$$

59.
$$\frac{30}{100} \text{ of } (B - A) = \frac{18}{100} \text{ of } (B + A)$$
$$\therefore \quad 30\,B - 30\,A = 18\,B + 18A$$
$$\therefore \quad -48A = -12\,B$$
$$\therefore \quad A : B = 12 : 48$$
$$= 1 : 4$$

60. Maximum marks = $\dfrac{100(125 + 40)}{33}$
$$= 500$$

61. Required % = $\dfrac{100 \times 10}{100 + 10}$
$$= \frac{1000}{110}$$
$$= 9\frac{1}{11}$$

62. A single discount = $\left(10 + 5 - \dfrac{10 \times 5}{100}\right)\%$
$$= 14.5\%$$

64. Part of the cistern filled in 3 minutes
$$= \frac{3}{12} + \frac{3}{15}$$
$$= \frac{15 + 12}{60} = \frac{9}{20}$$
Remaining part = $1 - \dfrac{9}{20} = \dfrac{11}{20}$
$$\therefore \quad \text{Required time} = \frac{11}{20} \times 15$$
$$= 8\frac{1}{4} \text{ minutes.}$$

65. Speed of second train = $\dfrac{364}{4} = 91$ km/hr
$$\therefore \text{ Speed of first train } = 91 \times \frac{6}{7}$$
$$= 78 \text{ km/hr}$$

66. Relative speed = $35 - 25$
$$= 10 \text{ km/hr}$$
$$= 10 \times \frac{5}{18}$$
$$= \frac{25}{9} \text{ m/sec}$$
Total distance = $80 + 120 = 200$ m
$$\therefore \quad \text{Required time} = 200 \times \frac{9}{25} = 72 \text{ sec.}$$

67.
$$2x = x\left(1+\frac{R}{100}\right)^3$$

$$\therefore \quad 2 = \left(1+\frac{R}{100}\right)^3$$

and
$$4 = \left(1+\frac{R}{100}\right)^y$$

$$\therefore \quad (2)^2 = \left(1+\frac{R}{100}\right)^6$$

$$= \left(1+\frac{R}{100}\right)^y$$

$$\therefore \quad y = 6 \text{ years.}$$

68.
$$\frac{1}{9}P = \frac{P \times R \times R}{100}$$

$$\therefore \quad R^2 = \frac{100}{9}$$

$$\therefore \quad R = \frac{10}{3} = 3\frac{1}{3}\%$$

69. Let the number of candidiates who apeared in the examination be x.

$$\therefore \quad x \times 45 = x \times 50 - 100(90-60)$$

$$\therefore \quad 45x = 50x - 3000$$

$$\therefore \quad x = 600$$

70. Let the weight of the student who left the class be x kg.

$$50 \times 45 = 49 \times (45 - 0.1) + x$$

$$2250 = 44.9 \times 49 + x$$

$$\therefore \quad x = 2250 - 2200.1 = 49.9 \text{ kg.}$$

71. Let the speed of current be y km/hr and the speed of the boat in still water be x km/hr.

$$\frac{25}{x-y} + \frac{36}{x+y} = 6$$

or
$$\frac{36}{x-y} + \frac{54}{x+y} = 9$$

and
$$\frac{36}{x-y} + \frac{24}{x+y} = \frac{13}{2}$$

$$\frac{30}{x+y} = \frac{5}{2}$$

$$\therefore \quad x + y = 12$$

and
$$x - y = 8$$

$$\therefore \quad y = 2 \text{ km/hr}$$

72. Average price of a pen

$$= \frac{510 - 150}{30} = ₹\,12$$

73. Required number $= 1060 + 920 = 1980$

74. Required number $= 1440$

75. Required number

$$= 800 + 1300 + 1060 + 920 + 1440 = 5520$$

■■

PRACTICE SET - 12

GENERAL INTELLIGENCE

Directions: In question no. 1 to 3, select the related word/letters/number from the given alternatives.

1. BKLP : DNPU : : SORT : ?

  (a) URVY   (b) VRUX

  (c) TQVX   (d) UQRY

2. NIKE : JEGA : : SALT : ?

  (a) OVHP   (b) OWHP

  (c) NWGN   (d) NVGP

3. 475 : 639 : : 382 : ?

  (a) 576   (b) 496

  (c) 582   (d) 676

4. Arrange the following words as per the order in the dictionary:

  (i) Ascend   (ii) Asceses

  (iii) Ascots   (iv) Ascetic

  (v) Asbestos

  (a) (v), (iv), (iii), (ii), (i)   (b) (v), (i), (ii), (iv), (iii)

  (c) (v), (i), (iv), (ii), (iii)   (d) (v), (iv), (ii), (iii), (i)

Directions: In question nos. 5 and 6, find the odd word /number/letters from the given alternatives.

5. (a) Telephone   (b) Newspaper

  (c) Podcast   (d) Television

6. (a) 217   (b) 126

  (c) 344   (d) 729

7. Which one of the following would be a meaningful order of the following states in descending order of area?

  (i) Rajasthan   (ii) Manipur

  (iii) Delhi   (iv) Uttar Pradesh

  (v) Tamil Nadu

  (a) (v), (i), (iv), (iii), (ii)

  (b) (i), (iv), (v), (ii), (iii)

  (c) (iv), (i), (v), (ii), (iii)

  (d) (i), (iv), (v), (iii), (ii)

Directions: In question nos. 8 to 11, a series is given, with one term missing. Choose the correct alternative from the given ones.

8. MLKS, ONMU, QPOW, ?.

  (a) SQPY   (b) SRQX

  (c) SRQY   (d) SQRY

9.

3	5	(−2)	8
6	7	(−1)	13
9	3	?	12
8	6	2	?

  (a) 6 and (−14)   (b) −6 and 14

  (c) 6 and 14   (d) (−6) and (−14)

10. 8, 15, 29, 57, 113, ?.

  (a) 225   (b) 228

  (c) 232   (d) 248

11. 4, 14, 18, 32, 50, ?.

  (a) 96   (b) 88

  (c) 82   (d) 92

12. Sandeep and Manish start from a certain point. Sandeep walks 3 km South, turns right and then walks 6 km. Manish walks 6 km West, turns right and walks 4 km. How far are they apart now?

  (a) 10 km   (b) 8 km

  (c) 7 km   (d) 6 km

13. If SELDOM is written as UCNBQK, how can BASKET be written?

  (a) ZCQMCV   (b) DYUIGR

  (c) DZUJGR   (d) ZBQMBV

14. From the given alternatives, select the word which can be formed using the letters of the given word.

PROBABLY

  (a) LABLE   (b) PROBATE

  (c) LOBBY   (d) BROAD

15. If 'P' means '+', 'Q' means '×', 'R' means '÷' and 'S' means '−' then

92 P 182 R 13 Q 3 S 18 =?

  (a) 303   (b) 116

  (c) 305   (d) 117

16. Which of the following interchange of sign/number would make the given equation **correct**?

$$(67 + 5) - 3 \div 2 \times 8 = 8$$

  (a) + and ×

  (b) 2 and 5

  (c) ÷ and −

  (d) 8 and 67

17. If North-east becomes West, South-east becomes North and so on, what will North become?

(a) South-west   (b) South-east

(c) North-east   (d) North-west

18. If TRACE is written as VTCEG, then what will be written as MULTY?

(a) KTJRW   (b) OWNVA

(c) KSJRW   (d) OVMVA

Directions: In the following question two statements are given followed by two conclusions I and II. You have to consider the statements to be true, even if they seem at variance from commonly known facts. You have to decide which of the given conclusions, if any, follow from the given statements.

19. Statement I: Some parrots are birds, some birds are mammals.

Statement II: All mammals are animals, all animals are social.

Conclusion I: Some social are mammals.

Conclusion II: Some birds are animals.

(a) Only conclusion I follows

(b) Only conclusion II follows

(c) Both conclusions I and II follow

(d) Neither conclusion I nor conclusion II follows

20. A cube painted black on the outer surface is of 4 cm edge. If it is cut into one-cm equal sized cubes. How many cubes are there which are black on only one side?

(a) 8   (b) 12

(c) 16   (d) 24

21. Identify the response figure in which the figures given are found.

Question Figure:

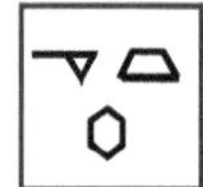

Answer Figures:

(a)   (b)   (c)   (d)

Directions: In the following question study the following diagram carefully and answer the questions based on it.

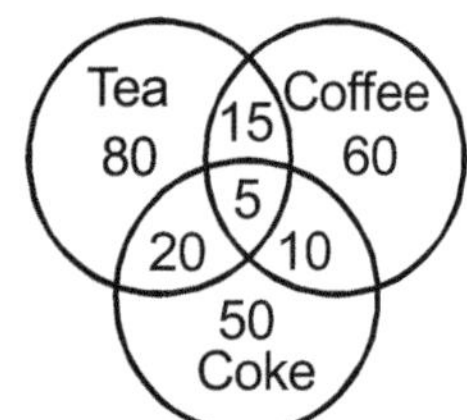

22. The diagram shows the survey in a class on a sample of 250 students with reference to their liking of Tea, Cofee and Coke. 20 students like

(a) Only Tea and Coke

(b) Only Cofee and coke

(c) Only Tea and Cofee

(d) Tea, Cofee and Coke

Directions: In the following question nos. 23 and 25, which answer figure will complete the pattern in the question figure?

23. Question Figure:

Answer Figures:

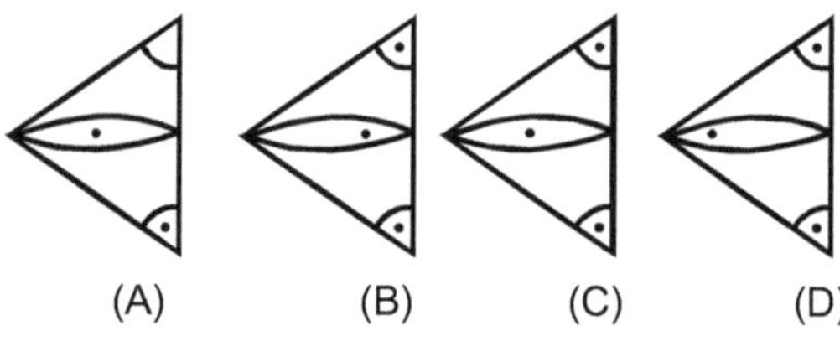

(A)   (B)   (C)   (D)

24. From the given answer figures, select the one in which the question figure is not hidden/embedded.

Question Figure:

Answer Figures:

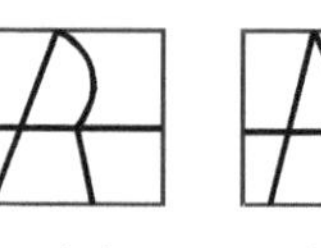 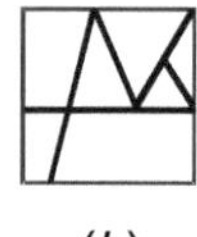  

(a)   (b)   (c)   (d)

25. A piece of paper is folded and punched as shown below in the question figures. From the given answer figures, indicate how it will appear when opened.

Question Figures:

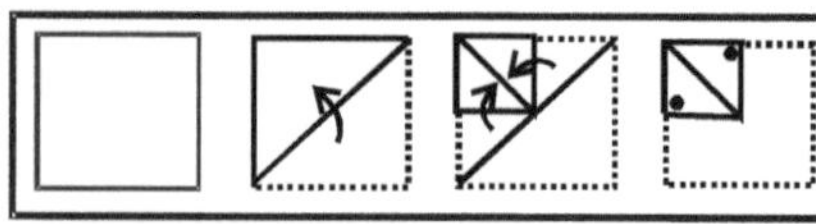

Answer Figures:

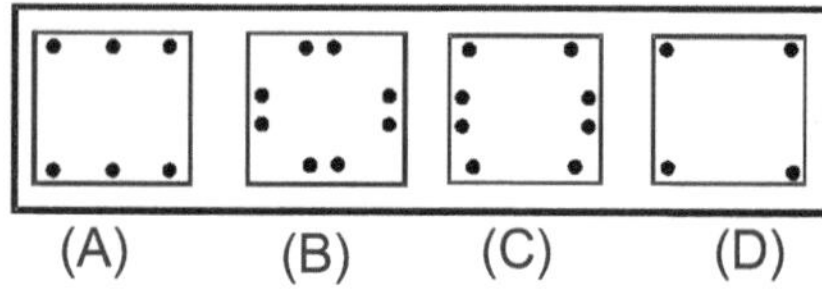

(A)   (B)   (C)   (D)

ENGLISH LANGUAGE

Directions: In question nos. **26** to **27**, out of the four alternatives, choose the one which best expresses the meaning of the given word and mark it in the answer sheet.

26. Pester

    (*a*) Console   (*b*) Disregard

    (*c*) Oblige   (*d*) Annoy

27. Sanctum

    (*a*) Pureness   (*b*) Selfishness

    (*c*) Shrine   (*d*) Baptizer

Directions: In question nos. **28** to **29**, in the following question choose the word opposite in meaning to the given word and mark it in the answer sheet.

28. Prudence

    (*a*) Elemental   (*b*) Watchful

    (*c*) Witti   (*d*) Carelessness

29. Exacerbate

    (*a*) Aggravate   (*b*) Exaggerate

    (*c*) Ease   (*d*) Understate

Directions: In question nos. **30** to **32**, out of the four alternatives, choose the one which can be substituted for the given words/sentences.

30. A person who is an expert in a particular subject

    (*a*) Gourmand   (*b*) Oenophile

    (*c*) Swill   (*d*) Connoisseur

31. Stamp collector

    (*a*) Numismatist   (*b*) Bibliophile

    (*c*) Antiquarian   (*d*) Philatelist

32. Cultivation of ornamental flowers

    (*a*) Orthodontic

    (*b*) Agriculture

    (*c*) Floriculture

    (*d*) Anthropology

Directions: In question nos. **33** to **35**, four alternatives are given for the idiom/phrase underlined in the sentence. Choose the alternative which best expresses the meaning of the given idiom/phrase.

33. Namit's boss has been <u>taking him to task</u> for his irresponsibility towards the work he was assigned.

    (*a*) to be angry at someone

    (*b*) to give additional work to someone

    (*c*) to criticize somebody

    (*d*) to be indifferent towards someone

34. Prashant was mesmerized by the beauty of the setting sun; it was <u>a sight for sore eyes</u>.

    (*a*) soothing for aching eyes.

    (*b*) long forgotten.

    (*c*) not seen before.

    (*d*) pleasant to look at.

35. The team surrendered without <u>putting up</u> much of a fight.

    (*a*) making or preparing something

    (*b*) engaging in something

    (*c*) raising something to a higher position

    (*d*) causing somebody trouble or difficulty

Direction: In the following question four words are given in each question, out of which only one word is spelt correctly. Find the correctly spelt word and mark your answer in the answer sheet.

36. (*a*) Conccession   (*b*) Concession

    (*c*) Concesion   (*d*) Conccesion

Directions: In question nos. **37** to **39**, some parts of the sentences have errors and some are correct. Find out which part of the sentence has an error and mark the answer corresponding to the appropriate letter (A,B,C). If a sentence is free from error, mark your answer as (*d*).

37. As mens work moved away from the home (*a*) / and into shops, the household became a new (*b*) / kind of place: a private, feminized domestic sphere. (*c*) / No error (*d*)

38. God loves each one of us as if he/she (*a*) / were the only person in the entire (*b*) /world to love. (*c*) / No error (*d*)

39. The judge decided to take (*a*) / the decision after closely (*b*) / consulting to the president. (*c*) / No error (*d*)

Directions: In question nos. **40** and **42**, sentences are given with blanks to be filled with an appropriate word(s). Four alternatives are suggested for each question. Choose the correct alternative out of the four.

40. The nation's economic growth swept many Americans into a/an _____ but unfamiliar "consumer society."

    (*a*) affluent   (*b*) bankrupt

    (*c*) frugal   (*d*) herculean

41. Ace badminton player Nishtha Trivedi has _____ her state level competitor.

    (*a*) tumbled   (*b*) upraised

    (*c*) collapsed   (*d*) toppled

42. I stopped _______ his place.

   (*a*) by   (*b*) for

   (*c*) with   (*d*) towards

Directions: In question nos. **43** to **45**, a sentence/ part of the sentence is underlined. Beneath each sentence four different ways of phrasing the underlined part are given. Choose the grammatically correct option. In case no improvement is needed, your answer should be option (*d*).

43. I want to help <u>every one of my cousins in her</u> work.

   (*a*) each one of my cousin in her

   (*b*) everyone of my cousins in their

   (*c*) each one of my cousins in there

   (*d*) No improvement

44. Either Siddhant or <u>me is</u> going to the mall with her.

   (*a*) me are

   (*b*) I am

   (*c*) I are

   (*d*) No improvement

45. When the school closed down, Mr. Pandey <u>will already be teaching</u> there for six years.

   (*a*) had already been teaching

   (*b*) was already teaching

   (*c*) had already taught

   (*d*) No improvement

Direction: In question nos. **46** to **50**, you have given a passage with 5 questions. Read the passage carefully and choose the best answer to each question out of the four alternatives.

Since the dawn of civilization mankind has always been plagued by some or the other form of disease. The number of lives accounted for by each disease has, through the decades, varied continually, though none of them can be singled out as the leading cause of death, collectively they are the leading cause of deaths. The origin or evolution of diseases has never been too clearcut a phenomenon, though some wishful dreamers even attribute it to Pandora's box of troubles.

A survey of the five leading causes of deaths during a period from the early 1900s to the mid 1900s shows a distinct and significant trend. In the early 1900s these causes in order of number of death's caused were:

  i. Tuberculosis,

  ii. Pneumonia,

  iii. Intestinal diseases,

  iv. Heart diseases,

  v. and Cerebral haemorrhage and thrombosis.

A decade later the only change was that heart disease had moved from fourth to fifth place, tuberculosis now being second, and pneumonia third.

Toward the later part of this period, however, the list had changed profoundly. Heart diseases were far out in front; cancer, which had come up from eighth place, was second; and cerebral haemorrhage and thrombosis, third. Fatal accidents, which had been well down the list, were now fourth, and nephritis was fifth. All of these are, of course, composites rather than single diseases, and it is significant that, except for accidents, they are characteristic of the advanced rather than the early or middle years of life.

46. On the basis of the passage, which of the following statements is most tenable?

   (*a*) A cure for cancer will be found within this decade.

   (*b*) Many of the medical problems of today are problems of the gerontologist (specialist in medical problems of old age).

   (*c*) Older persons are more accident prone than are younger persons.

   (*d*) Tuberculosis has been all but eliminated.

47. Which one of the following trends is least indicated in the passage?

   (*a*) As one grows older, one is more subject to debilitating disease.

   (*b*) Pneumonia has become less common.

   (*c*) Relative to mortality rates for acute intestinal diseases, the mortality rate for cancer has increased.

   (*d*) The incidence of heart disease has increased.

48. Which one of the following statements is most nearly correct?

   (*a*) Such mortality trends (stated in the passage) are caused by decreased infant mortality.

   (*b*) The changes in the data reported are a function of improved diagnosis and reporting.

   (*c*) The mortality data are based on the records of physicians who practised continuously from 1900 to 1950.

   (*d*) There appears to be a greater change in the mortality patterns from 1910 to 1950 than in the decade ending in 1910.

49. It can be inferred from reading this passage that

(a) longevity increased between 1900 and 1915.

(b) longevity increased steadily between 1915 and 1950.

(c) longevity increased significantly between 1900 and 1950.

(d) longevity was not a factor in these findings.

50. The word 'wishful', given in the passage, means

(a) skeptical (b) hopeful

(c) demanding (d) scruplous

QUANTITATIVE APTITUDE

51. The perimeter of a rectangular field is 240 m and area is 3456 m^2. The dimensions of the field are

(a) 48 m and 64 m (b) 44 m and 76 m

(c) 72 m and 48 m (d) 64 m and 56 m

52. A positive integer when divided by 248 gives a remainder 74. When the same number is divided by 31, the remainder will be

(a) 24 (b) 12

(c) 15 (d) 9

53. Mr. X can do a piece of work in 18 days. Mr. Y is 20% more efficient than Mr. X. How long would Mr.Y alone take to finish this work?

(a) 22 days (b) $6\frac{2}{3}$ days

(c) 15 days (d) $12\frac{1}{9}$ days

54. 3 men and 4 women can do a piece of work in 12 days while 4 men and 3 women can do the same work in 10 days. In how many days 2 men and 3 women can do the work?

(a) 15 days

(b) $17\frac{1}{2}$ days

(c) $20\frac{1}{2}$ days

(d) $18\frac{1}{3}$ days

55. Diameter of a circle is thrice the side of a square. Ratio of the area of circle and the square is

(a) $2\pi : 3$

(b) $9\pi : 4$

(c) $4\pi : 9$

(d) $2\pi : 9$

56. A shirt is marked at ₹2,000. The shopkeeper allows successive discounts of a%, 2b% and 3c% on it. The final selling price (in ₹) is

(a) $\dfrac{(100-a)(100-b)(100-c)}{200}$

(b) $\dfrac{(100-a)(100+b)(100-c)}{200}$

(c) $\dfrac{(100-a)(100+2b)(100-3c)}{1000}$

(d) $\dfrac{(100-a)(100-2b)(100-3c)}{500}$

57. The ratio of the number of balls in two bags A and B is 7 : 4. If 15 balls are taken out from the bag A and is dropped in bag B, the number of balls in each of the two bags is become same. The number of balls in each of the two bags now is

(a) 70 (b) 55

(c) 40 (d) 30

58. Out of the five numbers, average of first four is 24 and that of last four is 30. If the first number is 16, then the last number is

(a) 22 (b) 26

(c) 32 (d) 40

59. A dishonest shopkeeper sells his goods at 10% more than cost price and uses a false weight of 900 gm instead of 1 kg. His total gain percent is

(a) 20% (b) $21\frac{1}{9}\%$

(c) 21% (d) $22\frac{2}{9}\%$

60. A train 150 meters long crosses a cyclist travelling with a speed of 24 km/hr in the same direction of the train in 15 seconds and a other train of same length travelling in opposite direction in 10 seconds. The speed (in km/hr) of the second train is

(a) 126

(b) 60

(c) 48

(d) 45

61. Lines 3x + 4y = 12 and 2y – 6 = 0 intersect each other at the point

(a) (–4, 3)

(b) (–1, –4)

(c) (0, 3)

(d) (0, –3)

62. A fraction becomes $\dfrac{4}{5}$ when 3 is added to the numerator and 1 is added to the denominator. If 1 is subtracted from both the numerator and the denominator, the fraction becomes $\dfrac{1}{2}$. What is the original fraction?

(a) $\dfrac{5}{7}$ (b) $\dfrac{5}{9}$

(c) $\dfrac{7}{9}$ (d) $\dfrac{6}{11}$

63. If $\dfrac{x^2}{y}+\dfrac{y^2}{x}-\left(x+y\right)=0,$ then the value of x^2-y^2 is

(a) 1   (b) –1

(c) 0   (d) –2

64. If $x=7+5\sqrt{2},$ then the value of $x^2+x+\dfrac{1}{x}+\dfrac{1}{x^2}$ is

(a) $99+70\sqrt{2}$ (b) 198

(c) 212   (d) $198+10\sqrt{2}$

65. If a and b are positive real numbers and $ab^2 = 32$, then the minimum value of $(a + b)$ is

(a) 1   (b) 4

(c) 6   (d) 8

66. If θ is the positive acute angle and $6\left(\cos ec^2\theta+\cot^2\theta\right)=10,$ then which one is true?

(a) $\cos\theta = \sin(180°-3\theta)$

(b) $\sin\theta = \cos 3\theta$

(c) $\sin 2\theta = \cos 2\theta$

(d) $\cos 2\theta = \sin(3\theta + 30°)$

67. In $\triangle ABC$, the angle bisector of $\angle B$, meets AC at point D. If AB = 9 cm, CB = 12 cm and AD = 3 cm, then the perimeter of the $\triangle ABC$ is

(a) 22 cm   (b) 24 cm

(c) 28 cm   (d) 30 cm

68. If the inradius of an equilateral triangle is $6\sqrt{3}$ cm, then the height (in cm) of the triangle is

(a) $12\sqrt{3}$

(b) 18

(c) $18\sqrt{3}$

(d) 12

69. In $\triangle ABC$, G is the centroid and AD and BE are the two medians. If the area of the $\triangle ABC$ is 120 cm^2, then area of quadrilateral DGEC is

(a) 20 cm^2 (b) 40 cm^2

(c) 60 cm^2 (d) 45 cm^2

70. If $\cos\theta - 4\sec\theta = 3$, then the value of $\cos^3\theta + \sec^3\theta$ is

(a) 3   (b) –2

(c) 0   (d) $\dfrac{1}{3}$

71. The value of $6(\sin x + \cos x)^2 + 3(\cos x - \sin x)^4 + 6(\sin^4 x + \cos^4 x)$ is

(a) 1   (b) 6

(c) 12   (d) 15

72. The value of $\left(\dfrac{1}{\sin\theta}+\dfrac{1}{\tan\theta}\right)\left(\dfrac{1}{\sin\theta}-\dfrac{1}{\tan\theta}\right)$ is

(a) –1   (b) 0

(c) 1   (d) 2

Directions: The following bar graph shows the percentage of the number of mobile handsets of three brands– Nokia, Samsung and Micromax– sold in a city during the period 2008 to 2011. Examine the bar graph and answer the question nos. **73 – 75.**

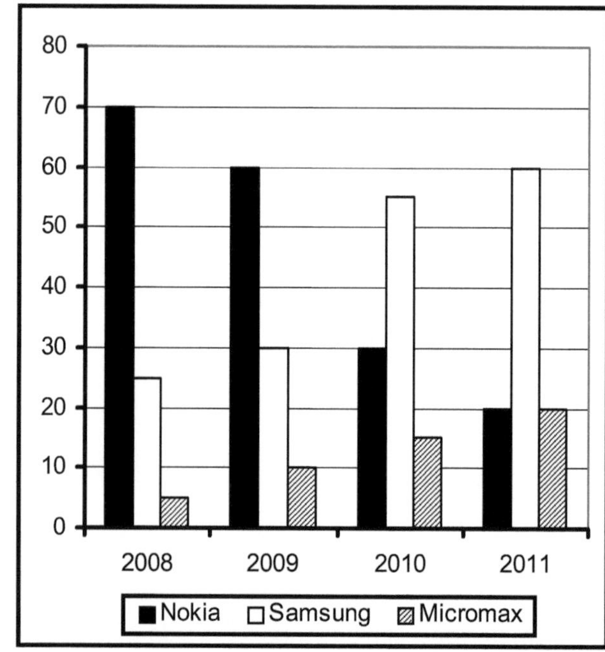

73. If the total number of mobile handsets sold in 2008 was 12 crores, then the total number of handsets sold by two brands Nokia and Micromax in that year was

(a) 6,40,00,000   (b) 7,80,00,000

(c) 8,40,00,000   (d) 9,00,00,000

74. If the total number of mobile handsets sold in 2009 was 12 crores, then the number of handsets sold by Samsung in that year was

(a) 4,40,00,000   (b) 2,80,00,000

(c) 3,60,00,000   (d) 4,40,00,000

75. Ratio of the number of mobile handsets sold by Nokia and Samsung in 2010 was

(a) 3 : 5   (b) 6 : 11

(c) 3 : 4   (d) 5 : 11

GENERAL AWARENESS

76. Recently Orkut launched a new social network called _______?

(a) Hi   (b) How are you

(c) Hello   (d) Hello world

77. Economic situation in which consumers spend less than their disposable income, not because they want to save but because the goods they seek are not available. This is known as

(a) Inflation   (b) Stagflation

(c) Forced savings   (d) None of these

78. Goods and services tax is

(a) Value added tax

(b) Corporate tax

(c) Modified alternate tax

(d) All of these

79. Which of the following statements is not true about Bal Gangadhar Tilak?

(a) Tilak started the home rule league.

(b) Tilak was a strong radical in Indian consciousness.

(c) Tilak was one of the first and strongest advocates of "Swaraj" (self-rule).

(d) None of the above

80. Which of the following article is related to adult franchise in Indian Constitution?

(a) Article 320   (b) Article 326

(c) Article 345   (d) Article 278

81. Which of the following article of Indian constitution deals with right to education?

(a) Article 19   (b) Article 20

(c) Article 21   (d) Article 32

82. Regulating Act 1773 deals with

(a) Act limited the dividends of the company

(b) Prohibited the servants from engaging in any private trade

(c) Both (a) and (b)

(d) None of these

83. Moplah rebellion took place in

(a) 1919   (b) 1920

(c) 1921   (d) 1922

84. Jogs falls are created by

(a) Narmada   (b) Sharavathi

(c) Tapi   (d) Periyar

85. Star fishes belong to

(a) Echinoderms   (b) Fishes

(c) Amphibians   (d) Reptiles

86. Carotenoids are found in

(a) Plants

(b) Human kidney

(c) Human hair and nails

(d) All of the above

87. Which of the following is responsible for the formulation of a computing problem to executable programs?

(a) Computer programming

(b) Computer memory

(c) Computer hardware

(d) Computer software

88. Which of the following is a fish?

(a) Silver fish   (b) Sea horse

(c) Star fish   (d) Devil Fish

89. Electrical conductivity is measured in

(a) Amperes   (b) Voltage

(c) Siemens/metre   (d) Ohm/metre

90. X-rays are

(a) Electromagnetic radiations

(b) Visible radiations

(c) Similar to infra red rays

(d) Infrasonic vibrations

91. Which of the following is the latest country to join Wrod Trade Organization?

(a) Yemen   (b) South Sudan

(c) Seychelles   (d) Angola

92. Graphene is an allotrope of

(a) Carbon   (b) Nitrogen

(c) Hydrogen   (d) Helium

93. German silver is an alloy of

(a) Copper

(b) Silver

(c) Gold

(d) None of these

94. Which of the following is a nitrogen fixing bacterium?

(a) Pseudomonas   (b) Spirogyra

(c) Rhizobacteria   (d) All of these

95. Who won the Bronze medal in the wrestling 58 kg category at Rio?
 (a) Sunita Jain
 (b) Sakshi Malik
 (c) Vinesh Phogat
 (d) Mrinal Miri

96. Which of the following cereals is/are a part of National Food Security Law?
 (a) Rice
 (b) Wheat
 (c) Millets
 (d) All of these

97. Who was the first person to achieve the Nobel Prize in chemistry?
 (a) Albert Einstein
 (b) Van't Hoff
 (c) Madam Curie
 (d) Both (b) and (c)

98. Who is the author of the book, "PaxIndica"?
 (a) Shashi Tharoor
 (b) Romesh Thapar
 (c) Arundhati Roy
 (d) Sitaram Yechury

99. Which of the following is not a permanent member of UN Security Council?
 (a) Germany
 (b) UK
 (c) France
 (d) China

100. Who is the present Prime Minister of Australia?
 (a) Julia Gillard
 (b) John Howard
 (c) Malcom Turnbull
 (d) Kevin Rudd

ANSWERS

1. (a)	**2.** (b)	**3.** (c)	**4.** (b)	**5.** (b)	**6.** (d)	**7.** (b)	**8.** (c)	**9.** (c)	**10.** (a)
11. (c)	**12.** (c)	**13.** (b)	**14.** (c)	**15.** (b)	**16.** (c)	**17.** (a)	**18.** (c)	**19.** (c)	**20.** (d)
21. (a)	**22.** (a)	**23.** (c)	**24.** (a)	**25.** (b)	**26.** (d)	**27.** (c)	**28.** (d)	**29.** (c)	**30.** (d)
31. (d)	**32.** (c)	**33.** (c)	**34.** (d)	**35.** (b)	**36.** (b)	**37.** (a)	**38.** (d)	**39.** (c)	**40.** (a)
41. (d)	**42.** (a)	**43.** (d)	**44.** (b)	**45.** (a)	**46.** (b)	**47.** (a)	**48.** (d)	**49.** (c)	**50.** (b)
51. (c)	**52.** (b)	**53.** (c)	**54.** (b)	**55.** (b)	**56.** (d)	**57.** (b)	**58.** (d)	**59.** (d)	**60.** (c)
61. (c)	**62.** (b)	**63.** (c)	**64.** (d)	**65.** (c)	**66.** (d)	**67.** (c)	**68.** (c)	**69.** (b)	**70.** (b)
72. (d)	**72.** (c)	**73.** (d)	**74.** (c)	**75.** (b)	**76.** (c)	**77.** (c)	**78.** (a)	**79.** (d)	**80.** (b)
81. (c)	**82.** (c)	**83.** (c)	**84.** (b)	**85.** (a)	**86.** (a)	**87.** (a)	**88.** (b)	**89.** (c)	**90.** (a)
91. (c)	**92.** (a)	**93.** (a)	**94.** (c)	**95.** (b)	**96.** (d)	**97.** (b)	**98.** (a)	**99.** (a)	**100.** (c)

EXPLANATIONS

1.
```
B    K    L    P
↓+2  ↓+3  ↓+4  ↓+5
D    N    P    U
```
Similarly,
```
S    O    R    T
↓+2  ↓+3  ↓+4  ↓+5
U    R    V    Y
```

2.
```
N    I    K    E
↓−4  ↓−4  ↓−4  ↓−4
J    E    G    A
```
Similarly,
```
S    A    L    T
↓−4  ↓−4  ↓−4  ↓−4
O    W    H    P
```

3.
$$4\ 7\ 5 \rightarrow 4 + 7 + 5 = 16$$
$$6\ 3\ 9 \rightarrow 6 + 3 + 9 = 18 \quad \bigg\}+2$$
Similarly,
$$3\ 8\ 2 \rightarrow 3 + 8 + 2 = 13$$
$$\text{and } 5\ 8\ 2 \rightarrow 5 + 8 + 2 = 15 \quad \bigg\}+2$$

4. As per the order in the dictionary, the correct sequence is (v), (i), (ii), (iv), (iii). Hence, option (B) is the correct answer.

5. Options (A), (C) and (D) are electronic media of communication, while option (B) is the print medium of communication. Hence, option (B) is the correct answer.

6. $217 = 6^3 + 1$

$126 = 5^3 + 1$

$344 = 7^3 + 1$

$729 = 9^3$

Hence, 729 is odd-one.

7. Rajasthan has the largest area, followed by Uttar Pradesh, Tamil Nadu, Manipur and Delhi. Hence, option (B) is the correct answer.

8.
```
M    L    K    S
↓+2  ↓+2  ↓+2  ↓+2
O    N    M    U
↓+2  ↓+2  ↓+2  ↓+2
Q    P    O    W
↓+2  ↓+2  ↓+2  ↓+2
S    R    Q    Y
```

9. $3\ 5\ 3 - 5 = -2\ 3 + 5 = 8$

$6\ 7\ 6 - 5 = -1\ 6 + 7 = 13$

$9\ 3\ 9 - 3 = \underline{6}\ 9 + 3 = 12$

$8\ 6\ 8 - 6 = 2\ 8 + 6 = \underline{14}$

10.
```
8      15      29      57      113     225
  +7 ×1   +7 × 2   +7 × 4   +7 × 8   +7 × 16
```

11. $4 + 14 = 18$

$14 + 18 = 32$

$18 + 32 = 50$

$32 + 50 = \underline{82}$.

12.
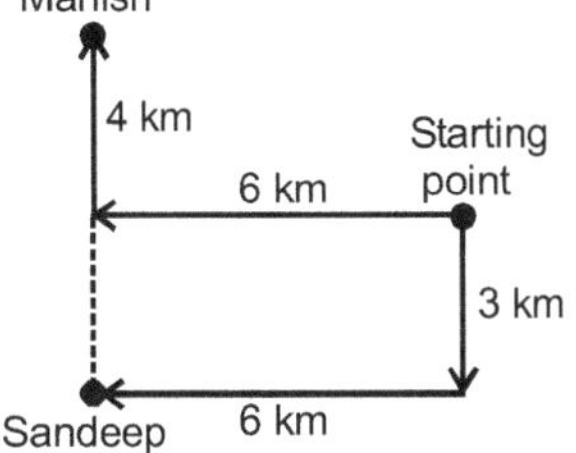

Hence, they are 7 km apart.

13.
```
S    E    L    D    O    M
↓+2  ↓−2  ↓+2  ↓−2  ↓+2  ↓−2
U    C    N    B    Q    K
```
Similarly,
```
B    A    S    K    E    T
↓+2  ↓−2  ↓+2  ↓−2  ↓+2  ↓−2
D    Y    U    I    G    R
```

14. The word 'LOBBY' can be formed using the letters of the given word. Hence, option (C) is the correct answer.

15. The given expression can be written as:

$92 + 182 \div 13 \times 3 - 18 = 92 + 14 \times 3 - 18$

$= 92 + 42 - 18 = 116$.

16. By interchanging the signs $\div$ and $-$, we have,

$(67 + 5) \div 3 - 2 \times 8 = 8$.

17. Since the direction changes by 135° in anti clockwise direction. Hence, North will become South-west.

18.
```
T    R    A    C    E
↓+2  ↓+2  ↓+2  ↓+2  ↓+2
V    T    C    E    G
```
Similarly,
```
K    S    J    R    W
↓+2  ↓+2  ↓+2  ↓+2  ↓+2
M    U    L    T    Y
```

19.
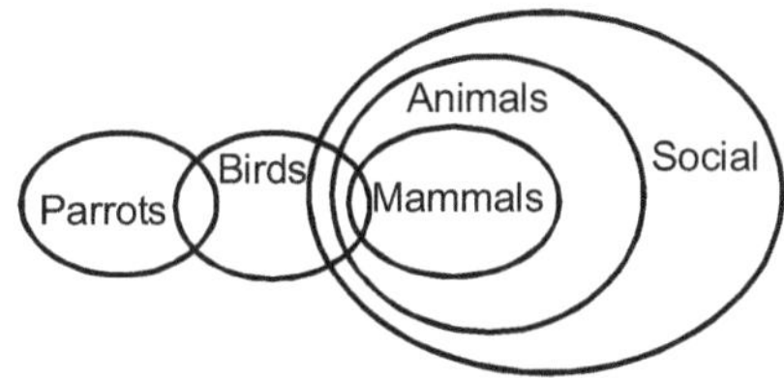

From the above Venn diagram it is evident that both the conclusions follow. Hence, option (C) is the correct answer.

20. On each of the six faces of the cube there will be 4 cubes with only one side painted.

Hence, total number of cubes which are painted black on one side = 4 × 6 = 24.

26. 'Pester' means to annoy or bother in a repeated way. Hence, option (D) is the correct answer.

27. 'Sanctum' refers to a holy place. 'Shrine' is a place, which is connected with a holy person or a holy event, where people go to worship. Hence, option (C) is the correct answer.

28. 'Prudence' refers to a careful, good judgment that allows you to avoid danger or risk. 'Carelessness' means not being careful. Hence, the correct answer is option (D).

29. 'Exacerbate' means to make a bad situation worse. Thus, its antonym will be 'ease'. Hence, the correct answer is option (C).

30. A person who knows a lot about a particular subject is called a 'connoisseur'. Hence, option (D) is the correct answer. 'Gourmand' is a person who loves to eat and drink. 'Oenophile' is a lover of wine. A 'swill' is unappealing drink or food.

31. A person who collects stamps is called 'Philatelist'. Hence, option (D) is the correct answer. A collector of coins is called 'Numismatist'. 'Bibliophile' is a person who collects books. An 'antiquarian' is someone who collects antiques.

32. 'Floriculture' refers to the cultivation of ornamental plants. Hence, option (C) is the correct answer. 'Orthodontic' means treatment of problems relating to teeth and jaws. 'Agriculture' refers to the science and occupation of farming. 'Anthropology' refers to the study of human race.

33. 'Take someone to task' means to criticize somebody strongly for something they have done. Hence, option (C) is the correct answer.

34. 'Sight for sore eyes' refers to something that is very pleasant to look at. Hence, option (D) is the correct answer.

35. 'Putting up' means to engage in something. Hence, option (B) is the correct answer.

36. The correct spelling is 'concession'. Hence, option (B) is the correct answer.

37. There is an error in part (A). 'Men' is plural. It should have been men's, which refers to the work done by men. Hence, option (A) is the correct answer.

38. The sentence is correct in its given form. It is a case of subjunctive, which is used to express a wish or desire. In such cases, we use the verb 'were'. Hence, option (D) is the correct answer.

39. 'Consulting' takes the preposition 'with' and not 'to'. The correct usage is 'consult with somebody about/ on something'. Hence, part (C) is the answer.

40. The sentence talks about economic growth. Therefore, the word that will fit in the meaning of the sentence will be a positive word. Thus, options (B) and (C) are incorrect. 'Affluent' means having a lot of money and a good standard of living. This makes the sentence grammatically and logically correct. Hence, option (A) is the correct answer. 'Herculean', which means needing a lot of strength and effort, does not fit in the meaning of the sentence.

41. The sentence means that NishthaTridevi has defeated her state level competitor. 'Topple' means to win a victory over someone in a war, contest, etc. Hence, option (D) is the correct answer. 'Tumble' means to slip or drop.

42. 'By his place' means near his place or beside his place. Hence, option (A) is the correct answer. Options (B), (C) and (D) will make the sentence grammatically incorrect.

43. The given sentence is correct. Words like 'everyone', 'everybody', 'everything', etc. are treated as singular pronouns. The pronoun he/she is used according to the context. Hence, the given sentence is correct, making option (D) the answer. Option (A) is incorrect since 'cousin' should be plural.

44. In the sentence, 'I' will be correct since it is the subject. 'Me' is used as an object of the verb. For example: She is taking me to the mall. Here, in this example, the subject is 'she' and the object of the verb is 'me'. When the subjects of a sentence joined by 'or' or 'nor' are of different persons, the verb agrees with the nearer. Therefore, the verb will be 'am' and not 'are'. Hence, option (B) is the correct answer.

45. Past perfect continuous tense is used for an action that began before a certain point in the past and continued up to that time. In the sentence, the action (teaching) began before the school closed down and continued up to that time. Hence, option (A) is the correct answer.

46. Towards the end of the passage it is clearly mentioned that with exception to accidents, the other diseases are more prone to advanced years or old age.

47. Options (B), (C) and (D) can all be clearly deduced from the passage which leaves only option (A) which has not been indicated at all.

48. As per the passage, during the decade after 1900s (upto 1910 or so) there were 5 main diseases which merely changed in order of importance. However, towards the latter part of the period from 1900 to 1950, the list of main diseases underwent profound change. Hence, option (D) is the correct answer.

49. The last few lines of the passage state that diseases that lead to death were predominant amongst elderly people (during the latter part of 1900 - 1950). Thus we can say longevity increased during this period.

50. 'Wishful' means 'expressive of a wish'; desirous. Hence, 'hopeful' is the most appropriate option.

51. Let the length and breadth of the rectangular field be l m and b m respectively. Then,

$2(l + b) = 240$

$\Rightarrow l + b = 120$ and $lb = 3456$

$\Rightarrow l - b = \sqrt{(l+b)^2 - 4lb} = \sqrt{120^2 - 4 \times 3456} = 24$

$\Rightarrow l = \dfrac{120 + 24}{2} = 72$ and $b = \dfrac{120 - 24}{2} = 48.$

52. Let the number be $248x + 74 = 31(8x + 2) + 12.$ When the number is divided by 31, then the remainder = 12.

53. Let the total work be 'w' units. Then, Mr. X does $\dfrac{w}{18}$ units of work in 1 day

$\therefore$ Mr.Y does $\left(1 + \dfrac{20}{100}\right) \times \dfrac{w}{18} = \dfrac{w}{15}$ units of work in 1 day

Hence, the required number of days = 15.

54. Let the work done by a man and a woman be 'm' and 'n' units respectively. Then,

$12(3m + 4w) = 10(4m + 3w)$

$\Rightarrow 2m = 9w$

Total work = $10(4m + 3w) = 210 w$

Hence, required number of days

$= \dfrac{210w}{2m + 3w} = \dfrac{210}{12} = 17\dfrac{1}{2}.$

55. Let the radius of the circle be x cm and the side of the square be y cm. Then, $2x = 3y$

Hence, required ratio $= \pi x^2 : y^2 = \pi x^2 : \left(\dfrac{2x}{3}\right)^2 = 9\pi : 4.$

56. The selling price after 1st discount

$= 2000\left(1 - \dfrac{a}{100}\right) = ₹20(100 - a)$

The selling price after 2nd discount

$= 20(100 - a)\left(100 - \dfrac{2b}{100}\right) = ₹\dfrac{(100 - a)(100 - 2b)}{5}$

The selling price after 3rd discount i.e., final price

$= \dfrac{(100 - a)(100 - 2b)}{5}\left(1 - \dfrac{3c}{100}\right)$

$= ₹\dfrac{(100 - a)(100 - 2b)(100 - 3c)}{500}.$

57. Let the number of balls in the bag A and B be 7x and 4x respectively. Then,

$7x - 15 = 4x + 15 \Rightarrow x = 10$

Hence, the number of balls in each of the two bags now = 4x + 15 = 55.

58. Let the 2nd, 3rd, 4th and 5th number be a, b, c and d. Then,

$\dfrac{16 + a + b + c}{4} = 24 \Rightarrow a + b + c = 80$ and $\dfrac{a + b + c + d}{4} = 30$

$\Rightarrow 80 + d = 120 \qquad\qquad \Rightarrow d = 40$

Hence, the last number is 40.

59. Let the cost price of shopkeeper of 900 gm of goods be ₹900, then he sells 900 gm as 1000 gm in ₹1000 ×1.1 = ₹1,100

$\therefore$ Cost price = ₹900, Selling price = ₹1,100

Hence, the profit percent = $\dfrac{1100 - 900}{900} \times 100 = 22\dfrac{2}{9}.$

60. Let the speed of the first and second trains be x km/hr and y km/hr respectively. Then,

$\left[(x - 24) \times \dfrac{5}{18}\right] \times 15 = 150$

$\Rightarrow (x - 24) = 36$

$\Rightarrow x = 60$

Now, $\left[(60 + y) \times \dfrac{5}{18}\right] \times 10 = 300$

$\Rightarrow (60 + y) = 108$

$\Rightarrow y = 48.$

61. $2y - 6 = 0$

$\Rightarrow y = 3$

Putting the value of y in the equation $3x + 4y = 12,$ we get

$x = 0$

Hence, the point is (0, 3).

62. Let the fraction be $\dfrac{x}{y}.$ Then,

$\dfrac{x + 3}{y + 1} = \dfrac{4}{5}$

$\Rightarrow 5x - 4y = -11 \qquad\qquad\qquad ...(i)$

and $\dfrac{x - 1}{y - 1} = \dfrac{1}{2}$

$\Rightarrow 2x - y = 1 \qquad\qquad\qquad ...(ii)$

On solving (i) and (ii), we get

x = 5 and y = 9

Hence, the required fraction is $\dfrac{5}{9}.$

63. $\dfrac{x^2}{y} + \dfrac{y^2}{x} = x + y$

$\Rightarrow x^3 + y^3 = x^2 y + y^2 x$

$\Rightarrow (x^3 + y^3)(x + y) = (x^2 y + y^2 x)(x + y)$

$\Rightarrow x^4 + y^4 = 2x^2 y^2 \Rightarrow x^2 - y^2 = 0.$

64. $\dfrac{1}{x} = \dfrac{1}{7+5\sqrt{2}} = \dfrac{\left(5\sqrt{2}-7\right)}{\left(7+5\sqrt{2}\right)\left(5\sqrt{2}-7\right)} = \left(5\sqrt{2}-7\right)$

$\therefore x^2 + x + \dfrac{1}{x} + \dfrac{1}{x^2} = \left(7+5\sqrt{2}\right)^2 + \left(7+5\sqrt{2}\right) + \left(5\sqrt{2}-7\right) + \left(5\sqrt{2}-7\right)^2$

$= \left(49+50+70\sqrt{2}\right) + \left(7+5\sqrt{2}\right) + \left(5\sqrt{2}-7\right) + \left(49+50-70\sqrt{2}\right)$

$= 198 + 10\sqrt{2}.$

65. $\dfrac{a + \dfrac{b}{2} + \dfrac{b}{2}}{3} \geq \sqrt[3]{\left(a \times \dfrac{b}{2} \times \dfrac{b}{2}\right)}$ (For positive real numbers,

Arithmetic mean = Geometric mean)

$\Rightarrow \dfrac{a+b}{3} \geq \sqrt[3]{\left(\dfrac{ab^2}{4}\right)}$

$\Rightarrow a+b \geq 3 \times \sqrt[3]{\left(\dfrac{ab^2}{4}\right)} \Rightarrow a+b \geq 3 \times \sqrt[3]{\dfrac{32}{4}} = 6$

Hence, the minimum value of $(a + b)$ is 6.

66. $6(\text{cosec}^2\theta + \cot^2 \theta) = 6(1 + 2\cot^2 \theta) = 10$

$(\because \text{cosec}^2\theta = 1 + \cot^2 \theta)$

$\Rightarrow \cot^2 \theta = \dfrac{1}{3}$

$\Rightarrow \cot \theta = \dfrac{1}{\sqrt{3}}$

$\Rightarrow \theta = 60°$

$\therefore \sin(3\theta + 30°) = \sin 210° = \sin\left(90° + 120°\right) = \cos 120° = \cos 2\theta.$

67.

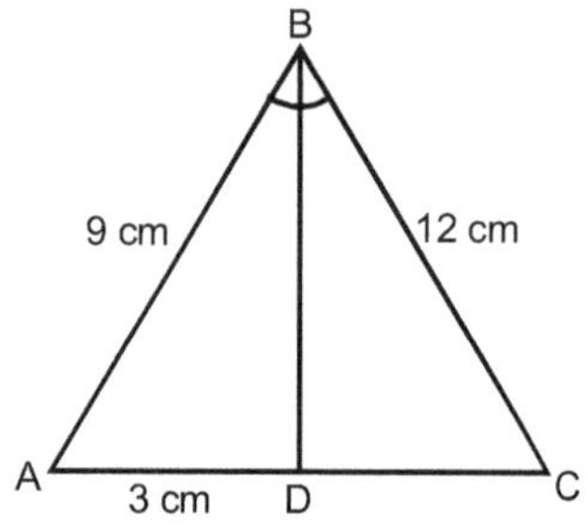

As BD is the angle bisector of $\angle$B, therefore,

$\dfrac{AD}{DC} = \dfrac{AB}{BC}$

$\Rightarrow \dfrac{3}{DC} = \dfrac{9}{12}$

$\Rightarrow DC = 4$ cm

$\therefore$ Perimeter of the $\triangle ABC$

$= AB + BC + DC + DA = 9 + 12 + 4 + 3 = 28$ cm.

68. Height of the equilateral triangle = 3 × Inradius

$= 3 \times 6\sqrt{3} = 18\sqrt{3}$ cm.

69.

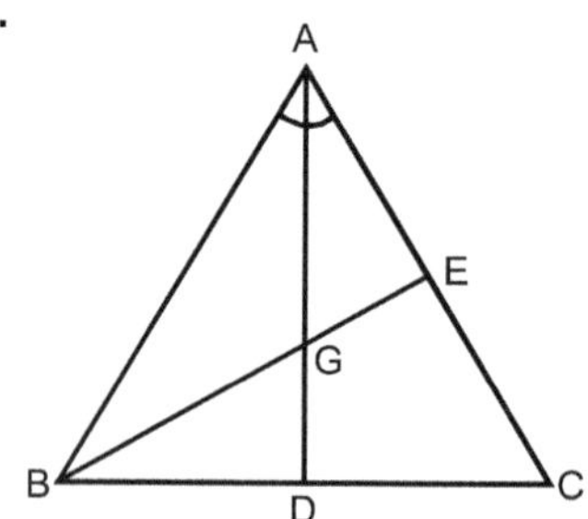

Area of $\triangle BEA = 60$ cm^2 (Median divides the area in two equal parts.)

2 × Area of $\triangle EAG$ = Area of $\triangle BAG$ (As bases BG and GE are in ratio 1 : 2 but the height is same)

$\therefore$ Area of $\triangle EAG$ = Area of $\triangle BGD$ = $\dfrac{1}{1+2} \times 60 = 20$ cm^2

and Area of $\triangle BAG = 40$ cm^2

$\therefore$ The required area = Area of $\triangle ABC - $ (Area of $\triangle BDG$ + Area of $\triangle BGA$ + Area of $\triangle AGE$)

$= 120 - (20 + 40 + 20) = 40$ cm^2.

70. $\cos\theta - \dfrac{4}{\cos\theta} = 3$

$\Rightarrow \cos^2 \theta - 3\cos \theta - 4 = 0 \Rightarrow (\cos\theta - 4)(\cos\theta + 1) = 0$

$\therefore \cos \theta = -1$ and $\sec \theta = -1$ [$\because \cos\theta$ cannot be 4]

Hence, $\cos^3\theta + \sec^3\theta = -1 - 1 = -2.$

71. $6(\sin x + \cos x)^2 + 3(\cos x - \sin x)^4 + 6(\sin^4 x + \cos^4 x)$

$= 6(1 + 2\sin x \cos x) + 3(1 - 2\sin x \cos x)^2 + 6(\sin^4 x + \cos^4 x)$

$= 6 + 12\sin x \cos x + 3 + 12\sin^2 x \cos^2 x - 12\sin x \cos x + 6 \sin^4 x + 6 \cos^4 x$

$= 6 + 3 + 12\sin^2 x \cos^2 x + 6\sin^4 x + 6\cos^4 x$

$= 9 + 6 \sin^2 x (\cos^2 x + \sin^2 x) + 6\cos^2 x (\sin^2 x + \cos^2 x)$

$= 9 + 6\sin^2 x + 6\cos^2 x = 9 + 6 = 15.$

72. $\left(\dfrac{1}{\sin \theta} + \dfrac{1}{\tan \theta}\right)\left(\dfrac{1}{\sin \theta} - \dfrac{1}{\tan \theta}\right)$

$= \left(\dfrac{1+\cos \theta}{\sin \theta}\right)\left(\dfrac{1-\cos \theta}{\sin \theta}\right) = \dfrac{1-\cos^2 \theta}{\sin^2 \theta} = \dfrac{\sin^2 \theta}{\sin^2 \theta} = 1.$

73. The total number of handsets sold by two brands Nokia and Micromax in 2008

$= \dfrac{70+5}{70+25+5} \times 12,00,00,000 = 9,00,00,000.$

74. The total number of handsets sold by Samsung in 2009

$= \dfrac{30}{60+30+10} \times 12,00,00,000 = 3,60,00,000.$

75. Ratio of the number of mobile handsets sold by Nokia and Samsung in 2010 = 30 : 55 = 6 : 11.

GENERAL INTELLIGENCE

1. If MEKLF is coded as 91782 and LLLJK as 88867, then how can IGHED be coded ?

  (a) 97854   (b) 64521

  (c) 53410   (d) 75632

2. Two statements are given below followed by four alternative inferences. Select the one which is most appropriate.

Statements :

(i) All radios sold in that shop are of high standard.

(ii) Some of murphy radios are sold in that shop.

Inferences :

1. All radios of high standard are manufactured by murphy company.

2. Some of the Murphy radios are of high standard.

3. None of the murphy radios is of high standard.

4. Some of the murphy radios of high standard are sold in that shop.

  (a) 1 and 2 inferences only

  (b) 2 and 4 inferences only

  (c) 1 and 3 inferences only

  (d) 1 and 4 inferences only

Direction (Q. 3) : *Select the missing number from the given responses :*

3.

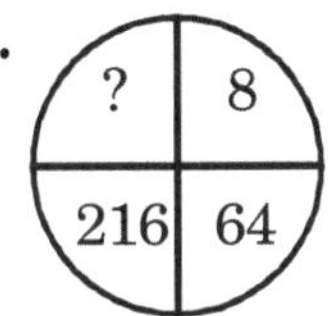

  (a) 343   (b) 512

  (c) 729   (d) 1000

4. If – stands for division, + for multiplication, ÷ for subtraction and × for addition, then which one of the following equations is correct ?

  (a) $19 + 5 - 4 \times 2 \div 4 = 11$

  (b) $19 \times 5 - 4 \div 2 + 4 = 16$

  (c) $19 \div 5 + 4 - 2 \times 4 = 13$

  (d) $19 \div 5 + 4 + 2 \div 4 = 20$

Directions (Q. 5-6) : *Select the related letter / word from the given alternatives.*

5. Country : President : : State : ?

  (a) Chief Minister   (b) Prime Minister

  (c) Speaker   (d) Governor

6. JIHK : PONQ : : WVUX : ?

  (a) KNML   (b) RSTU

  (c) HIGJ   (d) MLKN

Directions (Q. 7-8) : *Find the odd number / letters / number pair from the given alternatives.*

7. (a) Soft ball   (b) Base ball

  (c) Cricket   (d) Basket ball

8. (a) 125   (b) 789

  (c) 236   (d) 347

9. Find out the pair of numbers that does not belong to the group for lack of common property.

  (a) 16 – 18   (b) 56 – 63

  (c) 96 – 108   (d) 86 – 99

10. Which one of the given responses would be a meaningful order of the following ?

1. Sentence   2. Word

3. Chapter   4. Phrase

5. Paragraph

  (a) 4, 3, 1, 2, 5   (b) 2, 3, 5, 4, 1

  (c) 3, 5, 1, 4, 2   (d) 1, 3, 2, 4, 5

11. Arrange the following words as per order in the dictionary :

1. Inhabit   2. Ingenions

3. Inherit   4. Influence

5. Infatuation

  (a) 1, 2, 3, 4, 5   (b) 5, 4, 1, 2, 3

  (c) 4, 5, 2, 1, 3   (d) 5, 4, 2, 1, 3

12. Which one set of letters when sequentially placed at the gaps in the given letter series shall complete it ?

  __ ab __ b __ aba __ abab

  (a) a bb aa   (b) bb aa b

  (c) ab aa b   (d) a aa ba

13. In a row of trees, a tree is 7th from left end and 14th from the right end. How many trees are there in the row ?

  (a) 18

  (b) 19

  (c) 20

  (d) 21

14. There are 80 families in a small extension area. 20 per cent of these families own a car each 50 per cent of the remaining families own a motor cycle each. How many families in that extension do not own any vehicle ?

(a) 30   (b) 32

(c) 23   (d) 36

15. Sita is elder than Swapna. Lavanya is elder than Swapna but younger than Sita. Suvarna is younger than both Hari and Swapna, Swapna is elder than Hari. Who is the youngest ?

(a) Sita   (b) Lavanya

(c) Suvarna   (d) Hari

16. After 9'O clock at what time between 9 pm and 10 pm will the hour and minute hands of a clock point in opposite direction ?

(a) 15 minutes past 9

(b) 16 minutes past 9

(c) $16\dfrac{4}{11}$ minutes past 9

(d) $17\dfrac{1}{11}$ minutes past 9

17. Vivek and Ashok start from a fixed point Vivek moves 3 km north and turns right and the covers 4 km. Ashok moves 5 km west and turns right and walks 3 km. Now how far are they apart ?

(a) 10 km   (b) 9 km

(c) 8 km   (d) 6 km

18. From the given alternative words, select the word which can be formed using the letters of the given word :

STRANGULATION

(a) TRIANGLE   (b) GARLAND

(c) ROASTING   (d) TRAUMA

19. If in a certain Code, RAMAYANA is written as PYKYWYLY, then how MAHABHARATA can be written in that code ?

(a) NBIBCIBSBUB

(b) LZGZAGZQZSZ

(c) MCJCDJCTCVC

(d) KYFYZFYPYRY

20. Some equations have been solved on the basis of certain system. Find the correct answer for the unsolved equation on that basis.

If 94 + 16 = 42, 89 + 23 = 78, then 63 + 45 = ?

(a) 18

(b) 28

(c) 38

(d) 48

21. Which one of the following diagrams represents the correct relationship among 'Judge', 'Thief' and 'Criminal' ?

(a) 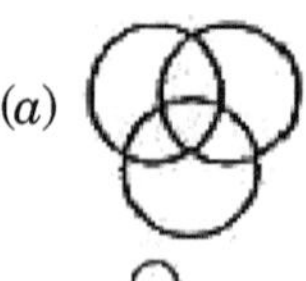   (b) 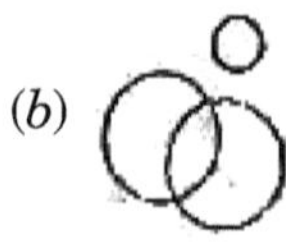

(c) 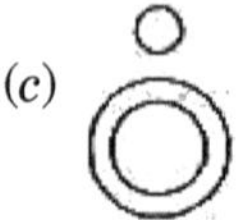   (d) 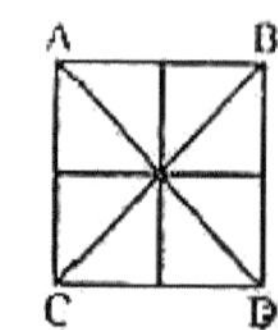

22. How many triangles are there in the given figure ?

(a) 16

(b) 14

(c) 8

(d) 12

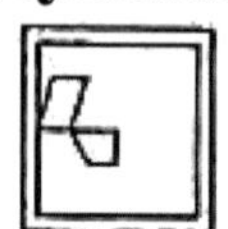

Direction : *From the given answer figures, select the one in which the question figure is hidden / embedded.*

23. Question figure

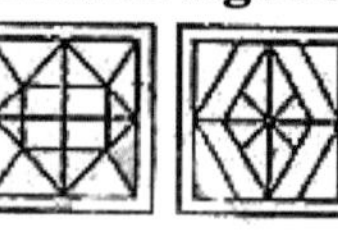

Answer figures

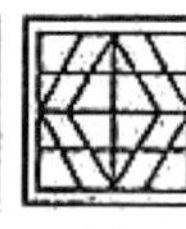

(a)   (b)   (c)   (d)

Direction : *If a mirror is placed on the line MN, then which of the answer figures is the right image of the given figure ?*

24. Question figure

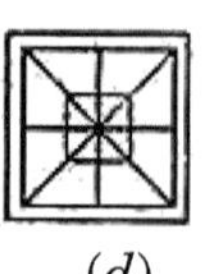

Answer figures

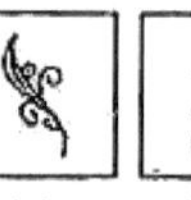

(a)   (b)   (c)   (d)

Direction : *A piece of paper is folded and cut as shown below in the question figures. From the given answer figures, indicate how it will paper when opened.*

25. Question figure

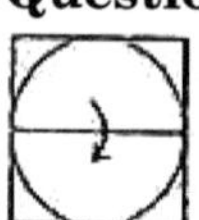

Answer figures

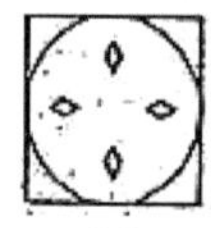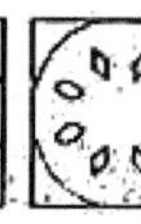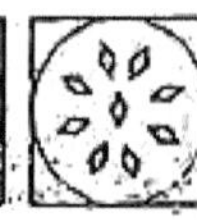

(a)   (b)   (c)   (d)

ENGLISH LANGUAGE

Directions (Q. 26-27) : *Out of the four alternatives, choose the one which best expresses the meaning of the given word and mark it in the Answer Sheet.*

26. Barren

    (a) good   (b) wholesome

    (c) unproductive   (d) profitable

27. Infamy

    (a) notoriety   (b) glory

    (c) integrity   (d) familiarity

Directions (Q. 28-29) : *Choose the word opposite in meaning to the given word and mark it in the Answer Sheet.*

28. Liberty

    (a) serenity   (b) slavery

    (c) seridom   (d) subordination

29. Disorderly

    (a) chaotic   (b) organized

    (c) adjusted   (d) arranged

Directions (Q. 30-32) : *Out of the four alternatives, choose the one which can be substituted for the given words / sentence and indicate it by blackening the appropriate rectangle in the Answer Sheet.*

30. An inscription on a tomb

    (a) espionage   (b) epilogue

    (c) epitaph   (d) elegy

31. Feeling inside you which tells you what is right and what is wrong

    (a) cleverness   (b) conscience

    (c) consciousness   (d) fear

32. Release of a prisoner from jail on certain terms and condition

    (a) Parole   (b) Parley

    (c) Pardon   (d) Acquittal

Directions (Q. 33-35) : *Four alternatives are given for the Idiom / Phase. Choose the alternative which best expresses the meaning of the Idiom / Phrase and mark it in the Answer Book.*

33. a damp squib

    (a) rainy weather

    (b) a disappointing result

    (c) a skirt in a laundry

    (d) none of the above

34. in cold blood

    (a) angrily   (b) deliberately

    (c) excitedly   (d) slowly

35. to take someone for a ride

    (a) to give a ride to someone

    (b) to deceive someone

    (c) to be indifferent

    (d) to disclose a secret

Direction (Q. 36) : *Groups of four words are given. In each group, one word is correctly spelt. Find the correctly spelt word and mark your answer in the Answer Sheet.*

36. (a) qestalt   (b) imbrolios

    (c) ampassc   (d) recondite

Directions (Q. 37-39): *Some of the sentences have errors and some are correct. Find out which part of a sentence has an error and blacken the rectangle corresponding to the appropriate letter (a, b, c). If a sentence is free from errors, blacken the rectangle corresponding to (d) in the Answer Sheet.*

37. A great many student (a)/ have been declared (b)/ successful (c)/No error (d)

38. We are going to launch (a)/ this three-crores project/(b) within the next few months (c)/No error (d)

39. I hope to go to shopping (a)/ this weekendy (b)/ if the weather permits/(c) /No error (d)

Directions (Q. 40-42) : *Sentences are given with blanks to be filled in with an appropriate word(s). Four alternatives are suggested for each question. Choose the correct alternative out of the four and indicate it by blackening the appropriate rectangle in the Answer Sheet.*

40. The company let me _____ time off work.

    (a) take   (b) taking

    (c) to take   (d) took

41. I assume _____ with me.

    (a) every one agreeing

    (b) that every one agrees

    (c) every one to agree

    (d) that every one to agree

42. the rain forests is very important, if we _____ do not want the flora and fauna found there to become extinct.

    (a) Reserving   (b) Destroying

    (c) Preserving   (d) Maintaining

Directions (Q. 43-45) : *A sentence is given which / a part of which may need improvement. Alternatives are given at (a), (b) and (c) below which may be a better option. In case no improvement is needed, your answer is (d). Blacken the appropriate rectangle in the Answer Sheet.*

43. What do you for go to school ?

    (a) For what do you go to school ?

    (b) What do you go for to school ?

    (c) What do you go to school ?

    (d) No improvement

44. He pleased the directors and this completed his report in good time.

    (a) He pleased the directors in good time and this completed his report

    (b) He completed his report in good time and this pleased the directors.

    (c) He pleased the directors and completed his report and this in good time

    (d) No improvement

45. The courtiers used to tell the King how efficient an administrator he was all day long.

    (a) The courtiers all day long used to tell the King how efficient an administrator he was

    (b) The courtiers used all day long to tell King how efficient an administrator he was

    (c) The courtiers used to tell the King all day long how efficient an administrator he was

    (d) No improvement.

Directions: In question nos. **46** to **50**, you have given a passages with 5 questions. Read the passage carefully and choose the best answer to each question out of the four alternatives.

The Black Death arrived in Europe by sea when 12 Genoese trading ships docked at the Sicilian port of Messina after a long journey through the Black Sea. The people who gathered on the docks to greet the ships were met with a horrifying surprise: Most of the sailors aboard the ships were dead, and those who were still alive were gravely ill. They were overcome with fever, unable to keep food down and delirious from pain. Strangest of all, they were covered in mysterious black boils that oozed blood and pus and gave their illness its name: the "Black Death." The Sicilian authorities hastily ordered the fleet of "death ships" out of the harbor, but it was too late: Over the next five years, the mysterious Black Death killed more than 20 million people in Europe–almost one-third of the continent's population.

Today, scientists understand that the Black Death, now known as the plague, is spread by a bacillus called Yersina pestis. They know that the bacillus travels from person to person pneumatically, or through the air, as well as through the bite of infected fleas and rats.

46. How did the sailors on the ship die?

    (a) They were suffering from fever.

    (b) They were suffering from an unknown disease.

    (c) The ships they sailed on were cursed.

    (d) The food they ate was poisonous.

47. Which of the following is not a symptom of the Black Death?

    (a) Pus filled swelling

    (b) High Pain

    (c) Fever

    (d) Inflamed and tender skin

48. Which of the following is a cause of the spread of Yersina pestis?

    (a) Touch   (b) Bite of infected flies

    (c) Air   (d) Unclean water

49. What is the meaning of the word 'fleet?

    (a) Group of people

    (b) Group of ships

    (c) Bundle of weapons

    (d) Group of diseased people

50. Find a synonym of the word 'delirious'.

    (a) Distraught   (b) Placid

    (c) Unperturbed   (d) Recollected

QUANTITATIVE APTITUDE

51. X sells two articles for ₹ 4,000 each with no loss and no gain in the interaction. If one was sold at a gain of 25% the other is sold at a loss of

    (a) 25%   (b) $18\frac{2}{9}\%$

    (c) $16\frac{2}{3}\%$ (d) 20%

52. 20% loss on selling price is what percent loss on the cost price ?

    (a) 25%   (b) 15%

    (c) $16\frac{2}{3}\%$ (d) $16\frac{1}{3}\%$

53. A reduction of 20% in the price of sugar enables me to purchase 5 kg more for ₹ 600. Find the price of sugar per kg before reduction of price.

    (a) ₹ 24

    (b) ₹ 30

    (c) ₹ 32

    (d) ₹ 36

54. The price of a commodity rises from ₹ 6 per kg to ₹ 7.50 per kg. If the expenditure cannot increase, the percentage of reduction in consumption is

    (a) 15

    (b) 20

    (c) 25

    (d) 30

55. First and second numbers are less than a third number by 30% and 37% respectively. The second number is less than the first by

(a) 7%   (b) 4%

(c) 3%   (d) 10%

56. Walking at $\dfrac{6^{th}}{7}$ of his usual speed a man is 25 minutes too late. His usual time to cover this distance is

(a) 2 hours 30 minutes

(b) 2 hours 15 minutes

(c) 2 hours 25 minutes

(d) 2 hours 10 minutes

57. A sum of ₹ 12,000 deposited at compound interest becomes double after 5 years. After 20 years, it will become

(a) ₹ 48,000   (b) ₹ 96,000

(c) ₹ 1,90,000   (d) ₹ 1,92,000

58. Simple interest on a certain sum for 6 year is $\dfrac{9}{25}$ of the sum. The rate of interest is

(a) 6%   (b) $6\dfrac{1}{2}\%$

(c) 8%   (d) $8\dfrac{1}{2}\%$

59. If $\dfrac{4\sqrt{3}+5\sqrt{2}}{\sqrt{48}+\sqrt{18}} = a + b\sqrt{6}$, then the values of a and b are respectively

(a) $\dfrac{9}{15}, \dfrac{4}{15}$ (b) $\dfrac{3}{11}, \dfrac{4}{33}$

(c) $\dfrac{9}{10}, \dfrac{2}{5}$ (d) $\dfrac{3}{5}, \dfrac{4}{15}$

60. If 17^{200} is divided by 18, the remainder is

(a) 1   (b) 2

(c) 16   (d) 17

61. The value of $3 + \dfrac{1}{\sqrt{3}} + \dfrac{1}{3+\sqrt{3}} + \dfrac{1}{\sqrt{3}-3}$ is

(a) $3 + \sqrt{3}$ (b) 3

(c) 1   (d) 0

62. If $x + y = y - x$, then $\dfrac{y^2 - x^2}{y^2 + 2xy + x^2}$ is

(a) 1   (b) 3

(c) 2   (d) 1

63. A student was asked to divide a number by 6 and add 12 to the quotient. He, however, first added 12 to the number and then divided it by 6, getting 112 as the answer. The correct answer should have been

(a) 124   (b) 122

(c) 118   (d) 114

64. Four runners started running simultaneously from a point on a circular track. They took 200 sec, 300 sec, 360 sec and 450 sec to complete one round. After how much time do they meet at the starting point for the first time ?

(a) 1800 seconds   (b) 3600 seconds

(c) 2400 seconds   (d) 4800 seconds

65. A work can be completed by P and Q in 12 days, Q and R in 15 days, R and P in 20 days. In how many days P alone can finish the work ?

(a) 10   (b) 20

(c) 30   (d) 60

66. A is thrice as good a workman as B and is therefore, able to finish a piece of work in 60 days less than B in what days they can finish work together?

(a) 22   (b) $22\dfrac{1}{2}$

(c) 23   (d) $23\dfrac{1}{4}$

67. A copper wire is bent in the form of square with an area of 121 cm². If the same wire is bent in the form of a circle, the radius (in cm) of the circle is

(Take $\pi = \dfrac{22}{7}$)

(a) 7   (b) 10

(c) 11   (d) 14

68. The areas of three consecutive faces of a cuboid are 12 cm², 20 cm² and 15cm², then the volume (in cm³) of the cuboid is

(a) 3600   (b) 100

(c) 80   (d) 60

69. The wheel of a motor car makes 1000 revolutions in moving 440 m. The diameter (in meter) of the wheel is

(a) 0.44   (b) 0.14

(c) 0.24   (d) 0.34

70. The sides of a triangle are in the ratio 2 : 3 : 4. The perimeter of the triangle is 18 cm. The area (in cm²) of the triangle is

(a) 9   (b) 36

(c) $\sqrt{42}$ (d) $3\sqrt{15}$

71. The ratio of the quantities of an acid and water in a mixture is 1 : 3. If 5 litres of acid is further added to the mixture, the new ratio becomes 1 : 2. The quantity of new mixture in litres is

(a) 32   (b) 40

(c) 42   (d) 45

72. If the cost price of 15 articles is equal to the selling price of 12 articles, find gain %.

(a) 20   (b) 25

(c) 18   (d) 21

Directions (Q. 73-75) : *The following graph shows the production of cotton bales of 100 kg each in lakhs by different states A, B, C, D and E over the years. Study the graph and answer the following question.*

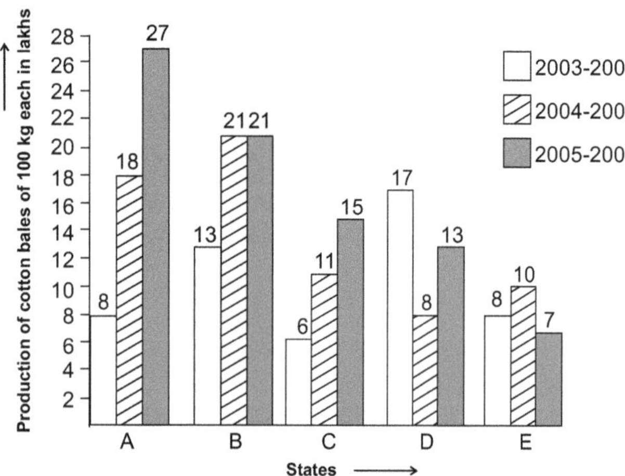

73. The production of State C in 2003-2004 is how many times its production in 2005-2006.

(a) 2.5   (b) 1.85

(c) 1.5   (d) 0.4

74. In which State(s) is there a steady increase in the production of cotton during the given period ?

(a) A and B   (b) B and D

(c) A and C   (d) D and E

75. How many kg of cotton was produced by State C during the given period ?

(a) 32,00,00,000 kg   (b) 42,50,00,000 kg

(c) 33,00,00,000 kg   (d) 35,00,00,000 kg

GENERAL AWARENESS

76. Who inaugurated the newly announced Goa Indian Institute of Technology's temporary Campus and will be mentored by IIT Mumbai?

(a) Narendra Modi   (b) Suresh Prabhu

(c) Sushma Swaraj   (d) Prakash Javdekar

77. The common tree species in Nilgiri hills is

(a) Sal   (b) Pine

(c) Eucalyptus   (d) Teak

78. The Buddhist monk who spread Buddhism in Tibet was

(a) Padmasambhava

(b) Nagarjuna

(c) Ananda

(d) Asanga

79. First Indian Prime Minister to visit Siachen has been

(a) Rajiv Gandhi

(b) Inder Kumar Gujaral

(c) Man Mohan Singh

(d) None of the above

80. Which of the following folk/tribal dances is associated with Karnataka ?

(a) Yakshagana   (b) Veedhi

(c) Jatra   (d) Jhora

81. "What is the Third Estate?" pamphlet – associated with the French Revolution, was written by

(a) Abbe Sieyes   (b) Marquis Lafayette

(c) Edmund Burke   (d) Joseph Foulon

82. Which of the following countries did not win any of the "FIFA World Cup" in 2002, 2006 & 2010 ?

(a) Brazil   (b) Argentina

(c) Spain   (d) South Africa

83. Who has clinched the first position in the category of Women's Champions in 2016 Australian Open Squash?

(a) Dipika Pallikal   (b) Madhura Radje

(c) Manohari Raji   (d) Deepika Kamrakar

84. Who was the first Indian to become member of British Parliament ?

(a) Bankim Chander Chatterjee

(b) W.C. Bannerjee

(c) Dadabhai Naoroji

(d) None of the above

85. BT seed is associated with

(a) Rice   (b) Wheat

(c) Cotton   (d) Oil seeds

86. The Headquarters of International Atomic Energy Agency is in

(a) Geneva   (b) Paris

(c) Vienna   (d) Washington

87. Gandhi's Salt Satyagraha was a part of

(a) Civil Disobedience Movement

(b) Champaran Satyagraha

(c) Quit India Movement

(d) Non-Cooperation Movement

88. If the Anglo-Indian community does not get adequate representation in the Lok Sabha, two members of the community can be nominated by the

(a) Prime Minister

(b) President

(c) Speaker

(d) President in consultation with the Parliament

89. For the election of President of India, a citizen should have completed the age of
(a) 25 years   (b) 30 years
(c) 35 years   (d) 18 years

90. In India, the Residuary Powers are vested in
(a) Union Government
(b) Sate Government
(c) Both (a) and (b)
(d) Local Government

91. The System of Dyarchy was introduced in India in
(a) 1909   (b) 1935
(c) 1919   (d) 1945

92. Which is the largest living bird on Earth ?
(a) Emu   (b) Ostrich
(c) Albatross   (d) Siberian Crane

93. The Headquarters of MCF (Master Control Facility) – the nerve centre of the entire space craft operations-in India is at
(a) Hderabad   – Andhra Pradesh
(b) Thumba   – Kerala
(c) Sriharikota   – Andhra Pradesh
(d) Hassan   – Karnataka

94. Which part becomes modified as the tusk of elephant ?
(a) Canine   (b) Premolar
(c) Second incisor   (d) Molar

95. Optical fibres are based on the phenomenon of
(a) Interference   (b) Dispersion
(c) Diffraction   (d) Total Internal Reflection

96. 'Mirage' is an example of
(a) refraction of light only
(b) total internal reflection of light only
(c) refraction and total internal reflection of light
(d) dispersion of light only

97. In which of the following areas, a spreadsheet software is more useful ?
(a) Psychology   (b) Publishing
(c) Statistics   (d) Message sending

98. Lens is made up of
(a) Pyrex glass   (b) Flint glass
(c) Ordinary glass   (d) Cobalt glass

99. 'Loktak" is a
(a) Valley   (b) Lake
(c) River   (d) Mountain Range

100. 2016 Nobel Prize for chemistry was awarded to Jean-Pierre Sauvage, Sir James Fraser Stoddart and Bernard L Feringa for the design and synthesis of which machines?
(a) Cyber
(b) Kinetic
(c) Molecular
(d) None of the above

ANSWERS

1. (c)	**2.** (b)	**3.** (b)	**4.** (c)	**5.** (d)	**6.** (d)	**7.** (d)	**8.** (d)	**9.** (d)	**10.** (c)
11. (d)	**12.** (d)	**13.** (c)	**14.** (b)	**15.** (c)	**16.** (d)	**17.** (b)	**18.** (c)	**19.** (d)	**20.** (b)
21. (c)	**22.** (a)	**23.** (c)	**24.** (b)	**25.** (c)	**26.** (c)	**27.** (a)	**28.** (b)	**29.** (d)	**30.** (c)
31. (b)	**32.** (a)	**33.** (b)	**34.** (a)	**35.** (b)	**36.** (d)	**37.** (a)	**38.** (b)	**39.** (a)	**40.** (a)
41. (b)	**42.** (c)	**43.** (c)	**44.** (b)	**45.** (c)	**46.** (b)	**47.** (d)	**48.** (c)	**49.** (b)	**50.** (a)
51. (c)	**52.** (a)	**53.** (b)	**54.** (b)	**55.** (d)	**56.** (a)	**57.** (d)	**58.** (a)	**59.** (d)	**60.** (a)
61. (b)	**62.** (a)	**63.** (b)	**64.** (b)	**65.** (c)	**66.** (b)	**67.** (a)	**68.** (d)	**69.** (b)	**70.** (d)
71. (d)	**72.** (b)	**73.** (a)	**74.** (c)	**75.** (a)	**76.** (d)	**77.** (c)	**78.** (a)	**79.** (c)	**80.** (a)
81. (a)	**82.** (d)	**83.** (a)	**84.** (c)	**85.** (c)	**86.** (c)	**87.** (a)	**88.** (b)	**89.** (c)	**90.** (a)
91. (c)	**92.** (b)	**93.** (d)	**94.** (c)	**95.** (d)	**96.** (a)	**97.** (c)	**98.** (b)	**99.** (b)	**100.** (c)

EXPLANATIONS

1. Given,

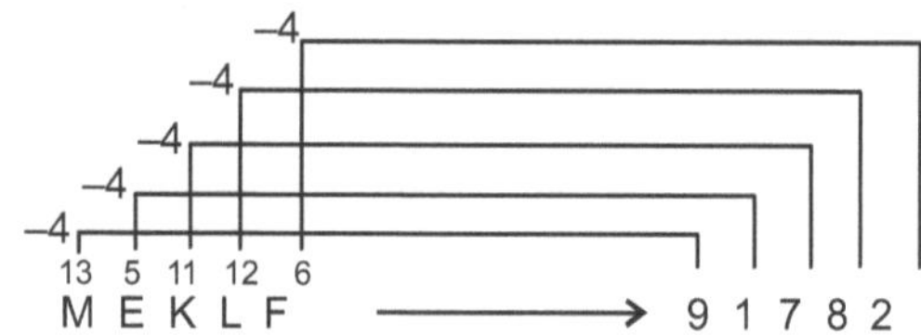

M E K L F ⟶ 9 1 7 8 2

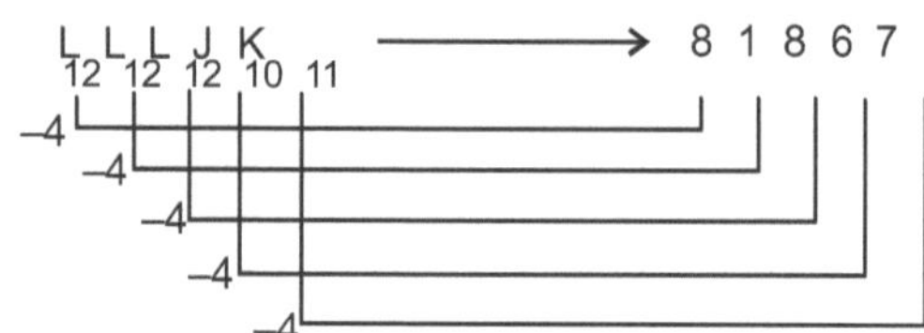

8 1 8 6 7

Similarly,

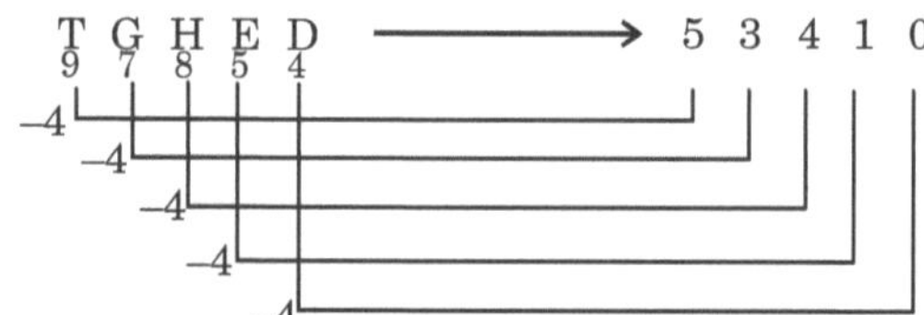

5 3 4 1 0

Hence, answer is option (c)

2.

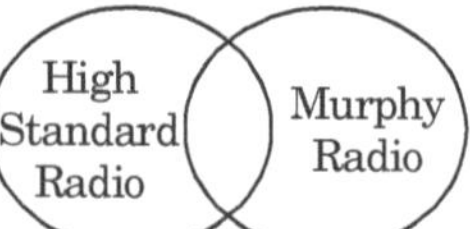

3. Given

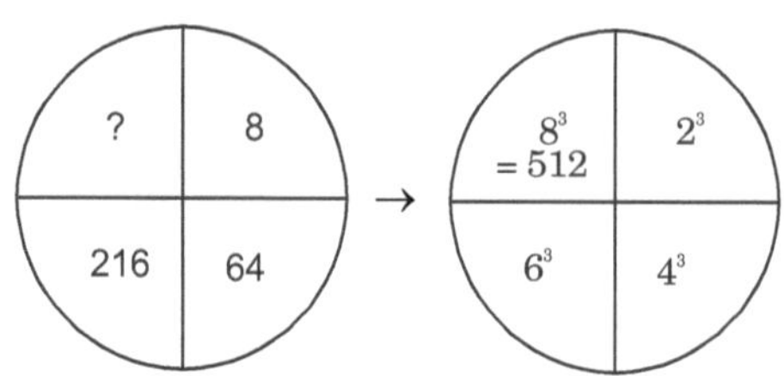

4. According to questin

$$19 - 5 \times 4 \div 2 + 4 = 13$$
$$19 - 5 \times 2 + 4 = 13$$
$$19 - 10 + 4 = 13$$
$$23 - 10 = 13$$
$$13 = 13$$
$$\text{L.H.S} = \text{R.H.S}$$

6. Given $\quad J \xrightarrow{-1} I \xrightarrow{-1} H \xrightarrow{+3} K$

$$P \xrightarrow{-1} O \xrightarrow{-1} N \xrightarrow{+3} Q$$

$$W \xrightarrow{-1} V \xrightarrow{-1} U \xrightarrow{+3} X$$

Similarly, $\quad M \xrightarrow{-1} L \xrightarrow{-1} K \xrightarrow{+3} N$

9. $\qquad 18 - 16 = 2$

$$63 - 56 = 7$$
$$108 - 96 = 12$$
$$99 - 86 = 13$$

All option's answer is prime number except 12.

12. The complete series is as follows

aaba̲b̲ / aaba̲b̲ / aabab

13. Tree rank from left = 7th

Tree rank from right = 14th

∴ Total number of trees = 14 + 7 − 1 = 20

14. Total number of families = 80

Number of families own a car

$$= \frac{20}{100} \times 80 = 16$$

Number of families own a motor cycle

$$= \frac{50}{100} \times (80 - 16) = \frac{1}{2} \times 64 = 32$$

Number of families not own any vehicle

$$= 80 - (16 + 32) = 80 - 48 = 32$$

15. Eldest ← Sita > Lavanya > Swapna > Hari > Suvarna → Younget

16. At 9 O'clock, hands are 45 minutes apart. They will be opposite to each other when there is a space of 30 minutes between then. This will happen when the minute hand gains (45 − 30) or 15 minute.

Now, the minute-hand losses 14 minutes in

$$= \frac{15 \times 60}{55} = \frac{180}{11} = 16\frac{4}{11} \text{ min}$$

Hence, the hands are opposite to each other at $16\frac{4}{11}$ min past 9.

18.

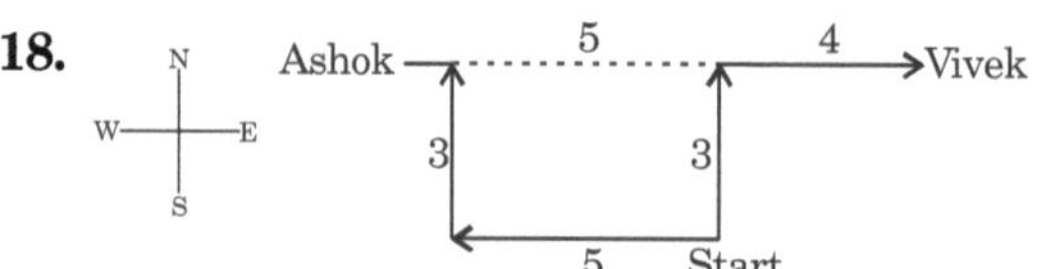

Distance between Ashok and Vivek

$$= (4 + 5) \text{ km} = 9 \text{ km}.$$

19. Given,

$$\text{RAMAYANA} \xrightarrow{-2} \text{RYKYWYLY}$$

Similarly,

$$\text{MAHABARATA} \xrightarrow{-2} \text{KYFYZFYPYRY}$$

20. Given pattern to solve equation is

$$(9 \times 4) + (1 \times 6) = 42$$
$$(8 \times 9) + (2 \times 3) = 78$$

Similarly, $\quad (6 \times 3) + (5 \times 4) = 38$

21.

51. Let cost price of 1st article = ₹x.

According to question.

$$x + \frac{25}{100}x = 4000$$

$$1.25x = 4000$$

$$x = ₹\,3200$$

∴   Gain = 4000 − 3200 = ₹ 800

As we know, x have no profit no loss

∴ cost price of IInd article

$$= 4000 + 800 = 4800$$

∴ Loss percentage of IInd article

$$= \frac{800}{4800} \times 100 = \frac{50}{3}\% = 16\frac{2}{3}\%$$

52. Let selling price = ₹ 100

According to question.

$$\text{Cost Price} = 100 + \frac{20}{100} \times 10 = ₹\,100$$

∴ Loss in cost price $= \frac{20}{120} \times 100 = \frac{50}{3} = 16\frac{2}{3}\%$

53. Let, price of sugar before reduction = ₹ x

total quantity purchase before reduction = y kg

According to question.

$$xy = 600 \text{ (Before reduction)}$$

$$\left(x - \frac{20}{100}x\right)(y + 5) = 600 \text{ (After reduction)}$$

$$0.8xy + 4x = 600$$

$$0.8(600) + 4x = 600$$

$$480 + 4x = 600$$

$$4x = 120$$

$$x = 30$$

∴ Price of sugar before reduction = ₹30.

54. Let total expenditure = ₹ 300

∴ Consumption at rate of ₹ 6 = 300 ÷ 6 = 50 kg

Similarly, consumption at rate of ₹ 7.5

$$= 300 \div 7.5 = 40 \text{ kg}$$

According to question.

Percentage of reduction

$$= \frac{(50 - 40)}{50} \times 100$$

$$= \frac{10}{50} \times 100 = 20\%$$

55. Let, III number be 100

∴ First Number = 100 − 30 = 71

Similary, Second Number = 100 − 37 = 63

According to question

$$= \frac{70 - 63}{70} \times 100 = \frac{7}{70} \times 100 = 10\%$$

56. Let usual speed of man = x

Let usual time = t

∴ Let distance = d

According to question.

$$\frac{6}{7}x = \frac{d}{t + 25}$$

$$\frac{6}{7}\left(\frac{d}{t}\right) = \frac{d}{t + 25} \left[x = \frac{d}{t}\right]$$

$$\frac{6}{7} = \frac{t}{t + 25}$$

$$6t + 150 = 7t$$

$$t = 150 \text{ min} = 2\text{hr. } 30 \text{ min.}$$

57. Given, $2P = P\left(1 + \dfrac{R}{100}\right)^5$

$$2 = \left(1 + \frac{R}{100}\right)^5 \quad \text{(Divide both side by P)}$$

$$2^4 = \left(1 + \frac{R}{100}\right)^{5 \times 4}$$

[Taking 4th power on both side]

$$16 = \left(1 + \frac{R}{100}\right)^{20}$$

$$16P = P\left(1 + \frac{R}{100}\right)^{20}$$

[Multiply both side by P]

So, that Amount after 20yrs

$$= 16 \times P = 16 \times 12000 = 192000$$

58. Let Princile and rate will be P and r respectively

According to question.

$$\frac{9}{25}P = \frac{P \times R \times 6}{100}; \quad \frac{9 \times 100}{25 \times 6} = R; \ R = 6\%$$

59.

$$a + b\sqrt{6} = \frac{4\sqrt{3} + 5\sqrt{2}}{\sqrt{48} + \sqrt{18}}$$

$$= \frac{4\sqrt{3} + 5\sqrt{2}}{4\sqrt{3} + 3\sqrt{2}}$$

$$= \frac{4\sqrt{3} + 5\sqrt{2}}{4\sqrt{3} + 3\sqrt{2}} \times \frac{4\sqrt{3} - 3\sqrt{2}}{4\sqrt{3} - 3\sqrt{2}}$$

$$= \frac{48 - 12\sqrt{6} + 20\sqrt{6} - 30}{48 - 18}$$

$$= \frac{18 + 8\sqrt{6}}{30}$$

$$= \frac{18}{30} + \frac{8}{30}\sqrt{6} = \frac{3}{5} + \frac{4}{15}\sqrt{6}$$

Comparing both side,

$$a = \frac{3}{5}, \ b = \frac{4}{15}$$

61. $3 + \dfrac{1}{\sqrt{3}} + \dfrac{1}{3+\sqrt{3}} + \dfrac{1}{\sqrt{3}-3}$

$$= 3 + \dfrac{1}{\sqrt{3}} + \dfrac{\sqrt{3}-3+\sqrt{3}+3}{3-9}$$

$$= 3 + \dfrac{1}{\sqrt{3}} - \dfrac{2\sqrt{3}}{6} = \dfrac{18\sqrt{3}+6-6}{6\sqrt{3}} = 3$$

63. Let divisior $= x$

According to question

$$(x + 12) \div 6 = 112$$
$$x + 12 = 672$$
$$x = 672 - 12 = 660$$

$\therefore$ Correct Answer $= (660 \div 6) + 12 = 110 + 12 = 122$

64. Time taken by

Ist runner $= 200$ sec

IInd runner $= 300$ sec

IIIrd runner $= 360$ sec

IVth runner $= 450$ sec

$\therefore$ L.C.M. of their time $= 1800$ sec.

So that they meet after 1800 second at starting point.

65. A work completed by P + Q = 12 day

(P + Q) work done in 1 day $= \dfrac{1}{12}$ ...(1)

Similarly,

(Q + R) work done in 1 day $= \dfrac{1}{15}$ ...(2)

(R + P) work done in 1 day $= \dfrac{1}{20}$ ...(3)

Adding equation (1), (2) & (3), we get

$\therefore\ 2(1 + Q + R) = \dfrac{1}{12} + \dfrac{1}{15} + \dfrac{1}{20}$

$$= \dfrac{5+4+3}{60} = \dfrac{12}{60} = \dfrac{1}{5}$$

$$P + Q + R = \dfrac{1}{10}$$

$$P + \dfrac{1}{15} = \dfrac{1}{5}$$

$$P = \dfrac{1}{10} - \dfrac{1}{15} = \dfrac{3-2}{30} = \dfrac{1}{30}$$

P work done in 1 day $= \dfrac{1}{30}$

work completed by P = 30 days

66. If A works 3 times as fast then B,

$$A = \dfrac{1}{3}B$$

According to question

$$B - A = 60$$

$$B - \dfrac{1}{3}B = 60$$

$$\dfrac{3B - B}{3} = 60$$

$$\dfrac{2B}{3} = 60$$

$$B = \dfrac{60 \times 3}{2} = 90$$

$\therefore \qquad A = \dfrac{1}{3} \times 90 = 30$

$\therefore$ A can do work per day $= \dfrac{1}{30}$

$\therefore$ B can do work per day $= \dfrac{1}{90}$

(A + B) work in 1 day $= \dfrac{1}{30} + \dfrac{1}{90} = \dfrac{3+1}{90} = \dfrac{4}{90}$

$\therefore$ A + B work together to finish work

$$= \dfrac{90}{4} \text{ days} = 22.5 \text{ days.}$$

71. Let quantity of acid $= x$

$\therefore$ quantity of water $= 3x$

According to question

$$\dfrac{x+5}{3x} = \dfrac{1}{2}$$
$$2x + 10 = 3x$$
$$x = 10$$

$\therefore$ Quantity of new mixture $= x + 3x + 5$

$$= 10 + 3 \times 10 + 5 = 45 \text{ ltrs.}$$

72. According to question

$$\text{Gain \%} = \dfrac{15-12}{12} \times 100$$

$$= \dfrac{3}{12} \times 100$$

$$= \dfrac{1}{4} \times 100 = 25\%$$

■■

GENERAL INTELLIGENCE

1. 25 * 2 * 6 = 4 * 11 * 0

Which set of symbols can replace * ?

(a) ×, – ×, + (b) +, –, ×, +

(c) ×, + , ×, – (d) ×, +, +, ×

2. Find the missing number from the given responses:

5	6	12
4	3	4
2	3	?
18	27	96

(a) 4 (b) 5

(c) 3 (d) 6

3. Peter walked 8 kms. west and turned right and walked 3 kms. Then again he turned right and walked 12 kms. How far is he from the starting point?

(a) 7 (b) 8

(c) 4 (d) 5

Directions (Q. 4 & 5) : *Select the related word / letters / number / figure from the given alternatives.*

4. FOX : CUNNING : : RABBIT : ?

(a) COURAGEOUS

(b) DANGEROUS

(c) TIMID

(d) FEROCIOUS

5. FLEXIBLE : RIGID : : CONFIDENCE : ?

(a) DIFFIDENCE

(b) INDIFFERENCE

(c) COWARDICE

(d) SCARE

Directions (Q. 6 & 7) : *Find the odd word / letters / number / figure from the given responses.*

6. (a) Room (b) Chamber

(c) Veranda (d) Cabin

7. (a) 6243 (b) 2643

(c) 8465 (d) 4867

8. From amongst the given alternatives, select the one in which the set of numbers in most like the set of numbers given below :

(6 , 14, 30)

(a) 4, 16, 28 (b) 7, 12, 22

(c) 6, 12, 22 (d) 5, 12, 20

9. Which one of the given responses would be a meaningful order of the following words?

1. Family 2. Community

3. Member 4. Locality

5. Country

(a) 3, 1, 4, 2, 5 (b) 3, 1, 2, 4, 5

(c) 3, 1, 2, 5, 4 (d) 3, 1, 4, 5, 2

10. Which set of letters when sequentially placed at the gaps in the given letter series shall complete it?

__ a __ aaaba __ __ ba __ ab __

(a) abaaaa (b) abaaba

(c) aababa (d) ababaa

Directions (Q. 11 &12) : *Find the missing number / letters / figure from the given responses:*

11. a, r, c, s, e, t, g, __, __

(a) x, z (b) u, i

(c) w, y (d) v, b

12. 36, 28, 24, 22, ?

(a) 18 (b) 19

(c) 21 (d) 22

13. Select the number which does NOT belong to the given series :

232, 343, 454, 564, 676

(a) 676 (b) 454

(c) 343 (d) 564

14. If the day after tomorrow is Sunday, what day was tomorrow's day before yesterday?

(a) Friday (b) Thursday

(c) Monday (d) Tuesday

15. A man is 3 years older than his wife and four times as old as his son. If the son becomes 15 years old after 3 years, what is the present age of the wife?

(a) 60 years (b) 51 years

(c) 48 years (d) 45 years

16. Suresh is 7 ranks ahead of Ashok in the class of 39 students. If Ashok's rank is 17th from the last, what is Suresh's rank from the start?

(a) 16th   (b) 23rd

(c) 24th   (d) 15th

17. A word/set of letters given in capital letters is followed by four answer words. Out of these only one **cannot** be formed by using the letters of the given word/set of letters. Find out that word :

INDETERMINATE

(a) DETERMINE   (b) RETINUE

(c) REMINDER   (d) RETINAL

18. A group of alphabets are given with each being assigned a numerical code. These have to be unscrambled into a meaningful word and the correct code so obtained may be indicated from the given responses :

R A H K S

1 2 3 4 5

(a) 5 1 2 3 4   (b) 5 4 2 1 3

(c) 5 3 2 1 4   (d) 5 3 1 2 4

19. Two statements are given followed by four conclusions, I, II, III and IV. You have to consider the statements to be true, even if they seem to be at variance from commonly known facts. You are to decide which of the given conclusions can definitely be drawn from the given statements. Indicate your answer.

Statements :

(A) No cow is a chair

(B) All chairs are tables

Conclusions :

I.   Some tables are chairs

II. Some tables are cows.

III. Some chairs are cows.

IV. No table is a cow.

(a) Either II or III follow

(b) Either II or IV follow

(c) Only I follows

(d) All conclusions follow

20. In a certain code SISTER is written as RHRSDQ. How is UNCLE written in that code?

(a) TMBKD

(b) TBMKD

(c) TVBOD

(d) TMKBD

21. Choose the correct figure that represents the given relation :

Blue eyed, females, doctors

(a) 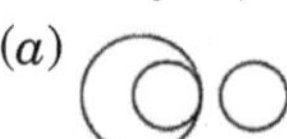

(b)

(c)

(d)

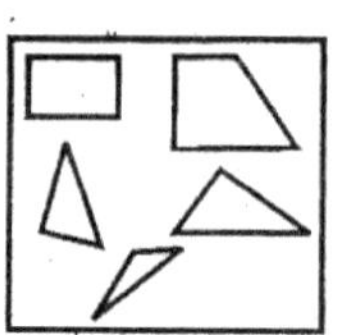

22. Among the four answer figures, which figure can be formed from the cut-pieces given below in the question figure?

Question Figure :

Answer Figures :

(a) 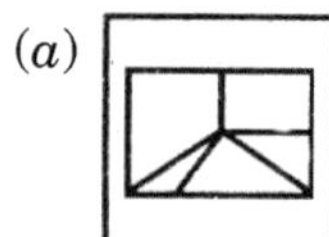   (b) 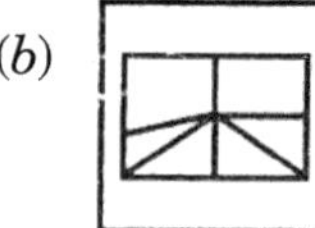

(c) 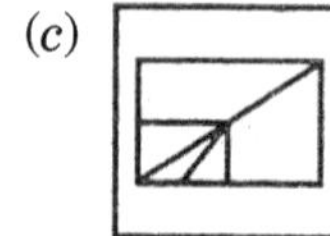   (d) 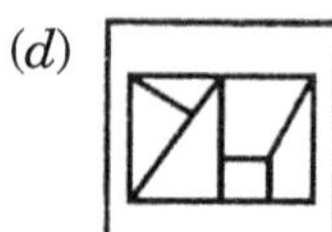

23. If a mirror is placed on the line LM, then which of the answer figures is the right image of the given question figure?

Question Figure :

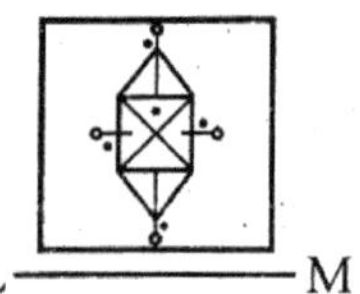

L—————M

Answer Figures :

(a) 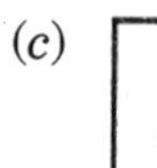   (b) 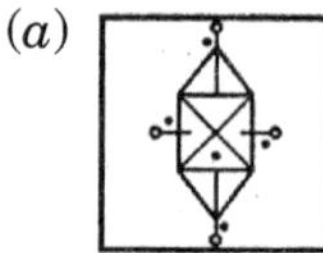

(c) 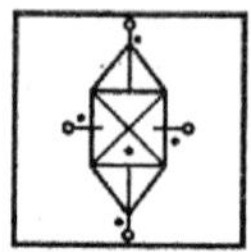   (d) 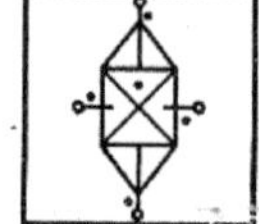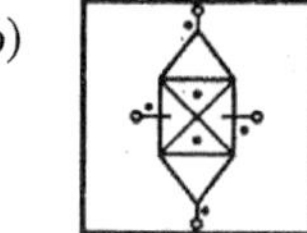

24. How many triangles are there in the following figure?

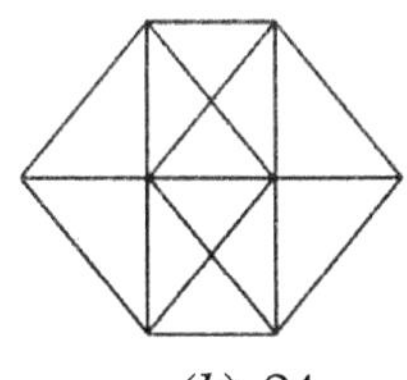

(a) 20   (b) 24
(c) 26   (d) 32

25. From the given answer figures, select the one in which the question figure is hidden/embedded.

Question Figure :

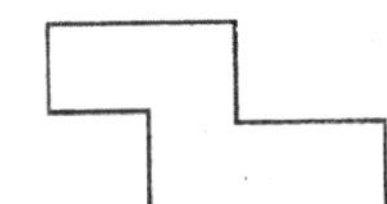

Answer Figures :

(a)
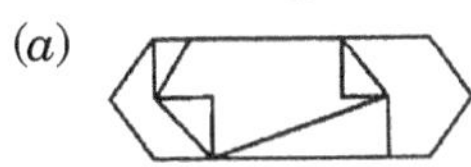

(b)
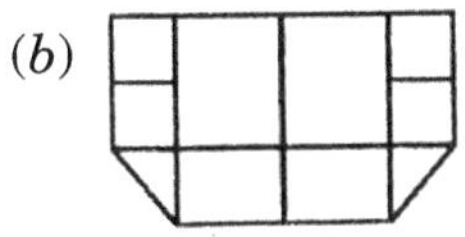

(c)
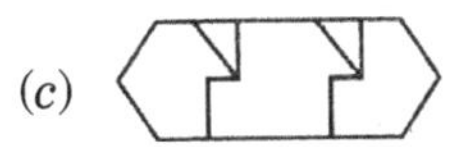

(d)
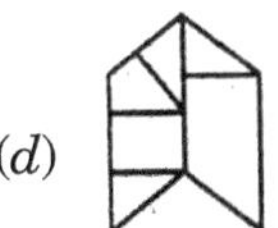

ENGLISH LANGUAGE

Directions (Q. 26-27): *In following questions out of the four alternatives, choose the one which best expresses the meaning of the given word and mark it in the Answer-Sheet.*

26. Debacle
(a) decline   (b) downfall
(c) discomfiture   (d) degeneration

27. Ostracise
(a) banish   (b) belittle
(c) beguile   (d) besiege

Directions (Q. 28-29): *Choose the word opposite meaning to the given word and mark it in the Answer-Sheet.*

28. Jettison
(a) accept   (b) reward
(c) preserve   (d) consent

29. Ameliorate
(a) improve   (b) depend
(c) soften   (d) worsen

Directions (Q. 30-32): *Out of the four alternatives, choose the one which can be substituted for the given words / sentence and indicate it by blackening the appropriate rectangle [/] in the Answer-Sheet.*

30. One who hides away on a ship to obtain a free passage
(a) compositor   (b) stoker
(c) stowaway   (d) shipwright

31. Clues available at a scene
(a) circumstantial   (b) derivative
(c) inferential   (d) suggestive

32. An unexpected piece of good fortune
(a) windfall   (b) philanthropy
(c) benevolence   (d) turnstile

Directions for questions 33 to 35: *Four alternatives are given for the Idiom / Phrase. Choose the alternative which best expresses the meaning of the Idiom / Phrase.*

33. Play ducks and drakes
(a) Back to original position
(b) To make friends
(c) To run away
(d) To squander one's wealth.

34. A dog's life
(a) To be extremely haughty
(b) To pretend sadness
(c) unhappy existence full of problems.
(d) Delaying tactics

35. My sincere advice to my maidservant *fell on stony ground.*
(a) was counter productive
(b) had a strong impact
(c) made one stubborn
(d) had little success

Direction (Q. 36): *Groups of four words are given. In each group, one word is correctly spelt. Find the correctly spelt word and mark your answer in the Answer-Sheet.*

36. (a) parapharnelia   (b) parsimonious
(c) peccadilo   (d) peadiatrics

Directions (Q. 37-39): *Some of the sentences have errors and some have none. Find out which part of a sentence has an error and blacken the rectangle [/] corresponding to the appropriate letter (a, b, c). If there is no error, blacken the rectangle [/] corresponding to (d) in the Answer-sheet.*

37. Judge in him / prevailed upon the father/
　　　　(a)　　　　　　　　(b)
and he sentenced his son to death / No error
　　　　(c)　　　　　　　　　　(d)

38. Nine tenths / of the pillar/ have rotted away/
　　　(a)　　　　(b)　　　　(c)
No error
(d)

39. One major reason/ for the popularity of television
      (a)   *(b)*

  is / that most people like to stay at home /
                      (c)

  No error
    (d)

Directions (Q. 40-42): *Sentences are given with blanks to be filled in with an appropriate word(s). Four alternatives are suggested for each question. Choose the correct alternative out of the four and indicate it by blackening the appropriate rectangle [/] in the Answer-sheet.*

40. The court _________ cognisance of the criminal's words.
- *(a)* took
- *(b)* made
- *(c)* gave
- *(d)* allowed

41. _________ wins this civil war there will be little rejoicing at the victory.
- *(a)* Whichever
- *(b)* Whoever
- *(c)* Whatever
- *(d)* Wherever

42. As he got older his belief in these principles did not _________ .
- *(a)* wither
- *(b)* shake
- *(c)* waver
- *(d)* dither

Directions (Q. 43-45): *A part of the sentence is underlined. Below are given alternatives to the underlined part at (a), (b) and (c) which may improve the sentence. Choose the correct alternative. In case no improvement is needed your answer is (d).*

43. To get into the building I'll <u>disguise as</u> a reporter.
- *(a)* disguise to be
- *(b)* disguise as one
- *(c)* disguise myself
- *(d)* No improvement

44. He denied that he <u>had not forged</u> my signature.
- *(a)* would not forget
- *(b)* had forged
- *(c)* did not forge
- *(d)* No improvement

45. If <u>I had played well,</u> I would have won the match.
- *(a)* I played well
- *(b)* I play well
- *(c)* I am playing well
- *(d)* No improvement

Directions (Q. 46-50) : *You have a brief passage with 5 questions following the passage. Read the passage carefully and choose the best answer to each question out of the four alternatives and mark it in the Answer Sheet.*

In May 1966, the World Health Organisation was authorised to initiate a global campaign to eradicate small-pox. The goal was to eradicate the disease in one decade. Because similar projects for malaria and yellow fever had failed, few believed that small-pox could actually be eradicated, but eleven years after the initial organisation of the campaign, no cases were reported in the field.

The strategy was not only to provide mass vaccinations, but also to isolate patients with active small-pox in order to contain the spread of the disease and to break the chain of human transmission. Rewards for reporting small-pox assisted in motivating the public to aid health workers. One by one, each small-pox victim was sought out, removed from contact with others and treated. At the same time, the entire village where the victim had lived was vaccinated.

Today small-pox is no longer a threat to humanity. Routine vaccinations have been stopped worldwide.

46. Which of the following is the best title for the passage?
- *(a)* The World Health Origanisation
- *(b)* The eradication of small-pox
- *(c)* Small-pox vaccinations
- *(d)* Infectious diseases

47. What was the goal of the campaign against small-pox ?
- *(a)* To decrease the spread of small-pox worldwide.
- *(b)* To eliminate small-pox worldwide in ten years.
- *(c)* To provide mass vaccinations against small-pox worldwide.
- *(d)* To initiate worldwide projects for small-pox, malaria and yellow fever at the same time.

48. According to the paragraph what was the strategy used to eliminate the spread of small-pox?
- *(a)* Vaccination of the entire village
- *(b)* Treatment of individual victims
- *(c)* Isolation of victims and mass vaccinations
- *(d)* Extensive reporting of outbreaks.

49. Which statement doesn't refer to small-pox?
- *(a)* Previous projects had failed
- *(b)* People are no longer vaccinated for it
- *(c)* The World Health Organisation mounted a worldwide campaign to eradicate the disease
- *(d)* It was a serious threat

50. It can be inferred that
- *(a)* no new cases of small-pox have been reported this year
- *(b)* malaria and yellow fever have been eliminated
- *(c)* small-pox victims no longer die when they contract the disease
- *(d)* small-pox is not transmitted from one person to another

QUANTITATIVE APTITUDE

51. The ratio of income and expenditure of a person is 11 : 10. If he saves ₹ 9,000 per annum, his monthly income is

(a) ₹ 8,000 (b) ₹ 8,800

(c) ₹ 8,500 (d) ₹ 8,250

52. A copper wire of length 36 m and diameter 2 mm is melted to form a sphere. The radius of the sphere (in cm) is

(a) 2.5 (b) 3

(c) 3.5 (d) 4

53. If the length of a rectangle is increased by 10% and its breadth is decreased by 10%, the change in its area will be

(a) 1% increase (b) 1% decrease

(c) 10% increase (d) No change

54. In how many years will a sum of money double itself at $6\frac{1}{4}$% simple interest per annum?

(a) 24 (b) 20

(c) 16 (d) 12

55. A sum of ₹ 12,000, deposited at compound interest becomes double after 5 years. How much will it be after 20 years?

(a) ₹ 1,44,000 (b) ₹ 1,20,000

(c) ₹ 1,50,000 (d) ₹ 1,92,000

56. In a 100 m race, Kamal defeats Bimal by 5 seconds. If the speed of Kamal is 18 km./hr., then the speed of Bimal is

(a) 15.4 km/hr (b) 14.5 km/hr

(c) 14.4 km/hr (d) 14 km/hr

57. A train, 240 m long, crosses a man walking along the line in opposite direction at the rate of 3 km/h in 10 seconds. The speed of the train is

(a) 63 km/h (b) 75 km/h

(c) 83.4 km/h (d) 86.4 km/h

58. A boatman rows 1 km in 5 minutes along the stream and 6 km in 1 hour against the stream. The speed of the stream is

(a) 3 km/hr (b) 6 km/hr

(c) 10 km/hr (d) 12 km/hr

59. A can complete $\frac{1}{3}$ of a work in 5 days and B $\frac{2}{5}$ of the work in 10 days. In how many days both A and B together can complete the work?

(a) 10 (b) $9\frac{3}{8}$

(c) $8\frac{4}{5}$ (d) $7\frac{1}{2}$

60. One pipe fills a water tank three times faster than another pipe. If the two pipes together can fill the empty tank in 36 minutes, then how much time will the slower pipe alone take to fill the tank?

(a) 1 hour 21 minutes

(b) 1 hour 48 minutes

(c) 2 hours

(d) 2 hours 24 minutes

61. If A's income is 25% less than B's income, by how much percent is B's income more than that of A?

(a) 25 (b) 30

(c) $33\frac{1}{3}$ (d) $66\frac{2}{3}$

62. $(1^2 + 2^2 + 3^2 + ... + 10^2)$ is equal to

(a) 380 (b) 385

(c) 390 (d) 392

63. A number, when divided by 136, leaves remainder 36. If the same number is divided by 17, the remainder will be

(a) 9 (b) 7

(c) 3 (d) 2

64. If $2p + \dfrac{1}{p} = 4$, the value of $p^3 + \dfrac{1}{8p^3}$ is

(a) 4 (b) 5

(c) 8 (d) 15

65. The least among the fractions

$\dfrac{15}{16}, \dfrac{19}{20}, \dfrac{24}{25}, \dfrac{34}{35}$ is

(a) $\dfrac{34}{35}$ (b) $\dfrac{15}{16}$

(c) $\dfrac{19}{20}$ (d) $\dfrac{24}{25}$

66. $1.\overline{27}$ in the form $\dfrac{p}{q}$ is equal to

(a) $\dfrac{127}{100}$ (b) $\dfrac{73}{100}$

(c) $\dfrac{14}{11}$ (d) $\dfrac{11}{14}$

67. $\dfrac{3.25 \times 3.20 - 3.20 \times 3.05}{0.064}$ is equal to

(a) 1 (b) $\dfrac{1}{2}$

(c) $\dfrac{1}{10}$ (d) 10

68. $\left\{ \dfrac{(0.1)^2 - (0.01)^2}{0.0001} + 1 \right\}$ is equal to

    (a) 1010 (b) 110

    (c) 101 (d) 100

69. If the cost price of 15 books is equal to the selling price of 20 books, the loss percent is

    (a) 16 (b) 20

    (c) 24 (d) 25

70. Successive discounts of 10%, 20% and 30% is equivalent to a single discount of.

    (a) 60% (b) 49.6%

    (c) 40.5% (d) 36%

71. The price of an article was first increased by 10% and then again by 20%. If the last increased price be ₹ 33, the original price was

    (a) ₹ 30 (b) ₹ 27.50

    (c) ₹ 26.50 (d) ₹ 25

72. The ratio of milk and water in mixtures of four containers are 5 : 3, 2 : 1, 3 : 2 and 7 : 4 respectively. In which container is the quantity of milk, relative to water, minimum?

    (a) First (b) Second

    (c) Third (d) Fourth

Directions (Q.73-75): *The pie chart, given here, shows the amount of money spent on various sports by a school administration in a particular year.*

Observe the pie chart and answer questions that follow:

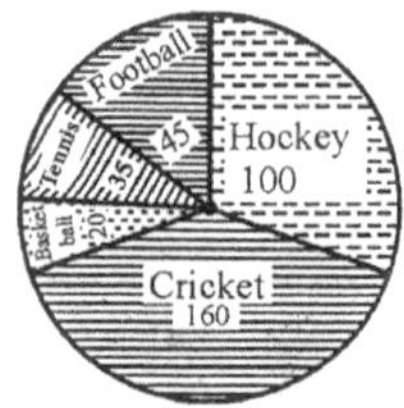

73. If the money spent on football was ₹ 9,000, how much more money was spent on hockey than on football?

    (a) ₹ 11,000 (b) ₹ 11,500

    (c) ₹ 12,000 (d) ₹ 12,500

74. If the money spent on football was ₹ 9,000, what amount was spent on Cricket?

    (a) ₹ 31,000 (b) ₹ 31,500

    (c) ₹ 32,000 (d) ₹ 32,500

75. If the money spent on football ₹ 9,000, then what was the amount spent on all sports?

    (a) ₹ 73,000 (b) ₹ 72,800

    (c) ₹ 72,500 (d) ₹ 72,000

GENERAL AWARENESS

76. Who has been conferred with the Academy Ratna in Oct 2016?

    (a) CV Ram (b) CV Singh

    (c) CV Chandra (d) CV Chandrashekhar

77. Pituitary gland is situated in

    (a) the base of the heart

    (b) the base of the brain

    (c) the neck

    (d) the abdomen

78. Who discovered cement?

    (a) Agassit (b) Albertus Magnus

    (c) Joseph Aspdin (d) Janseen

79. The nuclear particle having no mass and no charge, but only spin is

    (a) electron (b) proton

    (c) neutrino (d) meson

80. The technology that is used to establish wireless networking is

    (a) Bluetooth (b) TCP/IP

    (c) J2ME (d) MATLAB

81. TRIPS and TRIMS are the terms associated with

    (a) IMF (b) WTO

    (c) IBRD (d) IDA

82. A presidential Ordinance can remain in force

    (a) for three months

    (b) for six months

    (c) for nine months

    (d) indefinitely

83. What is USB?

    (a) Urgent Sent Bit

    (b) Ultimate Service Bit

    (c) Universal Sent Bit

    (d) Universal Serial Bus

84. How many year extension has secured Arundhati Bhattacharya as the chairperson of the State Bank of India (SBI)?

    (a) Half (b) Two

    (c) One (d) Three

85. Which one of the following states does <u>not</u> form part of Narmada River basin?

    (a) Madhya Pradesh (b) Rajasthan

    (c) Gujarat (d) Maharashtra

86. The exchange of commodities between two countries is referred as

    (a) balance of trade (b) bilateral trade

    (c) volume of trade (d) multilateral trade

87. Soil erosion on hill slopes can be checked by
(a) Afforestation
(b) Terrace cultivation
(c) Strip cropping
(d) Contour ploughing

88. Who coined the word 'Geography'?
(a) Ptolemy
(b) Eratosthenese
(c) Hecataus
(d) Herodatus

89. The art and science of map making is called
(a) Remote Sensing
(b) Cartography
(c) Photogrammetry
(d) Mapping

90. The monk who influenced Ashoka to embrace Buddhism was
(a) Vishnu Gupta
(b) Upa Gupta
(c) Brahma Gupta
(d) Brihadratha

91. The declaration that Democracy is a Government 'of the people, by the people; for the people' was made by
(a) George Washington
(b) Winston Churchill
(c) Abraham Lincoln
(d) Theodore Roosevelt

92. The Lodi dynasty was founded by
(a) Ibrahim Lodi
(b) Sikandar Lodi
(c) Bahlol Lodi
(d) Khizr Khan

93. India attained 'Dominion Status' on
(a) 15th January, 1947
(b) 15th August, 1947
(c) 15th August, 1950
(d) 15th October, 1947

94. Sarkaria Commission was concerned with
(a) Administrative Reforms
(b) Electoral Reforms
(c) Financial Reforms
(d) Centre-State relations

95. The terms "Micro Economics" and "Macro Economics" were coined by
(a) Alfred Marshall
(b) Ragner Nurkse
(c) Ragner Frisch
(d) J.M. Keynes

96. The isotope used for the production of atomic energy is
(a) U-235
(b) U-238
(c) U-234
(d) U-236

97. 'C' language is a
(a) low level language
(b) high level language
(c) machine level language
(d) assembly level language

98. NIS stands for
(a) national infectious diseases seminar
(b) national irrigation schedule
(c) national immunisation schedule
(d) national information sector

99. Ringworm is a ______ disease.
(a) Bacterial
(b) Protozoan
(c) Viral
(d) Fungal

100. Which of the following became first BCCI member to adopt Lodha panel recommendations?
(a) Railways Sports Promotion Board
(b) Vidarbha Cricket Association
(c) Baroda Cricket Association
(d) Services Sports Control Board

ANSWERS

1. (a)	**2.** (d)	**3.** (d)	**4.** (c)	**5.** (a)	**6.** (c)	**7.** (c)	**8.** (b)	**9.** (b)	**10.** (a)
11. (b)	**12.** (d)	**13.** (d)	**14.** (c)	**15.** (d)	**16.** (a)	**17.** (a)	**18.** (c)	**19.** (b)	**20.** (a)
21. (d)	**22.** (a)	**23.** (c)	**24.** (c)	**25.** (a)	**26.** (b)	**27.** (a)	**28.** (a)	**29.** (d)	**30.** (c)
31. (a)	**32.** (a)	**33.** (d)	**34.** (c)	**35.** (d)	**36.** (b)	**37.** (a)	**38.** (b)	**39.** (c)	**40.** (a)
41. (b)	**42.** (a)	**43.** (c)	**44.** (b)	**45.** (d)	**46.** (b)	**47.** (b)	**48.** (c)	**49.** (a)	**50.** (c)
51. (d)	**52.** (b)	**53.** (b)	**54.** (c)	**55.** (d)	**56.** (c)	**57.** (c)	**58.** (a)	**59.** (b)	**60.** (d)
61. (c)	**62.** (b)	**63.** (d)	**64.** (b)	**65.** (b)	**66.** (c)	**67.** (d)	**68.** (d)	**69.** (d)	**70.** (b)
71. (d)	**72.** (c)	**73.** (a)	**74.** (c)	**75.** (d)	**76.** (d)	**77.** (b)	**78.** (c)	**79.** (c)	**80.** (a)
81. (b)	**82.** (b)	**83.** (d)	**84.** (c)	**85.** (b)	**86.** (c)	**87.** (b)	**88.** (b)	**89.** (b)	**90.** (b)
91. (c)	**92.** (c)	**93.** (b)	**94.** (d)	**95.** (d)	**96.** (a)	**97.** (b)	**98.** (d)	**99.** (d)	**100.** (b)

EXPLANATIONS

1. The Correct statement is
$$25 \times 2 - 6 = 4 \times 11 + 0$$
$$50 - 6 = 44$$
$$44 = 44$$
$$\text{L.H.S} = \text{R.H.S}$$

2. The given sequence is
$$(5 + 4) \times 2 = 18$$
$$(6 + 3) \times 3 = 27$$
Similarly,
$$(12 + 4) \times x = 96$$
$$x = \frac{96}{16} = 6$$

3. 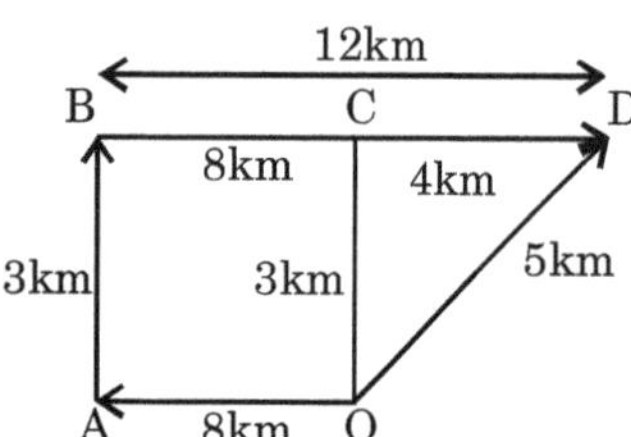

In $\triangle OCD$,
$$OC^2 + CD^2 = OD^2$$
$$(3)^2 + (4)^2 = OD^2$$
$$9 + 16 = OD^2$$
$$OD = \sqrt{25} = 5 \text{ km}$$

7. $6 + 2 + 4 + 3 = 15$
$2 + 6 + 4 + 3 = 15$
$8 + 4 + 6 + 5 = 23$
$4 + 8 + 6 + 7 = 25$

All above options are non-prime number except option (c).

8. Given
$$6 \xrightarrow{(6\times2+2)} 14 \xrightarrow{(14\times2+2)} 30$$
Similarly,
$$7 \xrightarrow{(7\times2-2)} 12 \xrightarrow{(12\times2-2)} 22$$

10. $\underline{aa}b\underline{a}$ / $\underline{aa}b\underline{a}$ / $\underline{aa}b\underline{a}$ / $\underline{aa}b\underline{a}$

11.
$$\overset{+2 \quad +2 \quad +2 \quad +2}{a_1 \ r_1 \ c_1 \ s_1 \ e_1 \ t_1 \ g_1 \ u \ i}$$
$$+1 \quad +1 \quad +1$$

12. $36 \xrightarrow{-8} 28 \xrightarrow{-4} 24 \xrightarrow{-2} 22 \xrightarrow{-1} \boxed{21}$

13. $232 \longrightarrow 343 \longrightarrow 454 \longrightarrow \boxed{564} \longrightarrow 676$
$(2+2)-3 = 1 \quad (3+3)-4 = 2 \quad (4+4)-5 = 3 \quad (5+4)-6 = 3 \quad (6+6)-7 = 5$

15. Let age of son $= x$
According to question
$$x + 3 = 15$$
$$x = 12 \text{ yrs}$$
$\therefore$ Age of man $= 4x = 4 \times 12$
$$= 48 \text{ yrs}$$
$\therefore$ Age of wife $= 4x - 3$
$$= 48 - 3$$
$$= 45 \text{ yrs.}$$

16. Ashok's rank from last $= 17$
$\therefore$ Sureh's rank from last $= 17 + 7 = 24$
Total no. student $= 39$
$\therefore$ Suresh's rank from start
$$= 39 - 24 + 1 = 16$$

18. 5 3 2 1 4
S H A R K

20. Given

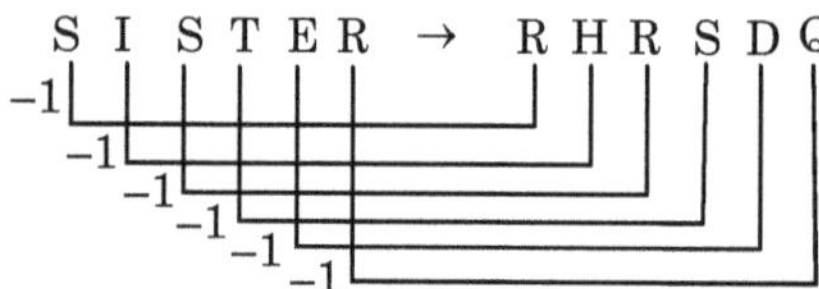

Similarly,

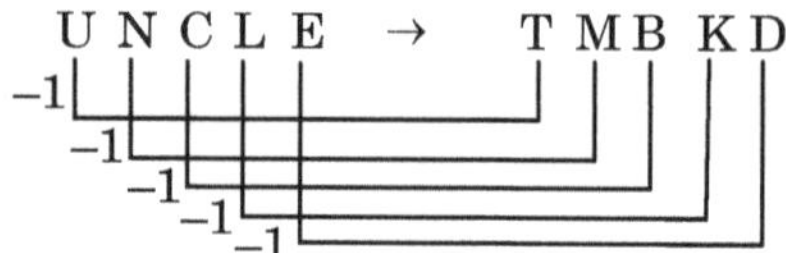

21.

51. Let the income and expenditure of a person $= 11x$ and $10x$
According to question
$$11x - 10x = 9{,}000$$
$$x = 9000$$
$\therefore$ Income of person $= 11 \times 9000$
$$= ₹ \ 99000 \text{ per annum.}$$
$\therefore$ Monthly income $= \dfrac{99{,}000}{12} = ₹ \ 8250$

53. Change in area $= 10 - 10 - \dfrac{10 \times 10}{100} = 1$

$\therefore$ Area decreased by 1%.

54. Let the money $= ₹\, x$

Simple interest $= 2x - x = ₹\, x$

According to question

$$x = \dfrac{x \times 25 \times time}{4 \times 100}$$

$$\text{Time} = \dfrac{400}{25} = 16 \text{ years}$$

55. $P\left[1 + \dfrac{r}{100}\right]^{s} = 2P$

After 20 year

$$P\left[1 + \dfrac{r}{100}\right]^{5 \times 4} = (2P)^4 = 16P$$

$\therefore$ After 20 year the sum of money

$$= 16 \times 12{,}000$$
$$= ₹\, 1{,}92{,}000$$

56. Let the speed of Bimal $= x$ m/s

Speed of Kamal $= 18 \times \dfrac{5}{18} = 5$ m/s

According to question

$$\dfrac{100}{x} - \dfrac{100}{5} = 5$$

$$\dfrac{500 - 100x}{5x} = 5$$

$$125x = 300$$

$$x = \dfrac{500}{125} = 4 \text{ m/s}$$

$\therefore$ $\qquad x = 4 \times \dfrac{18}{5} = 14.4$ km/hr.

57. Relative speed $= (3 + x)$ km/h.

$\qquad\qquad$ [Let x be the speed to train.]

According to question.

$$\dfrac{.240}{(3 + x)} = \dfrac{1\cancel{0}}{360\cancel{0}}$$

$\Rightarrow \qquad 3 + x = 86.4$

$\Rightarrow \qquad x = 83.4$ km/h.

58. Speed of boat man along the stream

$$= \dfrac{1}{\dfrac{5}{60}} = 12 \text{km/hr}$$

Speed of boat man against the stream

$$= \dfrac{6}{1} = 6 \text{ km/h}$$

Speed of stream $= \dfrac{12 - 6}{2} = \dfrac{6}{2} = 3$km/hr.

59. A complete $\dfrac{1}{3}$ work $= 5$ days

A complete 1 work in $= 15$ days

B complete $\dfrac{2}{5}$ work $= 10$ days

B complete 1 work $= \dfrac{5}{2} \times 10 = 25$ days

A + B complete work $= \dfrac{1}{15} + \dfrac{1}{25} = 9\dfrac{3}{8}$ days

60. Let first pipe takes $= n$ minuts

Second pipes takes $= \dfrac{n}{3}$ minuts

According to question

$$\dfrac{1}{n} + \dfrac{3}{n} = \dfrac{1}{36}$$

$$\dfrac{4}{n} = \dfrac{1}{36}$$

$$\dfrac{1}{n} = \dfrac{1}{36 \times 4}$$

$$n = 144 \text{ minuts}$$

$\therefore$ Slower pipes takes $= 2$ hours 24 minuts.

61. Income of B in comparison of A

$$= \dfrac{25}{75} \times 100 = 33\dfrac{1}{3}$$

62. Sum $= \dfrac{n(n + 1)(2n + 1)}{6} = \dfrac{10(10 + 1)(20 + 1)}{6}$

$$= \dfrac{10 \times 11 \times 21}{6} = 385$$

64. $2P + \dfrac{1}{P} = 4$

Divide both side by 2 we get

$$P + \dfrac{1}{2P} = 2$$

$$\left(P + \dfrac{1}{2P}\right)^3 = (2)^3$$

$$P^3 + \dfrac{1}{8P^3} + 3\dfrac{P1}{2P}\left(P + \dfrac{1}{2P}\right) = 8$$

$$P^3 + \frac{1}{8P^3} + \frac{3}{2}(2) = 8$$

$$P^3 + \frac{1}{8P^3} = 5$$

66. Let, $p/q = x = 1.\overline{27}$ ... (1)

$$100x = 127.\overline{27} \qquad ... (2)$$

Substracting equation (1) from (2), we get

$$99x = 126$$

$$x = \frac{126}{99}$$

$$\therefore \quad \frac{p}{q} = \frac{14}{11}$$

67. $\dfrac{3.25 \times 3.20 - 3.20 \times 3.05}{0.064} = \dfrac{10.4 - 9.76}{0.064} = 10$

68. $\dfrac{(0.1)^2 - (0.01)^2}{0.0001} + 1$

$$= \frac{0.01 - 0.0001}{0.0001} + 1$$

$$= \frac{0.01 - 0.\cancel{0}001 + 0.\cancel{0}001}{0.0001}$$

$$= \frac{0.01}{0.0001} = 100$$

69. Cost Price of 15 books = S.P of 20 book

$$\text{loss} = \frac{20 - 15}{20} \times 100 = 25\%$$

70. Successive discount of 10% and 20%

$$= 10 + 20 - \frac{10 \times 20}{200}$$

$$= 28\%$$

Successive discount of 28% and 30%

$$= 28 + 30 - \frac{28 \times 30}{100}$$

$$= 49.6\%$$

71. Original price $= 33 \times \dfrac{100}{110} \times \dfrac{100}{120} = ₹\, 25$

73. Let the total money spent $= ₹\, x$

$$x \times \frac{45}{360} = 9,000$$

$$x = ₹\, 72000$$

$\therefore$ Money spent on Hockey

$$= \frac{100}{360} \times 72000 = ₹\, 20000$$

Difference $= 20,000 - 9000 = ₹\, 11,000$

74. Money spent on cricket $= 72000 \times \dfrac{160}{360}$

$$= ₹\, 32,000$$

75. Amount spent on all sports $= ₹\, 72,000$

GENERAL INTELLIGENCE

Directions (Q. 1-3) : *Select the related letter/word/ number from the given alternatives:*

1. Zoology : Animal : : Psychology: ?

(a) Plant

(b) Animal

(c) Human-being

(d) Animal and human-being

2. Man : Mammal : : ?

(a) Liberty : Literate

(b) Hail : Snow

(c) Native : Inhabitant

(d) Offspring : Family

3. CFIL : XURO : : ORUX : ?

(a) MJFC   (b) ROLI

(c) RITO   (d) LIFC

Directions (Q. 4-5): *Find the odd number/word pair from the given alternatives.*

4. (a) 72

(b) 81

(c) 93

(d) 66

5. (a) Division   (b) Addition

(c) Subtract   (d) Multiplication

Directions (Q. 6-7) : *A series is given, with one term missing. Choose the correct alternative from the given ones that will complete the series.*

6. RAZ SBY TCX UDW VEV ?

(a) ZAT   (b) WFU

(c) FWU   (d) XGX

7. AAC BBD CCE DDF EEG F ?

(a) DG   (b) FG

(c) GH   (d) FH

8. *Which one set of letters when sequentially placed at the gaps in the given letter series shall complete it?*

a_ba_c_aad_aa_ea

(a) babbb   (b) babbd

(c) babbc   (d) bacde

9. It was Shriram's and Sreedevi's 12th Wedding Anniversary. Shriram said "When we got married, Sreedevi was 3/4th of my age, but now she is 5/6th of my age". What actually are their present ages?

(a) Shriram 38, Sreedevi 32

(b) Shriram 36, Sreedevi 30

(c) Shriram 30, Sreedevi 24

(d) Shriram 40, Sreedevi 34

10. Find the wrong number in the series from the given alternatives.

17, 36, 53, 68, 83, 92

(a) 92   (b) 53

(c) 68   (d) 83

11. If P denotes ÷, Q denotes ×, R denotes +, and S denotes –, then 18 Q 12 P 4 R 5 S 6 = ?

(a) 95   (b) 53

(c) 51   (d) 57

12. If DEAF is equal to 32, what will be LEAF = ?

(a) 56   (b) 48

(c) 50   (d) 52

13. In a certain code "CERTAIN" is coded as "XVIGZRM", "SEQUENCE" is coded as "HVJFVMXV". How would "REQUIRED" be coded?

(a) FJIVWVIR   (b) VJIFWTRV

(c) WVJRIFVI   (d) IVJFRIVW

14. In following question from the given alternatives select the word which **cannot** be formed using the letters of the given word.

'CONSTITUTIONAL'

(a) CONSULT

(b) LOCATION

(c) TUTION

(d) TALENT

15. *Select the missing number from the given responses.*

7	6	9
2	8	4
4	3	?
36	42	26

(a) 5   (b) 2

(c) 3   (d) 4

16. Sherly starting from a fixed point goes 15 m towards North and then after turning to his right he goes 15 m. Then he goes 10, 15 and 15 metres after turning to his left each time. How far is he from his starting point?

(a) 15 metres   (b) 5 metres

(c) 10 metres   (d) 20 metres

17. *Following questions have two statements are followed by 2 conclusions numbered I and II. Which one of the four alternatives is correct?*

Statements : I. All skaters are good swimmers.

                II. All good swimmers are runners.

Conclusions : I. Some runners are skaters.

                 II. Some skaters are good swimmers.

(a) Neither conclusion I nor II follow

(b) Only conclusion I follows

(c) Only conclusion II follows

(d) Both conclusion I and II follow

18. How many 9's are followed by and preceeded by numbers divisible by 2 ?

896535968349652699673729413794173

4984539761531957429685329574894 51

(a) 12   (b) 6

(c) 8   (d) 10

19. If LUXOR is coded as 30, then GUILDS will be coded as?

(a) 40   (b) 36

(c) 38   (d) 24

20. In the following list of English alphabets, one alphabet has not been used. Identify the same.

X N F A P S R W L T M D E X M G B

C X Q J L O P V R C Q J Z O H S G

O D I P T S M R A B E F G N U N E

(a) V   (b) I

(c) K   (d) J

21. Which answer figure will complete the question figure?

Question figure

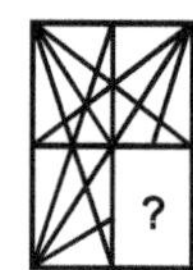

Answer figures

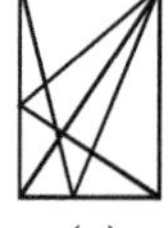 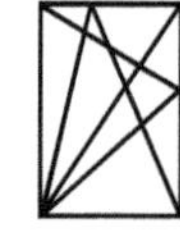 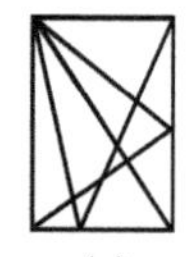 

  (a)   (b)   (c)   (d)

22. From the given answer figures, select the one in which the question figure is hidden/embedded

Question figure

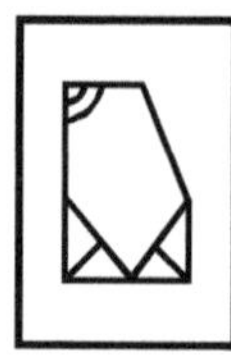

Answer figures

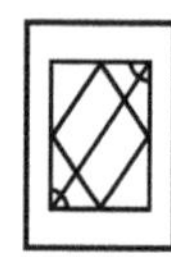  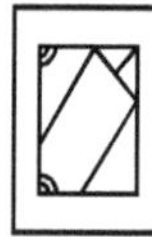 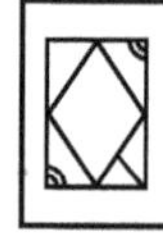

  (a)   (b)   (c)   (d)

23. If a mirror is placed on the line MN, then which of the answer figures is the right image of the given figure?

Question figure

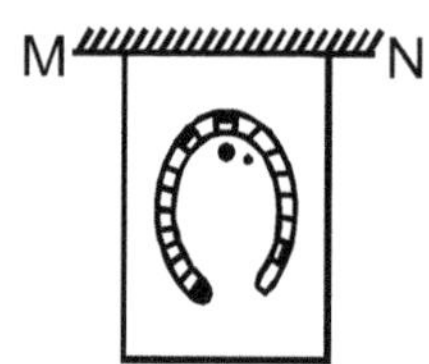

Answer figures

  (a)   (b)   (c)   (d)

24. A square sheet of paper has been folded and punched as shown below. You have a figure out from amongst the four response figures, how it will appear when opened?

Question figures

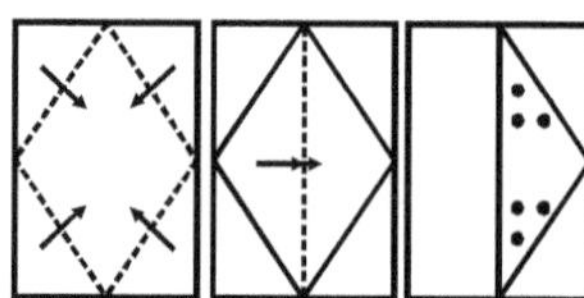

Answer figures

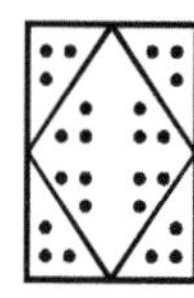 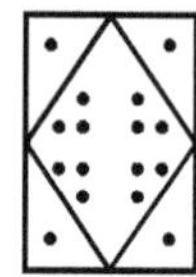  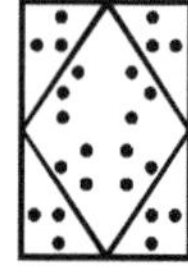

  (a)   (b)   (c)   (d)

Directions : *A word is represented by only one set of numbers as given in any one of the alternatives. The sets of numbers given in the alternatives are represented by two classes of alphabets as in two matrices given below. The columns and rows of Matrix I are numbered from 0 to 4 and that of Matrix II are numbered from 5 to 9. A letter from these matrix can be represented first by its row and next by its column, e.g., 'T' can be represented by 31, 76 etc. and 'S' can be represented by 14, 99, etc. Similarly, you have to identify the set for the word STAR.*

25.

Matrix-I					
	0	1	2	3	4
0	G	V	E	A	C
1	R	O	N	G	S
2	M	N	E	S	I
3	O	T	I	T	A
4	N	S	N	E	P

Matrix-II					
	5	6	7	8	9
5	R	E	O	N	G
6	N	P	V	E	S
7	M	T	I	O	N
8	E	A	I	C	O
9	N	T	A	R	S

   (a) 99, 31, 86, 98   (b) 23, 76, 33, 98
   (c) 14, 87, 98, 97   (d) 69, 96, 03, 56

ENGLISH LANGUAGE

Directions (Q. 26-27): *Out of the four alternatives, choose the one which best expresses the meaning of the given word and mark it in the Answer Sheet.*

26. Annexure
  (a) retirement
  (b) commencement
  (c) attachment
  (d) development

27. Errand
  (a) energy
  (b) task
  (c) mistake
  (d) blunder

Directions (Q. 28-29): *Choose the word opposite in meaning to the given word and mark it in the Answer Sheet.*

28. Amenable
  (a) Acquiescent   (b) Distrustful
  (c) Inattentive   (d) Unwilling

29. Conspicuous
  (a) blatant   (b) definite
  (c) obvious   (d) obscure

Directions (Q. 30-32) : *Out of the four alternatives choose the one which can be substituted for the given words / sentence.*

30. A raised place on which offerings to a God are made
  (a) rostrum   (b) church
  (c) altar   (d) mound

31. Something that cannot be explained :
  (a) unthinkable   (b) impregnable
  (c) mysterious   (d) inexplicable

32. A written declaration made on oath in the presence of a magistrate :
  (a) affidavit   (b) dossier
  (c) voucher   (d) document

Directions (Q. 33-35) : *Four alternatives are given for the idiom / phrase underlined in the sentence. Choose the alternative which best expresses the meaning of the Idiom / phrase and mark it in the Answer-Sheet.*

33. His speech has <u>taken the wind out of my sails</u>.
  (a) made my words or actions ineffective
  (b) made me depressed
  (c) made me think of the future
  (d) made me remember my past

34. There is no point in discussing the new project with him as he always <u>pours cold water on</u> any new ideas.
  (a) puts off   (b) dislikes
  (c) disapproves of   (d) postpones

35. Regardless of what her parents said, she wanted to <u>let her hair down</u> that night.
  (a) Really enjoy   (b) Wash her hair
  (c) Comb her hair   (d) Work till late

36. *Four words are given in each question, out of which only one word is correctly spelt. Find the correctly spelt word and indicate it in the Answer Sheet by blackening the appropriate rectangle [■].*
  (a) digresion   (b) digrestion
  (c) digression   (d) degression

Directions (Q. 37-39) : *Some parts of the sentences have errors and some have none. Find out which part of a sentence has an error and blacken the rectangle [■] corresponding to the appropriate letter (a, b, c). If a sentence is free from error, blacken the rectangle corresponding to (d) in the Answer Sheet.*

37. World is producing enough *(a)*/ for every citizen but still there is hunger and malnutrition *(b)*/ and it is continuing year after year *(c)*/ No error. *(d)*

38. The N.C.C. commandant along with his cadets *(a)*/ are going to Delhi *(b)*/ to participate in the Republic Day Parade. *(c)*/ No error. *(d)*

39. He did not succeed *(a)*/ to get the job *(b)*/ though he tried his level best *(c)*/ No error. *(d)*

Directions (Q. 40-42) : *Sentences are given with blanks to be filled in with an appropriate word(s). Four alternative are suggested for each question. Choose the correct alternative out of the four and indicate it by blackening the appropriate rectangle [■] in the Answer Sheet.*

40. The ladies black purse, which is on sale has a beautiful________carved on it.

   (a) motif   *(b)* patch

   (c) layout   *(d)* schematic

41. Who is the person you_____at the cinema last night?

   (a) where recognising

   (b) recognised

   (c) have recognised

   (d) had recognised

42. As you sow _______shall you reap.

   (a) when   *(b)* as

   (c) like   *(d)* so

Directions (Q. 43-45) : *A part of the sentence is underlined. Below are given alternatives to the underlined part at (a), (b), (c) which may improve the sentence. Choose the correct alternative. In case no improvement is needed your answer (d). Mark your answer in the Answer Sheet.*

43. It took her a long time to get <u>past</u> her failure in the medical examination.

   (a) through   *(b)* over

   (c) by   *(d)* No improvement

44. The boy wanted to ask his father for money, but waited for a <u>propitious</u> occasion.

   (a) protective   *(b)* prophetic

   (c) prospective   *(d)* No improvement

45. I did not agree with him; he appeared to be <u>so</u> bigoted for me to concur.

   (a) much   *(b)* very

   (c) too   *(d)* No improvement

Directions (Q. 46-50) : *Read the following passage carefully and choose the best answer to each question out of four alternatives and mark it the correct answer.*

"People very often complain that poverty is a great evil and that it is not possible to be happy unless one has a lot of money. Actually, this is not necessarily true. Even a poor man, living in a small hut with none of the comforts and luxuries of life, may be quite contented with his lot and achieve a measure of happiness. On the other hand, a very rich man, living in a palace and enjoying everything that money can buy, may still be miserable, if, for example, he does not enjoy good health or his only son has taken to evil was. Apart from this, he may have a lot of business worries which keep him on tenterhooks most of the time. There is a limit to what money can buy and there are may things which are necessary for man's happiness and which money cannot procure.

Real happiness is a matter of the right attitude and the capacity of being contented with whatever you have is the most important ingredient of this attitude".

46. The phrase "on tenterhooks" means :

   (a) in a state of thoughtfulness

   (b) in a state of anxiety

   (c) in a state of sadness

   (d) in a state of forgetfulness

47. It is true that :

   (a) money alone can give happiness

   (b) money always gives happiness

   (c) money seldom gives happiness

   (d) money alone cannot give happiness

48. A rich man's life may become miserable if he :

   (a) has evil son, bad health and business worries

   (b) does not enjoy good health

   (c) has business worries

   (d) has business worries and his only son has taken to evil ways

49. Which of the following is the most appropriate title to the passage?

   (a) Poverty, a great evil

   (b) The key of happiness

   (c) Contentment, the key to happiness

   (d) Money and contentment

50. Which of the following statement is true?

   (a) Only a poor but contented man can be happy

   (b) A poor but contented man can never be happy

   (c) A poor but contented man can be happy

   (d) A poor but contented man is always happy

QUANTITATIVE APTITUDE

51. If cotA + cosecA = 3 and A is an acute angle, then the value of cosA is :

(a) 4/5   (b) 1

(c) 1/2   (d) 3/4

52. A three-digit number 4a3 is added to another three-digit number 94 to give the four digit number 13b7 which is divisible by 11.

(a) 11

(b) 12

(c) 9

(d) 10

53. In a right-angled triangle ABC, $\angle$B is the right angle and AC = $2\sqrt{5}$ cm. If AB − BC = 2 cm, then the value of $(\cos^2 A - \cos^2 C)$ is :

(a) 2/5

(b) 3/5

(c) 6/5

(d) 3/10

54. The perimeter of an isosceles right-angled triangle is 2p unit. The area of the same triangle is :

(a) $(3 - 2\sqrt{2})p^2$ sq. unit

(b) $(2 + \sqrt{2})p^2$ sq. unit

(c) $(2 - \sqrt{2})p^2$ sq. unit

(d) $(3 - \sqrt{2})p^2$ sq. unit

55. $\triangle$ABC and $\triangle$DEF are similar and their areas be respectively 64 cm^2 and 121 cm^2. If EF = 15.4 cm, BC is

(a) 12.3 cm

(b) 11.2 cm

(c) 12.1 cm

(d) 11.0 cm

56. If G is the centroid of $\triangle$ABC and AG = BC, then $\angle$BGC is :

(a) 75°

(b) 45°

(c) 90°

(d) 60°

57. If $\tan(x + y) \tan(x - y) = 1$, then the value of tan x is :

(a) $\sqrt{3}$ (b) 1

(c) 1/2   (d) $\dfrac{1}{\sqrt{3}}$

58. In a partnership business, A invests $\dfrac{1}{6}$th of the capital for $\dfrac{1}{6}$ of the total time, B invests $\dfrac{1}{4}$ of the capital for $\dfrac{1}{4}$ of the total time and C, the rest of the capital for the whole time. Out of a profit of ₹ 19,400, B's share is :

(a) ₹ 2000   (b) ₹ 1200

(c) ₹ 1600   (d) ₹ 1800

59. A jar contains a mixture of two liquids A and B in the ratio of 4 : 1. When 10 litre of the mixture is replaced with liquid B, the ratio becomes 2 : 3. The volume of liquid A present in the jar earlier was :

(a) 20 litre   (b) 10 litre

(c) 16 litre   (d) 15 litre

60. If $a = \dfrac{\sqrt{3} - \sqrt{2}}{\sqrt{3} + \sqrt{2}}$, $b = \dfrac{\sqrt{3} + \sqrt{2}}{\sqrt{3} - \sqrt{2}}$, then the value of $\dfrac{a^2}{b} + \dfrac{b^2}{a}$ is :

(a) 900   (b) 970

(c) 1030   (d) 930

61. The next term of the series

−1, 6, 25, 62, 123, 214,____is :

(a) 345   (b) 143

(c) 341   (d) 343

62. If $ax + by = 6$, $bx - ay = 2$ and $x^2 + y^2 = 4$, then the value of $(a^2 + b^2)$ would be :

(a) 10   (b) 2

(c) 4   (d) 5

63. The mean of 19 observation is 24. If the mean of the first 10 observations is 17 and that of the last 10 observations is 24, find the 10th observation.

(a) 65   (b) 37

(c) 46   (d) 53

64. A watch is sold at profit of 30%. Had it been sold for ₹ 80 less, there would have been a loss of 10%. What is the cost price in rupees?

(a) 150   (b) 200

(c) 400   (d) 800

65. A train overtakes two persons who are walking in the same direction in which the train is running, at the rate of 2 kmph and 4 kmph and passes them completely in 9 and 10 seconds respectively. The length of the train (in metres) is :

(a) 72   (b) 45

(c) 54   (d) 50

66. If a commission of 10% is given on the market price of a work, the publisher gains 20%. If the commission is increased to 15%, the gain percent is

(a) 15%

(b) $16\dfrac{2}{3}\%$

(c) $13\dfrac{1}{3}\%$

(d) $15\dfrac{1}{6}\%$

67. If 12 men or 18 women can reap a field in 14 days, then working at the same rate, 8 men and 16 women can reap the same field in :

(a) 9 days   (b) 5 days

(c) 7 days   (d) 8 days

68. By selling 9 articles for a rupee, a man incurred a loss of 4%. To make a gain of 44%, the number of articles to be sold for a rupee is :

(a) 5   (b) 3

(c) 4   (d) 6

69. If $a^3 - b^3 = 56$ and $a - b = 2$, then the value of $(a^2 + b^2)$ is :

(a) -10 (b) -12

(c) 20   (d) 18

70. Area of the triangle formed by the graph of the line $2x - 3y + 6 = 0$ along with the coordinate axes is :

(a) 1/2 sq. units

(b) 3/2 sq. units

(c) 3 sq. units

(d) 6 sq. units

71. Prabhat took a certain amount as a loan from a bank at the rate of 8% p.a. simple interest and gave the same amount to Ashish as a loan at the rate of 12% p.a. If at the end of 12 years, he made a profit of ₹ 960 in the deal, then the original amount was :

(a) ₹ 3356   (b) ₹ 1000

(c) ₹ 2000   (d) ₹ 3000

72. If $a + \dfrac{1}{a+2} = 0$, then the value of

$(a + 2)^3 + \dfrac{1}{(a+2)^3}$ is

(a) 2   (b) 6

(c) 4   (d) 3

Directions (Q. 73-75) : *The number of mobile simcards in 4 states are given in multiple bar diagrams. Study the diagram and answer the question.*

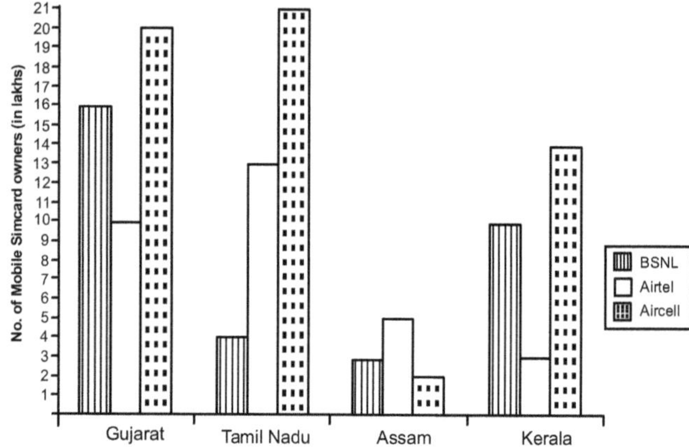

73. In Assam, the ratio of Aircell simcard and Airtel simcard sold is :

(a) 3 : 2   (b) 2 : 5

(c) 5 : 2   (d) 2 : 3

74. In which state are there the largest number of owners of Airtel simcard?

(a) Tamilnadu   (b) Gujarat

(c) Kerala   (d) Assam

75. Average of simcard sold in the four states in lakhs is

(a) 30.25   (b) 40.5

(c) 35   (d) 33.75

GENERAL AWARENESS

76. Reliance Industries Limited (RIL) has signed a shareholder agreement with which of the following Bank have signed Subscription and Shareholders' Agreement to set up payments bank?

(a) Punjab National Bank

(b) ICICI Bank

(c) IDBI Bank Ltd

(d) State Bank of India

77. The infective stage of Malaria is

(a) Gametocyte   (b) Ring stage

(c) Sporozoite   (d) Merozoite

78. The treaty of Versailles restored Alsace-Lorraine to:

(a) Italy   (b) Britain

(c) France   (d) Belgium

79. The Asokan Edicts were deciphered first by:

(a) Sir John Marshall

(b) Sir William Jones

(c) Charles Wilkins

(d) James Prinsep

80. Which of the following is meant for the ex-situ conservation of various species?
   (a) Sperm bank   (b) Blood bank
   (c) Germplasm bank (d) Herbarium

81. An algae type ocean deposit is :
   (a) Neritic remains   (b) Diatom Ooze
   (c) Pteropod Ooze   (d) Pelagic deposits

82. Photosynthetic vesicle found in bacteria is called a :
   (a) Mesosome   (b) Chromatophore
   (c) Genophore   (d) Pneumatophore

83. Name the renowned sculptor and painter who passed away in Vadodara, Gujarat following a brief illness recently.
   (a) KG Subramanyan
   (b) Amrita Shergill
   (c) Jatin Das
   (d) Harsh Goenka

84. Who said that the Directive Principles of State Policy are just like "a cheque on bank payable at the convenience of the bank".
   (a) Pandit Nehru   (b) K.T. Shah
   (c) B.R. Ambedkar   (d) N.G. Ranga

85. The proposal for the creation of new All-India Services can be considered only:
   (a) if majority of State Legislatures make such demand
   (b) if Lok Sabha passes a resolution by two-thirds majority
   (c) if the Rajya Sabha passes a resolution by two-thirds majority
   (d) None of the above

86. Value-added means value of
   (a) goods and services less cost of intermediate goods and services
   (b) output at factor cost
   (c) output at market prices
   (d) goods and services less depreciation

87. Tohra is the sacred book of :
   (a) Zoroastrianism
   (b) Confucianism
   (c) Taoism
   (d) Judaism

88. The red, orange and yellow colours of leaves are due to :
   (a) Carotenoids   (b) Aldehydes
   (c) Tannins   (d) Lignins

89. We receive sunlight on earth surface. What type of light beams are these?
   (a) Random
   (b) Parallel
   (c) Converging
   (d) Diverging

90. Earth is a very big magnet. In which direction does its magnetic field extend?
   (a) west to east
   (b) north to south
   (c) south to north
   (d) east to west

91. The authority to specify which castes shall be deemed to be scheduled castes rests with the :
   (a) Commissioner for Scheduled Castes and Tribes
   (b) Prime Minister
   (c) President
   (d) Governor

92. The ultimate source of energy in a hydroelectric power station is :
   (a) solar energy
   (b) the potential energy of water
   (c) the kinetic energy of water
   (d) the lectro-chemical energy of water

93. India making 'Double Taxation Avoidance Agreements' (DTAA) with other countries for the promotion of :
   (a) Bilateral trade
   (b) External commercial borrowings
   (c) Foreign direct investments
   (d) Foreign institutional

94. Brain drain has been caused by :
   (a) failure to recognise talent in the originating country
   (b) the lure of high living standards
   (c) lack of employment opportunities
   (d) socio-economic instability

95. The prose collection of the vedic poems are :
   (a) Samhitas   (b) Upanishads
   (c) Aranyakas   (d) Brahmanas

96. The study of population is known as_______.
   (a) Demography
   (b) Climatology
   (c) Petrology
   (d) Hydrology

97. The Union Cabinet has approved signing of a Memorandum of Understanding (MoU) between India and which of the following country for bilateral cooperation in water resources management and development?

(a) Russia (b) Bhutan

(c) Germany (d) Tanzania

98. Which is NOT a correct statement?

(a) Phenols are acidic

(b) In benzene all the atoms lie in one plane

(c) Methylated spirit contains only methanol

(d) Dilute solutions contain less amount of solute

99. What is m-commerce?

(a) machine commerce

(b) mobile commerce

(c) money commerce

(d) marketing commerce

100. The first speaker of Lok Sabha was :

(a) S.Radhakrishnan

(b) M. Ananthasayanam

(c) Sardar Hukam Singh

(d) G.V. Mavlankar

ANSWERS

1. (d)	**2.** (d)	**3.** (d)	**4.** (b)	**5.** (c)	**6.** (b)	**7.** (d)	**8.** (d)	**9.** (b)	**10.** (d)
11. (b)	**12.** (b)	**13.** (d)	**14.** (d)	**15.** (b)	**16.** (c)	**17.** (d)	**18.** (b)	**19.** (b)	**20.** (c)
21. (d)	**22.** (c)	**23.** (b)	**24.** (a)	**25.** (a)	**26.** (c)	**27.** (b)	**28.** (d)	**29.** (d)	**30.** (c)
31. (d)	**32.** (a)	**33.** (a)	**34.** (c)	**35.** (a)	**36.** (c)	**37.** (d)	**38.** (b)	**39.** (b)	**40.** (a)
41. (b)	**42.** (d)	**43.** (b)	**44.** (d)	**45.** (c)	**46.** (b)	**47.** (d)	**48.** (d)	**49.** (d)	**50.** (c)
51. (a)	**52.** (c)	**53.** (b)	**54.** (a)	**55.** (b)	**56.** (c)	**57.** (b)	**58.** (d)	**59.** (c)	**60.** (b)
61. (c)	**62.** (a)	**63.** (c)	**64.** (b)	**65.** (d)	**66.** (c)	**67.** (a)	**68.** (d)	**69.** (c)	**70.** (c)
71. (c)	**72.** (a)	**73.** (b)	**74.** (a)	**75.** (a)	**76.** (d)	**77.** (c)	**78.** (c)	**79.** (d)	**80.** (d)
81. (d)	**82.** (b)	**83.** (a)	**84.** (b)	**85.** (c)	**86.** (a)	**87.** (d)	**88.** (a)	**89.** (b)	**90.** (c)
91. (c)	**92.** (b)	**93.** (a)	**94.** (c)	**95.** (d)	**96.** (a)	**97.** (d)	**98.** (c)	**99.** (b)	**100.** (d)

EXPLANATIONS

1. Zoology → Study related to animals.

Psychology → animals and human beings.

2. Man : Mammal :: Offspring : Family

$\quad\uparrow\qquad\qquad\uparrow$

Content   Class

3. CFIL : XURO :: ORUX : LIFC

$\qquad$ reverse order

4. 81 → perfect square

5. Subtraction should be perfect ending with 'ion'.

6. middle term should be F

7. FH

8. a bb aa cc aa dd aa ee a

9. $t = 0\ \dfrac{3}{4}$ $S_r = S_d$

$t = 12\ \dfrac{5}{6}$ $(S_r + 12) = S_d + 12$

Solving above .(b)

10. Wrong Question

11. $18 \times 12 \div 4 + 5 - 6 = 53$ (bodmas)

12. double of sum of position = 48

13. E → V, R → I ⇒ (d)

14. E is not found in word 'CONSTITUTIONAL' to make 'TALENT'

15. $(7 + 2) \times 4 = 36$

$(9 + 4) \times 2 = 26 \Rightarrow$ (b)

16.

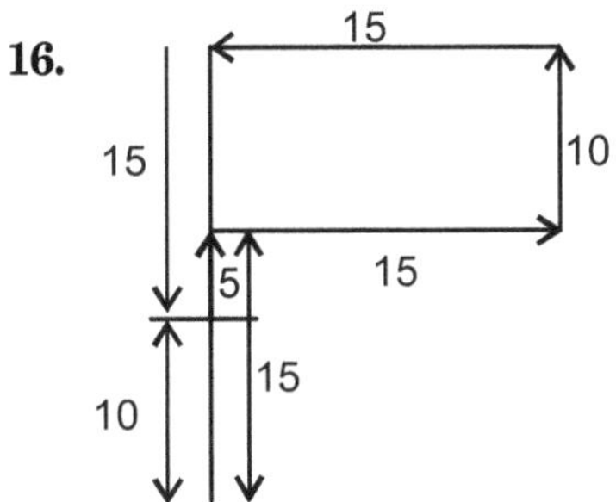

17. obvious both follows.

18. 9 come '6' times followed by and preceded by number divisible by 6 in this series.

19. Sum up position ÷ 3

i.e. $(7 + 21 + 9 + 12 + 4 + 19) \div 3 = 24$

20. K is not used

51.

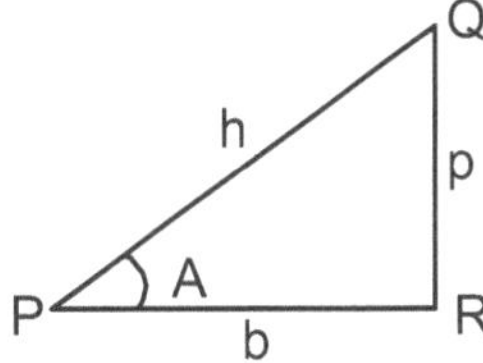

$$\cos A = \frac{b}{h}$$

$$\cot A + \csc A = 3$$

$$\frac{b}{p} + \frac{h}{p} = 3$$

$$b + h = 3p$$

$$= 3\sqrt{h^2 - b^2}$$

$$b^2 + h^2 + 2bh = 9h - 9b^2$$

$$10b^2 + 2bh - 8h^2 = 0$$

$$10b^2 + 10bh - 8bh - 8h^2 = 0$$

$$10b(b + h) - 8h(b + h) = 0$$

$$(10b - 8h)(b + h) = 0$$

$$\Rightarrow \qquad b = \frac{8h}{10}$$

$$\frac{b}{h} = \frac{8}{10}$$

$$= \frac{4}{5} = \cos A$$

53. Given, $AB - BC = 2$

$$c - a = 2$$

$$\Rightarrow a^2 + c^2 - 2ac = 4$$

By Pythagorous theorem

$$\sqrt{a^2 + c^2} = 2\sqrt{5}$$

$$\Rightarrow \quad 20 - 2ac = 4$$

$$\Rightarrow \qquad ac = 8$$

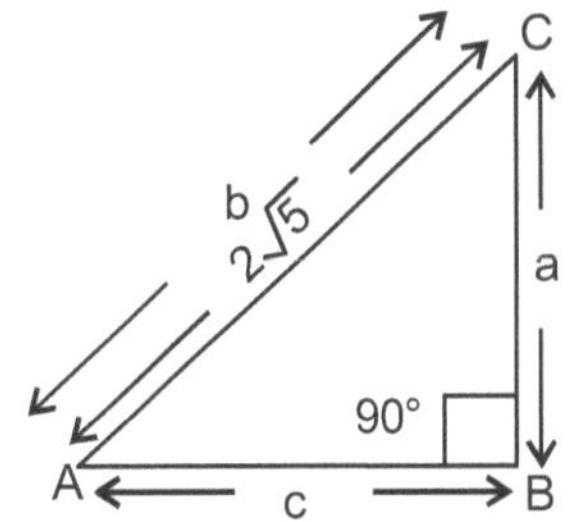

$$\therefore a^2 + c^2 + 2ac = (a + c)^2$$
$$= 20 + 16$$
$$= 36$$
$$\Rightarrow \quad a + c = 6 \qquad \ldots (1)$$
$$\Rightarrow \quad c = 4, a = 2$$
$$c - a = 2 \qquad \ldots (2)$$

By solving eq. (1) and (2), we get

$$b = 2\sqrt{5}$$

$$\therefore \cos^2 A - \cos^2 C = \frac{c^2}{b^2} - \frac{a^2}{b^2}$$

$$\Rightarrow \quad \frac{c^2 - a^2}{b^2} = \frac{12}{20} = \frac{3}{5}$$

54.

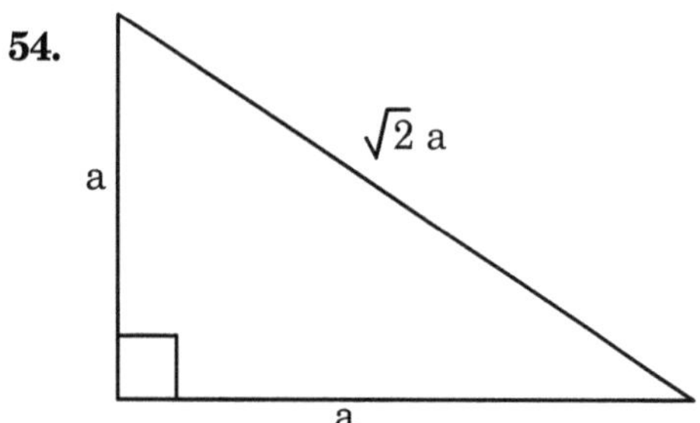

$$a + a + \sqrt{2}a = 2p$$
$$\left(2 + \sqrt{2}\right)a = 2p$$

$$\text{Area} = \frac{1}{2}a^2 = \frac{1}{2}\frac{4p^2}{\left(2 + \sqrt{2}\right)^2}$$

$$= \frac{p^2}{\left(\sqrt{2} + 1\right)^2}$$

$$= p^2\left(\sqrt{2} - 1\right)^2 = \left(3 - 2\sqrt{2}\right)p^2$$

55. $\dfrac{\text{Area } \Delta ABC}{\text{Area } \Delta DEF} = \dfrac{64}{121}$

$$\Rightarrow \quad \frac{BC}{EF} = \frac{\sqrt{64}}{\sqrt{121}}$$

$$= \frac{8}{11} = \frac{BC}{15.4}$$

$$\Rightarrow \quad BC = 11.2$$

56.

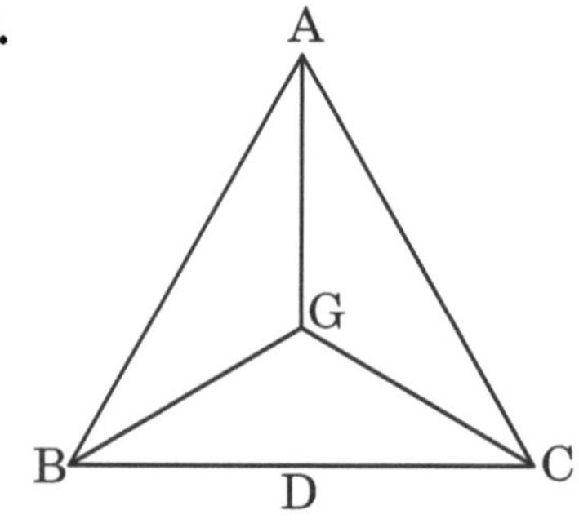

$$AG = BC = x$$
$$\Rightarrow \quad BD = DC$$

$$= \frac{x}{2} = GD$$

assume GD $\perp$
$$\Rightarrow \quad \angle BGD = 45° = \angle DGC$$
$$\Rightarrow \quad \angle BGC = 90°$$

57. $1 - \tan(x + y)\tan(x - y) = 0$

$$\frac{\tan(x + y) + \tan(x - y)}{\tan(x + y + x - y)} = 0$$

$$\Rightarrow \quad \tan 2x = \infty$$
$$\therefore \quad 2x = 90°$$
$$x = 45°$$
$$\therefore \quad \tan x = 1$$

58. Let total time be t A $= \dfrac{x}{6}, \dfrac{t}{6}$

total capital be x B $= \dfrac{x}{4}, \dfrac{t}{4}$

$$C = \frac{7}{12}x, t$$

$$\text{B's share} = \frac{\dfrac{x}{4} \cdot \dfrac{t}{4}}{\dfrac{x}{6} \cdot \dfrac{t}{6} + \dfrac{x}{4} \cdot \dfrac{t}{4} + \dfrac{7x}{12} \cdot t} \cdot 19400$$

$$= \frac{\dfrac{1}{16}}{\dfrac{1}{36} + \dfrac{1}{16} + \dfrac{7}{12}} \times 19400$$

$$= \frac{1}{16} \times \frac{144}{4 + 9 + 84} \times 19400$$

$$= 1800$$

59. A : B

$4x : 1x$

$$\frac{4x-8}{x-2+10} = \frac{2}{3}$$

$\Rightarrow \quad 12x - 24 = 2x + 16$

$\qquad\qquad x = 4$

$\therefore \qquad\quad 4x = 26 \ .(c)$

60.

$$a = 5 - 2\sqrt{6}$$

$$b = 5 + 2\sqrt{6}$$

$$\frac{a^2}{b} + \frac{b^2}{a} = \frac{a^3 + b^3}{25 - 24}$$

$$= \frac{2\times 5^3 + 3\times 5\times 2\sqrt{6}\left(5 + 2\sqrt{6} - 5 + 2\sqrt{6}\right)}{1}$$

$$= 250 + 720$$

$$= 970$$

61. $-1, \ 6, \ 25, \ 62, \ 123, \ 214, \circled{341}$

$7 \ \ 19 \ \ 37 \ \ 61 \ \ 91 \ \ \circled{127}$

$12 \ \ 18 \ \ 24 \ \ 30 \ \ \circled{36}$

62. Given, $ax + by = 6$ \qquad ... (1)

$\qquad\qquad bx - ay = 2$ \qquad ... (2)

$\qquad\qquad x^2 + y^2 = 4$ \qquad ... (3)

By solving equation (1) and (2), we get

$$y = \frac{6b - 2a}{a^2 + b^2}$$

Substituting value of x in eq. (3), we get

$$x = \frac{6a - 2b}{a^2 + b^2}$$

$$40(a^2 + b^2) = 4(a^2 + b^2)^2$$

$$a^2 + b^2 = 10$$

64. Cost Price $= x$

$\therefore$ Sold at $1.3x$

According to question

$\qquad 1.3x - 80 = .9x$

$\Rightarrow \qquad\quad .4x = 80$

$\qquad\qquad\quad x = ₹\ 200$

65. Speed of train $= s$ km/h.

Length of train $= l$ km

$$\frac{l}{s-2} = \frac{9}{3600} \ \bigg| \ \frac{l}{s-4} = \frac{10}{3600}$$

$\qquad 40l = 2$

$\Rightarrow \qquad\quad l = \dfrac{1}{20}$ km

$\qquad\qquad\quad = 50$m

66. Marked Price $= x$

10% commission $= \Rightarrow 9x$ gives 20% profit

$\qquad 1.2$ C.P. $= 9x$

$\qquad\quad$ C.P. $= .75x$

15% commission

$\Rightarrow .85x$

$\Rightarrow 13.33\%$ Profit

68. S.P. $= \dfrac{1}{9} \Rightarrow 4y.$ loss

$\Rightarrow \qquad$ C.P. $= \dfrac{1}{9} \times \dfrac{100}{96}$

for 44% + Profit S.P. $= \dfrac{1}{9} \times \dfrac{100}{96} \times 1.44$

$$= \frac{1}{6}$$

69. $\qquad a^3 - b^2 = 56$

$\qquad\qquad a - b = 2$

$\Rightarrow a^3 - b^3 - 3ab(a - b) = 8$

$\qquad 56 - 3ab\times 2 = 8$

$\qquad\qquad\quad ab = 8$

$\qquad\quad (a-b)^2 = a^2 + b^2 - 2ab$

$\qquad\qquad\quad 4 = a^2 + b^2 - 16$

$\Rightarrow \quad a^2 + b^2 = 20$

70.

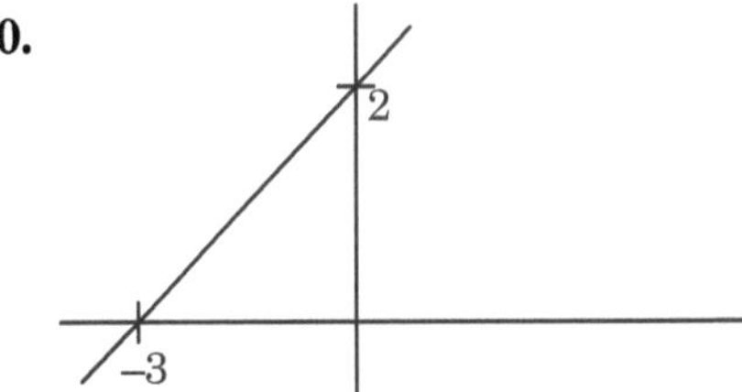

Area $= \dfrac{1}{2} \times 3 \times 2 = 3$ sq. units

71. Original amount = P

$$\text{Profit} = (12-8)\% \text{ of P} \times 12 = ₹960$$

$$\frac{4}{100}\text{P} \times 12 = 960$$

$$\Rightarrow \qquad \text{P} = ₹\,2000$$

72.
$$a + \frac{1}{a+2} = 0$$

$$\therefore \qquad \frac{1}{a+2} = -a$$

So that,

$$(a+2)^3 + \left(\frac{1}{a+2}\right)^3$$

$$= a + 8 + 6a(a+2) - a$$

$$= 6a^2 + 12a + 8$$

$$= 6a(a+2) + 8$$

$$= -6 + 8 = 2$$

73. $\dfrac{2}{5}$

74. Tamil Nadu

75. $\text{Avg} = \dfrac{\text{Total}}{4}$

$$= \frac{\begin{array}{c}16+10+20+4+13+21+3\\ +5+2+9+3+14\end{array}}{4}$$

$$= 30$$

GENERAL INTELLIGENCE

Directions 1: *In each of the following questions, a word is represented by only one set of numbers, as given in one of the alternatives. The set of numbers given in the alternatives are represented by two classes of alphabets as in the two matrices given below. The columns and rows of matrix I are numbered from 0 to 4 and that of matrix II from 5 to 9. A letter from the matrices can be represented first by its row number and then by its column number. E.g., 'R' can be represented by 69, 87, etc. 'X' can be represented by 20, 43, etc. Similarly, you have to identify the set for the word given in each question.*

MATRIX I

	0	1	2	3	4
0	E	X	S	T	W
1	W	T	X	S	E
2	X	S	E	W	T
3	S	W	T	E	X
4	T	E	W	X	S

MATRIX II

	5	6	7	8	9
5	R	Y	G	I	O
6	O	I	Y	G	R
7	G	O	I	R	Y
8	Y	G	R	O	I
9	I	R	O	Y	G

1. SWIG

(a) 02, 42, 95, 76   (b) 30, 23, 77, 99

(c) 44, 10, 89, 87   (d) 21, 03, 58, 68

2. From the given alternative words, select the word which can be formed using the letters of the given word:

HYPERTENSION

(a) Tension   (b) Tent

(c) Scent   (d) Reason

3. Which one of the given responses would be a meaningful order of the following words?

A. Eggs   B. Caterpillar

C. Larva   D. Adult Butterfly

E. Pupa

(a) A,B,C,D,E   (b) A,B,C,E,D

(c) B,C,A,D,E   (d) B,C,A,E,D

4. *Find the missing letters / numbers from the given responses.*

KUZ, MOX, OIV, QCT, ?

(a) SDR   (b) SXS

(c) SAQ   (d) SWR

5. What will come in place of the question mark (?)?

9	4	32
15	5	70
17	3	?

(a) 51   (b) 64

(c) 48   (d) 17

6. If today is Saturday, which day of the week will it be after 27 days?

(a) Monday   (b) Friday

(c) Saturday   (d) Sunday

7. How many squares does the following figure have?

(a) 10

(b) 18

(c) 22

(d) 24

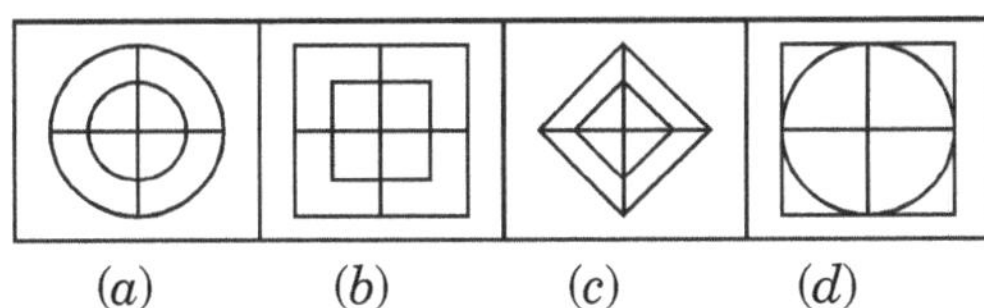

8. Find the mirror image of: KWALITY261C

(a) KMAꞱIⱢⱯƧ91Ɔ   (b) Ɔ162YTIⱢAWꓘ

(c) C162YTILAWK   (d) ƆⱣƷ6ꓓYTIⱢAWꓘ

9. Find the odd figure from the given responses.

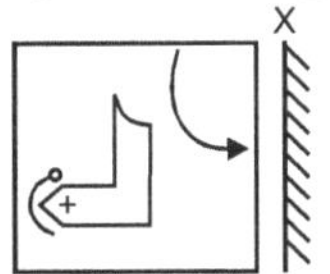

(a)   (b)   (c)   (d)

Directions for question 10: *Mark the alternative which closely resembles the mirror image of the question figure, when a mirror XY is placed along the line shown in the figure.*

10. Question figure

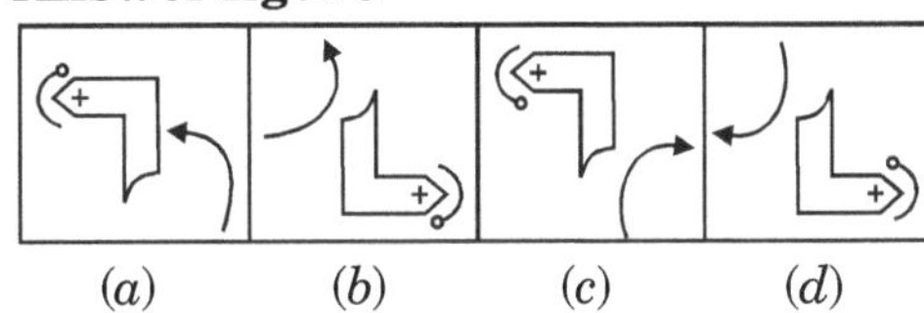

Answer figure

(a)   (b)   (c)   (d)

11. Question Figure is embedded in any one of the four alternative Answer figures. Find the alternative containing figure (x).

Question figure

Answer figures

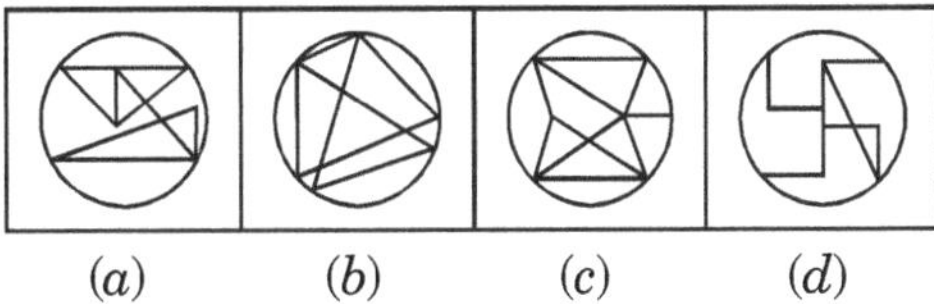

(a)   (b)   (c)   (d)

12. Which of the following sets of numbers follows the same pattern as the one given below follows?

(96, 48, 24)

(a) (44, 22, 12) (b) (42, 20, 10)

(c) (72, 36, 18) (d) (46, 22, 11)

Directions for questions 13 to 14: *In each of the following questions, four groups of letters / numbers / words are given. Three of them are alike in a certain way while one is different. Choose the odd one.*

13. (a) WTQ   (b) PMJ

 (c) JGD   (d) FDA

14. (a) vodka   (b) rum

 (c) wine   (d) water

15. If '–' stands for multiplication, '+' stands for division, '×' stands for addition and '÷' stands for subtraction, then which of the following equations is correct?

(a) $69 - 3 \times 7 + 2 \div 11 = 20$

(b) $69 \times 3 + 7 - 2 \div 11 = 20$

(c) $69 + 3 \times 7 \div 2 - 11 = 20$

(d) $69 + 3 \div 7 - 2 \times 11 = 20$

16. In a certain code language, '329' means 'su ka ni', '731' means 'su pa fa' and '169' means 'fa, cha, ni'. Which of the following digits stands for 'ka' in that language?

(a) 3   (b) 2

(c) 9   (d) 1

17. Three years ago, the average age of Yogesh and Ritu was 19 years. With Ayusha joining them now, their average age has reduced by 2 years. How old will Ayusha be after 5 years?

(a) 16 years (b) 18 years

(c) 21 years (d) 23 years

18. A paper is folded and a cut is made as shown in the figure given below. Choose the figure which would most closely resemble the unfolded form of the folded paper.

Question figures

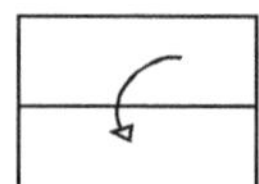 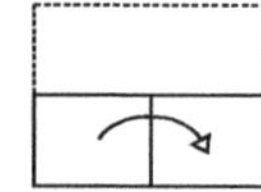 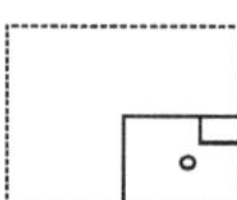

Answer figures

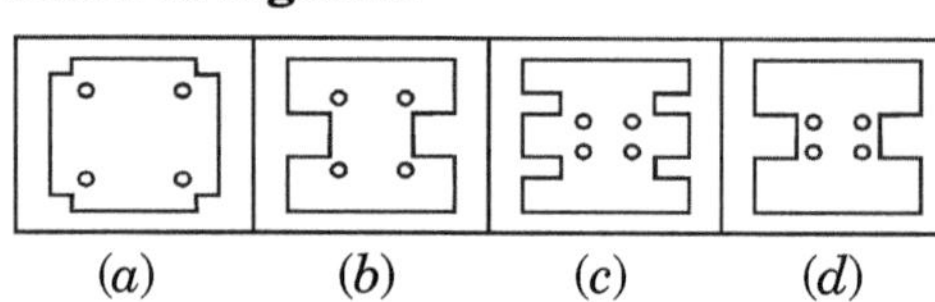

  (a)   (b)   (c)   (d)

19. In the expression given below, Δ stands for a mathematical operation. Which of the following sequences of mathematical operations, if substituted, will make the given expression correct?

$$48 \, \Delta \, 3 \, \Delta \, 16 \, \Delta \, 32$$

(a) ÷ = +   (b) = ÷ +

(c) ÷ + =   (d) + ÷ =

20. P is a city which is located $16\sqrt{2}$ km South–West of city A. While city Q is located 32 km East of P. Another city, R is located $16\sqrt{2}$ km South–West of Q, and city S is located $32\sqrt{2}$ km North–West of city R. What is the position of city A with respect to city S?

(a) North   (b) West

(c) South   (d) East

Directions for questions 21 to 22: *In each of the following questions, select the related letters / word / number from the given alternatives.*

21. PQRS : TSRQ : : ABCD : ?

(a) CDBA   (b) ECDB

(c) EDCB   (d) CBDA

22. Sloth : lethargy :: slovenly : ?

(a) Untidy   (b) Serenity

(c) Slander   (d) Retort

23. Arrange the following words according to the dictionary:

A. Positional   B. Poseidon

C. Positron   D. Positive

E. Possession

(a) B,A,D,C,E (b) B,A,D,E,C

(c) B,A,E,D,C (d) B,A,E,C,D

24. From the given alternative words, select the word which cannot be formed using the letters of the given word:

GLOOMINESS

(a) Gloom   (b) Mine

(c) Mint   (d) Slog

25. Two statements are given followed by four conclusions. You have to consider the statements to be true, even if they seem at variance with commonly known facts. You are to decide which of the given conclusions can definitely be drawn from the given statements.

Statement:

1. All negative is positive.

2. All positive is neutral.

Conclusions:

1. Some neutral is negative.

2. No negative is positive

3. No positive is neutral

4. Some positive is not neutral.

(a) Only 1 follows

(b) Either 2 or 3 follow

(c) Either 3 or 4 follow

(d) All conclusions follow.

ENGLISH LANGUAGE

Directions for questions 26 to 27 : *In each of the following questions, a word is followed by four options. Select the option that best expresses the meaning of the given word.*

26. Disinterested
  - (a) Endorse
  - (b) Indifferent
  - (c) Incorporate
  - (d) Exclude

27. Circumlocution
  - (a) Hide
  - (b) Verboseness
  - (c) Comprise
  - (d) Understand

Direction for questions 28 to 29: *In each of the following questions, a word is followed by four options. Select the option that is opposite in meaning to the given word.*

28. Preamble
  - (a) Epilogue
  - (b) Instinctive
  - (c) Loyalty
  - (d) Foreword

29. Proscribe
  - (a) Affectation
  - (b) Endorse
  - (c) Perishable
  - (d) Curb

Directions for questions 30 to 32: *Out of the four alternatives, choose the one which can be substituted for the given words.*

30. Am imitative work created to mock an original work.
  - (a) Parody
  - (b) Sonnet
  - (c) Leery
  - (d) Dirge

31. Likely to break easily.
  - (a) Potable
  - (b) Epiphanic
  - (c) Atavistic
  - (d) Brittle

32. In capable of being corrected.
  - (a) Irascible
  - (b) Incorrigible
  - (c) Gastronomic
  - (d) Corrigible

Directions for questions 33 to 35: *Four alternatives are given for the Idiom / Phrase. Choose the alternative which best expresses the meaning of the Idiom / Phrase.*

33. Black sheep
  - (a) Bad character
  - (b) More acceptable person
  - (c) Unique person
  - (d) To become angry

34. A live wire
  - (a) Dangerous wire
  - (b) Energetic person
  - (c) Invincible
  - (d) To be aloof

35. Bone to pick with some one
  - (a) To be angry
  - (b) To be perplexed
  - (c) Bribing someone
  - (d) To desire something strongly

Direction for question 36: *Groups of four words are given. In each group, one word is correctly spelt. Find the correctly spelt word.*

36.
  - (a) Pernickety
  - (b) Reconaissance
  - (c) Visisitudes
  - (d) Suculent

Directions for questions 37 to 39: *Some of the sentences have errors and some are correct. Find out the part of a sentence which has an error. If there is no error, mark your answer as (d).*

37. There were no less (a) / than forty boys (b) / in the class (c)./ No error (d)

38. No sooner did (a) / I reach (b) / Patna railway station than the train departed (c)./ No error (d)

39. The jury (a) / is (b) / fighting among them selves (c)./ No error (d)

Directions for questions 40 to 42: *Sentences are given with blanks to be filled in with an appropriate word. Four alternatives are suggested for each question. Choose the correct alternative out of the four.*

40. The bill ____ reduction in electroral expenses.
  - (a) admonishes
  - (b) rates
  - (c) forecloses
  - (d) rebukes

41. We must adapt ourselves ____ our circumstances.
  - (a) to
  - (b) in
  - (c) with
  - (d) for

42. Send the letter ____ post.
  - (a) in
  - (b) by
  - (c) through
  - (d) of

Directions (Q. 43-45): *In the following question, a part of the sentence is underlined Below are given alternatives to the underlined part at (a), (b) and (c) which may improve the sentence. Choose the correct alternative. In case no improvement is needed your answer is (d). Mark your answer in the Answer-Sheet.*

43. A citizen is expected to give <u>allegiance</u> to his country of origin,
  - (a) homage
  - (b) loyalty
  - (c) obedience
  - (d) No improvement

44. We were <u>with</u> daggers drawn despite attempts to understand each other,
  - (a) in
  - (b) on
  - (c) at
  - (d) No improvement

45. As soon as she noticed the workmen, she asked them <u>what they have been doing</u>.
  - (a) have done
  - (b) had been
  - (c) are doing
  - (d) No improvement

Direction: In question nos. **46** to **50**, you have a passage with 5 questions in following passage. Read the passages carefully and choose the best answer to each question out of the four alternatives.

With a mile and a half of Pacific Ocean sitting on their shoulders, ghost-pale crabs and fish forage among blood-red tube worms. Such communities flourish where super-heated water gushes from seafloor springs. Advances in the tools that scientists use to investigate deep-sea ecosystems are expanding knowledge of these creatures and their hostile environment.

Water heated as high as 760 F by magma from Earth's interior billows from a seafloor chimney. The surrounding ocean is just a few degrees above freezing. When the two fluids meet, iron sulfide precipitates, giving the "black smoker" its color. In these dark depths, chemosynthesis—based on thermal and chemical energy from the vents—is the primary mechanism sustaining life.

High-intensity lighting and high-resolution imaging technologies provide researchers with the equivalent of a microscope to examine life in the deep sea. These tools can reveal organisms that have always been part of vent communities but have been hidden until now.

46. Which 'creatures' does the passage refer to?

   (a) The ones who live among tube worms

   (b) The ones living in iron sulfide

   (c) The ones living around hydrothermal vents

   (d) The ones living in warm seas

47. The information presented in the passage is most likely to result from the work of which of the following types of scientist?

   (a) An ecologist   (b) An entomologist

   (c) An ornithologist   (d) A herpetologist

48. What does 'a mile and a half of Pacific Ocean sitting on their shoulders' refer to?

   (a) The mentioned creatures have no shoulders and hence, no relationship to the Ocean.

   (b) The creatures exist because of the depth of the Ocean.

   (c) The Ocean exists because of the mentioned creatures.

   (d) The Ocean is above the creatures.

49. Which of the following is true about the water in which ghost-pale crabs and fish flourish?

   (a) Extreme differences exist in temperature of the water in which they live and the surrounding water.

   (b) The water is black in colour.

   (c) A microscope is required to study that water.

   (d) The water gets light because of chemosynthesis.

50. What can tools 'equivalent to a microscope' do as per the passage?

   (a) Compare the details of organisms found in the deep sea

   (b) Find new species in the Pacific Ocean

   (c) Help in study of the seemingly hidden organisms in the deep sea vents

   (d) Clearly see the organisms living in the warm seas

QUANTITATIVE APTITUDE

51. The value of 1.333.... expressed in the form of $\dfrac{p}{q}$ is

   (a) $\dfrac{13}{10}$ (b) $\dfrac{1333}{1000}$

   (c) $\dfrac{4}{3}$ (d) $\dfrac{1}{9}$

52. One of the factors of $(49x^2 - 1) + (1 + 7x)^2$ is

   (a) $7 + x$ (b) $7 - x$

   (c) $7x + 1$ (d) $10x$

53. In the figure given below, three lines are concurrent at O. The value of x is

   (a) $30°$

   (b) $20°$

   (c) $70°$

   (d) $45°$

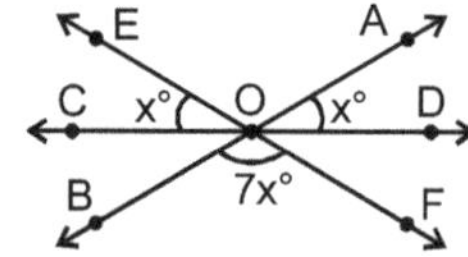

54. A scooter is purchased for ₹42,000. What will be its approximate value after 2 years, if it depreciates at 8% p.a.?

   (a) ₹40,000   (b) ₹35,800

   (c) ₹35,550   (d) ₹38,000

55. The perimeter of a rhombus with diagonals of length 6 cm and 8 cm is

   (a) 24 cm   (b) 20 cm

   (c) 40 cm   (d) 36 cm

56. Two sides of a triangle are 5 cm and 13 cm and its perimeter is 30 cm. The area of the triangle is

   (a) 30 cm^2 (b) 60 cm^2

   (c) 32.5 cm^2 (d) 65 cm^2

57. $\dfrac{4.40 \times 4.45 - 0.05 \times 4.40}{0.0011}$ is equal to

   (a) 1760   (b) 1.76×10^4

   (c) 176   (d) 1.76×10^2

58. If sum of two numbers is 84 and their H.C.F. and L.C.M. are 7 and 245 respectively, the smaller among the two numbers is

   (a) 39   (b) 35

   (c) 49   (d) 45

59. If a cube of side 2cm is melted and cost into a wire of diameter 0.002 cm, what is the length of the wire?

(a) 25400 m   (b) 22000 m

(c) 25000 m   (d) 24400 m

60. An article is sold with an offer of two successive discounts of 50% each. The ratio of M.P. to S.P. is

(a) 4 : 1   (b) 1 : 4

(c) 3 : 4   (d) 4 : 3

61. If $\sin\theta = \dfrac{a}{b}$, then $\cot\theta$ is equal to

(a) $\dfrac{b^2}{a^2 - b^2}$ (b) $\dfrac{\sqrt{b^2 - a^2}}{a}$

(c) $\dfrac{a}{b}$ (d) $\dfrac{a.b^2}{\sqrt{b^2 - a^2}}$

62. Walking at 3/5 th of his usual speed, a man, takes 2 hours more to cover a distance. How much time does he take usually to cover that distance?

(a) 2.5 hours   (b) 4 hours

(c) 3 hours   (d) 4.5 hours

63. If the radius of a cylinder is increased by 10% while its height is decreased by 20%, what is the effect on its volume?

(a) 3.2% increase   (b) 3.2% decrease

(c) 4.2% increase   (d) 4.2% decrease

64. The cost price of an article is 70% of its marked price. If the discount offered on the marked price is 15%, then the profit percentage is

(a) $22\dfrac{3}{17}\%$ (b) $22\dfrac{7}{13}\%$

(c) $22\dfrac{3}{7}\%$ (d) $21\dfrac{3}{7}\%$

65. If x is 80% of y, then what percent of 4x is y?

(a) 30%   (b) $31\dfrac{1}{4}\%$

(c) 31%   (d) $32\dfrac{1}{4}\%$

66. What will be the remainder when 19^{2000} is divided by 18?

(a) 5   (b) 17

(c) 1   (d) 15

67. Anil, Bijoy and Chandan can do a piece of work in 10, 12 and 15 days respectively. They start working alternately with Bijoy starting the work followed by Anil and Chandan in that order. Time taken to complete $\dfrac{3}{5}$th of the work will be

(a) 6 days   (b) $7\dfrac{1}{6}$ days

(c) $6\dfrac{1}{6}$ days   (d) $9\dfrac{3}{5}$ days

68. Find the number of sides and the measure of an interior angle of a regular polygon whose exterior angle is 40°.

(a) 6, 90°   (b) 8, 120°

(c) 9, 140°   (d) 5, 108°

69. Three pipes A, B and C can fill a tank in 20 minutes, 30 minutes and 40 minutes respectively. If A is opened first, followed by B after 5 minutes and by C after 10 minutes, how much time will they together take to fill the tank completely?

(a) 13 min   (b) $13\dfrac{1}{13}$ min

(c) $13\dfrac{1}{3}$ min   (d) 15 min

70. The greatest number among $\sqrt{2}, \sqrt[3]{3}, \sqrt[4]{5}$ and $\sqrt[6]{6}$ is

(a) $\sqrt{2}$ (b) $\sqrt[3]{3}$

(c) $\sqrt[4]{5}$ (d) $\sqrt[6]{6}$

71. If $3p + \dfrac{1}{p} = 12$, then the value of $p^3 + \dfrac{1}{27p^3}$ will be

(a) 24   (b) 60

(c) 64   (d) 56

72. By selling 15 books, a shopkeeper earns profit equal to the selling price of 3 books. His profit percentage is

(a) 10%   (b) 20%

(c) 25%   (d) 15%

Directions for questions 73 to 75: *The following line diagram represents the number of visitors during a day in two super markets X and Y. Answer the questions on the basis of the diagram.*

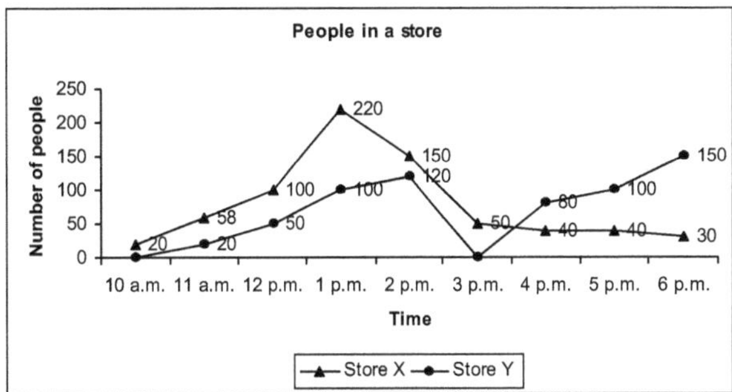

Note: No person remaind in store for more than 30 minutes.

73. What is the ratio of the number of visitors in stores X and Y from 2 p.m. to 5 p.m.?

(a) 7 : 4   (b) 4 : 7

(c) 14 : 15   (d) 15 : 14

74. By what percentage, the number of visitors are less in store Y as comapared to store X at 2 p.m.?

(a) 15 %   (b) 16.66 %

(c) 20 %   (d) 25 %

75. Average number of visitors during 1 p.m. to 3 p.m. visiting the store Y is

(a) 100   (b) 90

(c) 110   (d) 80

GENERAL AWARENESS

76. Which minister inaugurated the 5th International Buddhist Conclave in Varanasi-Sarnath by showcasing and project the Buddhist heritage and pilgrim sites of India?
(a) Ravi Shankar Prasad
(b) Suresh Prabu
(c) Mahesh Sharma
(d) Smriti Irani

77. Fa-hien visited India during the reign of
(a) Chandragupta II (b) Krishnadeva Raya
(c) Harshavardhana (d) Rudradaman

78. 'Arctic - Home of the Aryans' is a book written by
(a) G K Gokhale   (b) B G Tilak
(c) R C Dutt   (d) Mahatma Gandhi

79. Who was the first Turkish invader of India?
(a) Mahmud Gaznavi (b) Mohammad Ghori
(c) Sabuk tigin   (d) Mohammad Bin Qasim

80. Which of the following committee is related to education?
(a) Lawrence Committee
(b) Hartog Committee
(c) Strachey Committee
(d) Reading Committee

81. Earth hour is a worldwide event organized by
(a) UNO   (b) WWF
(c) WNEP   (d) UNICEF

82. Who would be honoured with the invitation of the Chief Guest at India's Republic Day parade for the first time?
(a) Mohammed Basha
(b) Sheikh Mohammed bin Zayed Al Nahyan
(c) Sheikh Ibrahim
(d) Mohammed Akhtar

83. World Sparrow Day is observed on
(a) 22 February   (b) 21 March
(c) 24 April   (d) 27 May

84. Glaucoma is a disease that affects:
(a) Eye   (b) Liver
(c) Lungs   (d) Ear

85. Who was the first African woman recipient of Nobel Prize?
(a) Allan Sirleaf   (b) Tawakkul Karman
(c) Wangari Mathai (d) Helen Osaba

86. Moniligaster Ivaniosi is a species of
(a) Earthworm   (b) Lizard
(c) Frog   (d) Cheetah

87. Strait of Hormuz lies between
(a) Gulf of Aden and Gulf of Oman
(b) Gulf of Aden and Persian Gulf
(c) Gulf of Carpentaria and Gulf of Bab-el-Mandab
(d) Persian Gulf and Gulf of Oman

88. Haber process is used to manufacture:
(a) Gum Powder   (b) Ammonia
(c) R.D.X.   (d) Ferric oxide

89. Oxide of which of the following oxide is called 'Heavy water'?
(a) Protinum   (b) Deuterium
(c) Tritium   (d) None of these

90. Which of the following is most electronegative?
(a) Chlorine   (b) Fluorine
(c) Bromine   (d) Iodine

91. Cotopaxi volcano is in which of the following countries?
(a) Nicaragua   (b) Ecuador
(c) Guatemala   (d) Chad

92. Who of the following is not a recipient of Jnanpith Award, the highest award of literate in India?
(a) Harivansh Rai Bachchan
(b) Mahadevi Verma
(c) Naresh Mehta
(d) Sri Lal Shukla

93. K computer has been developed by
(a) Sony   (b) Riken
(c) C-DAC   (d) Google

94. Which of the following river arises at verunag?
(a) Jhelum   (b) Beas
(c) Chenab   (d) Mandovi

95. Betla National Park is in which state?
(a) Jharkhand   (b) Orissa
(c) Madhya Pradesh (d) West Bengal

96. IMF introduced Special Drawing Right (SDR) in which of the following year?
(a) 1956   (b) 1969
(c) 1976   (d) 1982

97. Narora nuclear reactor is in which of the following states?
(a) Maharashtra   (b) Rajasthan
(c) Gujarat   (d) Uttar Pradesh

98. What is the capital of Ukraine?
(a) Belgrade   (b) Belfast
(c) Keiv   (d) Reykjavik

99. How many seats of Rajya Sabha are from Uttar Pradesh?
(a) 19   (b) 23
(c) 29   (d) 31

100. Who is the author of the book titled "Modi's Midas Touch in Foreign Policy" ?
(a) Smriti Irani   (b) Ravi Shankar Prasad
(c) Surendra Kumar (d) Venkaiah Naidu

ANSWERS

1. (b)	**2.** (a)	**3.** (b)	**4.** (d)	**5.** (c)	**6.** (b)	**7.** (b)	**64.** (d)	**65.** (d)	**66.** (d)
11. (b)	**12.** (c)	**13.** (d)	**14.** (d)	**15.** (d)	**16.** (b)	**17.** (c)	**18.** (b)	**19.** (c)	**20.** (d)
21. (c)	**22.** (a)	**23.** (a)	**24.** (c)	**25.** (a)	**26.** (b)	**27.** (b)	**28.** (a)	**29.** (b)	**30.** (a)
31. (d)	**32.** (b)	**33.** (a)	**34.** (b)	**35.** (a)	**36.** (a)	**37.** (a)	**38.** (d)	**39.** (b)	**40.** (c)
41. (a)	**42.** (b)	**43.** (b)	**44.** (c)	**45.** (b)	**46.** (c)	**47.** (a)	**48.** (d)	**49.** (a)	**50.** (c)
51. (c)	**52.** (c)	**53.** (b)	**54.** (c)	**55.** (b)	**56.** (a)	**57.** (b)	**58.** (b)	**59.** (a)	**60.** (a)
61. (b)	**62.** (c)	**63.** (b)	**64.** (d)	**65.** (b)	**66.** (c)	**67.** (b)	**68.** (c)	**69.** (b)	**70.** (c)
71. (b)	**72.** (c)	**73.** (c)	**74.** (c)	**75.** (c)	**76.** (c)	**77.** (a)	**78.** (b)	**79.** (c)	**80.** (b)
81. (b)	**82.** (b)	**83.** (b)	**84.** (a)	**85.** (c)	**86.** (a)	**87.** (d)	**88.** (b)	**89.** (b)	**90.** (b)
91. (b)	**92.** (a)	**93.** (b)	**94.** (a)	**95.** (a)	**96.** (b)	**97.** (d)	**98.** (c)	**99.** (d)	**100.** (c)

EXPLANATIONS

1. 'S' could be represented as 02, 13, 21, **30**, 44.

'W' could be represented as 04, 10, **23**, 31, 42.

'I' could be represented as 58, 66, **77**, 89, 95.

'G' could be represented as 57, 68, 75, 86, **99**.

∴ The correct option will be b.

2. The only word which can be formed using the letters of the given word is "tension".

3. The given options are stages in the life cycle of a butterfly.

4. $(11) K \xrightarrow{+2} (13) M \xrightarrow{+2} 15(O)$
$\xrightarrow{+2} (17) Q \xrightarrow{+2} (19) \mathbf{S}$

$(21) U \xrightarrow{-6} (15) O \xrightarrow{-6} (9) I$
$\xrightarrow{-6} (3) C \xrightarrow{-6} (23) \mathbf{W}$

$(26) Z \xrightarrow{-2} (24) X \xrightarrow{-2} (22) V$
$\xrightarrow{-2} (20) T \xrightarrow{-2} (18) \mathbf{R}$

5. Here,

$9 \times 4 - 4 = 32$

$15 \times 5 - 5 = 70$

∴ $17 \times 3 - 3 = 48$

6. Number of odd days in 27 days will be 6 days

∴ 6 days after Saturday will be Friday.

7. Total number of squares of 1 unit = 12

Total number of squares of 2 units = 6

Total = 18 squares.

9. In rest of the figures, outer and inner figure are same and concentric.

12. $96 \div 2 = 48$ and $48 \div 2 = 24$

Also, $72 \div 2 = 36$ $36 \div 2 = 18$

Hence, c is the correct option.

13. Here,

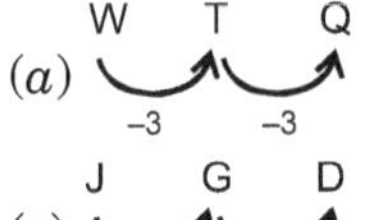

Hence, d is the correct option.

14. Options (a), (b), and (c) are alcoholic beverages.

15. By writing the expression with actual algebraic signs expression $(69 + 3 \div 7 - 2 \times 11 = 20)$

will be $69 \div 3 - 7 \times 2 + 11 = 23 - 14 + 11 = 20$

16. Given,

$su\ ka\ ni \equiv 329$ ...(i)

$su\ pa\ fa \equiv 731$ ...(ii)

$fa\ cha\ ni \equiv 169$ ...(iii)

From (i) and (ii), 'su' is coded as 3.

From (i) and (iii), 'ni' is coded as 9.

Hence code for 'ka' is 2.

17. Present average age of Yogesh and Ritu

$= 19 + 3 = 22$ years

∴ Sum of ages of Yogesh and Ritu

$= 22 \times 2 = 44$ years

Also, sum of ages of Yogesh, Ritu and Ayusha

$= (22 - 2) \times 3 = 60$ years

∴ Ayusha's present age

$= 60 - 44 = 16$ years

Ayusha's age after 5 years $= 16 + 5 = 21$ years.

18. Figure (b) resembles the unfolded form of the folded paper.

19. Since $48 \div 3 + 16 = 32$, "$- + =$" is the correct option.

20. Given information can be shown

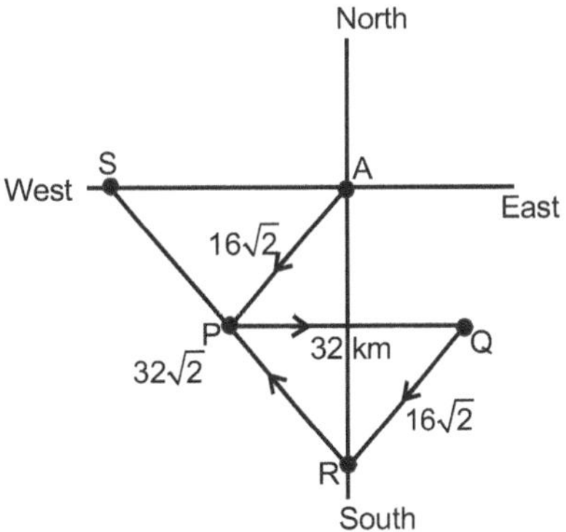

Therefore, city A is located towards East of city S.

21.

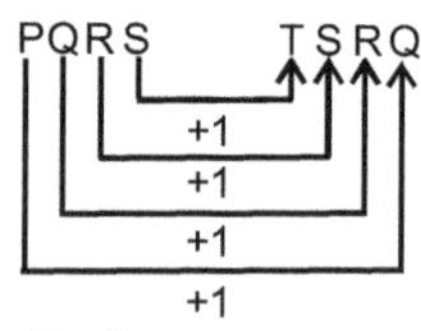

Similarly,

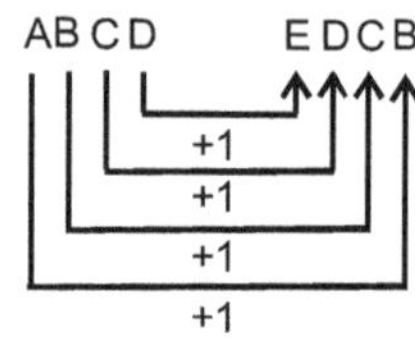

22. "Sloth" means "lethargy", likewise the synonym of "slovenly" is "untidy".

23. The correct order according to the dictionary is B,A,D,C,E

24. "Mint" cannot be formed using the letters of the given word because the given word does not have the letter "T"

25.

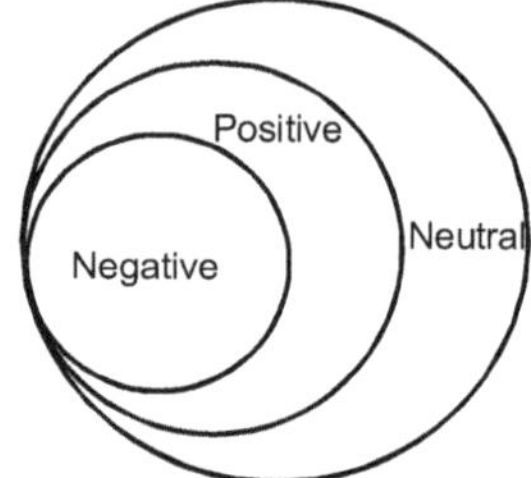

Thus some neutral is negative.

26. "Disinterested" means not having the mind or feelings engaged. "Endorse" means declare one's public approval or support of. "Indifferent" means having no particular interest or sympathy. "Incorporate" means put or take in (something) as part of a whole. "Exclude" means deny (someone) access to or bar (someone) from a place.

27. "Circumlocution" means the use of an unnecessarily large number of words to express an idea ."Verboseness" means containing more words than necessary. "Hide" means to put out of sight. "Comprise" means to include especially within a particular scope. "Understand" means to grasp the meaning of.

28. "Epilogue" means a concluding section that rounds out the design of a literary work.

"Preamble" means an introductory statement. "Instinctive" means prompted by natural instinct or propensity. "Loyalty" means the quality or state or an instance of being loyal. "Foreword" means prefatory comments.

29. "Proscribe" means to condemn or forbid as harmful or unlawful. "Endorse" means to approve openly. "Curb" means check. "Affectation" means speech or conduct not natural to oneself. "Perishable" means liable to perish.

30. "Parody" means a literary or musical work in which the style of an author or work is closely imitated for comic effect or in ridicule. "Leery" means suspicious. "Sonnet" means a fixed verse form of Italian origin consisting of 14 lines. "Dirge" means a song or hymn of grief or lamentation.

31. "Potable" means suitable for drinking. "Epiphany" means an appearance or manifestation especially of a divine being. "Atavistic" means recurrence of or reversion to a past style, manner, outlook, approach, or activity. "Brittle" means easily broken, cracked, or snapped.

32. "Irascible" means marked by hot temper and easily provoked anger. "Incorrigible" means incapable of being corrected. "Gastronomic" means from the standpoint of gastronomy. "Corrigible" means capable of being set right.

33. "Black sheep" is an idiom used to describe an odd or disreputable member of a group.

34. "A live wire" is a vivacious, alert, or energetic person.

35. "Bone to pick with some one" means something someone has done that has annoyed you.

36. The correct spelling of option (*b*) is "reconnaissance".The correct spelling of option (*c*) is vicissitudes. The correct spelling of option (*d*) is "succulent".

37. The correct sentence is "there were no fewer than forty boys in the class". As "fewer" is used to denote number or countable nouns and "less" is used to denote quantity, or uncountable nouns.

38. There is no error in the sentence.

39. The correct sentence is "the jury are fighting among themselves."A collective noun takes a singular verb when the collection is thought of as a whole;plural verb when the individuals of which it is composed are thought of.

40. The bill deals with reduction in electoral expenses. "Forecloses" means to deal with. "Rates" means to rebuke angrily. "Admonish" means to express warning. Option (*d*) is negated.

41. The correct sentence is "we must adapt ourselves to our circumstances".

42. The correct sentence is "send the letter by post". "Send by" means to dispatch.

51. $1.3333... = 1.\overline{3} = 1\dfrac{3}{9} = 1\dfrac{1}{3} = \dfrac{4}{3}.$

52. $(49x^2 - 1) + (1 + 7x)^2$

$$= [(7x)^2 - (1)^2] + (1 + 7x)^2$$
$$= (7x + 1)(7x - 1 + 7x + 1)$$
$$= 14x(7x + 1)$$

Hence, $(7x + 1)$ is a factor of the given expression.

53.

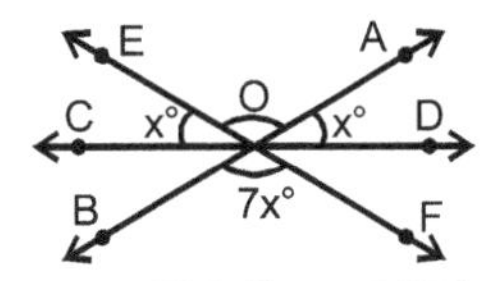

Here, $\angle EOC = \angle FOD = x$

$\angle AOD = \angle BOC = x$

$\angle BOF = \angle AOE = 7x$

Since sum of angles around a point is $360°$,

$2(x + x + 7x) = 360°$.

$\Rightarrow 18x = 360°$

$\therefore x = 20°$.

54. Value of the scooter after 2 years

$= 42000\,(1 - 0.08)^2$

$= 35548.8 \approx ₹35550$ (approx).

55.

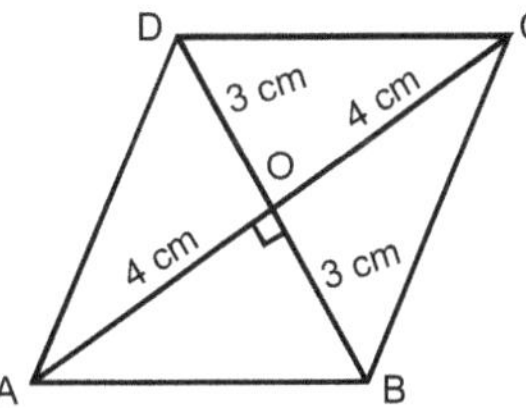

Diagonals of rhombus bisect each other at right angle.

In right angled triangle AOB,

$AB^2 = AO^2 + OB^2 = 4^2 + 3^2 = 25$

$\Rightarrow AB = \sqrt{25} = 5$ cm (Since, AB > 0)

$\therefore$ Perimeter of the rhombus ABCD $= 4 \times AB$

$= 4 \times 5 = 20$ cm.

56. Third side of the triangle $= 30 - (5 + 13) = 12$ cm

$$s = \frac{\text{Perimeter}}{2} = \frac{30}{2} = 15 \text{ cm}$$

$\therefore$ Area of the triangle

$= \sqrt{s(s-a)(s-b)(s-c)}$

$= \sqrt{15(15-13)(15-12)(15-5)}$

$= \sqrt{15 \times 2 \times 3 \times 10}$

$= \sqrt{2 \times 2 \times 3 \times 3 \times 5 \times 5} = 2 \times 3 \times 5 = 30 \text{ cm}^2$.

Alternate solution:

Since a triangle with sides 5, 12 and 13 forms a right triangle,

Area of the triangle $= \dfrac{1}{2}\,b \times h = \dfrac{1}{2} \times 12 \times 5 = 30 \text{ cm}^2$.

57. $\dfrac{4.40 \times 4.45 - 0.05 \times 4.40}{0.0011}$

$= \dfrac{4.40(4.45 - 0.05)}{0.0011} = \dfrac{4.40 \times 4.40}{0.0011}$

$= \dfrac{44 \times 44}{11} \times \dfrac{10^{-2}}{10^{-4}} = 176 \times 10^2 = 1.76 \times 10^4$.

58. Product of two numbers = L.C.M. $\times$ H.C.F.

Let one of the numbers be x.

$\therefore$ Other number $= 84 - x$

According to the question,

$$x(84 - x) = 1715$$

$\Rightarrow x^2 - 84x + 1715 = 0$

$\Rightarrow x^2 - 49x - 35x + 1715 = 0$

$\Rightarrow x(x - 49) - 35(x - 49) = 0$

$\Rightarrow (x - 35)(x - 49) = 0$

$\Rightarrow x = 35$ or $x = 49$

$\therefore$ Smaller number is 35.

59. Let the length of the wire be x m.

$\therefore$ Volume of the wire = volume of the cube

$\Rightarrow \pi r^2 x = 2 \times 2 \times 2$

$\Rightarrow \dfrac{22}{7} \times (0.001)^2 \times x = 8$

$\therefore x = \dfrac{8 \times 7 \times 10^6}{22} \approx 2.54 \times 10^6$ cm

$= 2.54 \times 10^4$ m = 25400 m.

60. Let M.P. of the article be x.

$\therefore$ S.P. of the article after two successive discounts of 50% each

$= x(1 - 0.5)(1 - 0.5) = 0.25x$

$\therefore$ M.P. : S.P. $= x : 0.25x = 4 : 1$.

61. $\sin \theta = \dfrac{a}{b}$

$\because \cot^2 \theta = \operatorname{cosec}^2 \theta - 1$

$\Rightarrow \cot^2 \theta = \dfrac{1}{\sin^2 \theta} - 1$

$\Rightarrow \cot^2 \theta = \dfrac{1}{\left(\dfrac{a}{b}\right)^2} - 1 = \dfrac{b^2}{a^2} - 1 = \dfrac{b^2 - a^2}{a^2}$

$\Rightarrow \cot \theta = \dfrac{\sqrt{b^2 - a^2}}{a}$.

62. Let the usual speed be 's' and time taken be 't'.

As speed becomes $\dfrac{3s}{5}$, time taken will be $\dfrac{5t}{3}$.

According to the question,

$$\dfrac{5t}{3} - t = 2$$

$\Rightarrow \dfrac{2t}{3} = 2 \qquad \therefore t = 3$ hrs.

63. Let the radius of the cylinder be 'r' and its height be 'h'.

$\therefore$ Volume, $V = \pi r^2 h$

Now, radius will be 1.1r and height will be 0.8h.

New volume $= \pi(1.1r)^2 \times 0.8h = 0.968\pi r^2 h$

$\therefore$ Volume decreases by $(100 - 96.8)$, i.e. 3.2%.

64. Let the marked price of the article be ₹x.

∴ Cost price = ₹$0.7x$

Selling price of the article = $x(1 - 0.15) = ₹\,0.85x$.

∴ Profit percentage

$$= \frac{0.85x - 0.7x}{0.7x} \times 100 = \frac{150}{7} = 21\frac{3}{7}\%.$$

65. $x = 80\%$ of $y = 0.8y$

∴ $$y = \frac{x}{0.8}$$

∴ Required percentage $= \dfrac{\dfrac{x}{0.8}}{4x} \times 100 = \dfrac{125}{4} = 31\dfrac{1}{4}\%.$

66. $$\frac{19^{2000}}{18} = \frac{(18+1)^{2000}}{18}$$

∴ Remainder will be 1.

67. Let the total unit of work be L.C.M. (10, 12, 15) *i.e.*, 60 units.

∴ Anil's 1 day work = $\dfrac{60}{10} = 6$ units

Bijoy's 1 day work = $\dfrac{60}{12} = 5$ units

Chandan's 1 day work = $\dfrac{60}{15} = 4$ units

Since they work alternately, total unit of work done in 3 days = $(6 + 5 + 4) = 15$ units

Also, total amount of work to be completed

$$= \frac{3}{5} \times 60 = 36 \text{ units.}$$

∴ $(15 \times 2) = 30$ units would be completed in 6 days.

Left over work = $36 - 30 = 6$ units

Out of these 6 units,

Bijoy will complete 5 units in one day and remaining 1 unit will be completed by Anil in $\dfrac{1}{6}$ days.

∴ Total time taken = $7\dfrac{1}{6}$ days.

68. Number of sides of the polygon = $\dfrac{360°}{40°} = 9$

∴ Measure of an interior angle

$$= \frac{(2n - 4)90°}{n} = \frac{14 \times 90°}{9} = 140°.$$

Alternate method:

Sum of exterior and interior angles of a polygon is 100°. Only option (c) satisfy the condition.

69. Let the total units to be filled up be the L.C.M. of (20, 30, 40), *i.e.*, 120 units.

Units filled by A in 10 minutes

$$= \frac{120}{20} \times 10 = 60 \text{ units}$$

Units filled by B in 5 minutes

$$= \frac{120}{30} \times 5 = 20 \text{ units}$$

∴ Total units filled in initial 10 minutes = 80 units

Remaining units to be filled = $120 - 80 = 40$ units

Now, these 40 units would have been filled by all the 3 pipes in $\dfrac{40}{13}$ minutes.

∴ Total time taken to fill the tank

$$= \left(10 + \frac{40}{13}\right) \text{min} \ i.e. \ 13\frac{1}{13} \text{ minutes.}$$

70. L.C.M. of orders of given surds, *i.e.*, (2, 3, 4 and 6) will be 12.

∴ $\sqrt{2} = \sqrt[2\times6]{2^6} = \sqrt[12]{64}$

$\sqrt[3]{3} = \sqrt[3\times4]{3^4} = \sqrt[12]{81}$

$\sqrt[4]{5} = \sqrt[4\times3]{5^3} = \sqrt[12]{125}$

$\sqrt[6]{6} = \sqrt[6\times2]{6^2} = \sqrt[12]{36}$

Hence, $\sqrt[4]{5}$ is the greatest number.

71. We have, $3p + \dfrac{1}{p} = 12.$

$\Rightarrow 3\left(p + \dfrac{1}{3p}\right) = 12$

∴ $p + \dfrac{1}{3p} = \dfrac{12}{3} = 4$

Taking cube on both the sides, we get

$$\left(p + \frac{1}{3p}\right)^3 = (4)^3 = 64$$

$\Rightarrow p^3 + \dfrac{1}{27p^3} + 3 \cdot p \dfrac{1}{3p}\left(p + \dfrac{1}{3p}\right) = 64$

$\Rightarrow p^3 + \dfrac{1}{27p^3} = 64 - 4 = 60.$

72. Let the selling price of each book be ₹x.

∴ Profit on selling 15 books = ₹$3x$

Selling price of fifteen books = ₹$15x$

∴ Cost price = $15x - 3x = ₹12x$

∴ Profit percentage $= \dfrac{3x}{12x} \times 100 = 25\%.$

73. Total number of visitors from 2 p.m. to 5 p.m. in store X = $150 + 50 + 40 + 40 = 280$

And, in store Y = $120 + 0 + 80 + 100 = 300$

∴ Required ratio = $\dfrac{280}{300} = 14 : 15.$

74. Required percentage $= \dfrac{150 - 120}{150} \times 100 = 20\%$.

75. Average number of visitors from 1 p.m. to 3 p.m. visiting the store Y

$$= \frac{100 + 120}{2} = 110.$$

■■

GENERAL INTELLIGENCE

1. The average height of students in a class of 20 is 105 cm. If 10 students of average height of 120 cm are added to the class, what will be the average height of the students in the class ?

(a) 117.5 cm

(b) 116 cm

(c) 110 cm

(d) 108 cm

2. Two statements are given followed by two conclusions I and II. You have to consider the two statements to be true even if they seem to be at variance from commonly known facts. You have to decide which one of the given conslusions is definitely drawn from the given statements.

Statements :

1. Sachin is a good cricketer.

2. Sachin's sister is a good singer.

Conclusions :

I. Sachin and his sister are good cricketers.

II. Sachin and his sister are talented.

(a) Only I follows

(b) Only II follows

(c) Neither I nor II follows

(d) Both I and II follow

3. Which one of the following figures represents the relationship among Horses, Mammals, Animals ?

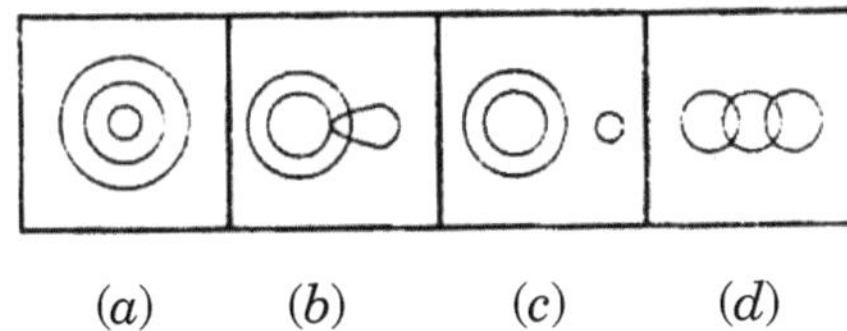

   (a)   (b)   (c)   (d)

4. There are 70 cycles in a cycle stand. 50 cycles have carriers, 35 have both bells and carriers, while some have only bells. Find out from the following Venn diagrams, which is the correct way of representing the above problem.

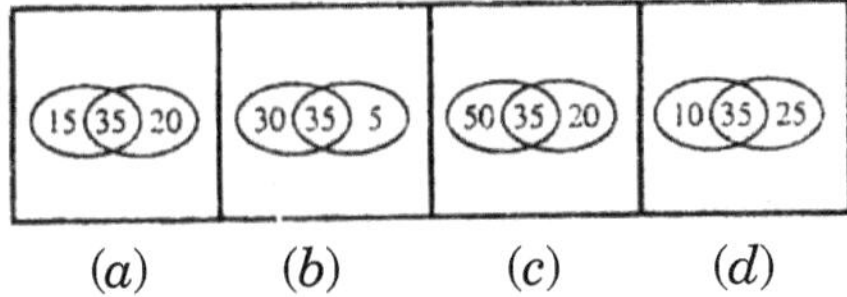

   (a)   (b)   (c)   (d)

5. In the following figures, four different views of a dice are given. Find the number of dots on the face opposite to the face with one dot.

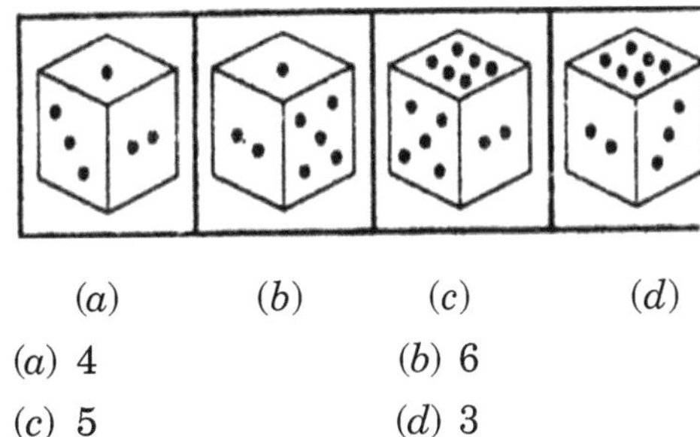

   (a)   (b)   (c)   (d)

(a) 4   (b) 6

(c) 5   (d) 3

6. A piece of paper is folded and punched as shown below. From the given responses, indicate how it will appear when opened.

Question

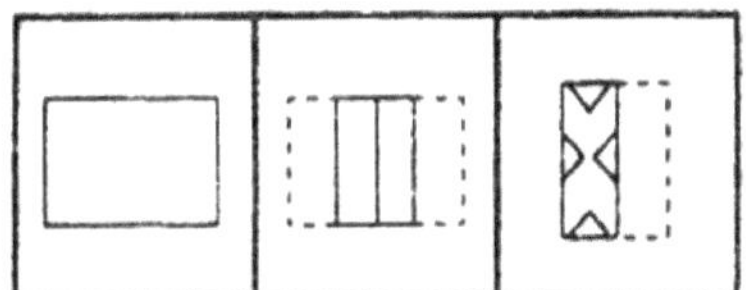

Answer :

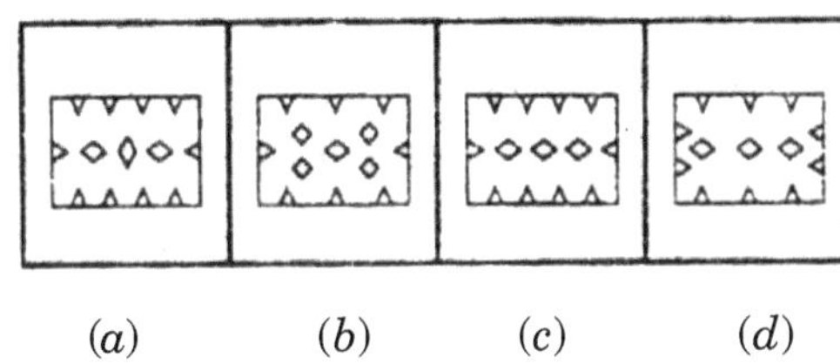

   (a)   (b)   (c)   (d)

7. Which of the answer figures shall complete the question figure ?

Question

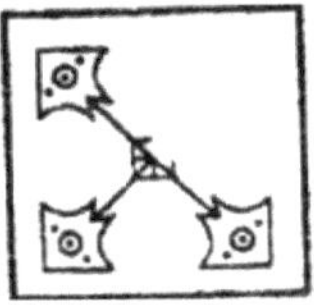

Answer :

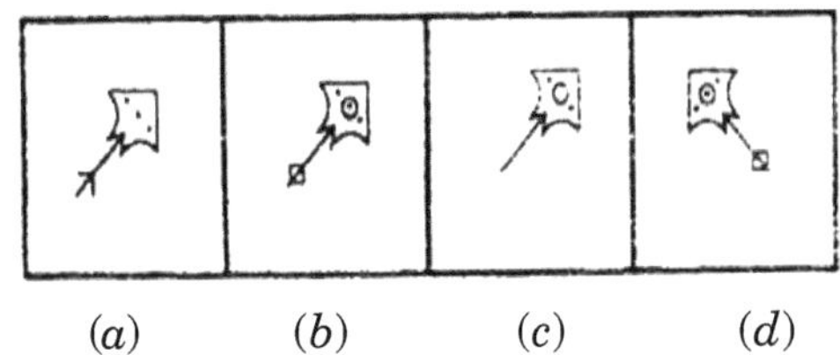

   (a)   (b)   (c)   (d)

8. In which answer figure is the question figure embedded ?

Question

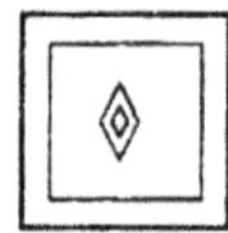

Answer :

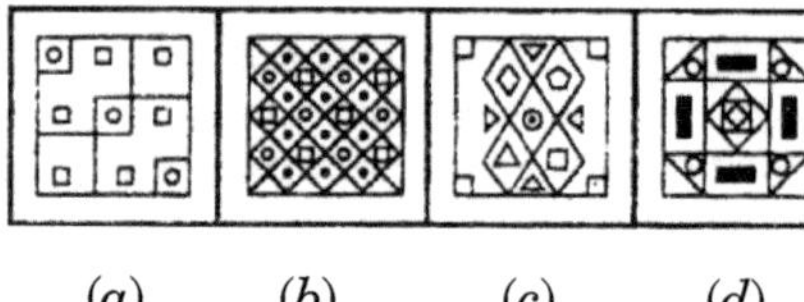

(a)   (b)   (c)   (d)

Directions(Q. 9-11) : *Select the related word / letters / numbers / figure from the given responses.*

9. Sculptor : Statue : : Poet : ?

(a) Poem

(b) Music

(c) Painting

(d) Dance

10. ABCD : FGIH : : DEGF : ?

(a) STRP

(b) MNPO

(c) DEFG

(d) XYZA

11. Question

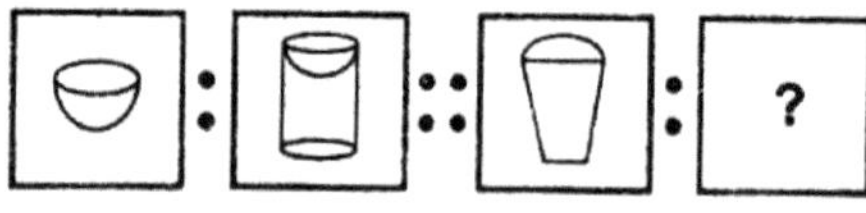

Answer :

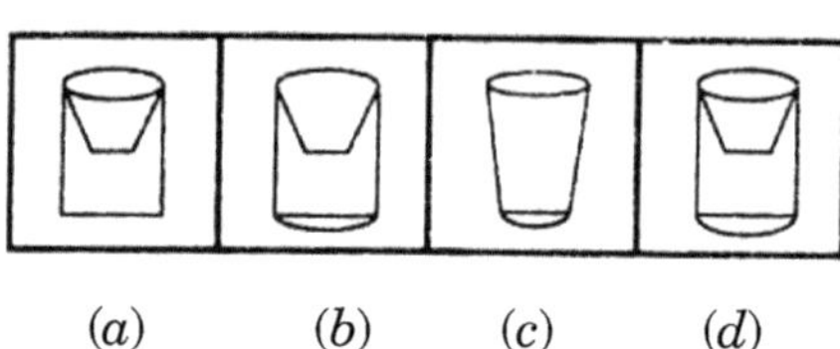

(a)   (b)   (c)   (d)

Directions (Q. 12 - 13) : *Find the odd word / letters / numbers / figure from the given responses.*

12. (a) Violin

(b) Sitar

(c) Harp

(d) Flute

13. (a) JLMK

(b) SUVT

(c) SVUT

(d) GIJH

14. Which one of the given responses would be a meaningful order of the following words ?

1. Digest

2. Cook

3. Chew

4. Swallow

5. Taste

(a) 5, 2, 3, 4, 1

(b) 2, 5, 3, 4, 1

(c) 3, 5, 2, 4, 1

(d) 2, 5, 4, 3, 1

15. Arrange the following words according to dictionary

1. Counter

2. Courier

3. Courage

4. Counsel

5. Country

(a) 4, 1, 2, 3, 5

(b) 4, 1, 5, 3, 2

(c) 5, 1, 4, 2, 3

(d) 5, 4, 2, 1, 3

Directions(Q. 16-19): *Find the missing letters / number / figure from the given respones*

16. WAB, XCD, YEF,.....?.....

(a) CMN

(b) ZGH

(c) BKL

(d) AIJ

17. 18, 30, 48, 72,.....?......

(a) 106

(b) 115

(c) 120

(d) 102

18. Question

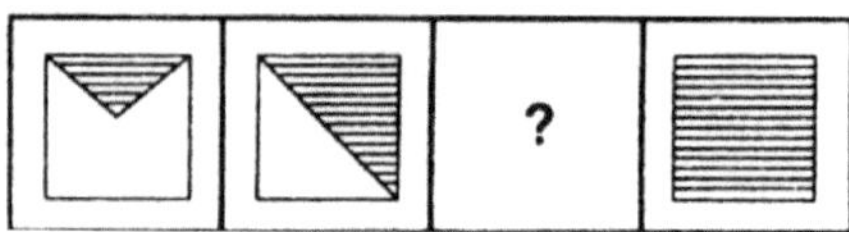

Answer :

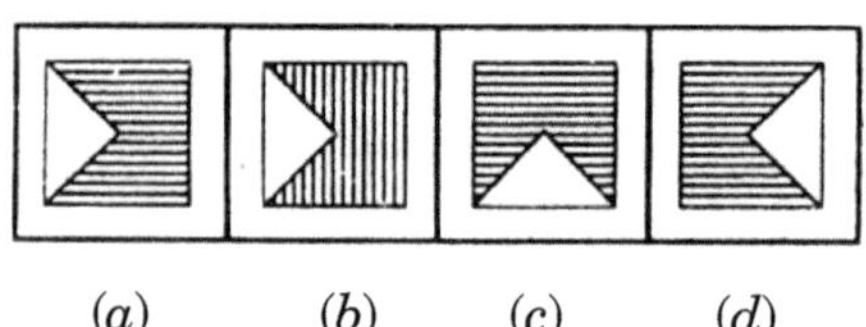

(a)   (b)   (c)   (d)

19. Question

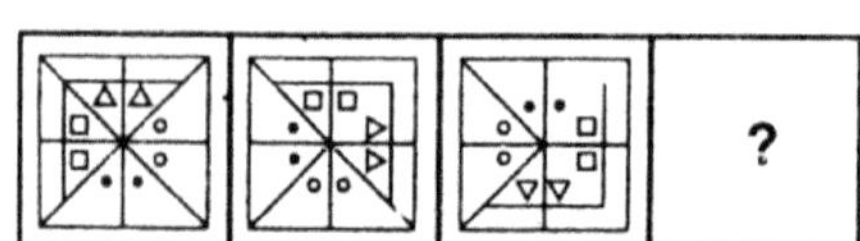

Answer :

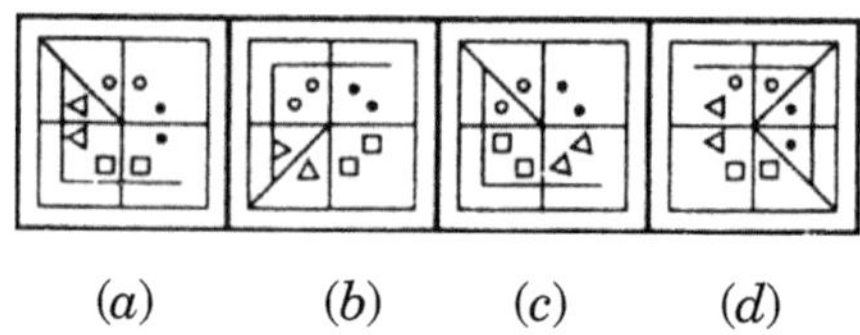

(a)   (b)   (c)   (d)

20. Which one set of letters when sequentially placed at the gaps in the given letter series shall complete it ?

D – – N – – N N D M – N

(a) N D M N M

(b) M N D M N

(c) M D M N M

(d) D M N N M

Directions (Q. 21): *Find the missing number from the given responses*

21.

(a) 165 (b) 164
(c) 177 (d) 169

22. In the following question, you have to identify the correct response from the given premises stated according to following symbols

If − means ×, × means +, + means ÷ and ÷ means −, then

$14 - 10 \div 4 \times 16 + 8 = ?$

(a) 142 (b) 138
(c) 19 (d) 6

23. If TABLE is written as GZYOV, how is JUICE written ?

(a) OZLFJ (b) QFRXV
(c) HOFAD (d) QZHMT

24. In a certain code the following number are coded in a particular way by assigning signs

1 2 3 4 5 6 7 8 9
⌐ ¬ ‖ ≡ ∧ ∨ ÷ × ◊

Which number can be decoded from the following?

× ≡ ◊ ∧ ÷

(a) 84975 (b) 84957
(c) 84597 (d) 84795

25. A word given in capital letters is followed by four words. Out of these only one cannot be formed by using the letters of the given word. Find out that word

CONSTANTINOPLE

(a) NAPLES (b) CONSTANT
(c) COUP (d) TIPTOE

ENGLISH LANGUAGE

Directions (Q. 26-27): *In the following question, out of the four alternatives, choose the one which best expresses the meaning of the given word and mark it in the Answer-Sheet.*

26. Vociferous
   (a) violent (b) loud
   (c) secret (d) true

27. Fictional
   (a) genuine (b) authentic
   (c) fanciful (d) real

Directions (Q. 28-29): *In the following question, choose the word opposite in meaning to the given word and mark it in the Answer-Sheet.*

28. Cultivated
   (a) Crude (b) Gentel
   (c) Suave (d) Refined

29. Impertinent
   (a) Insolent (b) Impudent
   (c) Cheeky (d) Courteous

Directions (Q. 30-32): *In the following question, out of the four alternatives, choose the one which can be substituted for the given words / sentence.*

30. A round or cylindrical container used for storing things such as food, chemicals or rolls of film
   (a) tankard (b) canister
   (c) vessel (d) casket

31. A place of permanent residence
   (a) abode (b) dormitory
   (c) domicile (d) apartment

32. That cannot be altered or withdrawn
   (a) irrevocable (b) irretrievable
   (c) irrefutable (d) irresistible

Directions (Q. 33-35): *In the following questions, four alternatives are given for the idiom / phrase and bold italicised in the sentence. Choose the alternative which best expresses the meaning of the idom / phrase and mark it in the Answer-Sheet.*

33. Once the case reached the court, the police **washed their hands** off it.
   (a) waited for a response to
   (b) claimed credit for
   (c) disassociated themselves from
   (d) seemed eager to continue

34. She wanted to go hitch-hiking but her mother ***put her foot down*** now she's going by bus,
   (a) took a firm stand
   (b) expressed her displeasure
   (c) scolded her badly
   (d) got irritated

35. Adolescence is a period of ***halcyon days.***
   (a) hard days
   (b) of mental pressure
   (c) happy days
   (d) days of preparation

Direction (Q. 36): *In the following question four words are given in each question, out of which only one word is correctly spelt, Find the correctly spelt word and indicate it in the Answer-Sheet by blackening the appropriate rectangle [■].*

36. (a) garulous
    (b) garrulous
    (c) garullous
    (d) garrullous

Directions (Q. 37-39): *In the following some parts of the sentences have errors and some have none. Find out which part of a sentence has an error and blacken the rectangle [■] corresponding to the appropriate letter (a, b, c). If there is no error, blacken, the rectangle [■] corresponding to (d) in the Answer-Sheet.*

37. Air pollution, together with littering, / (a) are causing many problems / (b) in our cities / (c) No error. (d)

38. The accused refused / (a) to answer to the policeman / (b) on duty. / (c) No error. / (d)

39. What is / (a) the use of me / (b) attending the session? / (c) No error. / (d)

Directions (Q. 40-42): In the following question. *Sentences are given with blanks to be filled in with word(s). Four correct alternatives are suggested for each question. Choose the correct alternative out of the four and indicate it by blackening the appropriate rectangle [■] in the Answer-Sheet.*

40. ______ pollution control measures are expensive, many industries hesitate to adopt them.
    (a) Although   (b) However
    (b) However   (d) Despite

41. It is not ______ for a man to be confined to the pursuit of wealth.
    (a) healthy   (b) easy
    (c) possible   (d) common

42. ______ his being innocent of the crime, the judge sentenced him to one year imprisonment.
    (a) Inspite of   (b) In case of
    (c) On account of   (d) In the event of

Directions (Q. 43-45): *In the following question, a part of the sentence is underlined Below are given alternatives to the underlined part at (a), (b) and (c) which may improve the sentence. Choose the correct alternative. In case no improvement is needed your answer is (d). Mark your answer in the Answer-Sheet.*

43. You <u>shall have attended</u> if the court had instructed you to do so.
    (a) would have had to attend
    (b) would at lend
    (c) would have to
    (d) No improvement

44. The relics of Greece <u>over which</u> such a great deal of evidence has been collected should be preserved.
    (a) from which   (b) on which
    (c) ascent which   (d) No improvement

45. When the beverage was ready, they drank <u>posssibly as much as they could</u>.
    (a) as much as they possibly could
    (b) as much as possibly they could
    (c) as much as they could possibly
    (d) No improvement

Directions (Q. 46-50): *In the following question, you have brief passages with 5 questions. Read the passages carefully and choose the best answer to each question out of the four alternatives and mark it by blackening the appropriate rectangle [■] the Answer-Sheet.*

Stuck with the development dilemma ? Stay away from management courses. Seriously, one of the biggest complaints that organisations have about management courses is that they fail to impact the participants' on-the-job behaviour. Some management trainers stress the need for follow-up and reinforcement on the job. Some go so far as briefing the participants' managers on what behaviour they should be reinforcing back on the job. Others include a follow-up training day to review the progress of the participants. None of this is really going far enough.

The real problem is that course promoters view development as something which primarily, takes place in a classroom. A course is an event and events are, by definition limited in time. When you talk about follow-up after a course, it is seen as a nice idea, but not as an essential part of the participants, development programme.

Any rational, empowered individual should be able to take what has been learnt in a course and transfer it to the work place — or so the argument goes, Another negattive aspect of the course mindset is that, primarily, development is thought to be about skill-acquisition.

So, it is felt that the distinction between taking the course and behaving differently in the work place parallels the distinction between skill-acquisition and skill-application. But can such a sharp distinction be maintained? Skills are really acquired only in the context of applying them on the job, finding them effective and, therefore, reinforcing them.

The problem with courses is that they are events, while development is an on-going process which involves, within a complex environment continual interaction, regular feedback and adjustment. As we tend to equate development with a one-off event, it is difficult to get seriously motivated about the follow-up. Anyone paying for a course tends to look at follow-up as an unnecessary and rather costly frill.

46. What is the passage about ?

   (*a*) personal management

   (*b*) development dilemma

   (*c*) management courses

   (*d*) course promoters' attitude

47. Which of the following statements is false ?

   (*a*) Some management trainers stress the need for follow-up and reinforcement on the job

   (*b*) Some suggest a follow-up training day to review the progress of the participants

   (*c*) Some go to the extent of briefing the participants' managers on what behaviour they should be reinforcing back on the job

   (*d*) The real problem is that course promoters view development as something which does not take place during a course

48. The writer's attitude, as reflected in the passage, is

   (*a*) critical   (*b*) ironic

   (*c*) sympathetic   (*d*) philosophical

49. The course promoters' attitude is

   (*a*) self-righteous   (*b*) indifferent

   (*c*) easy-going   (*d*) unprogressive

50. The word 'mindset' here means

   (*a*) a determined mind

   (*b*) a (fixed) attitude of mind

   (*c*) an open mind

   (*d*) mindful

QUANTITATIVE APTITUDE

51. How much per cent more than the cost price should a shopkeeper mark his goods so that after allowing a discount of 12.5%, he still gains 5% ?

   (*a*) 15   (*b*) 20

   (*c*) 25   (*d*) 30

52. If 10% discount is allowed on the marked price of an article, the profit of a dealer is 20%. If he allows a discount of 20%, his profits will be

   (*a*) $4\dfrac{1}{3}\%$ (*b*) 5%

   (*c*) $6\dfrac{2}{3}\%$ (*d*) 8%

53. A tank can be filled by two pipes A and B separately in 3 hours and 3 hours and 45 minutes respectively. A third pipe C can empty the full tank in 1 hour. When the tank was exact half-filled, all the three pipes are opened. The tank will become empty in

   (*a*) 1 hour and 15 minutes

   (*b*) 2 hours and 30 minutes

   (*c*) 3 hours and 15 minutes

   (*d*) 4 hours and 10 minutes

54. A and B together can do a piece of work in 36 days. If A word alone for the last 10 days, it is completed in 40 days. B alone can do the work in

   (*a*) 45 days   (*b*) 60 days

   (*c*) 75 days   (*d*) 90 days

55. 30 carpenters working 6 hours a day can make 750 chairs in 12 days. How many days will it take for 24 carpenters working 9 hours a day to make 1125 similar chairs ?

   (*a*) 18   (*b*) 15

   (*c*) 16   (*d*) 20

56. A train of length 150 m takes 10 seconds to pass another 100 m long train coming from the opposite direction. If the speed of the first train be 30 km/hr, the speed of the second train is

   (*a*) 36 km/hr   (*b*) 54 km/hr

   (*c*) 60 km/hr   (*d*) 62 km/hr

57. A boat covers a certain distance downstream in 8 hours and comes back upstream in 10 hours. If the speed of the current be 1 km/hr, the distance (in km) of the one-way journey is

   (*a*) 60   (*b*) 70

   (*c*) 80   (*d*) 90

58. A thief, seeing a policemen from a distance of 200 metres, starts running with a speed of 8 km/hr. The policeman gives chase immediately with a speed of 9 km/hr and the thief is caught. The distance run by the thief is

   (*a*) 2000 m   (*b*) 1800 m

   (*c*) 1600 m   (*d*) 1500 m

59. By selling an article at 80% of the marked price, there is a loss of 10%. If the article is sold at the marked price, the profit percent will be

   (*a*) 18.4   (*b*) 20

   (*c*) 12.5   (*d*) 15

60. By selling toffees at a rate of 20 for ₹ 10, a man loses 4%. To gain 20%, how many toffees must be sold for ₹ 10 ?

   (*a*) 16   (*b*) 20

   (*c*) 24   (*d*) 25

61. If the cost price of 12 articles is equal to the selling price of 9 articles, the gain per cent is

   (*a*) 20   (*b*) 25

   (*c*) $33\dfrac{1}{3}$ (*d*) $36\dfrac{4}{11}$

62. If A be the area of a right-angled triangle and b is the length of one of the sides containing the right angle, then the length of the altitude on the hypotenuse is

(a) $\dfrac{2Ab}{\sqrt{b^2 + 4A^2}}$ (b) $\dfrac{2Ab}{b^2 + 4A^2}$

(c) $\dfrac{2Ab}{\sqrt{b^4 + 4A^4}}$ (d) $\dfrac{2Ab}{\sqrt{b^4 + 4A^2}}$

63. The diagonal of a square is $16\sqrt{2}$ cm. Its perimeter is

(a) 48 cm   (b) 56 cm

(c) 64 cm   (d) 72 cm

64. The length, breadth and height of a room are respectively 5 metres, 4 metres and 3 metres. The length of the longest bamboo stick, that can be kept entirely into the room, is

(a) 5 m   (b) 60 m

(c) 7 m   (d) $5\sqrt{2}$ m

65. If the length of a rectangle is increased by one-third and its width is decreased by one-third, the percentage of decrease in its area will be

(a) $66\dfrac{2}{3}$ (b) $33\dfrac{1}{3}$

(c) $16\dfrac{2}{3}$ (d) $11\dfrac{1}{9}$

66. A right circular cylinder is formed by rolling a rectangular sheet of metal of length 24 cm and breadth 22 cm along its length. The volume of the cylinder is $\left(\text{use } \pi = \dfrac{22}{7} \right)$

(a) 924 cm³   (b) 462 cm³

(c) 264 cm³   (d) 528 cm³

Directions (Q. 67-69) : *A constituency was divided into four regions A, B, C and D. Two candidates X and Y contested the election from that constituency. The adjoining graph gives the breakup of voting in the four regions.*

Study the graph and answer the following questions

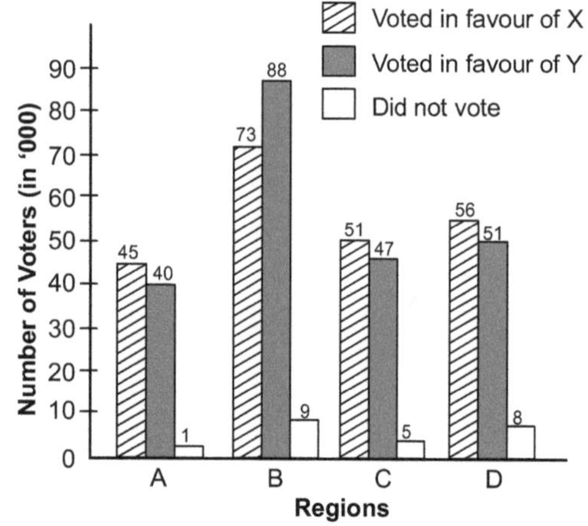

67. In which regions (s) did Y get more than 50% votes?

(a) A, C and D   (b) B

(c) A   (d) None of these

68. How many votes, in all, were there in the constituency ?

(a) 474   (b) 2,26,000

(c) 4,74,000   (d) 5,74,000

69. In which region of the constituency, the percentage of voters, who did not vote, was highest ?

(a) A   (b) B

(c) C   (d) D

70. In an examination, a student is awarded 4 marks for every correct answer and loses 2 marks for every wrong answer. If a student attempted all 75 questions and secured 150 marks, the number of question he attemped is

(a) 45   (b) 50

(c) 55   (d) 48

71. If $x = 8 + 2\sqrt{15}$, the value of $\sqrt{x} + \dfrac{1}{\sqrt{x}}$ is

(a) $2\sqrt{3}$ (b) $2\sqrt{5}$

(c) $\dfrac{3}{2}\sqrt{5} + \dfrac{\sqrt{3}}{2}$ (d) $\dfrac{\sqrt{5}}{2} + \dfrac{3}{2}\sqrt{3}$

72. The HCF and LCM of two numbers are respectively 12 and 2448. If the difference of the numbers is 60, their sum is

(a) 348   (b) 284

(c) 248   (d) 204

73. $\dfrac{1.\bar{3} \times 1.\bar{3} \times 1.\bar{3} - 1}{1.\bar{3} + 1.\bar{3} \times 1.\bar{3} + 1}$ is simplified to

(a) $\dfrac{1}{3}$

(b) $1\dfrac{1}{3}$

(c) $\dfrac{37}{91}$

(d) $\dfrac{27}{91}$

74. $\dfrac{0.73 \times 0.73 \times 0.73 + 0.27 \times 0.27 \times 0.27}{0.73 \times 0.73 - 0.73 \times 0.27 + 0.27 \times 0.27}$ is equal to

(a) 1   (b) 10

(c) 100   (d) 1000

75. The number of digits in $(48^4 \times 5^{12})$ is

(a) 18

(b) 16

(c) 14

(d) 12

GENERAL AWARENESS

76. How many scientists awarded with The 2016 Nobel Prize for their work on exotic states of matter?

(a) 5

(b) 2

(c) 4

(d) 3

77. Which one of the following countries *does not* have a common border with Iraq ?

(a) Jordan

(b) Syria

(c) Turkey

(d) Lebanon

78. In India, agricultural income is calculated by

(a) output method

(b) income method

(c) expenditure method

(d) commodity flow method

79. The Blue Revolution is related with

(a) fish production

(b) food grain production

(c) oilseed production

(d) milk production

80. The famous Kruger National Park is in

(a) Saudi Arabia

(b) South Africa

(c) Sudan

(d) Tanzania

81. "Interest is the reward for abstinence." Who says this ?

(a) Keynes

(b) Marshall

(c) Malthus

(d) David Ricardo

82. Which bank was earlier called the Imperial Bank of India ?

(a) RBI

(b) SBI

(c) UBI

(d) PNB

83. The Second Five Year Plan was based on

(a) Mahalanobis Model

(b) Vakil and Brahmananda's Wag Good Model

(c) Harrod-Domar Growth Model

(d) Solow Growth Model

84. Which International Airport has become First Asia-Pacific and one of the world's few airports to achieve a "Carbon Neutral" Status?

(a) Chatrapathi Shivaji

(b) Sardar Vallabhai Patel

(c) Kempegowda

(d) Indira Gandhi

85. The concept of Judicial Review in our Constitution has been taken from the Constitution of

(a) England

(b) USA

(c) Canada

(d) Australia

86. The Constitution of India was adopted on

(a) 26th January, 1950

(b) 26th January, 1949

(c) 26th November, 1949

(d) 15th August, 1947

87. In India, the Prime Minister remains in office so long as he enjoys the

(a) support of armed forces

(b) confidence of Rajya Sabha

(c) confidence of Lod Sabha

(d) support of the people

88. Who considered the Right to Constitutional Remedies as very 'heart and soul' of the Indian Constitution ?

(a) M.K. Gandhi

(b) J.L. Nehru

(c) B.R. Ambedkar

(d) Dr.Rajendra Prasad

89. Who decides whether a bill is a Money Bill or not?

(a) Speaker of the Lok Sabha

(b) The President

(c) The Prime Minister

(d) The Parliamentary Select Committee

90. Which one of the following writings is *not* related to Mahatma Gandhi ?

(a) My Experiments with Truth

(b) Harijan

(c) The Holy Family

(d) Hind Swaraj

91. SEZ stands for

(a) Southern Economic Zone

(b) South European Zone

(c) Special Economic Zone

(d) Special Eastern Zone

92. The highest score in an innings in Test Cricket has so far been made by

(a) Matthew Hayden

(b) Don Bradman

(c) Mahela Jayavardhane

(d) Drian Lara

93. Stethoscope works on the principle of
  (a) Conversion of current to sound
  (b) Conversion of sound to current
  (c) Reflection of sound
  (d) Reflection of light

94. In which phylum, octopus, snail, sepia and unio are included ?
  (a) Porifera   (b) Annelida
  (c) Mollusca   (d) Arthropoda

95. What is the scientific name of National Animal of India ?
  (a) Panthera leo   (b) Panthera tigris
  (c) Elephas indicus   (d) Bos domesticus

96. 27th June is the
  (a) World AIDS Day
  (b) World Diabetes Day
  (c) World Environment Day
  (d) World Population Day

97. Which of the following was **not** one of the titles assumed by the Chola King Rajendra ?
  (a) Tyagasamudra   (b) Gangikonda
  (c) Mudikonda   (d) Pandita Chola

98. What was the Capital of Kanishka ?
  (a) Purushapura   (b) Mathura
  (c) Taxila   (d) Pataliputra

99. Match the founders in List - I with the Bhakti Sects in List - II and select the correct answer using the code given below the Lists

List-I
  (a) Shankardeva
  (b) Jagjivan
  (c) Lalgin or Lalbeg
  (d) Govinda Prabhu

List-II
  1. Mahanubhava Panth
  2. Alakhnami
  3. Satnami
  4. Ek–Sarana–Dharma

Codes :

	A	B	C	D
(a)	4	3	2	1
(b)	4	2	1	3
(c)	1	4	3	2
(d)	1	2	4	3

100. Who has been awarded the 'Lata Mangeshkar Award for Lifetime Achievement' instituted by the Maharashtra government?
  (a) A R Rahman   (b) Uttam Singh
  (c) Maniratnam   (d) Premji

ANSWERS

1. (c)	**2.** (b)	**3.** (a)	**4.** (a)	**5.** (b)	**6.** (c)	**7.** (b)	**8.** (c)	**9.** (a)	**10.** (b)
11. (d)	**12.** (d)	**13.** (c)	**14.** (b)	**15.** (b)	**16.** (b)	**17.** (d)	**18.** (a)	**19.** (a)	**20.** (b)
21. (b)	**22.** (b)	**23.** (b)	**24.** (b)	**25.** (c)	**26.** (b)	**27.** (c)	**28.** (a)	**29.** (d)	**30.** (b)
31. (c)	**32.** (a)	**33.** (c)	**34.** (a)	**35.** (c)	**36.** (b)	**37.** (a)	**38.** (b)	**39.** (b)	**40.** (c)
41. (c)	**42.** (a)	**43.** (d)	**44.** (b)	**45.** (a)	**46.** (c)	**47.** (d)	**48.** (a)	**49.** (d)	**50.** (b)
51. (b)	**52.** (c)	**53.** (a)	**54.** (d)	**55.** (b)	**56.** (c)	**57.** (c)	**58.** (c)	**59.** (c)	**60.** (a)
61. (c)	**62.** (d)	**63.** (c)	**64.** (d)	**65.** (d)	**66.** (a)	**67.** (b)	**68.** (c)	**69.** (d)	**70.** (b)
71. (c)	**72.** (a)	**73.** (a)	**74.** (a)	**75.** (b)	**76.** (d)	**77.** (d)	**78.** (a)	**79.** (a)	**80.** (b)
81. (b)	**82.** (b)	**83.** (a)	**84.** (d)	**85.** (b)	**86.** (c)	**87.** (c)	**88.** (c)	**89.** (a)	**90.** (c)
91. (c)	**92.** (d)	**93.** (c)	**94.** (c)	**95.** (b)	**96.** (b)	**97.** (c)	**98.** (a)	**99.** (a)	**100.** (b)

EXPLANATIONS

1. Total height of 20 students $= 20 \times 105$
$$= 2100 \text{ cm}$$
Total height of 10 new students $= 10 \times 120$
$$= 1200 \text{ cm.}$$
$\therefore$ Total height of 30 students
$$= 2100 + 1200$$
$$= 3300 \text{ cm.}$$
$\therefore$ Average height of 30 students
$$= \frac{3300}{30} = 110 \text{ cm.}$$

3. 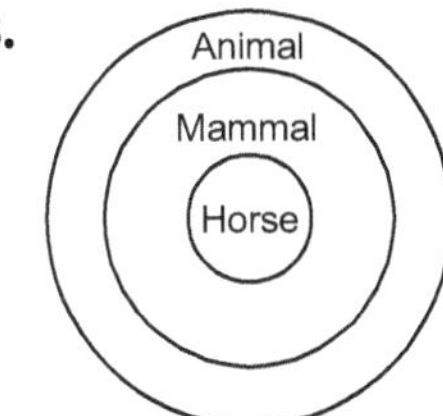

5. If in two different positions of a dice, the position of a common face be same then the opposite faces of the remaining faces are in the same position. As in the given question among the four positions in I and III the faces having two dots, are in same position. Therefore on the face opposite to the face with one dot, the number of dots will be 6.

9. As 'statue' is made by 'sculptor' similarly 'poem' is made by 'poet'.

10. As,　　　　　　　Similarly,

　　$A \xrightarrow{+5} F$　　　$D \xrightarrow{+9} M$

　　$B \xrightarrow{+5} G$　　　$E \xrightarrow{+9} N$

　　$D \xrightarrow{+5} I$　　　$G \xrightarrow{+9} P$

　　$C \xrightarrow{+5} H$　　　$F \xrightarrow{+9} O$

13. J L M K　S U V T　S V·U T　G I J H

16. W A B , X C D , Y E F , Z G H

17. 18 , 30 , 48 , 72 　(102)
　　　　+12　+18　+24　+30

18. In each subsequent figure $\frac{1}{4}$ part (shaded region) is increasing clockwise.

19. In each subsequent figure all the inner designs are shifting 90° clockwise. Inner design Γ is also shifting in the same direction 90°

20. D **M N N** | D **M N N** | D **M N N**

21. $5^2 + 7^2 + 3^2 + 4^2 = 99$
$7^2 + 6^2 + 2^2 + 5^2 = 114$
Similarly　　$? = 3^2 + 9^2 + 5^2 + 7^2$
$$= 164$$

22. $14 - 10 \div 4 \times 16 + 8 \rightarrow 14 \times 10 - 4 + 16 \div 8$
$$= 140 - 4 + 2 = 138.$$

23. Each letter in the word 'TABLE' is replaced by the letter which occupies the same position from the other end of the alphabet to obtain the code 'GZYOV'.

25. The letter 'U' of the word 'COUP' is not present in the word 'CONSTANTINOPLE'. Hence from the given word, 'CQUP' cannot be formed.

51. Let C.P. of goods $= ₹ \, P$ and shopkeeper marked $x\%$ more than the cost price.

From the question,

$$P \left(\frac{100 + x}{100} \right) \times \left(\frac{100 - 12.5}{100} \right) = P \, \frac{(100 + 5)}{100}$$

$\therefore \quad \dfrac{(100 + x)}{100} = 105 \times \dfrac{2}{175} = \dfrac{6}{5}$

$\Rightarrow \quad 100 + x = 120$

$$x = 120 - 100 = 20\%$$

52. Let cost price and market price of an article be $₹ \, x$ and $₹ \, P$ respectively.

Then, $\dfrac{(100 - 10)}{100} \times P = \dfrac{(100 + 20)}{100} \times x$

$\Rightarrow \qquad P = \dfrac{12}{9} x = \dfrac{4}{3} x$

Again, S.P. at a discount of 20%

$$= \frac{(100 - 20)}{100} \times P$$

$$= \frac{4}{5} P$$

$$= \frac{4}{5} \times \left(\frac{4}{3} x \right) = \frac{16}{15} x$$

$\therefore$ Required profit $= \dfrac{\left(\dfrac{16}{15} x - x \right)}{x} \times 100\%$

$$= \frac{100}{15} \%$$

$$= 6 \frac{2}{3} \%$$

53. If all the three pipes are opened,

$\because$ Part of the tank emptied in 1 hour

$$= 1 - \left(\frac{1}{3} + \frac{4}{15}\right) = 1 - \frac{9}{15} = \frac{2}{5}$$

$\Rightarrow$ Time taken to empty the full filled tank

$$= \frac{1}{\left(\frac{2}{5}\right)} = \frac{5}{2} \text{ hour}$$

$\therefore$ Time taken to empty the exact half filled tank

$$= \frac{1}{2} \times \frac{5}{2} \text{ hours}$$
$$= 1 \text{ hour } 15 \text{ minutes}$$

54. Work of (A + B) for 1 day $= \dfrac{1}{36}$

$\Rightarrow$ Work of (A + B) for 30 days $= 30 \times \dfrac{1}{36} = \dfrac{5}{6}$

$\therefore$ Remaining work after 30 days $= 1 - \dfrac{5}{6} = \dfrac{1}{6}$

Since work of A alone for 10 days $= \dfrac{1}{6}$

$\Rightarrow$ Work of A for 1 day $= \dfrac{1}{10} \times \dfrac{1}{6} = \dfrac{1}{60}$

$\Rightarrow$ Work of B alone for 1 day $= \dfrac{1}{36} - \dfrac{1}{60}$

$$= \frac{5 - 3}{180} = \frac{1}{90}$$

Hence B alone can do the work in 90 days.

55. Let number of required days $= D_2$

$\therefore \dfrac{M_2 \times D_2 \times H_2}{W_2} = \dfrac{M_1 \times D_1 \times H_1}{W_1}$

$\Rightarrow \dfrac{24 \times D_2 \times 9}{1125} = \dfrac{30 \times 12 \times 6}{750}$

$\therefore D_2 = \dfrac{72 \times 1125}{25 \times 24 \times 9}$

$$= \frac{45}{3} = 15 \text{ days}$$

56. Let speed of the second train $= x$ km/hr.

Since both the trains are running in opposite directions, therefore

relative speed of any train

$$= (30 + x) \text{ km/hr}$$
$$= (30 + x) \times \frac{5}{18} \text{ m/sec.}$$

Time taken to pass another train

$$= \frac{\text{Sum of lengths of both trains in metres}}{\text{Relative speed in m/sec}}$$

$\therefore \quad 10 = \dfrac{(150 + 100)m}{(30 + x) \times \dfrac{5}{18}}$

$\Rightarrow (30 + x) = \dfrac{250 \times 18}{10 \times 5} = 90$

$\Rightarrow x = 90 - 30 = 60 \text{ kms/hour}$

57. Let speed of the boat in still water $= U$ kmph

According to question,

$$(U + 1) \times 8 = (U - 1) \times 10$$

$\therefore \quad 4U + 4 = 5U - 5$

$\Rightarrow \quad U = 5 + 4 = 9 \text{ kmph}$

$\therefore$ Required distance of the one-way journey

$$= (9 + 1) \times 8$$
$$= 80 \text{ kms}$$

58. Relative speed of police-man with respect to thief

$$= (9 - 8) \text{ km/hr}$$
$$= 1 \times \frac{5}{18} \text{ m/sec.}$$

Time taken by police man to caught the thief

$$= \frac{200}{\left(\dfrac{5}{18}\right)}$$
$$= 40 \times 18 = 720 \text{ seconds}$$

$\therefore$ Distance run by the thief

$$= \text{Speed} \times \text{Time}$$
$$= \left(8 \times \frac{5}{18}\right) \times 720$$
$$= 40 \times 40 = 1600 \text{ metres}$$

59. Let cost-price and marked price of an article be ₹ x and ₹ y respectively,

$\therefore \quad y \times \dfrac{80}{100} = \dfrac{(100 - 10)}{100} \times x$

$$y = \frac{5}{4} \times \frac{9}{10} \times x$$
$$= \frac{9}{8} x$$

$\therefore$ Required profit per cent $= \dfrac{y - x}{x} \times 100\%$

$$= \frac{\dfrac{9}{8} x - x}{x} \times 100\%$$
$$= \frac{1}{8} \times 100\% = 12.5\%$$

60. Let x toffees must be sold for ₹ 10 to gain 20%

$\therefore$ S.P. of one toffee $= ₹ \dfrac{10}{x}$

Let cost price of one toffee $= ₹ y$

According to question,

$$\frac{(100-4)}{100}y = ₹\,\frac{1}{2}$$

$$\Rightarrow \qquad y = \frac{25}{24}\times\frac{1}{2} = ₹\,\frac{25}{48}$$

Since $\qquad \dfrac{10}{x} = \dfrac{(100+20)}{100}\times y$

$$= \frac{6}{5}\times\left(\frac{25}{48}\right) = \frac{5}{8}$$

$$\therefore \qquad x = \frac{10\times 8}{5} = 16$$

61. Required gain per cent $= \dfrac{12-9}{9}\times 100\%$

$$= \frac{1}{3}\times 100\% = 33\frac{1}{3}\%$$

62. Let length of one side and the altitude on the hypotenuse be x and p respectively.

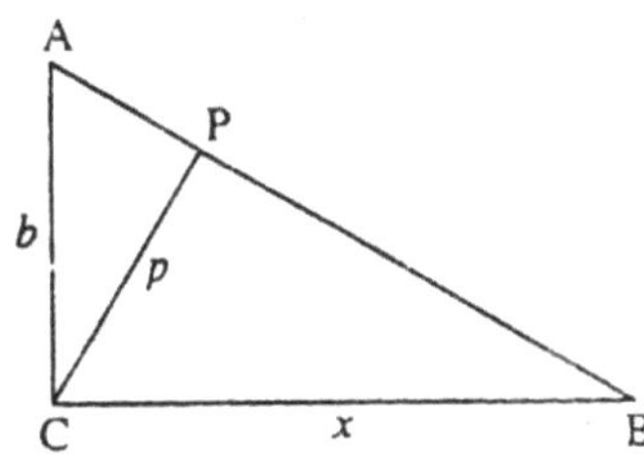

Area of $\triangle ABC = A = \dfrac{1}{2}\times b \times x$

$$= \frac{1}{2}\times p \times AB$$

$$\therefore \qquad x = \frac{2A}{b}$$

and $\qquad p = \dfrac{2A}{AB}$

But, $\quad AB^2 = x^2 + b^2$

$$\Rightarrow \quad AB = \sqrt{x^2 + b^2} = \sqrt{\left(\frac{2A}{b}\right)^2 + b^2}$$

$$\therefore \qquad p = \frac{2A}{\sqrt{x^2 + b^2}}$$

$$= \frac{2A}{\sqrt{\left(\frac{2A}{b}\right)^2 + b^2}}$$

$$= \frac{2A}{\sqrt{\frac{1}{b^2}(4A^2 + b^4)}}$$

$$= \frac{2A.b}{\sqrt{b^4 + 4A^2}}$$

63. Let length of one side of the square $= a$ cm

$\therefore$ Length of diagonal of square $= a\sqrt{2}$

$$= 16\sqrt{2}$$

$$\Rightarrow \qquad a = 16$$

$\therefore$ Perimeter of square $= 4 \times a$

$$= 4 \times 16$$

$$= 64 \text{ cm}$$

64. Length of the longest bamboo stick

$$= \sqrt{l^2 + b^2 + h^2}$$

$$= \sqrt{5^2 + 4^2 + 3^2}$$

$$= \sqrt{25 + 16 + 9}$$

$$= 5\sqrt{2} \text{ metres}$$

65. Percentage of decrease in area

$$= \frac{l\times b - \left(\frac{4}{3}l\right)\times\left(\frac{2}{3}b\right)}{l\times b}\times 100$$

$$= \frac{\left(1-\frac{8}{9}\right)}{1}\times 100 = \frac{100}{9} = 11\frac{1}{9}$$

66. Let radius of the circular cylinder $= R$ cm

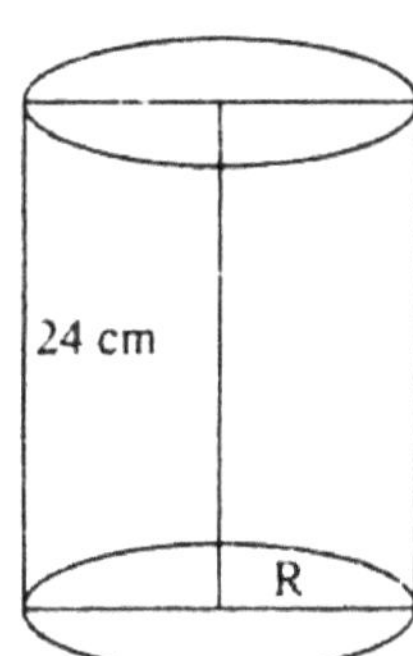

Since cylinder is formed by rolling the rectangular sheet along its length.

$\therefore 2\pi R = $ Breadth of the rectangular sheet

$$\Rightarrow \quad 2\times\frac{22}{7}\times R = 22 \text{ cm}^3$$

$$\therefore \qquad R = \frac{7}{2} \text{ cm}$$

$\therefore$ Volume of the cylinder $= \pi R^2 \times h$

$$= \frac{22}{7}\times\left(\frac{7}{2}\right)^2 \times 24$$

$$= 11 \times 7 \times 12$$

$$= 924 \text{ cm}^3$$

67. In region B, 'Y' got the votes

$$= \frac{88}{(73+88+9)} \times 100\% = \frac{8800}{170}\%$$

$$= 51.76\% \text{ (More than 50\% votes)}$$

68. Total number of voters in the constituency

$$= [86 + 170 + 103 + 115] \text{ (in thousand)}$$
$$= 474 \text{ thousands} = 474000$$

69. Percentage of voters, who did not vote in each constituency was as follows:

% in region A $= \dfrac{1}{86} \times 100\% = 1.16\%$

% in region B $= \dfrac{9}{170} \times 100\% = 5.29\%$

% in region C $= \dfrac{3}{103} \times 100\% = 4.85\%$

% in region D $= \dfrac{8}{115} \times 100\% = 6.95\%$

Hence highest percentage of voters, who did not vote was in the region = D

70. Let number of questions attempted correctly $= x$

Number of wrong answered questions

$$= (75 - x)$$

According to question,

Marks secured $= 4 \times x - 2 \times (75 - x)$

$$\therefore \quad 150 = 4x - 150 + 2x$$
$$\Rightarrow \quad 6x = 150 + 150 = 300$$
$$x = \frac{300}{6} = 50$$

71.
$$x = 8 + 2\sqrt{15}$$
$$= (5 + 3 + 2\sqrt{5 \times 3})$$
$$= (\sqrt{5} + \sqrt{3})^2$$
$$\therefore \quad \sqrt{x} = (\sqrt{5} + \sqrt{3})$$

$$\sqrt{x} + \frac{1}{\sqrt{x}} = (\sqrt{5}+\sqrt{3}) + \frac{1}{(\sqrt{5}+\sqrt{3})} \times \frac{(\sqrt{5}-\sqrt{3})}{(\sqrt{5}-\sqrt{3})}$$

$$= (\sqrt{5}+\sqrt{3}) + \frac{1}{2}(\sqrt{5}-\sqrt{3})$$

$$= \frac{3}{2}\sqrt{5} + \frac{\sqrt{3}}{2}$$

72. Let two numbers are x and y

According to question

Difference : $x - y = 60$ ...(1)

Product : $x \times y =$ H.C.F. $\times$ L.C.M

$$= 12 \times 2448 \quad ...(2)$$

Hence their sum

$$= x + y$$
$$= \sqrt{(x-y)^2 + 4x.y}$$
$$= \sqrt{(60)^2 + 4 \times (12 \times 2448)}$$
$$= \sqrt{(12 \times 5)^2 + (4 \times 12 \times 12 \times 204)}$$
$$= 12\sqrt{25 + 816}$$
$$= 12\sqrt{841} = 12 \times 29 = 348$$

73. $1.\overline{3} = 1 + \dfrac{3}{9} = 1 + \dfrac{1}{3} = \dfrac{4}{3}$

$\therefore$ Given Expression $= \dfrac{1.\overline{3} \times 1.\overline{3} \times 1.\overline{3} - 1}{1.\overline{3} + 1.\overline{3} \times 1.\overline{3} + 1}$

$$= \frac{\left(\dfrac{4}{3}\right)^3 - 1}{\left(\dfrac{4}{3}\right) + \left(\dfrac{4}{3}\right)^2 + 1}$$

$$[\because a^3 - b^3 = (a-b)(a^2 + ab + b^2)]$$

$$= \frac{\left(\dfrac{4}{3} - 1\right)\left[\left(\dfrac{4}{3}\right)^2 + \left(\dfrac{4}{3}\right) + 1\right]}{\left[\left(\dfrac{4}{3}\right)^2 + \left(\dfrac{4}{3}\right) + 1\right]}$$

$$= \frac{4}{3} - 1 = \frac{1}{3}$$

74. Given Expression

$$= \frac{0.73 \times 0.73 \times 0.73 + 0.27 \times 0.27 \times 0.27}{0.73 \times 0.73 - 0.73 \times 0.27 + 0.27 \times 0.27}$$

$$= \frac{(0.73)^3 + (0.27)^3}{(0.73)^2 - (0.73) \times (0.27) + (0.27)^2}$$

$$= \frac{a^3 + b^3}{a^2 - a.b + b^2} \text{ (Here } 0.73 = a \text{ and } 0.27 = b)$$

$$= \frac{(a+b)(a^2 - ab + b^2)}{(a^2 - ab + b^2)}$$

$$= a + b = 0.73 + 0.27$$
$$= 1.00 = 1$$

75. Given Number $= 48^4 \times 5^{12}$

$$= (3 \times 2^4)^4 \times 5^{12} = 3^4 \times 2^{16} \times 5^{12}$$
$$= 3^4 \times 2^4 \times 2^{12} \times 5^{12}$$
$$= 6^4 \times 10^{12} = 1296 \times 10^{12}$$
$$= 1296000000000000$$

$\therefore$ Number of digit in $(48^4 \times 5^{12}) = 4 + 12 = 16$

PRACTICE SET – 18

GENERAL INTELLIGENCE

1. In the following question, the number of letters skipped in between adjacent letters in the series is 5. Which of the following series observes this rule ?

   (a) X D I P V
   (b) X D K P V
   (c) X D J O U
   (d) X D J P V

Directions : *From among the given alternatives select the one in which the set of numbers is most like the set of numbers given in the question.*

2. Given set (3, 4, 5)

   (a) (6, 8, 10)
   (b) (9, 12, 15)
   (c) (6, 7, 8)
   (d) (12, 16, 20)

Directions : *Arrange the following words in a meaningful order.*

3. (1) Rain   (2) Vaporization
   (3) Water   (4) Condensation
   (5) Cloud

   (a) 1, 3, 2, 4, 5
   (b) 5, 3, 4, 1, 2
   (c) 3, 2, 5, 4, 1
   (d) 2, 3, 5, 4, 1

Directions : *In question 5, which one set of letters when sequentially placed at the gaps in given letter series shall complete it?*

4. ca – bd – ec – fd – ge?

   (a) b, c, d, e
   (b) b, d, c, e
   (c) b, c, e, d
   (d) d, b, c, e

Directions (Q. 5 – 7) : *Find the missing number letters / figure from the given responses.*

5. $\dfrac{A}{5}, \dfrac{D}{9}, \dfrac{H}{15}, \dfrac{M}{22}, ?$

   (a) $\dfrac{R}{30}$
   (b) $\dfrac{S}{30}$
   (c) $\dfrac{Q}{31}$
   (d) $\dfrac{Q}{30}$

6. ZCBA, YFED, XIHG,?

   (a) WLKM
   (b) WJKL
   (c) WKLJ
   (d) WLKJ

7. **Question figures**

Answer figures

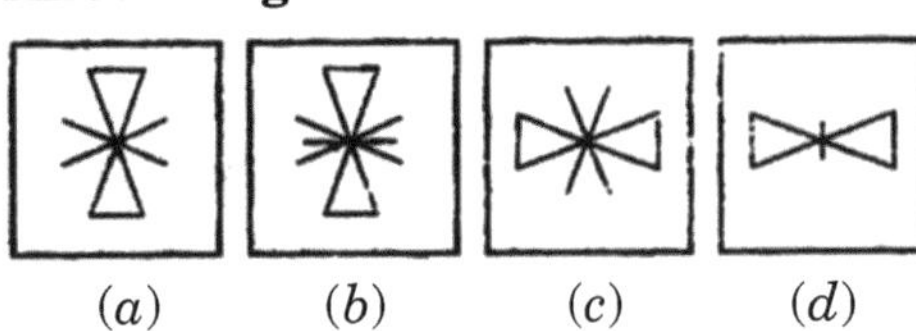

(a)   (b)   (c)   (d)

8. A is father of C and D is son of B. E is brother of A. If C is sister of D how is B related to E?

   (a) Sister-in-law
   (b) Sister
   (c) Brother
   (d) Brother-in-law

9. The difference between a mother's age and the sum of her two daughter's age is 6. The average age of two daughters is 22. What is the age of mother?

   (a) 40
   (b) 44
   (c) 46
   (d) 50

10. Of the six members of a panel sitting in a row, X is to the left of Q but on the right of P. Y is on the right of Q but is on the left of Z, Z is to the left of R. Find the members who are at the extreme?

    (a) QZ
    (b) XZ
    (c) PR
    (d) QY

Directions (Q. 11): *A word given in Capital Letters is followed by four answer words. Out of these only one cannot be formed by using the letters of the given words. Find out that word.*

11. INTEGRAL

    (a) ENTREATY
    (b) TRIANGLE
    (c) RELATING
    (d) ALERTING

12. If PALE is coded as 2134, EARTH is CODED as 41590, how is PEARL coded in that code?

    (a) 29530
    (b) 24153
    (c) 25413
    (d) 25430

13. Which one of the following is correct?

    6* 4* 9* 15

    (a) ×, =, –
    (b) ×, –, =
    (c) =, ×, –
    (d) –, ×, =

Directions (Q. 14) : *Find the missing number from the given responses*

14.

5	20	6	9
4	8	15	3
9	25	7	9
22	7	8	?

  (a) 7   (b) 8

  (c) 9   (d) 10

15. Ravi started walking from his house east direction to Bus stop which is 3 km away. Then he set off in the bus straight towards his right to the school 4 km away. What is the crow flight distance from his house to the school?

  (a) 1 km

  (b) 5 km

  (c) 7 km

  (d) 12 km

16. Choose from the four answer figures the figure that will be formed when question figure is folded into a box.

Question figures

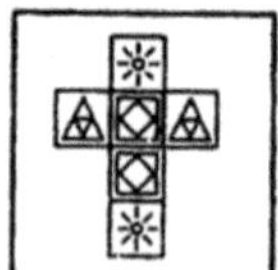

Answer figures

    (a)   (b)   (c)   (d)

17. Two positions of a cube are given. Based on them find out which number is found opposite number 4 in a given cube?

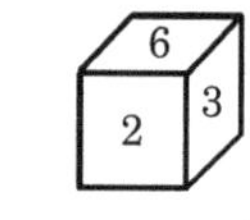 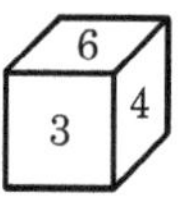

  (a) 1   (b) 2

  (c) 3   (d) 4

Directions : *In question 27, a statement is followed by two conclusions I and II. You have to consider the statement to be true, even if it seems to be at variance from commonly known facts. You are to decide which of the given conclusions can definitely be drawn from the given statements. Indicate your answer.*

18. Statements :

  Happiness derived from external materials in momentary. Everlasting happiness has to come from within.

Conclusions :

  I. Nobody can experience happiness from outside.

  II. Happiness experienced happiness from cinema is not lasting.

  (a) Only I follows

  (b) Only II follows

  (c) Neither I nor II follow

  (d) Both I and II follow

19. Select the diagram which best represents the relationship between educated people, unemployed and teachers

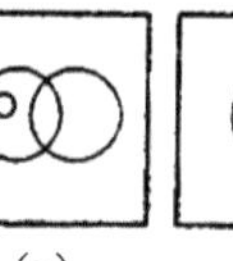 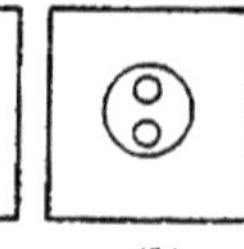 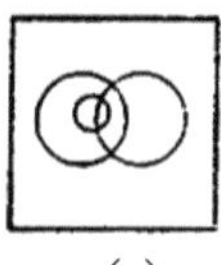 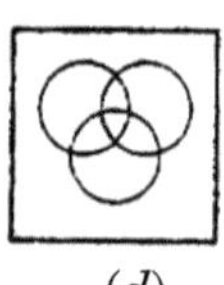

    (a)   (b)   (c)   (d)

20. Which Answer figure will complete the Question figure?

Question figure

Answer figures

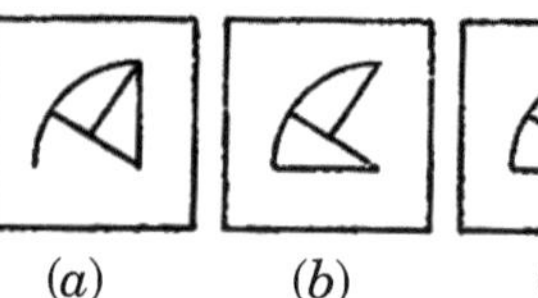

    (a)   (b)   (c)   (d)

Directions : *In question No. 32, from the given Answer figures, select the one in which the Question figure is hidden / embedded.*

21. Question figure

Answer figures

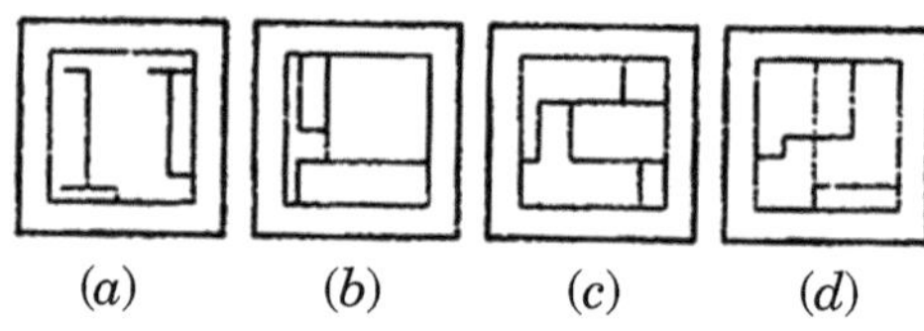

    (a)   (b)   (c)   (d)

Directions(Q. 22 – 23) : *Select the related letters / word / number / figure from the given alternatives.*

22. Framework : House : : Skeleton : ?

  (a) Ribs

  (b) Skull

  (c) Body

  (d) Grace

23. Question figures

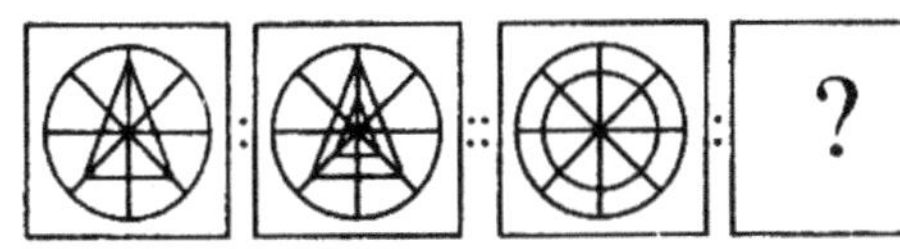

Answer figures

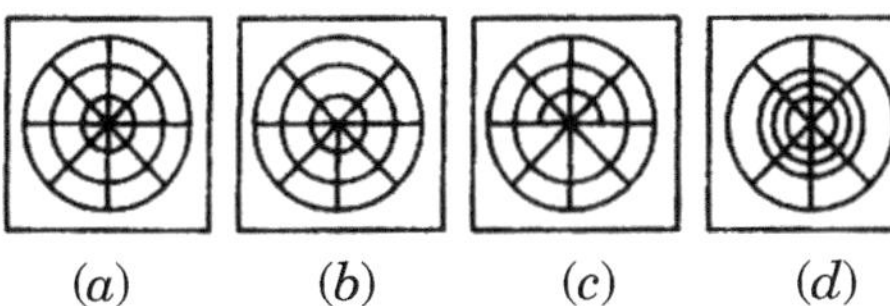

(a) (b) (c) (d)

Directions(Q. 24) : *Find the odd word / letters / number / figure from the given responses.*

24. (a) 1023 – 1046 (b) 1169 – 1192

(c) 1494 – 1517 (d) 1899 – 1921

Directions : *A series of figures is given which can be grouped into classes. Select the group into which the figures can be classified from the given responses.*

25.

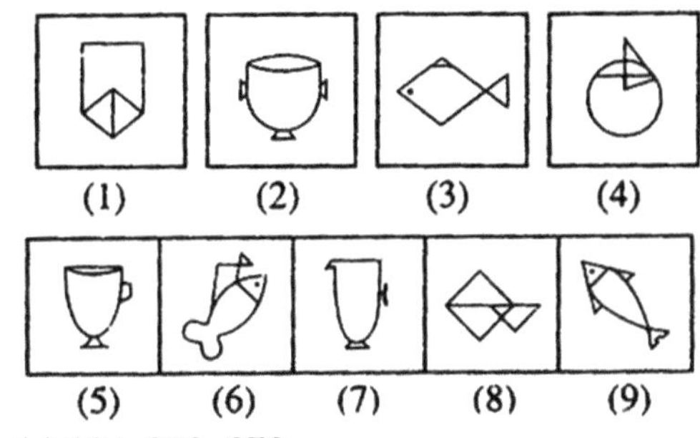

(a) 134, 259, 678

(b) 148, 257, 369

(c) 256, 348, 179

(d) 348, 235, 167

ENGLISH LANGUAGE

Directions (Q. 26-27) : *Out of the four alternatives, choose the one which best expresses the meaning of the given word and mark it in the Answer sheet.*

26. Forbearance

(a) relevance (b) deliverance

(c) patience (d) extravagance

27. Bequeath

(a) surround (b) give

(c) disclose (d) scold

Directions (Q. 28-29) : *Choose the word opposite in meaning to the given word and mark it in the Answer Sheet.*

28. Niggard

(a) Miserly

(b) Extravagant

(c) Revolve

(d) Generous

29. Amenable

(a) Unwilling (b) Acquiescent

(c) Distrustful (d) Inattentive

Directions (Q. 30-32) : *Out of the four alternatives choose the one which can be substituted for the given words / sentence.*

30. A person who thinks only about himself and not about others' needs:

(a) egocentric (b) egomaniacal

(c) egoistic (d) egotistic

31. Something that cannot be explained:

(a) inexplicable (b) unthinkable

(c) impregnable (d) mysterious

32. A written declaration made on oath in the presence of a magistrate:

(a) document (b) affidavit

(c) dossier (d) voucher

Directions (Q. 33-35) : *Four alternatives are given for the Idiom / phrase underlined in the sentence. Choose the alternative which best expresses the meaning of the Idiom / phrase and mark it in the Answer-Sheet.*

33. She didn't realize that the clever salesman was <u>taking her for a ride</u>.

(a) forcing her to go with him

(b) trying to trick her

(c) taking her in a car

(d) pulling her along

34. I <u>jumped out of my skin</u> when the explosion happened.

(a) was angry (b) was in panic

(c) was excited (d) was nervous

35. There is no point in discussing the new project with him as he always <u>pours cold water on</u> any new ideas.

(a) postpones (b) puts off

(c) dislikes (d) disapproves of

Direction (Q. 36) : *Four words are given in each question, out of which only one word is correctly spelt. Find the correctly spelt word and indicate it in the Answer Sheet by blackening the appropriate rectangle [■] .*

36. (a) veterinerian

(b) vaterinerian

(c) veterinarian

(d) vetarinerian

Directions (Q. 37-39) : *In following questions some parts of the sentences have errors and some have none. Find out which part of a sentence has an error and blacken the rectangle [■] corresponding to the appropriate letter (a, b, c). If a sentence is free from error, blacken the rectangle corresponding to (d) in the Answer Sheet.*

37. The N.C.C commandant along with his cadets (*a*)/are going to Delhi (*b*)/ to participate in the Republic Day Parade. (*c*)/ No error. (*d*)

38. World is producing enough (*a*)/ for every citizen but still there is hunger and malnutrition (*b*)/ and it is continuing year after year. (*c*)/ No error. (*d*)

39. Many of the famous (*a*)/ advertising offices (*b*)/ are located at Madison Avenue. (*c*)/ No error. (*d*)

Directions (Q. 40-42): *Sentences are given with blanks to be filled in with an appropriate word(s). Four alternatives are suggested for each question. Choose the correct alternative out of the four and indicate it by blackening the appropriate rectangle [■] in the Answer Sheet.*

40. As you sow _______ shall you reap.
    (*a*) so
    (*b*) when
    (*c*) as
    (*d*) like

41. It took him a long time _______ the candidate's application.
    (*a*) to consider and to weigh
    (*b*) to considering
    (*c*) to consider and weigh
    (*d*) considering weighing

42. Who is the person you _______ at the cinema last night?
    (*a*) had recognised
    (*b*) were recognising
    (*c*) recognised
    (*d*) have recognised

Directions (Q. 43-45) : *A part of the sentence is underlined. Below are given alternatives to the underlined part at (a), (b), (c) which may improve the sentence. Choose the correct alternative. In case no improvement is needed your answer is (d). Mark your answer in the Answer Sheet.*

43. It took her a long time to get <u>past</u> her failure in the medical examination.
    (*a*) through
    (*b*) over
    (*c*) by
    (*d*) No improvement

44. He was asleep before the mother tucked him <u>off</u>.
    (*a*) through
    (*b*) away
    (*c*) in
    (*d*) No improvement

45. I did not agree with him; he appeared to be <u>so</u> bigoted for me to concur.
    (*a*) much
    (*b*) very
    (*c*) too
    (*d*) No improvement

Directions (Q. 46-50) : *You have a brief passages with 5 questions. Read the passages carefully and choose the best answer to each question out of the four alternatives and mark it by blackening the appropriate rectangle [■] in the Answer Sheet.*

"People very often complain that poverty is a great evil and that it is not possible to be happy unless one has a lot of money. Actually, this is not necessarily true. Even a poor man, living in a small hut with none of the comforts and luxuries of life, may be quite contented with his lot and achieve a measure of happiness. On the other hand, a very rich man, living in a palace and enjoying everything that money can buy, may still be miserable, if, for example, he does not enjoy good health or his only son has taken to evil ways. A part from this, he may have a lot of business worries which keep him on tenterhooks most of the time. There is a limit to what money can buy and there are many things which are necessary for a man's happiness and which money cannot procure.

Real happiness is a matter of the right attitude and the capacity of being contented with whatever you have is the most important ingredient of this attitude".

46. Which of the following is the most appropriate title to the passage?
    (*a*) Money and contentment
    (*b*) Poverty, a great evil
    (*c*) The key of happiness
    (*d*) Contentment, the key to happiness

47. Which of the following statement is true?
    (*a*) A poor but contented man is always happy
    (*b*) Only a poor but contented man can be happy
    (*c*) A poor but contented man can never be happy
    (*d*) A poor but contented man can be happy

48. It is true that:
    (*a*) money alone cannot give happiness
    (*b*) money alone can give happiness
    (*c*) money always gives happiness
    (*d*) money seldom gives happiness

49. A rich man's life may become miserable if he:
    (*a*) has business worries and his only son has taken to evil ways
    (*b*) has evil son, bad health and business worries
    (*c*) does not enjoy good health
    (*d*) has business worries

50. The phrase "on tenterhooks" means:

(a) in a state of forgetfulness

(b) in a state of thoughtfulness

(c) in a state of anxiety

(d) in a state of sadness

QUANTITATIVE APTITUDE

51. If a sum of money at simple interest doubles in 12 years, the rate of interest per annum is

(a) $16\frac{2}{3}\%$

(b) 7.5%

(c) $8\frac{1}{3}\%$

(d) 10%

52. In what time will ₹ 10,000 amount to ₹ 12,310 at 20% per annum compounded half yearly?

(a) $1\frac{1}{2}$ years

(b) 2 years

(c) $2\frac{1}{2}$ years

(d) 3 years

53. A shopkeeper marks his goods 30% above his cost price but allows a discount of 10% at the time of sale. His gain is

(a) 21%

(b) 20%

(c) 18%

(d) 17%

54. An article is sold at a discount of 20% and an additional discount of 30% is allowed on cash payment. If Vidya purchased the article by paying ₹ 2,240 in cash, the marked price of the article was

(a) ₹ 4,000

(b) ₹ 4,368

(c) ₹ 4,400

(d) ₹ 4,480

55. A shopkeeper earns a profit of 12% on selling a book at 10% discount on the printed price. The ratio of the cost price and the printed price of the book is

(a) 99 : 125

(b) 25 : 37

(c) 50 : 61

(d) 45 : 56

56. Working 5 hours a day, A can complete a work in 8 days and working 6 hours a day, B can complete the same work in 10 days. Working 8 hours a day, they can jointly complete the work in

(a) 3 days

(b) 4 days

(c) 4.5 days

(d) 5.4 days

57. 40 men can complete a work in 40 days. They started the work together. But at the end of each 10th day, 5 men left the job. The work would have been completed in

(a) $56\frac{2}{3}$ days

(b) $53\frac{1}{3}$ days

(c) 52 days

(d) 50 days

58. A tank has a leak which would empty the completely filled tank in 10 hours. If the tank is full of water and a tap is opened which admits 4 litres of water per minute in the tank, the leak takes 15 hours to empty the tank. How many litres of water does the tank hold?

(a) 2,400

(b) 4,500

(c) 1,200

(d) 7,200

59. A and B started at the same time from the same place for a certain destination. B walking at $\frac{5}{6}$ of A's speed reached the destination 1 hour 15 minutes after A. B reached the destination in

(a) 6 hours 45 minutes

(b) 7 hours 15 minutes

(c) 7 hours 30 minutes

(d) 8 hours 15 minutes

60. Two trains started at the same time, one from A to B and the other from B to A. If they arrived at B and A respectively 4 hours and 9 hours after they passed each other, the ratio of the speeds of the two trains was

(a) 2 : 1

(b) 3 : 2

(c) 4 : 3

(d) 5 : 4

61. Two men start together from the same place in the same direction to go round a circular path. If one takes 10 minutes and the other takes 15 minutes to make one complete round they will meet after

(a) 30 minutes

(b) 33 minutes

(c) 40 minutes

(d) 45 minutes

62. A moving train crosses a man standing on a platform and a bridge 300 metres long in 10 seconds and 25 seconds respectively. What will be the time taken by the train to cross a platform 200 metres long?

(a) $16\frac{2}{3}$ seconds

(b) 18 seconds

(c) 20 seconds

(d) 22 seconds

63. A man goes downstream with a boat to some destination and returns upstream to his original place in 5 hours. If the speed of the boat in still water and the stream are 10 km/hr and 4 km/hr respectively, the distance of the destination from the starting place is

(a) 16 km (b) 18 km

(c) 21 km (d) 25 km

64. A businessman sells a commodity at 10% profit. If he had bought it at 10% less and sold if for ₹ 2 less, then he would have gained $16\dfrac{2}{3}\%$. The cost price of the commodity is

(a) ₹ 32 (b) ₹ 36

(c) ₹ 40 (d) ₹ 48

65. A sells an article to B at a profit of 10%. B sells the article back to A at a loss of 10%. In this transaction

(a) A neither loses nor gains

(b) A makes a profit of 11%

(c) A makes a profit of 20%

(d) B loses 20%

66. The ratio, in which tea costing ₹ 192 per kg is to be mixed tea costing ₹ 150 per kg so that the mixed tea, when sold for ₹ 194.40 per kg, gives a profit of 20%, is

(a) 2 : 5

(b) 3 : 5

(c) 5 : 3

(d) 5 : 2

67. On the basis of selling price of an article, the loss is calculated to be 25%. The percentage of loss on the basis of cost price is

(a) 18

(b) 20

(c) 22

(d) 25

68. If the difference between areas of the circumcircle and the incircle of an equilateral triangle is 44 cm², then the area of the triangle is $\left(\text{Take } \pi = \dfrac{22}{7}\right)$

(a) 28 cm²

(b) $7\sqrt{3}$ cm²

(c) $14\sqrt{3}$ cm²

(d) 21 cm²

69. A wire, when bent in the form of a square, encloses a region having area 121 cm². If the same wire is bent into the form of a circle, then the area of the circle is $\left(\text{Take } \pi = \dfrac{22}{7}\right)$

(a) 144 cm² (b) 180 cm²

(c) 154 cm² (d) 176 cm²

70. If the area of a circle inscribed in a square is 9π cm², then the area of the square is

(a) 24 cm² (b) 30 cm²

(c) 36 cm² (d) 81 cm²

71. The total surface area of a solid hemisphere is 108π cm². The volume of the hemisphere is

(a) 72π cm³ (b) 144π cm³

(c) $108\sqrt{6}$ cm³ (d) $54\sqrt{6}$ cm³

Directions (Q. 72 –74) : *The table given above depicts the export of a commodity through four ports in the year 1998 and 1999.*

Port	Export in 1998 (in crore rupees)	Export in 1999 (in crore rupees)
A	57	61
B	148	160
C	229	234
D	146	150

72. The percentage increase in the export of the commodity from the year 1998 to 1999 was the hightest from which port?

(a) A (b) B

(c) C (d) D

73. What was the change in the aggregate export of the commodity in the year 1999 as compared to the year 1998?

(a) Nearly 4.3% increase

(b) Nearly 4.3% decrease

(c) Nearly 0.04% increase

(d) Nearly 0.04% decrease

74. What was the average increase in the export of the commodity from the ports in the year 1999 as compared to the year 1998?

(a) ₹ 8,25,00,000 (b) ₹ 8,00,000,00

(c) ₹ 7,50,00,000 (d) ₹ 6,25,000,00

75. $\dfrac{(5.624)^3 + (4.376)^3}{5.624 \times 5.624 - (5.624 \times 4.376) + 4.376 \times 4.376}$

(a) 10 (b) 1.248

(c) 20.44 (d) 1

GENERAL AWARENESS

76. Who took charge as a Chief Coach of the table tennis national team after Rio Olympics?

(a) Tom Lodziak

(b) Jiang Yongning

(c) Peter Karlsson

(d) Massimo Costantini

77. Why two thin shirts can keep us warmer than a single thick shirt in winter?

(a) Two thin shirts become thicker so prevent transmission of heat

(b) Air layer between two shirts works as good conductor

(c) Air layer between two shirts behaves like insulating media

(d) No radiation of heat takes place

78. Which layer of the earth's atmosphere reflect back radio waves to the earth's surface?

(a) Ionosphere

(b) Stratosphere

(c) Mesosphere

(d) Exosphere

79. Sound cannot pass through

(a) Water

(b) Steel

(c) Air

(d) Vacuum

80. Helium gas is used in gas balloons instead of hydrogen gas because it is

(a) lighter than hydrogen

(b) more abundant than hydrogen

(c) non-combustible

(d) more stable

81. The gas used in the artificial of fruits is

(a) acetylene

(b) methane

(c) ethane

(d) butane

82. Which of the following pairs is incorrent?

(a) Amirkhusro   – Sarod

(b) Bhim Sen Joshi   – Vocal music

(c) Utpal Dutt   – Films

(d) Shambhu Maharaj – Kathak

83. Which of the following country had moved out of the SAARC summit in Pakistan in November, citing an "unsuitable environment" for the annual gathering of South Asian leaders?

(a) Bangladesh

(b) Bhutan

(c) Afghanistan

(d) All the above

84. In a photocell light energy is converted into

(a) potential energy

(b) chemical energy

(c) heat energy

(d) electrical energy

85. According to WHO, the bird flu virus cannot be transmitted through food cooked beyond

(a) 60 degrees celsius

(b) 70 degrees celsius

(c) 90 degrees celsius

(d) 100 degrees celsius

86. The science of map-making is

(a) Cartography

(b) Geography

(c) Carpology

(d) Geology

87. Who is known as 'the father of Indian missile technology'?

(a) Dr. U. R. Rao

(b) Dr. A.P. J Abdul Kalam

(c) Dr. Chidambaram

(d) Dr. Homi Bhabha

88. Who is the author of 'A River Sutra' ?

(a) V.S. Naipaul

(b) Nirad C. Choudhuri

(c) Gita Mehta

(d) Vikram Seth

89. The capital of IMF is made up by contribution of the

(a) credit

(b) deficit financing

(c) member nations

(d) borrowings

90. Where is the National Academy of Agricultural Research Management located?

(a) Dehradun

(b) Hyderabad

(c) New Delhi

(d) Itanagar

91. Which Amendment Act introduced changes in the preamble to the Indian Constitution?

(a) The 38th Amendment Act, 1975

(b) The 40th Amendment Act, 1976

(c) The 42nd Amendment Act, 1976

(d) The 44th Amendment Act, 1979

92. The original name of Tansen, the most famous musician at the court of Akbar was

(a) Lal Kalwant

(b) Banda Bahadur

(c) Ramatanu Pande

(d) Markandey Pande

93. Who was the Governor-General of India during the Revolt of 1857?

(a) Lord Dalhousie

(b) Lord Canning

(c) Lord Mayo

(d) Lord Ripon

94. Which one of the following is an abiotic and renewable resource?

(a) Iron ore

(b) Livestock

(c) Water

(d) Forests

95. The capital of Tanzania is

(*a*) Nairobi   (*b*) Lusaka

(*c*) Kampala   (*d*) Dar-es-Salaam

96. The Andaman group and Nicobar group of islands are separated from each other by

(*a*) Ten Degree Channel

(*b*) Great Channel

(*c*) Bay of Bengal

(*d*) Andaman Sea

97. The vitamin that helps in blood clotting is

(*a*) Vitamin C   (*b*) Vitamin D

(*c*) Vitamin E   (*d*) Vitamin K

98. Which of the following is a perfect match?

(*a*) Coronary attack–Vascular dilation

(*b*) Atherosclerosis – Blockage of arteries

(*c*) Hypertension – Low blood pressure

(*d*) Hypotension – Heart attack

99. 'IC Chips' for computers are usually made of

(*a*) chromium   (*b*) silicon

(*c*) lead   (*d*) copper

100. Which country has passed a bill giving its small Hindu Minority the right to register marriages?

(*a*) United States   (*b*) Afghanistan

(*c*) Pakistan   (*d*) Russia

ANSWERS

1. (*d*)	**2.** (*c*)	**3.** (*c*)	**4.** (*a*)	**5.** (*b*)	**6.** (*d*)	**7.** (*a*)	**8.** (*a*)	**9.** (*d*)	**10.** (*c*)
11. (*a*)	**12.** (*b*)	**13.** (*b*)	**14.** (*a*)	**15.** (*b*)	**16.** (*d*)	**17.** (*b*)	**18.** (*b*)	**19.** (*a*)	**20.** (*b*)
21. (*b*)	**22.** (*c*)	**23.** (*a*)	**24.** (*d*)	**25.** (*b*)	**26.** (*c*)	**27.** (*b*)	**28.** (*d*)	**29.** (*a*)	**30.** (*a*)
31. (*a*)	**32.** (*b*)	**33.** (*b*)	**34.** (*b*)	**35.** (*d*)	**36.** (*c*)	**37.** (*b*)	**38.** (*d*)	**39.** (*c*)	**40.** (*a*)
41. (*c*)	**42.** (*a*)	**43.** (*b*)	**44.** (*c*)	**45.** (*c*)	**46.** (*d*)	**47.** (*d*)	**48.** (*a*)	**49.** (*b*)	**50.** (*c*)
52. (*c*)	**52.** (*a*)	**53.** (*d*)	**54.** (*a*)	**55.** (*d*)	**56.** (*a*)	**57.** (*a*)	**58.** (*d*)	**59.** (*c*)	**60.** (*b*)
61. (*a*)	**62.** (*c*)	**63.** (*c*)	**64.** (*c*)	**65.** (*b*)	**66.** (*a*)	**67.** (*b*)	**68.** (*c*)	**69.** (*c*)	**70.** (*c*)
71. (*b*)	**72.** (*b*)	**73.** (*a*)	**74.** (*d*)	**75.** (*a*)	**76.** (*d*)	**77.** (*c*)	**78.** (*a*)	**79.** (*d*)	**80.** (*a*)
81. (*a*)	**82.** (*a*)	**83.** (*d*)	**84.** (*d*)	**85.** (*b*)	**86.** (*a*)	**87.** (*b*)	**88.** (*c*)	**89.** (*c*)	**90.** (*b*)
91. (*c*)	**92.** (*c*)	**93.** (*b*)	**94.** (*c*)	**95.** (*d*)	**96.** (*a*)	**97.** (*d*)	**98.** (*d*)	**99.** (*b*)	**100.** (*c*)

EXPLANATIONS

1. X $\xrightarrow{+5}$ D $\xrightarrow{+5}$ J $\xrightarrow{+5}$ P $\xrightarrow{+5}$ V

2. 3 $\xrightarrow{+1}$ 4 $\xrightarrow{+1}$ 5 and 6 $\xrightarrow{+1}$ 7 $\xrightarrow{+1}$ 8

4. ca<u>b</u> | bd<u>c</u> | ec<u>d</u> | fd<u>e</u> | ge

5. $\dfrac{A}{4} \xrightarrow{+3} \dfrac{D}{9} \xrightarrow{+5} \dfrac{H}{15} \xrightarrow{+7} \dfrac{M}{22} \xrightarrow{+9} \dfrac{S}{30} \xrightarrow{+11}$

6. Z $\xrightarrow{-1}$ Y $\xrightarrow{-1}$ X $\xrightarrow{-1}$ W

C $\xrightarrow{+3}$ F $\xrightarrow{+3}$ I $\xrightarrow{+3}$ L

B $\xrightarrow{+3}$ E $\xrightarrow{+3}$ H $\xrightarrow{+3}$ K

A $\xrightarrow{+3}$ D $\xrightarrow{+3}$ G $\xrightarrow{+3}$ J

7. In each subsequent problem figure the design moves through 90° and one line is increased.

8.

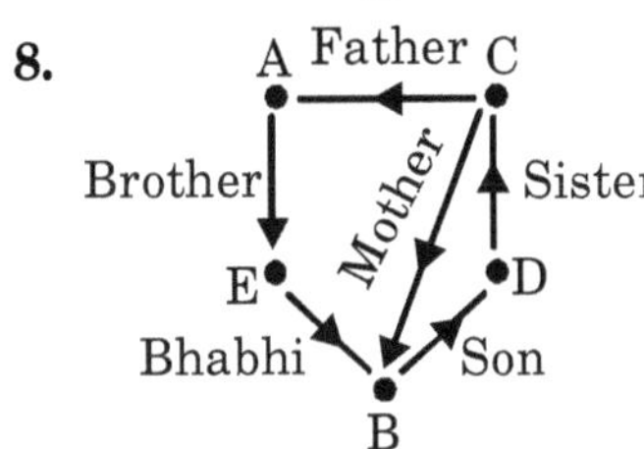

9. Let ages of daughters be x years and y years respectively.

$\therefore \qquad x + y = 2 \times 22 = 44$

$\therefore$ Age of mother = $44 + 6 = 50$ years

10.
●   ●   ●   ●   ●   ●
R   Z   Y   Q   X   P

11. There is no Y in the given word.

12.

P →	2	E →	4
A →	1	A →	1
L →	3	R →	5
E →	4	T →	9
		H →	0

Hence P → 2, E → 4, A → 1, R → 5, L → 3

13. $6 \times 4 - 9 = 15$

14. In row I $\quad 5 + 6 + 9 = 20$

In row II $\quad 4 + 8 + 3 = 15$

In row III $\quad 9 + 7 + 9 = 25$

In row IV $\quad 7 + 8 + \boxed{7} = 22$

15.

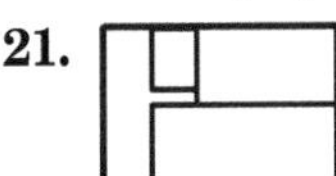

$AC = \sqrt{(3)^2 + (4)^2} = \sqrt{9 + 16} = \sqrt{25} = 5$ km

19.

All teachers are literate and some educated are unemployed.

21.

23. From problem figure (1) to problem figure (2) one Δ is increased. Similarly from problem figure (3) to problem figure (4) one circle is increased.

24. 1023 $\xrightarrow{+23}$ 1046,   1169 $\xrightarrow{+23}$ 1192

1494 $\xrightarrow{+23}$ 1517,   1899 $\xrightarrow{+22}$ 1921

25. In each of 1, 4, 8 there is Δ.

In each of 2, 5, 7 there is U

and in each of 3, 6, 9 there is fish.

51. $\text{Rate} = \dfrac{(n-1) \times 100}{p} = \dfrac{(2-1) \times 100}{12} = 8\dfrac{1}{3}\%$

Here, $p = 12$ and $n = 2$

52. $13310 = 10000\left(1 + \dfrac{10}{100}\right)^n$

$\Rightarrow \dfrac{13310}{10000} = \left(\dfrac{11}{10}\right)^n$

$\Rightarrow \left(\dfrac{11}{10}\right)^3 = \left(\dfrac{11}{10}\right)^n$

$\therefore \qquad n = 3 \text{ Half years} = 1\dfrac{1}{2}$ years

53. $30 = \dfrac{(10 + \text{gain}\%) \times 100}{100 - 10}$

$\therefore \dfrac{30 \times 90}{100} = 10 + \text{gain}\%$

$\Rightarrow \text{Gain}\% = \dfrac{30 \times 90}{100} - 10 = 17\%$

54. Equivalent discount $= 20 + 30 - \dfrac{20 \times 30}{100}$

$$= 20 + 30 - 6 = 44\%$$

$\therefore$ M.P. of the article $= \dfrac{2240 \times 100}{100 - 44} = ₹\ 4000$

55. Let M.P. of the book be $₹\ x$

$\therefore$ S.P. of the book $= \dfrac{x \times 90}{100} = ₹\ 0.9x$

and C.P. of the book $= \dfrac{0.9x \times 100}{100 + 12} = ₹\ \dfrac{90x}{112}$

$\therefore$ Required ratio $= \dfrac{90x}{112} : x = 90 : 112 = 45 : 56$

56. Work of A for 1 day for 1 hour

$$= \dfrac{1}{8 \times 5} = \dfrac{1}{40}$$

Work of B for 1 day for 1 hour

$$= \dfrac{1}{6 \times 10} = \dfrac{1}{60}$$

$\therefore$ Work of (A + B) for 1 day for 1 hour

$$= \dfrac{1}{40} + \dfrac{1}{60} = \dfrac{1}{24}$$

$\therefore$ Work of (A + B) for 1 day for 8 hour

$$= \dfrac{1}{24} \times 8 = \dfrac{1}{3}$$

Hence jointly working 8 hr. per day they complete the work in 3 days.

57. Work of 40 men for first 10 days $= \dfrac{10}{40} = \dfrac{1}{4}$

Work of 35 men for next 10 days $= \dfrac{10}{40} \times \dfrac{35}{40} = \dfrac{7}{32}$

Work of 30 men for next 10 days $= \dfrac{10}{40} \times \dfrac{30}{40} = \dfrac{3}{16}$

Work of 25 men for first 10 days $= \dfrac{10}{40} \times \dfrac{25}{40} = \dfrac{5}{32}$

Work of 20 men for next 10 days $= \dfrac{10}{40} \times \dfrac{20}{40} = \dfrac{1}{8}$

$\therefore$ Work for 50 days $= \dfrac{1}{4} + \dfrac{7}{32} + \dfrac{3}{16} + \dfrac{5}{32} + \dfrac{1}{8} = \dfrac{15}{16}$

$\therefore$ Remaining work $= 1 - \dfrac{15}{16} = \dfrac{1}{16}$

$\therefore \dfrac{1}{16}$ work will do 15 men in

$$= \dfrac{40}{15} \times 40 \times \dfrac{1}{16} = \dfrac{20}{3}\ \text{days}$$

Hence complete work will be done in $50 + 6\dfrac{2}{3}$ in $56\dfrac{2}{3}$ days.

58. Let capacity of the tank be x litres

$\therefore \qquad \dfrac{x}{10} = \dfrac{x}{15} + 4 \times 60$

$\therefore \qquad \dfrac{x}{10} - \dfrac{x}{15} = 240$

$\therefore \qquad \dfrac{x}{30} = 240$

$\therefore \qquad x = 240 \times 30$

$$= 7200\ \text{litres}$$

59. Let total distance be x km and the speed of A be y km/hr.

$\therefore$ Speed of B $= \dfrac{5y}{6}$ km/hr

$$\dfrac{x}{\dfrac{5y}{6}} - \dfrac{x}{y} = \dfrac{5}{4}$$

$$\dfrac{6x}{5y} - \dfrac{x}{y} = \dfrac{5}{4}$$

$$\dfrac{6x - 5x}{5y} = \dfrac{5}{4}$$

$\therefore \qquad \dfrac{x}{5y} = \dfrac{5}{4}$

$\therefore \qquad \dfrac{6x}{5y} = \dfrac{5}{4} \times 6$

$$= 7\ \text{hrs. } 30\ \text{min.}$$

60. Let distance between a $A\ \overset{\underset{\displaystyle x \quad (d-x)}{\bullet\!\!-\!\!\bullet\!\!-\!\!\bullet}}{}\ B$

P

If speeds of the trains from A and from B be u km/hr respectively and v km/hr respectively. And they meet each other at P.

$\therefore \qquad \dfrac{x}{u} = t = \dfrac{d-x}{v} \qquad \qquad …(1)$

$\Rightarrow \qquad d - x = 4u$

and $\qquad x = 9v \qquad \qquad …(2)$

$\therefore \qquad \dfrac{9v}{u} = t = \dfrac{4u}{v}$

$\Rightarrow \qquad \dfrac{u^2}{v^2} = \dfrac{9}{4}$

$\therefore \qquad \dfrac{u}{v} = \dfrac{3}{2} = 3 : 2$

61. L.C.M. of 10 and 15 = 30

Hence they will meet after 30 minutes.

62. Let length of the train be x metres and its speed by y m/sec.

$$\therefore \quad \frac{x}{y} = 10$$

and $\quad \dfrac{x+300}{y} = 25$

$$\therefore \quad x - 10y = 0$$

and $\quad x - 25y = -300$

$$\therefore \quad 15y = 300$$

$$\Rightarrow \quad y = 20 \text{ m/sec.}$$

and $\quad x = 10 \times 20 = 200$ m

$\therefore$ Reqd. time to cross a platform

$$= \frac{200 + 200}{20} = 20 \text{ secs.}$$

63. Let the distance of the destination from the starting place be x km.

$$\therefore \quad \frac{x}{10+4} + \frac{x}{10-4} = 5$$

$$\Rightarrow \quad \frac{x}{14} + \frac{x}{6} = \frac{3x+7x}{42} = 5$$

$$\therefore \quad x = \frac{5 \times 42}{10} = 21 \text{ km}$$

64. C.P. of commodity

$$= \frac{x}{\left(\dfrac{100+A}{100}\right) \times \left(\dfrac{100+B}{100}\right) - \left(\dfrac{100+C}{100}\right)}$$

(Here, $x = -2$, $A = -10$, $B = \dfrac{50}{3}$ and $C = 10$)

$$= \frac{-2}{\left(\dfrac{100-10}{100}\right) \times \left(\dfrac{100+\dfrac{50}{3}}{100}\right) - \left(\dfrac{100+10}{100}\right)}$$

$$= \frac{-2}{\dfrac{90}{100} \times \dfrac{350}{300} - \dfrac{110}{100}} = \frac{-2}{1.05 - 1.1} = \frac{-2}{-0.05} = ₹ 40$$

65. Suppose A purchased the article for ₹ 100

$\therefore \quad$ S.P. for A $= 100 + 10 = ₹ 110$

$\therefore \quad$ C.P. for B $= ₹ 110$

$\therefore \quad$ S.P. for A $= \dfrac{110(100-10)}{100} = \dfrac{110 \times 90}{100} = ₹ 99$

$\therefore$ In the whole transaction profit for A

$$= (110 - 99) = 11\%$$

66. Let the reqd. ratio be $1 : x$

$\therefore$ Cost price of the mixture $= ₹ (192 \times 1 + 150 \times x)$

and S.P. price of the mixture $= ₹ 194.40 \times (1 + x)$

$$\therefore \quad 194.40 (1 + x) = (192 + 150x) \times \frac{120}{100}$$

$$\therefore \quad 19440 (1 + x) = (192 + 150x) \times 120$$

$$\therefore \quad 19440 + 19440x = 23040 + 18000x$$

$$\therefore \quad 19440x - 18000x = 23040 - 19440$$

$\therefore \quad 1440x = 3600$

$\therefore \quad x = \dfrac{3600}{1440} = \dfrac{5}{2}$

$\therefore \quad$ Reqd. ratio $= 2 : 5$

67. Let the S.P. of the article be ₹ 100

$\therefore$ C.P. of the article $= ₹ (100 + 25) = ₹ 125$

$\therefore$ % of loss on the basis of C.P.

$$= \frac{25 \times 100}{125} = 20\%$$

68. If each side of Δ be a cm.

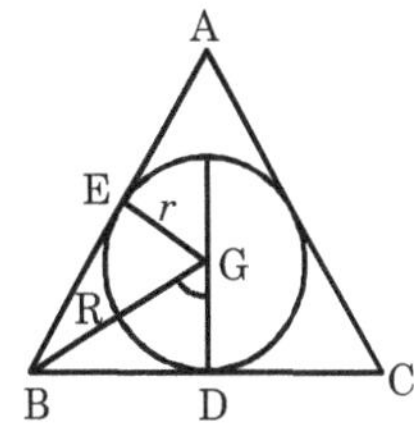

Then, $\quad$ AD $= \sqrt{AB^2 - BD^2}$

$$= \sqrt{a^2 - \left(\frac{a^2}{4}\right)} = \frac{\sqrt{3}a}{2} \text{ cm}$$

$$\therefore \quad \text{AG} = \frac{\sqrt{3}}{2}a \times \frac{2}{3} = \frac{a}{\sqrt{3}} \text{ cm}$$

$$\therefore \quad \text{R} = \sqrt{\left(\frac{a}{2}\right)^2 + \left(\frac{\sqrt{3}a}{2} \times \frac{1}{3}\right)^2}$$

$$= \sqrt{\frac{a^2}{4} + \frac{a^2}{12}} = \sqrt{\frac{a^2}{3}} = \frac{a}{\sqrt{3}} \text{ cm.}$$

and $\quad r = \sqrt{AG^2 - AE^2} = \sqrt{\frac{a^2}{3} - \frac{a^2}{4}} = \frac{a}{2\sqrt{3}} \text{ cm}$

$$\therefore \quad \pi R^2 - \pi r^2 = 44$$

$$\therefore \quad \frac{22}{7}\left(\frac{a^2}{3} - \frac{a^2}{12}\right) = 44$$

$$\therefore \quad \frac{a^2}{4} = 44 \times \frac{7}{22}$$

$$\therefore \quad a^2 = 44 \times \frac{7}{22} \times 4 = 56$$

$\therefore$ Required area of $\Delta = \dfrac{\sqrt{3}}{4} \times 56 = 14\sqrt{3} \text{ cm}^2$

69. One side of the square $= \sqrt{121} = 11$ cm

$\therefore$ Perimeter of the square $= 4 \times 11 = 44$ cm

$\therefore \quad$ Circumference of circle $= 44$ cm.

$$\therefore \quad \text{Radius of circle} = \frac{44 \times 7}{2 \times 22} = 7 \text{ cm}$$

$$\therefore \quad \text{Area of circle} = \frac{22}{7} \times 7 \times 7 = 154 \text{ cm}^2$$

70. If one side of the square be a cm.

Then, area of the circle $= \pi\left(\dfrac{a^2}{4}\right)$

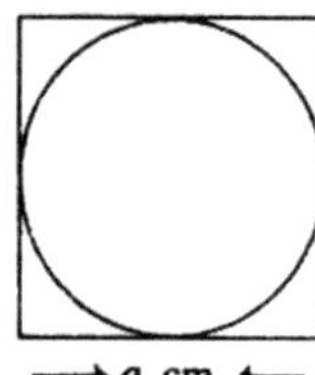

$\therefore \qquad 9\pi = \dfrac{\pi a^2}{4}$

$\therefore \qquad a^2 = 36$

$\therefore \qquad$ Area of the square $= 36$ cm²

71. Let the radius of hemisphere be r cm.

$\therefore \qquad 2\pi r^2 + \pi r^2 = 108\pi$

$\therefore \qquad 3r^2 = 108$

$\therefore \qquad r = \sqrt{\dfrac{108}{3}} = 6$ cm

$\therefore$ Vol. of the hemisphere

$\qquad = \dfrac{2}{3} \times \pi \times 6 \times 6 \times 6 = 144\pi$ cm³

72. % increase in the export from A

$\qquad = \dfrac{61 - 57}{57} \times 100 = 7.02$

% increase in the export from B

$\qquad = \dfrac{160 - 148}{148} \times 100 = 8.108$

% increase in the export from C

$\qquad = \dfrac{234 - 229}{229} \times 100 = 2.183$

% increase in the export from D

$\qquad = \dfrac{150 - 146}{146} \times 100 = 2.739$

73. Reqd. change $= \dfrac{\substack{(61 + 160 + 234 + 150) \\ -(57 + 148 + 229 + 146)}}{(57 + 148 + 229 + 146)} \times 100$

$\qquad = \dfrac{2500}{580} = 4.3\%$ nearly increase

74. Average increase $= ₹ \dfrac{4 + 12 + 5 + 4}{4}$ crores

$\qquad = ₹\ 6.25$ crores $= ₹\ 62500000$

75. $= \dfrac{(5.624)^3 + (4.376)^3}{(5.624)^2 - (5.624 \times 4.376) + (4.376)^2}$

$\qquad = \dfrac{(5.624 + 4.376)[(5.624)^2 - (5.624) \times 4.376 + (4.376)^2]}{(5.624)^2 - (5.624 \times 4.376) + (4.376)^2}$

$\qquad = 5.624 + 4.376 = 10$

PRACTICE SET – 19

GENERAL INTELLIGENCE

1. There are three baskets of fruits. First basket has twice the number of fruits in the 2nd basket. Third basket has $\frac{3}{4}$ th of the fruits in the first. The average of the fruits in all the baskets is 30. What is the number of fruits in the first basket?

(a) 20   (b) 30

(c) 35   (d) 40

2. From the given alternative words, select the word which *cannot* be formed using the letters of the given word:

REFORMATION

(a) REFRAIN   (b) MOTION

(c) REFRACT   (d) FORMAT

Directions (Q.3-4): *From the given alternative words, select the word which can be formed using the letters of the given word.*

3. MANUFACTURE

(a) FRACTURE

(b) MANNER

(c) MATTER

(d) FACE

4. If in a certain code, 95789 is written as EGKPT and 2436 is written as ALUR, the how will 24539 be written in that code?

(a) ALEUT   (b) ALGTU

(c) ALGUT   (d) ALGRT

5. A statement is given followed by four alternative arguments. Select on which is most appropriate.

Statement : White clothes are women more often is summer because

(a) they are thin and cool

(b) they are bad absorbers of heat

(c) they can be easily washed

(d) they are easily available in summer

Directions (Q.6-7) : *Select the related letter/word/number from the given alternatives.*

6. PROCESSION : ROUTE : : EARTH : ?

(a) Space

(b) Sun

(c) Orbit

(d) Highway

7. IC : 6 : : DP : ?

(a) 14   (b) 10

(c) 12   (d) 16

Directions (Q. 8-9) : *Find the odd word from the given alternatives.*

8. (a) Ladder   (b) Staircase

(c) Bridge   (d) Escalator

9. Find out the set of numbers amongst the four sets of numbers given in the alternatives which is most like the set given in the question.

Given set: (8, 56, 72)

(a) (7, 56, 63)   (b) (3, 15, 24)

(c) (6, 42, 54)   (d) (5, 30, 35)

Directions: *Arrange the following words as per order in the dictionary.*

10. 1. Noble   2. Nobilitary

3. Noblesse   4. Nobility

5. Nobble

(a) 1, 4, 3, 2, 5

(b) 3, 4, 1, 2, 5

(c) 5, 2, 4, 1, 3

(d) 2, 4, 3, 5, 1

11. Which one of set of letters when sequentially placed at the gaps in the given letter series shall complete it?

an _ nn _ ana _ na _ nan _ a

(a) Annan   (b) Aanan

(c) Nanna   (d) Naana

Directions (Q. 12-13): *A series is given with one/two term missing. Choose the correct alternative from the given ones that will complete the series.*

12. 5 9 ? = 84

8 6 4 = 56

7 3 7 = 70

(a) 4   (b) 7

(c) 5   (d) 6

13. Find the wrong number in the series.

7, 28, 63, 124, 215, 342

(a) 28   (b) 63

(c) 124   (d) 342

14. In a class Rajan got the 11th rank and he was 31st from the bottom of the list of boys passed. Three boys did not take the examination and one failed. What is the total strength of the class?

(a) 32
(b) 42
(c) 45
(d) 46

15. In a family, mother's age is twice that of daughter's age. Father is 10 years older than mother. Brother is 20 years younger than his mother and 5 years older than his sister. What is the age of the father?

(a) 62 years

(b) 60 years

(c) 58 years

(d) 55 years

16. Rahul and Robin are brothers. Pramod is Robin's father. Sheela is Pramod's sister. Prema is Pramod's niece. Shubha is Sheela's granddaughter. How is Rahul related to Shubha?

(a) Brother

(b) Cousin

(c) Uncle

(d) Nephew

17. Mr. and Mrs. Gopal have 3 daughters and each daughter has one brother. How many persons are there in the family?

(a) 5
(b) 6
(c) 7
(d) 8

18. Select the missing number from the given responses.

1	2	3
4	5	6
7	8	9
27	28	?

(a) 49
(b) 50
(c) 51
(d) 52

19. If '×' means 'addition', '–' means 'division', '÷' means 'subtraction' and '+' means 'multiplication', then which of the following equations is correct?

(a) $16 + 5 - 10 \times 4 \div 3 = 9$

(b) $16 - 5 \times 10 \div 4 + 3 = 12$

(c) $16 + 5 \div 10 \times 4 - 3 = 9$

(d) $16 \times 5 \div 10 \div 4 - 3 = 19$

20. A man starts from a point, walks 8 km towards North, turns right and walks 12 km, turns left and walks 7 km, turns and walks 24 km towards South, turns right and walks 12 km. In which direction is he from the starting point?

(a) North
(b) South
(c) West
(d) East

21. Which diagram correctly represents the relationship between *Human beings, Teachers, Graduates?*

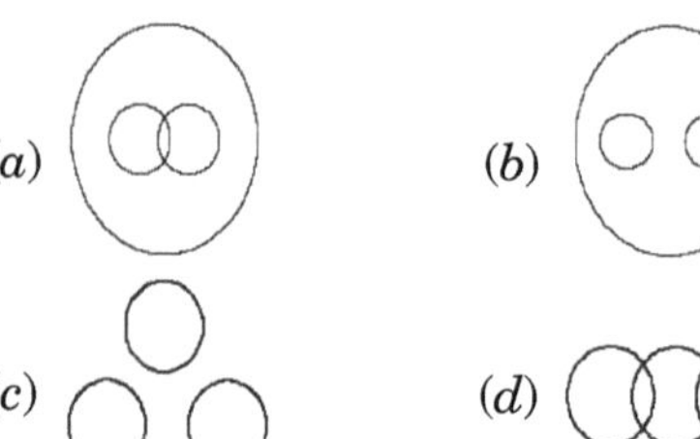

22. How many triangles are there in the given figures?

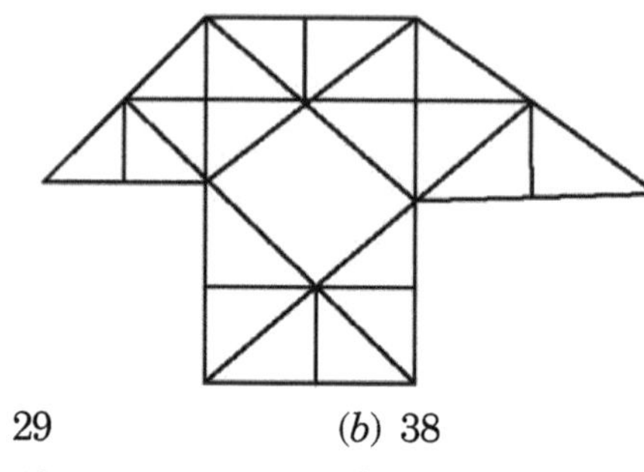

(a) 29
(b) 38
(c) 40
(d) 35

23. From the given answer figures, select the one in which the question figures is hidden/ embedded.

Question figure

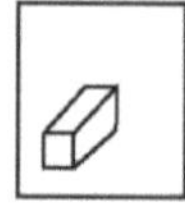

Answer figures

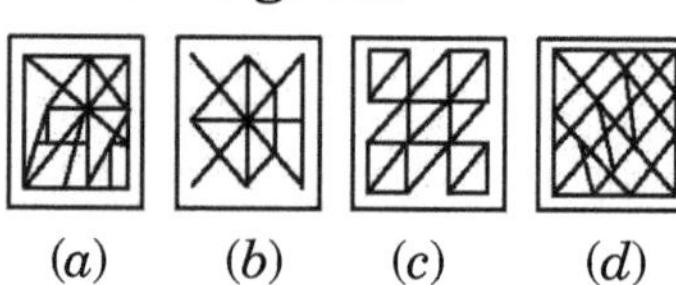

(a)   (b)   (c)   (d)

24. In a mirror is placed on the line MN, the which of the answer figures is the right image of the given figure?

Question figure

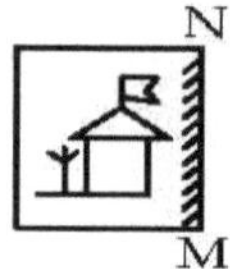

Answer figures

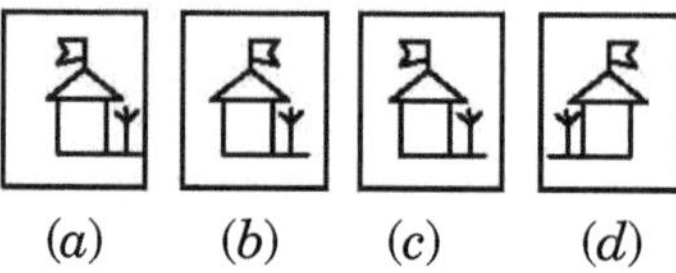

(a)   (b)   (c)   (d)

25. A piece of paper is folded and cut as shown below in the question figures. From the given answer figures, indicate how it will appear when opened.

Question figures

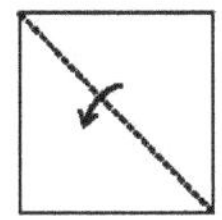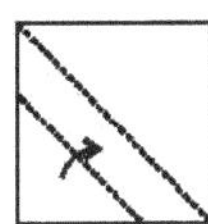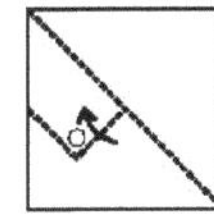

Answer figures

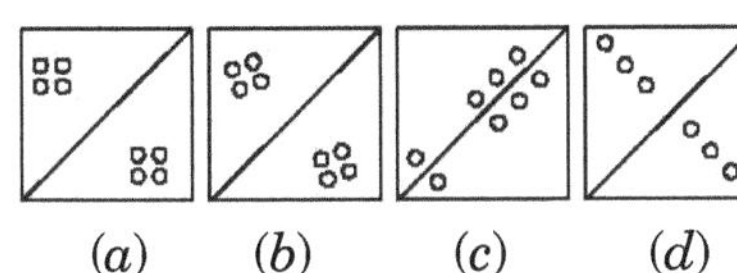

(a)   (b)   (c)   (d)

ENGLISH LANGUAGE

Directions (Q. 26-27) : *Out of the four alternatives, choose the one which best expresses the meaning of the given word and mark it in the Answer Sheet.*

26. Poignant
 (a) showy   (b) sad
 (c) silly   (d) snobbish

27. Querulous
 (a) critical   (b) curious
 (c) complaining   (d) ambiguous

Directions (Q. 28-29) : *Choose the word opposite in meaning to the given word and mark in the Answer Sheet.*

28. Autonomous
 (a) self-government
 (b) dependent
 (c) defensive
 (d) neutral

29. Deceitful
 (a) sincere   (b) useful
 (c) plain   (d) honest

Directions (Q. 30-32) : *Out of the four alternatives, choose the one which can be substituted for the given words / sentence and indicate it by blackening the appropriate rectangle [☐] in the answer Sheet.*

30. A person who has no money to pay off his debts
 (a) Insolvent   (b) Poor
 (c) Destitute   (d) Pauper

31. Words uttered impiously about God
 (a) amoral
 (b) philosophy
 (c) logic
 (d) blasphemy

32. Quibble
 (a) Premeditate
 (b) Prenominate
 (c) Prevaricate
 (d) Preponderate

Directions (Q. 33-35) : *Four alternatives are given for the Idiom / Phrase and bold italicized in the sentence. Choose the alternative which best expresses the meaning of the Idiom / Phrase and mark it in the Answer Sheet.*

33. To strain every nerve
 (a) to make utmost efforts
 (b) to feel weak and tired
 (c) to be a diligent worker
 (d) to be methodical in work

34. To flog a dead horse
 (a) to whip a dead horse
 (b) to attempt to do the impossible
 (c) waste one's efforts
 (d) to take advantage of a weakness

35. To show a clean pair of heels
 (a) to hide   (b) to escape
 (c) to pursue   (d) to follow

36. Groups of four words are given in one word is correctly spelt. Find the correctly spelt word and mark your answer in the Answer Sheet.
 (a) persistence
 (b) thesaurus
 (c) conspicous
 (d) renaissance

Directions (Q. 37-39) : *In the following questions, some of the sentences have errors and some are correct. Find out which part of a sentence has an error. The number of that part is your answer. If a sentence is free from errors, then your answer is (d) i.e., No error.*

37. If you had told (a)/ I would have helped you (b)/ solve the problem. (c)/ No error (d).

38. "The Arabian Nigh" (a)/ are indeed (b)/ an interesting book. (c)/ No error (d).

39. He (a)/ lover her (b)/ despite of himself (c)/ No error (d).

Directions (Q. 40-42) : *In the following questions, sentences are given with blanks to be filled in with an appropriate words. Four alternatives are suggested for each question. Choose the correct alternative out of the four.*

40. ____ your instructions, we have closed you bank account.

(a) In lieu of   (b) With regard to

(c) In accordance with (d) On account of

41. ____ she is cleaver, she often makes mistakes.

(a) Despite   (b) Since

(c) Although   (d) Yet

42. Do you prefer ____ or traditional art forms?

(a) archaic   (b) contemporary

(c) foreign   (d) simultaneous

Directions (Q. 43-45) : *A sentence is given which may need improvement. Alternatives are given at (a), (b) and (c) below which may be a better option. In case no improvement is needed, your answer is (d). Blacken the appropriate rectangle [▭] in the Answer Sheet.*

43. A taller Sikh rushed forward than any of his comrades.

(a) A Sikh, taller than any of this comrades, rushed forward

(b) A Sikh rushed forward taller than any of his comrades

(c) A Sikh rushed forward than any of his comrades taller

(d) No improvement

44. An author is the reign of Question Anne who was famous lived in a cottage.

(a) An author in the reign, who was famous, of Queen Anne lived in a cottage

(b) In the reign of Queen Anne, an author lived in a cottage, who was famous

(c) An author who was famous in the reign of Queen Anne lived in a cottage

(d) No improvement

45. In the absence of your support, he would have lost the election.

(a) Lacking your support, he would have lost the election

(b) But for your support, he would have lost the election

(c) He would have lost the election, if you had not support him

(d) No improvement

Directions (Q. 46-50) : *Read the following passage carefully and choose the best answer to each question out of four alternatives and mark it the correct answer.*

If an opinion contrary to your own makes you angry, that is a sign that you are subconsciously aware of having no good reason for thinking as you do. If someone maintains that two and two are five, or that Iceland is on the Equator, you feel pity rather than anger, unless you know so little of arithmetic or geography that his opinion shakes your own contrary conviction.

46. If someone else's opinion makes us angry, it means that

(a) we are subconsciously aware of having no good reason for becoming angry

(b) there may be good reasons for his opinion but we are not consciously aware of them

(c) out own opinion is not based on good reason and we know this subconsciously

(d) we are not consciously aware of any reason for our own opinion

47. "Your own contrary conviction" refers to

(a) the fact that you feel pity rather than anger

(b) the opinion that two and two are four and that Iceland is a long way from the Equator

(c) the opinion that two and two are five and that Iceland is on the Equator

(d) the fact that you know so little about arithmetic or geography

48. Conviction means

(a) persuasion

(b) disbelief

(c) strong belief

(d) ignorance

49. The writer says if someone maintains that two and two are five you feel pity because you

(a) have sympathy

(b) don't agree with him

(c) want to help the person

(d) feel sorry for his ignorance

50. The second sentence in the passage

(a) builds up the argument of the first sentence by restating it from the opposite point of view

(b) makes the main point which has only been introduced by the first sentence

(c) simply adds a further point to the argument already stated in the first sentence

(d) illustrates the point made in the first sentence

QUANTITATIVE APTITUDE

51. A reduction of 20% in the price of an apple enables a man to buy 10 apples more for ₹ 54. The reduced price of apple per dozen is

(a) ₹ 4.32

(b) ₹ 12.96

(c) ₹ 10.80

(d) ₹ 14.40

52. Price of a commodity has increased by 60%. By what per cent must a consumer reduce the consumption of the commodity so as not to increase the expenditure?

(a) 37

(b) 37.5

(c) 40.5

(d) 60

53. The cost of an apple is twice that of a banana and the cost of a banana is 25% less than that of a guava. If the cost of each type of fruit increase by 10%, then the percentage increase in cost of 4 bananas, 2 apples and 3 guavas is

(a) 10%

(b) 12%

(c) 16%

(d) 18%

54. Walking $\frac{6}{7}$ th of his usual speed, a man is 12 minutes too late. The usual time taken by him to cover that distance is

(a) 1 hour

(b) 1 hour 12 minutes

(c) 1 hour 15 minutes

(d) 1 hour 20 minutes

55. If I walk at 5 km/hour, I miss a train by 7 minutes. If, however, I walk at 6 km/hour, I reach the station 5 minutes before the departure of the train. The distance (in km) between my house and the station is

(a) 6

(b) 5

(c) 4

(d) 3

56. ₹ 800 becomes ₹ 956 in 3 years at a certain rate of simple interest. If the rate of interest is increased by 4%, what amount will ₹ 800 become in 3 years?

(a) ₹ 1020.80

(b) ₹ 1025

(c) ₹ 1052

(d) ₹ 1050

57. Simple interest on a certain sum is $\frac{16}{25}$ of the sum. The rate per cent if the rate per cent and time (in years) are equal, is

(a) 6%

(b) 8%

(c) 10%

(d) 12%

58. A hemisphere and a cone have equal bases. If their heights are also equal, the ratio of their curved surface will be

(a) $1 : \sqrt{2}$

(b) $\sqrt{2} : 1$

(c) $1 : 2$

(d) $2 : 1$

59. If x = $\dfrac{\sqrt{5}+1}{\sqrt{5}-1}$, then, the value of $5x^2 - 5x - 1$ is

(a) 0

(b) 3

(c) 4

(d) 5

60. Find the unit digit in the product $(4387)^{245} \times (621)^{72}$

(a) 1

(b) 2

(c) 5

(d) 7

61. The value of $\dfrac{(3.2)^3 - 0.008}{(3.2)^2 + 0.64 + 0.04}$ is

(a) 0

(b) 2.994

(c) 3.208

(d) 3

62. If $\sqrt{a + \dfrac{x}{961}} = \dfrac{32}{31}$, then the value of x is

(a) 63

(b) 61

(c) 65

(d) 64

63. A and B working separately can do a piece of work in 9 and 12 days respectively. If the work for a day alternately with a beginning, the work would be completed in

(a) $10\frac{2}{3}$ days

(b) $10\frac{1}{2}$ days

(c) $10\frac{1}{4}$ days

(d) $10\frac{1}{3}$ days

64. A and B together can do a work in 10 days. B and C together can do the same work in 6 days. A and C together can do the work in 12 days. Then A, B and C together can do the work in

(a) 28 days

(b) 14 days

(c) $5\frac{5}{7}$ days

(d) $8\frac{2}{7}$ days

65. If a wire is bent into the shape of a square, then the area of the square so formed is 81cm². When the wire is rebent into a semicircular shape, then the area (in cm²) of the semicircle will be

(Take $\pi = \dfrac{22}{7}$)

(a) 22

(b) 44

(c) 77

(d) 154

66. An alloy contains copper, zinc and nickel in the ratio of 5 : 3 : 2. The quantity of nickel in kg that must be added to 100 kg of this alloy to have the new ratio 5 : 2 : 3, is

(a) 8

(b) 10

(c) 12

(d) 15

67. The incomes of A, B and C are in the ratio 7 : 9 : 12 and their spending are in the ratio 8 : 9 : 15. If A saves $\dfrac{1}{4}$ th of his income, then the saving of A, B and C are in the ratio of

(a) 69 : 56 : 48

(b) 47 : 74 : 99

(c) 37 : 72 : 49

(d) 56 : 99 : 69

68. The average of 25 observations is 13. It was later found that an observation 73 was wrongly entered as 48. The new average is

(a) 12.6 (b) 14

(c) 15 (d) 13.8

Direction (Q. 69-71) : *The following graph shows the production of wheat flour (in 1000 tonnes) by three companies X, Y and Z over the years. Study the graph and answer given questions.*

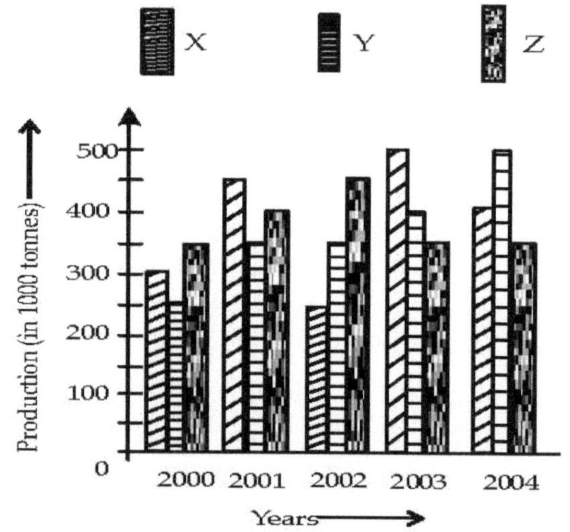

69. What is the different between the production of company Z in 2004 and company Y in 2000 (in thousand tonnes)?

(a) 2000 (b) 200

(c) 20 (d) 100

70. What is the ratio of the average production of Company X in the period 2002-2004 to the average production of company Y in the same period?

(a) 1 : 1 (b) 15 : 17

(c) 25 : 23 (d) 27 : 29

71. What is the percentage increase in the production of company Y from 2002 to 2003?

(a) $14\dfrac{2}{7}$ (b) $16\dfrac{6}{7}$

(c) 25 (d) 40

72. If $2 - \cos^2 \theta = 3\sin\theta\cos\theta,\ \sin\theta \neq \cos\theta$, then $\tan\theta$ is

(a) $\dfrac{1}{2}$ (b) 0

(c) $\dfrac{2}{3}$ (d) $\dfrac{1}{3}$

73. If $\sin\theta + \cos\theta = \sqrt{2}\cos(90 - \theta)$, then $\cot\theta$ is

(a) $\sqrt{2} + 1$

(b) 0

(c) $\sqrt{2}$

(d) $\sqrt{2} - 1$

74. The side BC of $\triangle$ABC is produced to D. If $\angle$ACD $= 108°$ and $\angle$B $= \dfrac{1}{2}\angle$A, then $\angle$A is

(a) 36° (b) 72°

(c) 108° (d) 59°

75. If the length of the sides PQ of the rhombus PQRS is 6 cm and $\angle$PQR $= 120°$, then the length of QS, in cm, is

(a) 4 (b) 6

(c) 3 (d) 5

GENERAL AWARENESS

76. Lambert's law is related to

(a) Reflection

(b) Refraction

(c) Interference

(d) Illumination

77. The coral reefs are the marine counterparts of

(a) Temperate forest

(b) Tropical rain forests

(c) Savannahs

(d) Scrubland

78. The Refrigerant 'FREON' is

(a) Calcium Tetra Fluoride

(b) Difluoro Dichloro Methane

(c) Fluorspar and Felspar

(d) Hydrofluosilicic acid

79. Who decides a 'bill' is a money bill?

(a) President

(b) Prime Minister

(c) Speaker of Lok Sabha

(d) Chairman of Rajya Sabha

80. WIKILEAKS, a whistleblowers website is an international organisation based in

(a) U.S.A.　　　　(b) U.K.

(c) Sweden　　　　(d) Norway

81. Which of the following countries is regarded as the home of 'Fabian Socialism'?

(a) Italy　　　　(b) Russia

(c) England　　　　(d) France

82. LIC Mutual Fund Asset Management Company has inked a tie-up with which of the following co-operative Banks for distribution of its mutual fund products through the bank's 140 branches across India recently?

(a) Bihar State Co-operative Bank

(b) Cosmos Co-operative Bank

(c) Bharat Co-operative Bank

(d) Kerala State Co-operative Bank

83. Which of the following folk dances is associated with Jammu and Kashmir?

(a) Jhora　　　　(b) Veedhi

(c) Rauf　　　　(d) Suisini

84. Who invented the Jet Engine?

(a) Karl Benz

(b) Sir Frank Whittle

(c) Thomas Savery

(d) Michael Faraday

85. ______________ a communist nation in East Asia, has completed installation of the world's largest telescope in Guizhou province. The 500 metre-diameter telescope covers an area larger than 30 football pitches.

(a) China　　　　(b) Japan

(c) India　　　　(d) South Korea

86. Stagflation refers to a situation which is characterised by

(a) inflation and rising unemployment

(b) stagnant employment and deflation

(c) deflation and rising unemployment

(d) inflation and rising employment

87. The demand for necessities is

(a) perfectly elastic

(b) elastic

(c) perfectly inelastic

(d) inelastic

88. The 'break-even' points where

(a) marginal revenue equals marginal cost

(b) average revenue equals average cost

(c) total revenue equals total cost

(d) none of the above

89. The method of Impeachment of the President of India is adopted from

(a) U.S.A.　　　　(b) U.K.

(c) U.S.S.R.　　　　(d) France

90. Indian Parliament Means

(a) Rajya Sabha – Lok Sabha

(b) Rajya Sabha – Lok Sabha – Prime Minister

(c) President of India – Rajya Sabha – Lok Sabha

(d) President of India – Vise President of India – Lok Sabha – Rajya Sabha

91. Hiuen Tsang visited India during the reign of

(a) Chandragupta I

(b) Chandragupta II

(c) Harshavardhana

(d) Rudradaman

92. The Muslim adventurer who destroyed the Nalanda University was

(a) Alla-ud-din Khilji

(b) Muhammad-bin-Tughlak

(c) Muhammad-bin-Bhaktiyar

(d) Muhammad-bin-Quasim

93. Painting reached its highest level of development during the region of

(a) Akbar

(b) Aurangzeb

(c) Jahangir

(d) Shah Jahan

94. Sea breeze is formed during
- (a) Day time
- (b) Night time
- (c) Both (a) and (b)
- (d) Seasonal

95. Which one of the following rivers of India does not make a delta?
- (a) Ganges
- (b) Godavari
- (c) Mahanandi
- (d) Tapti

96. Which country was unanimously elected as the 39th Associate Member of International Cricket Council's (ICC) during its full council meeting in Edinburgh, Scotland?
- (a) UAE
- (b) Malaysia
- (c) China
- (d) Saudi Arabia

97. Normal fasting blood sugar level per 100 ml. of blood in man is
- (a) 30 – 50 mg
- (b) 50 – 70 mg
- (c) 80 – 100 mg
- (d) 120 – 140 mg

98. The vector of disease sleeping sickness is
- (a) sand-fly
- (b) house-fly
- (c) fruit-fly
- (d) tse-tse fly

99. Microsoft Office's personal information manager is
- (a) Outlook
- (b) Internet Explorer
- (c) Organizer
- (d) Access

100. Which is the most stable eco-system?
- (a) Desert
- (b) Ocean
- (c) Mountain
- (d) Forest

ANSWERS

1. (d)	**2.** (c)	**3.** (d)	**4.** (c)	**5.** (b)	**6.** (c)	**7.** (c)	**8.** (c)	**9.** (c)	**10.** (c)
11. (b)	**12.** (d)	**13.** (a)	**14.** (c)	**15.** (b)	**16.** (c)	**17.** (d)	**18.** (c)	**19.** (a)	**20.** (b)
21. (a)	**22.** (c)	**23.** (c)	**24.** (c)	**25.** (b)	**26.** (b)	**27.** (c)	**28.** (b)	**29.** (d)	**30.** (a)
31. (d)	**32.** (c)	**33.** (a)	**34.** (b)	**35.** (b)	**36.** (b)	**37.** (d)	**38.** (b)	**39.** (c)	**40.** (c)
41. (c)	**42.** (b)	**43.** (a)	**44.** (c)	**45.** (c)	**46.** (c)	**47.** (d)	**48.** (c)	**49.** (d)	**50.** (d)
51. (b)	**52.** (b)	**53.** (a)	**54.** (b)	**55.** (a)	**56.** (c)	**57.** (b)	**58.** (b)	**59.** (c)	**60.** (d)
61. (d)	**62.** (a)	**63.** (c)	**64.** (c)	**65.** (c)	**66.** (b)	**67.** (d)	**68.** (b)	**69.** (d)	**70.** (c)
71. (a)	**72.** (a)	**73.** (d)	**74.** (b)	**75.** (b)	**76.** (d)	**77.** (b)	**78.** (b)	**79.** (c)	**80.** (c)
81. (c)	**82.** (b)	**83.** (c)	**84.** (b)	**85.** (a)	**86.** (a)	**87.** (d)	**88.** (c)	**89.** (a)	**90.** (c)
91. (c)	**92.** (c)	**93.** (c)	**94.** (b)	**95.** (d)	**96.** (d)	**97.** (c)	**98.** (d)	**99.** (a)	**100.** (a)

EXPLANATIONS

1. The ratio of Ist and IInd basket is $2 : 1$

$$= 4 : 2$$

The ratio of Ist and IIIrd basket is $1 : \dfrac{3}{4}$

$$= 4 : 3$$

$\therefore$ The ratio of 1st, IInd, IIIrd is, $4 : 2 : 3$.

Let total number of fruit is x.

$\therefore$ According to question:-

$$\frac{4x + 2x + 3x}{3} = 30$$

$$9x = 90$$

$$x = 10$$

$\therefore$ Number of fruit in 1st basket

$$= 4 \times 10 = 40.$$

4. Given

9 5 7 8 9   2 4 3 6
E G K P T and A L U R

   2 4 5 3 9
$\therefore$ A L G U T

7. I C : 6
 9 3

$\therefore \qquad 9 - 3 = 6$

Similarly,

D P : ?
4 16

$\therefore \qquad 16 - 4 = 12$

9. The pattern is:-

$(8, 8 \times 7 = 56, 8 \times 9 = 72)$

similarly,

$(6, 6 \times 7 = 42, 6 \times 9 = 54)$

11. The series is

ananna / ananna / ananna

12. Given,

$$(8 + 6) \times 4 = 56$$

$$(7 + 3) \times 7 = 70$$

Similarly,

$$(5 + 9) \times x = 84$$

$$x = \frac{84}{14}$$

13. Rajan rank from top = 11th

Rajan rank from bottom = 31st

Number of boys did not take examination = 3

Number of boy failed in examination = 1

According to question

Total number of student

$$= 31 + 11 + 3 + 1 - 1$$

$$= 45.$$

15. Let the age of daughter $= x$ yrs

$\therefore$ Age of mother $= 2x$ yrs

$\therefore$ Age of father $= 10 + 2x$ yrs

$\therefore$ Age of brother $= 2x - 20$ yrs $= 5 + x$ yr.

$$2x - 20 = 5 + x$$

$$x = 25$$

$\therefore$ Age of Father $= 10 + 2x$ yrs

$$= 10 + 2 \times 25 \text{ yrs} = 60 \text{ yrs.}$$

16. 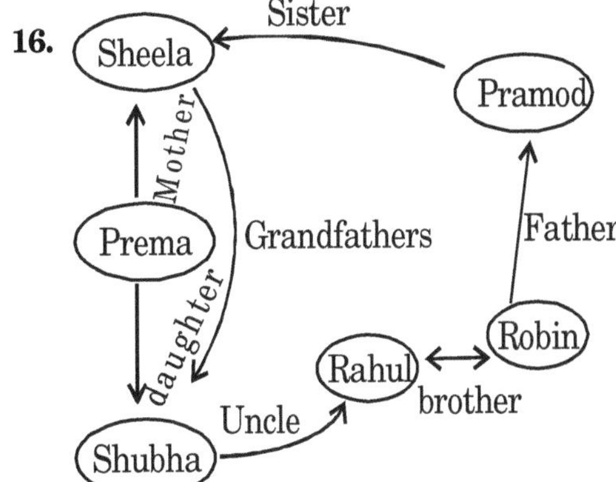

17. 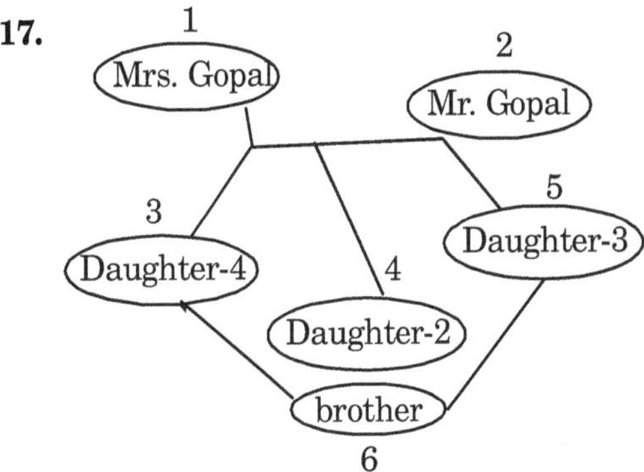

19. The correct equation is

$$16 \times 5 \div 10 + 4 - 3 = 9$$

$$16 \times \frac{1}{2} + 4 - 3 = 9$$

$$8 + 4 - 3 = 9$$

$$9 = 9$$

$$\text{L.H.S} = \text{R.H.S.}$$

20.

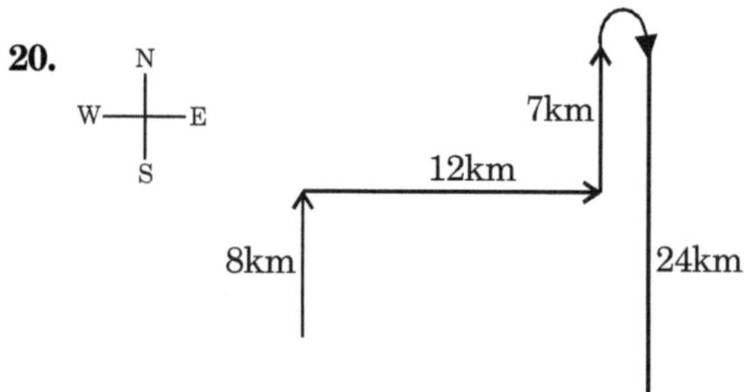

21.

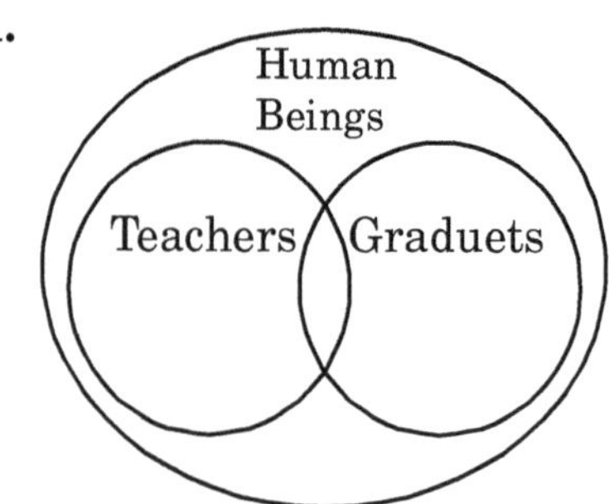

24.

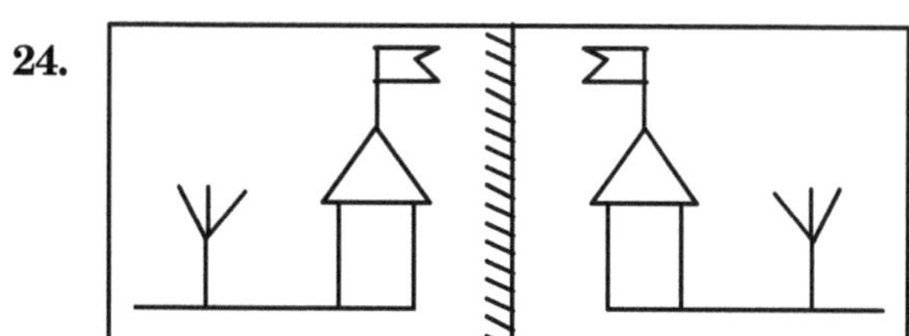

51. Reduced prize of an apple $= \dfrac{20}{100} \times \dfrac{54}{10} = 1.08$

reduced prize of apple per dozen

$\qquad = 1.08 \times 12$

$\qquad = ₹\ 12.96.$

52. Reduce percentage $= \dfrac{60}{160} \times 100 = 37.5$

53. Let Price of Guava = 100

Then price of Banana = 75

and Price of Apple $= 2 \times 75 = 150$

Total cost of 4 bananas, 2 apples and 3 guavas.

$= 4 \times 75 + 3 \times 100 + 2 \times 150$

$= 900$

Total cost after 10% increase in cost

$= 4 \times 75 \times \dfrac{110}{100} + 3 \times 100 \times \dfrac{110}{100} + 150 \times 2 \times \dfrac{110}{100}$

$\qquad = 330 + 330 + 330$

$\qquad = 990$

% increment $= \dfrac{990 - 900}{900} \times 100$

$\qquad = \dfrac{90}{900} \times 100$

$\qquad = 10\%$

54. Let time taken by man $= x$ min

time taken by man with $\dfrac{6}{7}$

of usual speed $= \dfrac{7}{6}x$

$\therefore \qquad \dfrac{7}{6}x - x = 12$

$\qquad x = 72$ min

$\qquad = 1$ hour 12 minutes.

55. Total distance $= \dfrac{6 \times 5}{6 - 5} \times \dfrac{12}{60} = 6$km

56. SI $= 956 - 800 = 156$

$156 = \dfrac{800 \times 3 \times R}{100}$

$R = \dfrac{156}{24} = \dfrac{13}{2}\%$

New Rate (R) $= 4 + \dfrac{13}{2} = \dfrac{21}{2}\%$

New S.I. $= \dfrac{800 \times 21}{100 \times 2} \times 3 = 252$

Total amount $= 800 + 252 = ₹\ 1052$

57. Let the sum $= x$

S.I. $= \dfrac{16}{25}x$

Rate (R) = Time (T)

S.I. $= \dfrac{x \times R \times T}{100}$

$\dfrac{16}{25}x = \dfrac{x \times R \times R}{100}$

$\dfrac{16 \times 100}{25} = R^2$

$R = 8\%$

58. Ratio $= \dfrac{\text{curved surface area of hemisphore}}{\text{curved surface area of cone}}$

$= \dfrac{2\pi r^2}{\pi r \sqrt{r^2 + h^2}} \qquad [\because r = h]$

$= \sqrt{2} : 1$

60. $(4387)^{245} \times (621)^{72}$

unit place for 4387 = 7

and unit place for 621 = 1

$\therefore$ unit digit of product $= 7 \times 1 = 7$

61. $\dfrac{(32)^3 - (0.2)^3}{(3.2)^3 + 0.64 + 0.04}$

$$(a^3 - b^3) = \dfrac{(a-b)(a^2 + b^2 + ab)}{a^2 + b^2 + ab}$$
$$= a - b$$
$$= (3.2 - 0.2) = 3$$

62. $\sqrt{1 + \dfrac{x}{961}} = \dfrac{32}{31}$

squaring both side

$$1 + \dfrac{x}{961} = \left(\dfrac{32}{31}\right)^2$$

$$\dfrac{961 + x}{961} = \dfrac{1024}{961}$$

$$961 + x = 1024$$
$$x = 1024$$
$$x = 63$$

63. Work done by A in 1 day $= \dfrac{1}{9}$

Work done by B in 1 day $= \dfrac{1}{12}$

A + B complete work in 2 day $= \dfrac{1}{9} + \dfrac{1}{12}$

$$= \dfrac{12 + 9}{108} = \dfrac{21}{108} = \dfrac{7}{36}$$

we know $= 5 \times \dfrac{7}{30} = \dfrac{35}{30}$ (less than)

Therfore they work in pair of 5 therefore they work for 10 days.

Remaining work $= 1 - \dfrac{35}{30}$

$$= \dfrac{1}{36} \text{ work completed by}$$

A worked $= \dfrac{9}{36} = \dfrac{1}{4}$ day.

$\therefore$ Total days $= 10 + \dfrac{1}{4} = 10\dfrac{1}{4}$

64. (A + B) work in 1 day $= \dfrac{1}{10}$

B + C work in 1 day $= \dfrac{1}{6}$

C + A work in 1 day $= \dfrac{1}{12}$

$$2(A + B + C) \text{ work} = \dfrac{1}{10} + \dfrac{1}{6} + \dfrac{1}{12}$$

A + B + C work $= \dfrac{21}{160}$

$$\dfrac{6 + 10 + 5}{60} = \dfrac{21}{60}$$

A + B + C work $= \dfrac{120}{21} = 5\dfrac{5}{7}$ day

65. Area of square $a^2 = 81$ km^2

$\therefore \qquad a = 9$ cm

Perimeter of square $= 4 \times a$
$$= 4 \times 9 = 36 \text{ cm}$$
Perimeter of semi circle $= \pi r + 2r$
$$36 = r(\pi + 2)$$
$$36 = r\left(\dfrac{36}{7}\right)$$
$$r = 36 \times \dfrac{7}{30} = 7$$

Area of semicircle $= \dfrac{1}{2}\pi r^2$

$$= \dfrac{1}{2} \times \dfrac{22}{7} \times 7 \times 7 = 77 \text{ cm}^2$$

66. Let copper $= 5x$; zinc $= 3x$ and nickel $= 2x$

$$5x + 3x + 2x = 100$$
$$x = 10$$
$\therefore \qquad$ copper $= 50$ kg
$$\text{zinc} = 30 \text{ kg}$$
$$\text{nickel} = 20 \text{ kg}$$
$$\text{new ratio} = 5 : 2 : 3$$
$$= 5x, 2x, 3x$$
$\therefore 5x + 2x + 3x = 100$
$$x = 10$$
$$\text{nickel} = 3 \times 10 = 30$$
Quality of nickel added $= 30 - 20 = 10$ kg

67. Let the income of A, B and C $= 7x, 9x, 12x$

and spending of A, B and C $= 8y, 9y, 15y$

According to question

$$7x - 8y = \dfrac{1}{4}7x$$

$$7x \dfrac{7}{4}x = 8y$$

$$21x = 32y$$

$$\frac{x}{y} = \frac{\text{total salery}}{\text{spending}} = \frac{32}{21}$$

saving of A, B and C

$= (7x - 8y) : (9x - 9y) : (2x - 5y)$

$= 7 \times 32 - 8 \times 21 : (9 \times 32 - 9 \times 21) :$

$$(2 \times 32 - 15 \times 21)$$

$= 56 : 99 : 69$

69. Difference $= 350 - 2500$

$$= 100 \text{ thousand tonnes}$$

70. Average of $X = \dfrac{250 + 500 + 500}{3} = \dfrac{1250}{3}$

average of $Y = \dfrac{350 + 400 + 400}{3} = \dfrac{1150}{3}$

ratio $X : Y = \dfrac{1250}{1150} = \dfrac{25}{23}$

71. Percentage $= \dfrac{450 - 350}{350} \times 100 = 14\dfrac{2}{7}\%$

72. $2 - \cos^2 \theta = 3 \sin \theta . \cos \theta$

Divide by $\cos^2 \theta$

$\quad 2\sec^2 \theta - 1 = 3\tan \theta$

$2(1 + \tan^2 \theta) - 1 = 3\tan \theta$

$2\tan^2 \theta - 3\tan \theta + 1 = 0$

$$\tan \theta = \frac{1}{2} \text{ or } \tan \theta = 1$$

73. $\sin \theta + \cos \theta = \sqrt{2} \cos(90 - \theta) = \sqrt{2} \sin \theta$

Squaring both side

$\sin^2 \theta + \cos^2 \theta + 2\sin \theta \cos \theta = 2\sin^2 \theta$

$\cos^2 \theta = \sin^2 \theta - 2\cos \theta \sin \theta$

Divide by $\sin^2 \theta$

$$\cot^2 \theta = 1 - 2\cot \theta$$

$$\cot^2 \theta + 2\cot \theta - 1 = 0$$

$$\cot \theta = \frac{-2 \pm \sqrt{4 + 4}}{2}$$

$$\cot \theta = \sqrt{2} - 1 \text{ or } \cot \theta = -\sqrt{2} - 1$$

74.

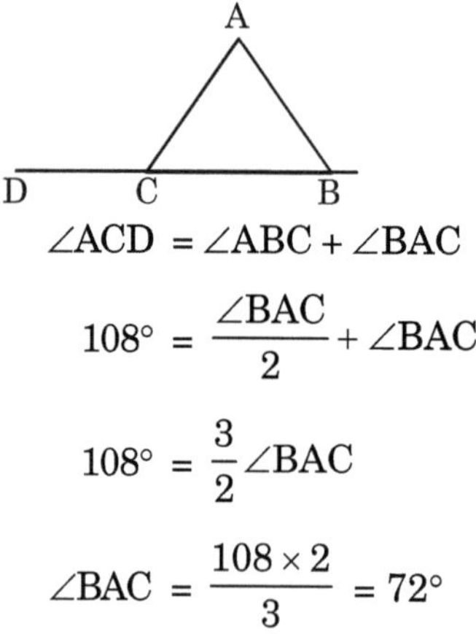

$\angle ACD = \angle ABC + \angle BAC$

$$108° = \frac{\angle BAC}{2} + \angle BAC$$

$$108° = \frac{3}{2} \angle BAC$$

$$\angle BAC = \frac{108 \times 2}{3} = 72°$$

75.

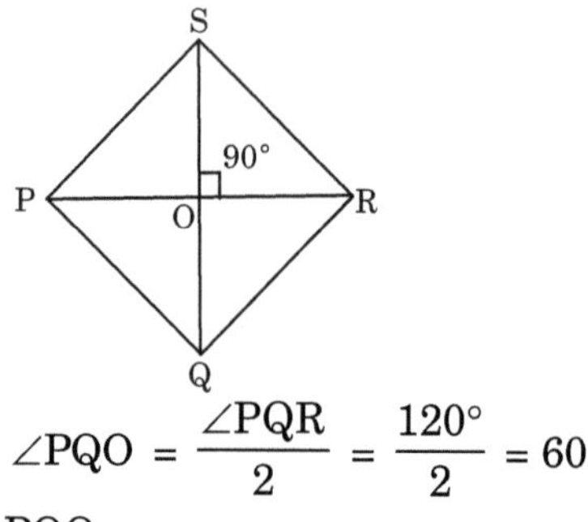

$$\angle PQO = \frac{\angle PQR}{2} = \frac{120°}{2} = 60°$$

From $\triangle POQ$

$$\angle OPQ = 180° - 90° - 60° = 30°$$

$$\sin \angle OPQ = \frac{DQ}{PQ}$$

$$OQ = PQ \sin 30° = 6\left(\frac{1}{2}\right) = 3$$

$\therefore \qquad QS = 2(OS) \qquad [OS = OQ]$

$$= 2 \times 3 = 6 \text{ cm}$$

GENERAL INTELLIGENCE

Directions for questions 1: *A series is given, with one term missing. Choose the corect alternative.*

1. 2, 7, 27, 107, ?

   (a) 327   (b) 427

   (c) 227   (d) 127

2. E is the sister of B. A is the father of C. B is the son of C. How is A related to E?

   (a) Grandfather

   (b) Granddaughter

   (c) Father

   (d) Great grandfather

3. Which of the following diagrams correctly represents the relationship among husband, wife and family?

   (a) 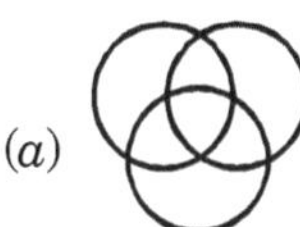   (b) 

   (c)    (d) 

4. In which answer figure is the given question figure embedded?

   Question figure

   Answer figures

   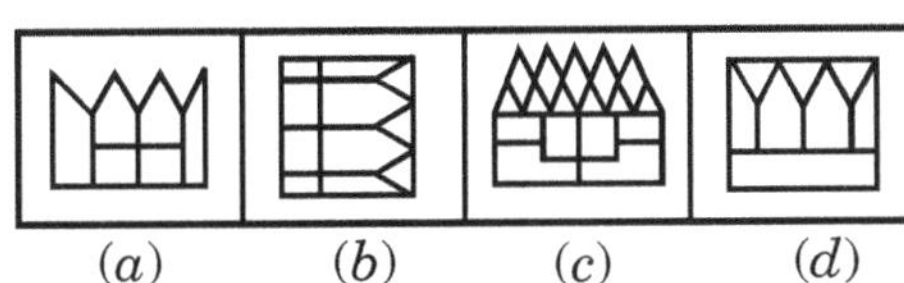

      (a)   (b)   (c)   (d)

5. A paper is folded as shown in the given figures and cut is made. How will it appear after opening?

   Question figure

   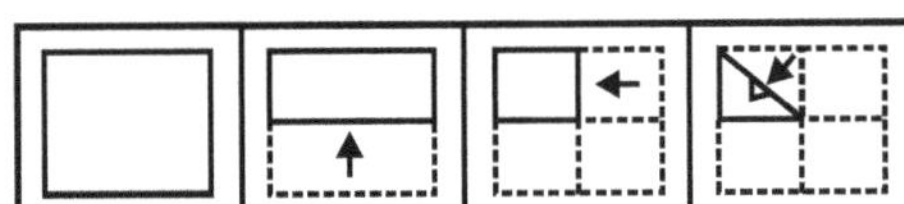

   Answer figures

   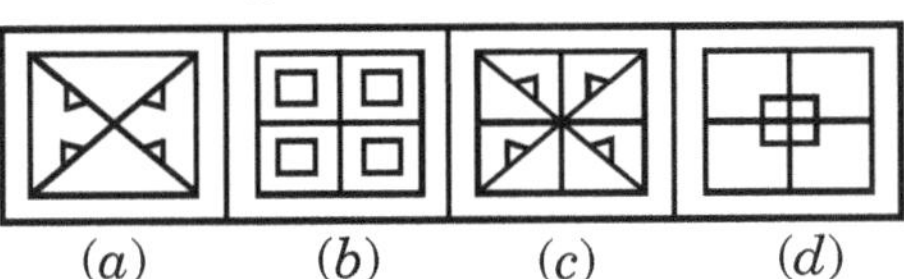

      (a)   (b)   (c)   (d)

Directions for questions 6 to 7: *Find the odd number / letter / word from the given alternatives.*

6. (a) Badminton

   (b) Lawn Tennis

   (c) Table Tennis

   (d) Soccer

7. (a) 40 – 5

   (b) 126 – 17

   (c) 128 – 16

   (d) 72 – 9

Directions for questions 8: *From the given alternatives, select the one in which the set of numbers is most similar to the set of numbers given in the questions.*

8. Given set : (7, 35, 39)

   (a) (12, 60, 63)   (b) (11, 55, 53)

   (c) (9, 48, 52)   (d) (13, 65, 69)

Directions for questions 9: *Select the missing number from the given responses.*

9. 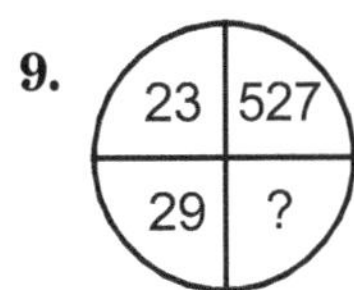

   (a) 829   (b) 837

   (c) 841   (d) 839

10. If 'EDUCATION' is 769143285 and 'REFER' is coded as 47374, what will be the code for the word 'FRANCE'?

    (a) 344517   (b) 344217

    (c) 344516   (d) 342516

11. Which one of the following sets of letters when sequentially placed in the gaps in the given letter series shall complete it?

    _ abbaa _ c _ ad _ aae _

    (a) acade   (b) acedc

    (c) bebde   (d) babce

12. Riya is facing North-west. She turns in clockwise direction by 90°, then 180° in the anti-clockwise direction and then another 90° in the same direction. Which direction is she facing now?

    (a) South-west   (b) West

    (c) South-east   (d) South

13. If a mirror is placed on the line AB, then which of the answer figures is the right image of the given figure.

Question figure:

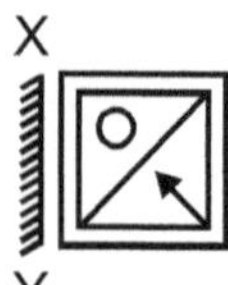

Answer figures:

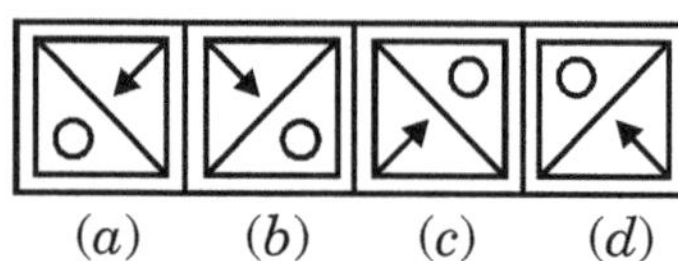

  (a) (b) (c) (d)

14. How many triangles are there in the following figure?

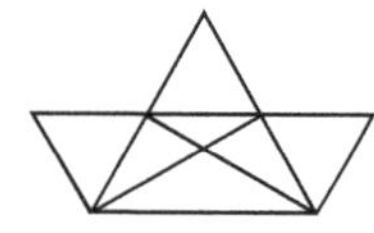

(a) 17   (b) 16

(c) 15   (d) 14

15. Select the related figure from the given alternatives.

Question figure:

Answer figure:

  (a) (b) (c) (d)

16. In the following question, among the four answer figures, which one can be formed from the cut out pieces given below?

Question figures

Answer figures

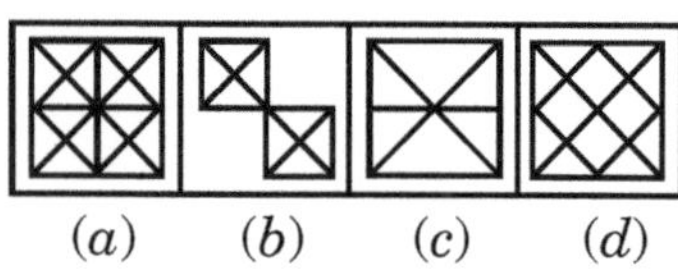

  (a) (b) (c) (d)

Directions for questions 17: *In each of the following questions select the related letter / word / number from the given alternatives.*

17. Ignominious:Disreputable :: Supercilious: ?

(a) Haughty   (b) Humble

(c) Cringing   (d) Deferential

Direction for question 18: *In the following question you have to identify the correct response from the given premises stated according to following symbols.*

18. If > = ÷, ∨ = ×, < = +, ∧ = −, + = =, × = <, − = >

(a) 8 > 4 ∧ 16 ∨ 2 > 7 × 38

(b) 8 < 4 > 16 ∧ 2 ∨ 7 − 38

(c) 8 > 4 ∨ 16 ∧ 2 < 7 × 38

(d) 8 < 4 ∧ 16 > 2 ∨ 7 + 38

Directions for questions 19: *A series is given, with a missing term. Choose the correct alternative.*

19. F 1 G, H 2 J, K 3 N, O 4 S, _?_

(a) T 5 X   (b) T 4 Y

(c) T 5 Y   (d) T 4 W

20. Which one of the given responses would be a meaningful order of the following words?

A. District

B. State

C. City

D. Continent

E. Country

(a) A,C,B,D,E (b) A,C,E,B,D

(c) A,C,E,D,B (d) A,C,B,E,D

21. From the given alternative words,select the word which cannot be formed using the letters of the given word:

SATISFACTORY

(a) Fact   (b) Factory

(c) Fist   (d) Tractor

22. From the given alternative words,select the word which can be formed using the letters of the given word:

ADMINISTERED

(a) Deter   (b) Alter

(c) Sinister   (d) Terminate

23. A statement is given followed by two assumptions, (1) and (2).You have to consider the statement to be true ,even if it seems to be at variance with commonly known facts. You are to decide which of the given assumptions can definitely be drawn from the given statement.

Statement: Some states continue to rely on nuclear weapons for their security, while others seek them to dominate their neighbors and maintain great power status

Assumptions:

1. States that rely on nuclear weapons for their security,do not rely on alternate security measures.

2. The States that seek to acquire nuclear weapons to maintain great power status do not rely on these weapons for their security.

(a) If only assumption 1 is implicit

(b) If only assumption 2 is implicit.

(c) If both 1 and 2 are implicit.

(d) If both 1 and 2 are not implicit.

24. Arrange the following words according to the dictionary:

A. Furnace

B. Furlough

C. Furniture

D. Furnish

E. Furor

(a) B,A,D,E,C

(b) B,A,D,C,E

(c) B,A,C,D,E

(d) B,A,C,E,D

25. Two statements are given followed by four conclusions. You have to consider the statements to be true, even if they seem at variance with commonly known facts. You are to decide which of the given conclusions can definitely be drawn from the given statements.

Statements:

A. Some paper is charcoal.

B. All charcoal is black.

Conclusions:

1. Some black is paper.

2. No paper is black.

3. No charcoal is paper.

4. Some charcoal is not black.

(a) Only 1 follows

(b) Both 1 and 2 follow

(c) Either 3 or 4 follow

(d) All conclusions follow

ENGLISH LANGUAGE

Directions for questions 26 to 27: *In each of the following questions, a word is followed by four options.* Select the option that best expresses the meaning of the given word.

26. Abstemious

(a) Realization

(b) Frugal

(c) Temporary

(d) Day-dream

27. Abjure

(a) Kind

(b) Rumour

(c) Admit

(d) Renounce

Directions for questions 28 to 29: *In each of the following questions, a word is followed by four options. Select the option that is opposite in meaning to the given word.*

28. Fatuous

(a) Brilliant

(b) Stationary

(c) Vague

(d) Enthusiastic

29. Brackish

(a) Saline

(b) Unappetizing

(c) Flavorful

(d) Nauseating

Directions for questions 30 to 33: *Out of the four alternatives, choose the one which can be substituted for the given words.*

30. Plurality of wives

(a) Polygyny

(b) Polyandry

(c) Misogyny

(d) Polyglot

31. A person who uses both hand equally skillfully

(a) Knackwurst

(b) Ambidexterous

(c) Parable

(d) Amputate

32. Devotion to pleasures of the senses

(a) Cassandra

(b) Hedonist

(c) Rubric

(d) Oaf

33. Easy to carry over long distance

(a) Manumit

(b) Maelstrom

(c) Niggardly

(d) Portable

Directions for questions 34 to 36: *Four alternatives are given for the Idiom / Phrase. Choose the alternative which best expresses the meaning of the Idiom / Phrase.*

34. Up to snuff

(a) Heated argument

(b) Meeting the minimum requirements

(c) Cancelled programme

(d) Extremely comfortable

35. To give someone cold shoulder

(a) To ignore someone

(b) To pass on the responsibility

(c) To treat someone affectionately

(d) To make someone curious

36. To hit the nail on the head.

(a) To hit someone violently

(b) To argue endlessly

(c) To make someone obey the order

(d) To state the truth exactly

Directions for questions 37 : *Groups of four words are given. In each group, one word is correctly spelt. Find the correctly spelt word.*

37. (a) Hautuer   (b) Feasible

     (c) Pusillannimous   (d) Paparazi

Directions for questions 38 to 40: *Some of the sentences have errors and some are correct. Find out the part of a sentence which has an error. If there is no error, mark your answer as (d).*

38. The (a) / dog (b) / scratched (c)./ No error (d)

39. We rented (a) / a house in Chelsea, (b) / London (c)./ No error (d)

40. The rich (a) / has (b) / to help the poor (c)./ No error (d)

Directions for questions 41 to 43: *Sentences are given with blanks to be filled in with an appropriate word. Four alternatives are suggested for each question. Choose the correct alternative out of the four.*

41. I have dispensed ____his services.

     (a) by   (b) of

     (c) off   (d) with

42. I slept after dinner ___ the armed chair.

     (a) in   (b) between

     (c) on   (d) over

43. He deals ____ fruit these days.

     (a) in   (b) over

     (c) about   (d) on

Directions for questions 44 to 45: *In the following questions, a sentence is given which /a part of which may need improvement. Alternatives are given (a), (b) and (c) below which may be a better option. In case no improvement is needed, your answer is (d).*

44. We distressed very little about the astonishing echo the guide talked so much about.

     (a) We distressed little about the astonishing echo the guide talked so much about.

     (b) We distressed very little the guide who talked so much about the astonishing echo.

     (c) We distressed ourselves very little about the astonishing echo the guide talked so much about.

     (d) No improvement.

45. Brought up as a boy, it was natural to resent household chores.

     (a) For a person brought up as a boy, it was natural to resent household chores.

     (b) Brought up as a boy, was natural to resent household chores.

     (c) Brought up as a boy, they was natural to resent household chores.

     (d) No improvement.

Directions (Q. 46-50) : *You have a brief passage with 5 questions. Read the passage carefully and choose the best answer to each question out of the four alternatives and mark it by blackening the appropriate rectangle [■] in the Answer Sheet.*

The problem of water pollution by pesticides can be understood only in context, as part of the whole to which it belongs - the pollution of the total environment of mankind. The pollution entering our waterways comes from many sources, radioactive wastes from reactors, laboratories, and hospitals; fallout from nuclear explosions; domestic wastes from cities and towns; chemical wastes from factories. To these is added a new kind of fallout - the chemical sprays applied to crop lands and gardens, forests and fields. Many of the chemical agents in this alarming melange initiate and augment the harmful effects of radiation, and within the groups of chemicals themselves there are sinister and little - understood interactions, transformations, and summations of effect.

Ever since the chemists began to manufacture substances that nature never invented, the problem of water purification have become complex and the danger to users of water has increased. As we have seen, the production of these synthetic chemicals in large volume began in the 1940's. It has now reached such proportion that an appalling deluge of chemical pollution is daily poured into the nation's waterways. When inextricably mixed with domestic and other wastes discharged into the same water, these chemicals sometimes defy detection by the methods in ordinary use by purification plants. Most of them are so complex that they cannot be identified. In rivers, a really incredible variety of pollutants combine to produce deposits that sanitary engineers can only despairingly refer to as "gunk".

46. Water pollution can only be understood:

     (a) in relation to the number of pesticides that exist

     (b) in relation to world contamination

     (c) by the whole human race

     (d) in context

47. Water contamination has become serious:

     (a) since businessmen authorised the use of chemicals

     (b) since water pollution was difficult to assess

     (c) since nature has taken a hand in pollution

     (d) since chemists began to use new substances

48. All the following words mean 'chemicals' except:

(a) deposits   (b) sands

(c) substances   (d) pesticides

49. The main argument of paragraph 1 is :

(a) that pesticides are dangerous

(b) that there are sinister interaction in the use of chemicals

(c) that there are numerous reasons for contamination of water supplies

(d) that there are many dangers from nuclear fallout

50. The word 'gunk' in the last line refers:

(a) to the domestic water supplies

(b) to the waste products deposited by sanitary engineers

(c) to the debris found in rivers

(d) to unidentifiable chemicals found in water

QUANTITATIVE APTITUDE

51. After obtaining two successive discounts of 30% and x%, a person saves ₹555. If the marked price of the article is ₹1500, the value of x is :

(a) 20%   (b) 12%

(c) 10%   (d) None of these

52. A pipe can fill /of a cistern in 12 hrs while another one can make it half empty in 24 hrs. Find the time taken to fill the tank if both pipes are opened simultaneously.

(a) 18 hr   (b) 16 hr

(c) 24 hr   (d) 30 hr

53. The speed of a train is 96 km/hr excluding stoppages while 80 km/hr including the stoppages. What is the total stoppage time in a 10-hour journey?

(a) 2 hr 10 min   (b) 1 hr 10 min

(c) 1 hr 40 min   (d) 50 min

54. By selling 15 toffees for ₹3, a shopkeeper loses 10%. At what rate should he sell the toffees so as to make a profit of 80%?

(a) 6 for ₹19   (b) 5 for ₹2

(c) 3 for ₹5   (d) 3 for ₹1

55. The area of a regular polygon with an external angle 60° and side 5 cm would be

(a) $\dfrac{125\sqrt{3}}{4}$ cm²   (b) $\dfrac{75\sqrt{3}}{4}$ cm²

(c) $\dfrac{75\sqrt{3}}{2}$ cm²   (d) $\dfrac{125\sqrt{3}}{2}$ cm²

56. The greatest number which when divides 4036 and 4319 leaves remainder 4 and 7 respectively is

(a) 112   (b) 28

(c) 56   (d) 48

57. The edges of a cuboid are increased by 10%, 20% and 30% respectively. Find the percentage change in its volume.

(a) 60%   (b) 50%

(c) 71.6%   (d) 72%

58. Amit sells an article at 20% profit. Had he bought it for ₹100 less and sold it for 20% more his gain would have been 60%. C.P. of the article is

(a) ₹600   (b) ₹720

(c) ₹500   (d) ₹1000

59. Evaluate : $\sqrt{12+\sqrt{12+\sqrt{12+......}}}$

(a) 1   (b) 4

(c) 3   (d) Cannot be determined

60. Area of a parallelogram with sides 8 unit and 12 unit such that angle between the adjacent sides is 45°, will be

(a) 24 sq. unit   (b) $24\sqrt{2}$ sq. unit

(c) $48\sqrt{2}$ sq. unit   (d) 48 sq. unit

61. A circular wire is bent to form a rectangle such that its sides are in the ratio of 7:4. If the length of the wire is 110 cm, what is area of the rectangle so formed?

(a) 750 cm²   (b) 780 cm²

(c) 700 cm²   (d) 720 cm²

62. If $\sqrt{\dfrac{1+\sqrt{2x}}{125}} = \dfrac{3}{5}$, then the value of x is:

(a) 968   (b) 1064

(c) 864   (d) 786

63. Two numbers are in the ratio of 3 : 2. If 6 is subtracted from each one of them, the ratio becomes 5 : 3. Sum of the two numbers is:

(a) 60   (b) 50

(c) 80   (d) 100

64. If a man travels at $\dfrac{5}{6}$ th of his usual speed for his office, he gets late by an hour. What is the usual time taken by the man to reach his office?

(a) 5 hrs

(b) 6 hrs

(c) 4 hrs 30 minutes

(d) 3 hrs

65. A number is 40% more than the second number and 30% less than the third number. By what percent is the second number more or less than the third number?

(a) 100% less

(b) 100% more

(c) 50% less

(d) $33\dfrac{1}{3}\%$ more

66. It takes 24 days to complete a piece of work when P, Q and R work together. In how many days will Q complete $\dfrac{1}{4}$th of the work if P and R working together can complete the same work in 48 days?

(a) 16

(b) 12

(c) 18

(d) 24

67. The difference between simple interest and compound interest on the amount of ₹10000 for 2 years is ₹64. The rate of interest is:

(a) 8%

(b) 10%

(c) 12%

(d) 6%

68. A roller of diameter 3.5 m and length 6 m takes 1000 revolutions to roll a cricket ground. The area of the ground in hectare is:

(a) 5.6 hectare

(b) 6.6 hectare

(c) 5 hectare

(d) 6 hectare

69. If $x+\dfrac{1}{x}=3$, then the value of $\dfrac{x+1}{\sqrt{x}}$ is:

(a) 2

(b) $\sqrt{5}$

(c) 1

(d) $\sqrt{2}$

70. 12 men and 16 women can do a piece of work in 6 days. How long will 16 men and 32 women take to complete the work, if work done by 12 men equal to that done by 16 women?

(a) 3.5 days

(b) $3\dfrac{3}{5}$ days

(c) $3\dfrac{2}{5}$ days

(d) 4 days

71. The price of a child's ticket in a bus is half of that of an adult. If tickets of 4 children and 7 adults cost ₹261, what will be the cost of tickets of 3 adults and 2 children?

(a) ₹112

(b) ₹216

(c) ₹116

(d) ₹206

72. The average of five consecutive odd numbers is 53. The product of 2nd and 4th number is

(a) 2600

(b) 2700

(c) 2800

(d) 2805

Directions for questions 73 to 75: *Answer the following questions on the basis of the given information.*

The given table represents the annual production (in million tonnes) of wheat, rice and barley in five different states.

State \ Crop	Wheat	Rice	Barley
Gujarat	24	32	82
Maharashtra	84	76	41
Punjab	82	82	60
Haryana	72	70	28
Tamil Nadu	38	90	39

73. The ratio of total production of all the three types of crops is:

(a) 6 : 7 : 5

(b) 6 : 6 : 7

(c) 7 : 5 : 8

(d) 6 : 7 : 10

74. The annual production of Rice in Haryana is what percent of the production of Barley produced in Maharashtra and Tamil Nadu?

(a) 70%

(b) 84.6%

(c) 77.5%

(d) 87.5%

75. If 20% of Wheat in Punjab and 18% of the total crops in Gujarat were destroyed due to flood, by what amount has the total production decreased (in million tonnes)?

(a) 16.4

(b) 24.84

(c) 41.24

(d) 44.24

GENERAL AWARENESS

76. Who has received the Norwegian Nobel Peace Prize for the year 2016?

(a) Juan Manuel Santos

(b) Mathews Samuels

(c) Julias Caesar

(d) John Kath

77. Which of the following gas is called laughing gas?

(a) Sulphurous oxide

(b) Titanium nitrate

(c) Ferrous sulphate

(d) Nitrous oxide

78. Which of the following river originates at Amar Kantak?

(a) Narmada

(b) Tapti

(c) Shipra

(d) Mahi

79. LIC was established in which of the following year?

(a) 1949

(b) 1953

(c) 1956

(d) 1961

80. In which year first census was conducted in India?

(a) 1861

(b) 1872

(c) 1881

(d) 1901

81. Bihar was excluded from having a minister for tribal affairs by
(a) 93rd Amendment Act
(b) 94th Amendment Act
(c) 96th Amendment Act
(d) 98th Amendment Act

82. Which of the following is not a land locked country?
(a) Afghanistan
(b) Uzbekistan
(c) Nepal
(d) Denmark

83. 1 Gigabyte (GB) equals
(a) 876 MB
(b) 964 MB
(c) 1024 MB
(d) 1176 MB

84. Shimla Agreement in 1945 A.D. took place under which viceroy?
(a) Lord Linlithgow
(b) Lord Wavell
(c) Lord Mountbatten
(d) None of these

85. Which place is called the 'Orchid of India'?
(a) Jammu Kashmir
(b) Himachal Pradesh
(c) Uttarakhand
(d) Meghalaya

86. Which is world's first packet switching network?
(a) ARPANET
(b) ALVAC
(c) ELPO
(d) COBOL

87. The two day State Power Ministers Conference held in which city ?
(a) New Delhi
(b) Mumbai
(c) Bhuvaneshwar
(d) Vadodara

88. India's first bamboo mission has been inaugurated in which of the following states?
(a) Tamil Nadu
(b) Himachal Pradesh
(c) Orissa
(d) Jammu & Kashmir

89. Which of the following mission of NASA is directed towards moon?
(a) Antilia
(b) Cheron
(c) Octopus
(d) GRAIL

90. Who was the first recipient of World Food Prize?
(a) M S Swaminathan
(b) Lula Da Silva
(c) Norman Borlaug
(d) None of these

91. Fujita scale is used to measure
(a) Strength of tornadoes
(b) Intensity of earthquake
(c) Bitterness of chillies
(d) Viscosity of liquids

92. Which of the following article of constitution corresponds to emergency provisions?
(a) Article 323
(b) Article 346
(c) Article 349
(d) Article 352

93. The concept of 'Rule of Law' has been adopted in our constitution from which country?
(a) UK
(b) France
(c) Canada
(d) Australia

94. Who is the first Indian to be appointed as the Governor of a province during British Rule in India?
(a) Satyendra Prasad Sinha
(b) S N Tagore
(c) Sarojini Naidu
(d) T B Sapru

95. Constitution of India is divided into how many parts?
(a) 18
(b) 22
(c) 26
(d) 32

96. Endosulfan is a/an
(a) Steroid
(b) Fertilizer
(c) Insecticide
(d) Hybrid seed

97. H1N1 virus causes which of the following disease?
(a) Encephalitis
(b) Kala Azar
(c) Swine flu
(d) Rabies

98. EXIM Bank was established in which of the following year?
(a) 1976
(b) 1979
(c) 1982
(d) 1986

99. Which of the following category of gold is referred as 'Primary gold'?
(a) 18 carat
(b) 20 carat
(c) 22 carat
(d) 24 carat

100. How many athletes participated from India to the 2016 Paralympics in Rio De Janeiro?
(a) 20
(b) 19
(c) 16
(d) 18

ANSWERS

1. (b)	**2.** (a)	**3.** (d)	**4.** (c)	**5.** (b)	**6.** (d)	**7.** (b)	**8.** (d)	**9.** (d)	**10.** (a)
11. (a)	**12.** (c)	**13.** (c)	**14.** (b)	**15.** (a)	**16.** (d)	**17.** (a)	**18.** (c)	**19.** (c)	**20.** (d)
21. (d)	**22.** (a)	**23.** (d)	**24.** (b)	**25.** (a)	**26.** (b)	**27.** (d)	**28.** (a)	**29.** (c)	**30.** (a)
31. (b)	**32.** (b)	**33.** (d)	**34.** (b)	**35.** (a)	**36.** (d)	**37.** (b)	**38.** (c)	**39.** (d)	**40.** (b)
41. (d)	**42.** (a)	**43.** (a)	**44.** (c)	**45.** (a)	**46.** (d)	**47.** (d)	**48.** (b)	**49.** (b)	**50.** (d)
51. (c)	**52.** (c)	**53.** (c)	**54.** (b)	**55.** (c)	**56.** (c)	**57.** (c)	**58.** (d)	**59.** (b)	**60.** (c)
61. (c)	**62.** (a)	**63.** (a)	**64.** (a)	**65.** (c)	**66.** (b)	**67.** (a)	**68.** (b)	**69.** (b)	**70.** (b)
71. (c)	**72.** (d)	**73.** (a)	**74.** (d)	**75.** (c)	**76.** (a)	**77.** (d)	**78.** (a)	**79.** (c)	**80.** (b)
81. (b)	**82.** (d)	**83.** (c)	**84.** (b)	**85.** (a)	**86.** (a)	**87.** (d)	**88.** (b)	**89.** (d)	**90.** (a)
91. (a)	**92.** (d)	**93.** (a)	**94.** (a)	**95.** (b)	**96.** (c)	**97.** (c)	**98.** (c)	**99.** (d)	**100.** (b)

EXPLANATIONS

1. The given series is

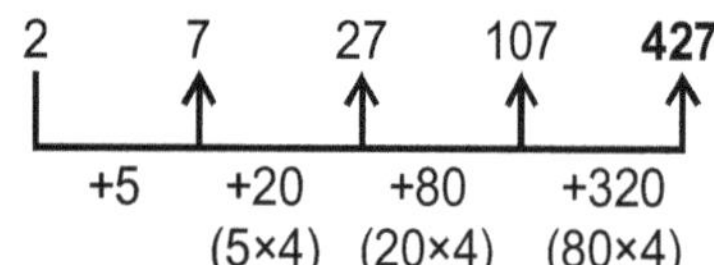

Hence, the next term is 427.

2. The given relationship can be shown as

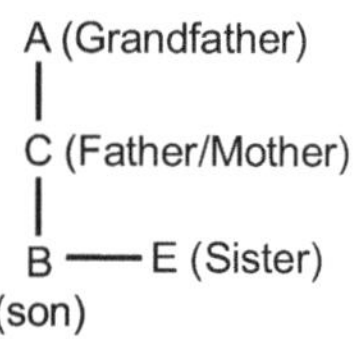

A (Grandfather)
|
C (Father/Mother)
|
B —— E (Sister)
(son)

∴ A is Grandfather of E.

3.

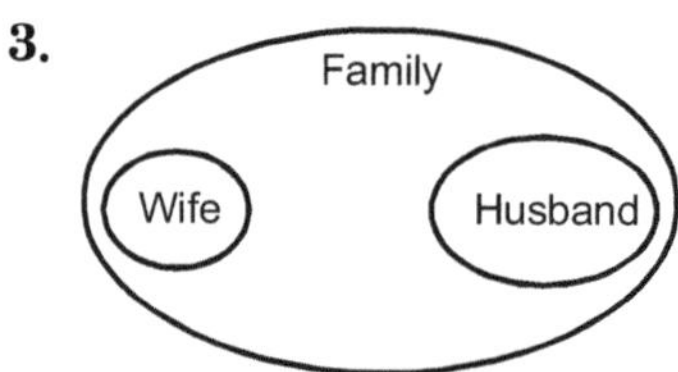

4.

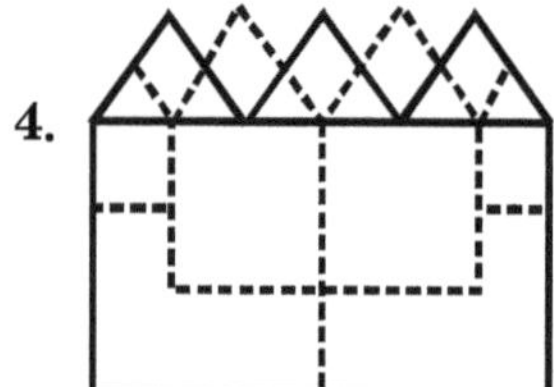

5. Every quarter of the sheet will contain a square in the middle.

6. The odd word out is "soccer" because in the rest of the games one requires a racket to play.

7.
$$5 \times 8 = 40$$
$$17 \times 8 = \mathbf{136}$$
$$16 \times 8 = 128$$
$$9 \times 8 = 72$$

8. Given :

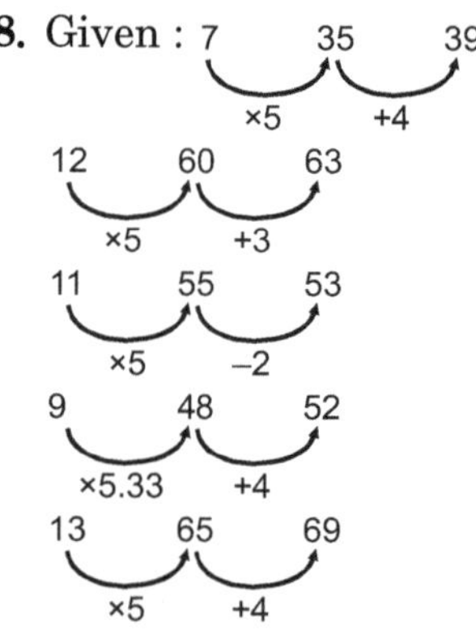

Hence, correct solution is (13, 65, 69).

9. $23^2 - 2 = 527$

$29^2 - 2 = \mathbf{839}$

10. F → 3

R → 4

A → 4

N → 5

C → 1

E → 7

11. The given series is

a̲abb / aa̲c̲c̲ / a̲add̲ / aae̲e̲

12. Riya is facing South-east direction.

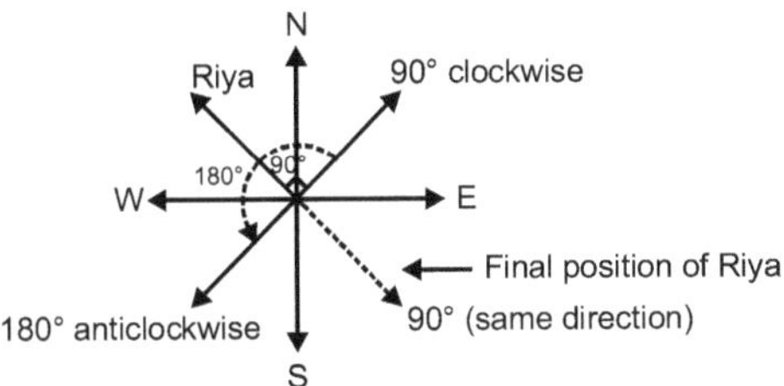

13. Answer figure (c) is the mirror image of the question figure.

14. 16 traingles.

15. The figure is enclosed in a new figure with one more number of sides and the upper vertex of both figures coincide.

16. The four cut pieces will join to give answer figure (d).

17. "Ignominious" means deserving or causing public disgrace or shame. "Disreputable" is a synonym of "ignominious". "Supercilious" means coolly and patronizingly haughty.

18. In option (c), after applying given rule,

$$8 \div 4 \times 16 - 2 + 7 < 38$$

$$\text{LHS} = \frac{8}{4} \times 16 - 2 + 7 = 37 \text{, which is less than 38.}$$

19. F (6) + 1 → G (7)

H (8) + 2 → J (10)

K (11) + 3 → N (14)

O (15) + 4 → S (19)

T (20) + 5 → Y (25)

∴ The missing term is T5Y.

20. The city is divided into districts, a state is divided into cities, a country is divided into states and so on.

21. The word "tractor" cannot be formed because the given word does not have an additional "R".

22. "Deter" is the only word that can be formed from the letters of the given word.

23. We cannot assume the first assumption because the question statement is silent on the fact that whether states rely on alternate security measures or not. The assumption (2) states that the states that seek to acquire nuclear weapons to maintain great power status do not rely on these weapons for their security. We cannot assume this because the question statement is silent on the fact whether these states rely on nuclear weapons for their security.

24. The correct order of the given words according to the dictionary is B,A,D,C,E

25.

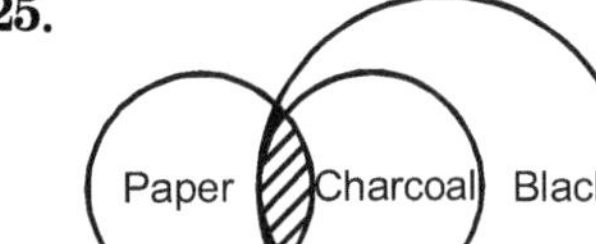

Some paper is charcoal. All charcoal is black. Thus some black is paper. Only 1 follows.

26. "Abstemious" means marked by restraint especially in the consumption of food or alcohol. The word most similar in meaning to the given word is "frugal". "Realization" means the action of realizing. "Temporary" means lasting for a limited time. "Day-dream" means a pleasant visionary usually wishful creation of the imagination.

27. "Abjure" means to renounce upon oath. "Rumour" means talk or opinion widely disseminated with no discernible source. "Admit" means to concede as true or valid. "Kind" means fundamental nature or quality. "Renounce" is the word most similar in meaning to the given word.

28. "Fatuous" means complacently or inanely foolish. "Brilliant" is the word most opposite in meaning to the given word. "Stationary" means fixed in a station. "Vague" means not clearly expressed. "Enthusiastic" means filled with or marked by enthusiasm.

29. "Brackish" means saline and not appealing to the taste. "Unappetizing" means not appetizing, insipid and unattractive. Option (a) and (d) are negated as well. "Flavorful" which means the blend of taste and smell sensations evoked by a substance in the mouth is the correct answer.

30. "Polygyny" is a form of marriage in which a man has two or more wives at the same time. "Polyandry" refers to a form of marriage in which a woman has two or more husbands at the same time. "Polyglot" is a person having a speaking, reading, or writing knowledge of several languages. "Misogyny" is hatred of women.

31. "Ambidextrous" means using both hands with equal ease. "Parable" means a short allegorical story designed to illustrate or teach some truth or moral lesson. "Knackwurst" may refer to a variety of different sausage types, depending on the geographical region. "Amputate" means to remove by or as if by cutting.

32. "Hedonist" is a person who believes that pleasure or happiness is the sole or chief good in life. "Rubric" means an authoritative rule. "Oaf" means a big clumsy slow-witted person. "Cassandra" is a daughter of Priam endowed with the gift of prophecy but fated never to be believed.

33. "Portable" means capable of being carried or moved about. "Manumit" means to release from slavery. "Maelstrom" means a powerful often violent whirlpool sucking in objects within a given radius. "Niggardly" means grudgingly mean about spending.

34. "Up to snuff" means up to the required standard.

35. "To give someone cold shoulder" means a show of intentional unfriendliness or rejection.

36. "To hit the nail on the head" means to find exactly the right answer.

37. The correct spelling for option (a) is "hauteur". The correct spelling for option (c) is "pusillanimous". The correct spelling for option (d) is "paparazzi"

38. The correct sentence is "the dog scratched itself". For verbs used reflexively like "scratched" there must be a reflexive pronoun after the verb.

39. There is no error in the sentence.

40. A collective noun is always plural and requires a plural verb. The correct sentence is "the rich have to help the poor."

41. The correct phrasal verb is "dispense with" which means to stop using something or get rid of something because one no longer needs it.

42. Preposition "on" indicates that the position of an object is defined with respect to a surface on which it rests. Preposition "in" indicates that an object lies within the confines of a volume.

43. The correct phrasal verb is "deals in". If a shop deals in a particular type of goods ,it buys and sells those goods.

44. For verbs used reflexively like "distressed" there must be a reflexive pronoun "ourselves" after the verb.

45. "Brought up as a boy" is a dangling modifier that illogically modifies "it". We need a subject for the clause "brought up as a boy".

51. Value of first discount = 30% of 1500

$$= ₹450$$

Also, total discount = ₹555

∴ x% discount is equivalent to $(555 - 450) = ₹105$

According to question,

$$x\% \text{ of } (1500 - 450) = 105$$

$$∴ \quad x = \frac{105 \times 100}{1050} = 10\%.$$

52. Time taken by the first pipe to make it completely fill the cistern

$$= \frac{12}{3/4} = 16 \text{ hours}$$

Also, time taken by the second pipe to empty it

$$= \frac{24}{1/2} = 48 \text{ hours}$$

If both pipes are opened simultaneously, part of the cistern filled in one hour

$$= \frac{1}{16} - \frac{1}{48} = \frac{3-1}{48} = \frac{2}{48} = \frac{1}{24}$$

Therefore, time taken to fill the tank will be 24 hours.

53. Total distance travel by the train

$$= \text{speed} \times \text{time}$$
$$= 80 \times 10 = 800 \text{ km}$$

If the train travels without stoppage for 10 hrs, then distance covered

$$= 96 \times 10 = 960 \text{ km}$$

Therefore, total stoppage time

$$= \frac{960 - 800}{96} = \frac{160}{96}$$

$$= \frac{10}{6} = 1\frac{2}{3} \text{ hrs}$$

i.e., 1 hr 40 minutes.

54. Selling price of 1 toffee $= \frac{3}{15} = ₹\frac{1}{5}$

∴ Cost price of 1 toffee if loss is 10%

$$= \frac{1/5}{1 - 0.1} = \frac{1}{5 \times 0.9} = ₹\frac{2}{9}$$

∴ Selling price at a profit of 80%

$$= \frac{2}{9}(1 + 0.8) = 0.4 = ₹\frac{2}{5}$$

∴ One must sell 5 toffees for ₹2.

55.

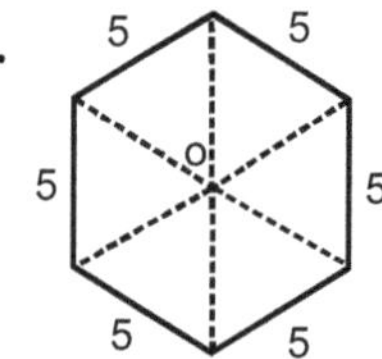

Number of sides in the regular polygon

$$= \frac{360°}{60°} = 6$$

∴ Area of the polygon so formed

$$= 6 \times \text{Area of equilateral triangle of side 5 cm}$$

$$= 6 \times \frac{\sqrt{3}}{4} \times (5)^2$$

$$= \frac{75\sqrt{3}}{2} \text{ cm}^2.$$

56. Required number

$$= \text{HCF}[(4036 - 4), (4319 - 7)],$$

i.e. HCF (4032, 4312), which is 56.

57. Let the edges of cuboid be l, b and h respectively.

$\therefore$ Volume when each of the edge changes

$$= 1.1\, l \times 1.2\, b \times 1.3\, h$$
$$= 1.716\ lbh.$$

$\therefore$ Percentage change

$$= \frac{(1.716 - 1)}{lbh}\, lbh \times 100 = 71.6\%$$

58. Let C.P. of the article is ₹x.

S.P. at a profit of 20% = 1.2x.

If bought at ₹100 less, then C.P. = x – 100

New selling price will be (1.2x × 1.2) = 1.44x

According to question,

$$(x - 100)(1 + 0.60) = 1.44x$$
$$\Rightarrow\ 1.6x - 160 = 1.44x$$
$$\Rightarrow\ x = 1000.$$

59. Let $x = \sqrt{12 + \sqrt{12 + \sqrt{12 + \ldots\ldots}}}$

$\therefore\ x = \sqrt{12 + x}$

$\Rightarrow\ x^2 = 12 + x$

$\Rightarrow\ x^2 - x - 12 = 0$

$\Rightarrow\ x^2 - 4x + 3x - 12 = 0$

$\Rightarrow\ x(x - 4) + 3(x - 4) = 0$

$\Rightarrow\ (x - 4)(x + 3) = 0$

$\therefore\ x = 4\ $ or $\ -3$

Since x cannot be negative, therefore $x = 4$.

60. Here, In right $\triangle$ADM

$$\sin 45° = \frac{DM}{AD} = \frac{h}{8}$$

$\therefore\ h = 8 \times \dfrac{1}{\sqrt{2}} = \dfrac{8}{\sqrt{2}}$ units.

$\therefore$ Area of parallelogram = Base × Height

$$= AB \times h = 12 \times \frac{8}{\sqrt{2}}$$
$$= 48\sqrt{2}\ \text{units.}$$

61. Let the sides of rectangle be 7k and 4k

According to question,

circumference of wire

$$= \text{perimeter of rectangle}$$
$$110 = 2\,(7k + 4k)$$
$$\Rightarrow\quad \frac{110}{2} = 11k$$
$$\Rightarrow\quad\quad k = 5$$

Thus, sides of rectangle are 7 × 5 = 35 cm and 4 × 5 = 20 cm.

$\therefore\quad$ Area = 35 × 20 = 700 cm².

62. $\sqrt{\dfrac{1 + \sqrt{2x}}{125}} = \dfrac{3}{5}$

Squaring both sides, we get

$$\frac{1 + \sqrt{2x}}{125} = \left(\frac{3}{5}\right)^2 = \frac{9}{25}$$

$\Rightarrow\ 1 + \sqrt{2x} = 45$

$\Rightarrow\ \sqrt{2x} = 45 - 1 = 44$

$\therefore\ 2x = (44)^2$

$\therefore\ x = \dfrac{44 \times 44}{2} = 22 \times 44 = 968.$

63. Let the numbers be 3x and 2x respectively.

According to question,

$$\frac{3x - 6}{2x - 6} = \frac{5}{3}$$

$\Rightarrow\quad 9x - 18 = 10x - 30$

$\Rightarrow\quad 10x - 9x = 30 - 18 = 12$

$\therefore\quad\quad x = 12$

$\therefore$ Sum of the numbers would be

$$3x + 2x = 5x,$$

i.e., $\quad\quad 5 \times 12 = 60.$

64. Let the usual time taken is 't' while the speed is 's'.

$\therefore$ Distance = st

Now, Speed = $\dfrac{5s}{6}$

$\therefore$ Time taken = $\dfrac{st}{5s/6} = \dfrac{6t}{5}$

According to question, $\dfrac{6t}{5} - t = 1$

$\therefore\ t = 5\text{hrs.}$

65. Let first, second and third, numbers be x, y and z.

Then, $x = (1 + 0.4)y = 1.4y$

Also, $x = (1 - 0.3)z = 0.7z$

$\Rightarrow\ x = 1.4y = 0.7z = k$

$\therefore\ x = k$

$$y = \frac{5}{7}k\ \text{ and }\ z = \frac{10}{7}k$$

Difference between y and z $= \dfrac{10}{7}k - \dfrac{5}{7}k = \dfrac{5}{7}k$

$\therefore$ Percentage by which y is less than z

$$= \frac{(5/7)k}{(10/7)k} \times 100 = 50\%$$

Hence, second number is 50% less than the third number.

66. Let the total amount of work be

LCM (24 and 48) = 48 units.

Work done by P, Q and R in one day

$$= \frac{48}{24} = 2 \text{ units}.$$

Work done by P and R in one day

$$= \frac{48}{48} = 1 \text{ unit}.$$

$\therefore$ Work done by Q in one day = 2 − 1 = 1 unit.

Time taken by Q to complete $\frac{1}{4}$th of the work

$$= \frac{1}{4} \times \frac{48}{1} = 12 \text{ days}.$$

67. Let the rate of interest be R%.

$$P\left(\frac{R}{100}\right)^2 = 64$$

$$\Rightarrow \frac{R^2}{100 \times 100} = \frac{64}{10000}$$

$$\Rightarrow R^2 = \frac{64 \times 100 \times 100}{10000} = 64$$

$$\therefore R = \sqrt{64} = 8\% \text{ p.a.}$$

68. Area of the ground = Curved surface area of cylinder × Number of revolutions

$$= 2\pi r h \times 1000 = 2 \times \frac{22}{7} \times \frac{3.5}{2} \times 6 \times 1000$$

$$= 66000 \text{ m}^2 = 6.6 \text{ hectare}.$$

69. $x + \dfrac{1}{x} = 3$

Adding 2 on both sides

$$\Rightarrow (\sqrt{x}) + \left(\frac{1}{\sqrt{x}}\right)^2 + 2 \cdot \sqrt{x} \cdot \frac{1}{\sqrt{x}} = 3 + 2$$

$$\Rightarrow \left(\sqrt{x} + \frac{1}{\sqrt{x}}\right)^2 = 5$$

$$\Rightarrow \sqrt{x} + \frac{1}{\sqrt{x}} = \sqrt{5} \Rightarrow \frac{(\sqrt{x})^2 + 1}{\sqrt{x}} = \sqrt{5}$$

$$\Rightarrow \frac{x+1}{\sqrt{x}} = \sqrt{5}.$$

70. (12 men + 16 women) can do a piece of work in 6 days.

$\because$ 12 men $\equiv$ 16 women

$\therefore$ 1 men $\equiv \dfrac{16}{12}$ women

$\therefore$ 16 men $\equiv \dfrac{16}{12} \times 16 = \dfrac{64}{3}$ women

$\because$ 32 women can do the work in 6 days.

$\therefore$ 1 women can do the work in 6 × 32 days

$\therefore \left(32 + \dfrac{64}{3}\right)$ women can do it in $\dfrac{32 \times 6}{160/3} = \dfrac{18}{5}$

$$= 3\frac{3}{5} \text{ days}.$$

71. Let the ticket price for a child is ₹x and that for an adult is ₹2x.

According to question, 4x + 7 × 2x = 261

$$\Rightarrow 18x = 261 \Rightarrow x = \frac{261}{18} = \frac{29}{2} = ₹14.5$$

$\therefore$ Cost of 3 adults and 2 children

$$= 3 \times 2x + 2x = 8x = 8 \times 14.5 = ₹116.$$

72. Let the odd numbers be $2n + 1, 2n + 3, 2n + 5, 2n + 7$ and $2n + 9$.

$$\therefore \text{Average} = \frac{\begin{array}{c}2n+1+2n+3+2n+5\\+2n+7+2n+9\end{array}}{5}$$

$$= \frac{10n + 25}{5} = 2n + 5$$

$$\Rightarrow 53 = 2n + 5$$

$\therefore$ n = 24

$\therefore$ Product of 2nd and 4th number

$$= (2n + 3)(2n + 7) = 51 \times 55 = 2805.$$

Solution for 73 to 75:

State\Crop	Wheat	Rice	Barley	Total
Gujarat	24	32	82	138
Maharashtra	84	76	41	201
Punjab	82	82	60	224
Haryana	72	70	28	170
Tamil Nadu	38	90	39	167
Total	300	350	250	900

73. Wheat : Rice : Barley = 300 : 350 : 250

$$= 6 : 7 : 5$$

74. Amount of Barley produced in Maharashtra and Tamil Nadu = (41 + 39) = 80 million tonnes.

Amount of Rice produced in Haryana

$$= 70 \text{ million tonnes}.$$

$\therefore$ Required percentage $= \dfrac{70}{80} \times 100 = 87.5\%$.

75. Amount of Wheat damaged in Punjab = 20% of 82 million tonnes = 16.4 million tonnes.

Amount of crops damaged in Gujarat = 18% of 138 million tonnes = 24.84 million tonnes.

$\therefore$ Decrease in the total production of crops = (16.4 + 24.84) = 41.24 million tonnes.

GENERAL INTELLIGENCE

Directions (Q. 1-4) : *Select the related letter / word / number from the given alternatives.*

1. 8 : 12 : : 6 : ?

   (a) 8   (b) 11

   (c) 5   (d) 7

2. APPLE : 50 : : ORANGE : ?

   (a) 60   (b) 69

   (c) 61   (d) 63

3. Accommodation : Rent : : Journey : ?

   (a) Freight   (b) Octroi

   (c) Fare   (d) Expense

4. Fire : Smoke : : ?

   (a) Children : School

   (b) Cloud : Rain

   (c) Moon : Sky

   (d) Shoe : Polish

Directions (Q. 5-6) : *Find the odd number / letters / word / number pair from the given alternatives.*

5. (a) SP   (b) NL

   (c) ZW   (d) TQ

6. (a) (132, 5)   (b) (125, 8)

   (c) (124, 7)   (d) (112, 4)

Directions (Q. 7-8) : *A series is given, with one term missing. Choose the correct alternative from the given ones that will complete the series.*

7. D9Y, J27S, P81M, V243G, ?

   (a) A324B   (b) C729B

   (c) B729A   (d) A729B

8. Which one set of letters when sequentially placed at the gaps in the given letter series shall complete it?

_c_bd_cbcda_a_db_a

   (a) daabbc   (b) bdcba

   (c) adabcd   (d) cdbbca

9. Identify wrong number in the series.

    9, 19, 40, 83, 170, 340

   (a) 83   (b) 40

   (c) 340   (d) 170

10. Some relationships have been express through symbols which are explained below

   o = greater than;   Δ = not equal to

   × = not less than;   + = equal to

   ϕ = not greater than; ∇ = less than

   $a \nabla b \nabla c$, implies

   (a) $a \Delta b \phi c$ (b) $a \phi b + c$

   (c) $a\ o\ b + c$ (d) $a\ o\ b \times c$

11. If 54 + 43 = 2, 60 + 51 = 10, then 62 + 72 = ?

   (a) 30   (b) 18

   (c) 20   (d) 9

12. If   L denotes ×

       M denotes ÷

       P denotes +

       Q denotes –

   then 16 P 24 M 8 Q 6 M 2 L 3 = ?

   (a) 10   (b) 9

   (c) 12   (d) 11

13. In this question, from the given alternatives select the word which **cannot** be formed by using the letters of the given word.

APPROPRIATE

   (a) PIRATE

   (b) APPROVE

   (c) PROPER

   (d) RAPPORT

14. If FLATTER is coded as 7238859 and MOTHER is coded as 468159, then how is MAMMOTH coded?

   (a) 4344681   (b) 4344651

   (c) 4146481   (d) 4346481

15. Select missing number from the given responses.

10	11	15
12	12	8
4	12	10
10	5	13
18	20	?

   (a) 21   (b) 20

   (c) 23   (d) 22

16. Satish start from A and walks 2 km east upto B and turns southwards and walks 1 km upto C. At C he turns to east and walks 2 km upto D. He then turns northwards and walks 4 km to E. How far is he from his starting point?

(a) 5 km   (b) 6 km

(c) 3 km   (d) 4 km

17. In given question one/two statements are given, followed by two conclusions I and II. You have to consider the statements to be true, even if they seem to be at variance from commonly known facts. You have to decide which of the given conclusions, if any, follow from the given statements.

Statements :

1. Temple is a place of worship.
2. Church is also a place of worship.

Conclusions :

I. Hindus and Christians use the same place for worship.

II. All churches are temples.

(a) Neither conclusion I nor II follows

(b) Both conclusions I and II follows

(c) Only conclusion I follows

(d) Only conclusion II follows

18. In the following letter series how many times do PQR occur in such away that Q is in the middle of P and R.

QMPNPQRROPQNOPPQRPMQROPQRPPRRPQRP

(a) 5   (b) 6

(c) 4   (d) 3

19. Volume of a sphere is equal to the volume of a hemisphere. If the radius of the hemisphere is

$3\sqrt[3]{2}$ cm, then the radius of the sphere is equal to

(a) $9\sqrt[3]{2}$ cm   (b) $6\sqrt[3]{2}$ cm

(c) 27 cm   (d) 3 cm

20. A sheet of paper has been folded as shown by the question figure. You have to figure out from amongst the four answer figures how it will appear when opened?

Question figures:

Answer figures:

  (a)   (b)   (c)   (d)

21. Which of the answer figures is exactly the mirror image of the question figure if a mirror is placed on the line MN?

Question figure:

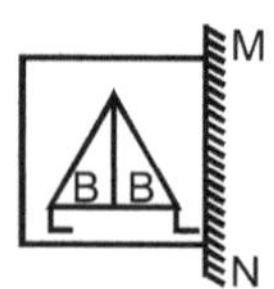

Answer figures:

 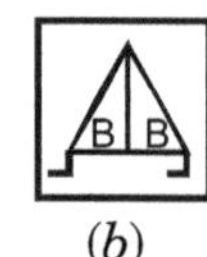  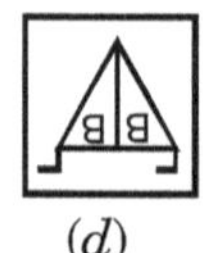

  (a)   (b)   (c)   (d)

22. In SEARCH is coded as TFBSDI, how will PENCIL be coded?

(a) RGPEN   (b) LICNEP

(c) QFODJM   (d) QDMBHK

23. Which answer figure completes the form in the question figure?

Question figure:

Answer figures:

 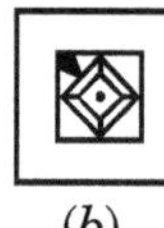  

  (a)   (b)   (c)   (d)

24. From the answer figures, select the one in which the question figure is hidden/embedded.

Question figure:

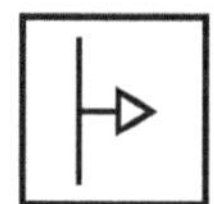

Answer figures:

 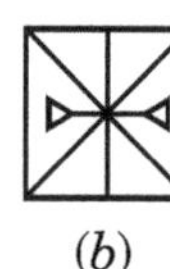  

  (a)   (b)   (c)   (d)

25. A word is represented by only one set of numbers as given in any one of the alternatives. The sets of numbers given in the alternatives are represented by two classes of alphabets as in two matrices given below. The columns and rows of Matrix I are numbered from 0 to 4 and that of Matrix II are numbered from 5 to 9. A letter from these matrices can be represented *first by its row* and *next by its column, e.g.,* 'A' can be represented by 10, 33, etc., and H can be represented by 59, 78 etc. Similarly, you have to identify the set for the word GUIDE.

MATRIX I

	0	1	2	3	4
0	I	E	A	O	U
1	A	O	U	I	E
2	E	I	O	U	A
3	O	U	E	A	I
4	U	A	I	E	O

MATRIX II

	5	6	7	8	9
5	F	D	B	G	H
6	B	G	H	F	D
7	D	F	G	H	B
8	G	H	D	B	F
9	H	B	F	G	O

(a) 85, 23, 21, 87, 32

(b) 58, 31, 12, 57, 41

(c) 77, 13, 42, 99, 32

(d) 66, 31, 43, 78, 14

ENGLISH LANGUAGE

Directions (Q. 26-27) : *Out of the four alternatives, choose the one which best expresses the meaning of the given word and mark it in the Answer Sheet.*

26. Nexus

(a) connection   (b) distance

(c) deficit   (d) difference

27. Mammoth

(a) straight   (b) huge

(c) wild   (d) greedy

Directions (Q. 28-29) : *Choose the word opposite in meaning to the given word and mark it in the Answer Sheet.*

28. Impeccable

(a) faulty   (b) tedious

(c) flashy   (d) boring

29. Amalgamate

(a) separate   (b) combine

(c) assimilate   (d) integrate

Directions (Q. 30-32) : *Out of the four alternatives, choose the one which can be substituted for the given words / sentence.*

30. One who loves books

(a) Bibliophile   (b) Bibliophagist

(c) bibliophoebe   (d) Bibliographer

31. Speaking without preparation

(a) Deliberate   (b) Fluent

(c) Loquacious   (d) Extempore

32. Special trial of the Head of State by Parliament

(a) Impingement   (b) Infringement

(c) Impeachment   (d) Impediment

Directions (Q. 33-35): *Four alternatives are given for the idiom / phrase underlined in the sentence. Choose the alternative which best expresses the meaning of the idiom / phrase and mark it in the Answer Sheet.*

33. Ram is very calculative and always has an axe to grind.

(a) has no result

(b) works for both sides

(c) has a private agenda

(d) fails to arouse interest

34. The police looked all over for him but drew a blank.

(a) did not find him   (b) put him in prison

(c) arrested him   (d) took him to court

35. On the issue of marriage, Sarita put her foot down.

(a) stood up   (b) was firm

(c) got down   (d) walked fast

36. There are four different words out of which one is correctly spelt. Find the correctly spelt word.

(a) pleintive   (b) sustein

(c) villain   (d) alleince

Directions (Q. 37-39): *In question some parts of the sentences have errors and some have none. Find out which part of a sentence has an error and blacken the rectangle [■] corresponding to appropriate letter (a, b, c). If a sentence is free from error, blacken the rectangle [■] corresponding to (d) in the Answer Sheet.*

37. You do not (a)/ look as (b)/ your brother. (c)/ No error (d)

38. My elder brother (a)/ is six (b)/ foot high. (c)/ No error. (d)

39. Without no proof of your guilt (a)/ the only course open to me (b)/ is to dismiss the case. (c)/ No error. (d)

Directions (Q. 40-42): *Sentences are given with blanks to be filled in with an appropriate word(s). Four alternatives are suggested for each question. Choose the correct alternative out of the four and indicate it by blackening the appropriate rectangle [■] in the Answer Sheet.*

40. The Union Budget is likely to be presented on February 26, two days ahead of the_____date.

(a) critical   (b) conventional

(c) suitable   (d) convenient

41. I am sorry_____the mistake.

(a) from   (b) with

(c) for   (d) at

42. He_____her that she would pass.

(*a*) insured   (*b*) ensured

(*c*) assumed   (*d*) assured

Directions (Q. 43-45): *A part of the sentence is underlined. Below are given alternatives to the underlined part at (a), (b) and (c) which may improve the sentence. Choose the correct alternative. In case no improvement is needed, your answer is (d).*

43. Sordid and sensational books tend to <u>vitiate</u> the public tastte.

(*a*) divide   (*b*) distract

(*c*) distort   (*d*) No improvement

44. <u>By studying</u> AIDS has engaged many researchers in the last decade.

(*a*) Important study

(*b*) Now that the study

(*c*) The study of

(*d*) No improvement

45. His master's thesis <u>was highly estimated</u> and is now being prepared for publication.

(*a*) was highly discussed

(*b*) was highly commended

(*c*) is highly appraised

(*d*) No improvement

Directions (Q. 46-50) : *Read the following passage carefully and choose the best answer to each question out of four alternatives and mark it the correct answer.*

Two years later, in November 1895, he signed his final will. He left the bulk of his fortune, amounting to about £1,75,000 to a trust fund administered by Swedish and Norwegian trustees. The annual interest shall be awarded as prizes to those persons who during the previous year have rendered the greatest services to mankind. The interest shall be divided into five equal parts — now amounting to about £8,000 each — one of which shall be awarded to the person who has made the most important discovery or invention in the realm of physics, one to the person who has made the most important chemical discovery or improvement, one to the person who has made the most important physiological or medical discovery, one to the person who has produced the most outstanding work of literature, idealistic in character, and one to the person who has done the best work for the brotherhood of nations, the abolition or reduction of standing armies, as well as for the formation or popularization of peace congress.

46. The said prize is awarded

(*a*) once in 5 years   (*b*) every year

(*c*) once in 4 years   (*d*) once in 2 years

47. Which is the prize that is referred to in the passage?

(*a*) Nobel Prize

(*b*) Magsaysay Award

(*c*) Pulitzer Prize

(*d*) Booker Prize

48. The number of prizes in the field of science are

(*a*) Four   (*b*) One

(*c*) Three   (*d*) Five

49. Total annual prize money amounts to

(*a*) £ 8,000   (*b*) £ 1,750,000

(*c*) £ 350,000   (*d*) £ 40,000

50. Prize is awarded for outstanding work in

(*a*) Chemistry

(*b*) Literature

(*c*) Physics

(*d*) All the above

QUANTITATIVE APTITUDE

51. P and Q are two points observed from the top of a building $10\sqrt{3}$ m high. If the angles of depression of the points are complementary and PQ = 20 m, then the distance of P from the building is

(*a*) 25 m   (*b*) 45 m

(*c*) 30 m   (*d*) 40 m

52. If A and B are complementary angles, then the value of sinA cosB + cosA sin B – tanA tanB + $\sec^2 A - \cot^2 B$ is

(*a*) 2   (*b*) 0

(*c*) 1   (*d*) – 1

53. The least value of $2\sin^2\theta + 3\cos^2\theta$ is

(*a*) 3   (*b*) 5

(*c*) 1   (*d*) 2

54. A, O, B are three points on a line segment and C is a point not ying on AOB. If $\angle AOC = 40°$ and OX, OY are the internal and external bisectors of $\angle AOC$ respectively, then $\angle BOY$ is

(*a*) 70°   (*b*) 80°

(*c*) 72°   (*d*) 68°

55. If $4x = \sec\theta$ and $\dfrac{4}{x} = \tan\theta$, then $8\left(x^2 - \dfrac{1}{x^2}\right)$ is

(a) $\dfrac{1}{16}$ (b) $\dfrac{1}{8}$

(c) $\dfrac{1}{2}$ (d) $\dfrac{1}{4}$

56. In the following figure, O is the centre of the circle and XO is perpendicular to OY. If the area of the triangle XOY is 32, then the area of the circle is

(a) 64π (b) 256π

(c) 16π (d) 32π

57. Two circles of radii 4 cm and 9 cm respectively touch each other externally at a point and a common tangent touches them at the point P and Q respectively. Then the area of a square with one side PQ, is

(a) 97 sq. cm   (b) 194 sq. cm

(c) 72 sq. cm   (d) 144 sq. cm

58. Two tangents are drawn from a point P to a circle at A and B. O is the centre of the circle. If $\angle AOP = 60°$, then $\angle APB$ is

(a) 120°   (b) 90°

(c) 60°   (d) 30°

59. If $x^4 + \dfrac{1}{x^4} = 23$, then the value of $\left(x - \dfrac{1}{x}\right)^2$ will be

(a) 7   (b) -7

(c) -3 (d) 3

60. The value of $\sqrt{[6 + \sqrt{6 + \sqrt{\{(6 + \cdots \text{upto } \infty)\}}]}}$ is equal to

(a) 3   (b) 10

(c) 8   (d) 2

61. If $x + \dfrac{1}{x} = 3$, the value of $x^5 + \dfrac{1}{x^5}$ is

(a) 123   (b) 126

(c) 113   (d) 129

62. The average age of four boys, five years ago was 9 years. On including a new boy, the present average age of all the five is 15 years. The present age of the new boy is

(a) 14 years   (b) 6 years

(c) 15 years   (d) 19 years

63. The cost of a piece of diamond varies with the square of its weight. A diamond of ₹ 5,164 value is cut into 3 pieces whose weights are in the ratio $1 : 2 : 3$. Find the loss involved in the cutting.

(a) ₹ 3,068   (b) ₹ 3,088

(c) ₹ 3,175   (d) ₹ 3,168

64. A discount of 30% on the marked price of a toy reduces its selling price by ₹ 30. What is the new selling price (in ₹)?

(a) 70   (b) 21

(c) 130   (d) 100

65. The capacities of two hemispherical vessels are 6.4 litres and 21.6 litres. The ratio of their inner radii is

(a) $4 : 9$ (b) $16 : 81$

(c) $\sqrt{2} : \sqrt{3}$ (d) $2 : 3$

66. Pipe A alone can fill a tank in 8 hours. Pipe B alone can fill it in 6 hours. If both the pipes are opened and after 2 hours Pipe A is closed, then the other pipe will fill the tank in

(a) 6 hours   (b) $3\dfrac{1}{2}$ hours

(c) 4 hours   (d) $2\dfrac{1}{2}$ hours

67. The population of a town is 15000. If the number of males increases by 8% and that of females by 10%, then the population would increase to 16300. Find the number of females in the town.

(a) 4000   (b) 6000

(c) 3000   (d) 5000

68. If ₹ 5,000 becomes ₹ 5,700 in a year's time, what will ₹ 7,000 become at the end of 5 years at the same rate of simple interest?

(a) ₹ 10,500   (b) ₹ 11,900

(c) ₹ 12,700   (d) ₹ 7,700

69. A thief is noticed by a policeman from a distance of 200m. The thief starts running and the policeman chases him. The thief and the policeman run at the rate of 10 km and 11 km per hour respectively. The distance (in metres) between them after 6 minutes is

(a) 190   (b) 200

(c) 100   (d) 150

70. 'A' sells an article to 'B' at a profit of 20% and 'B' sells it to 'C' at a profit of 25%. If 'C' pays ₹ 1,200, the cost price of the article originally (in ₹) is

(a) 700   (b) 600

(c) 1,000   (d) 800

71. A farmer divided his herd of n cows among his four sons, so that the first son gets one-half the herd, the second one-fourth, the third son $\dfrac{1}{5}$ and the fourth son 7 cows. Then the value of n is

(a) 240 (b) 100

(c) 180 (d) 140

72. The least number which when divided by 35, 45, 55 leaves the remainder 18, 28, 38 respectively is

(a) 3448 (b) 3482

(c) 2468 (d) 3265

Directions (Q. 73-75) : *The graph shows Income and Expenditure of a company. Study the graph and answer the questions.*

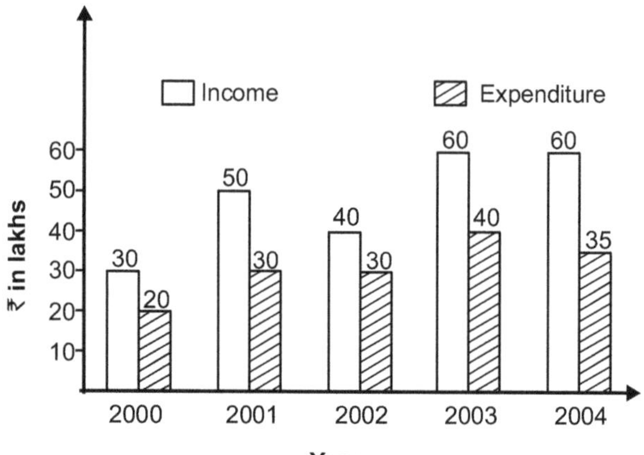

73. The expenditure from 2002 to 2003 increased by

(a) $33\dfrac{1}{3}\%$ (b) 40%

(c) 10% (d) 20%

74. The income in 2002 was equal to the expenditure in the year

(a) 2003 (b) 2004

(c) 2000 (d) 2001

75. The profit was maximum in the year

(a) 2003 (b) 2004

(c) 2001 (d) 2002

GENERAL AWARENESS

76. The National Commission for Minorities was constituted in the year

(a) 1990 (b) 1992

(c) 1980 (d) 1989

77. In which of the following systems of government is biocameralism an essential feature?

(a) Federal system

(b) Unitary system

(c) Parliamentary system

(d) Presidential system

78. Economic planning is an essential feature of

(a) Socialist economy

(b) Capitalist economy

(c) Mixed economy

(d) Dual economy

79. The National Policy for Empowerment of Women was adopted in the year

(a) 2001 (b) 2005

(c) 1991 (d) 1995

80. Ballots were first used in

(a) Australia (b) USA

(c) Ancient Greece (d) England

81. Fertilization occurs normally in the

(a) Cervix (b) Vagina

(c) Fallopian tube (d) Uterus

82. People consuming alcohol in heavy quantities generally die of

(a) liver or stomach cancer

(b) weakening of heart muscles leading to cardiac arrest

(c) blood cancer

(d) cirrhosis

83. The organisms at the base of the grazing food-chain are

(a) Carnivores (b) Decomposers

(c) Producers (d) Herbivores

84. Who among the following was credited with the destruction of 'Chihalgani', a group of powreful nobles?

(a) Balban (b) Qutb-ud-din Aibak

(c) Iltutmish (d) Razia Sultan

85. Bombay was given away as dowry to the English King Charles II for marrying the Princess of

(a) France (b) Portugal

(c) Holland (d) Denmark

86. Airports Authority of India (AAI) has signed an agreement with which of the following State Government for developing seven airports in the state recently?

(a) Bihar (b) West Bengal

(c) Assam (d) Uttar Pradesh

87. Name the Maratha Saint who was a contemporary of Shivaji.

(a) Saint Eknath

(b) Saint Tukaram

(c) Saint Dhyaneshwar

(d) Namdev

88. The study of lakes is called
- (a) Topology
- (b) Hydrology
- (c) Limnology
- (d) Potomology

89. A series of lines connecting places having a quake at the same time are called
- (a) Homoseismal lines
- (b) Seismolines
- (c) Coseismal lines
- (d) Isoseismal lines

90. Which of the state government has decided to ban "electronic cigarette' in view of studies claiming that its use can cause various health issues, including cancer and heart ailments?
- (a) Kerala
- (b) Maharashtra
- (c) Andhra Pradesh
- (d) Bihar

91. Which of the following items is *not* used in Local Area Networks (LANs)?
- (a) Interface Card
- (b) Cable
- (c) Computer
- (d) Modem

92. Vitamin A is rich in
- (a) Carrot
- (b) Lime
- (c) Beans
- (d) Rice

93. Which of the following cereals was among the first to be used by man?
- (a) Rye
- (b) Wheat
- (c) Barley
- (d) Oat

94. Which one of the following forces is a 'dissipative force'?
- (a) Electrostatic force
- (b) Magnetic force
- (c) Gravitational force
- (d) Frictional force

95. If a magnetic has a third pole, then the third pole is called
- (a) defective pole
- (b) consequent pole
- (c) extra pole
- (d) arbitrary pole

96. _____________ collided with Mercedes team-mate Nico Rosberg on the last lap before passing him to win a thrilling Austrian Grand Prix recently?
- (a) Lewis Hamilton
- (b) Jenson Button
- (c) Sebastian Vettel
- (d) Valtteri Bottas

97. The latest book '*Kurukshetra to Kargil*' is written by
- (a) Suryanath Singh
- (b) Kunal Bhardwaj
- (c) Karan Singh
- (d) Kuldip Singh

98. The organisation involved primarily with environmental planning is
- (a) CIFRI
- (b) ICAR
- (c) CSIR
- (d) NEERI

99. The sweet taste of fruits is due to
- (a) Lactose
- (b) Fructose
- (c) Maltose
- (d) Ribose

100. The brightest planet is
- (a) Venus
- (b) Mercury
- (c) Jupiter
- (d) Mars

ANSWERS

1. (a)	**2.** (a)	**3.** (c)	**4.** (b)	**5.** (b)	**6.** (a)	**7.** (c)	**8.** (c)	**9.** (c)	**10.** (a)
11. (d)	**12.** (a)	**13.** (b)	**14.** (a)	**15.** (c)	**16.** (a)	**17.** (a)	**18.** (a)	**19.** (d)	**20.** (a)
21. (d)	**22.** (c)	**23.** (b)	**24.** (d)	**25.** (a)	**26.** (a)	**27.** (b)	**28.** (a)	**29.** (a)	**30.** (a)
31. (d)	**32.** (c)	**33.** (c)	**34.** (a)	**35.** (b)	**36.** (c)	**37.** (b)	**38.** (c)	**39.** (a)	**40.** (a)
41. (c)	**42.** (d)	**43.** (d)	**44.** (c)	**45.** (b)	**46.** (b)	**47.** (a)	**48.** (c)	**49.** (d)	**50.** (d)
51. (c)	**52.** (c)	**53.** (d)	**54.** (b)	**55.** (c)	**56.** (a)	**57.** (d)	**58.** (c)	**59.** (d)	**60.** (a)
61. (a)	**62.** (a)	**63.** (d)	**64.** (a)	**65.** (d)	**66.** (d)	**67.** (d)	**68.** (b)	**69.** (c)	**70.** (d)
71. (d)	**72.** (a)	**73.** (a)	**74.** (a)	**75.** (b)	**76.** (b)	**77.** (a)	**78.** (a)	**79.** (a)	**80.** (c)
81. (c)	**82.** (d)	**83.** (c)	**84.** (c)	**85.** (b)	**86.** (d)	**87.** (b)	**88.** (c)	**89.** (d)	**90.** (a)
91. (d)	**92.** (a)	**93.** (c)	**94.** (d)	**95.** (a)	**96.** (a)	**97.** (d)	**98.** (d)	**99.** (b)	**100.** (a)

EXPLANATIONS

1. Given 8 : 12 : : 6 : ?

$$8 \times 2 - 4 = 12$$
$$6 \times 2 - 4 = 8$$

2.

A – 1	similarly	O – 15	
P – 16		R – 18	
P – 16		A – 1	
L – 12		N – 14	
E – 5		G – 7	
E – 5			
Total 50		**60**	

3. We pay rent for accommodation as well as we pay fare for journey.

4. Smoke occure due to fire. Similarly rain occure due to cloud.

5. S P   N L   Z W   T Q
     3   2   3   3

6. $1 + 3 + 2 = 6$

$1 + 2 + 5 = 8$

$1 + 2 + 4 = 7$

$1 + 1 + 2 = 4$

7. D9Y   J27S   P81M   V243G   B729A

3^2 3^3 3^4 3^5 3^6

D $\xrightarrow{+6}$ J $\xrightarrow{+6}$ P $\xrightarrow{+6}$ V $\xrightarrow{+6}$ B

Y $\xrightarrow{-6}$ S $\xrightarrow{-6}$ M $\xrightarrow{-6}$ G $\xrightarrow{-6}$ A

9. Given 9, 19, 40, 83, 170, 340

$$9 \times 2 + 1 = 19$$
$$19 \times 2 + 2 = 40$$
$$40 \times 2 + 3 = 83$$
$$83 \times 2 + 4 = 170$$
$$170 \times 2 + 5 = 345$$

So, 340 is wrong.

10. $a \nabla b \nabla c \to a < b < c$

$a \neq b \,;\, b \not> c$

So $a \Delta b \phi c$

11. $5 - 4 = 1 \,;\, 4 - 3 = 1 \Rightarrow 1 + 1 = 2$

$6 - 0 = 6 \,;\, 5 - 1 = 4 \Rightarrow 6 + 4 = 10$

$6 - 2 = 4 \,;\, 7 - 2 = 5 \Rightarrow 4 + 5 = 9$

12. $L \to \times \,;\quad M \to \div \,;\quad P \to + \,;\quad Q \to -$

16 P 24 M 8 Q 6 M 2 L 3

$\therefore 16 + 24 \div 8 - 6 \div 2 \times 3 = 10$

13. There is no, 'V' letter in word APPROPRIATE. So, APPROVE is not made from word APPROPRIATE.

14.

F - 7	M - 4 so	M → 4
L - 2	O - 6	A → 3
A - 3	T - 8	M → 4
T - 8	H - 1	M → 4
T - 8	E - 5	O → 6
E - 5	R - 9	T → 8
R - 9		H → 1

15. 1st column $= \dfrac{10 + 12 + 4 + 10}{2} = 18 \leftarrow$ Last number

2nd column $= \dfrac{11 + 12 + 12 + 5}{2} = 20$

3rd column $= \dfrac{15 + 8 + 10 + 13}{2} = 23$

16.

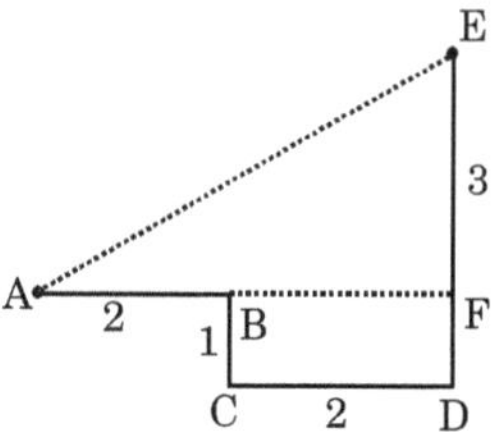

$$AE = \sqrt{(AF)^2 + (EF)^2} = \sqrt{(4)^2 + (3)^2}$$
$$AE = 5 \text{ km}$$

17. Temple and Church are different places for worship not same. So both conclusion are wrong.

19. Volume of sphere $= \dfrac{4}{3} \pi r_1^3$

Volume of hemisphere $= \dfrac{2}{3} \pi r_2^3$

According to question,

$$\frac{4}{3} \pi r_1^3 = \frac{2}{3} \pi r_2^3$$

$$r_1 = \left(\frac{r_2^3}{2} \right)^{\frac{1}{3}}$$

Given $r_2 = 3\sqrt[3]{2}$ cm

$\therefore$ $r_1 = 3$ cm

22. S E A R C H → T F B S D I

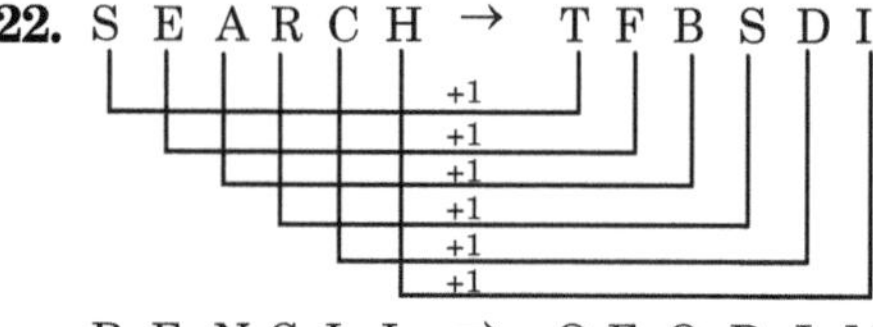

P E N C I L → Q F O D J M

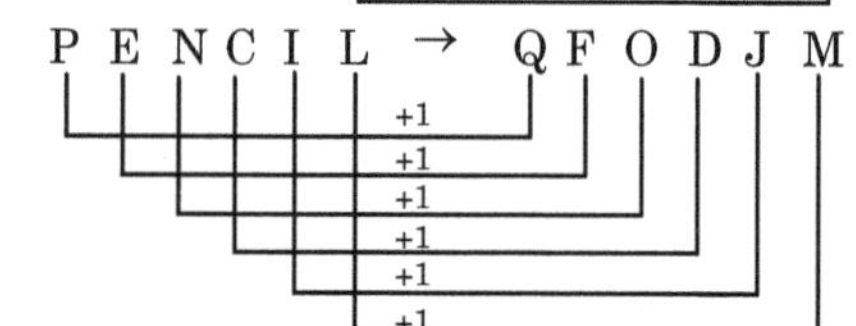

25. From Matrix

G → 58, 66, 77, 85, 98

U → 04, 12, 23, 31, 40

I → 00, 13, 21, 34, 42

D → 56, 09, 75, 87, 99

E → 01, 14, 20, 32, 43

Match the options.

GUIDE → 85, 23, 21, 87, 32

51.
$$\tan \theta = \frac{10\sqrt{3}}{x+20}$$

$$\tan (90 - \theta) = \frac{10\sqrt{3}}{x}$$

$$\cot \theta = \frac{10\sqrt{3}}{x}$$

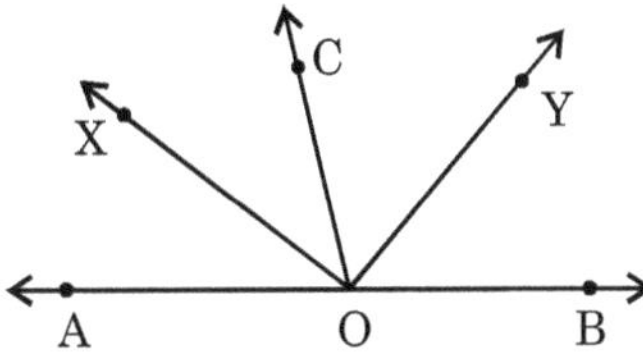

So,
$$\frac{10\sqrt{3}}{x+20} = \frac{x}{10\sqrt{3}}$$

$$x^2 + 20x - 300 = 0$$

$x = 10$ or $x = -3$ (x can not be negative)

∴ $x = 10$ meter.

52. A and B are complementary angles.

So, A + B = 90 ; A = 90 − B

sin A = sin (90 − B) = cos B

cos A = cos (90 − B) = sin B

tan A = tan (90 − B) = cot B

cot A = cot (90 − B) = tan B

Given,

sin A cos B + cos A sin B − tan A tan B + $\sec^2 A - \cot^2 B$

$= \sin^2 A + \cos^2 B - \cot B \tan B + \sec^2 A - \tan^2 A$

$= 1 - 1 + 1 = 1$

53. $2\sin^2 \theta + 3 \cos^2 \theta = 2 + \cos^2 \theta$

So least value = 2   ∵ $(\cos^2 \theta \geq 0)$

54.

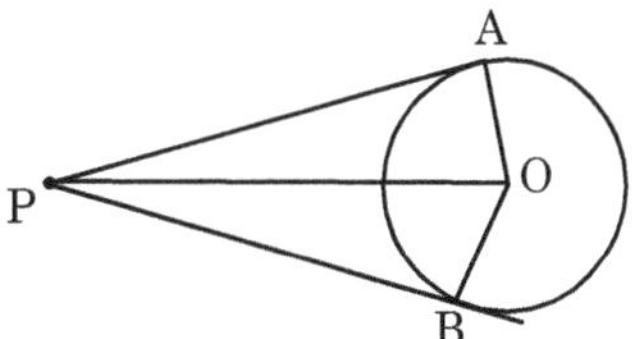

OX is the bisector of ∠AOC

∴   ∠AOC = 2∠COX

OY is the bisector of ∠BOC

∴   ∠BOC = 2∠COY

∠AOC + ∠BOC = 2∠COY + 2 ∠COX = 180°

∴   ∠XOY = 90

∠AOX + ∠XOY + ∠BOY = 180°

∠BOY = 180° − 90° − 20° = 70°

55. Given $4x = \sec \theta \Rightarrow x = \dfrac{\sec \theta}{4}$

$$\frac{4}{x} = \tan \theta$$

$$\Rightarrow \frac{1}{x} = \frac{\tan \theta}{4}$$

$$\therefore \quad 8\left(x^2 - \frac{1}{x^2}\right) = 8\left(\frac{\sec^2 \theta}{16} - \frac{\tan^2 \theta}{16}\right) = \frac{1}{2}$$

56. ∠XOY = 90° ; OX = OY = R

ΔXOY is right angle triangle

So, $\dfrac{1}{2}$(OX)(OY) = 32

$$R^2 = 64 = 8$$

Area of circle $= \pi R^2 = 64 \pi$

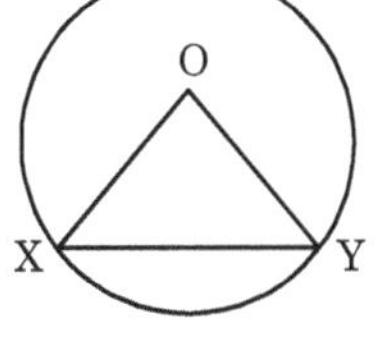

57.

$R_1 + R_2 = 13$

$R_2 - R_1 = 9 - 4 = 5$

$PQ = \sqrt{(AB)^2 - (R_2 - R_1)^2}$

$PQ = \sqrt{13^2 - 5^2} = 12$ cm

58.

AP = PB; OA = OB = radius;

OP = OP

So,   ΔOAP = ΔOPB

     ∠AOP = ∠POB

     ∠APO = ∠OPB

∴   ∠APO = 180° − 90° − 60° = 30°

     ∠APB = 2 × 30 = 60°

59. $x^4 + \dfrac{1}{x^4} = 23$

$$\left(x^2 + \frac{1}{x^2}\right)^2 - 2 = 23 \; ; \; x^2 + \frac{1}{x^2} = 5$$

$$\left(x^2 - \frac{1}{x^2}\right)^2 = x^2 + \frac{1}{x^2} - 2 = 5 - 2 = 3$$

60. Let $y = \sqrt{6 + \sqrt{6 + \sqrt{6 + \ldots \infty}}}$

$$y = \sqrt{6 + y}$$

$$y^2 = 6 + y$$

$$y^2 - y - 6 = 0$$

$y = 3$ or $y = -2$ (y can not be negative)

∴ $y = 3$

61. $x + \dfrac{1}{x} = 3$ ... (1)

by squaring

$$x^2 + \dfrac{1}{x^2} + 2 = 9$$

$$x^2 + \dfrac{1}{x^2} = 7 \qquad ... (2)$$

Taking cube on both side, to equation (1)

$$\left(x + \dfrac{1}{x}\right)^3 = 27$$

$$x^3 + \dfrac{1}{x^3} + 3\left(x + \dfrac{1}{x}\right) = 27$$

$$x^3 + \dfrac{1}{x^3} = 27 - 3 \times 3 = 18 \qquad ... (3)$$

From equation (2) and (3)

$$\left(x^2 + \dfrac{1}{x^2}\right)\left(x^3 + \dfrac{1}{x^3}\right) = 18 \times 7$$

$$x^5 + \dfrac{1}{x^5} + x + \dfrac{1}{x} = 126$$

$$x^5 + \dfrac{1}{x^5} = 126 - 3 = 123$$

62. Sum of present age of four boys $= 9 \times 4 + 20 = 56$
sum of total five boys $= 15 \times 5 = 75$
So, age of new boy $= 75 - 56 = 19$ years.

63. Let weight of a piece of diamond is $6y$.
Let original price of one piece $= ₹\ x$
So $x(6y)^2 = 5184$
New price $= x(y^2 + 4y^2 + 9y^2)$

$$= 14\ xy^2 = \dfrac{14 \times 5184}{36} = ₹\ 2016$$

Loss $= 5184 - 2016 = ₹\ 3168$

64. $30\% = ₹\ 30$
$100\% = ₹\ 100$
New selling price $= 100 - 30 = ₹\ 70$

65. Volume of hemisphere $= \dfrac{2}{3}\pi r^3$

So, $\dfrac{\frac{2}{3}\pi r_1^3}{\frac{2}{3}\pi r_2^3} = \dfrac{6.4}{21.6}$

$$\left(\dfrac{r_1}{r_2}\right)^3 = \dfrac{64}{216} = \left(\dfrac{4}{6}\right)^3$$

$$\dfrac{r_1}{r_2} = \left(\dfrac{4}{6}\right) = \dfrac{2}{3}$$

66. Part of the tank filled by both pipes in two hour

$$= 2\left(\dfrac{1}{8} + \dfrac{1}{6}\right) = 2\left(\dfrac{3+4}{24}\right) = \dfrac{7}{12}$$

Remaining part $= 1 - \dfrac{7}{12} = \dfrac{5}{12}$

Time taken by B to fill the remaining part

$$= \dfrac{5}{12} \times 6 = 2\dfrac{1}{2}\ \text{hours}$$

67. If number of females $= a$
then number of males $= 15000 - a$

$$\therefore\ a \times \dfrac{10}{100} + (15000 - a) \times \dfrac{8}{100} = 16300 - 15000$$

$$10a + 120000 - 8a = 130000$$

$$2a = 130000 - 120000$$

$$2a = 10000$$

$$a = 5000$$

68. Interest $= 5700 - 5000 = ₹\ 700$

$$\text{Rate} = \dfrac{700 \times 100}{5000 \times 1} = 14\%$$

$$\text{Now Interest} = \dfrac{7000 \times 5 \times 14}{100} = ₹\ 4900$$

Total amount $= 7000 + 4900 = ₹\ 11900$

69. Relative speed $= 11 - 10 = 1$ km/hour

$$\text{Distance covered in 6 min} = \dfrac{1000}{60} \times 6$$

$$= 100\ \text{meter}$$

Remaining distance $= 200 - 100 = 100$ meter.

70. Effective profit percent

$$= \left(20 + 25 + \dfrac{20 \times 25}{100}\right) = 50\%$$

$$\text{Original C.P.} = \dfrac{100}{150} \times 1200 = ₹\ 800$$

71. Total cows $= n$

Given $\dfrac{n}{2} + \dfrac{n}{4} + \dfrac{n}{5} + 7 = n$

$$\dfrac{10n + 5n + 4n + 140}{20} = n$$

$$n = 140$$

72. $35 - 18 = 17$
$45 - 28 = 17$
$55 - 38 = 17$
LCM of 35, 45, and 55 $= 3465$
Number $= 3465 - 17 = 3448$

73. % increase $= \dfrac{40 - 30}{30} \times 100 = \dfrac{100}{3} = 33\dfrac{1}{3}\%$

74. Income in 2002 $= ₹\ 40$ Lakhs.
Expanditure of company in 2003 $= ₹\ 40$ Lakhs

75. Profit in 2004 $= ₹\ 25$ Lakhs

GENERAL INTELLIGENCE

Directions (Q. 1-2) : *In questions select the related letters / words / numbers from the given alternatives.*

1. 6 : 64 : : 11 : ?

   (a) 144   (b) 169

   (c) 121   (d) 124

2. Writer : Pen : : ?

   (a) Needle : Tailor   (b) Artist : Brush

   (c) Painter : Canvas   (d) Teacher : Class

Directions (Q. 3) : *In questions find the odd number / letters / word from the given alternatives.*

3. (a) Flute   (b) Violin

   (c) Guitar   (d) Sitar

4. Find out the pair of numbers that does not belong to the group for lack of common property.

   (a) 11 – 115   (b) 10 – 90

   (c) 9 – 72   (d) 8 – 56

5. Arrange the following words as per order in the dictionary.

   1. Dissident   2. Dissolve

   3. Dissent   4. Dissolute

   5. Dissolution

   (a) 3, 1, 4, 5, 2   (b) 3, 2, 1, 4, 5

   (c) 3, 1, 4, 2, 5   (d) 3, 2, 4, 5, 1

6. Which one set of letters when sequentially placed at the gaps in the given letter series shall complete it ?

   _cd_cab_baca_cba_ab

   (a) cabcb   (b) abccb

   (c) bacbc   (d) bcaba

Directions (Q. 7) : *In questions a series is given, with one / two terms(s) missing. Choose the correct alternative from the given ones that will complete the series.*

7. 4, 196, 16, 169, ?, 144, 64

   (a) 21   (b) 81

   (c) 36   (d) 32

8. Find the wrong number in the series.

   6, 9, 15, 22, 51, 99

   (a) 99   (b) 51

   (c) 22   (d) 15

9. At what time are the hands of clock together between 6 and 7?

   (a) $32\dfrac{8}{11}$ min. past 6   (b) $34\dfrac{8}{11}$ min. past 6

   (c) $30\dfrac{8}{11}$ min. past 6   (d) $32\dfrac{5}{7}$ min. past 6

10. Out of 100 families in the neighbourhood, 50 have radios, 75 have TVs and 25 have VCRs Only 10 families have all three and each VCR owner also has a TV. If some families have radio only, how many have only TV?

   (a) 30   (b) 35

   (c) 40   (d) 45

11. Suresh was born of 4th October 1999. Shashikanth was born 6 days before Suresh. The Independence day of that year fell on Sunday. Which day was Shashikanth born ?

   (a) Tuesday   (b) Wednesday

   (c) Monday   (d) Sunday

12. From the given alternative words, select the word which **cannot** be formed using the letters of the given word :

   'CONCENTRATION'

   (a) CONCERN   (b) NATION

   (c) TRAIN   (d) CENTRE

13. Ganesh cycles towards South-West a distance of 8 m, then he moves towards East a distance of 20 m. From there he moves towards North-East a distance of 8 m, then he moves towards West a distance of 6 m. From there he moves towards North-East a distance of 2 m. Then he moves towards West a distance of 4 m and then towards South-West 2 m and stops at that point. How far is he from the starting point?

   (a) 12 m   (b) 10 m

   (c) 8 m   (d) 6 m

14. Two statements are given followed by four inferences. Select the alternative which is most appropriate.

Statements :

India is becoming industrialised.

Pollution is a problem associated with industralisation.

Inferences :

   I. All industrial centres are polluted.

   II. India is polluted.

   III. Polluted nations are industrialised.

   IV. India may become polluted

   (a) All are appropriate

   (b) None is appropriate

   (c) Only IV is appropriate

   (d) Only II is appropriate

15. From the given alternative words, select the word which can be formed using the letters of the given word :

'DETERMINATION'

(a) DECLARATION (b) NATIONAL

(c) TERMINATED (d) DEVIATION

16. If in a certain code HYDROGEN is written as JCJZYSSD, then how can ANTIMONY be written in that code?

(a) CPVKOQPA (b) CRZQWABO

(c) ERXMQSRC (d) GTZOSUTE

17. If DELHI coded as 73541 and CALCUTTA as 82589662, then how can CALICUT be coded?

(a) 5279431 (b) 5978013

(c) 8251896 (d) 8543691

Directions (Q. 18-19) : *In questions select the missing number from the given responses.*

18.

2	7	9
7	3	4
9	8	?
126	168	216

(a) 8 (b) 3

(c) 6 (d) 36

19.

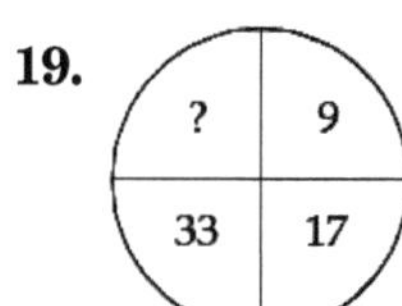

(a) 60 (b) 68

(c) 55 (d) 65

20. How many rectangles are there in the given diagram?

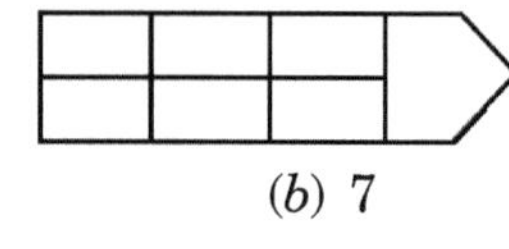

(a) 4 (b) 7

(c) 9 (d) 18

21. Which of the following diagrams represents the relationship among Sun, Moon and Star ?

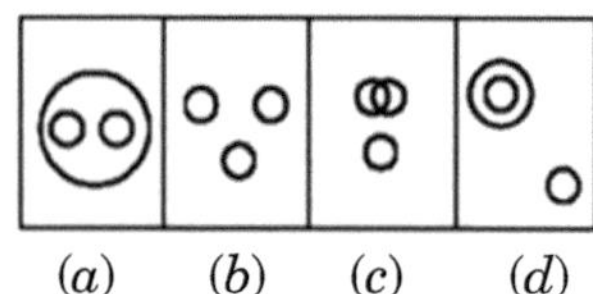

(a) (b) (c) (d)

22. If '−' stand for '÷', '+' stand for '×', '÷' for '−' and '×' for '+', which one of the following equations is correct?

(a) $30 - 6 + 5 \times 4 \div 2 = 27$

(b) $30 + 6 - 5 \div 4 \times 2 = 30$

(c) $30 \times 6 \div 5 - 4 + 2 = 32$

(d) $30 \div 6 \times 5 + 4 - 2 = 40$

Directions : *From the given answer figures, select the one in which the question figure is hidden / embedded.*

23. Question figure.

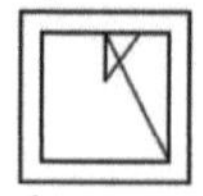

Answer figures.

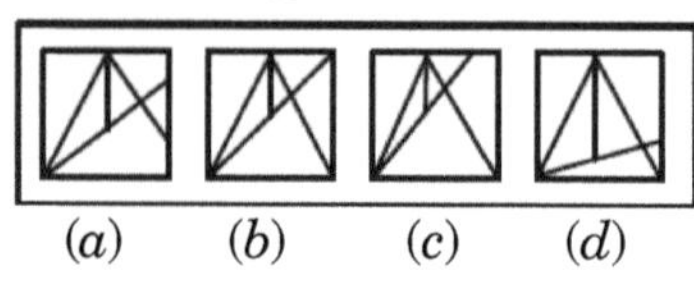

(a) (b) (c) (d)

Directions : *If a mirror is placed on the line MN, then which of the answer figures is the correct image of the given question figures?*

24. Question figure.

Answer figures.

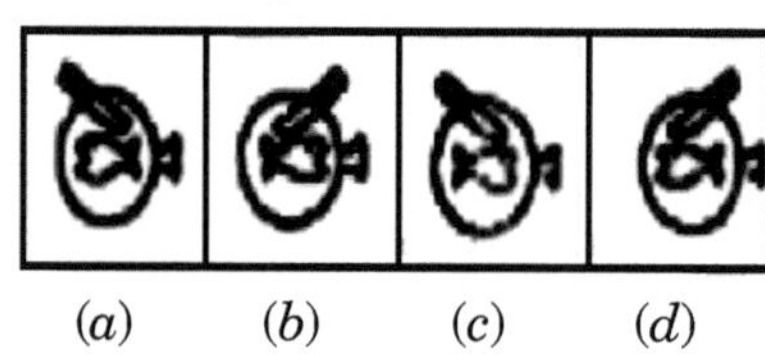

(a) (b) (c) (d)

Directions : *A piece of paper is folded and cut as shown below in the question figures. From the given answer figures, indicate how it will appear when opened.*

25. Question figures :

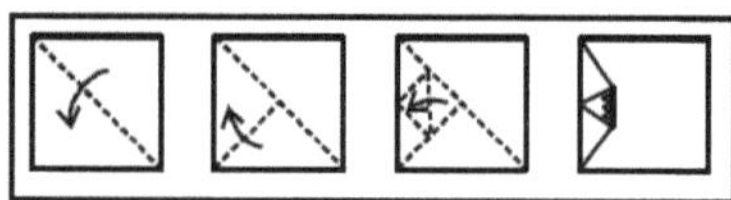

Answer figures :

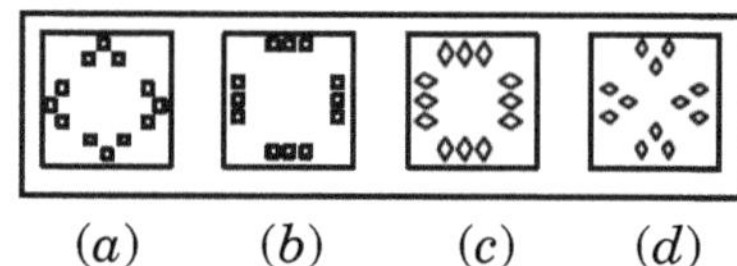

(a) (b) (c) (d)

ENGLISH LANGUAGE

Directions (Q. 26 - 27) : *Out of the four alternatives, choose the one which best expresses the meaning of the given word and mark it in the Answer Sheet.*

26. GENIAL

(a) Cordial (b) Unselfish

(c) Careful (d) Specific

27. ACCRUE

(a) Accumulate

(b) Accommodate

(c) Grow

(d) Suffice

Directions (Q. 28 - 29) : *Choose the word opposite in meaning to the given word and mark it in the Answer Sheet.*

28. SYNTHETIC

    (*a*) Natural   (*b*) Plastic

    (*c*) Cosmetic   (*d*) Apathetic

29. ACCORD

    (*a*) Disagreement   (*b*) Welcome

    (*c*) Disrespect   (*d*) Conformity

Directions (Q. 30-32) : *Out of the four alternatives, choose the one which can be substituted for the given words / sentence and indicate it by blackening the appropriate rectangle [▭] in the Answer Sheet.*

30. Pertaining to cattle

    (*a*) Canine   (*b*) Feline

    (*c*) Bovine   (*d*) Verminous

31. To look at someone in an angry or threatening way

    (*a*) Glower   (*b*) Gnaw

    (*c*) Gnash   (*d*) Grind

32. A post with little work but high salary

    (*a*) Director   (*b*) Trustee

    (*c*) Sinecure   (*d*) Ombudsman

Directions (Q. 33 - 35) : *Four alternatives are given for the meaning of the given Indiom / Phrase. Choose the alternative which best express the meaning of the Indiom / Phrase and mark it in the Answer Sheet.*

33. To be all at sea

    (*a*) a family voyage

    (*b*) lost and confused

    (*c*) in the middle of the ocean

    (*d*) a string of islands

34. To take to one's heels

    (*a*) to walk slowly   (*b*) to run away

    (*c*) to march forward   (*d*) to hop and jump

35. To bite the dust

    (*a*) eat voraciously   (*b*) have nothing to eat

    (*c*) eat roots   (*d*) none of the above

Direction (Q. 36) : *Group of four words are given. In each group, one word is correctly spelt. Find the correctly spelt word and mark your answer in the Answer Sheet.*

36. (*a*) malaign

    (*b*) arraign

    (*c*) asigne

    (*d*) degine

Directions (Q. 37 - 39) : *Some of the sentences have errors and some are correct. Find out which part of a sentence has an error and blacken the rectangle [▭] corresponding to the appropriated letter (a, b, c). If a sentence is free from errors, blacken the rectangle corresponding to (d) in the Answer Sheet.*

37. His son | is working | very hardly | No error.
    (*a*)   (*b*)   (*c*)   (*d*)

38. Do you know that it was I | who has done
    (*a*)   (*b*)

    this piece of beautiful work ? | No error.
    (*c*)   (*d*)

39. The company has ordered | some
    (*a*)   (*b*)

    new equipments. | No error.
    (*c*)   (*d*)

Directions (Q. 40 - 42) : *Sentences are given with blanks to the filled in with an appropriate word(s). Four alternatives are suggested for each question. Choose the correct alternative out of the four and indicate it by blackening the appropriate rectangle [▭] in the Answer Sheet.*

40. If you had followed the rules, you ____ disqualified.

    (*a*) will not be

    (*b*) would not be

    (*c*) will not have been

    (*d*) would not have been

41. The housewife _______ the cakes burning, and ran to switch off the oven.

    (*a*) smell   (*b*) smells

    (*c*) smelt   (*d*) smelling

42. _______ and old legend, King Shirham lived in India.

    (*a*) In the event of   (*b*) Due to

    (*c*) According to   (*d*) In reference to

Directions (Q. 43-45) : *A sentence or underlined part thereof is given which many need improvement. Alternatives are given of (a), (b) and (c) below, which may be a better option. In case no improvement is needed, your answer is (d). Blacken the appropriate rectangle [▭] in the Answer Sheet.*

43. My friend lives in a nearly street <u>whose name</u> I have forgotten.

    (*a*) the name of which

    (*b*) which name

    (*c*) of which name

    (*d*) No improvement

44. He both won a medal and a scholarship.

    (*a*) He won a medal and a scholarship both.

    (*b*) Both he won a medal and a scholarship.

    (*c*) He won both a medal and a scholarship.

    (*d*) No improvement

45. He has for good left India.

    (*a*) He has left for good India.

    (*b*) He has left India for good.

    (*c*) Good he has left India.

    (*d*) No improvement

Directions (Q. 46-50): *In the following question, you have a brief passage with 5 questions. Read the passage carefully and choose the best answer to each question out of the four alternatives and mark it by blackening the appropriate rectangle [■] the Answer-Sheet.*

One may look at life, events, society, history, in another way. A way which might, at a stretch, be described as the Gandhian way, though it may be from times before Mahatma Gandhi came on the scene. The Gandhian reaction to all the grim, poverty, squalor and degradation of the human being would approximate to effort at self-change and self-improvement, to a regime of living regulated by discipline from within. To change society, the. individual must first change himself. In this way of looking at life and society, words too begin to mean differently. Revolution, for instance, is a term frequently used, but not always in the sense it has been in the lexicon of the militant. So also with words like peace and struggle. Even society may mean differently, being some kind of organic entity for the militant, and more or less a sum of individuals for the Gandhian. There is yet another way, which might, for want of a better description, be called the mystic. The mystic's prespective measures these concerns that transcend political ambition and the dynamism of the reformer, whether he be militant or Gandhian. The mystic measures the terror of not knowing the remorseless march of time; he seeks to know what was before birth, what comes after death. The continuous presence of death, of the consciousness of death, sets his priorities and values : militants and Gandhians, kings and prophets, must leave all that they have built; all that they have unbuilt and depart when messengers of the buffalo-riding Yama come out of the shadows. Water will to water, dust to dust, Think of impermanence. Everything passes.

46. The Gandhian reaction to poverty is

    (*a*) a total war on poverty

    (*b*) self-discipline

    (*c*) self-abnegation

    (*d*) a regulated distribution of wealth

47. According to Gandhianism, the individual who wants to change society

    (*a*) should destroy the existing society

    (*b*) must re-form society

    (*c*) must change himself

    (*d*) may change society without changing himself

48. Who, according to the passage, finds new meaning for words like revolutions, peace and struggle ?

    (*a*) A Gandhian who believes in non-violent revolution

    (*b*) A militant

    (*c*) A mystic

    (*d*) A Gandhian who disciplines himself from within

49. The expression 'water will to water, dust to dust' means

    (*a*) water and dust can mix well

    (*b*) man will become water after death

    (*c*) man will one day die and become dust

    (*d*) man will become dust and water after death

50. What does society mean to a Gandhian ?

    (*a*) a sum of individuals

    (*b*) an organic entity

    (*c*) a regime of living regulated by discipline from within

    (*d*) a disciplined social community

QUANTITATIVE APTITUDE

51. The value of

$$\frac{3\sqrt{2}}{\sqrt{3}+\sqrt{6}} - \frac{4\sqrt{3}}{\sqrt{6}+\sqrt{2}} + \frac{\sqrt{6}}{\sqrt{3}+\sqrt{2}} \text{ is}$$

    (*a*) 4   (*b*) 0

    (*c*) $\sqrt{2}$ (*d*) $3\sqrt{6}$

52. $\sqrt{6+\sqrt{6+\sqrt{6+\ldots}}} = ?$

    (*a*) 2.3   (*b*) 3

    (*c*) 6   (*d*) 6.3

53. The square root of $\dfrac{\sqrt{3}+\sqrt{2}}{\sqrt{3}-\sqrt{2}}$ is

    (*a*) $\sqrt{3}+\sqrt{2}$ (*b*) $\sqrt{3}-\sqrt{2}$

    (*c*) $\sqrt{2}\pm\sqrt{3}$ (*d*) $\sqrt{2}-\sqrt{3}$

54. The remainder when 3^{21} is divided by 5 is

    (*a*) 1

    (*b*) 2

    (*c*) 3

    (*d*) 4

55. The last digit of $(1001)^{2008} + 1002$ is

   (*a*) 0   (*b*) 3

   (*c*) 4   (*d*) 6

56. If $x * y = (x + 3)^2 (y - 1)$, then the value of $5 * 4$ is

   (*a*) 192   (*b*) 182

   (*c*) 180   (*d*) 172

57. $\dfrac{(0.05)^2 + (0.41)^2 + (0.073)^2}{(0.005)^2 + (0.041)^2 + (0.0073)^2}$ is

   (*a*) 10   (*b*) 100

   (*c*) 1000   (*d*) None of these

58. A and B can complete a piece of work in 8 days, B and C can do it in 12 days, C and A can do it in 8 days. A, B and C together can complete it in

   (*a*) 4 days   (*b*) 5 days

   (*c*) 6 days   (*d*) 7 days

59. X is 3 times as fast as Y and is able to complete the work in 40 days less than Y. Then the time in which they can complete the work together is

   (*a*) 15 days   (*b*) 10 days

   (*c*) $7\dfrac{1}{2}$ days   (*d*) 5 days

60. A copper wire is bent in the shape of a square of area 81 cm². If the same wire is bent in the form of a semicircle, the radius (in cm) of the semicircle is $\left(\text{Take } \pi = \dfrac{22}{7} \right)$

   (*a*) 16   (*b*) 14

   (*c*) 10   (*d*) 7

61. The volume (in m³) of rain water that can be collected from 1.5 hectares of ground in a rainfall of 5 cm is

   (*a*) 75   (*b*) 750

   (*c*) 7500   (*d*) 75000

62. A river 3 m deep and 40 m wide is following at the rate of 2 km per hour. How much water (in litres) will fall into the sea in a minute ?

   (*a*) 4,00,000   (*b*) 40,00,000

   (*c*) 40,000   (*d*) 4,000

63. The L.C.M. of three different numbers is 120. Which of the following **cannot** be their H.C.F. ?

   (*a*) 8

   (*b*) 12

   (*c*) 24

   (*d*) 35

64. In an examination a student scores 4 marks for every correct answer and loses 1 mark for every wrong answer. If he attempts all 75 questions and secures 125 marks, the number of questions he attempts correctly is

   (*a*) 35   (*b*) 40

   (*c*) 42   (*d*) 46

65. The mean of 50 numbers is 30. Later it was discovered that two entries were wrongly entered as 82 and 13 instead of 28 and 31.

Find the correct mean.

   (*a*) 36.12   (*b*) 30.66

   (*c*) 29.28   (*d*) 38.21

66. A man can row 6km/h in still water. If the speed of the current is 2 km/h, it takes 3 hours more in upstream than in the downstream for the same distance. The distance is

   (*a*) 30 km   (*b*) 24 km

   (*c*) 20 km   (*d*) 32 km

67. While selling a watch, a shopkeeper gives a discount of 5%. If he gives a discount of 6%, he earns ₹ 15 less as profit. What is the marked price of the watch?

   (*a*) ₹ 1,250   (*b*) ₹ 1,400

   (*c*) ₹ 1,500   (*d*) ₹ 750

68. A trader bought two horses for ₹ 19,500. He sold one at a loss of 20% and the other at a profit of 15%. If the selling price of each horse is the same, then their cost prices are respectively

   (*a*) ₹ 10,000 and ₹ 9,500

   (*b*) ₹ 11,000 and ₹ 8,000

   (*c*) ₹ 12,000 and ₹ 7,500

   (*d*) ₹ 10,500 and ₹ 9,000

69. When the price of sugar decreases by 10%, a man could buy 1 kg more for ₹ 270. Then the original price of sugar per kg is

   (*a*) ₹ 25   (*b*) ₹ 30

   (*c*) ₹ 27   (*d*) ₹ 32

70. If the price of sugar is raised by 25%, find by how much percent a householder must reduce his consumption of sugar so as not to increase his expenditure ?

   (*a*) 10

   (*b*) 20

   (*c*) 18

   (*d*) 25

71. A sum of money placed at compound interest doubles itself in 4 years. In how many years will it amount to four times itself ?

(a) 12 years   (b) 13 years

(c) 8 years   (d) 16 years

72. The simple interest on a sum of 5 years is one-fourth of the sum. The rate of interest per annum is

(a) 5%   (b) 6%

(c) 4%   (d) 8%

Directions (Q. 73 - 75) : *The following graph shows the demand and production of cotton by 5 companies A, B, C, D and E. Study the graph and answer question.*

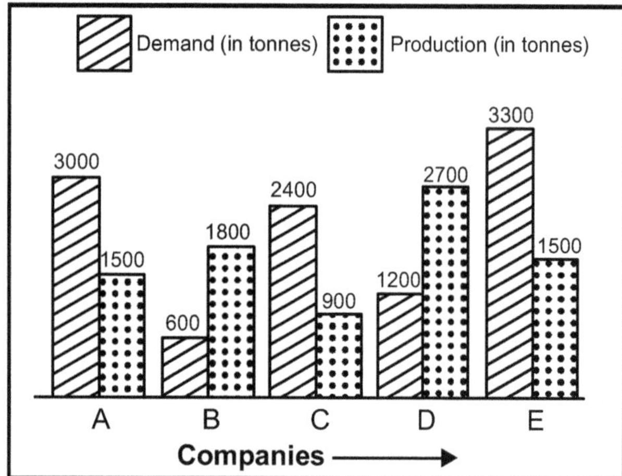

73. The production of company D is how many times that of the production of the company A ?

(a) 1.8

(b) 1.5

(c) 0.5

(d) 0.4

74. The demand for company B is what percent of the demand for company C?

(a) 1.5

(b) 2.5

(c) 25

(d) 30

75. What is the ratio of companies having more demand than production to those having more production than demand ?

(a) 2 : 3

(b) 4 : 1

(c) 3 : 2

(d) 1 : 4

76. Rio Olympic bronze medal winner Sakshi Malik has been appointed as the brand ambassador of which state?

(a) Maharashtra   (b) Uttar Pradesh

(c) Bihar   (d) Haryana

77. Judicial review in the Indian Constitution is based on

(a) Rule of Law

(b) Due process of Law

(c) Procedure established by Law

(d) Precedents and Conventions

78. The Drafting of the Constitution was completed on

(a) 26th January 1950

(b) 26th December 1949

(c) 26th November 1949

(d) 30th November 1949

79. Who was the President of the Constituent Assembly?

(a) Pt. Jawahar Lal Nehru

(b) Sardar Patel

(c) Dr. Rajendra Prasad

(d) Dr. B.R. Ambedkar

80. Which innovative discussion process is introduced by the Indian Parliament to the World Parliamentary systems ?

(a) Question hour   (b) Zero hour

(c) Resolutions   (d) Presidential speech

81. The Judges of the Supreme Court retire at the age of

(a) 60 years   (b) 65 years

(c) 62 years   (d) 58 years

82. Inflation redistributes income and wealth in favour of

(a) Pensioners   (b) Poor

(c) Middle class   (d) Rich

83. Who among the following British persons admitted the Revolt of 1857 as a national revolt?

(a) Lord Dalhousie

(b) Lord Canning

(c) Lord Ellenborough

(d) Disraeli

84. The Greek ambassador sent to Chandragupta Maurya's court was

(a) Kautilya   (b) Selecus Nicator

(c) Megasthenes (d) Justin

85. The call of "Back to the Vedas" was given by

(a) Swami Vivekananda

(b) Swami Dayanand Saraswati

(c) Aurobindo Ghosh

(d) Raja Ram Mohan Roy

86. Simon Commission was boycotted by the nationalist leaders of India because

(a) they felt that it was only an eyewash

(b) all the numbers of the Commission were english

(c) the members of the Commission were biased against India

(d) it did not meet the demands of the Indians

87. Who has won the German Grand Prix with 19 points lead championship over his teammate?

(a) Daniel Ricciardo

(b) Nico Rosberg

(c) Lewis Hamilton

(d) Max Verstappen

88. The lowest layer of the atmosphere is

(a) Stratosphere (b) Thermosphere

(c) Troposphere (d) Mesosphere

89. The Konkan Railway connects

(a) Goa—Mangalore

(b) Roha—Mangalore

(c) Kanyakumari—Mangalore

(d) Kanyakumari—Mumbai

90. Bark of this tree is used as a condiment–

(a) Cinnamon   (b) Clove

(c) Neem   (d) Palm

91. Which of the following is called the 'shrimp capital of India'?

(a) Mangalore

(b) Nagapatnam

(c) Kochi

(d) Nellore

92. River Indus originates from

(a) Hindukush range (b) Himalayan range

(c) Karakoram range (d) Kailash range

93. The first computer made available for commercial use was

(a) MANIAC   (b) ENIAC

(c) UNIVAC   (d) EDSAC

94. Who was the architect of North and South Blocks of the Central Secretariat in Delhi ?

(a) Sir Edward Lutyens

(b) Hebert Baker

(c) Robert Tor Russell

(d) Antonin Raymond

95. Saliva helps in the digestion of

(a) Fats   (b) Starch

(c) Proteins   (d) Vitamins

96. The longest bone in the human body is

(a) Ulna   (b) Humerus

(c) Femur   (d) Tibia

97. Red data book gives information about species which are

(a) extinct   (b) endangered

(c) dangerous   (d) rare

98. Indoform is used as an

(a) antipyretic (b) analgesic

(c) antiseptic   (d) anaesthetic

99. Which of the following folk/tribal dances is associated with Uttar Pradesh ?

(a) Veedhi

(b) Thora

(c) Tamasha

(d) Rauf

100. What is the theme of Swachh Bharat special campaign is being organized by The Ministry of Drinking Water and Sanitation throughout August 2016?

(a) Liberation from Open Excretion

(b) Freedom from Open Excretion

(c) Freedom from Open Defecation

(d) Liberation from Open Defecation

ANSWERS

1. (b)	**2.** (b)	**3.** (a)	**4.** (a)	**5.** (a)	**6.** (c)	**7.** (c)	**8.** (c)	**9.** (a)	**10.** (c)
11. (a)	**12.** (d)	**13.** (b)	**14.** (c)	**15.** (c)	**16.** (b)	**17.** (c)	**18.** (c)	**19.** (d)	**20.** (d)
21. (d)	**22.** (a)	**23.** (c)	**24.** (c)	**25.** (c)	**26.** (a)	**27.** (a)	**28.** (a)	**29.** (a)	**30.** (c)
31. (a)	**32.** (c)	**33.** (b)	**34.** (b)	**35.** (d)	**36.** (b)	**37.** (c)	**38.** (b)	**39.** (b)	**40.** (d)
41. (c)	**42.** (c)	**43.** (a)	**44.** (c)	**45.** (b)	**46.** (b)	**47.** (c)	**48.** (d)	**49.** (d)	**50.** (a)
51. (b)	**52.** (b)	**53.** (a)	**54.** (c)	**55.** (b)	**56.** (a)	**57.** (b)	**58.** (c)	**59.** (a)	**60.** (d)
61. (b)	**62.** (b)	**63.** (d)	**64.** (b)	**65.** (c)	**66.** (b)	**67.** (c)	**68.** (b)	**69.** (b)	**70.** (b)
71. (c)	**72.** (a)	**73.** (a)	**74.** (c)	**75.** (c)	**76.** (d)	**77.** (c)	**78.** (c)	**79.** (c)	**80.** (b)
81. (b)	**82.** (d)	**83.** (d)	**84.** (c)	**85.** (b)	**86.** (b)	**87.** (c)	**88.** (c)	**89.** (b)	**90.** (a)
91. (d)	**92.** (d)	**93.** (c)	**94.** (b)	**95.** (b)	**96.** (c)	**97.** (b)	**98.** (c)	**99.** (b)	**100.** (c)

EXPLANATIONS

1. $6 : 64$

$\Rightarrow 6 : (6 + 2)^2 = 64$

$11 : ?$

$\Rightarrow 11 : (11 + 2)^2 = 169$

2. Writer use pen to write so, Artist use brush to make painting.

3. All the instrument have strings to play except option (a).

4.

$11 \rightarrow 115$

$10 \rightarrow 10 \times 9 \neq 90$

$9 \rightarrow 9 \times 8 \rightarrow 72$

$8 \rightarrow 8 \times 7 \rightarrow 56$

6. b c b a c a / b c b a c a / b c b a c a / b

7. 4, 196, 16, 169, ____, 144, 64

So, series is 4, 16, ___, 64

also, $(2)^2, (4)^2, (6)^2, (8)^2$

$\therefore \quad 6^2 = 36$

8. All the number divide by 3 except option (c).

9. At 6 o'clock the hour hand is at 6 and minute hand is at 12. It means that they are 30 minute space apart.

$\therefore$ 30 minute gain $= \dfrac{60}{55} \times 30 = \dfrac{12}{11} \times 30$

$= \dfrac{360}{11} = 32\dfrac{8}{11}$ minutes

Therefore, the hands will be together at

$32\dfrac{8}{11}$ minutes part 6.

10. The vendiagram of given data is:-

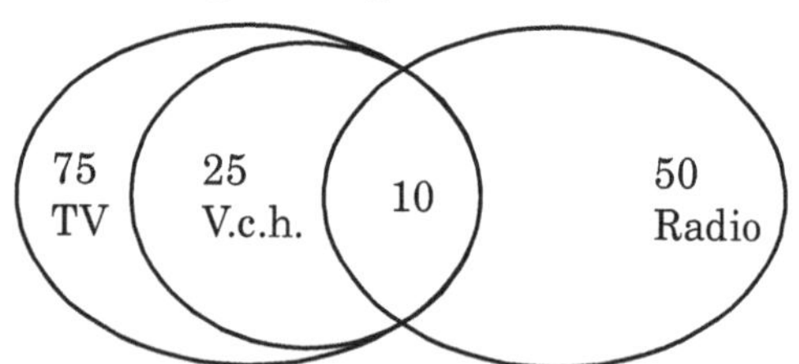

$\therefore$ Families have T.V. only

$= 75 - (25+10)$

$= 40$

11. Suresh data of Birth = 4th oct 1999

$\therefore$ Shashikant data of Birth = 28 sep 1999

Given, 15 Aug 1999 is sunday.

Therefore, Sunday dates between 15 August and 28 Ocober on

(i) 22 August

(ii) 29 August

(iii) 5 September

(iv) 12 September

 (v) 19 September

(vi) 26 September

So, that 28 september is Tuesday.

12. All the given option can be formed from letter CONCENTRATION except Centre becaue it has 'E' twice.

13.

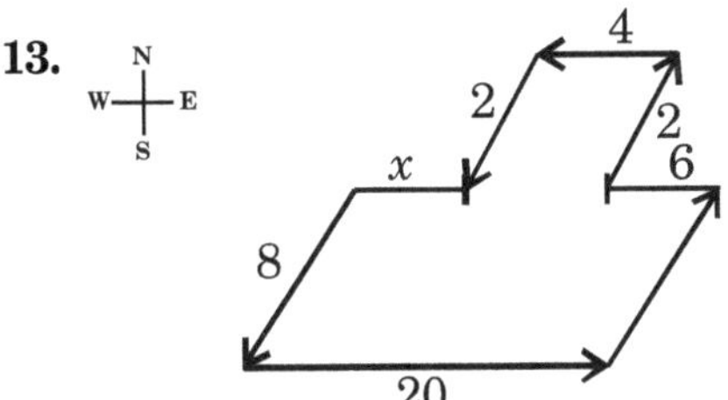

From diagram

∴ distance from starting point

$$= 20 - (6 + 4)$$

$$= 20 - 10$$

$$= 10 \text{ m.}$$

16.

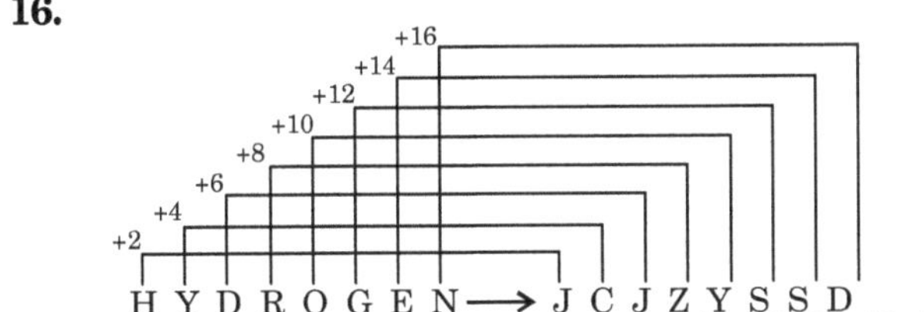

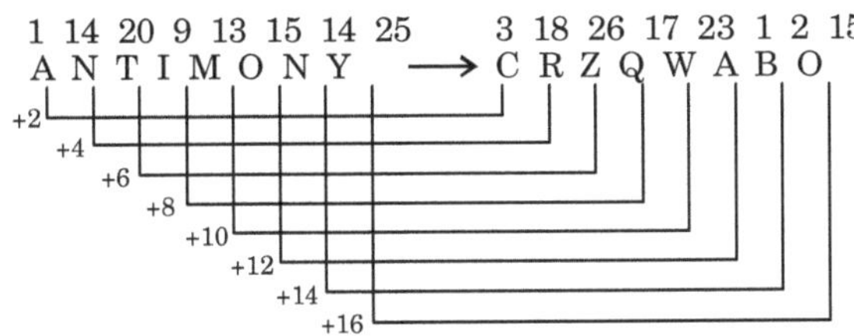

17. D E L H I   and

 7 3 5 4 1

 C A L C U T T A

 8 2 5 8 9 6 6 2

∴ C A L I C U T

   8 2 5 1 8 9 6

18. $2 \times 7 \times 9 = 126$

   $7 \times 3 \times 8 = 168$

∴ $9 \times 4 \times 6 = 216$

19.

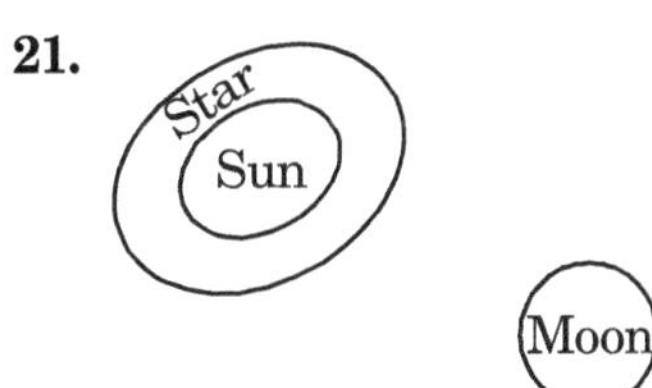

21.

Hence, answer is (d).

22. The correct equation is

$$30 \div 6 \times 5 + 4 - 2 = 27$$

$$\Rightarrow 5 \times 5 + 4 - 2 = 27$$

$$\Rightarrow \quad 25 + 4 - 2 = 27$$

$$\Rightarrow \qquad 29 - 2 = 27$$

$$\Rightarrow \qquad\qquad 27 = 27$$

$$\text{L.H.S} = \text{R.H.S}$$

51. $\dfrac{3\sqrt{2}}{\sqrt{3}+\sqrt{6}} - \dfrac{4\sqrt{3}}{\sqrt{6}+\sqrt{2}} + \dfrac{\sqrt{6}}{\sqrt{3}+\sqrt{2}}$ ...(1)

Applying rationalization method

$$= \frac{3\sqrt{2}}{\sqrt{3}+\sqrt{6}} \times \frac{\sqrt{3}-\sqrt{6}}{\sqrt{3}-\sqrt{6}}$$

$$= \frac{3\sqrt{2}}{\sqrt{3}+\sqrt{6}} \times \frac{\sqrt{3}-\sqrt{6}}{\sqrt{3}-\sqrt{6}}$$

$$= \frac{3\sqrt{6}-3\sqrt{12}}{3-6}$$

$$= \frac{3\sqrt{12}-3\sqrt{6}}{3}$$

$$= \sqrt{12} - \sqrt{6}$$

$$= \frac{4\sqrt{3}}{\sqrt{6}+\sqrt{8}} \times \frac{\sqrt{6}-\sqrt{2}}{\sqrt{6}-\sqrt{2}}$$

$$= \frac{4\sqrt{18}-4\sqrt{6}}{\left(\sqrt{6}\right)^2-\left(\sqrt{2}\right)^2} \qquad ...(2)$$

$$= \frac{4\sqrt{18}-4\sqrt{6}}{4}$$

$$= \sqrt{18}-\sqrt{6} \qquad ...(3)$$

$$= \frac{\sqrt{6}}{\sqrt{3}+\sqrt{2}} \times \frac{\sqrt{3}-\sqrt{2}}{\sqrt{3}-\sqrt{2}}$$

$$= \frac{\sqrt{18}-\sqrt{12}}{\left(\sqrt{3}\right)^2-\left(\sqrt{2}\right)^2}$$

$$= \sqrt{18}-\sqrt{12} \qquad ...(4)$$

From equation (1), (2), (3), (4), we get

$$= \sqrt{12}-\sqrt{6}-\sqrt{18}+\sqrt{6}+\sqrt{18}-\sqrt{12}$$

$$= 0$$

52. $\sqrt{6+\sqrt{6+\sqrt{6+...}}}$

$$\sqrt{3 \times 2} = 3$$

53. $\dfrac{\sqrt{3}+\sqrt{2}}{\sqrt{3}-\sqrt{2}}$

Rationalizing it $= \dfrac{\sqrt{3}+\sqrt{2}}{\sqrt{3}-\sqrt{2}} \times \dfrac{\sqrt{3}+\sqrt{2}}{\sqrt{3}-\sqrt{2}}$

$$= \frac{\left(\sqrt{3}+\sqrt{2}\right)^2}{\left(\sqrt{3}\right)^2-\left(\sqrt{2}\right)^2}$$

$$= \left(\sqrt{3}+\sqrt{2}\right)^2$$

taking square root of it $= \sqrt{3}+\sqrt{2}$

54. 3^{21}

the power of unit place '3' is 21

So last digit will be 3

Hence after dividing by 5, we get remainder 3

55. $(1001)^{2008}+1002$

the power of unit place '1' is 2008

$$1 + 1002 = 3$$

therefore the last digit is '3'

56.
$$x \times y = (x+3)^2 (y-1)$$
$$5 \times 4 = (5+3)^2 (4-1)$$
$$= (8)^2 (3)$$
$$= 64 \times 3$$
$$= 192$$

57. $\dfrac{(0.05)^2+(0.041)^2+(0.073)^2}{(0.005)^2+(0.041)^2+(0.0073)^2}$

$$= \frac{\left(\frac{5}{100}\right)^2+\left(\frac{41}{100}\right)^2+\left(\frac{7.3}{100}\right)^2}{\left(\frac{5}{1000}\right)^2+\left(\frac{41}{1000}\right)^2+\left(\frac{7.3}{1000}\right)^2}$$

$$= \frac{\left(\frac{1}{100}\right)^2+(51)^2+(41)^2+(7.3)^2}{\left(\frac{1}{100}\right)^2 (5)^2+(41)^2+(7.3)^2}$$

$$= 100$$

58. A + B complete a work = 8 day

B + C complete a work = 12 day

C + A complete a work = 8 days

$$A + B + C \text{ complete a work} = \frac{1}{8}+\frac{1}{12}+\frac{1}{8}$$

$$2(A+B+C) = \frac{3+2+3}{24}$$

$$A+B+C = \frac{8}{24 \times 2}$$

$$A+B+C = \frac{1}{6}$$

A + B + C complete work in = 6 days.

59. X is faster than Y, 3 times. Therefore if x complete a work in 1 day y take 3 days to complet it.

Therefore the difference between the working days is 2.

But in this case the difference is 40 days.

Therefore A completes a work in 20 day and B completes the work in 60 day.

A and B together competes a work

$$= \frac{1}{20} + \frac{1}{60}$$

$$= \frac{3+1}{60}$$

$$= \frac{1}{15}$$

$$= 15 \text{ days}$$

60. Area of square $(a^2) = 81$

$$a = 9$$

Perimeter of square $= 4a = 4 \times 9 = 36$

Perimeter of semicircle $= \pi r + 2r$

$$\pi r + 2r = 36$$

$$r(\pi + 2) = 36$$

$$r\left(\frac{36}{7}\right) = 36$$

$$r = 7$$

61. We know

$$1 \text{ hectar } = 10{,}000 \text{m}^2$$

Area of the ground

$$= 1.5 \times 10000 \text{m}^2$$

$$= 15000 \text{m}^2$$

Volume of rain water collected

$$= 15000 \times 5 \times 10^{-2}$$

$$= 150 \times 5$$

$$= 750 \text{m}^3$$

62. Flow of water in (m/min)

$$= \frac{2 \times 1000}{60}$$

$$= \frac{100}{3}$$

Fall of water into the sea in one minute

$$= 3 \times 40 \times \frac{100}{3}$$

$$= 4000 \text{ litre}$$

64. Let the correct answer $= x$

and incorrect anger $= y$

$$x + y = 75$$

$$\underline{4x - y = 125}$$

$$5x = 200$$

$$x = 40$$

The no. of question attempt correctly = 40

65. Mean of 50 number = 30

sum of 50 number $= 30 \times 50 = 1500$

wrongly entered no. 82 and 13

$$\therefore 1500 - (82 + 13) = 1500 - 95 = 1405$$

correctly entered no. is

$$= 1405 + (28 + 31)$$

$$= 1405 + 59$$

$$= 1465$$

mean of 1465 is $= \dfrac{1465}{50}$

$$= 29.28$$

66. Speed of man in still water = 6 km/h

speed of current = 2 km/h

speed of man in upstream

$$= 6 - 2 = 4 \text{ km/hr.}$$

speed of man in down stream

$$= 6 + 2 = 8 \text{ km/hr.}$$

Let the total distance $= x$ km

$$\frac{x}{4} - \frac{x}{8} = 3$$

$$\frac{x}{8} = 3$$

$$x = 24 \text{ km}$$

67. Let the market prize of watch $= ₹\ x$

$$x \times \frac{95}{100} - x \times \frac{94}{100} = 15$$

$$\frac{x}{100} = 15$$

$$x = ₹\ 1500$$

68. Let the cost price of first horse $= ₹\ x$

cost price of second horse $= ₹\ (19500 - x)$

According to question

$$x \times \frac{80}{100} = (19500 - x) \times \frac{115}{100}$$

$$80x = 19500 \times 115 - 115x$$

$$80x + 115x = 19500 \times 115$$

$$195x = 19500 \times 115$$

$$x = \frac{19500 \times 115}{195}$$

$$= ₹\ 11500$$

Cost price of second horse

$$= 19500 - 11500$$

$$= ₹\ 8000$$

69. Original price of sugar = ₹ x/kg

According to question,

$$\frac{270}{x} + 1 = \frac{270}{0.9x}$$

$$\Rightarrow \frac{300}{x} - \frac{270}{x} = 1$$

$$\Rightarrow x = ₹\ 30/\text{kg}.$$

70. Percentage to reduce his consumption

$$= \frac{25}{125} \times 100 = 20\%$$

71. ₹ x double it self y in 4 year

$2x$ four times it self y in next 4 years

therefore it takes 8 years for amount four times itself.

72. Let the sum = x

According to question

$$\frac{x}{4} = \frac{x \times 5 \times r}{100}$$

$$r = \frac{20}{4} = 5\%$$

73. Production of company D

$$= \frac{2700}{1500} \times \text{production of company A}$$

$$= 1.8 \times \text{production of company B}$$

74. Percentage $= \dfrac{600}{2400} \times 100$

$$= 25\%$$

75. Number of companies whose demand is more than production = 3

Number of companies whose production is more than demand = 2

∴ Ratio = 3 : 2

GENERAL INTELLIGENCE

1. In the following question, select the related word from the given alternatives.

ACEG : SUWY : : BDFH : ?

(a) TVZX   (b) RTZV

(c) TVXZ   (d) RTVZ

2. In the following question select the one which is different from the other three responses.

(a) Heat   (b) Light

(c) Bulb   (d) Electricity

3. Arrange the following words according to the dictionary ?

1. Inventory   2. Involuntary

3. Invisible   4. Invariable

5. Investigate

(a) 4, 2, 5, 3, 1

(b) 4, 5, 1, 3, 2

(c) 2, 5, 4, 1, 3

(d) 4, 1, 5, 3, 2

4. Which one set of letters when sequentially placed at the gaps in the given letter series shall complete it ?

a _ b _ a _ _ n _ bb _ abbn

(a) abnabb   (b) bnbban

(c) bnbbna   (d) babban

5. Find out a set of numbers amongst the four sets of numbers given in the alternatives, which is the most similar to the numbers given in the question.

Given: (6, 30, 90)

(a) 6, 42, 86   (b) 7, 42, 218

(c) 6, 24, 70   (d) 8, 48, 192

6. Arrange the following in the meaningful/logical order :

1. Exhaust   2. Night

3. Day   4. Sleep

5. Work

(a) 1, 3, 5, 2, 4

(b) 3, 5, 1, 4, 2

(c) 3, 5, 1, 2, 4

(d) 3, 5, 2, 1, 4

7. In the following question, a series is given with one term missing. Choose the correct alternative from the given ones that will complete the series.

3, 4, 7, 11, 18, 29 ?

(a) 31   (b) 39

(c) 43   (d) 47

8. M is the son of P. Q is the grand daughter of O who is the husband of P. How is M related to O ?

(a) Son   (b) Daughter

(c) Mother   (d) Father

9. From the given alternative words, select the word which **cannot** be formed using the letters of the-given word :

Given : IMPASSIONABLE

(a) IMPASSABLE   (b) IMPOSSIBLE

(c) IMPASSIVE   (d) IMPASSION

10. Only one meaningful word can be formed by rearranging the letter of the given Jumbled word. Find out that word. Given : MUSPOPAPOTIH

(a) METAMORPHIC

(b) PHILANTHROPIST

(c) HIPPOCAMPUS

(d) HIPPOPOTAMUS

11. Which number is **wrong** in the given series ?

1, 9, 25, 50, 81

(a) 1   (b) 25

(d) 50   (d) 81

12. If the day before yesterday was Sunday, what day will it be three days after the day after tomorrow ?

(a) Sunday   (b) Monday

(c) Wednesday   (d) Saturday

Directions : *In the following question, one statement is given followed by two assumptions I and II. You have to consider the statement to be true even if it seems to be at variance from commonly known facts. You have to decide which of the given assumptions if any, follow from the given statement.*

13. Statement : Politicians become rich by the votes of the people.

Assumptions :

I. People vote to make politicians rich.

II. Politicians become rich by their virtue.

(a) Only I is implicit

(b) Only II is implicit

(c) Both I and II are implicit

(d) Both I and II are not implicit

Directions : *In the following question, two statements P and Q are given followed by four conclusions I, II, III and IV. You have to consider the two statements to be true even if they seem to be at variance from commonly known facts. You have to decide which of the given conclusions, if any, follow the given statements.*

14. Statements :   P. All men are women.

                  Q. All women are crazy.

Conclusion :   I. All men are crazy,

             II. All the crazy are men.

             III. Some of the crazy are men.

             IV. Some of the crazy are women.

(a) None of the conclusions follows

(b) All the conclusions follow

(c) Only I, III and IV follow

(d) Onlv II and III follow

15. If HOSPITAL is written as 32574618 In a certain code, how would POSTAL be written in that code ?

(a) 752618   (b) 725618

(c) 725188   (d) 725661

16. Find the missing number from the given resnonses.

173 (24) 526; 431 (18) 325; 253 (?) 471

(a) 22   (b) 42

(c) 30   (d) 06

17. After interchanging + and +, 12 and 18, which one of the following equations becomes correct ?

(a) $(90 \times 18) + 18 = 60$

(b) $(18 + 6) + 12 = 2$

(c) $(72 + 18) \times 18 = 72$

(d) $(12 + 6) \times 18 = 36$

18. In the following question, Δ stands for any of the mathematical signs at different places, which are given as choices under each question. Select the choice with the correct sequence of aigns which when substituted makes the question as a correct equation.

        $24 \, \Delta \, 4 \, \Delta \, 5 \, \Delta \, 4$

(a) $\times + =$ (b) $= \times +$

(c) $+ \times =$ (d) $= + \times$

19. What is the number missing from the third target ?

5	9	15
16	29	?
49	88	147

(a) 45   (b) 48

(c) 51   (d) 54

20. K is a place which is located 2 km away in the north-west direction from the capital P, R is another place that is located 2 km away in the south-west direction from K. M is another place and that is located 2 km away in the north-west direction from R. T is yet another place that is located 2 km away in the South-west direction from M. In which direction is T located in relation to P ?

(a) South-west   (b) North-west

(c) West   (d) North

21. Find out which of the diagrams given in the alternatives correctly represents the relationship stated in the question.

Sharks, Whales, Turtles.

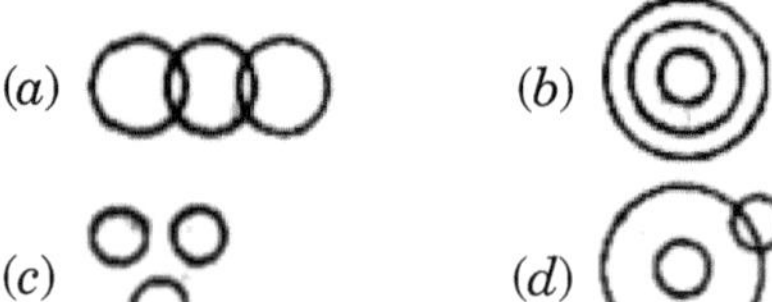

Direction : *In this questions, among the four answer figures, which figure can be formed from the cut-pieces given below in the question figure.*

22. Question Figure

Answer Figures

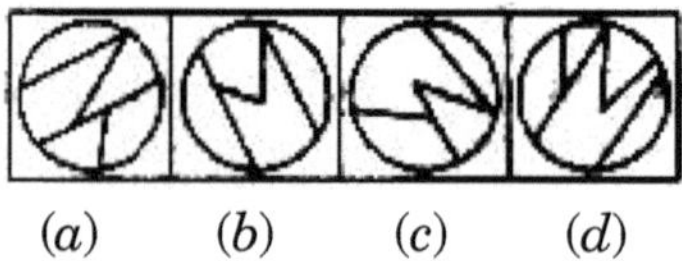

   (a)   (b)   (c)   (d)

23. How many triangles are there in the following figure ?

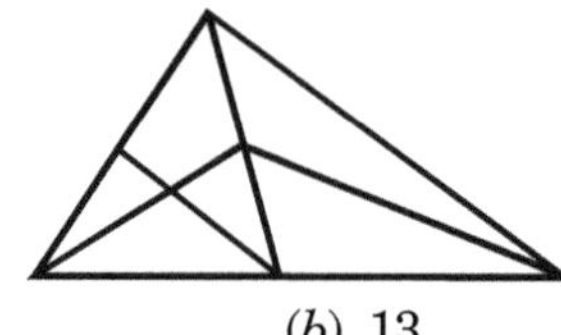

(a) 11   (b) 13

(c) 9   (d) 15

24. From the given answer figures, select the one in which the question figure is hidden/embedded in the same direction.

Question Figure

Answer Figures

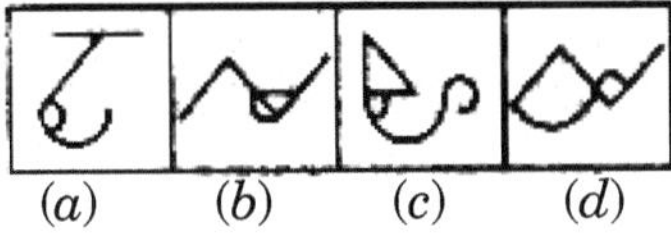

(a)   (b)   (c)   (d)

25. Which answer figure is the exact mirror image of the given question figure when the mirror is held from the right at PQ ?

Question Figure

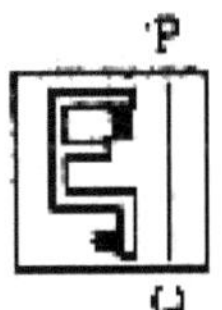

Answer Figures

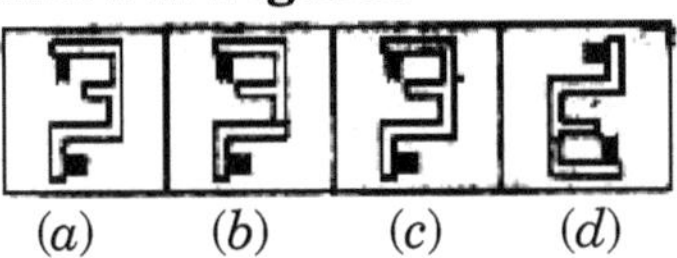

(a)   (b)   (c)   (d)

ENGLISH LANGUAGE

Directions (Q. 26-27) : *In the following questions out of the four alternatives, choose the one which best expresses the meaning of the given word.*

26. LUXURIANT

(a) Luxury-loving   (b) Lovely

(c) Rich   (d) Abundant

27. CANTANKEROUS

(a) Cancerous   (b) Ferocious

(c) Quarreisome   (d) Fissiparous

Directions (Q. 28-29) : *In the following questions choose the word opposite in meaning to the given word.*

28. FLORID

(a) Weak   (b) Pale

(c) Monotonous   (d) Ugly

29. VERITY

(a) Sanctity   (b) Reverence

(c) Falsehood   (d) Rarity

Directions (Q. 30-32) : *In the following questions. out of the four as ternatives. Choose the one which can be substituted for the given words / sentence.*

30. An underhand device resorted to in order to justify misconduct

(a) subterfuge   (b) Manoenvp

(c) Stratagem   (d) Complicity

31. Impossible to describe

(a) Miraculous   (b) Ineffable

(c) Stupendous   (d) Appalling

32. One who criticises popular beliefs which he thinks is mistaken or unwise

(a) Philistine   (b) Iconoclast

(c) Imposter   (d) Cannibal

Directions (Q. 33-35): *Four alternatives are given for the idiom / phrase underlined in the sentence. Choose the alternative which best expresses the meaning of the idiom / phrase and mark it in the Answer Sheet.*

33. His investments helped him <u>make a killing</u> in the stock market.

(a) lose money quickly

(b) plan a murder quickly

(c) murder someone quickly

(d) make money quickly

34. There is <u>no gainsaying</u> the fact that the country is in difficulties.

(a) ignoring   (b) hiding

(c) forgetting   (d) denying

35. To die in harness

(a) premeditated murder

(b) dying young in an accident

(c) to die while in service

(d) to be taken by surprise

36. In the following question, groups of four words are given. In each group, one word is correctly spelt. Find the correctly spell word.

(a) collaborate   (b) comemorate

(c) colate   (d) choclate

Directions (Q. 37-39) : *In the following questions, some of the sentences have errors and some have none. Find out which part of a sentence has an error. The number of that part is your answer. Your answer is (d) i.e.. No error.*

37. He is a university professor (a)/ but of his three sons (b)/ neither has any merit, (c)/ No error (d)

38. After knowing truth, (a)/ they took the right decision (b)/ in the matter (c)/ No error (d)

39. It is time you (a)/ decide on your next (b)/ course of action. (c)/ No error (d)

Directions (Q. 40 - 42) : *Sentences are given with blanks to be filled in with an appropriate word (s). Four alternatives are suggested for each question. Choose the correct alternative out of the four.*

40. The hotel was not too expensive ___ .

   (a) was it ?   (b) wasn't it ?

   (c) is it ?   (d) isn't it ?

41. Like humans, zoo animals must have a dentist ___ their teeth.

   (a) fill   (b) filled

   (c) filling   (d) to be filled

42. It was very kind of you to do the washing-up, but you ___ it.

   (a) didn't have to do

   (b) hadn't to do

   (c) mightn't have done

   (d) mustn't have done

Directions (Q. 43-45) : *In the following questions a part of the sentence is **bold**. Below are given alternatives to the bold part at (a), (b) and (c) which may improve the sentence. Choose the correct alternative. In case no Improvement is needed your answer is (d).*

43. Obviously he isn't **cut up** to be a good teacher.

   (a) cut out   (b) cut in

   (c) cut for   (d) No improvement

44. Power got with money is the most **craved for** today.

   (a) sought after   (b) wished for

   (c) welcomed for   (d) No improvement

45. The brown shirt **wants washing**

   (a) has to wash   (b) is in need of a wash

   (c) requires a wash   (d) No improvement

Directions (Q. 46-50): *Read the following passage carefully and choose the best answer to each question out of four alternatives and mark it the correct answer.*

Every profession or trade, every art and every science has its technical vocabulary, the function of which is partly to designate things or processes which have no names in ordinary English and partly to secure greater exactness in nomenclature. Such special dialects or jargons are necessary in technical discussion of any kind, Being universally understood by the devotees of the particular science or art, they have the precision of a mathematical formula. Besides, they save time, for it is much more economical to name a process than to describe it. Thousands of these technical terms are very properly included in every large dictionary, yet, as a whole, they are rather on the outskirts of the English language than actually within its borders.

Different occupation, however, differ widely in the character of their handicrafts and other vocations like farming and fishing that have occupied great numbers of men from remote times, the technical vocabulary is very old. An average man now uses these in his own vocabulary. The special dialects of law, medicine, divinity and philosophy have become familiar to cultivated persons.

46. Special words used in technical discussion

   (a) may become part of common speech

   (b) never last long

   (c) should resemble mathematical formula

   (d) should be confined to scientific fields

47. The writer of this article is

   (a) a scientist   (b) a politician

   (c) a linguist   (d) a businessman

48. This passage is primarily concerned with

   (a) various occupations and professions

   (b) technical terminology

   (c) scientific undertakings

   (d) a new language

49. It is true that

   (a) various professions and occupations often interchange words

   (b) there is always a non-technical word that may be substituted for the technical word

   (c) the average man often uses in his own vocabulary what was once technical language not meant for him

   (d) everyone is interested in scientific findings

50. In recent years, there has been a marked increase in the number of technical terms in the nomenclature of

   (a) Farming   (b) Fishing

   (c) Sports   (d) Government

QUANTITATIVE APTITUDE

51. $\dfrac{0.125 + 0.027}{0.25 - 0.15 + 0.09}$ is equal to

   (a) 0.3   (b) 0.5

   (c) 0.8   (d) 0.9

52. A number, when divided by 114, leaves remainder 21. If the same number is divided by 19, then the remainder will be

   (a) 1   (b) 2

   (c) 7   (d) 17

53. If $a = 11$ and $b = 9$, then the value of $\left(\dfrac{a^2 + b^2 + ab}{a^3 - b^3} \right)$ is

   (a) $\dfrac{1}{2}$ (b) 2

   (c) $\dfrac{1}{20}$ (d) 20

54. If a and b be positive integers such that $a^2 - b^2 = 19$, then the value of a is

(a) 19   (b) 20

(c) 9   (d) 10

55. If the ratio of cost price and selling price of an article be as 10 : 11 the percentage of profit is

(a) 8   (b) 10

(c) 11   (d) 15

56. A shopkeeper earns a profit of 12% on selling a book at 10% discount on the printed price. The ratio of the cost price and the printed price of the book is

(a) 45 : 56   (b) 45 : 51

(c) 47 : 56   (d) 47 : 51

57. By selling an article a man makes a profit of 25% of its selling price. His profit per cent is

(a) 20   (b) 25

(c) $16\frac{2}{3}$ (d) $33\frac{1}{3}$

58. Two natural numbers are in the ratio 3 : 5 and their product is 2160. The smaller of the numbers is

(a) 36   (b) 24

(c) 18   (d) 12

59. Two successive price increases of 10% and 10% of an article are quivalent to a single price increase of

(a) 19%   (b) 20%

(c) 21%   (a) 22%

60. An equilateral triangle of side 6 cm has its corners cut off to form a regular hexagon. Area (in cm²) of this regular hexagon will be

(a) $3\sqrt{3}$ (b) $3\sqrt{6}$

(c) $6\sqrt{3}$ (d) $\dfrac{5\sqrt{3}}{2}$

61. If ₹ 1000 is divided between A and B in the ratio 3 : 2. then A will receive

(a) ₹ 400   (b) ₹ 500

(c) ₹ 600   (d) ₹ 800

62. At what rate per cent per annum will a sum of ₹ 1,000 amount to ₹ 1, 102,50 in 2 years at compound interest ?

(a) 5   (b) 5.5

(c) 6   (d) 6.5

63. What annual payment wll discharge a debt of ₹ 6,450 due in 4 years at 5% per annum simple interest ?

(a) ₹ 1.400   (b) ₹ 1.1500

(c) ₹ 1.550   (d) ₹ 1.600

64. In a family, the average age of a father and a mother is 35 years. The average age of the father, mother and their only son is 27 years What is the age of the son ?

(a) 12 years   (b) 11 years

(c) 10.5 years   (d) 10 years

65. If A and B together can complete a piece of work in 15 days and B alone in 20 days. In how many days can A alone complete the work ?

(a) 60   (b) 45

(c) 40   (d) 30

66. A can complete a piece of work in 18 days, B in 20 days and C in 30 days, B and C together start the work and are forced to leave after 2 days. The time taken by A alone to complete the remaining work is

(a) 10 days   (b) 12 days

(c) 15 days   (d) 16 days

67. A train, 300m long, passed a man, walking along the line in the same direction at the rate of 3 km/hr in 33 seconds. The speed of the train is

(a) 30 km/h   (b) 32 km/h

(c) $32\frac{8}{11}$ km/h   (d) $35\frac{8}{11}$ km/h

Directions (Q. 68-70) : *The piechart, given here, represents the number of valid votes obtained by four students who contested election for school leadership. The total number of valid votes polled was 720.*

Observe the chart and answer the questions based on it.

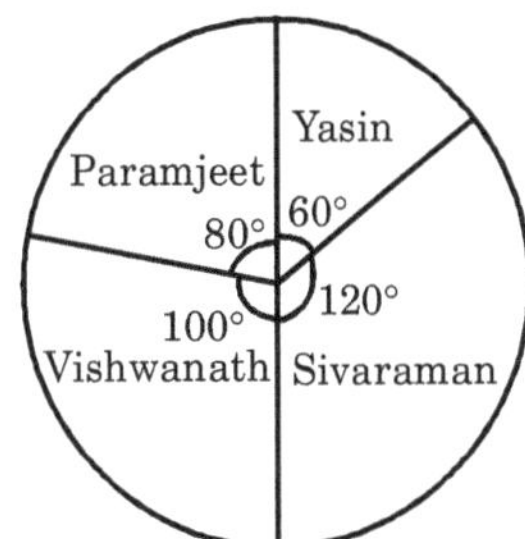

68. What was the minimum number ol votes obtained by any candidate ?

(a) 100   (b) 110

(c) 120   (d) 130

69. What was the winner ?

(a) Sivaraman   (b) Paramjeet

(c) Yasin   (d) Vishwanath

70. By how many votes did the winner defeat his nearest rival ?

(a) 40   (b) 45

(c) 48   (d) 50

71. If $x\sin^3\theta + y\cos^3\theta = \sin\theta\cos\theta$

and $x\sin\theta = y\cos\theta$,

$\sin\theta \neq 0$, $\cos\theta \neq 0$, then $x^2 + y^2$ is

(a) $\dfrac{1}{\sqrt{2}}$ (b) $\dfrac{1}{2}$

(c) 1   (d) $\sqrt{2}$

72. $\sec^4\theta - \sec^2\theta$ is equal to

(a) $\tan^2\theta - \tan^4\theta$ (b) $\tan^2\theta + \tan^4\theta$

(c) $\cos^4\theta + \cos^2\theta$ (d) $\cos^2\theta + \cos^4\theta$

73. If each interior angle is double of each exterior angle of a regular polygon with n sides, then the value of n is

(a) 8   (b) 10

(c) 5   (d) 6

74. The angle formed by the hour-hand and the minute-hand of a clock at 2 : 15 p.m. is

(a) $27\dfrac{1}{2}°$ (b) $45°$

(c) $22\dfrac{1}{2}°$ (d) $30°$

75. Two sides of a triangle are of length 4 cm and 10 cm. If the length of the third side is 'a' cm, then

(a) $a > 5$ (b) $6 \leq a \leq 12$

(c) $a < 6$ (d) $6 < a < 14$

GENERAL AWARENESS

76. A concave lens always forms an image which is

(a) real and erect

(b) virtual and erect

(c) real and inverted

(d) virtual and inverted

77. A vitamin requires cobalt for its activity. The vitamin is

(a) Vitamin B_{12} (b) Vitamin D

(c) Vitamin B_2 (d) Vitamin

78. One of the constituents of tear gas is

(a) Ethane   (b) Ethanol

(c) Ether   (d) Chloroplerin

79. The modulus of rigidity is the ratio of

(a) longitudinal stress to longitudinal strain

(b) Volume stress to volume strain

(c) shearing stress to shearing strain

(d) tensile stress to tensile strain

80. An atomic clock is based on transitions in

(a) Sodium   (b) Caesium

(c) Magnesium   (d) Aluminium

81. The World Bank, in its latest once-in-two-yearLogistics Performance Index (LPI), India is now ranked __________ as against the 54th spot it occupied in the previous 2014 report.

(a) 20th   (b) 25th

(c) 35th   (d) 45th

82. Plasma membrane in eukaryotic cells is made up of

(a) Phospholipid

(b) Lipoprotein

(c) Phospholipo-protein

(d) Phospho-protein

83. Arrange the following in chroma logical order :

1. Tughlaqs   2. Lodis
3. Saiyids   4. Ubari Turks
5. Khiljis

(a) 1, 2, 3, 4, 5   (b) 5, 4, 3, 2, 1

(c) 2, 4, 5, 3, 1   (d) 4, 5, 1, 3, 2

84. The book titled 'The Indian War of Independence' was written by

(a) Krishna Verma   (b) Madame Cama

(c) B.G. Tilak   (d) V.D. Savarkar

85. Who was the founder of the 'Servants of India Society' ?

(a) G.K Gokhale   (b) M.G. Ranade

(c) B.G.Tilak   (d) Bipin Chandra Pal

86. The term 'Caste' was derived from

(a) Portuguese   (b) Dutch

(c) German   (d) English

87. Seismic sea waves which approach the coasts at greater force are known as

(a) Tides   (b) Tsunami

(c) Current   (d) Cyclone

88. Depression formed due to deflating action of winds are called

(a) Playas   (b) Yardang

(c) Ventifacts   (d) Sand dunes

89. India's leading food products company __________ has signed up as the official sponsor for the Indian contingent to the Rio Olympics 2016.

(a) Mother Dairy   (b) Rajdhani Group

(c) Amul   (d) KRBL Limited

90. Indian Standard Time relates to

(a) 75.5° E longitude   (b) 82.5° E longitude

(c) 90.5° E longitude   (d) 0° longitude

91. Who is rightly called the "Father of Local Self Government" In India ?

(a) Lord Mayo   (b) Lord Ripon

(c) Lord Curzon   (d) Lord Clive

92. Which is the second nearest star to the Earth after the Sun ?
- (*a*) Vega
- (*b*) Sirius
- (*c*) Proxima Centauri
- (*d*) Alpha Centauri

93. Which is not an All India Service ?
- (*a*) Indian Administration Service
- (*b*) Indian Police Service
- (*c*) Indian foreign Service
- (*d*) Indian Forest Service

94. Noise is measured in
- (*a*) Watt
- (*b*) REM
- (*c*) Centigrade
- (*d*) Decibel

95. The Union Agriculture & Farmers' Welfare Minister, Shri Radha Mohan Singh has launched Crop Manager for Rice-based Systems (CMRS) a web-based App for better crop and Nutrient management released for...........?
- (*a*) Uttar Pradesh
- (*b*) Bihar
- (*c*) Madhya Pradesh
- (*d*) Gujarat

96. An Intelligent terminal
- (*a*) has a microprocessor, but can not be programmed by the user
- (*b*) can process small data processing jobs. with the use of a large CPU
- (*c*) interacts with the user in English
- (*d*) cannot take data from the user

97. The monetary policy is India is formulated by
- (*a*) Central Government
- (*b*) Industrial Financial Corporation of India
- (*c*) Reserve Bank of India
- (*d*) Industrial Development Bank of India

98. WTO basically promotes
- (*a*) Financial support
- (*b*) Global peace
- (*c*) Unilateral trade
- (*d*) Multilateral trade

99. Price theory is also known as
- (*a*) Macro Economics
- (*b*) Development Economics
- (*c*) Public Economics
- (*d*) Micro Economics

100. National Income is the
- (*a*) Net National Product at market price
- (*b*) Net National Product at factor cost
- (*c*) Net Domestic Product at market price
- (*d*) Net domestic Product at factor cost

ANSWERS

1. (*c*)	**2.** (*c*)	**3.** (*d*)	**4.** (*b*)	**5.** (*d*)	**6.** (*c*)	**7.** (*d*)	**8.** (*a*)	**9.** (*c*)	**10.** (*d*)
11. (*c*)	**12.** (*a*)	**13.** (*d*)	**14.** (*c*)	**15.** (*b*)	**16.** (*a*)	**17.** (*d*)	**18.** (*)	**19.** (*b*)	**20.** (*c*)
21. (*c*)	**22.** (*c*)	**23.** (*b*)	**24.** (*d*)	**25.** (*c*)	**26.** (*d*)	**27.** (*c*)	**28.** (*b*)	**29.** (*c*)	**30.** (*b*)
31. (*b*)	**32.** (*b*)	**33.** (*d*)	**34.** (*d*)	**35.** (*c*)	**36.** (*a*)	**37.** (*c*)	**38.** (*a*)	**39.** (*b*)	**40.** (*a*)
41. (*a*)	**42.** (*d*)	**43.** (*a*)	**44.** (*d*)	**45.** (*c*)	**46.** (*c*)	**47.** (*c*)	**48.** (*b*)	**49.** (*c*)	**50.** (*d*)
51. (*c*)	**52.** (*b*)	**53.** (*a*)	**54.** (*d*)	**55.** (*b*)	**56.** (*a*)	**57.** (*d*)	**58.** (*a*)	**59.** (*c*)	**60.** (*c*)
61. (*c*)	**62.** (*a*)	**63.** (*b*)	**64.** (*b*)	**65.** (*a*)	**66.** (*c*)	**67.** (*d*)	**68.** (*c*)	**69.** (*a*)	**70.** (*a*)
71. (*c*)	**72.** (*b*)	**73.** (*d*)	**74.** (*c*)	**75.** (*d*)	**76.** (*b*)	**77.** (*a*)	**78.** (*d*)	**79.** (*b*)	**80.** (*b*)
81. (*c*)	**82.** (*a*)	**83.** (*d*)	**84.** (*d*)	**85.** (*a*)	**86.** (*a*)	**87.** (*b*)	**88.** (*b*)	**89.** (*c*)	**90.** (*b*)
91. (*b*)	**92.** (*c*)	**93.** (*c*)	**94.** (*d*)	**95.** (*b*)	**96.** (*a*)	**97.** (*c*)	**98.** (*d*)	**99.** (*d*)	**100.** (*b*)

EXPLANATIONS

1. 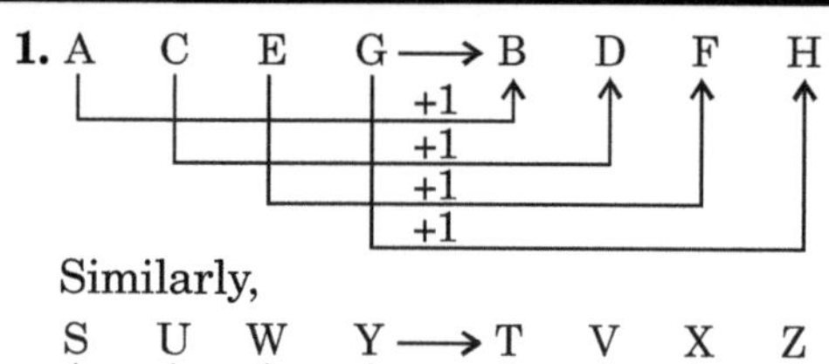

Similarly,

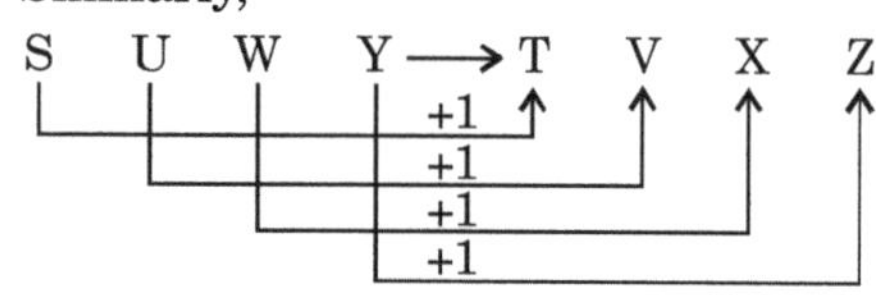

2. Bulb is an item while all other are phenomena.

3. Arrangement of words according to the Dictionary :

(4)	Invariable
	↓
(1)	Inventory
	↓
(5)	Investigate
	↓
(3)	Invisible
	↓
(2)	Involuntary

4. a $\boxed{b}$ b $\boxed{n}$ / a $\boxed{bb}$ n / $\boxed{a}$ bb $\boxed{n}$ / abbn

5. $6 \times 5 = 30$; $30 \times 3 = 90$, $8 \times 6 = 48$, $48 \times 4 = 192$

6. Meaningful order of the words :

3. Day → 5. Work → 1. Exhaust →
2. Night → 4. Sleep

7. $3 + 1 = 4$; $3 + 4 = 7$; $4 + 7 = 11$; $7 + 11 = 18$;

$11 + 18 = 29$; $18 + 29 = \boxed{47}$

8. O is the husband of P. M is the son of P.
Therefore, M is the son of O.

9. There is no 'V' letter in word IMPASSIONABLE
to make IMPASSIVE.

10. Meaningful word ⇒ HIPPOPOTAMUS

11.

1	9	25	49	81
↓	↓	↓	↓	↓
$(1)^2$	$(3)^2$	$(5)^2$	$(7)^2$	$(9)^2$

Therefore, the number 50 is wrong in the series.

12. Day before yesterday was Sunday.
Therefore, today is Tuesday.
Day after tomorrow will be Thursday.
Thursday + 3 = Sunday

13. The statement implies that politicians win elections by the votes of people. Therefore, neither of the assumptions is implicit in the statement.

14. Both the Premises are Universal Affirmative (A-type).
All men are women.

All women are crazy.

$A + A \Rightarrow A$ – type of Conclusion.
"All men are crazy"
This is Conclusion I.
Conclusion III is the Converse of it.
Conclusion IV is the Converse of Statement Q.

15.

H	O	S	P	I	T	A	L
↓	↓	↓	↓	↓	↓	↓	↓
3	2	5	7	4	6	1	8

So,

P	O	S	T	A	L
↓	↓	↓	↓	↓	↓
7	2	5	6	1	8

16. $1 + 7 + 3 + 5 + 2 + 6 = 24$
$4 + 3 + 1 + 3 + 2 + 5 = 18$
∴ $2 + 5 + 3 + 4 + 7 + 1 = 22$

17. $(12 + 6) \times 18 = 36$
$\Rightarrow (18 \div 6) \times 12 = 36$ $\Rightarrow 3 \times 12 = 36$

18. Option (2); $24 = 4 \times 5 + 4$ $\Rightarrow 24 = 20 + 4$
Option (4); $24 = 4 + 5 \times 4$ $\Rightarrow 24 = 4 + 20$
Both options (2) and (4) are correct.

19. $5 \times 3 + 1 = 16$; $16 \times 3 + 1 = 49$; $9 \times 3 + 2 = 29$
$29 \times 3 + 2 = 89$

Similarly, $15 \times 3 + 3 = \boxed{48}$; $48 \times 3 + 3 = 147$

20.

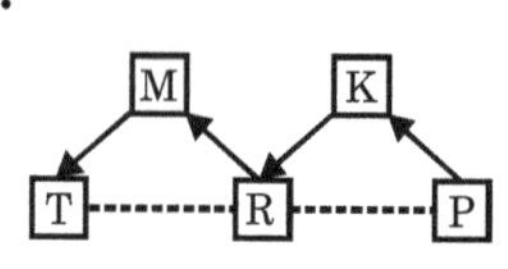

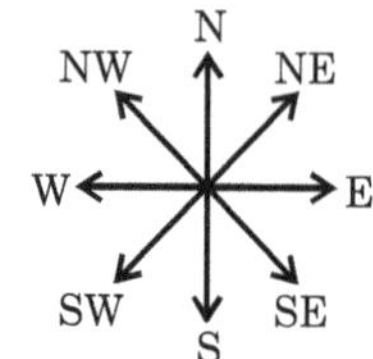

It is clear that T is located to the West of P.

21. Sharks belong to class pisces whale is a mammal and Turtle belong to class reptillia.

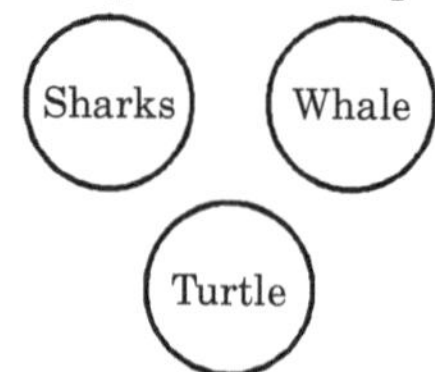

22. 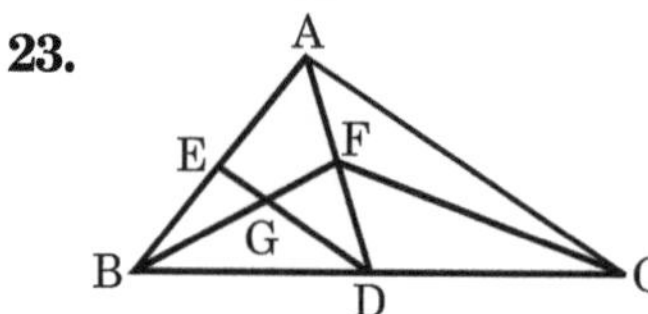

The triangles are :

ΔABC : ΔABD : ΔADC : ΔAFC

ΔFDC : ΔAFB : ΔFDF : ΔFBC

ΔGBD : ΔADE : ΔGBE : ΔFDG

ΔDBE :

24. 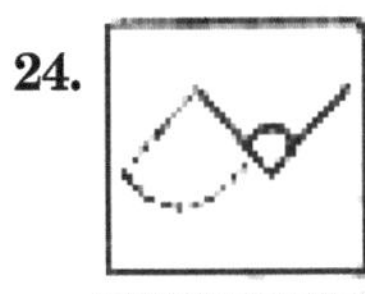

25. 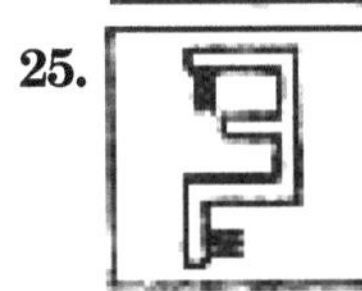

26. Neither is used for two things. For more than two things none should be used.

27. After knowing the truth will be a correct usage

28. It is time/It is high time is followed by the clause in simple past that shows present time Hence, **decided on your next** should be used.

32. The word **Florid (Adjective)** means rosy; gaudy; ornate; red ; having too much decoration or detail.

The word **Pale (Adjective)** means : light in colour not strong or bright; having skin that is almost white because of illness.

Hence the words **florid** and **pale** are antonymous

33. The world **Verity (Noun)** means : a belief or principle about life that is accepted as true : truth.

Hence the words **verity** and **falsehood** are antonymous.

34. The word **Luxuriant (Adjective)** means; growing thickly and strongly; rich in something that is pleasant or beautiful; abundant.

35. The word **Cantankerous (Adjective)** means : bad tempered and always complaining

Hence, the words **cantankerous** and **quarrelsome** are synonymous.

36. Phrase 'cut out' means : to have the qualitles and abilities needed for something.

51. Tricky approach

If $0.5 = a$ and $0.3 = b$ then,

$$\text{Expression} = \frac{a^3 + b^3}{a^2 - ab + b^2}$$

$$= \frac{(a+b)(a^2 - ab + b^2)}{a^2 - ab + b^2} = a + b$$

$$= 0.5 + 0.3 = 0.8$$

52. Tricky approach

If the first divisor is a multiple of second divisor, then the remainder in second case = remainder obtained by dividing the first remainder by the second divisor.

∴ Remainder = 21 − 19 = 2

53. Tricky approach

$$\frac{a^2 + b^2 + ab}{a^3 - b^3} = \frac{a^2 + b^2 + ab}{(a-b)(a^2 + b^2 + ab)}$$

$$= \frac{1}{a-b} = \frac{1}{11-9} = \frac{1}{2}$$

54. Tricky approach

$a^2 - b^2 = 19$; $\Rightarrow 10^2 - 9^2 = 19$; $\Rightarrow a = 10$

55. Gain = $11x - 10x = ₹\, x$

$$\therefore \text{Gain \%} = \frac{\text{Gain} \times 100}{\text{Cost price}} \times 100 = \frac{x}{10x} \times 100 = 10$$

56. Let the C.P. be ₹ 100.

∴ SP = ₹ 112

If the marked price be x, then 90% of $x = 112$

$$\Rightarrow x = \frac{112 \times 100}{90} = ₹\, \frac{1120}{9}$$

$$\therefore \text{Required ratio} = 100 : \frac{1120}{9} = 900 : 1120 = 45 : 56$$

57. If the S.P. of article be ₹ x

then its CP $= x - \dfrac{x}{4} = ₹\, \dfrac{3x}{4}$

$$\therefore \text{Gain \%} = \frac{\dfrac{x}{4}}{\dfrac{3x}{4}} \times 100 = \frac{100}{3} = 33\frac{1}{3}\%$$

58. Let the numbers be $3x$ and $5x$

∴ $3x \times 5x = 2160$

$$\Rightarrow x^2 = \frac{2160}{3 \times 5} = 144 = 12 \times 12 \Rightarrow x = 12$$

∴ Smaller number = $3x = 3 \times 12 = 36$

59. Tricky approach

Single equivalent percentage increase in price

$$= \left(10 + 10 + \frac{10 \times 10}{100}\right) \text{q/n} = 21\%$$

60. Tricky approach

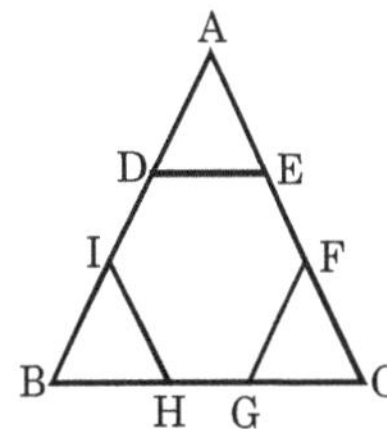

side of the regular hexagon $= \dfrac{1}{3} \times 6 = 2$ cm

$$\therefore \text{Area of the hexagon} = \frac{3\sqrt{3}}{2} a^2 = \frac{3\sqrt{3}}{2} \times 2 \times 2$$

$$= 6\sqrt{3} \text{ sq.cm.}$$

61. Tricky approach

A's share = ₹ $\left(\dfrac{3}{5} \times 1000\right)$ = ₹ 600

62. $A = P\left(1 + \dfrac{R}{100}\right)^T \Rightarrow \dfrac{110250}{1000} = \left(1 + \dfrac{r}{100}\right)^2$

$\Rightarrow \dfrac{11025}{10000} = \left(1 + \dfrac{r}{100}\right)^2 \Rightarrow \left(\dfrac{105}{100}\right)^2 = \left(1 + \dfrac{r}{100}\right)^2$

$\Rightarrow 1 + \dfrac{r}{100} = \dfrac{105}{100} \Rightarrow \dfrac{r}{100} = \dfrac{5}{100}$

$\Rightarrow r = 5\%$

63. Let the annual instalment be ₹ x

$\therefore \left(x + \dfrac{x \times 3 \times 5}{100}\right) + \left(x + \dfrac{x \times 2 \times 5}{100}\right) + \left(x + \dfrac{x \times 1 \times 5}{100}\right) + x$

$$= 6450$$

$\Rightarrow \dfrac{115x}{100} + \dfrac{110x}{100} + \dfrac{105x}{100} + x = 6450$

$\Rightarrow 115x + 110x + 105x + 100x = 6450 \times 100$

$\Rightarrow 430\,x = 6450 \times 100$

$\therefore x = \dfrac{6450 \times 100}{430} = ₹\ 1500$

64. Father + mother = $2 \times 35 = 70$ years

Fater + mother + son = $27 \times 3 = 81$ years

$\therefore$ Son's age = $81 - 70 = 11$ years

65. Tricky approach

(A + B)'s 1 day's work = $\dfrac{1}{15}$

B's 1 day's work = $\dfrac{1}{20}$

$\therefore$ A's 1 day's work = $\dfrac{1}{15} - \dfrac{1}{20} = \dfrac{4-3}{60} = \dfrac{1}{60}$

$\therefore$ A alone will do the work in 60 days.

66. [B + C]'s 2 days's work

$= 2\left(\dfrac{1}{20} + \dfrac{1}{30}\right) = 2\left(\dfrac{3+2}{60}\right) = \dfrac{1}{6}$ part

Remaining work $= 1 - \dfrac{1}{6} = \dfrac{5}{6}$ part

$\therefore$ Time taken by A to complete this part of work

$= \dfrac{5}{6} \times 18 = 15$ days

67. If the speed of the train be x kmph then relative

speed $= (x - 3)$ kmph. $= (x - 3) \times \dfrac{5}{18}$ m/sec

$\therefore \dfrac{300}{(x-3) \times \dfrac{5}{18}} = 33$

$\Rightarrow 5400 = 33 \times 5\ (x - 3)$

$\Rightarrow \quad 360 = 11\,(x - 3) \quad \Rightarrow 11x - 33 = 360$

$\Rightarrow \quad x = \dfrac{393}{11} = 35\dfrac{8}{11}$ kmph

68. Yasin got the minimum votes.

$\because \quad 360° = 720$

$\therefore \quad 60° = \dfrac{720}{360} \times 60 = 120$

69. Sivaraman got the maximum votes. i.e.

$\dfrac{720}{360} \times 120 = 240$ votes

He was the winner.

70. Angle of the difference of votes of the winner and the nearest rival = $120 - 100 = 20°$

$\therefore \quad 360° = 720$

$\therefore \quad 20° = \dfrac{720}{360} \times 20 = 40$

71. $x \sin^3 \theta + y \cos^3 \theta = \sin \theta . \cos \theta$

$(x \sin \theta) \sin^2 \theta + (y \cos \theta) \cos^2 \theta = \sin \theta \cos \theta$

$\because \quad x \sin \theta = y \cos \theta$

$\therefore x \sin \theta\ (\sin^2 \theta + \cos^2 \theta) = \sin \theta \cos \theta$

$x = \cos \theta$

$x \sin \theta = y \cos \theta$

$y = \sin \theta$

so $\quad x^2 + y^2 = \sin^2 \theta + \cos^2 \theta = 1$

72. $\sec^4 \theta - \sec^2 \theta = \sec^2 \theta\ (\sec^2 \theta - 1)$

$= (1 + \tan^2 \theta)(1 + \tan^2 \theta - 1)$

$= \tan^2 \theta + \tan^4 \theta$

73. $\dfrac{(2n - 4) \times 90°}{n} = \dfrac{360°}{n} \times 2$

$(2n - 4)90° = 720$

$2n - 4 = 8\ ;\ 2n = 12 = 6$

74. Angle formed by hour hand in an hour = $30°$

Angle formed in 2 : 15 hours $\left(\dfrac{9}{4} \text{hour}\right)$

$= \dfrac{9}{4} \times 30° = \dfrac{135°}{2}$

Angle formed by minute hand in 60 minutes = $360°$

$\therefore$ Angle formed in 15 minute $= \dfrac{360}{60} \times 15 = 90°$

$\therefore$ Angle formed by hour and minute hand

$= 90° - \dfrac{135}{2} = \dfrac{45}{2} = 22\dfrac{1}{2}$

75.

AB + BC > CA

AB − BC < CA

$10 + 4 > a$

$a < 14$

$10 - 4 < a$

$6 < a$

So, $\quad 6 < a < 14$

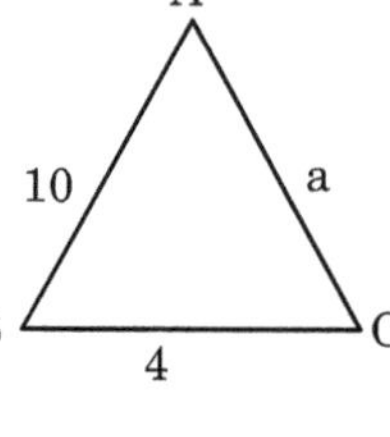

PRACTICE SET – 24

GENERAL INTELLIGENCE

Directions (Q. 1 – 2): *Select the related word / letters / number from the given alternatives.*

1. FLRX : DJPV : : EKQW : __?__
   - (a) WQKE
   - (b) BHMT
   - (c) CIOU
   - (d) AGMS

2. 4 : 17 : : 7 : __?__
   - (a) 51
   - (b) 48
   - (c) 49
   - (d) 50

Direction (Q. 3): *Find the odd words / letters / number pair from the given alternatives.*

3. (a) Radish
   (b) Carrot
   (c) Potato
   (d) Beetroot

4. Which one of the given responses would be a meaningful order of the following ?
   1. Ploughing
   2. Weeding
   3. Sowing
   4. Harvesting
   - (a) 1, 2, 4, 3
   - (b) 1, 2, 3, 4
   - (c) 1, 3, 2, 4
   - (d) 2, 3, 1, 4

5. Arrange the following words according to the English Dictionary :
   1. Voyage
   2. Voice
   3. Vocation
   4. Volume
   - (a) 2, 4, 3, 1
   - (b) 3, 2, 4, 1
   - (c) 2, 3, 4, 1
   - (d) 3, 4, 2, 1

6. Which one set of letters when sequentially placed at the gaps in the given letter series shall complete it?

   a_bab_ab_abb
   - (a) bba
   - (b) baa
   - (c) aaa
   - (d) bbb

7. Find out the set among the four sets which is like the given get.

   (11 – 18 – 25)
   - (a) (9 – 14 – 24)
   - (b) (4 – 12 – 16)
   - (c) (19 – 26 – 33)
   - (d) (18 – 28 – 33)

8. If day before yesterday was Sunday, what day will fall on day after tomorrow?
   - (a) Tuesday
   - (b) Wednesday
   - (c) Thursday
   - (d) Friday

9. If A = 1, AIR = 28, then RIB = ?
   - (a) 26
   - (b) 28
   - (c) 29
   - (d) 35

10. Sarika is 19th from either end of a row of girls. How many girls are there in that row?
    - (a) 19
    - (b) 38
    - (c) 39
    - (d) 37

11. If 'ETHICS' can be written as 'SECTIH', then how can 'AFECTION' be written?
    - (a) NAOFITCE
    - (b) NAOFETIC
    - (c) NAOFICTE
    - (d) NAOFIETC

12. Some letters are given below in the first line and numbers are given below them in the second line. Numbers are the codes for the alphabets and vice-versa. Choose the correct number-code for the given set of alphabets.

A	F	E	H	I	K	O	M	U	R
9	3	8	4	0	5	1	6	2	7

    M A E I O U
    - (a) 698201
    - (b) 698102
    - (c) 698012
    - (d) 698210

13. From the given alternatives select the word which can be formed using the letters given in the word.

    ONSLAUGHT
    - (a) STRONG
    - (b) HOUSE
    - (c) GHOST
    - (d) ENOUGH

Directions (Q. 14): *Select the missing number from the given responses.*

14.
4	5	8
3	?	2
4	10	4
48	200	64
    - (a) 4
    - (b) 185
    - (c) 40
    - (d) 20

15. 'A' walks 10 m towards East and then 10 m to his right. Then every time turning to his left, he walks 5, 15 and 15 m, respectively. How far is he now from his starting point?
    - (a) 20 m
    - (b) 5 m
    - (c) 10 m
    - (d) 15 m

16. Select the correct combination of mathematical signs to replace '*' signs and to balance the given equation.

    6 * 5 * 8 * 4 * 32
    - (a) – + × ×
    - (b) + + + =
    - (c) ÷ + × +
    - (d) × + ÷ =

17. Seema started early in the morning on the road towards the Sun. After some time she turned to her left. Again after some time she turned to her right. After moving some distance she again turned to her right and began to move. At this time, in what direction was she moving?

(a) South   (b) North-West

(c) North-East   (d) East

Direction (Q. 18): *In the following question two statements are given, followed by two conclusions I and II. You have to consider the statements to be ture, even if they seem to be at variance from commonly known facts. You have to decide which of the given conclusions, if any, follow from the given statements. Indicate your answer.*

18. Statements :

This world is neither good nor bad. Each individual manufactures world for himself.

Conclusions :

I. Some people find the world quite good.

II. Some people find the world quite bad.

(a) Neither conclusion I nor II follows

(b) Only conclusion I follows

(c) Only conclusion II follows

(d) Both conclusions I and II follow

19. Five girls E, F, G, H and I are standing in a row. H is on the right of G, I is on the left of G, but is on the right of F. H is on the left of E. Who is standing on the extreme right?

(a) E   (b) F

(c) G   (d) H

20. Choose the correct alternative from the given ones that will complete the series.

Question Figures :

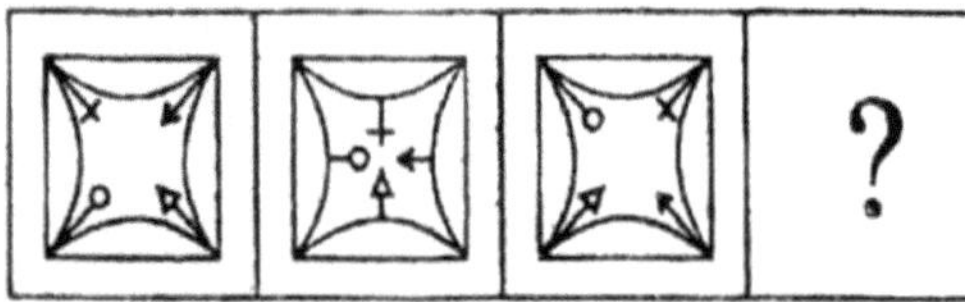

Answer Figures :

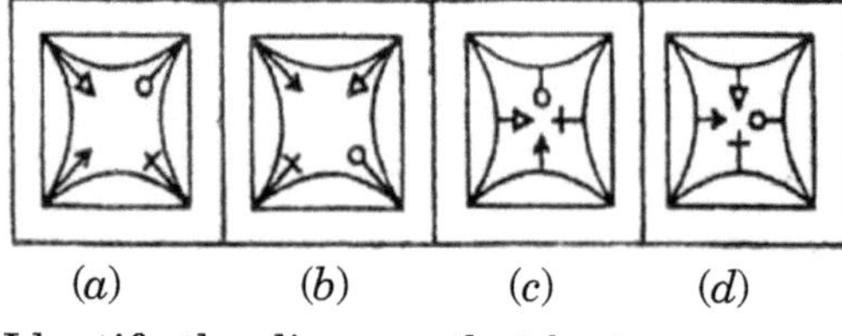

(a)   (b)   (c)   (d)

21. Identify the diagram that best represents the relationship among the classes given below:

     Potato, Vegetables and Eatables

(a) 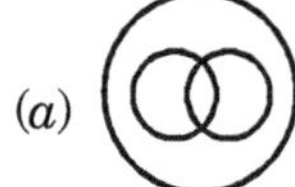   (b) 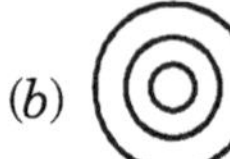

(c) 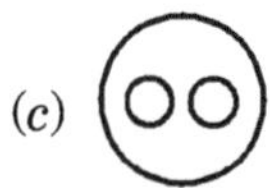   (d) 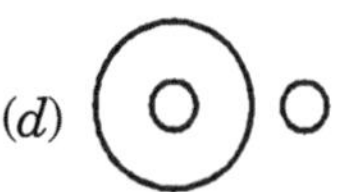

22. Which answer figure will complete the pattern in the question figure?

Question figure :

Answer figures :

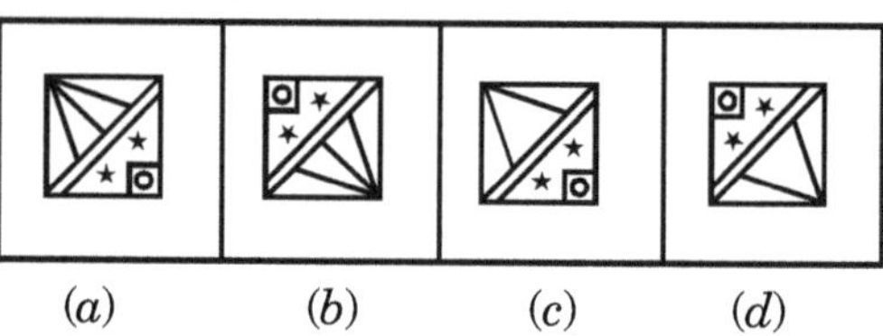

(a)   (b)   (c)   (d)

23. Find the missing number from the given responses.

(a) 98

(b) 7

(c) 192

(d) 193

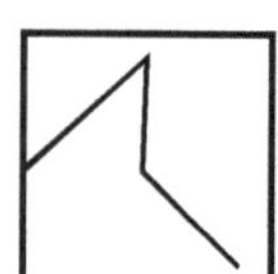

24. From the given answer figures, select the one in which the question figure is hidden/embedded.

Question figure :

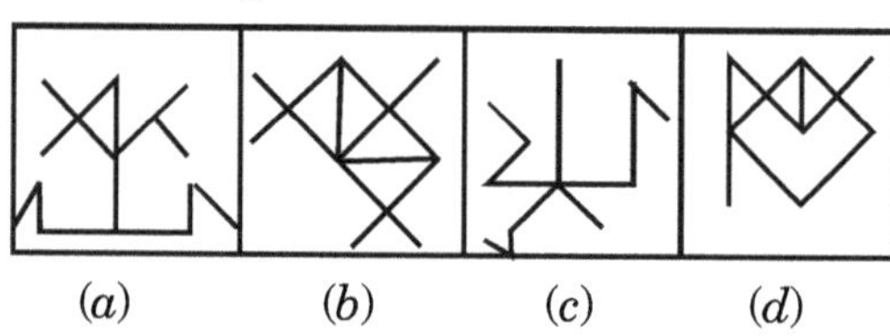

Answer figures :

(a)   (b)   (c)   (d)

25. A piece of paper is folded and cut/punched as shown below the question figures. From the given answer figures, indicate how it will appear when opened.

Question figures :

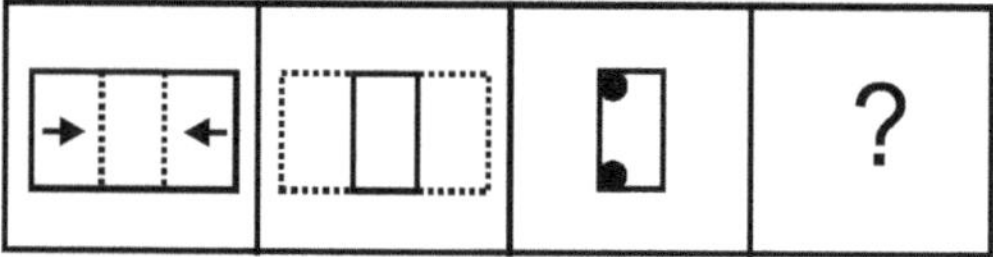

Answer figures :

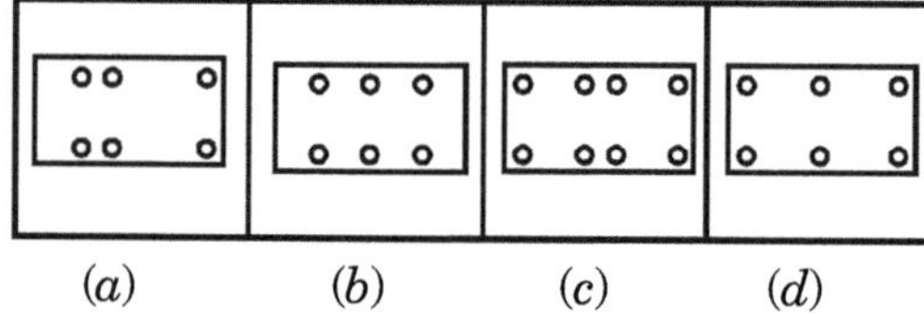

(a)   (b)   (c)   (d)

ENGLISH LANGUAGE

Directions (Q. 26 – 27): *In following questions out of the four alternatives, choose the one which best expresses the meaning of the given word and mark it in the Answer Sheet.*

26. Forsake
    - (*a*) Separate
    - (*b*) Abandon
    - (*c*) Forego
    - (*d*) Disintegrate

27. Stratagem
    - (*a*) Strait
    - (*b*) Stratum
    - (*c*) Ruby
    - (*d*) Trick

Directions (Q. 28 – 29): *Choose the word opposite in meaning to the given word and mark it in the Answer Sheet.*

28. Keen
    - (*a*) Immobile
    - (*b*) Impassioned
    - (*c*) Indifferent
    - (*d*) Clever

29. Dreary
    - (*a*) Interesting
    - (*b*) Solitary
    - (*c*) Dribble
    - (*d*) Unusual
    - (*d*) hippopatemus

Directions (Q. 30 – 32): *In following questions, out of the four alternatives choose the one which can be substituted for the given words / sentence.*

30. That which cannot be consumed by fire
    - (*a*) Invincible
    - (*b*) Inflammable
    - (*c*) Inexhaustible
    - (*d*) Incombustible

31. A place of shelter for ships.
    - (*a*) Barrack
    - (*b*) Helipad
    - (*c*) Port
    - (*d*) Harbour

32. A shopkeeper who sells fresh and green vegetables.
    - (*a*) Greengrocer
    - (*b*) Butcher
    - (*c*) Shopkeeper
    - (*d*) Vendor

Directions (Q. 33 – 35): *In following question, four alternatives are given for the Idiom / Phrases underlined in the sentence. Find the alternative which best expresses the meaning of Idioms / Phrases and mark it in the answer sheet.*

33. They earn so little that it is very difficult for them to <u>keep the wolf from the door</u>.
    - (*a*) to display the wolf before the door
    - (*b*) have less money to avoid hunger and need
    - (*c*) have enough money to avoid hunger and need
    - (*d*) to hide the wolf behind the door

34. Arvind finally got through with his doctoral thesis.
    - (*a*) was awarded his doctaral degree
    - (*b*) finally cleared his last examination.
    - (*c*) left the thesis half way through
    - (*d*) finally finishe his thesis after hard toil

35. We could sit here and talk <u>till the cows come home</u>.
    - (*a*) if the cows come home slowly
    - (*b*) for a very long time
    - (*c*) for a very short span of time
    - (*d*) if the cows come home quickly

Direction (Q. 36): *In following question four words are given in each question, out of which only one word is correctly spelt. Find the correctly spelt word and mark you answer in the Answer Sheet.*

36. (*a*) hippopotomous
    (*b*) hipopotamus
    (*c*) hippopotamus
    (*d*) hippopatemus

Directions (Q. 37 – 39): *In following questions some parts of the sentences have errors and some are correct. Find out which part of a sentence has an error and blacken the oval(●) corresponding to the appropriate letter (a, b, c). If a sentence is free from error, blacken the oval corresponding to (d) in the Answer Sheet.*

37. My mother made/ the servant to/ complete the
    (*a*)   (*b*)   (*c*)
    work/ No error.
    (*d*)

38. I want to get/ a M.A. degree/ from a reputed
    (*a*)   (*b*)
    university located in India./ No error.
    (*c*)   (*d*)

39. Not only she makes/home-made cakes/ she also
    (*a*)   (*b*)
    sells them. / No error.
    (*c*)   (*d*)

Directions (Q. 40 – 42): *In following questions sentences are given with blanks to be filled in with an appropriate word(s). Four alternatives are suggested for each question. Choose the correct alternative out of the four and indicate it by blackening the appropriate oval (●) in the Answer Sheet.*

40. They tried to bribe the peon but he _____ them.
    - (*a*) was clever for
    - (*b*) has been too clever for
    - (*c*) was too clever for
    - (*d*) was being clever for

41. She asked me ___________.
(a) what the time was   (b) what was the time
(c) what is the time   (d) what was time

42. A legislation was passed to punish brokers who____ their clients' funds.
(a) defalcate   (b) devastate
(c) devour   (d) embezzle

Directions (Q. 43 – 44): *In following questions a part of the sentence is underlined. Below are given alternatives to the underlined part at (a), (b), (c) which may improve the sentence. Choose the correct alternative. In case no improvement is needed your answer is (d). Mark your answer in the Answer Sheet.*

43. <u>When describing</u> the accident, he was in tears.
(a) When he was describing
(b) As describing
(c) In describing
(d) No improvement

44. Historians feel there is an <u>earnest</u> need for the review of history books every five years and a revision of the same every ten years.
(a) urgent
(b) imperative
(c) indispensable
(d) No improvement

Direction (Q. 45): *A sentence or underlined part thereof is given which may need improvement. Alternatives are given at (a), (b) and (c) below, which may be a better option. In case no improvement is needed, blacken the rectangle [▭] corresponding to (d) in the Answer Sheet.*

45. I in black and white must have been your terms down.
(a) I must have in black and white your terms down.
(b) I must have your terms in black and white down.
(c) I must have your terms down in black and white.
(d) No improvement

Directions (Q. 46 – 50): *You have a brief passage with 5 questions following the passage. Read the passage carefully and choose the best answer to each question out of the four alternatives and mark it by blackening the appropriate oval (●) in the Answer Sheet.*

I could not help thinking, as I looked at the works of Shakespeare on the shelf, that it would have been impossible, completely and entirely, for any woman to have written the plays of Shakespeare in the age of Shakespeare. Let me imagine, since facts are so hard to come by, what would have happened had shakespeare had a wonderfully gifted sister, called Judith, let us say. Shakespeare himself went, very probably — his mother was an heiress — to the grammar school, where he may have learnt Latin — Ovid, Virgil and Horace — and the elements of grammar and logic. He was, it is well known, a wild boy who poached rabbits, perhaps shot a deer, and had, rather sooner than he should have done, to marry a woman in the neighbourhood, who bore him a child rather quicker than was right. That escapade sent him to seek his fortune in London. He had, it seemed, a taste for the theatre; he began by holding horses at the stage door.

46. Shakespeare's sister was
(a) ordinary
(b) wise
(c) imaginary
(d) famous

47. Which of the following statements is true?
(a) Judith was Shakespeare's wife.
(b) Shakespeare's mother was poor.
(c) Shakespeare's learnt Roman.
(d) Shakespeare did not have a sister.

48. "Come by" means
(a) search
(b) maintain
(c) manage to get
(d) invent

49. the passage is about
(a) Shakespeare's life
(b) Shakespeare's sister
(c) Shakespeare's theatre
(d) Shakespeare's writing

50. Shakespeare's marriage reveals that he was
(a) stealthy
(b) impulsive
(c) talented
(d) wise

QUANTITATIVE APTITUDE

51. The value of $\dfrac{1}{1+\cot^2\alpha}+\dfrac{1}{1+\tan^2\alpha}$ is equal to

(a) 2

(b) 1

(c) $\dfrac{1}{4}$

(d) $\dfrac{1}{2}$

52. The angles of depression of the top and the bottom of a building of height h units, from the top of a monument of height H units are complementary. If the distance between the building and the monument is 'a' units, then it is always true that

(a) $\dfrac{H+a}{H-a}=\dfrac{H}{h}$

(b) $\dfrac{h}{a}=\dfrac{a}{H-h}$

(c) $\dfrac{H+a}{H}=\dfrac{h}{a-H}$

(d) $\dfrac{H}{a}=\dfrac{a}{H-h}$

53. If $\dfrac{\sec\theta+\tan\theta}{\sec\theta-\tan\theta}=\dfrac{2+\sqrt{3}}{2-\sqrt{3}}$, then the value of θ in circular measure will be

(a) $\dfrac{\pi}{6}$

(b) $\dfrac{\pi}{4}$

(c) $\dfrac{\pi}{12}$

(d) $\dfrac{\pi}{3}$

54. If $\cos 43° = \dfrac{x}{\sqrt{x^2+y^2}}$, then the value of $\tan 47°$ is

(a) $\dfrac{x}{\sqrt{x^2-y^2}}$

(b) $\dfrac{y}{\sqrt{x^2+y^2}}$

(c) $\dfrac{y}{x}$

(d) $\dfrac{x}{y}$

55. A wall 9 m long, 6 m high and 20 cm thick is to be constructed using bricks of dimension 30 cm × 15 cm × 10 cm. How many bricks will be required?

(a) 2400

(b) 2800

(c) 3600

(d) 3200

56. The base of pyramid of volume $48\sqrt{3}$ c.c. is an equilateral triangle. If the height of the pyramid is 4 cm, then each side of the equalateral triangle at the base is

(a) 12 cm

(b) 3 cm

(c) 4 cm

(d) 6 cm

57. In a triangle ABC, AB = 3 cm, BC = 4 cm and $\angle$ABC = 90°. The triangle is first rotated around the side AB and then around the side BC. The volume of the first cone, thus formed, is $x\%$ more than second cone. Then x is equal to

(a) $33\dfrac{1}{2}$

(b) 25

(c) $33\dfrac{1}{3}$

(d) 20

58. The base of a right-angled triangle is 5 units and hypotenuse is 13 units. Then the area is

(a) 60 sq. units

(b) 15 sq. units

(c) 30 sq. units

(d) 12 sq. units

59. If in a triangle PQR, PQ = 3 cm, QR = 5 cm and PR = 4 cm, then the angles of the triangle in descending order of magnitude are

(a) $\angle Q > \angle R > \angle P$

(b) $\angle P > \angle Q > \angle R$

(c) $\angle Q > \angle P > \angle R$

(d) $\angle P > \angle R > \angle Q$

60. If $x - \dfrac{1}{x} = 2$, then the value of $x^4 + \dfrac{1}{x^4}$ is

(a) 34

(b) 4

(c) 8

(d) 12

61. If $x = \dfrac{1}{1+\sqrt{2}}$, then the value of $x^2 + 2x + 3$ is

(a) 1

(b) 3

(c) 0

(d) 4

62. If $a + b + c = 4$, then $a^3 + b^3 + c^3 - 12c^2 + 48c - 64$ is equal to

(a) $abc + 12ab$

(b) $3abc$

(c) $3abc - 12ab$

(d) $3abc + 12ab$

63. The length of a wire is 66 m. Then the number of circles of circumference 1.32 cm that can be made from this wire is

(a) 5000

(b) 50

(c) 100

(d) 1000

64. Suppose O is the incentre of $\triangle$ABC and the circle touches the sides BC, CA and AB at the points P, Q, R respectively. If $\angle$A = 60°, then the magnitude of $\angle$QPR is

(a) 100°

(b) 60°

(c) 90°

(d) 120°

65. The average of 15 numbers is 7. If the average of the first 8 numbers is 6.5 and the average of the last 8 numbers is 8.5, then the middle number is

(a) 15   (b) 10

(c) 23   (d) 13

66. A's salary is 30% higher than B's salary. The percent that B's salary is less than A's salary is

(a) 25%   (b) 30%

(c) $23\dfrac{1}{13}\%$ (d) 20%

67. 8 men can finish a piece of work in 40 days. If 2 more men join with them, then the work will be completed in

(a) 25 days   (b) 30 days

(c) 32 days   (d) 36 days

68. A producer of tea blends two varieties of tea from two tea gardens, one costing ₹ 240 per kg and the other ₹ 300 per kg. in the ratio 5 : 3. If he sells the blended variety at ₹ 315 per kg then his gain percent is

(a) $11\dfrac{1}{9}$ (b) 10

(c) 20   (d) $16\dfrac{2}{3}$

69. A shopkeeper earns a profit of 15% on selling a book at 10% discount on the printed price. The ratio of the cost price and the printed price is

(a) 18 : 23   (b) 16 : 21

(c) 18 : 21   (d) 17 : 23

70. The selling price of an article is ₹ 39. If its cost price is numerically equal to its profit percent, then its cost price (in ₹) is

(a) 37   (b) 25

(c) 30   (d) 35

71. A number when divided by 5, 9, 13 leaves remainders 2, 6 and 10 respectively. The least such number is

(a) 582   (b) 572

(c) 692   (d) 602

72. The base of a prism is an equilateral triangle of side 12 cm. If the volume of the prism is 1080 cc, then the total surface area of the prism in sq. cm is

(a) 1080

(b) $72\sqrt{3}$

(c) $360\sqrt{3}$

(d) $432\sqrt{3}$

Directions (Q. 73 – 74): *In follownig questions the histogram below shows the marks of 50 students in an examination. Examine the diagram and answer the questions that follow.*

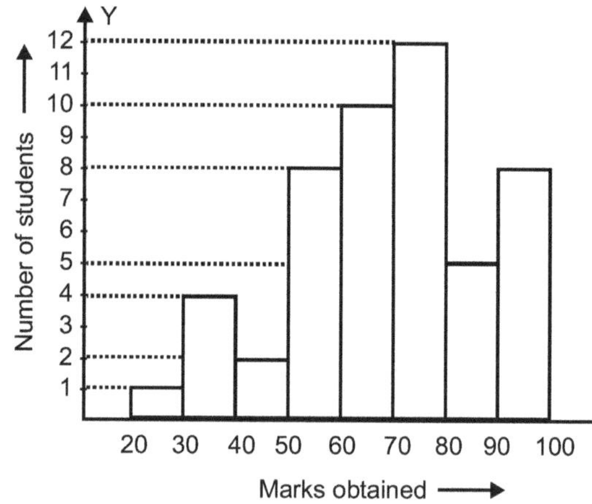

73. If the minimum marks for getting scholarship is 80, how many students will get it?

(a) 11   (b) 13

(c) 12   (d) 10

74. How many students obtained less than 40 ?

(a) 5

(b) 2

(c) 6

(d) 4

Direction (Q. 75): *The following pie-chart shows the result of an examination of 360 students. Study the chart and answer the questions that follow.*

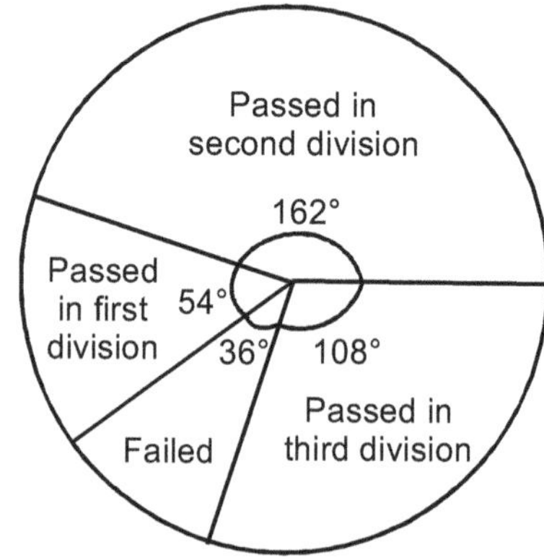

75. The number of students who passed in second division is more than that in third division by

(a) 64

(b) 54

(c) 50

(d) 51

GENERAL AWARENESS

76. Prime Minister Narendra Modi launched a series of works dedicated to the philosophy of ______________ in New Delhi on October 9 2016.

(a) Mahatma Gandhi

(b) Pandit Rama Bhai

(c) Pandit Jawaharlal Nehru

(d) Pandit Deendayal Upadhyay

77. The first Governor of the Portuguese in India was

(a) De Almeida   (b) Vasco-da-Gama

(c) Bartholomew Diaz   (d) Albuquerque

78. Which one of the following reformative measures was not introduced by William Bentinck?

(a) Suppression of thugs

(b) Abolition of Sati

(c) Removal of disabilities due to change of religion

(d) Abolition of slavery

79. Which work of Thomas Paine inspired the colonial people to fight against Britain during the American War of Independence?

(a) Social Contract

(b) What is the Third Estate?

(c) Common Sense

(d) The Spirit of the Laws

80. Which of the following commission is not a constitutional body?

(a) Union Public Service Commission

(b) Staff Selection Commission

(c) Election Commission

(d) Finance Commission

81. An index number measuring the average price of consumer goods and services purchased by households is

(a) Wholesale price index

(b) Consumer price index

(c) Human development index

(d) Cost of living index

82. Oligopoly consists of

(a) Few sellers

(b) Two sellers

(c) Three sellers

(d) Single seller

83. National Income in India is estimated by the

(a) product and income methods

(b) product method

(c) income method

(d) expenditure method

84. The fixed cost in the short-run for a producing firm will be

(a) always fluctuating

(b) always declining

(c) always constant and fixed

(d) always increasing

85. Machine tool is an example of ______ goods.

(a) intermediary   (b) consumer

(c) capital   (d) free

86. Gandhara art was the combination of

(a) Indian and Persian styles of sculptures

(b) Indian and Chinese styles of sculptures

(c) Indian and Greek styles of sculptures

(d) None of these

87. The Supreme Court stayed the Commercial release of the genetically modified variety of which Vegetable till October 2017?

(a) Custard   (b) Brinjal

(c) Tomato   (d) Mustard

88. Duncan Passage separates

(a) Little Andamans and Car Nicobar Islands

(b) North and Middle Andamans

(c) Middle and South Andamans

(d) South Andamans and Little Andamans

89. In biology, water soluble substances are referred to as

(a) hydrodynamic   (b) hydrophobic

(c) hydrophilic   (d) hydrokinetic

90. Amoeba acquires its food through the process of

(a) Exocytosis and endocytosis

(b) Exocytosis

(c) Endocytosis

(d) Plasmolysis

91. Which among the following is symbiotic Nitrogen-fixing bacteria?

(a) *Azotobacter*   (b) *Xanthomonas*

(c) *Pseudomonas*   (d) *Rhizobium*

92. How much time is given to Rajya Sabha to pass a Money Bill?

(a) 15 days   (b) 12 days

(c) 13 days   (d) 14 days

93. The electoral college to elect the President composes
    - (a) Elected members of both the Houses of Parliament and Legislative Assemblies
    - (b) All members of both the Houses of Parliament
    - (c) All elected members of both the Houses of Parliament
    - (d) All members of Parliament and all members of Legislative Assemblies and Councils

94. Rocks having large quantity of underground water and permitting ready flow of water are called
    - (a) Permeable
    - (b) Aqucludes
    - (c) Aquifers
    - (d) Porous

95. In DOS, the DIR Command is used to
    - (a) display contents of a files
    - (b) delete files
    - (c) display list of files and subdirectories
    - (d) copy files

96. _______ is the amount of work that the system is able to do per unit time
    - (a) Turnaround
    - (b) Output
    - (c) Transfer rate
    - (d) Throughput

97. In medicine bottles containing tablets or capsules, a small pouch of silica gel is kept to
    - (a) keep the bottle warm
    - (b) kill bacteria
    - (c) absorb moisture
    - (d) absorb gases

98. Match the two lists containing the names of poets and the language in which they wrote Ramayana:

Poets	*Language in which Ramayana was written*
A. Kamban	1. Bengali
B. Krittivasa	2. Hindi
C. Madhava Kandali	3. Tamil
D. Tulsi Das	4. Assamese

	A	B	C	D
(a)	3	4	1	2
(b)	2	3	1	4
(c)	3	1	4	2
(d)	4	2	1	3

99. Which country has given asylum to Julian Assange, WikiLeaks founder ?
    - (a) Ecuador
    - (b) Russia
    - (c) Cuba
    - (d) None of these

100. Union Government decided to suspend Indus water commission talks with which country because of unlawful actions ?
    - (a) China
    - (b) Pakistan
    - (c) Afghanistan
    - (d) Japan

ANSWERS

1. (c)	**2.** (d)	**3.** (c)	**4.** (c)	**5.** (b)	**6.** (d)	**7.** (c)	**8.** (c)	**9.** (c)	**10.** (d)
11. (d)	**12.** (c)	**13.** (c)	**14.** (a)	**15.** (b)	**16.** (d)	**17.** (a)	**18.** (a)	**19.** (a)	**20.** (c)
21. (b)	**22.** (b)	**23.** (d)	**24.** (b)	**25.** (a)	**26.** (b)	**27.** (d)	**28.** (c)	**29.** (a)	**30.** (d)
31. (d)	**32.** (a)	**33.** (c)	**34.** (d)	**35.** (b)	**36.** (c)	**37.** (b)	**38.** (b)	**39.** (a)	**40.** (c)
41. (a)	**42.** (d)	**43.** (a)	**44.** (a)	**45.** (c)	**46.** (c)	**47.** (d)	**48.** (c)	**49.** (a)	**50.** (b)
51. (b)	**52.** (d)	**53.** (d)	**54.** (d)	**55.** (a)	**56.** (a)	**57.** (c)	**58.** (c)	**59.** (b)	**60.** (a)
61. (d)	**62.** (c)	**63.** (a)	**64.** (b)	**65.** (a)	**66.** (c)	**67.** (c)	**68.** (c)	**69.** (a)	**70.** (c)
71. (a)	**72.** (d)	**73.** (b)	**74.** (a)	**75.** (b)	**76.** (d)	**77.** (a)	**78.** (d)	**79.** (c)	**80.** (b)
81. (b)	**82.** (a)	**83.** (a)	**84.** (c)	**85.** (c)	**86.** (c)	**87.** (d)	**88.** (d)	**89.** (c)	**90.** (c)
91. (d)	**92.** (d)	**93.** (a)	**94.** (c)	**95.** (c)	**96.** (d)	**97.** (c)	**98.** (c)	**99.** (a)	**100.** (b)

EXPLANATIONS

1.

F L R X
$-2\downarrow$ $-2\downarrow$ $-2\downarrow$ $-2\downarrow$
D J P V

Similarly,

E K Q W
$-2\downarrow$ $-2\downarrow$ $-2\downarrow$ $-2\downarrow$
C I O U

2. $(4)^2 + 1 = 17$

Similarly,

$(7)^2 + 1 = 50$

3. Except potato all other are roots

4. Ploughing $\rightarrow$ Sowing $\rightarrow$ Weeding $\rightarrow$ Harvesting

5. Vocation
$\downarrow$
Voice
$\downarrow$
Volume
$\downarrow$
Voyage.

6. a ḇ b / a b ḇ / a b ḇ / abb

7. $11 + 7 \rightarrow 18 + 7 \rightarrow 25$

Similarly,

$19 + 7 \rightarrow 26 + 7 \rightarrow 33$

9. A = 1

A I R = 1 + 9 + 18 = 28

Similarly,

R I B = 18 + 9 + 2 = $\boxed{29}$

10. Sarika is 19th from either end of the row

∴ Total number of girls in a row = 18 + 18 + 1 = 37.

Hence there are total 37 girls in that row.

11.

E T H I C S

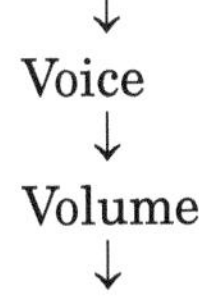

S E C T I H

Similarly,

A F E C T I O N

N A O F I E T C

12.

M A E I O U
$\downarrow\downarrow\downarrow\downarrow\downarrow\downarrow$
6 9 8 0 1 2

13. The word 'GHOST' can be formed from the given letters of the word.

14. $4 \times 3 \times 4 = 48$

$8 \times 2 \times 4 = 64$

Similarly,

$5 \times ? \times 10 = 200$

∴ $? = \dfrac{200}{50} = 4$

15.

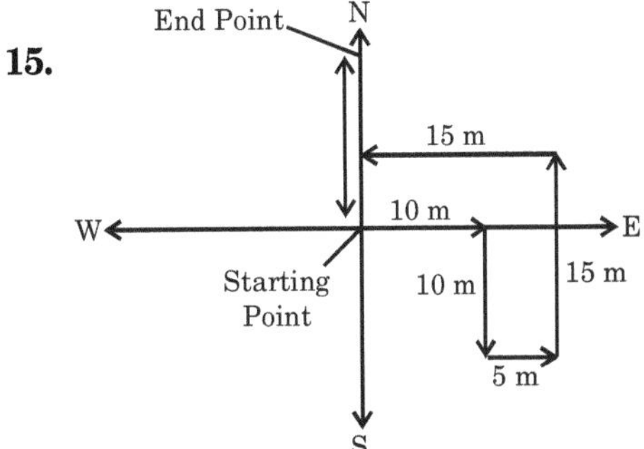

He is 5 m away from the starting point.

16. From option (*d*),

$6 \times 5 + 8 \div 4 = 32$.

L.H.S.

$(6 \times 5) + (8 \div 4) = 30 + 2 = 32 = $ R.H.S

∴ Option (*d*) is correct.

17.

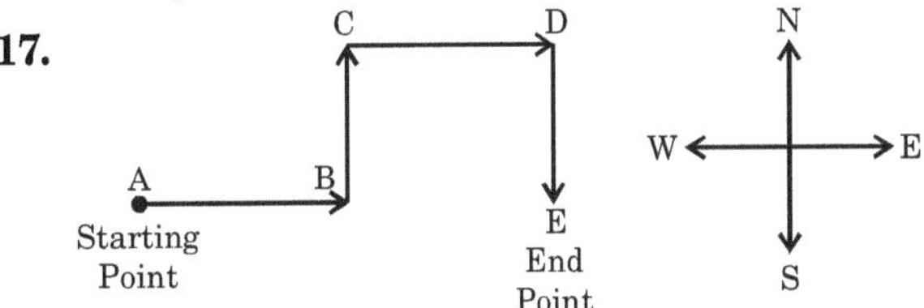

She was moving in south direction.

19.

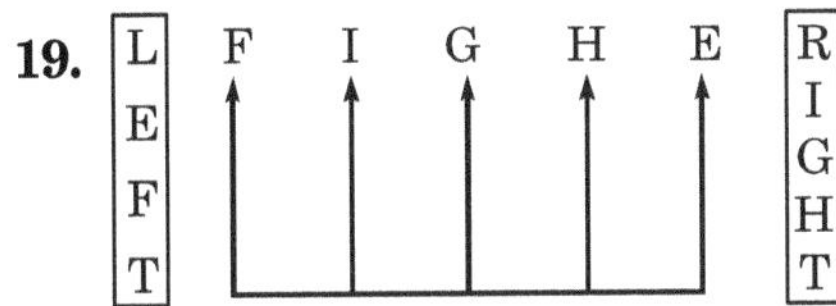

21.

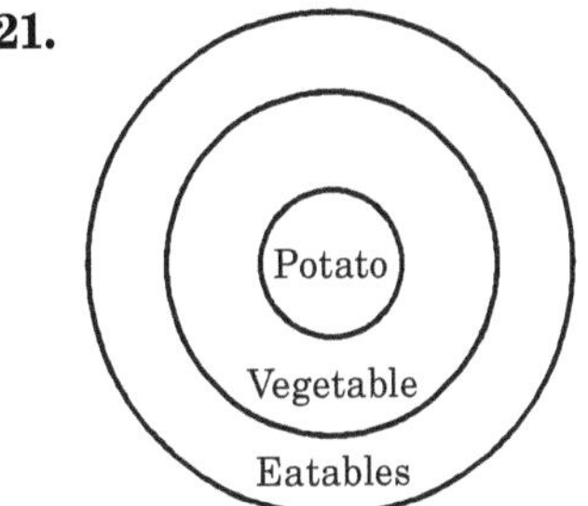

23. $7 \times 2 = 14$ and $14 - 1 = 13$

$13 \times 2 = 26$ and $26 - 1 = 25$

$25 \times 2 = 50$ and $50 - 1 = 49$

$49 \times 2 = 98$ and $98 - 1 = 97$

$97 \times 2 = 194$ and $194 - 1 = \boxed{193}$

51. $\dfrac{1}{1+\cot^2\alpha} + \dfrac{1}{1+\tan^2\alpha} = \dfrac{1}{\csc^2\alpha} + \dfrac{1}{\sec^2\alpha}$

$= \sin^2\alpha + \cos^2\alpha = 1$

52. In $\triangle$ ABC;

$$\tan(90 - \theta) = \frac{H}{a}$$

$$\therefore \qquad \cot\theta = \frac{H}{a} \qquad \qquad ...(i)$$

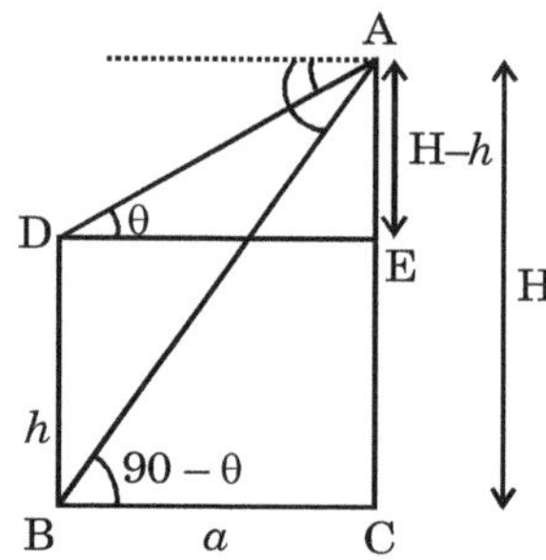

In $\triangle$ ADE;

$$\tan\theta = \frac{H-h}{a} \qquad \qquad ...(ii)$$

$$\tan\theta \times \cot\theta = \frac{H-h}{a} \times \frac{H}{a} = 1$$

$$\therefore \qquad \frac{H}{a} = \frac{a}{H-h}$$

53.
$$\frac{\sec\theta + \tan\theta}{\sec\theta - \tan\theta} = \frac{2+\sqrt{3}}{2-\sqrt{3}}$$

$$\frac{\dfrac{1}{\cos\theta} + \dfrac{\sin\theta}{\cos\theta}}{\dfrac{1}{\cos\theta} - \dfrac{\sin\theta}{\cos\theta}} = \frac{2+\sqrt{3}}{2-\sqrt{3}}$$

$$2 - \sqrt{3} + 2\sin\theta - \sqrt{3}\sin\theta$$
$$= 2 + \sqrt{3} - 2\sin\theta - \sqrt{3}\sin\theta$$

$$4\sin\theta = 2\sqrt{3}$$

$$\sin\theta = \frac{\sqrt{3}}{2}$$

$$\theta = \sin^{-1}\left(\frac{\sqrt{3}}{2}\right)$$

$$\therefore \qquad \theta = 60° = \frac{\pi}{3}$$

54. In $\triangle$ABC,

$$\cos 43° = \frac{x}{\sqrt{x^2 + y^2}} = \frac{B}{H}$$

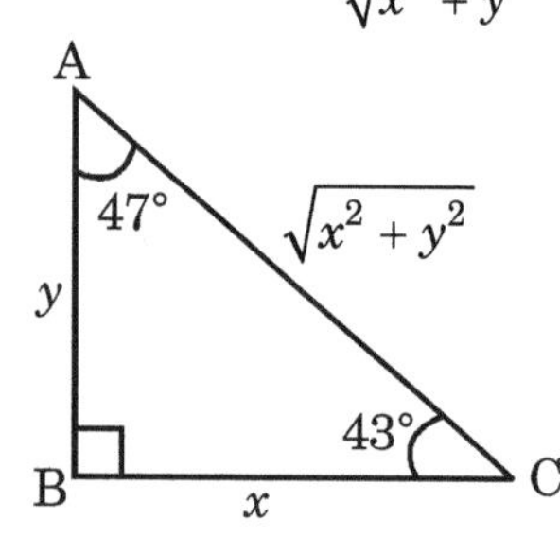

In $\triangle$CBA,

$$\tan 47° = \frac{x}{y} = \frac{P}{B}$$

55. Number of bricks $= \dfrac{900 \times 600 \times 20}{30 \times 15 \times 10} = 2400$

56. Volume of Pyramid $= \dfrac{1}{3} \times$ Area of base $\times$ height.

$$48\sqrt{3} = \frac{1}{3} \times \text{Area of base} \times 4.$$

$$\text{Area of base} = \frac{48\sqrt{3} \times 3}{4} = 36\sqrt{3}$$

$$\text{Area of equilateral triangle} = \frac{\sqrt{3}}{4}(\text{Side})^2$$

$$\therefore \qquad \frac{\sqrt{3}}{4}(\text{Side})^2 = 36\sqrt{3}$$

$$(\text{Side})^2 = 36 \times 4 = 144$$

$$\text{Side} = \sqrt{144} = 12 \text{ cm}$$

57. In triangle ABC, $\angle$B = 90°

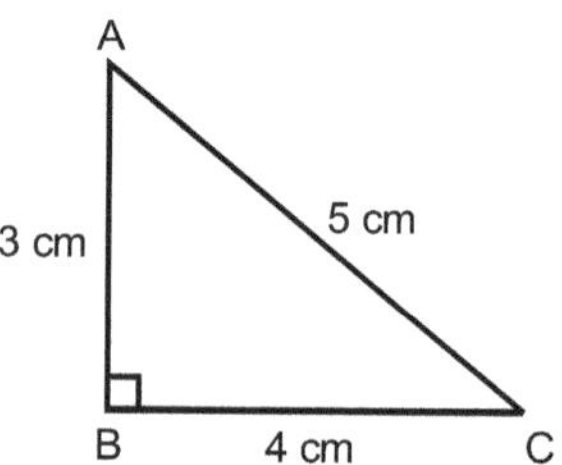

By, using pythagoras theorem,

$$AC = 5 \text{ cm.}$$

Now, when triangle is rotated around the side AB

$$\therefore \quad h = 3 \text{ cm and } r = 4 \text{ cm}$$

$$\therefore \quad \text{Volume of first cone} = \frac{1}{3}\pi r^2 h$$

$$= \frac{1}{3}\pi(4)^2 \times 3 = 16\,\pi$$

Now, when triangle is rotated around side BC

$$\therefore \quad h = 4 \text{ cm and } r = 3 \text{ cm}$$

$$\therefore \quad \text{Volume of second cone} = \frac{1}{3}\pi r^2 h$$

$$= \frac{1}{3}\pi(3)^2 \times 4 = 12\,\pi$$

Now, according to Question,

$$x = \frac{16\pi - 12\pi}{12\pi} \times 100$$

$$\therefore \qquad x = \frac{100}{3} = 33\frac{1}{3}\%$$

$$\therefore \quad \text{Option } (c) \text{ is correct.}$$

58. $AB = \sqrt{(13)^2 - (5)^2}$

$$= \sqrt{169 - 25}$$

$$= \sqrt{144}$$

$$AB = 12 \text{ unit}$$

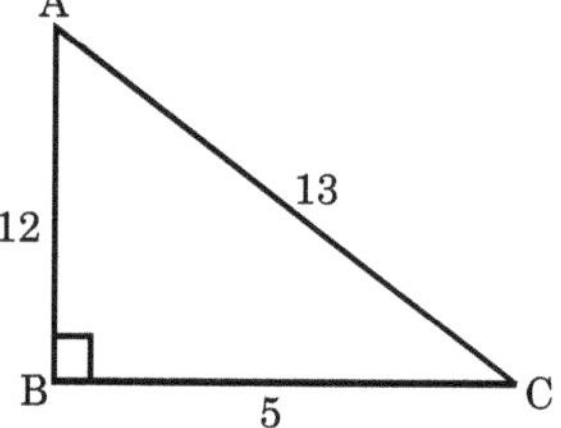

$$\text{Area of triangle } = \frac{1}{2} \times BC \times AB$$
$$= \frac{1}{2} \times 5 \times 12$$
$$= 30 \text{ sq. unit}$$

59. $QR > PR > PQ$.

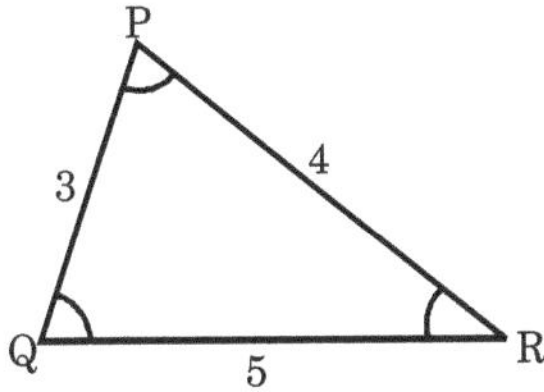

$$\therefore \quad \angle P > \angle Q > \angle R.$$

60. $x - \dfrac{1}{x} = 2$.

Squaring on both sides we get,

$$\left(x - \frac{1}{x}\right)^2 = (2)^2$$
$$x^2 + \frac{1}{x^2} - 2 = 4$$

Again squaring on both sides we get,

$$\left(x^2 + \frac{1}{x^2}\right)^2 = (6)^2$$
$$x^4 + \frac{1}{x^4} + 2 = 36$$
$$x^4 + \frac{1}{x^4} = 36 - 2 = 34$$

61. $x = \dfrac{1}{1+\sqrt{2}}$

$$\therefore \quad x = \frac{1}{1+\sqrt{2}} \times \frac{\sqrt{2}-1}{\sqrt{2}-1} = \frac{\sqrt{2}-1}{2-1} = \sqrt{2}-1$$

Now $\quad x^2 + 2x + 3$
$$= (\sqrt{2}-1)^2 + 2(\sqrt{2}-1) + 3$$
$$= 2 + 1 - 2\sqrt{2} + 2\sqrt{2} - 2 + 3$$
$$= 4$$

62. $a + b + c = 4$

Put $a = 1; b = 2$ and $c = 1$
$$(1)^3 + (2)^3 + (1)^3 - 12(1)^2 + 48(1) - 64$$
$$= 1 + 8 + 1 - 12 + 48 - 64$$
$$= -18$$

From option (c);
$$3abc - 12ab = 3 \times 1 \times 2 \times 1 - 12 \times 1 \times 2$$
$$= 6 - 24 = -18$$

$\therefore$ Option (c) satisfied the values.

63. Length of wire = 66 m = 6600 cm

$$\therefore \quad \text{Number of circles} = \frac{6600}{1.32} = 5000$$

64.

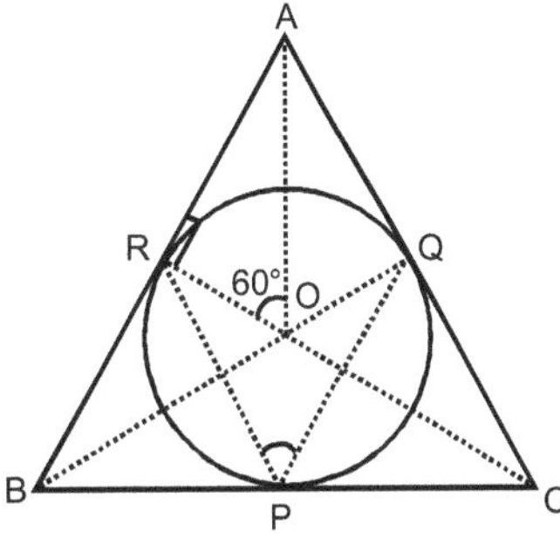

The point of intersection of angle bisector is the incentre of triangle

Now $\angle BAC = 60°$

$\therefore \quad \angle BAO = 30°$ ($\because$ AO is the angle bisector)

Now, In $\triangle ARO$
$$\angle A + \angle R + \angle O = 180°$$
$$\therefore \quad 30° + 90° + \angle O = 180°$$
$$\therefore \quad \angle O = 60°$$

Similarly $\angle AOQ = 60°$

Now $\angle QPR = \dfrac{1}{2} \angle ROQ$

$$\therefore \quad \angle QPR = \frac{1}{2} \times (120°) = 60°$$
$$\therefore \quad \angle QPR = 60°$$

65. Sum of first 8 number = $6.5 \times 8 = 52$

Sum of last 8 number = $8.5 \times 8 = 68$

Sum of all numbers = $15 \times 7 = 105$

$$\therefore \quad \text{Middle number} = [(52 + 68) - 105]$$
$$= [120 - 105]$$
$$= 15$$

66. A's salary = $\dfrac{130}{100}$ B's salary.

$$\text{Percentage} = \frac{30}{130} \times 100 = 23\frac{1}{13}\%$$

67. By Formula,
$$M_1 D_1 = M_2 D_2$$
$$8 \times 40 = 10 \times D_2$$
$$D_2 = \frac{8 \times 40}{10} = 32 \text{ days}$$

68. Cost price of tea $= \dfrac{240 \times 5 + 300 \times 3}{8}$
$$= \frac{1200 + 900}{8}$$
$$= \frac{2100}{8} = ₹\,262.5$$

Selling price = ₹ 315

$$\% \text{ profit} = \left[\frac{315 - 262.5}{262.5}\right]\% \times 100 = 20\%$$

69. Let printed price = ₹ 100

cost price = $100 \times \dfrac{90}{100} \times \dfrac{100}{115} = \dfrac{90 \times 20}{23}$

Cost price : Printed price = 18 : 23

70. Let cost price = ₹ x

∴   % profit = $x\%$ [∵ cost price = % profit]

$$39 \times \dfrac{100}{100 + x} = x$$

$$x^2 + 100x - 3900 = 0$$

$$x = 30$$

∴   Cost price = ₹ 30

71. L.C.M. of 5, 9, 13 = 585

$$5 - 2 = 9 - 6$$

$$= 13 - 10 = 3$$

∴ Smallest number = 585 − 3 = 582

72. Total surface area of prism = $2 \times b + ph$

Area of equilateral triangle = $\dfrac{\sqrt{3}}{4}(12)^2 = 36\sqrt{3}$

∴ Height = $\dfrac{1080}{36\sqrt{3}} = \dfrac{30}{\sqrt{3}} = 10\sqrt{3}$

Perimeter of base = 3 × 12 = 36

Total surface area of prism = $2 \times 36\sqrt{3} + 10\sqrt{3} \times 36$

$$= 72\sqrt{3} + 360\sqrt{3}$$

$$= 432\sqrt{3} \text{ cm}^2$$

Q. 73 – 74 :

Marks interval	No of Students
20 – 30	1
30 – 40	4
40 – 50	2
50 – 60	8
60 – 70	10
70 – 80	12
80 – 90	5
90 – 100	8

73. Number of students getting scholarship

$$= 5 + 8 = 13$$

74. Number of students getting less than 40 marks

$$= 1 + 4 = 5$$

75. Difference = $\left[\dfrac{162° - 108°}{360°}\right] \times 360° = 54$

■■

PRACTICE SET – 25

GENERAL INTELLIGENCE

Directions (Q. 1-3) : *Select the related word / letters / number from the given alternatives.*

1. ABCXYZ : DEFUVW : : GHIRST : ?
   - (a) JKLOPQ
   - (b) JOKPLN
   - (c) JNOPKL
   - (d) MNOLKJ

2. 5 : 28 : : 8 : ?
   - (a) 25
   - (b) 67
   - (c) 40
   - (d) 64

3. Doctor : Hospital : : Teacher : ?
   - (a) School
   - (b) Industry
   - (c) Field
   - (d) Laboratory

Directions (Q. 4-5) : *Find the odd word / letters / number from the given alternatives.*

4. (a) 2, 3
   - (b) 20, 21
   - (c) 9, 10
   - (d) 24, 25

5. (a) Flute
   - (b) Piano
   - (c) Violin
   - (d) Sitar

6. Arrange the following in ascending order :
   1. Centimeter
   2. Kilometre
   3. Decimetre
   4. Metre
   - (a) 3, 1, 2, 4
   - (b) 4, 2, 1, 3
   - (c) 1, 3, 4, 2
   - (d) 2, 4, 3, 1

7. Which one of the given responses would be a meaningful order of the following ?
   1. House
   2. Palace
   3. Bungalow
   4. Hut
   - (a) 3, 2, 1, 4
   - (b) 4, 1, 3, 2
   - (c) 1, 2, 3, 4
   - (d) 2, 3, 1, 4

Direction (Q. 8): *Which one set of letters when sequentially placed at the gaps in the given letter series shall complete it ?*

8. a_ba_b_b_a_b
   - (a) b b a b b
   - (b) a b b a b
   - (c) a b a a b
   - (d) a a b b a

Directions (Q. 9-10): *A series is given, with one term missing. Choose the correct alternative from the given ones that will complete the series.*

9. 1, 6, 13, 22, 33, ?
   - (a) 46
   - (b) 44
   - (c) 47
   - (d) 43

10. BY, GT, LO, ?, VE
    - (a) Q K
    - (b) QP
    - (c) PJ
    - (d) Q J

11. In a code language 'FORGE' is written as 'FPTJI'; how should 'CULPRIT' be written in the same code ?
    - (a) CVMQSTU
    - (b) CXOSULW
    - (c) CVNSVNZ
    - (d) CSJNPGR

12. Ann is 300 days older than Varun and Sandeep is 50 weeks older than Ann. If Sandeep was born on Tuesday, on which day was Varun born ?
    - (a) Wednesday
    - (b) Friday
    - (c) Monday
    - (d) Thursday

13. From the given alternatives, select the word which can be formed using the letters of the given word,

    IMMEASURABLE
    - (a) MEAT
    - (b) BIBLE
    - (c) BAILABLE
    - (d) BLUE

14. The question given below is based upon the following set of codes :

    Digit : 1 3 5 4 6 0 8 7 2

    Code : A O Z L D T N H Q

    Find the code for 21500
    - (a) SLOPH
    - (b) QAZTT
    - (c) SLPHO
    - (d) SHLPO

Direction (Q. 15): *Select the missing number from the given responses.*

15.
13	9	24
11	?	6
16	20	10
   - (a) 19
   - (b) 16
   - (c) 11
   - (d) 20

16. Mr. Das started his journey from his house straight to his friend's house at a distance of 12 km. On returning he walked 8 km in the same route and turned right and walked 4 km, then he turned to his left and walked 4 km. Finally he turned to his left and walked 2 km. How far was he from his house?
    - (a) 6 km
    - (b) 2 km
    - (c) 8 km
    - (d) 4 km

17. A is B's sister. C is B's mother. D is C's father. E is D's mother. Then how is A related to D ?
    - (a) Daughter
    - (b) Granddaughter
    - (c) Grandmother
    - (d) Grandfather

18. Which conclusion is true with respect to the given statements ?

Statements :

Anand is an artist

Artists are beautiful

Conclusions :

(a) Anand is not beautiful

(b) Beautiful persons are not artists

(c) All beautiful persons are artists

(d) Anand is beautiful

19. Which answer figure will complete the pattern in the question figure ?

Question figure :

Answer figures :

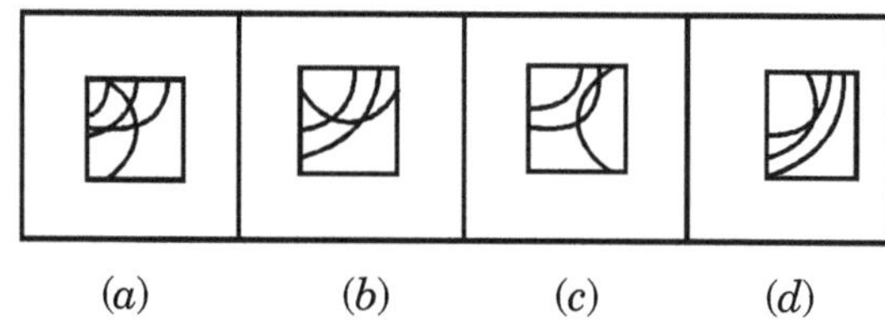

    (a)   (b)   (c)   (d)

20. Identify the diagram that best represents the relationship among the classes given below.

oxygen, Carbondioxide and Atmosphere

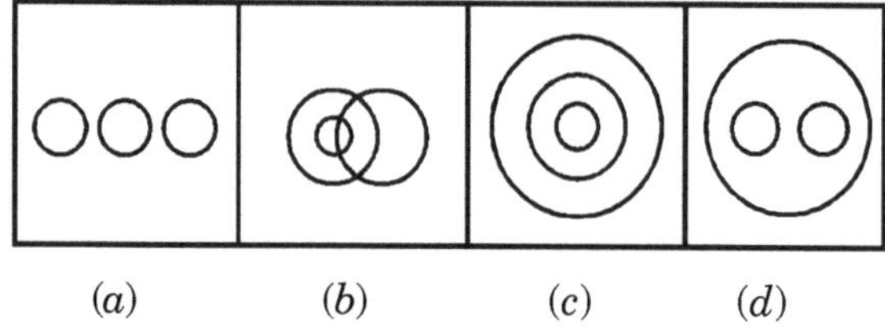

    (a)   (b)   (c)   (d)

21. Which statement is true with respect to the Venn diagram ?

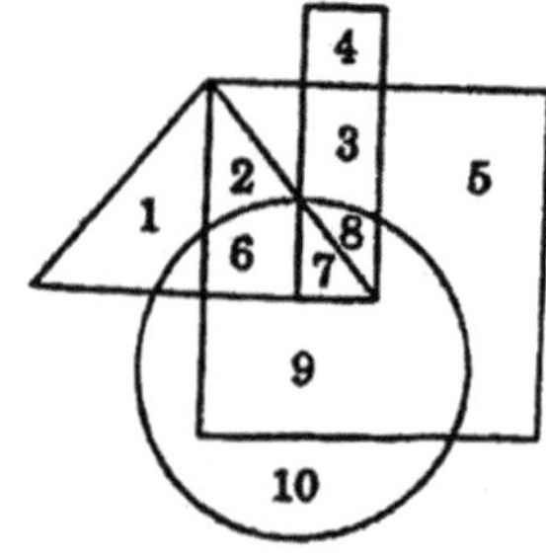

(a) 1, 9 and 10 are in all the figure

(b) 1, 2 and 6 are in the triangle

(c) 6, 7 and 8 are in all the figure

(d) 1,5, and 9 are in all the figures.

22. A piece of paper is folded and cut as shown below in the question figures. From the given answer figures, indicate how it will appear when opened:

Question figures :

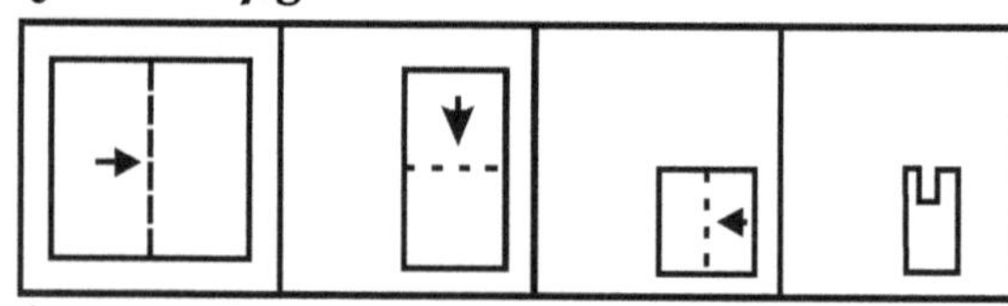

Answer figures :

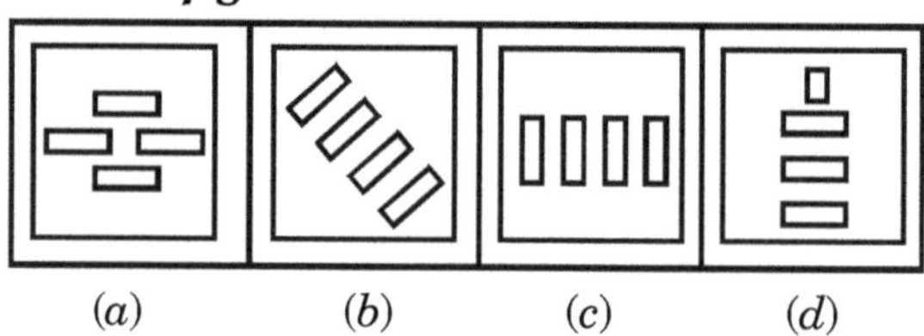

    (a)   (b)   (c)   (d)

23. Which of the answer figures is embedded in the question figure ?

Question figure :

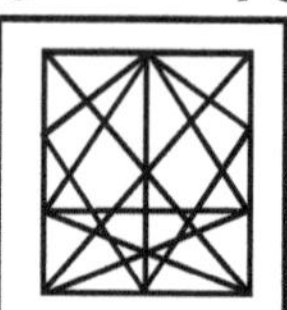

Answer figures :

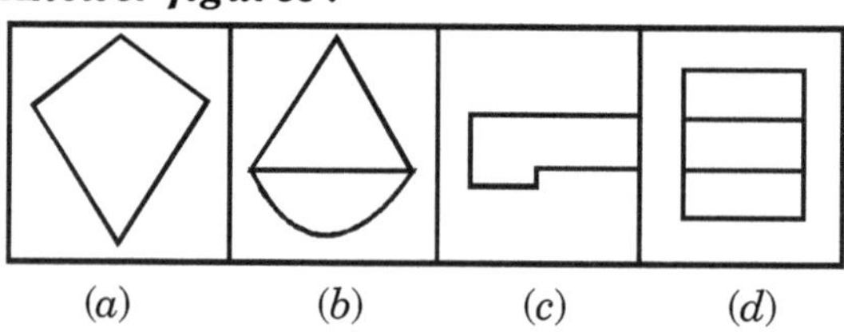

    (a)   (b)   (c)   (d)

24. A word is represented by only one set of numbers as given in any one of the alternatives. The sets of numbers given in the alternatives are represented by two classes of alphabets as in the two matrices given below. The columns and rows of Matrix I are numbered from 1 to 5 and that of Matrix II are numbered from 6 to 10. A letter from these matrices can be represented first by its row and next by its column, e.g., 'A' can be represented by 11, 23, etc., and 'G' can be represented by 67, 78, etc. Similarly, you have to identify the set for the word given below.

BEE

Matrix I

	1	2	3	4	5
1	A	B	C	D	E
2	E	D	A	B	C
3	B	C	D	E	A
4	D	A	E	C	D
5	C	E	B	A	B

Matrix II

	6	7	8	9	10
6	F	G	H	I	J
7	J	I	G	H	F
8	F	H	I	J	G
9	G	J	F	G	I
10	H	E	J	F	E

(a) 12, 15, 33

(b) 21, 12, 22

(c) 12, 15, 41

(d) 12, 21, 15

25. Identify the alternative which resembles the mirror- image of the given word.

D L 9 Q 3 5 7 4

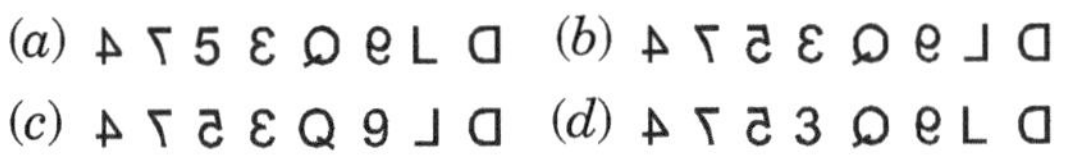

ENGLISH LANGUAGE

Directions (Q. 26-27): *Out of the four alternatives, choose the one which best expresses the meaning of the given word and mark it in the Answer Sheet.*

26. Spurious
(*a*) Particular (*b*) Fake
(*c*) Fictional (*d*) True

27. Latent
(*a*) Obstruct (*b*) Confuse
(*c*) Hidden (*d*) Expose

Directions (Q. 28-29): *Choose the word opposite in meaning to the given word and mark it in the Answer Sheet.*

28. Discrimination
(*a*) Motivation (*b*) Replenishment
(*c*) Bias (*d*) Equality

29. Endangered
(*a*) Abundant (*b*) Blissful
(*c*) Protected (*d*) Livening up

Directions (Q. 30-32): *Out of the for alternatives, choose the one which can be substituted for the given words / sentence.*

30. The schedule of travel
(*a*) Travel book (*b*) Guide book
(*c*) Itinerary (*d*) Time-table

31. Poem in short stanzas narrating a popular story
(*a*) Ballas (*b*) Sonnet
(*c*) Ballet (*d*) Epic

32. Design made by putting together coloured pieces of glass or stones
(*a*) Relief (*b*) Olegraph
(*c*) Tracery (*d*) Mosaic

Directions (Q. 33-35): *Four alternatives are given for the Idiom / Phrase underlined in the sentence. Choose the alternative, which best expresses the meaning of the Idiom / Phrase and mark it in the Answer Sheet.*

33. Despite the doctor's advice he still <u>eats like a horse</u>.
(*a*) does not like to eat (*b*) swallows his food
(*c*) eats slowly (*d*) eats a lot of food

34. The two friends are now <u>at daggers drawn</u> over a petty issue.
(*a*) enemies (*b*) competitors
(*c*) angry (*d*) frustrated

35. His work seems to be a <u>Penelope's web</u>
(*a*) declining (*b*) in his best form
(*c*) endless (*d*) difficult

Direction (Q. 36): *Four words are given in each question, out of which only one word is correctly spelt. Find the correctly spelt word and mark your answer in the Answer Sheet.*

36. (*a*) Machiavelian (*b*) Machaivelian
(*c*) Machiavilian (*d*) Machiavellian

Directions (Q. 37-39): *Some parts of the sentences have errors and some are correct. Find out which part of a sentence has an error and blacken the oval (⬬) corresponding to the appropriate letter (a, b, c). If a sentence is free from errors, blacken the oval corresponding to (d) in the Answer Sheet.*

37. The crime rate increases inspite (*a*) / formal moral education (*b*) / given in schools (*c*) ./ No error (*d*)

38. As soon as they (*a*) / entered the temple (*b*) / they prayed to the gods on bent knees (*c*) / No error (*d*)

39. Three-fourths of the men (*a*) / has gone (*b*) / to war (*c*) ./ No error (*d*)

Directions (Q. 40-42): *Sentences are given with blanks to be filled in with an appropriate word(s). Four alternatives are suggested for each question. Choose the correct alternative out of the four and indicate it by blackening the appropriate oval (⬬) in the Answer Sheet.*

40. If left unattended, even a small cut can turn into a __________.
(*a*) sore (*b*) ore
(*c*) soar (*d*) sour

41. My neighbour is very ______ for he believes that nothing good will happen to him.
(*a*) pessimistic (*b*) optimistic
(*c*) reasonable (*d*) forward-looking

42. She was aware of what was going______ her father's mind.
(*a*) in (*b*) by
(*c*) through (*d*) on

Directions (Q. 43-45): *In questions, a part of the sentence is underlined. Below are given alternatives to the underlined part at (a), (b), (c), which may improve the sentence. Choose the correct alternative. In case no improvement is needed your answer is (d). Mark your answer in the Answer Sheet.*

43. Walk carefully <u>lest you do not fall</u>

   (a) lest you fall

   (b) lest you should not fall

   (c) lest you might not fall

   (d) No improvement

44. Please tell the story <u>in a nutshell</u> .

   (a) in the nutshell   (b) in nutshells

   (c) in nutshell   (d) No improvement

45. The housing problem in Mumbai <u>becomes</u> more serious

   (a) has become   (b) become

   (c) is becoming   (d) No improvement

Directions (Q. 46-50) : You have given passage with 5 questions. Read the passage carefully and choose the best answer to each question out of the four alternatives given.

The positive nutritional effects led the Olmec to believe chocolate drink possessed mystic qualities, so it was generally reserved for important figures at sacred ceremonies. The Olmec passed the chocolate drink on to the Maya civilization, who found that chocolate was a mood enhancer and energy booster. They passed it on to perhaps the beverage's most famous historical forefathers, the Aztecs. Legendary Aztec leader Montezuma II was known to demand cacao beans from conquered peoples and supposedly drank five goblets of hot chocolate every day in a display of power and opulence. Besides his own enjoyment of the beverage, he only allowed those who contributed military service to drink chocolate. When Hernan Cortes and his soldiers encountered the Aztecs, one of his men wrote about Montezuma's consumption of the curious cacao-made drink and how the Spanish themselves were also served the beverage "all frothed up." Ultimately, Cortes conquered the Aztecs, and brought the popular drink to Spain, from which it spread throughout Europe and, eventually, the world.

46. Which of the following civilizations might not have enjoyed a chocolate drink?

   (a) Maya civilization   (b) Aztec

   (c) Olmec   (d) Cortes

47. Who among the following must not have been allowed to drink chocolate during the rule of Montezuma II?

   (a) Soldiers

   (b) Important figures

   (c) The Aztec leader of the time

   (d) Visitors

48. Find an option that is same in meaning to the word given in bold.

   Opulence

   (a) Authority   (b) Wealth

   (c) Political control   (d) Greatness

49. Which of the following is not a characteristic of the chocolate drink?

   (a) Energy booster   (b) Mood enhancer

   (c) Nutritional   (d) Intoxicating

50. What made Montezuma II drink five goblets of chocolate each day?

   (a) He wanted to show how great he was.

   (b) He wanted to assert his authority.

   (c) He wanted to suppress his people.

   (d) He felt energized after taking the drink.

QUANTITATIVE APTITUDE

51. The difference between the circumference and diameter of a circle is 150m. The radius of that circle is (Take $\pi = \dfrac{22}{7}$)

   (a) 30 m   (b) 40 m

   (c) 25 m   (d) 35 m

52. If the radius of a sphere be doubled, then the percentage of increase in volume is

   (a) 600%   (b) 800 %

   (c) 500%   (d) 700%

53. A merchant offers 8% discount on all his goods and still makes a profit of 15%. If an item is marked ₹ 250, then its cost price is

   (a) ₹ 230   (b) ₹ 187

   (c) ₹ 180   (d) ₹ 200

54. A box contains 280 coins of one-rupee, 50-paise and 25-paise. The values of each kind of the coins are in the ratio of 8 : 4 : 3. Then the number of 50-paise coins is

   (a) 80   (b) 90

   (c) 70   (d) 60

55. The average age of P,Q and R is 5 years more than R's age. If the total ages of P and Q together is 39 years, then R's age is

   (a) 16 years   (b) 14 years

   (c) 12 years   (d) 24 years

56. The simplified value of

$$(0.2)^3 \times 200 \div 2000 \text{ of } (0.2)^2 \text{ is}$$

   (a) $\dfrac{1}{10}$ (b) 1

   (c) $\dfrac{1}{100}$ (d) $\dfrac{1}{50}$

57. The next number of the sequence
$\dfrac{1}{2}, \dfrac{3}{4}, \dfrac{5}{8}, \dfrac{7}{16}, \ldots$ is

(a) $\dfrac{9}{24}$ (b) $\dfrac{9}{32}$

(c) $\dfrac{10}{24}$ (d) $\dfrac{11}{32}$

58. Two pipes A and B can separately fill a tank in 2 hours and 3 hours respectively. If both the pipes are opened simultaneously in the empty tank, then the tank will be filled in

(a) 1 hour 15 minutes (b) 1 hour 20 minutes

(c) 1 hour 12 minutes (d) 2 hours 30 minutes

59. The perimeter of a triangle is 54 m and its sides are in the ratio of $5 : 6 : 7$. The area of the triangle is

(a) $27\sqrt{2}\ \text{m}^2$ (b) $25\ \text{m}^2$

(c) $18\ \text{m}^2$ (d) $54\sqrt{6}\ \text{m}^2$

60. If the ratio of an external angle and an internal angle of a regular polygon is $1 : 17$, then the number of sides of the regular polygon is

(a) 36   (b) 12

(c) 20   (d) 18

61. A bicycle wheel has a diameter (including the tyre) of 56 cm. The number of times the wheel will rotate to cover a distance of 2.2 km is (Assume $\pi = \dfrac{22}{7}$)

(a) 1875   (b) 2500

(c) 625   (d) 1250

62. A tree of height 'h' metres is broken by a storm in such a way that its top touches the ground at a distance of 'x' metres from its root. Find the height at which the tree is broken, (Here $h > x$).

(a) $\dfrac{h^2 + x^2}{4h}$ metres   (b) $\dfrac{h^2 - x^2}{4h}$ metres

(c) $\dfrac{h^2 + x^2}{2h}$ metres   (d) $\dfrac{h^2 - x^2}{2h}$ metres

63. If $x^2 + ax + b$ is a perfect square, then which one of the following relations between a and b is true?

(a) $b^2 = 4a$ (b) $b^2 = a$

(c) $a^2 = b$ (d) $a^2 = 4b$

64. A car travels at a speed of 60 km/hr and covers a particular distance in one hour. How long will it take for another car to cover the same distance at 40 km/hr ?

(a) $\dfrac{3}{2}$ hours   (b) 1 hours

(c) $\dfrac{5}{2}$ hours   (d) 2 hours

65. In $\triangle\, ABC$, $\angle A = \angle B = 60°$, $AC = \sqrt{13}$ cm. The lines AD and BD intersect at D with $\angle D = 90°$. If DB = 2cm, then the length of AD is

(a) 4 cm   (b) 4.7 cm

(c) 3 cm   (d) 3.5 cm

66. In $\triangle\, ABC$, the medians AD, BE and CF intersect each other at the point G. If the area of $\triangle\, ABC$ is 36 sq.cm, then the area (in sq.cm) of the quadrilateral BDGF is equal to

(a) 18   (b) 24

(c) 6   (d) 12

67. If $\tan(A + B) = \sqrt{3}$ and $\tan(A - B) = \dfrac{1}{\sqrt{3}}$, $\angle(A + B) < 90°$, $A \geq B$, then $\angle A$ is

(a) 45°   (b) 60°

(c) 90°   (d) 30°

68. The value of $\dfrac{\sin\theta - 2\sin^3\theta}{2\cos^3\theta - \cos\theta}$ is equal to

(a) $\tan\theta$ (b) $\cot\theta$

(c) $\sin\theta$ (d) $\cos\theta$

69. If $a + b + c + d = 4$, then the value of
$$\dfrac{1}{(1-a)(1-b)(1-c)} + \dfrac{1}{(1-b)(1-c)(1-d)} +$$
$$\dfrac{1}{(1-c)(1-d)(1-a)} + \dfrac{1}{(1-d)(1-a)(1-b)} \text{ is}$$

(a) 1   (b) 4

(c) 0   (d) 5

70. The side BC of a triangle ABC is extended to D. If $\angle ACD = 120°$ and $\angle ABC = \dfrac{1}{2}\angle CAB$, then the value of $\angle ABC$ is

(a) 60°   (b) 20°

(c) 80°   (d) 40°

71. Two circles having radii r units intersect each other in such a way that each of them passes through the centre of the other. Then the length of their common chord is

(a) $r\sqrt{5}$ units   (b) r units

(c) $r\sqrt{2}$ units   (d) $r\sqrt{3}$ units

72. The angle of elevation of the top of a tower from a point on the ground is 30° and moving 70 metres towards the tower it becomes 60°. The height of the tower is

(a) $10\sqrt{3}$ metres   (b) $35\sqrt{3}$ metres

(c) 10 metres   (d) $\dfrac{10}{\sqrt{3}}$ metres

Directions (Q. 73-75) : *The bar-graph given below shows the percentage distribution of total expenditures of a company under various expense heads during 2013. Study the graph and answer the question.*

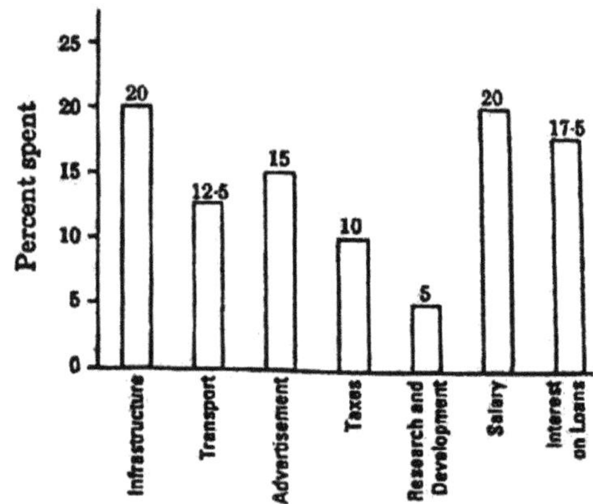

73. The ratio of the total expenditure on infrastructure and transport to the total expenditure on taxes and interest on loans is

(a) 9 : 7   (b) 13 : 11

(c) 5 : 4   (d) 8 : 7

74. If the expenditure on advertisement is ₹ 2.10 crores, then the difference between the expenditures on transport and taxes is

(a) ₹ 65 lakhs   (b) ₹ 95 lakhs

(c) ₹ 25 lakhs   (d) ₹ 35 lakhs

75. If the total amount of expenditure of the company is N times the expenditure on research and development, then the value of N is

(a) 20   (b) 27

(c) 5   (d) 18

GENERAL AWARENESS

76. Which place hold the 7th meeting of SAARC Immigration Authorities on August 2nd 2016?

(a) Kabul, Afghanistan (b) London, United States

(c) Beijing, China   (d) Islamabad, Pakistan

77. Universal adult franchise shows that India is a country which is

(a) Democratic   (b) Sovereign

(c) Secular   (d) Socialist

78. How many fundamental duties are there in our Indian Constitution?

(a) 12   (b) 8

(c) 11   (d) 9

79. The World Trade Organisation (W.T.O.) came into effect in

(a) 1995   (b) 1997

(c) 1990   (d) 1993

80. Which Article of the Constitution enjoins the State to establish village Panchayat?

(a) Article 44   (b) Article 57

(c) Article 32   (d) Article 40

81. The word 'Buddha' means

(a) An Enlightened one (b) A Wanderer

(c) A Conqueror   (d) A Liberator

82. What is meant by 'Capital Gain'?

(a) Appreciation in the money value of assets

(b) Additions to the capital invested in a business

(c) Part of profits added to the capital

(d) None of these

83. Which of the following listed is not a feature of organic farming?

(a) Use of synthetic fertilizers

(b) Very less energy consumption

(c) The non-use of chemical fertilizers and pesticides

(d) Soil is nurtured for future use by maintaining micro-organisms

84. Indian economy is a

(a) Capitalistic economy

(b) Centralised economy

(c) Mixed economy

(d) Communistic economy

85. Which Bollywood celebrity received the 'Outstanding Celebrity Woman of the Year' award while featuring among Outlook Business' 19 outstanding women?

(a) Aishwarya Rai Bachchan

(b) Deepika Padukone

(c) Priyanka Chopra

(d) Katrina Kaif

86. The longest river in the world is

(a) Brahmaputra   (b) Amazon

(c) Ganga   (d) Nile

87. The harmful substances produced by the microbes are known as

(a) Hormones   (b) Toxins

(c) Antibiotics   (d) Pollutants

88. For immediate energy production in cells, one should take

(a) Vitamin C   (b) Sucrose

(c) Glucose   (d) Proteins

89. Which one of the following types of malaria is pernicious malaria?

(a) Tertian   (b) Malignant

(c) Vivax   (d) Relapse

90. U.N.O. was founded in the year
  (a) 1950   (b) 1953
  (c) 1945   (d) 1946

91. Niyamgiri hill is located in Kalahandi district of
  (a) Punjab   (b) Kerala
  (c) Orissa   (d) West Bengal

92. The previous name of Zaire was
  (a) Congo   (b) Sierra Leone
  (c) Benin   (d) Liberia

93. The largest fresh water lake in India is
  (a) Wular Lake   (b) Nainital Lake
  (c) Dal Lake   (d) Bhimtal Lake

94. A solution is
  (a) a solid dissolved in water
  (b) a mixture of two liquids
  (c) a homogeneous mixture of two or more substances
  (d) a solid dissolved in a liquid

95. The buffer action of blood is due to the presence of
  (a) Cl^- and HCO_3^-
  (b) HCO_3^- and H_2CO_3
  (c) HCl and $NaCl$
  (d) Cl^- and CO_3^{2-}

96. A metal ball and a rubber ball, both having the same mass, strike a wall normally with the same velocity. The rubber ball rebounds and the metal ball does not rebound. It can be concluded that
  (a) Both suffer the same change in momentum
  (b) The initial momentum of the rubber ball is greater than that of the metal ball
  (c) The rubber ball suffers greater change in momentum
  (d) The metal ball suffers greater change in momentum

97. If a body moves with a constant speed in a circle
  (a) no acceleration is produced in it
  (b) its velocity remains constant
  (c) no work is done on it
  (d) no force acts on it

98. Name the oldest Indian civilization.
  (a) Mesopotamian civilization
  (b) Egyptian civilization
  (c) Indus Valley civilization
  (d) None of these

99. Who is called Rawalpindi Express?
  (a) Rahul Dravid   (b) Imran Khan
  (c) Sachin Tendulkar (d) Shoaib Akhtar

100. Union Government has extended Anti-Dumping duty on which country products for five years?
  (a) Pakistan   (b) Afghanistan
  (c) China   (d) Sri Lanka

ANSWERS

1. (a)	**2.** (b)	**3.** (a)	**4.** (a)	**5.** (a)	**18.** (c)	**19.** (d)	**20.** (a)	**22.** (a)	**25.** (d)
11. (c)	**12.** (a)	**13.** (d)	**14.** (b)	**15.** (c)	**39.** (b)	**40.** (b)	**41.** (d)	**44.** (a)	**45.** (d)
21. (b)	**22.** (c)	**23.** (a)	**24.** (d)	**25.** (b)	**26.** (b)	**27.** (c)	**28.** (d)	**29.** (c)	**30.** (c)
31. (a)	**32.** (d)	**33.** (d)	**34.** (a)	**35.** (c)	**36.** (d)	**37.** (a)	**38.** (c)	**39.** (b)	**40.** (a)
41. (a)	**42.** (c)	**43.** (a)	**44.** (d)	**45.** (a,c)	**46.** (d)	**47.** (b)	**48.** (b)	**49.** (d)	**50.** (b)
51. (d)	**52.** (d)	**53.** (d)	**54.** (a)	**55.** (c)	**56.** (d)	**57.** (b)	**58.** (c)	**59.** (d)	**60.** (a)
61. (d)	**62.** (d)	**63.** (d)	**64.** (a)	**65.** (c)	**66.** (d)	**67.** (a)	**68.** (a)	**69.** (c)	**70.** (d)
71. (d)	**72.** (b)	**73.** (b)	**74.** (d)	**75.** (a)	**76.** (d)	**77.** (a)	**78.** (c)	**79.** (a)	**80.** (d)
81. (a)	**82.** (c)	**83.** (a)	**84.** (c)	**85.** (a)	**86.** (d)	**87.** (b)	**88.** (c)	**89.** (c)	**90.** (c)
91. (c)	**92.** (a)	**93.** (a)	**94.** (c)	**95.** (b)	**96.** (c)	**97.** (c)	**98.** (c)	**99.** (d)	**100.** (c)

EXPLANATIONS

1. 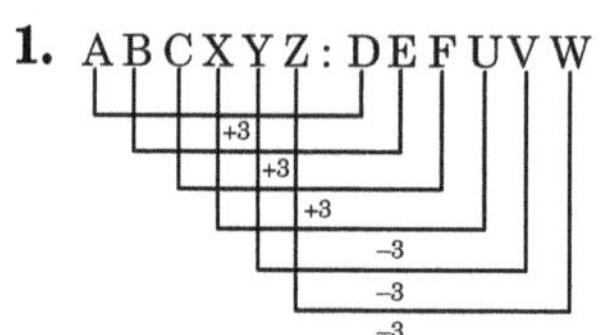

Similarly,

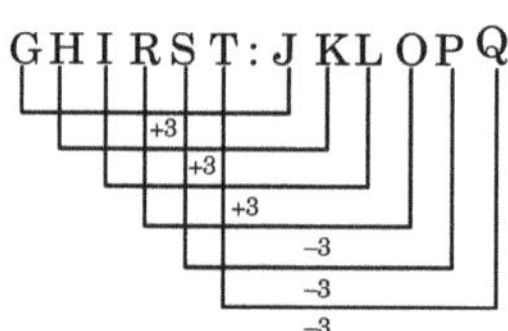

2. $5^3 + 3 = 28;$ $8^3 + 3 = 67$

3. A doctor works in a hospital, similarly, a teacher works in a school.

Hence, option (a) is the correct answer.

4. From the given options, option (a) is odd because a pair of given numbers is prime.

5. Piano, Violin and Sitar are played by hands (Percussion Instruments), while flute is played by mouth (Wind Instrument).

Hence, option (a) is the correct answer.

6. The correct order is Centimeter (0.01 meter)- Decimeter (0.1 meter)- Meter (1 meter)- Kilometer (1000 meter).

Hence, option (c) is the correct answer.

7. The correct order according to the size of the accommodation is Palace- Bungalow- House- Hut.

Hence, option (d) is the correct answer.

8. $a\boxed{b}b, a\boxed{b}b, \boxed{a}b\boxed{b}, a\boxed{b}b$

9. 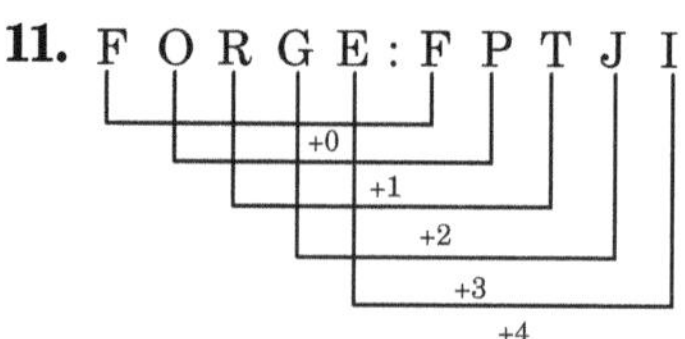

10. B Y, G T, L O, **Q J**, V E

11. F O R G E : F P T J I

Similarly,

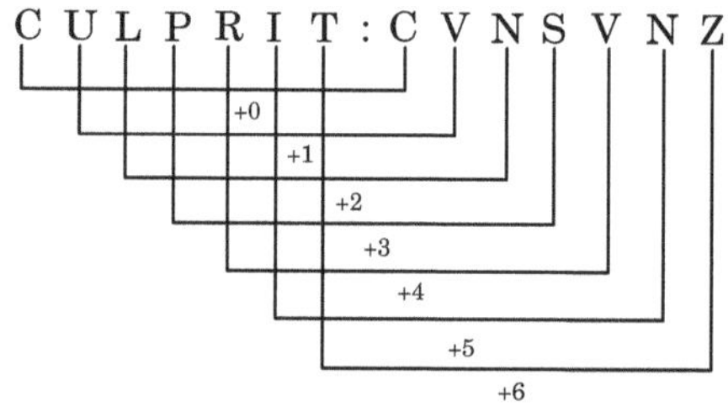

12. According to the question,

$$\text{Ann} = 300 + \text{Varun} \qquad ...(i)$$

and $\text{Sandeep} = 50 \times 7 + \text{Ann}$ [1 week = 7 days]

$$\text{Sandeep} = \text{Ann} + 350 \qquad ...(ii)$$

From equations (i), and (ii), we get

$$\text{Sandeep} = 300 + \text{Varun} + 350 = 650 + \text{Varun}$$

Hence, if Sandeep was born on Tuesday then Varun would born on Wednesday.

13. 'BLUE' can be formed by using the letters of the word 'IMMEASURABLE'. Hence, option (d) is the correct answer.

14. 2 1 5 0 0
Q A Z T T

15. $13 + 11 + 16 = 40;$ $9 + ? + 20 = 40$

$\therefore ? = 40 - 29 = 11;$ $24 + 6 + 10 = 40$

16. 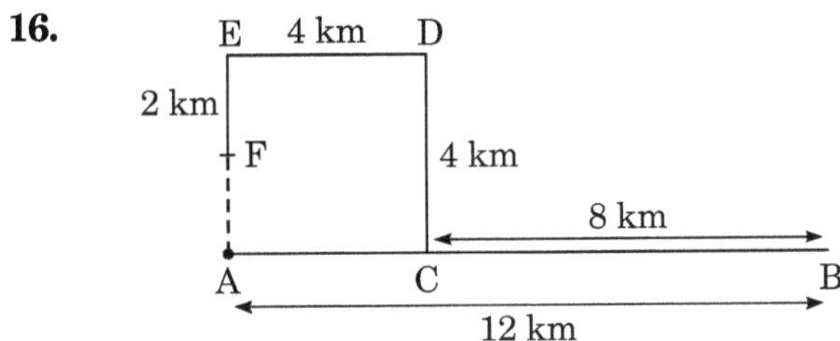

Now distance AF = 4 – 2 = 2 km

So, Mr. Das is 2 km far from his house.

17. 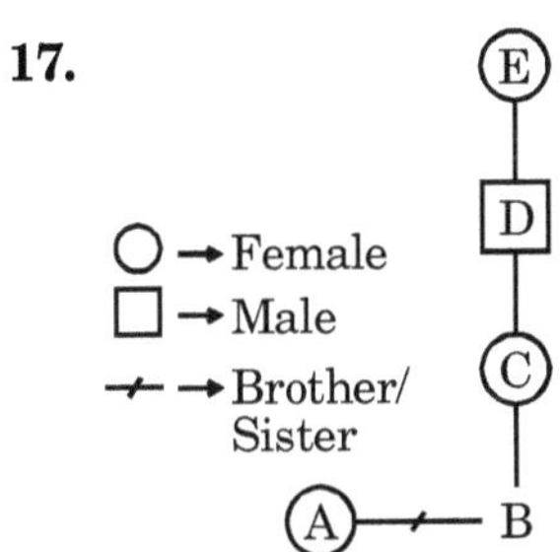

From figure it is clear that A is the grand daughter of D.

18. 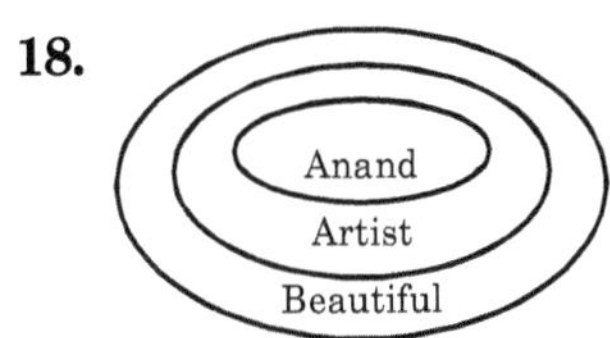

From the Venn Diagram, we can conclude that 'Anand is beautiful'. Hence, option (d) is the correct answer.

19. From the given answer figure option (a) will complete the given question figure.

20. Oxygen and Carbon-dioxide are a part of atmosphere. Therefore, both these entities lie inside the atmosphere domain. Hence, option (d) is the correct answer.

21. From (a), 1, 9 and 10 are in all the figures are false because only 7 is in all figures.

From option (b), 1, 2 and 6 are in the triangle is true.

23. In the given question figure option (a) is hidden/embedded.

24. From option (d)

12 21 15
B E E

25. Option (b) is the mirror image of the given word, when the given word keep near mirror, all the letters and number on the left side is appear on the right side.

26. Something false or inauthentic is 'spurious'. Therefore, 'fake' is synonymous to 'spurious'. 'Fictional' is incorrect as it covers all the creative fabrications that arise out of a person's imagination. Hence, option (b) is the correct ans..

27. 'Latent' is used to describe something that exists but cannot be seen. Therefore, 'hidden' is similar in meaning to 'latent'. Hence, option (c) is the correct answer.

28. 'Discrimination' means an unfair system that treats one group of people worse than another. 'Equality' is opposite in meaning to 'discrimination'. 'Bias' is used to describe unfair prejudices. 'To replenish' means to fill or build up something again. Hence, option (d) is the correct answer.

29. 'Endangered' means close to extinction. 'Protected' is an antonym of 'endangered'. 'Blissful' means completely happy and contended. Hence, option (c) is the correct answer.

30. An itinerary is a travel diary which contains schedule of travel. Hence, option (c) is the correct answer.

31. 'Ballad' is the correct answer as it refers to a poem that tells a story. 'Sonnet' is a poem made up of 14 lines that rhyme in a fixed pattern. 'Ballet' is a kind of dancing that is performed on a stage to depict a story. 'Epic' is a long poem that tells the story of a hero's adventures. Hence, option (a) is the correct answer.

32. 'Mosaic' is the correct answer as it is a decoration on a surface made by pressing small pieces of colored glass or stone into a soft material to make pictures or patterns. 'Oleograph' is a chromolithograph printed on cloth to imitate an oil painting. 'Tracery' is a decorative pattern made in stone in some church windows. 'Relief' is a mode of sculpture in which forms and figures are distinguished from a surrounding plane surface. Hence, option (d) is the correct answer.

33. The idiom 'eat like a horse' means to eat large amounts of food. Hence, option (d) is the correct answer.

34. The idiom 'at daggers drawn' means in state of extreme unfriendliness or hostility. Hence, option (a) is the correct answer.

35. The idiom 'Penelope's web' refers to an endless job. Hence, option (c) is the correct answer.

36. The correct spelling is 'Machiavellian'. Someone 'Machiavellian' is sneaky, cunning, and lacking a moral code. Hence, option (d) is the correct answer.

37. The error is in part (a) of the sentence. 'Increased' should be used in place of 'increases'. Since the given sentence talks of the past, therefore 'increased' is the correct usage. Hence, option (a) is the correct answer.

38. The error is in part (c) of the sentence. The correct phrase is 'they prayed to the gods on bended knees'. The phrase 'on bended knees' means 'humbly'. This expression alludes to a traditional attitude of supplication. Hence, option (c) is the correct answer.

39. The error is in part (b) of the sentence. According to subject-verb agreement rules, the verb agrees with the preceding noun or clause (three-fourths of the men). Therefore, 'have' should be used in place of 'has'. Hence, option (b) is the correct answer.

40. 'Sore' is the correct answer as it refers to a sore or painful spot on the body. Options (b) and (d) are logically incorrect as 'ore' refers to a source from which valuable matter is extracted and 'sour' refers to something that is unpleasant or unfriendly. 'Soar' is incorrect usage as it means to ascend to a higher or more exalted level. Hence, option (a) is the correct answer.

41. 'Pessimistic' is the correct answer because the given sentence talks about negative ideology of the neighbour. To be pessimistic means you believe evil outweighs the good and that bad things are more likely to happen. Options (b), (c) and (d) are incorrect as they carry a positive connotation. Hence, option (a) is the correct answer.

42. 'Through' is the correct preposition. 'Going through her father's mind' refers to the thoughts going through her father's mind. Hence, option (c) is the correct answer.

43. The correct phrase is 'lest you fall'. 'Lest' is used when you are saying something in order to prevent something from happening. Hence, option (a) is the correct answer.

44. The sentence is grammatically correct. Hence, option (d) is the correct answer.

45. The correct phrase is 'has become'. 'Is becoming' is also correct in the given context. Hence, both options (a) and (c) are correct.

46. 'Cortes' was not a civilization. He was a person whose army conquered the Aztecs. Hence, option (d) is the correct answer.

47. The passage says that when the chocolate was passed to the Aztecs, their leader Montezuma II, drank five goblets of hot chocolate and only those who contributed towards military service were allowed to drink it. Therefore, Options (a) and (c) are incorrect. The passage further states that the drink was served to Hernan Cortes and his soldiers, the Spaniyards, when they encountered the Aztecs. This means that visitors were also served the drink. Thus, we can say that option (b), important figures is the correct answer.

48. 'Opulence' means wealth, riches, capital or fortune. Hence, option (b) is the correct answer.

49. Option (c) can be inferred from the first sentence of the passage. The passage further states that the Mayans found that the chocolate drink was a mood enhancer and energy booster. Nothing is said about the drink being intoxicating. Hence, option (d) is the correct answer.

50. Look at the line "Legendary Aztec leader Montezuma II .display of power and opulence." It says that Montezuma II drank five cups of chocolate drink each day because he wanted to display his power and wealth. Hence, option (b) is the correct answer.

51. According to the question, $2\pi r - d = 150$

(Here r is the radius and d is the diameter of a circle)

$$2\pi r - 2r = 150 \qquad (r = \frac{d}{2})$$

$$\Rightarrow \quad 2r(\pi - 1) = 150$$

$$\Rightarrow \quad 2r\left(\frac{22}{7} - 1\right) = 150 \quad \Rightarrow \quad \frac{2r \times 15}{7} = 150$$

$$\therefore \qquad r = 35 \text{ m}$$

52. If r is the radius of a sphere, then volume $= \frac{4}{3}\pi r^3$

Let R is the radius of a new sphere
According to the question,

$$R = 2r$$

then volume of the new sphere

$$= \frac{4}{3}\pi R^3 = \frac{4}{3}\pi(2r)^3 = 8 \times \frac{4}{3}\pi r^3$$

% increase in volume

$$= \left(\frac{8 \times \frac{4}{3}\pi r^3 - \frac{4}{3}\pi r^3}{\frac{4}{3}\pi r^3} \times 100\right)\%$$

$$= \left(\frac{7 \times \frac{4}{3}\pi r^3}{\frac{4}{3}\pi r^3} \times 100\right)\% = 700\%$$

53. Marked price = ₹ 250

Selling price the item at 8% discount

$$= \frac{100 - \text{discount}}{100} \times \text{Marked price}$$

$$= \frac{100 - 8}{100} \times 250$$

$$= \frac{92}{100} \times 250$$

$$= ₹\ 230$$

Cost price of the item $= \frac{100}{115} \times 230 = ₹\ 200$

54. Given the ratio of one rupee, 50 paise and 25 paise of coins $\ \ 8 : 4 : 3$

Now the number of coins of one rupee, 50 paise and 25 paise will be

$$8 : 4 \times 2 : 3 \times 4 = 8 : 8 : 12 = 2 : 2 : 3$$

The number of 50 paise coins

$$= \frac{2}{2 + 2 + 3} \times 280 = \frac{2}{7} \times 280 = 80$$

55. Let age of R be x.

According to question

$$\frac{P + Q + R}{3} = R + 5$$

$$\frac{39 + x}{3} = x + 5$$

$$\Rightarrow \qquad 39 + x = 3x + 15$$

$$\Rightarrow \qquad 2x = 24$$

$$\therefore \qquad x = 12$$

So the age of R = 12 years

56. $(0.2)^3 \times 200 \div 2000 \text{ of } (0.2)^2$

$$= (0.2)^3 \times 200 \div 2000 \times \frac{2}{10} \times \frac{2}{10}$$

$$= (0.2)^3 \times 200 \div 80$$

$$= (0.2)^3 \times \frac{200}{80}$$

$$= \frac{2}{10} \times \frac{2}{10} \times \frac{2}{10} \times \frac{200}{80}$$

$$= \frac{1}{50}$$

57. Here the numerator of the given numbers is increased by 2 and denominator of the given numbers is multiple of 2 and each time power of 2 is increasing by 1.

58. Two pipes A and B can separately fill a tank in 2 hrs and 3 hrs.

Part filled by pipe A in 1 hr. $= \dfrac{1}{2}$

Part filled by pipe B in 1 hr. $= \dfrac{1}{3}$

Now if both pipes are opened, then part of tank filled in 1 hour $= \dfrac{1}{2} + \dfrac{1}{3} = \dfrac{5}{6}$ part

So, total time taken $= \dfrac{1}{\frac{5}{6}} = \dfrac{6}{5}$ hrs = 1 hr 12 minutes

So the tank will be filled in 1 hour 12 minutes

59. Let the sides of a triangle be $5x$, $6x$ and $7x$.

According to question,

$$5x + 6x + 7x = 54$$

$$18x = 54$$

$$x = 3 \text{ m}$$

So sides of the triangle = 15 m, 18 m and 21 m.

Now $\qquad S = \dfrac{a + b + c}{2} = \dfrac{54}{2} = 27 \text{ m}$

Area of the triangle $= \sqrt{S(S - a)(S - b)(S - c)}$

$$= \sqrt{27 \times 12 \times 9 \times 6}$$

$$= \sqrt{9 \times 3 \times 6 \times 2 \times 6 \times 9}$$

$$= 54\sqrt{6} \text{ m}^2$$

60. According to question,

$$\frac{\frac{360}{n}}{\frac{(n - 2)180}{n}} = \frac{1}{17}$$

Here n is the number of sides of regular polygon.

$$\Rightarrow \qquad \frac{2}{n - 2} = \frac{1}{17} \quad \Rightarrow 34 = n - 2$$

$$\therefore \qquad n = 36$$

So number of sides of regular polygon is 36.

61. Radius of the bicycle wheel $(r) = \dfrac{56}{2} = 28 \text{ cm}$

In one rotation bicycle covers $2\pi r$ distance

According to question,

Number of times wheel will rotate to cover distance 2.2 km

$$= \frac{2200 \times 100}{2\pi(28)} \qquad [1 \text{ km} = 1000 \text{ m}]$$

$$= \frac{2200 \times 100 \times 7}{2 \times 22 \times 28} = 1250$$

62.

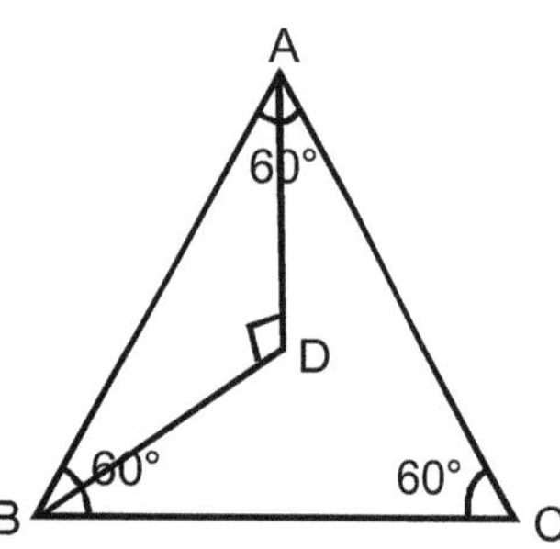

Let height AB of a tree be h.

$$AD = y \qquad \text{(say)}$$

So $\quad BD = CD = h - y \qquad$ (from figure)

$$AC = x$$

In right angle triangle DAC

$$CD^2 = AC^2 + AD^2$$
$$(h - y)^2 = x^2 + y^2$$
$$h^2 + y^2 = x^2 + y^2 + 2\,hy$$
$$h^2 - x^2 = 2\,hy$$

$$\therefore \qquad y = \frac{h^2 - x^2}{2h} \text{ metres}$$

63. Given $x^2 + ax + b$ is a perfect square then discriminant equal to zero.

$$x^2 + ax + b = 0$$
$$D = 0$$
$$\Rightarrow \quad a^2 - 4b = 0 \qquad [D = b^2 - 4\,ac]$$
$$\therefore \quad a^2 = 4b$$

64. Total distance covered by a car in 1 hr

$$= 60 \times 1 = 60 \text{ km}$$

Now total time taken by another car to cover same distance

$$= \frac{60}{40} = \frac{3}{2} \text{ hours}$$

65.

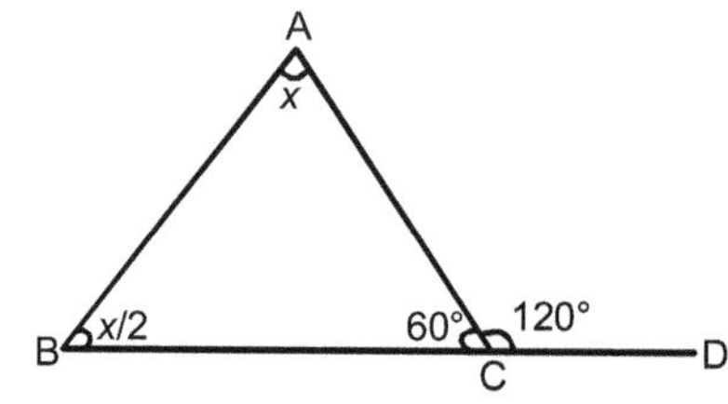

Given in $\triangle ABC$, $\angle A = \angle B = 60°$, so $\angle C$ will be $60°$. Therefore given triangle ABC is equilateral triangle.

$$\therefore \qquad AC = AB = BC = \sqrt{13} \text{ cm}$$

In $\triangle ADB$, $\angle D = 90°$ so, it is a right angle triangle.

$$DB = 2 \text{ cm}$$
$$(AB)^2 = (AD)^2 + (DB)^2$$
$$(\sqrt{13})^2 = (2)^2 + (AD)^2$$
$$(AD)^2 = 9$$
$$AD = 3 \text{ cm}$$

66.

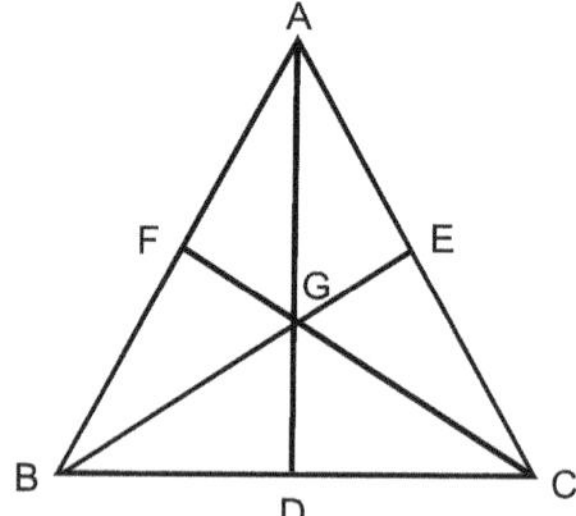

If area of $\triangle ABC$ is 36 sq. cm, then the area of the quadrilateral BDGF

$$= \frac{1}{3} \times \text{ area of } \triangle ABC = \frac{36}{3} = 12 \text{ sq. cm}$$

67.
$$\tan (A + B) = \sqrt{3} = \tan 60°$$

or $\qquad A + B = 60° \quad ...(i)$

and $\qquad \tan (A - B) = \dfrac{1}{\sqrt{3}} = \tan 30°$

$$A - B = 30° \quad ...(ii)$$

Adding equations (i) and (ii), we get

$$2A = 90°$$
$$A = 45°$$

68. $\dfrac{\sin\theta\left(1 - 2\sin^2\theta\right)}{\cos\theta\left(2\cos^2\theta - 1\right)}$

$$= \tan\theta \qquad \left(\because 1 - 2\sin^2\theta = 2\cos^2\theta - 1\right)$$

69. Given expression is equal to:

$$\frac{1 - a + 1 - b + 1 - c + 1 - d}{(1-a)(1-b)(1-c)(1-d)} = \frac{4 - (a + b + c + d)}{(1-a)(1-b)(1-c)(1-d)}$$

$$= \frac{4 - 4}{(1-a)(1-b)(1-c)(1-d)} = 0$$

70.

If	$\angle ACD = 120°$

$\therefore \qquad \angle ACB = 180° - 120°$

$\qquad\qquad \angle ACB = 60°$

In $\qquad \triangle ABC, \angle ACB = 60°$

and $\qquad \angle ABC = \dfrac{1}{2} \angle CAB$

Let $\qquad \angle CAB = x$

$\therefore \qquad \angle ABC = \dfrac{1}{2} x$

In $\triangle ABC \quad \angle A + \angle B + \angle C = 180°$

$$x + \dfrac{x}{2} + 60° = 180°$$

$$\dfrac{3x}{2} = 120°$$

$$x = 80°$$

$\therefore \qquad \angle ABC = \dfrac{x}{2} = 40°$

71.

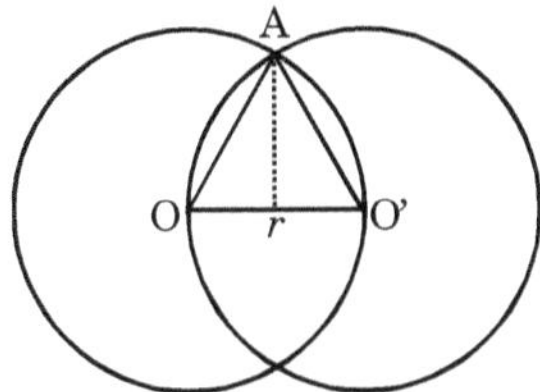

In $\triangle OAO'$;

$\qquad$ OA = O'A = OO' = r units

So; it is an equilateral triangle.

$\therefore$ AB $= \dfrac{\sqrt{3}r}{2}$

$\left(\text{Median of equilateral triangle} = \dfrac{\sqrt{3}}{2} \times \text{side}\right)$

So, length of common chord

$$= 2AB = \dfrac{2\sqrt{3}r}{2} = \sqrt{3}r \text{ units}$$

72.

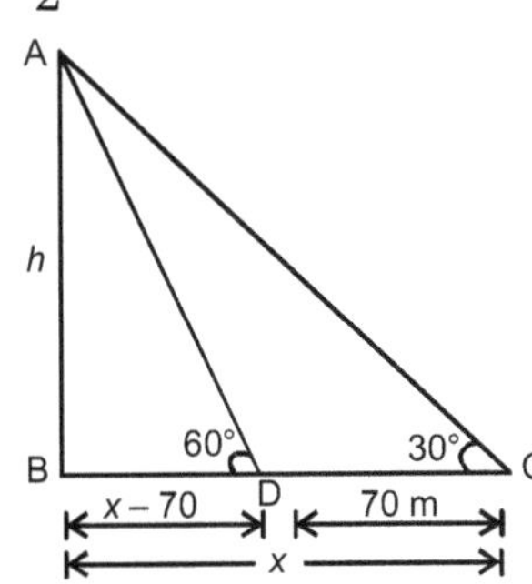

Let height of a tower be h.

In $\triangle ABC$, let BC = x

$$\tan 30° = \dfrac{h}{x}$$

$$\dfrac{1}{\sqrt{3}} = \dfrac{h}{x}$$

$$x = \sqrt{3}\, h$$

Again in $\triangle ABD$,

$$\tan 60° = \dfrac{h}{x - 70}$$

$$\sqrt{3} = \dfrac{h}{\sqrt{3}h - 70}$$

$$3h - 70\sqrt{3} = h$$

$$2h = 70\sqrt{3}$$

$$h = 35\sqrt{3} \text{ metres}$$

73. If total expenditure be x, then ratio of the total expenditure on infrastructure and transport to the total expenditure on taxes and interest on loans is

x of $(20 + 12.5)\% : x$ of $(10 + 17.5)\%$

$$\dfrac{x \times 65}{2 \times 100} : \dfrac{x \times 55}{2 \times 100} = 13 : 11$$

74. If total expenditure be x, then 15% of x.

$$= 2.10 \times 10000000$$

$$x = \dfrac{2.10 \times 10000000}{15}$$

Now difference between the expenditures on transport and taxes

$$= (12.5 - 10)\% \text{ of } \dfrac{2.10 \times 10000000}{15}$$

$$= \dfrac{2.10 \times 10000000}{15} \times \dfrac{5}{2 \times 100} = 35 \text{ lakhs}$$

75. Let total amount of expenditure of the company be x.

According to question,

$$x = N \times 5\% \text{ of } x$$

$$N = \dfrac{100}{5} = 20$$

■■

Printed by Libri Plureos GmbH in Hamburg,
Germany